# Bangalore
## &Karnataka

**Consulting Editor:** Priti David
**Assistant Editor:** Aravinda Anantharaman
**Writer:** Rajita Gadagkar
**Section Contributors:** Sreya Urs (Business & Children), Susheela Nair (Around Karnataka & Accommodation) & Sneha Koshi (Shopping).
**Sub Editors:** Raka Chaudhuri & Anirvanjyoti Chaudhuri.
**Researchers:** Apurvo Rao Parthasarathy, Amit M Panjabi, Shruti Rastogi, Sindhu Menon, Gautam R Kini, Prashanth M & Beena BS.

**Photo Editor:** Mahesh Bhat
**Resident Photographer:** DP Somashekar
**Contributing Photographers:** Mahesh Bhat, Shuvendu, KG Somsekhar, V Nagaraj & Anantica Singh.

**Art Director:** Pradeep Kumar KG
**Associate Art Directors:** George Jacob & Santhosh K
**Graphic Designers:** Adil Pasha S, Kannan Madhavan, Syam OR, Mahesh M & Saju James.

**Production Consultant:** KR Nagaraj
**Production Manager:** Soman N

**Cover Design**: Design Difference, Cochin

**Consultants:** Suryanath Kamath & Girija Chandran.

**Cartography:** Street Atlas Company, Bangalore

**Concept & Design:** Stark Communications Pvt. Ltd.

**Infinitum Publishing Pvt. Ltd.**
**Chairman:** TK Harshan
**Directors:** PN Shanavas, BR Swarup & Roy V Mathew.
**General Manager:** Sumit Chatterjee
**Accounts Manager:** Nagaraj G

**Corporate Office**
173 Penthouse, 9th cross,
Indiranagar I Stage, Bangalore 560038
Tel: 91-80-5125 5036
Fax: 91-80-5125 5037
Email: response@starkworld.net
www.starkworld.net

**Offices**
•Bangalore •New Delhi •Mumbai •Chennai
•Trivandrum •Kochi •Dubai

ISBN 81-902505-0-7
2005 Edition 1

# STARK WORLD

# Bangalore
## &Karnataka

*This is the first ever comprehensive book on Bangalore & Karnataka!*
*Regular guide books that cover India offer at best a passing glimpse of Bangalore and Karnataka. The subject is either appended among southern states or highlighted as India's pin-up city. Some books just list the best deals and the fastest getaways. Others are trapped by the cliché, missing the wood for the trees, the urban edge for the garden city. All told, that's a grave injustice and one that we at Stark World are doing our best to correct!*

*Stark World - Bangalore & Karnataka* is a wide angle look at the subject. Culture and history, food and fun, travel and entertainment are only a few pages apart. All the information presented, is current and researched by our team of 'insiders', people who know the ins and outs of the city and state.

Most travellers to the state already know about the two Unesco World Heritage sites located here, the highest waterfall in Asia and top rated forest destinations. We've tried to go beyond that. Where did the name 'Bangalore' first appear? Which is the best stretch of silver sand in Karnataka? Where will you find north Karnataka food in Bangalore? Where can you take children on holiday in the city? Queries that routinely trip off tourists' tongues and others that don't, are answered here.

*Stark World - Bangalore & Karnataka* has been widely researched and documented by an enthusiastic team of contributors, researchers, photographers and writers. Together, we have travelled miles and spent hours to gather and process information. The result is a book that will help you explore the state and the city, bone up on its history and plan a trip.

You could be an armchair traveller or an intrepid one. Someone who's never set foot here before or someone who's lived here all your life. Either way, you will find this book an exciting and complete guide to everything you ever wanted to know and things you never knew existed!

## Why we need a book on Bangalore & Karnataka

Once a quiet pensioner's paradise, today Bangalore has caught the attention of the world. It's at the forefront of information technology, biotech and other emerging industries. What's more, it is consistently rated as one of the best cities in Asia to live and work in. The weather is fabulous and the shopping, schools, entertainment and other facilities are on par with the bigger Indian metros.

The state of Karnataka too, is full of exciting opportunities for the traveller. Heritage sites lie alongside beaches, mountains and waterfalls. Spiritual retreats, forests and plantations open their doors to visitors from around the world. The highways are improving, the trains have speeded up and airports are opening across the state.

Together, they make for a great combination of the urbane and the rustic, the modern and the ancient. Pack your bags!

## About the Book

Within these pages you will find everything you need to know about the history of Karnataka and Bangalore, Business, Food & Drink, Shopping, Accommodation, Real Estate, Entertainment, Sports, Adventure & Fitness, Spiritual Matters, Health & Wellness, Children, The Arts, and most importantly, travel Around Karnataka. Each section is comprehensive with well-researched text, detailed listings, informative special features, colourful photographs, helpful tips and resources.

For easy reading, the book is divided into sections. For example, **Shopping** covers everything from what to buy, the best places to shop and listing information like **Open, Cards** accepted etc. If that doesn't satisfy you, try **Children** (for shops selling children's toys, clothing and books) and **Sports, Adventure & Fitness** for where to buy adventure gear. All manner of **Entertainment** from game arcades to pubs and parks to music may be found in the section by the same name. Turn to **Food & Drink** and even **The Arts** if your needs are more specific.

## Special Features

We've tried to go beyond the big picture with our Special Features – interesting insights about people and places of note. For example, the history of the Kodavas, the International Technology Park, Ayurveda Brief and so on. Each section carries at least a few of these in-depth stories.

## Listings

If anyone were to ask us what the toughest job has been, the answer would undoubtedly be 'listings'! Ferreting out new places, visiting and reviewing them, telephoning, verifying and re-checking is what makes this book a valuable and current guide. You are looking at a set of comprehensive lists with relevant information like where to Shop, where to Eat, Sights to See, Hotels and Serviced Apartments, Hospitals and Spiritual Centres. There are some unusual ones like Concept Stores, Aero Sports, Japanese cuisine and Social Dancing.

Useful contact information including *Tel*ephone numbers, **Open**, address and **Cards** accepted is provided. For example, the section on **Accommodation** carries listings of luxury, business and budget hotels, guesthouses, serviced apartments and resorts with tariff ranges and check in/check out timings. If you are looking for something specific like Tennis Academies, turn to **Sports, Adventure & Fitness**. **Food & Drink** lists the city's best restaurants categorised cuisine-wise with helpful information on lunch and dinner timings, whether alcohol is served or not and price of an average meal for two.

## Photos

*Stark World - Bangalore & Karnataka* is a visual treat with more than 750 fabulous pictures. Our photographers have travelled far and wide to capture people and places, monuments, wildlife and arresting images of Bangalore and Karnataka. We hope it whets your appetite and sends you on a journey like no other.

## Maps

Maps of the state have been divided into North, South, and West Karnataka. Area-wise maps of Bangalore city have been provided. Maps of Bangalore and Mysore city sights and getaways are also included.

## Books

In our research we came across a number of books on Bangalore and Karnataka. We have chosen to profile a few for the benefit of those readers who may want to explore the subject even further. A number of writers have spent time and energy exploring the history, geography, sociology and culture of the area and their books may be found in the section, Books. Besides factual information they also offer a glimpse into the life and customs prevalent within the state.

## A to Z Resources

For the rest, turn to A to Z Resources. All the useful/vital information that a traveller to the city needs has been placed here. The resources and facilities available are listed alphabetically, from Moneychangers and Helplines to Airlines and 24-Hour Medical Shops.

## Write to Us

The team at *Stark World - Bangalore & Karnataka* has made every effort to ensure that the information presented here is accurate and up-to-date. But rates change, schedules get rearranged and good places sometimes don't stay good! So, if you find our contents in anyway misleading or our information outdated, please drop us a line or email us. We would be delighted to hear from you and will incorporate your suggestions in our next edition. Letters, postcards, emails and phone calls from travellers and readers is valuable feedback for our team. And you may expect to see your name in our next edition, unless otherwise stated!

We hope you enjoy the book and find it a valuable companion in your travels across Bangalore and Karnataka. Go ahead, turn the pages, and begin your journey...

# CONTENTS

World Heritage Site, Hampi

Mysore was once the royal capital of the Wodeyar dynasty. Proof is the opulent Amba Vilas Palace, built in the Indo-Saracenic style with four grand arched entrances capped with gold domes. The city of Mysore regains its erstwhile grandeur during the Dasara festival held in October. The royal festival has been celebrated with pomp and splendour at the Mysore Palace for centuries. During the 10-day festivities cultural programmes are lined up and the city is bedecked with lights.

# Karnataka

Washed by the warm waters of the **Arabian Sea**, ringed by the **Deccan Plateau** and nurtured by the erstwhile **Mysore kingdom**, the state of Karnataka lies as a bridge between the north and south of India. The southern states of Tamil Nadu, Andhra Pradesh and Kerala share its borders in the east and the south, while the western states of Maharashtra and Goa lie to the north.

Pattadakal was the coronation city of the Chalukya kings.

Stretching from the burning, rock strewn plains of Gulbarga and Bijapur to the lush and cool forests of Bandipur, Karnataka presents an exciting contrast in landscape, people, food and cultures. Its capital city Bangalore is a homogenous mix of people from all over the country.

For the first time visitor to Karnataka, there is a fascinating array of sights to choose from. Along its snaking coastline are strung a number of beaches and temple towns. Its northern plains are strewn with the remains of Deccani Sultans' forts and tombs. The rest of the state boasts two World Heritage sites, scores of temples and historical monuments spanning 1,500 years of history and more. For the intrepid tourist, adventure sports beckon at every corner. From rappelling to rafting, gliding to golfing, the state has it all.

Karnataka's deep forests and priceless natural heritage have been mentioned in ancient texts. Over the centuries some rulers maintained these as private hunting grounds and protected them from pillage. Modern India turned them into reserves and sanctuaries where tropical evergreen, deciduous forests and scrubland are still home to an exciting range of wildlife. Its many sanctuaries are contiguous and together they are referred to as the Nilgiri Biosphere, offering important migratory corridors for protected species. Wildlife enthusiasts may expect to see tigers, Asian elephants, sloth bears, bonnet macaques, four-horned antelopes, sambars, spotted deers, reptiles and some 230 varieties of birds.

Hospitable people, a great climate and exciting opportunities have attracted citizens of all faiths and communities. The state's historical advantage in silk, sandalwood,

coffee and mining has been strengthened by a lead in hi-tech industries like information technology and aerospace. Over the last decade there has been an influx of IT companies, both domestic and global, who have sought Karnataka's hi-tech climate to build their businesses. Sunrise sectors like biotech and business process outsourcing have followed suit.

## Landscape and Climate

Karnataka presents great topographical and climatic diversity, unmatched across the Indian subcontinent. It has warm beaches of sparkling white sand, wet tropical hills covered with dense forest and dry, black and rocky plains within its borders. In a matter of hours, travelling through the state could expose you to all three geo-climatic regions!

The name 'Karnataka', derived from ancient Tamil 'karunat', is said to mean 'elevated land', or 'land above the Eastern Ghats'. Karnataka is predominantly a land of black soil, found in the northern regions of the state in areas like Gulbarga, Bidar and Bijapur.

This is predominantly found in the northern regions of the state in areas like Gulbarga, Bidar and Bijapur. The semi-arid plains stretch all the way to the rocky outcrops of the Deccan Plateau. To the west lie the verdant, fertile land of the Western Ghats, sloping down to a rich, 320 kilometre long coastline where several rivers empty into the sea. The districts of Dakshina Kannada, Uttara Kannada and Udupi lie along this fertile belt. In the south lie the cool, hilly forests and vast coffee plantations of Coorg or Kodagu.

A fifth of the state's nearly 2,00,000 sqkms is forest. Three major rivers – the Tungabhadra, Cauvery and Krishna – wind through the state, irrigating vast tracts of agricultural land of both black and red soil. With such variation in topography, it's not surprising that temperatures across the state differ by 10 to 25 degrees. Night temperatures in all the cooler regions are likely to drop a few degrees and if it's raining, could sink even lower.

Summer begins early in the month of February. The northern plains heat up quickly, and temperatures soar to over 40 degrees Celsius in arid areas. Fortunately, the rest of the state is better off. The capital city of Bangalore enjoys a temperate climate, and when the mercury rises to 38 degrees in summer, it makes the front pages of local dailies! By April, early monsoon showers are expected and matters cool down. But in Kodagu and areas of higher elevation, summers pass without a murmur.

Winters are pleasant throughout the state. Bangalore's elevation (920 metres above sea level) makes for nippy mornings and cold nights. The odd but entirely expected rain in the month of January brings down the average temperature and sends everyone scuttling inside. In the winter months, the most fabulous weather is enjoyed by Karnataka's coastal belt, the tourist high season here.

The monsoon months, between June and September are especially wet on the western coast. The hilly, forested ranges of the Western Ghats and the coastal strip on its western flank, witness torrential downpours. However, the eastern flank of the Western Ghats remains dry as it slopes towards the arid Deccan Plateau.

Kabini Reservoir

# The People of Karnataka

The Kodava, the Konkani, the Bunt and the Bangalorean are just some of the people who call Karnataka their home; they speak Coorgi, Konkani, Tulu and Kannada respectively. The two major communities in Karnataka are the Lingayats and the Vokkaligas. The Lingayats are followers of the 12th century saint, Basavanna who preached the importance of equality above all else and disagreed with several traditional beliefs and practices. His teachings on religion and education continue to influence his followers even today. Their contribution to society may be seen in the large number of educational institutions and charitable organisations set up by them. They are also known for their prose-poetry.

The Vokkaligas are essentially agriculturists, their name originating from the word, 'okkalu', meaning to thresh. They are numerically and economically significant in Karnataka and many of the state's political leaders hail from this community. The Vokkaligas mainly inhabit the regions of Shimoga, Chikmagalur, Kolar, Mandya, Hassan and Bangalore.

The Kodavas, natives of Kodagu or Coorg, which lies in the southwest corner of the state, share a unique history. In physical appearance they stand out as fairer and taller than their neighbours and are often referred to as the Kashmiris of the south. Legend has it that their ancestors were Greeks or Aryans! And their martial abilities and physical build seem

to tie-in with this theory. The Kodavas worship Goddess Cauvery and Lord Iguthappa and unlike Hindu weddings, Kodava weddings are solemnised by the elders of the family.

Another community, the Navayats of Bhatkal are believed to be descendants of Arabs while the Siddis of Uttara Kannada are of African origin. In the last century, five Tibetan settlements have been set up across Karnataka adding to the state's reputation as the melting pot of cultures. The Tulu speaking Bunts are an agricultural community with their own distinct rituals, residing in Dakshina Kannada.

Immigration from the neighbouring states of Tamil Nadu and Andhra Pradesh led to many settlers like the Sanketis. Originally Tamil Brahmins, they are believed to have migrated about a thousand years ago. Their dialect is a mix of both Tamil and Kannada.

Karnataka is also home to nearly seven million Muslims. It is said that Arab traders brought Islam to Karnataka centuries ago. Historically, Muslims are credited with introducing coffee, incense sticks and paper to the state. Karnataka has also been ruled by powerful and benevolent Muslim rulers, from the Bahmani Sultans of Bijapur to Tipu Sultan in Mysore. The evolution of Islamic architecture is seen in its many mosques and mausoleums.

Mangalore has a large Catholic population as is evident from their ancient churches, established in the 16th century. With their origins in South Kanara, most of them are either traders using Mangalore's ports or are involved in the agricultural processing industry.

## A Long and Turbulent History...

The region that is present-day Karnataka was once home to the earliest signs of life in peninsular India, dating to the period 3,000 BC. Agricultural communities thrived in the area that is now northern Karnataka. They grew millet, wheat and gram, a practice continued even today. In the coming centuries, the Deccan and further south would be ruled by many powerful dynasties, exerting their control from both the north and south and leaving behind a number of exquisite architectural monuments and towns, which have survived to this day. Many of the temples continue to be used for worship, hundreds of years later.

By the 4th century BC, the region had come under the Mauryan Empire, with Kanakagiri as its southern capital. Legend has it that the emperor Chandragupta Maurya embraced Jainism, renounced his worldly possessions and retired to Shravanabelagola. A Jain settlement sprung up in the area and some of it is visible even today.

The Mauryan empire faded out and brought in the Satkarnis who extended their reach from the Vindhyas in the north to the entire Deccan in the south. From the 4th to the 10th centuries, the Western Gangas ruled southern Mysore. Their territory was conquered by the Cholas. Under the Chalukyas and the Rashtrakutas, Jainism and Hinduism flourished side by side. Amazing architectural marvels sprung up during this time: Superb rock-cut sandstone and cave temples surrounded by landscaped gardens, flowing rivers and large lakes. Today, Pattadakal is acknowledged as a Unesco World Heritage Site.

The Rashtrakutas were overthrown by the later Chalukyas who set up a new capital, Kalyana, and built ornamental temples across Gadag, Itagi and Lakkundi. Their feudatories, the Hoysalas ruled in the south, using the weakening of the neighbouring Chola dynasty to assert their power and extend their rule. Halebid and Belur were their capitals and Hoysala king Vishnuvardhan is credited with building a number of temples in Belur. Soft soapstone was used to create rich and dense decoration depicting Hindu deities, sages, stylised animals, birds and even friezes illustrating the life of Hoysala kings.

The most famous Hindu dynasty to rule the region of present-day Karnataka was the Vijayanagar empire. Hampi was their citadel, lying on the banks of the mighty Tungabhadra river. Its ruins, now another Unesco World Heritage Site, may be seen even today. For 200 years it was the centre of power and influence, surrounded by rocky ridges acting as natural defences.

Islamic winds of change had been blowing through the south for a while now. The Bahmani kings of Gulbarga were extending their influence in the north and the Vijayanagar empire was feeling the heat. By the mid 1500s, the Muslim empire had shattered into five parts and was grabbed by the sultanates of Bijapur, Berar, Golconda, Ahmadnagar and Bidar. A couple of decades later the Mughals took over the north defeating the Muslim Sultans. The Wodeyars rose to occupy Mysore and surrounding areas that had disintegrated from the erstwhile Vijayanagar kingdom.

In the year 1761, the Mysore Wodeyars lost their kingdom to Hyder Ali. He used his position as commander-in-chief to overthrow them. In the next few years he waged many wars against the British with the aid of French mercenaries, winning them with his tactical brilliance. The Mysore kingdom

# Mysore State to Karnataka

Mysore Palace

The Wodeyars were the last monarchs of Mysore, ruling from 1399 to 1947. Their descendants live in Mysore even today. The Mysore state they once ruled included Mysore city and its districts, parts of Tamil Nadu, districts of Dakshina Kannada and Dharwad. Srirangapatna was the state's capital for long. It later shifted to Mysore and finally to Bangalore in 1831.

Indian Independence in 1947 threw open boundaries and states. In 1956 the States Reorganization Act was passed, and the country was organised on a linguistic basis.

All Kannada-speaking districts in the country united under Mysore State with Bangalore as state capital. Parts of the former Madras and Bombay presidencies and Hyderabad state merged with the new state of Karnataka, with Kannada as the main language. The Maharaja stepped out and a governor, installed by the President of India, took office.

The present state of Karnataka was created in 1956 by bringing all Kannada-speaking regions together around the nucleus of the erstwhile princely state of Mysore. Every year the 1st of November is celebrated as Karnataka Rajyotsava Day.

extended from Dharwad in the north to Dindigul in the south, an area of 300,000 sqkms, far more than present-day Karnataka!

His son Tipu Sultan was barely 13 years old when he made his first journey into war. His early military training helped in the many wars he and his father would wage against the British, earning him the nickname: Tiger of Mysore. But finally in 1799 in Srirangapatna, Tipu fell and the British annexed half his kingdom. Some of the northern territories were given out as rewards to British supporters like the Nizam of Hyderabad. Most importantly, the Mysore throne was handed back to the dispossessed Maharaja of Mysore, the Wodeyar descendent.

His family would rule until Indian Independence, barring a few upsets with the British. With Independence in 1947, the Mysore government took charge of the Cantonment, and in 1949 the City of Bangalore and the Cantonment of Bangalore were brought together under the Bangalore City Corporation. Seven years later, the state of Karnataka was born and Bangalore became its capital city.

## Karnataka Today

The state today is a far cry from the war stricken province and colonial hangout it once was. Its transition as the country's scientific and technological capital has been a steady one. Well before Independence, the state already had in its fold the Indian Institute of Science, a college of engineering (present day UVCE) in Bangalore and a medical college that was shifted to Mysore in 1930. The small town of Manipal was

emerging as a university town in its own right. This rich legacy of educational institutions laid the foundation for its development and even today Karnataka's schools, colleges and universities draw students from all over the country and abroad.

Karnataka is the second mineral rich state in India, producing gold, iron ore, bauxite and magnesite. In the 60s and 70s several public sector undertakings in the state provided employment to skilled labour. Hindustan Machine Tools, Hindustan Aeronautics Limited, Bharat Earthmovers, Indian Telephone Industries, Bharat Electronics were just some of them. The state also produces 70 per cent of the country's raw silk and it's the largest producer of coffee, more than half of which comes from Coorg.

In the 80s and 90s, the state moved to occupy a prominent spot on the world map of information technology – India's Silicon Valley. Since then, IT Parks have also been opened in Mysore, Mangalore and Hubli.

Biotech is the most recent industry to make it to the news. Poised to grow in a big way, this is good news for a once agriculture-driven state like Karnataka.

Karnataka is consistently rated as a great state for business and education. It is the acknowledged leader in information technology and the champion of the biotech industry. It's emerging as a health destination and a spiritual retreat of sorts. Its tourist destinations stretch from verdant hills and coffee plantations to lush coastal hideaways and important heritage towns. Welcome to Karnataka! May your journey and stay be rich and rewarding!

# State of Education

May is a month of sweltering heat throughout India. But anxious students and their parents could not care less. Most of them will be winging their way to Karnataka – undisputed leader in the field of higher education. Engineers, doctors, architects, lawyers, corporate managers, accountants, communication experts and fashion designers graduate every year from the state's numerous institutes of higher education. Karnataka's reputation attracts people from all over the country as well as the state.

The impetus for higher education came almost a century ago when the Mysore government started the UVCE (University Visveswaraya College of Engineering) in Bangalore in 1917, for high quality education in modern technology. In 1929, the first medical college was started in Bangalore and within a year was shifted to Mysore.

Karnataka has over 250 medical and engineering colleges, not counting the polytechnic and vocational training institutes. Universities for agricultural sciences have been set up in Bangalore and Dharwad. The major universities are Bangalore University, Mysore University, Karnatak University, Gulbarga University and Mangalore University. The varsities of Gulbarga, Mysore and Bangalore have been awarded five-star status by the National Assessment and Accreditation Council.

Good education is always followed by good academics and the state is dotted with many research institutes. Some of the national level ones like the Indian Institute of Science was built as early as in 1909 while the Indian Institute of Management came much later in 1973. The National Law School of India, the National Institute of Mental Health and Neuro Sciences, the Indian Space Research Organisation, Raman Research Institute, National Aeronautical Laboratory, Institute for Social and Economic Change, Central Food Technological Research Institute, National Institute of Astrophysics, National Institute of Advanced Studies, National Institute of Biological Sciences, Indian Statistical Institute and the National Institute for Sports are prominent research institutions in the state.

Karnataka is one the few states that allows private enterprise in education. Many groups set up colleges and universities, the most notable being the Manipal group which set up the Manipal Academy of Higher Education (MAHE). It has acquired the status of a deemed university with degrees in engineering, hotel management, medicine and mass communication. The Kasturba Medical College is now half a century old and one of the state's premier colleges of medicine.

Karnataka is a flourishing centre of sericulture.

**325 AD** The Pallava domination of the region we now know as Karnataka, ended. They were overthrown by local dynasties like the Kadambas of Banavasi and the Gangas of Kolar, who proceeded to divide the spoils.

**325-540** The area was ruled by the Kadambas of Banavasi, a dynasty founded by Mayurasharma who won part of north Karnataka from the Pallavas.

**325-999** The Gangas of Kolar ruled south Karnataka and later shifted their capital to Talakad. The monolithic Gomateshwara statue in Shravanabelagola is their creation.

**510-757** This was a significant period as the Chalukyas of Badami brought the whole of present day Karnataka under a single ruler and the Gangas continued to govern as their subordinates. Pulikeshin II (609-42) built a vast empire extending from river Narmada

in the north to river Cauvery in the south. The Chalukyan empire included not only the whole of present day Karnataka and Maharashtra, but the greater part of Gujarat, Madhya Pradesh and Andhra Pradesh, and parts of Orissa and Tamil Nadu. This empire continued to flourish under the Rashtrakutas and the Kalyana Chalukyas. Badami's Chalukyan kings built beautiful rock-cut temples at Badami, Aihole and Pattadakal.

**757 - 973** In 753, Dantidurga, the Rashtrakuta feudatory of the Chalukyas, overthrew the Chalukya king Keerthivarma II and the Rashtrakutas became rulers of Karnataka.

**973 - 1198** The Chalukyas of Kalyana overthrew the Rashtrakutas. Someshwara I, succeeded in resisting the efforts of the Cholas to subdue Karnataka, and he built a new capital, Kalyana (modern Basavakalyan in Bidar District).

**1198 - 1312** The Yadavas of Devagiri or Daulatabad became a sovereign power. Bhillama V captured Kalyana in 1186.

**1000 - 1346** The Hoysala rulers defeated the last of the Chalukyas and warred against the Yadava rulers, securing a foothold in Tamil Nadu. Ballala III, the last Hoysala king, had to struggle hard to hold his own against the invasion of the Delhi Sultan. He died in battle but his commanders Harihara and Bukka founded the Vijayanagar kingdom

**1336 - 1565** Harihara and Bukka succeeded in resisting the southern march of the Delhi Sultanate. The rule of Krishnadevaraya saw a period of peace and great prosperity.

**1347 - 1527** The Bahmanis ruled over parts of Karnataka, first from Gulbarga and later from Bidar. A number of Indo-Saracenic monuments were built under their patronage.

**1489 - 1686** The Sultans of Bijapur took over parts of the Bahmani territory when they broke up and Bijapur became their stronghold. The mausoleum Ibrahim Roza and the massive Gol Gumbaz are some of their finest monuments.

**1499 - 1763** The Mysore Wodeyars ruled as chieftains under the Vijayanagar empire. They gained independence under the rule of Ranadhira Kantirava Narasaraja Wodeyar (1638 - 1659 AD). Raja Wodeyar captured Srirangapatna and made it his capital. Ranadhira Kantirava defended his kingdom against the Bijapur Sultans.

**1500 - 1763** The Nayaks of Keladi ruled over the Malnad areas in the coastal region. The most famous of them is Rani Chennamma of Keladi who fought against Aurangzeb. He waged war against her for sheltering a Maratha prince Rajaram, son of Shivaji.

**1761 - 1799** Hyder Ali, commander-in-chief of the Wodeyars, unseated the Wodeyars. He expanded his territory with Srirangapatna as his capital. His son, Tipu Sultan continued to rule from there.

**1799 - 1831** Following Tipu Sultan's death in 1799, the British handed over power to Krishnaraja Wodeyar III. He shifted his capital to Mysore. The British shifted their cantonment to Bangalore in 1808.

**1956 -** All Kannada speaking districts in the country were united under the state of Mysore following the States Reorganization Act.

**1973 -** Mysore State was renamed Karnataka.

**1986 -** Bandipur and Nagarhole were included as part of Niligiri Biosphere Reserve.

**1989 -** Veteran artist KK Hebbar won the Padma Bhushan.

**1992 -** Eminent playwright Girish Karnad was awarded the Padma Bhushan.

**1995 -** Kannada matinee idol Dr. Rajkumar was awarded Dadasaheb Phalke Award.

**1996 -** 'Son of the Soil' Deve Gowda became the Prime Minister of India, leading the United Front coalition government.

**1996 -** The IT Park was started in Mysore.

**1998 -** Renowned writer, Prof. UR Ananthamurthy was awarded the Padma Bhushan.

**2000 -** One of India's oldest gold mines, Kolar Gold Fields closed down.

**2001 -** IT Park commenced operations in Mangalore.

**2002 -** The Software Technology Park was inaugurated at Hubli.

bbon Park, located in the heart of the city, spreads across 300 lush acres.

# Bangalore

Bangalore is the aerospace capital of the country with a number of prestigious institutions located here. Naturally, the city hosts the biennial Aero India show where global aerospace and aviation firms showcase aircrafts, products and technologies. The five day event is billed as one of the biggest shows in South Asia.

Bangalore is the most cosmopolitan city in the country, home to people from all parts of the country. On the day celebrated as Vijayadashmi, the idol of Durga is immersed amidst great excitement by the city's sizeable Bengali community.

*Pret a porter, haute couture...* Bangalore's designers are right up there with others in the fashion industry. Fashion shows are held around the year and promise to be high profile evenings filled with socialites, trendsetters and the city's glitterati.

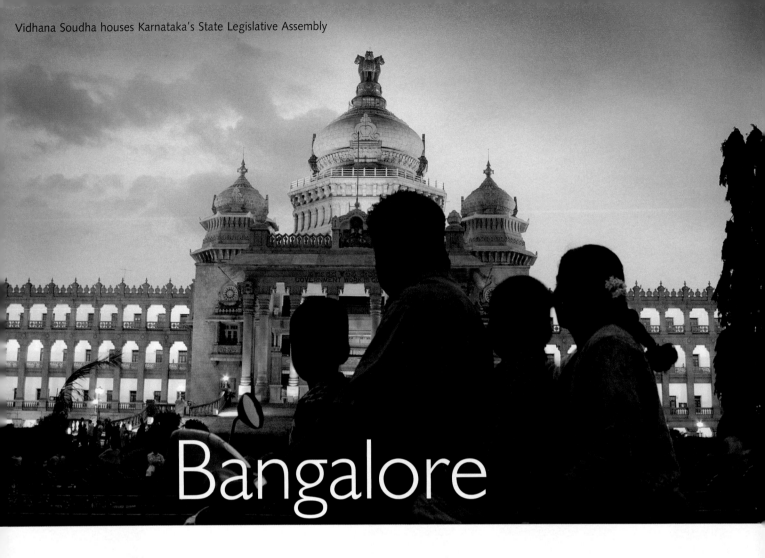

# Bangalore

Bangalore is the most **exciting** and **eclectic** city in India.

The city has many **parks**; the whole city is a park.

Some people work **all day**, others work **all night.**

**Women jockeys** win races on horses owned by women.

**Electric cars** run on the streets and street kids act in plays.

Modern **Spas** embrace ancient **Ayurveda** and Yoga is taught in hi-tech gyms.

CEO's chauffeurs are millionaires and **millionaires** drive their own cars.

International **rock stars** land here first and local bands make it to the charts.

Citizens manage the city and the Chief Minister goes online.

Children learn **Vedic chants** and grandmothers **bungee jump.**

It's a **small town** with a **big heart.**

It's a big city with a little attitude.


**Welcome to Bangalore!**

An urban sprawl of fascinating diversity, where the young and the old, the traditional and the modern, the **native** and the **neo-native** live together celebrating their differences, forging a uniquely urban identity. The **fifth largest city** in India and the **fastest growing.**

Ruled by Hindu kings, captured by a Muslim ruler and annexed by the British, Bangalore's identity is hard to pin down. There are churches that draw Hindu and Muslim believers, and temples and dargahs visited by people of all faiths. Ethnic identity is hard to isolate. The city of Bangalore is a microcosm of India. Only a third of the population have their roots within the state, the rest are migrants from all over the country. There is a fair percentage of foreigners too. Its history as a military town and location for public sector companies no doubt accounts for this. Both bring in people from all over, regardless of language and origin. The result is a city for everyone, a city that makes you feel welcome at once.

It carries its colonial legacy proudly, not bothering to 'Indianise' street names and suburbs. Murphy Town, Richmond Town, Cooke Town are as much a part of the city as Jayanagar and Raj Mahal Vilas. English is spoken widely and no one will penalise you for not speaking Kannada. This is also a reflection of Bangalore's multi-lingual and multi-ethnic status. Your neighbour could be from anywhere in India, and in some areas, from anywhere in the world! No wonder new restaurants and food stores flourish. You're more likely to find a dish of pasta listed on a menu than a local Bisi Bele Bhath! Food stores stock 'north' Indian vegetables alongwith 'European' ones like broccoli and asparagus.

## Number 1 City

Bangalore is consistently rated as one of the best cities to live in India, and one of the top ten tech cities in the world. International newsmagazine *Newsweek* has hailed Bangalore as one of the world's fastest growing big cities, and one of the better managed in Asia. A recent survey on Urbania by a business magazine said: 'Bangalore is even better than Mumbai. It's cheap, has great weather, nice pubs and it's a global tech centre.' It ranked second on jobs and income and third on health. Not just IT companies but multinationals too find the business climate stimulating. It's the regional headquarters of companies in hi-tech, garments, textiles, watches, biscuits, ice creams and so on. Professionals like the relaxed pace, the important amenities like schools and housing for their families, the invigorating weather and finally the high quality living.

Delhi lies on the banks of river Yamuna, while Kolkata, Chennai and Mumbai began life as ports of great importance. Most of the great cities of the world were either located on the banks of a river or were important trading ports. Bangalore has no river running through it and no sea for miles. Its salubrious climate, a rarity in Indian weather, exerts the greatest pull. (It was the reason why the British Commissioner wanted to move out of Srirangapatna!) More recently, it has attracted transnational companies looking for a base in India. Their executives are willing to travel twice a week out of Bangalore just for the privilege of living here!

# Garden City

Purple and blue jacarandas, flaming red Gulmohar, scarlet Flame of the Forest, golden Acacias and the cool emerald green spread of the Rain Tree are just some of the characteristic sights of urban Bangalore. These flowering trees bloom across the city – at busy traffic junctions, on broad avenues and in quiet neighbourhood parks, earning it its best loved sobriquet of 'Garden City'.

History has it that the German architect, Krumbiegel, under the guidance of the Maharaja of Mysore planted a variety of select saplings ranging from Tecomas to Cassias that flowered sequentially through every season. Bangalore also blossomed in the hands of John Cameron, Javaraya and Dr. Mari Gowda who planned the city's gardens and avenues.

But it was perhaps Hyder Ali who really set the tone for the Garden City with a 140-acre park laid more than two centuries ago. He named it 'Lal Bagh' for the profusion of red roses it housed. Inspired by the Mughal gardens of Sira, it is home to India's largest collection of rare tropical and sub-tropical plants and ancient trees from Europe, Afghanistan and Persia. Lalbagh even has a Glass House modelled on the Crystal Palace in London, venue for the bi-annual flower show. A hundred years later, the British laid out Cubbon Park in the Cantonment area and added yet another famous garden with flowering trees and shrubs. The British, must also be credited with the many wide avenues cooled by the spread of the dark green Rain Tree, the residential roads carpeted with blossoms round the year and a number of parks dense with trees.

The roots of Bangalore's flowering trees go back further than the British. Blossoming boughs frame sculptures in the ancient temples at Halebid and Belur. And the area that is now Karnataka was once a dense, semi-tropical forest filled with a profusion of flowering trees. Even today, most village houses across Karnataka sport a Sampige (Champak) and Mallige (Jasmine) garden in their frontyard.

The bi-annual flower show at Lalbagh Botanical Garden

# Churchill's Dues!

The Bangalore Club

A story oft repeated in Bangalore's club society relates to the late Winston Churchill, former Prime Minister of England. He arrived in Bangalore as a young bachelor and lived the typical life of a junior British officer. He shared accommodation with others like himself and the establishment was run by the butler who was handed a bag of silver rupees at the beginning of the month.

Churchill is supposed to have breakfasted often at The Victoria, under the cool shade of its many trees, within shouting distance of MG Road, then South Parade Road.

The Bangalore Club, then known as the Bangalore United Services Club, was a popular meeting place in the Cantonment. The club still has on record a charge of dues for the princely sum of Rs 1, owed by none other than Winston Churchill! It was written off only a decade ago.

## Young Population

Bangalore is the youngest metro in India, both historically and demographically. It gained the public eye only 200 years ago when British troops moved here. Now it's catching up in double quick time. A new airline touches down every few months, bringing the rest of the world closer and closer. City limits change everyday as new housing colonies spring up on roads leading out of the city. Flyovers and ring roads bring them closer and spur fresh building activity.

Old commercial districts are having their boundaries redrawn, rewriting traditional office addresses. The IT denizens have their own fiefdom now, an IT corridor that connects the two big spaces – Electronics City and ITPL. Biotech is getting its own corridor and one is being planned for agritech as well. The new suburbs are emerging as attractive addresses and rising land prices is proof of this.

The world thinks of Bangalore as a 'young' city and rightly so. The large numbers of graduates that the state produces have Bangalore firmly in their sights. The sobriquet of Pensioner's Paradise has given way to Silicon Valley of India, a name that attracts young professionals in droves.

## It's IT

Shenzen is a city in China that says it aims to be China's 'Bangalore'! The rapid development in information technology and its related services is something Bangalore is justifiably proud of. Today, it is an accepted fact that Bangalore (and Karnataka) has an edge in information technology and the lead in neo-IT like biotechnology, business process outsourcing and information technology enabled services. At least two new companies set up shop in the city every fortnight, hoping to cash in on the city's business-friendly reputation. The city offers the space for large campuses within its precincts, an unaffordable option anywhere else. The daily newspaper's classified section is filled with ads for 'techies' who stand a good chance of landing a job at the many hundreds of IT companies.

The most recent growth has come from the business process outsourcing (BPO) industry. Call centres have sprung up in and around the city, absorbing the thousands of graduates who seek employment every year.

## Ra Ra Bangalore

The IT boom has created an estimated 100,000 jobs. This in turn, has fuelled the city's economy. New stores and malls open every month and quality residential properties are snapped up before the advert is out. According to some reports, Bangalore sold the highest number of Mercedes cars! Not just cars, but big buys like home theatre systems and other top-end durables record higher than expected sales in the city. Fashion shows and new

product launches add to Bangalore's image as a 'happening' city. Even the hotel industry has something to cheer about – the highest per room earning came from a Bangalore hotel!

Bangalore rates high on regular entertainment – pubs, parks, horse racing, golfing, museums, riding schools, game arcades etc dot the city. It's slowly gaining a reputation for the unusual and the unexpected – sky diving, aero sports, modern dance classes, Ashtanga Yoga and so on. If nothing else, the city's many cafes and now tearooms offer a place to just 'sit and chill'. For children, besides the planetarium, there's a sports village and a library cum activity centre that is educative and fun.

Bangalore is ideally located for short breaks into the hills or on the coast. Coorg, BR Hills, Mangalore and Karwar lie within easy reach. Neighbouring Tamil Nadu and Kerala have many exciting spots that are a few hours drive from the city.

## Who's Who

Bangalore's list of who's who makes for interesting reading. It features information technology chiefs, space scientists, actors, playwrights, writers and musicians: NR Narayana Murthy, Azim Premji, Raja Ramanna, Roddam Narasimha, UR Ananthamurthy, Girish Karnad, Mahesh Dattani, Anita Nair and Amit Heri are some of them. It even boasts billionaire sons like Sabeer Bhatia who went to school here!

What gives the city its unique flavour are the contributions of citizens in areas ranging from social work to the arts and public utility. Quietly and with little fuss, public toilets are built, slum kids get a school, lakes

# The Beginnings of Bangalore

The Kempegowda watchtower in Lalbagh Botanical Garden

The earliest reference to Bangalore can be traced to a 9th century Ganga inscription which refers to it as 'Bengaluru'. The present day name 'Bangalore' is believed to be the anglicised version of this ancient name. It appears to have been derived from the tree 'Benga' that once abounded in the region. A popular legend suggests that Benguluru originated from the term 'benda kalu', or boiled beans. Prince Hoysala Ballala was lost and famished during his travels and came across a small hut, the home of an old woman. She offered the hungry prince boiled beans or benda kalu. Ballala christened the land around her, Bendakaluru, after the beans and the name stuck. Over the years it would change from Bengaluru to the more anglicised Bangalore. More theories abound: The words Benda-kadu-uru refer to a burnt forest, implying that a forest was burnt to accommodate the town. Playing yet more with the syntax brings forth Bengallu-uru or granite city!

Kempegowda is credited with the birth of the town Bangalore. A small feudatory of the Vijayanagar empire, Kempegowda built a town enclosed by a fort in 1537 and named it Bengaluru, after the village to which his mother belonged. His son went on to build four watch towers (now within the city) to mark the boundaries of his capital. He stopped at nothing to beautify the city, placing lakes and temples alongside planned residential areas and creating irrigation tanks to water the city.

In 1638 the rulers of Bijapur conquered Bangalore and handed it over to Shahji, Shivaji's father. In 1687, the Mughal Subedar of the Sira province leased out Bangalore to Chikkadevaraja Wodeyar of Mysore. In 1759, Hyder Ali was presented Bangalore as a jagir from Krishnaraja Wodeyar II. He took great pride in his new property and built the Delhi and Mysore Gates, but he is best remembered for Lalbagh Botanical Gardens which he conceptualised and created. Hyder Ali's son Tipu Sultan continued the good work, but on his death in the fourth Mysore war in 1799 the British returned Bangalore and Mysore to Krishnaraja Wodeyar the Third.

In 1809 the British troops moved from Srirangapatna to Halsoorpet (Ulsoor), on land given to them by the Mysore Maharaja. They quickly settled in, laying roads, residential areas and public offices. In 1831, Bangalore became the capital of Mysore state under the commissioner. In 1881, the Maharaja formally handed over the area to the British and it came to be known as the Civil and Military Station of Bangalore. The British Resident governed it.

Shortly after Independence, in 1949, the city of Bangalore and the Cantonment of Bangalore were brought together under the Bangalore City Corporation. Seven years later, the state of Karnataka was born and Bangalore became its capital.

get cleaned up and a hundred other civic problems are tackled. These are the people who give the city its moral quotient, the heroes who make every Bangalorean proud.

## Citizen & State Team Up

In the matter of state and citizen initiative to improve the city, Bangalore has once more shown the way to other metros. The state government has come up with the Bangalore Agenda Task Force (BATF) to improve infrastructure, and the private sector is an equal partner, empowered to work with government agencies to make a real difference to the life of residents. It works together with Janaagraha, a citizens' movement committed to increasing citizen participation in local governance. The result has been some great strides in waste management, Ward Works, where residents of each ward decide how the Bangalore municipality spends the funds allocated to it and PROOF or Public Record of Operations and Finance that aims to increase the level of transparency in state projects.

A 100 per cent people's movement, all of Janaagraha's work is carried out through volunteers, who are associated with one of three volunteer programs – Bala Janaagraha for school students, Yuva Janaagraha for college students and Corporate Janaagraha for corporate volunteers. Janaagraha has 250 associations in its fold, all striving to improve local living conditions. This initiative is now being cited as the way forward for other cities, not just in India, but across Asia as well.

Garbage collection and solid waste management are no longer the headache of only the municipal corporation. Citizens do their bit by separating biodegradable and non-biodegradable waste right at home. Residents join hands to take it further by offering a door-to-door facility for removal, working together with municipal bodies.

Bangalore once had an astounding 262 lakes within city limits. Urbanisation has killed off some, but now there is a movement to rejuvenate them, with the state and citizen's bodies coming together. The government has started a Lake Development Authority to look into Bangalore's water bodies.

Welcome to Bangalore! A big city and growing, but with its heart in the right place!

The Janaagraha team

# Bangalore through the Ages

**1537 -** Kempegowda, a feudal lord, in charge of Yelahanka province, built a mud fort, the first in the city. He also established trading outposts in Balepet, Doddapet, Chikpet and Taragupet within the fort. Five centuries later, they continue to serve as major commercial centres in the city.

His successor and son, Kempegowda II erected four watch towers to mark the boundaries of the city at Halsur (present day Ulsoor), Lalbagh, Kempambudhi Tank at Gavipuram Guttahalli and Vyalikaval.

**1638 -** Bangalore was conquered by Adil Shah, Sultan of Bijapur who leased it to Shahji, the father of Maratha king Shivaji.

**1686 -** The Mughal rulers conquered Sira and Bangalore.

**1689 -** The Mughals leased out Bangalore and Mysore to ruler Chikkadevaraya.

**1759 -** Hyder Ali received Bangalore as a jagir from Krishnaraja Wodeyar II. He fortified the southern fort and made Bangalore an army town.

**1799 -** Following Tipu Sultan's death, the British returned Bangalore to Krishnaraja Wodeyar III.

**1800 -** Bangalore General Post Office opened.

**1809 -** The British Cantonment was established.

**1812 -** St. Mark's Cathedral was built at one end of MG Road.

**1831 -** Alleging misrule by Krishnaraja Wodeyar III, the British took over the administration of Mysore kingdom again. Under their rule, Bangalore became the capital of Mysore State and acquired modern amenities like railways, telegraph and police services and grew into a flourishing administrative centre.

**1864 -** Bangalore was connected by rail to Madras.

**1867 -** The Attara Kacheri was built by Commissioner Bowring.

**1881 -** The British returned Bangalore to the Wodeyars.

**1892 -** Bangalore's first suburbs appeared in Chamrajpet and Sheshadripuram. They were named after Chamarajendra Wodeyar and Dewan Sheshadri Iyer respectively.

**1898 -** The outbreak of plague caused an exodus from central areas, leading to the creation of Basavanagudi and Malleswaram.

**1905 -** Bangalore was the first city in India to boast electric lights on its streets.

**1909 -** The Indian Institute of Science came up.

**1921-1931** The areas of Kalasipalayam and Gandhinagar were marked out.

**1947 -** India attained Independence. A government was formed in Mysore and was headed by KC Reddy.

**1948 -** Jayanagar, the largest residential layout in South Asia was inaugurated.

**1956 -** The States Reorganisation Act was passed. According to the Act, states were formed on linguistic lines. Mysore State (later renamed Karnataka) united the Kannada-speaking areas of the country and Bangalore was made the state capital. S Nijalingappa was the first Chief Minister of Karnataka.

**1954 -** The Vidhana Soudha was built.

**1976 -** The Karnataka State Electronics Development Corporation Limited (Keonics) was established, with the objective of promoting the electronics industry in Karnataka.

**1978 -** Electronics City was laid out.

**1981 -** Software Technology Parks of India (STPI) was established. Infosys set up its first office in Bangalore.

**1987 -** The National Law School of India University came up.

**1994 -** Information Technology Park Limited (ITPL) was incorporated as a company on 13th January 1994

**1999 -** The first flyover was opened in Bangalore from Sirsi Circle to TCM Royan Road.

**2000 -** The Cyber Park Technology Incubation Centre, a first of its kind, was set up to promote the growth of the IT sector.

**2001 -** Reva, India's first electric car was made commercially available.

**2002 -** Bill Gates opened the first Microsoft Software Development Centre outside the US, in Bangalore.

# A Culture of Capaciousness – Ramachandra Guha

Gol Gumbaz, Bijapur

Ramachandra Guha

Writers in Kannada have won seven Jnanpith awards, a record equalled only by one other language, Hindi. But then there are many more speakers of Hindi. And of the seven Kannada awardees, three did not even grow up speaking that language. This DR Bendre's mother tongue was Marathi. Masti Venkateswara Iyengar's first language was Tamil. Girish Karnad spoke Konkani to his parents. And of the four authentically 'Kannadiga' Jnanpith winners, two, VK Gokak and UR Ananthamurthy, were by profession teachers of English. Growing up on the West Coast, Shivarama Karanth most likely heard, and spoke, as much Tulu and Konkani as he did Kannada. Of all the Kannada Jnanpith winners, only the poet KV Puttappa (Kuvempu) spoke the language in the home, in the street, and in the classroom as well.

The culture of Karnataka is a culture of capaciousness. Just as one does not have to be a Hindu to be a proudly patriotic Indian, one does not have to be a speaker of Kannada to count as an honoured resident of Karnataka. Just as Indian nationalism, at its best, was never xenophobic, the best among the Kannadigas have always been open to influences from outside. While open to the world, the resident of Karnataka remains proud of his own culture, lovingly elaborated over the centuries. In the west of the state was developed the still vibrant tradition of dance-drama known as Yakshagana. In the north of the state are some superb Hindu temples, as at Aihole and Pattadakal, some fine illustrations of Islamic architecture, such as the Gol Gumbaz at Bijapur, and, above all, the great medieval city of Hampi. The south of the state can boast of its jewels too, notably the Hoysala temples at Belur, Halebid, and (my own particular favourite) Somnathpur.

In the realms of art and architecture the state of Karnataka can comfortably hold its own. And in terms of natural beauty it is well endowed. It has a staggeringly beautiful coastline, dense tropical forests, and a river (the Kaveri) that literally sings to you as it flows. But then other parts of India are lovely too. What marks out Karnataka is what I have called its culture of capaciousness, the ability, manifested down the ages, to harmoniously incorporate and integrate elements from other parts of India and the world.

This culture survives into the present. Consider thus the village of Heggodu, in Shimoga district, the home of an extraordinary experiment in the creative arts. Years ago, a farmer from Heggodu named KV Subbana went to study in Mysore with the poet Kuvempu. After he graduated he returned home, and started a publishing house named Akshara, which came to publish the best in Kannada writers. Next he started a theatre school, and a repertory company known as 'Ninasam'. Then, with the aid of UR Ananthamurthy, he conceived of an annual cultural workshop, consisting of two weeks of intensive discussion around film, drama, art, literature and politics.

Held in October, now in its twentieth year, the Heggodu workshop is a remarkable exercise in the democratisation of culture. Its participants, chosen through open competition, have included teachers and students, but also carpenters and bricklayers. They come to the village to see films by Ray and Goddard, and discuss books by Fukayama and Said, these introduced by a faculty of eminent critics. Every year, at this workshop, the Ninasam repertory performs three plays. One is an original play in Kannada, another a Kannada translation of a play written in another Indian language, a third, a translation of a play by a Western playwright. Thus one might see, on successive days, plays by P Lankesh, Mohan Rakesh and Anton Chekov. After these plays are premiered in Heggodu, a bus takes the cast on a trip through the state. Ninasam stages about one hundred and fifty performances annually, in towns big and small, and in villages as well.

The work of Ninasam is only the most vivid illustration of the unique capacity of the Kannadiga to creatively link his own milieu to the wider world. No state in India is less chauvinistic. Its open-ness is manifest in its art, its literature, its music and its sport. And in the realm of commerce too. Thus the most successful software entrepreneur in Bangalore is a Gujarati Muslim, Azim Premji. He has made his money in Karnataka and he has spent it in Karnataka, by contributing large amounts to philanthropic causes such as education and health. There is a lesson here for all of us, but perhaps especially for those who live in Azim Premji's home state. It is this – chauvinism literally does not pay.

*Ramachandra Guha is a historian, biographer, and cricket writer. His works include 'Environmentalism: A Global History' and 'A Corner of a Foreign Field', which won the Daily Telegraph/Cricket Society Award for the best cricket book of 2002. Guha has been described in the New York Times as 'perhaps the best among India's non-fiction writers'.*

The Chennakesava temple in Somnathpur is an exquisite example of Hoysala architecture.

# It's Great To Be In Bangalore

... with a little help from

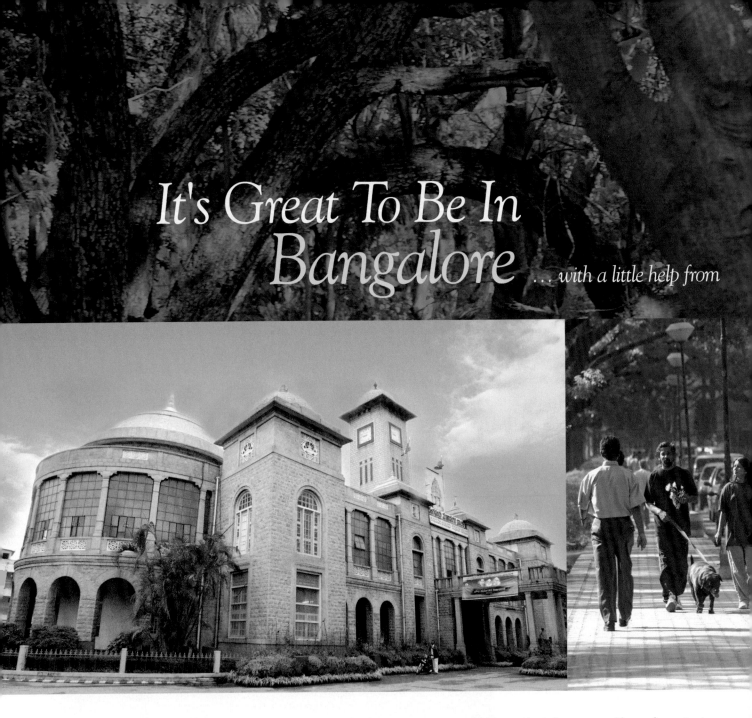

Bangalore is undoubtedly one of India's great cities... and increasingly a 'world city' that attracts tourists, investors and corporates from around the world. Now, a 'world city' needs world-class infrastructure. And that takes a lot of planning, resources and effort.

Bangalore Mahanagara Palike (BMP), the city corporation, is mandated to provide basic amenities and citizen services to a fast-growing Bangalore. That is a demanding task, as the explosive growth of the city creates ever-increasing needs and pressures on civic infrastructure and services.

BMP provides infrastructure like roads, sanitation, primary healthcare, education and recreation. Over 4000 km of roads and 2000 km of storm water drains are maintained. Everyday, over 2000 tonnes of garbage is collected and disposed.

Interestingly, Bangalore Mahanagara Palike has responded to the needs of the city though numerous innovative and creative initiatives, many of which have become models for other city administrations

www.bmponline.org

# Bangalore Mahanagara Palike

**Drinking Water Programmes** are established to provide drinking water and UGD facilities in 27 new wards at an investment of Rs. 113.40 crores, in partially new wards at a cost of Rs. 16.94 crores and in other wards at a cost of Rs. 4.09 crores. In all, Rs. 154 crores is being invested to ensure adequate water supply and underground drainage facility in every ward in Bangalore.

**Aesthetic Bus Shelters** have been set up in 550 locations. The shelters are well-lit and attractively designed, with railings, seating and route maps and is free of vandalism.

**Modern Road Networks** that can accommodate the rapidly growing transportation needs have been laid. BMP has concretized and upgraded most roads and developed sidewalks.

**Citizen-centric Initiatives** that have been launched successfully, include the computerization of birth and death registration and a centralized redressal cell. Self-assessment of property tax has been introduced and the payment of tax has been computerized. Applying for khata has been simplified and centralized. Trade licenses have become easy to obtain through the 'Sarala Partavanagi' Scheme.

**Public-Private Partnerships** that involve prominent citizens, corporate houses and private institutions in the activities of civic governance and development of amenities have resulted in successful initiatives such as the Bangalore Agenda Task Force (BATF).

**Reforming Accounting Systems** has led to greater transparency and accountability. BMP's Fund Based Accounting System (FBAS) is the first of its kind in the country and has enabled BMP to become the first civic body in India to have produced and publicly presented annual balance sheets of the corporation.

Traffic junctions, flyovers and underpasses in high-traffic areas have been constructed. Grade Separators are being developed at a cost of Rs. 50.96 crores.

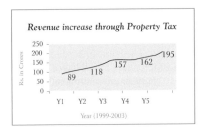

*Revenue increase through Property Tax*

Rs. in Crores

250
200
150
100
50
0

89  118  157  162  195

Y1  Y2  Y3  Y4  Y5

Year (1999-2003)

A subway is being constructed at Sujatha Talkies at a cost of Rs. 75 lakhs. Road Over Bridges are coming up at Lingapura at a cost of Rs. 15 crores, at Banaswadi at a cost of Rs. 8 crores and Road Under Bridges at Madhavanagar at a cost of Rs. 2.19 crores and at Cantonment Railway Station at a cost of Rs. 2.20 crores. A Rs 8.00 crore flyover is coming up at National College. About 1000 km of roads are being asphalted in Bangalore City at a total investment of Rs. 105.78 crores.

Over 270 km of footpath are also being developed. In fact, BMP is the first to develop a 'Pavement Condition Index' to aid road maintenance.

*Nirmala Bangalore* is an ambitious project that will contribute to higher levels of sanitation in Bangalore. These pay-and-use toilets that were initially launched with private funding from Mrs. Sudha Murty have been adopted by BMP and over 100 Nirmala pay-and-use toilet facilities are coming up in select areas.

*City Beautification* has been taken up proactively by BMP, beginning with the restoration of Bangalore's lakes and the development of parks in each neighbourhood. Sankey Tank, Yediyur Lake and Ulsoor Lake have been destilted and are today picturesque spots that are the pride of Bangalore. Byrasandra Tank is being restored at an investment of Rs. 1.20 crores.

A park has been developed in each ward. An 'Adopt A Park' Scheme has been created and the maintenance of these parks has been handed over to private entrepreneurs. The MN Krishna Rau Park, a heritage park in Basavangudi, Tavarekere Park, JP Park and Deer Park have been spruced up and opened to the public.

*Pay & Park Facilities* are helping decongest the city in a planned manner, and provide safe and secure parking. Several multi-level automated car parks have been planned as joint ventures.

*Clean Neighbourhoods* with 'Swachha Bangalore' is a BMP-BATF initiative that involves door-to-door collection of waste, rationalization of bins, minimal handling of wastes… all with active citizens' participation. Private businesses help with infrastructure, clearing of debris and night-cleaning in commercial areas. The 'Suchi Mitra' Scheme is also being undertaken successfully with citizen volunteers.

| Initiative | Investment in lakhs (Rs.) | Initiative | Investment in lakhs (Rs.) |
|---|---|---|---|
| Grade Separator at Rajajinagar | 1440 | RUB at Cantonment | 220 |
| Construction of subway near Sujatha Talkies | 75 | ROB at Lingarajapura | 1500 |
| Modi Road, Chord Road Grade | 1500 | ROB at Banaswadi | 800 |
| Construction of SWD in Hebbal Valley from Mathikere Main Road upto New BEL Road | 199 | Asphalting of 1000 km of roads | 10578 |
| Construction of Parking-cum-Commercial Complex at KG Road | 900 | Drinking water supply and UGD facilities in | |
| Construction of flyover at National College | 800 | a) 27 new wards | 11340.00 |
| | | b) Partially new wards | 1694.00 |
| Restoration of Byrasandra Tank | 120 | c) Missing bits in various wards | 409.00 |
| RUB at Madhavanagar | 218.75 | Providing basic amenities to slums under Vambay Scheme (9 works) | 384.98 |

## Freedom Park
### CENTRAL JAIL REDEVELOPMENT COMPETITION

A 'Freedom Park' is being developed on land that formerly housed the Central Jail. Set in 20 acres of land, this BMP-BATF initiative will be an iconic landmark of Bangalore.

BMP has also actively initiated a variety of programmes to provide good education, health and sanitation facilities in the poorer areas of the city.

Truly, for most Bangaloreans there is no place they would rather be in than Bangalore; and BMP has played its part in contributing to the beauty and conveniences of this wonderful city. Indeed, *'It's Great To Be In Bangalore'* as BMP's advertising line says.

India's City Of The Future, managed by

**Bangalore Mahanagara Palike**

*Citizens First. Always.*

Headquarters of software giant Infosys, one of the pioneers of India's IT revolution.

**Business**

Chikpet is one of Bangalore's oldest business districts where jewellers, cloth merchants, wholesale traders and pawnbrokers sit crammed together. Crowded lanes bustle with shoppers looking for a good deal on just about anything, from silk saris to second hand books.

Bangalore is the floriculture capital of the country, accounting for almost 70 per cent of India's total flower exports. Red roses, gladioli, anthurium and gerbera are grown across the state. The International Flower Auction Bangalore (IFAB), a state-of-the-art flower auction centre is planned.

From fixing computers to solving credit card problems, Bangalore's call centres have a say around the world. The job demands 24/7 work hours, learning to speak in a variety of accents and servicing global customers. The business process outsourcing (BPO) industry is growing at a fast clip and Bangalore is a forerunner.

The International Technology Park
at Whitefield, Bangalore

# Business

The next time you drink a cup of coffee, use a computer, log on to your bank's online service or dress up in your best silk, think Karnataka! These products and services were most likely produced or developed here. **Karnataka** is **Asia's El Dorado** – the land of opportunity and promise. Its riches are widespread – it contributes 70 per cent of India's **silk** and **coffee**, 20 per cent of electronic **hardware** and 35 per cent of **software exports**.

**Rich** in **natural resources** and **human talent**, Karnataka attracts the **third largest amount** of foreign and domestic direct **investment** in India: In 2003-04, the state received nearly Rs 4,000 crores in investment – a figure that has trebled in just two years, supporting the fact that Karnataka is the **darling of investors.** It is the most favoured destination not just for information technology, but engineering, electronics, automobiles, readymade garments and textiles, food processing and biotechnology among others.

The state plans to achieve an **industrial growth** of 10 to 12 per cent and has instituted a number of projects and policies in line with this. An IT corridor in Bangalore, a new international airport and a keen eye on infrastructure and civic amenities has ensured that the state capital keeps its place in the top ranking cities not just in India but around the world.

Karnataka is more than Bangalore city. Recognising the **latent** power of the state's other major towns, the government is pushing ahead with projects for Mysore, Hubli and others. **Mysore**, for one, boasts the presence of over **40 IT companies** including big names like Infosys and Wipro. IBM has signed an MoU with the state government to establish a Linux software development centre in **Hubli**. The city's huge engineering base – 5,000 students graduate in this discipline every year – makes it an ideal spot for IT related industries. The regions of **Dakshina Kannada**, **Udupi** and **Uttara Kannada** will each become Coastal Special Economic Zones. And an Export Promotion Park at **Mangalore** will ensure that this large coastal town is not forgotten in the IT race.

Agro food processing is a big industry and the state's abundant agricultural produce is a major revenue earner. To focus on this sector **Agro Foods Technology Parks** have been planned in Bagalkot, Belgaum, Dharwad, Chitradurga, Jewargi, Mallur and Maddur.

## Bangalore – Capital Gains

The **heart** of Karnataka's thriving economic and industrial world is Bangalore. It is the hub of **leading technology** companies. Most of what makes your life easier, from computer chips to banking software to detergent enzymes is developed in the city. It's rated as one of the top ten tech cities in the world! German publication Diezet called Bangalore '**City of the Future**', while Shenzhen, a town in China is advertising itself as '**China's Bangalore!**"

At least three companies set up operations in the state every fortnight, and foreign equity is pouring in. It's not just software services that have benefited but

IT enabled services and business processing as well. In fact the latter has seen growth of a whopping 275 per cent!

After India's independence, Bangalore was chosen as the base for a large number of **public sector units** (PSUs) that provided thousands of jobs to people from all over the country. The major PSUs based in Bangalore include watchmaker HMT, telecom giant ITI, Bharat Electronics Ltd., Bharat Earth Movers Ltd., Bharat Heavy Electronics Ltd., the Centre for Airborne Systems, the Aeronautical Development Agency and the Wheel and Axle Plant. The presence of so many technology-driven, research-based agencies gave Karnataka an early start in the hi-tech race. Seeing the success of information technology companies, other corporates were encouraged to join the scene.

Bangalore is a **world-class metro** that offers the best facilities comparable to any of its Asian counterparts. It's also the **fastest growing city** in south India with by far the highest concentration of hi-tech companies based here. All the **big brands** in any industry from information technology to textiles are based here. From Tommy Hilfiger to Microsoft to Levi Strauss to

Toyota – Bangalore is their address. An investment-friendly approach to industry has meant that a number of **multinational companies** have set up base in the state. These include IT majors IBM, Microsoft, Texas Instruments, Oracle, Novell, Sun Microsystems and Intel to apparel majors like Levi Strauss, Tommy Hilfiger and Allen Solly, to biotech companies like the US-based Alltech Biotechnology.

## Aerospace Capital

Aircraft design, **development** and **manufacture** along with national-level **space research**, form a major backdrop to Bangalore's image as a technology hub. **Hindustan Aeronautics, National Aerospace Laboratories, Indian Space Research Organisation** and the **Aeronautical Development Agency** are some of India's foremost aerospace institutions, based in Bangalore. Karnataka has nearly 100 engineering colleges and another 100 R&D institutions which act as feeders into these industries. And the Indian Institute of Science, the only one of its kind in India, is a major landmark.

Hindustan Aeronautics Limited (HAL) makes aircraft for the Indian Air Force and is the country's first

# Air Power

Hindustan Aeronautics Ltd. or HAL, is one of Asia's largest aeronautics company. Bangalore's hi-tech status owes a lot to the fact that HAL is headquartered here. Started as a joint venture between industrialist Walchand Hirachand and the Mysore government to make aircrafts under license, HAL today supplies a large chunk of the Indian Air Force's demand for aircraft, parts and services.

Initially known as Hindustan Aircraft Ltd., the company had a tie-up with the US-based Inter Continental Aircraft Company to make the Harlow trainer, Curtiss Hawk fighter and Vultee attack bomber. In the year 1941 the first flight of a Harlow trainer took place followed by the flight of India's first indigenous effort, a ten-seater glider designed by Dr. VM Ghatage. After World War II, the Indian government took over HAL, rechristening it Hindustan Aeronautics Ltd.

The company's successes include the design, development and manufacture of the Light Combat Aircraft (LCA) that recently flew successfully in Bangalore. HAL's other projects include the Advanced Light Helicopter and the Intermediate Jet Trainer. The company makes 20 types of aircraft including the MiG fighter aircraft, the Surya Kirans, Pushpak, Avro and Dornier airplanes. Eleven of these are of indigenous design. So far HAL has manufactured over 3,000 aircrafts and 600 helicopters.

aircraft manufacturing company. Initially a private company set up in the early 40s, HAL was taken over by the government after Independence. It makes a range of aircraft including the **Surya Kirans** and the **MiG** fighters. Its most recent launch has been the Light Combat Aircraft, designed and developed by HAL. Meanwhile, the National Aerospace Laboratories (NAL) has made Asia's first locally developed and designed 18-seater commercial aircraft, the **Saras**. NAL has already designed and developed a two-seater civilian trainer aircraft, the **Hansa** and is on its way to developing a four-seater variant.

Bangalore is also home to India's space research industry. The Indian Space Research Organization (ISRO) is headquartered here and is at the helm of the country's space technology industry. ISRO has launched a number of space systems that have helped India's communication, broadcasting and meteorological services. Its most recent launch was India's exclusive communication satellite **INSAT-3E** in September 2003.

Other national-level bodies in aerospace are the Aeronautical Development Agency (ADA), Aeronautical Development Establishment (ADE), Centre for Airborne Systems (CABS) and the Gas Turbine Research Establishment. Indian Air Force units like the Training Command, Air Force Technical College and Aircraft Systems Testing Establishment (ASTE) are also based here.

Reva, India's first electric car is manufactured in Bangalore.

## Business in Brief

 With successful initiatives in drug discovery, clinical development, bioprocessing and global marketing, Biocon is an integrated biotechnology enterprise focused on the development of biopharmaceuticals. A scientific knowledge pool, proprietary technologies and world-class facilities power the research and manufacture of high value biopharmaceuticals ranging from small molecules to biologicals and dosage forms – products and solutions used in over 50 countries. Biocon also is the first enzyme company globally to receive the ISO 9001 accreditation for their expertise in manufacturing and marketing a broad range of industrial enzymes, food additives and process aids. Headed by Dr. Kiran Mazumdar-Shaw, Biocon is biotech's Infosys and is rated among the top five pharma-stocks ranking alongside biggies like Ranbaxy, Dr Reddy's, Cipla and Sun. Educated in Bangalore and Australia, Mazumdar-Shaw started Biocon in 1978 in collaboration with an Irish firm.

 Karnataka's pre-eminent position as an industrial and commercial hub is reflected in the number of banks that have sprung up in the state over the past 100 years. These include public sector banks like Canara Bank, Corporation Bank, Syndicate Bank and Vijaya Bank – which are all nationalised. And then there is Vysya Bank – now known as ING Vysya, it is one of the largest private banks in the country. Karnataka received the third largest amount of foreign direct investment in 2003 with over Rs 1,300 crores coming in from overseas investors.

 The Himalaya Drug Company, is one of the country's leading Ayurvedic pharmaceutical and personal care products maker. Headquartered in Bangalore, Himalaya's most well known brand is Liv.52, a medicine used to improve the working of the liver. In 1999, the company launched its Himalaya Herbal Healthcare range of natural personal care products.

# Night Birds

Customers around the world call their service agency for help all the time. But as Bangalore's role in business process outsourcing (BPO) grows, callers for services as varied as car maintenance and telebanking will be answered by someone right here in one of Karnataka's numerous call centres.

One of the fastest growing segments in the software services industry is BPO and information technology-enabled services or ITES. While software exports grew by 26 per cent in 2002-2003, the BPO-ITES segment witnessed a jump of nearly 60 per cent. And Karnataka, which is the country's IT hub, saw the BPO-ITES sector grow by nearly 300 per cent during the same period.

Currently, BPO-ITES accounts for nearly Rs 1,000 crore of the state's total IT exports of almost Rs 14,000 crores. In 2002, 41 new BPO companies set up shop in Karnataka. The state IT department is working with industry bodies and consultancy firms to chalk out a strategy to improve Karnataka's position in the BPO-ITES industry. This is expected to create one million jobs in the sector by the year 2010. The state's large pool of qualified manpower makes Karnataka an ideal location. The state government was one of the first in the country to implement an entrance test developed by the Board for Information Technology Education Standards that evaluates the communication, accent, clarity and other skills of BPO employees. Laws that prohibit women working night-shifts have also been removed. The Karnataka state government is promoting Mangalore, Udupi, Mysore, Gulbarga and Hubli as BPO centres. The IT corridor in Bangalore, which stretches from Whitefield to Electronics City will open up 8,000 hectares of land for them to set up shop.

Some of the big BPO-ITES players in the state include 24x7 Customer.com, Convergys, ICICI oneSource, iSeva, Progeon, iGate, HCL Technologies BPO Service and Hinduja TMT Ltd.

## IT Dream Run

Bangalore is India's biggest earner in terms of IT exports. The groundwork for this achievement was laid in 1997 when the state government launched an IT Policy, the very first in the country. Today, the capital city of Bangalore is home to over a 1,000 software firms and nearly 50 hardware firms, exports nearly $3 billion worth of software services and nearly half a billion dollars worth of hardware. Other cities and towns in Karnataka like Mysore, Hubli and Dharwad are being developed as alternate centres of growth and by the year 2008, Karnataka's IT exports are expected to touch $10 billion.

The city is home to nearly 50 business process outsourcing (BPO) firms and there are plans to ramp up BPO operations from the current Rs 1,000 crore per annum. The IT industry employs over 1,00,000 people. Apart from highly skilled software and hardware engineers, people from all walks of life are enjoying the benefits of the IT boom. The BPO industry hires people with varied backgrounds. Young 18-year old students and 50-year old housewives have found lucrative employment in call centres around Bangalore.

Some big international names in the IT sector that have set up shop in Bangalore include Dell Computers, IBM, Texas Instruments, Intel, Sun, Oracle, Motorola, Microsoft, Lucent, Novell, Compaq and HP. And of course, India's two biggest IT success stories, Wipro and Infosys, are based in Bangalore. Intel is investing nearly Rs 200 crore in a chip design and development facility in the city. More such investments are expected in the future.

The state has many **technology parks** spread over the state to accommodate and nurture IT and IT enabled services. **Electronics City** in Bangalore was the first park of its size to come up anywhere in India and many big names that started there have multiplied their businesses. The **International Technology Park Ltd.** (ITPL) emerged as the pin-up park for the industry. It is now the swank address of some high profile international names. The state government has been quick to address the growing need for space of the IT industry and has created an IT corridor, stretching from Electronics City to ITPL.

Customer First, a BPO in the city

## Business in Brief

 The 100-year old **Amalgamated Bean Coffee** (ABC) set up the first cyber café in Bangalore in the mid-90s. The company, headed by VG Siddhartha, now has over 100 Café Coffee Day outlets across the country, a popular hangout for young people. ABC plans to open another 300 Café Coffee Day outlets across the country over the next few years and increase turnover to Rs 500 crore by the year 2006.

Karnataka wins hands down as the country's largest producer of **coffee**: of the 2,75,000 tonnes of coffee that India produces annually, **200,000** tonnes come from Karnataka. Legend has it that a Muslim pilgrim from India, Baba Budan, smuggled coffee beans from Mecca to India in the 17th century. He landed in Karnataka and planted the beans on his plantations in Chikmagalur district, the wet, green hills of the Western Ghats. That was the first coffee plantation on Indian soil and its subsequent success encouraged others to start coffee cultivation along the Western Ghats, in the Coorg and Chikmagalur regions.

Karnataka plans to attract **Rs 10,000** crores into the **food processing industry** over the next 10 years. Several international food companies are located in the state. These include Nestlè, Unilever, Global Green, Danone, Wrigleys, Heinz, PepsiCo, Coca Cola and Nissin.

The state government plans to float a joint venture company called Food Karnataka Ltd. to help develop markets for processed food both in local as well as international markets. **Six food technology parks** will be set up over the next five years at Mallur, Bagalkot, Belgaum, Maddur, Jewargi and Chitradurga. The state also plans to set up an agri-export zone in the state to sell Karnataka's produce abroad.

# 3.5 LAKH SQ. FT. OF INTELLIGENT IT SPACE IN THE COCHIN SPECIAL ECONOMIC ZONE

Technopolis, Kerala's first private IT park. Unmatched operational freedom, infrastructure and cost advantages. Making it the perfect destination for IT entrepreneurs and global players looking to expand. all +91 98470 01211 today, to become part of an intelligent revolution.

**Connectivity:** SEA-ME-WE-3 and SAFE submarine cable landings ▮ 15GBps bandwidth with least latency ▮ VSNL gateway in the zone through forty-six core fibre cables

**Infrastructure:** 3.5 lakh sq. ft. of intelligent space ▮ Among the top two ITES destinations in the country (NASSCOM "Super Nine" ITES destinations) ▮ One of the top destinations for hardware in India (MAIT rating)

**Autonomy:** Located in Cochin Special Economic Zone (CSEZ) a special enclave run directly by the Government of India ▮ Ten-year Corporate Income Tax exemption ▮ Exemption from Service Tax ▮ On-site customs facilitation ▮ Single Window Clearance Board

**Location:** Located along Seaport-Airport Highway ▮ Just 23 kms away from the Cochin International Airport and 12 kms from International Seaport

## Technopolis
### A Muthoot Pappachan IT Park
www.muthootechnopolis.com

Completion date: June 2005

Designed by Jurong Infrastructure (India) Ltd.          Promoted by The Muthoot Pappachan Group

## Biotech – The New IT

Karnataka's hi-tech reputation doesn't end with IT. The state is a pioneer in **biotechnology** as well. The Mysore-based Central Food Technologies Research Institute (CFTRI), has played an important role in shaping the country's development of food technology. Its most recent success has been to create bio-sensors that help the industry improve standards. CFTRI's achievements are now joined by Karnataka's biotech force. **Bangalore** has emerged as a **leader** in the **Indian biotech** field with over 85 companies headquartered here who employ over 8,000 people. These firms contribute over Rs 1,400 crore in turnover every year. The country's largest biotech firm, **Biocon**, and the third largest biotech company, **Wipro Health Sciences**, are based here. Bio-pharma, therapeutics and bio-industrial products like enzymes are being developed here.

Similarly, companies like **Avestha Gengraine Technologies Pvt. Ltd.**, are at the cutting edge of genetically modified rice and other plant-related research. While a lot of biotech is aimed at the pharmaceutical and agricultural industries, enzymes used for washing, food processing and leather tanning are equally important.

Biotech is being touted as the **new IT** and taking cognisance of this, Karnataka has drafted a biotech policy. A biotech corridor is also being developed on similar lines as the IT corridor. By the year 2005, the **Biotech Park** on Hosur Road, named **Bangalore Helix**, will come up at a cost of Rs 60 crore.

# Biocon

Biocon, India's largest biotech company is a fully integrated biotechnology enterprise focused on biopharmaceuticals, clinical research and enzymes. In business since 1978, Biocon's enzymes are exported to international markets and used in baking products, fruit juice, wine, grain processing, textile, pulp and paper industries. Started by India's biotech queen, Kiran Mazumdar-Shaw, this multibillion-rupee company has diversified from the manufacture of enzymes to drugs. Statins, Biocon's flagship product, has aided the company's foray into drug manufacture. Biocon also manufactures immunosuppressants, insulin and drugs to help fight cancer, heart disease and renal failure. The company has a state-of-the-art manufacturing base in Bangalore. Syngene, a subsidiary of Biocon provides customised R&D services to the pharmaceutical and biotechnology sectors. Clinigene, another Biocon subsidiary, aids biotechnology and pharmaceutical majors in drug development. Biocon also works closely with the Karnataka state government in helping boost the biotech industry in the state.
**Web** www.biocon.com

Kiran Mazumdar-Shaw

Courtesy: Pallon Daruwala

## Kiran Mazumdar-Shaw

Born and brought up in Bangalore, Kiran Mazumdar-Shaw is one of the city's most prominent business people. As Chairman and Managing Director of India's first and largest biotech company, Biocon Ltd., Mazumdar-Shaw is known for her tireless promotion of biotechnology in the country and acknowledged as the catalyst behind Bangalore's emergence as a bio-hub. Educated in Bangalore and Australia, Mazumdar-Shaw started Biocon in 1978 in collaboration with an Irish firm. Her efforts have led to Biocon's transition from an enzyme company to an integrated biopharmaceutical. Her role as chairperson of Karnataka's Vision Group on Biotechnology has helped the state draw up its policy on the biotech industry.
Shaw is respected not only for her business achievements but also her unstinting support to improve civic amenities and services. Her book on the brewing families of the world was well received.

A Café Coffee Day outlet at The Forum.

## Manufacturing Destination

It's not only hi-tech industries that enjoy the benefits of Karnataka's investment-friendly approach, but manufacturing companies too are making a beeline for the state. For example, the **TVS group**, which has a motorbike manufacturing unit in Mysore, is setting up a second plant to make two, three and four-wheelers with an investment of Rs 500 crore. **Volvo** has a unit to make trucks and buses just outside the Bangalore, and so does **Toyota Kirloskar**. India's first electric car, the **Reva**, was designed and produced right here by the Bangalore-based **Maini Group**. Not just automobiles, but even major watch manufacturers who have set the country on time, have their headquarters and factories in and around the state capital.

# Complete Wealthcare

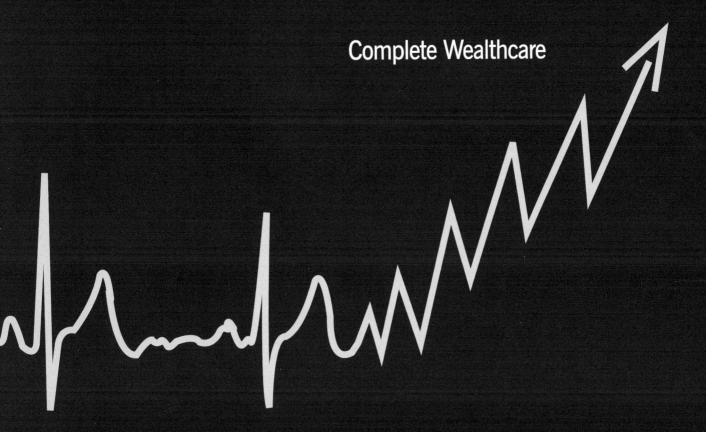

The most professional healthcare for your wealth. Wealth Solutions.

• Liability Management • Debt Syndication • Private Equity Placement

• M&A Advisory • Business Consulting • Investment Advisory • Wealth Management • Risk Management

Karnataka is renowned for its sandalwood products.

## Naturally Karnataka

Karnataka's natural resources include its aromatic, **high quality coffee** and **sandalwood**. The state produces two-thirds of the country's coffee in the salubrious Coorg and Chikmagalur districts. Legend has it that a Muslim pilgrim from India, Baba Budan, smuggled coffee beans from Mecca to India in the 17th century. He landed in Karnataka and planted the beans on his plantations in Chikmagalur district, on the green hills of the Western Ghats. That was the first coffee estate on Indian soil. Karnataka accounts for the bulk of coffee produced in the country. Out of the 2,75,000 tonnes of coffee produced in India, Karnataka produces nearly 200,000 tonnes. The **Coffee Board** helps planters market coffee around the world. As a leading producer of coffee, Karnataka is home to a number of coffee brands that source beans from the state. It has also witnessed the growth of the country's premier retail coffee chain – Café Coffee Day – owned by Amalgamated Bean Coffee Limited (ABCL).

Karnataka is famous for its **silk industry**. The state produces nearly **10,000 metric tonnes** of silk annually. Historically, Mysore silk, as the state's silk is known, has enjoyed a premium in the world market. The **Silk Board**, established in 1954, helps silk growers and weavers keep abreast with the latest technology.

The state is also home to over a **1,000 garment manufacturing units**. Karnataka is a major producer of **cotton** – nearly 2,00,000 tonnes of cotton annually. Many leading apparel manufacturers have set up shop in the state. These include Tommy Hilfiger, Levi Strauss, Arrow, Allen Solly and Lacoste. In 2001, **garment exports** touched nearly **$1 billion**. The state government has been trying to encourage the industry by setting up **apparel parks** that offer all facilities needed to start a garment unit.

And last but not least, **sandalwood** is **synonymous** with Karnataka. Sandalwood was one of the catalysts of the state's industrialisation programme. In the early 1900s, the Sandal Oil Factory was set up to add value to the sandalwood trade. Later, the Mysore Soaps and Detergents Limited produced the world famous Mysore Sandal soaps, popular even today.

*To turn the pressures of life down, turn to page 417.*

WEEKEND VITALISERS
IN GOD'S OWN COUNTRY

To turn the pressures of life down, turn to page 417.

## Business in Brief

Karnataka is famous for its **grapes, mangoes, pomegranates, gherkins, limes** and the **Bangalore rose onion**.

Karnataka has one major port, the **New Mangalore Port** – the nineth largest port in the country – and nine other minor ports at **Karwar, Bellikeri, Tadri, Honavar, Bhatkal, Malpe, Old Mangalore, Hagarakatta** and **Kundapura**. The New Mangalore Port handles nearly 35 million tonnes of cargo – mainly iron ore, crude oil, steel products and coal.

 Most of the **silk** produced in India is made in Karnataka. The state produces nearly **10,000 metric tonnes** of silk every year.

Karnataka is home to over a **1,000 garment manufacturing units**, and is a major producer of cotton with nearly **2,00,000 tonnes** grown annually. Many leading apparel manufacturers have set up shop in the state. These include Tommy Hilfiger, Levi Strauss, Arrow, Allen Solly and Lacoste. In 2001, garment exports touched nearly $1 billion.

The state government has set up apparel parks to encourage the industry.

 The Karnataka government's initiative in information technology began in the 90s when it formulated an IT policy. Bangalore was the first city to set up a **satellite earth station** offering high-speed communication links. This came as a boon to software exporters who needed dependable communication lines to run their businesses.
To help boost IT in the state, the Karnataka government encouraged a number of **IT parks** to come up in and around Bangalore. Software

# MetLife India

Headquartered in Bangalore, MetLife India is the largest life insurer in North America, servicing more than 12 million individuals with $2.5 trillion of life insurance in force. MetLife is headquartered in New York and operates in 11 countries, across the Americas and Asia.

MetLife India Insurance is a joint venture between MetLife International Holdings Inc, The Jammu and Kashmir Bank, M Pallonji Pvt. Ltd. and other private investors. It made its formal entry in India in 2001 and is headquartered in Bangalore with offices in 12 cities: Mumbai, Delhi, Kolkata, Chennai, Bangalore, Hyderabad, Kochi, Trivandrum, Thrissur, Coimbatore, Jammu and Srinagar. MetLife's distribution partners have taken it further to over thousand locations across the country.

MetLife aims to empower people to feel protected, guided and hopeful about their lives with financial freedom for all. Corporate values emphasise innovation, integrity, fairness and financial prudence. MetLife believes that the Indian customer is discerning, informed and exacting. It gets potential customers to ask questions about how life insurance can realise their personal long term goals and improve the quality of life. The accumulation and protection of wealth and creation of a legacy for the customer's family are equally important. Insurance at MetLife India is designed to protect members and their wealth in accordance with their special needs.

In addition to its portfolio of financial products and services, MetLife India is also associated with Snoopy, one of the world's best loved cartoon characters. Snoopy and the other Peanuts characters created by Charles M Schulz have been associated with MetLife since 1985. Snoopy is today recognised as MetLife's ambassador and is licensed for use by MetLife India.

*Web* www.metlifeindia.com

## Karnataka's History of Corporate Excellence

Karnataka has always enjoyed a pre-eminent position among other states. Called Mysore State, it was rechristened Karnataka on November 1st 1973. Famed for its abundant resources, the land was rich with **sandalwood, teak, rosewood, rice** and **coffee**. Water resources were ample, helping the kingdom's agrarian economy to flourish. The prosperity of Mysore ensured that its cultural and academic institutions received valuable patronage from its rulers – the **Wodeyars**. The Wodeyar dynasty ensured that the state was at the forefront of industrial development in the subcontinent. In June 1902, India's **first hydroelectric power plant** at the **Shivasamudram** Falls on the Cauvery river, 25 kilometres from Mysore, was opened. Christened the Kaveri Electric Power Scheme, it received 100 per cent backing from the Maharani-Regent, Kempananjammanni Avaru and the then Dewan, Sir K Seshadri Iyer.

The industrialisation of Mysore was kick-started under the rule of HH Krishnaraja Wodeyar IV at the turn of the 20th century. He appointed **Sir M Visveswaraya**, known as the **father of industrialisation** in Karnataka, as Dewan of Mysore. During Visveswaraya's tenure from 1912 to 1918, Mysore made the big shift from an agricultural to an industrial economy. Sir M Visveswaraya founded the Mysore Bank, the Chamarajendra Technical Institute, the Mechanical Engineering School and the Agricultural University. He believed that a sound educational policy would put Mysore state on the right track to development. Today, the result is there for all to see. Most companies, especially hi-tech ones, look to Karnataka as a source of highly educated manpower. For example, the **Jayachamrajendra College in Mysore** has one of the best computer engineering courses in the country. Similarly HH Krishnaraja Wodeyar IV, donated a large expanse of land for a science institute – what is today the **Indian Institute of Science**, it has produced some of India's finest scientists and scientific research. This early nurturing laid the foundation for a strong and vital workforce, which gave the state a head start in hi-tech fields like aerospace, engineering, information technology and biotechnology.

## Sir M Visveswaraya

Mokshagundam Visveswaraya is known as the father of industrialisation in Karnataka. His most famous line, 'industrialise or perish', helped the erstwhile princely state of Mysore become an industrial powerhouse in the early 20th century. Born on August 28 1860, Sir Visveswaraya became Dewan of Mysore State under the rule of HH Krishnaraja Wodeyar IV in the years 1912 to 1918. Under his initiative, Mysore's economy made the big shift from an agricultural to an industrial economy.

What set Visveswaraya on the fast track to industrialisation was a commodity – albeit a valuable one – sandalwood. The Dewan was worried about the price vagaries of sandalwood in the post-World War I market. Sandalwood was one of Mysore's biggest money spinners. After forming a Chamber of Commerce in Mysore in 1915, to tackle such issues, Visveswaraya went on to start the Sandal Oil Factory in Bangalore in May 1916 and another one in Mysore the following year.

The success of sandalwood oil produced by the Sandal Oil Factory, which was used in soaps and perfumes, gave the impetus to set up other industries that would exploit Mysore's natural resources.

Sir M Visveswaraya also founded the Mysore Bank, the Chamarajendra Technical Institute, the Mechanical Engineering School and the Agricultural University. He believed that churning out professionals, would help Mysore's development. Today, the result is there for all to see. Most companies, especially hi-tech ones, look to Karnataka as a source of highly educated manpower.

Known as much for his astuteness as his strictly disciplined personal life, Sir Visveswaraya passed away in April 1962 at the age of 102.

# Youthful.
# Enthusiastic.
# Energetic.

# And, did we mention,
# 136 years old?

The MetLife family of companies, with its 136* year-old history, has transformed the lives of 40 million people around the globe. With unlimited optimism and enthusiasm, as well as the energy of an 18-year old. And, of course, financial solutions that turned dreams worth US$ 2.4 trillion** in policies into reality.

Now, MetLife India is here to help you secure your financial freedom through its life insurance solutions.

So, you can enjoy the wisdom of age along with the optimism of youth.

To know more, call Toll Free: 1-600-44-6969 (9 am-6 pm, Mon-Fri) or visit us at www.metlifeindia.com

**have you met life today?**

# Wipro

Few are aware of the fact that Santoor sandalwood soap, Sunflower cooking oil, a range of infant products and light bulbs are made by the same company that is also one of the world's largest IT majors – Wipro. In the early 80s Wipro diversified into information technology and set up an IT base in Bangalore. Ever since, the group, founded in 1945, with interests in consumer care, lighting, engineering and healthcare products, has grown from strength to strength.

The multi-billion rupee Wipro, has its corporate office on a sprawling campus on Sarjapur Road.

Headed by Azim Premji, who is regularly on the world's richest men lists, Wipro is the first IT company in the world to get the SEI CMM Level 3 certification. It is also the world's first PCMM Level 5 company. Wipro Ltd. is also listed on the New York Stock Exchange.

Wipro was ranked the seventh best software services company by Business Week in 2002. It has 30 offices worldwide and nearly 20,000 employees. Its customer base stretches across the United States, Europe and Japan. **Web** www.wipro.com

## Azim Hasham Premji

India's richest man with an estimated worth of $6.7 billion, Azim Hasham Premji, chairman of Wipro Corporation, is probably the most humble man on the Forbes's 100 list of the richest people in the world. An alumnus of Stanford University, Premji joined Wipro at the age of 21 in 1966, after his father suddenly passed away. He went on to transform a Rs 70 million company making hydrogenated cooking oil to a corporation with a turnover of over a billion dollars. With interests in technology, consumer products and services and an impressive client list, Wipro is today one of the top 10 Indian companies in terms of market capitalisation and is considered one of the best run in the country.

Premji focuses on building the company through investing in the people who work for him. Personally, Premji lives a simple life, known for his business acumen as well as his personal integrity around the world.

Courtesy: Wipro

## Business in Brief

Software technology parks were set up in Mysore, Manipal, Mangalore and Hubli. One of the first was the Software Technology Parks of India or STPI, a national body, which set up a software park at **Electronics City** in Bangalore. This offered space, communication lines and consultancy services to companies starting up operations.

By the late 90s, the demand for exclusive software hubs was drying out commercial space within the city. In August 2000 the Cyber Park Technology Incubation Centre, a first of its kind, was set up in Bangalore to promote IT units around Karnataka. The state government has also formulated an Information Technology policy to encourage further investment in this sector.

Projects like the **International Technology Park** (ITPL) in Whitefield, Bangalore, gave the industry a new address and helped meet growing demand. Home to nearly 100 companies, the ITPL offers world-class infrastructure and services. Built around the plug and play concept, companies can move in and be assured of adequate power, communication lines, a building management system and help in setting up shop in a new city.

Karnataka has over **80 private IT parks** – with the offer to start business with the minimum hassle. The government now proposes to set up an **IT corridor** between ITPL and Electronics City in Bangalore. Plans are also underway to develop high-speed data communication links at other centres in the state.

Karnataka hopes to export $10 billion worth of software by 2008. There are over 1,000 software firms in the state employing more than 1,00,000 people.

GO BEYOND...

# W O R K + L I V E + P L A Y

Armed with the most strategic locales, sound financial strength and access to the most mission critical building technologies; DivyaSree handles the complete life-cycle of a project and maintains its competitive edge in providing the next level of facility standards.

Your work place environment is more than a sum of its parts. Studies have revealed that well designed offices result in higher employee morale, leading to superior performances that eventually translate to success for the organization.

DivyaSree's campuses blend facilities like captive power, redundant connectivity solutions, specialized cooling, with amenities like on-site housing, supermarkets, medical and banking facilities. Recreational areas like landscaped gardens, water bodies, health-clubs, food courts etc., further add to an attractive and creative environment that nurses and inspires the best talent in the world.

At DivyaSree's campuses, work will feel like an endless holiday.

**DivyaSree**
DEVELOPERS (P) LTD
*Building Values*

*Phone:* 080-2221 3344 *email:marketing@divyasree.com*    *www.divyasree.com*

# Infosys

Infosys Technologies Limited is the pin-up company of Indian software and largely responsible for Bangalore's reputation as the Silicon Valley of Asia. Started in the early 80s by a group of seven software engineers under the leadership of NR Narayana Murthy, Infosys has grown to become a billion dollar company in 2004. It was the first Indian company to be listed on NASDAQ in 1999.

Infosys hurtled into the big league in the early 90s with major off-shore contracts in the United States. Today, while the US continues to be the company's major market, it has earned its stripes in other important markets like Europe and Asia.

Infosys has moved from doing only off-shore projects to creating software products with its banking software suite. The bulk of the company's products are aimed at the banking and financial sectors. The company is equally famous for its pioneering human resource management systems. Its 25,000 employees enjoy a fabulous campus with basketball courts, gyms, cafeterias and other leisure activities. But one of the most attractive elements has been the Employee Stock Options (ESOPS) that has turned many Infoscians into proud millionaires.
**Web** *www.infosys.com*

## NR Narayana Murthy

Born on August 20 1946, in Karnataka, NR Narayana Murthy is the Chairman and Chief Mentor of Infosys Technologies. He studied in Mysore and later in the Indian Institute of Technology, Kanpur. Today, his company is ranked right up there with other global leaders in software and his genius in software entrepreneurship is widely acknowledged. Most importantly, Murthy's reputation as a simple, unassuming man of high integrity, warms the hearts of middleclass Indians.

Murthy has consistently ensured that Infosys keeps abreast with the latest corporate practices. From global accounting practices to the latest HR developments, Murthy ensures that Infosys sets an example among other Indian software firms.

As a member of the Technology Task Force of India, Murthy is active in promoting India's role as a software powerhouse.

## Business in Brief

 India's first electricity-fuelled car, the **Reva** was launched by the Bangalore-based **Maini Group** in 2000 and is a matter of great national pride. It was initiated in 1994 by Chetan Maini, managing director of the Reva Electric Car Company. RECC, a joint venture between the Maini Group and US-based AEVT Inc, aims at providing a trustworthy and environment-friendly car. The little cars in hundreds of customised colours can be seen zipping around Bangalore.

RECC has the capacity to produce 6,000 cars annually. The car can do 80 kilometres per charging and has a maximum speed of 60 kilometres per hour. RECC plans to introduce more powerful variants that will be able to run for longer periods between charging, and at higher speeds. The car now enjoys a tax exemption from the government, bringing the price of the basic model Reva to a little below Rs 2 lakh.

The Reva has attracted the attention of the international market. Enquiries are pouring in from countries like the United Kingdom, Israel, United States, Malaysia and Indonesia.

 **Himatsingka Seide** is probably the best known silk exporter from Karnataka. The multi-billion rupee company exports silk yarns and fabrics across Europe, Australia and the United States. The company's Bangalore unit, is one of the largest integrated silk mills in the world.

Himatsingka Seide's silk fabrics are known for their designs and quality and its manufacturing unit has an ISO 9001 certification. Dinesh and Aditya Himatsingka, who run the company, make sure that their high quality silks continue to demand a premium in global furnishing and fashion houses.

# Tracing Bangalore's IT Success – MK Shankaralinge Gowda, IAS

Bangalore today is a much sought after destination both for investors and professionals. Ranked fourth among technology clusters in the world, after Silicon Valley, Boston and London, Bangalore plays host for Asia's largest ICT event. The State Government has successfully implemented e-Governance in the citizen interface fields. The city has turned out to be a hot destination for job seekers and has a lot of promise for providing employment to both technical & non-technical workers.

To go back, it all began in 1984 when Texas Instruments came into Bangalore. The government saw the possibility of an emerging tech industry. There was little development immediately there after but, 1997 saw the beginning of what could be termed as a huge revolution. The industry grew in leaps and bounds and changed the face of Bangalore.

Global developments in the field of information technology encouraged the state government to give it the required attention. The growth of home-grown companies, Wipro and Infosys, in the nineties provided the initial critical mass. They held much promise, encouraging the government to turn its focus to IT. The possibilities of more employment were a huge attraction.

Karnataka was the first state to announce an IT policy, in 1997, intent on bringing in investments. Concessions were provided in sales and entry tax, power tariffs and land allotments. The state's advantage was in its skilled manpower and to boost

this, the government established more engineering colleges and increased the number of seats available – from 15,000 seats in 1997 to 45,000 in 2004. The presence of prestigious institutions like Indian Institute of Science, Indian Institute of Management, National Institute of Biological Sciences, National Aeronautical Institute and others have firmly put Bangalore on the map as a knowledge centre. This was extended to create skilled manpower that could avail the employment opportunities that IT now brought. A state-of-the-art Indian Institute of Information Technology was established in 1999 working in partnership with IT corporates.

The consequent success and growth of Bangalore as an IT super power is, as they say, history. IT exports grew from 500 million USD in 1999 to 4.2 billion USD in 2004. Estimated exports for 2007 from IT and IT-enabled Services are 10 billion USD. Bangalore's stronghold continues to be software but we are making efforts for the growth and development of hardware industry also. In fact, two thirds of the UPS production for American Power Conversion (APC) is from Bangalore. The hardware industry has seen a 20% growth and a new policy is being brought out this year, to attract investments in this sector.

The government set up IT parks in Bangalore and Hubli and earth stations in Mysore and Mangalore. Providing plug and play facility, the IT parks house some of the biggest players in the industry. Way back in the 1980s Electronic City was established and is the headquarters of Infosys. The

International Technology Park (ITPL) was established in 1997. It holds the distinction of being the largest in the country, with 12 lakh sqft space which is being expanded. A special IT corridor is being planned in and around Bangalore. The Export Promotion Industrial Park (EPIP) is a 288 acres park designed for export-oriented industries.

IT-enabled Services (ITES) were the next big thing. Bangalore caught up in double quick time despite a late start in 2001-02. Business process outsourcing (BPO) is the latest buzzword and has created a large opportunity for employment. IT and ITES combined employ 2,40,000 people in the city. Bangalore is gearing itself to provide quality back office support with the availability of skilled manpower – lawyers, pharmacists, commerce graduates and so on. Contrary to popular belief, call centres are only a part of the large BPO sector, employing 40% of the entire BPO workforce.

The Government has taken initiatives to ensure quality human resource by introducing the B-SAT (BPO Skill Assessment and Training) certification, in the secondary cities of Mysore, Mangalore, Davangere, Shimoga, Belgaum, Hubli and Hassan. The Government serves as a facilitator between the employer and job seekers. Prospective employees are assessed to check skill levels. Those requiring training are provided six weeks of training after which the associate partners employ them.

The success story continues as Bangalore attracts more and more foreign equity (FE) companies: The year 2003-04 saw an average of two FE companies entering Bangalore per week. There are 1,372 IT and ITES companies in Bangalore and the number is growing. It is no longer a concession driven industry but one that

Part of the growing IT and ITES industry

It's a thin line that  separates the best from the rest

Internet connected flat screen personal computers in every Plaza room. Just one among the many thoughtful touches that make The Muthoot Plaza the finest business hotel in Trivandrum.

Wi-Fi zones | Express check in | Airport transfer (2 way)

𝓣𝓱𝓮 𝓜𝓾𝓽𝓱𝓸𝓸𝓽 𝓟𝓵𝓪𝔃𝓪
THE FINEST BUSINESS HOTEL

TRIVANDRUM

❚ A Muthoot Pappachan Group Concern ❚ A Sarovar Park Plaza Hotel | Tel: 0471 2337733 email: muthoot@eth.net www.themuthootplaza.com

demands better social infrastructure. The city's attraction no doubt is its cosmopolitan culture, an inviting ambience and the many conveniences – good schools, housing blocks, and adequate entertainment. Information technology has provided increased revenue through exports, direct and indirect employment and increased purchasing power with the consumer.

IT.com, the event that Bangalore looks forward to each year was first held in 1998. In seven years, it has grown as much as the industry itself: From a small event at the ITPL to the largest IT event in Asia it has seen over 300 companies and over a dozen prominent foreign countries participating. The event is the venue for high level conferences discussing current trends, future developments and analysis of IT growth.

Government initiatives have been in using IT as a tool to simplify services like taxation, land registration etc. E-governance is now a reality and the government has numerous schemes: Bhoomi for computerised land records in rural areas, Nondani for land registration, Mukhya Vahini for monitoring various projects. The treasuries have been computerised and IT is now in use in the areas of education, telemedicine and rural development. Yuva.com is a training programme designed to bring IT education to the rural youth. A pilot project is on in Mysore to improve land usage. The government has also introduced online transactions in the silk market, bringing in transparency in market operations.

## Biotechnology

Biotechnology is a field that is showing plenty of promise. Bangalore is home to the richest Indian woman entrepreneur, Kiran

Simplifying bill payments with a 24-hour kiosk

The campus of National Centre for Biological Sciences

Mazumdar-Shaw who heads Biocon, the country's leading biotech company. There's plenty of R&D activity in this field and global developments have reaffirmed the same. Clinical research, new medicines for diabetes, breakthrough in cardiac medicine and vaccines can be attributed to the emergence of biotechnology. Bangalore based Indian Institute of Science has driven the research and development activity in India. The success of Biocon, a homegrown company has provided the 'critical mass' for the growth of the biotech sector.

The State Government was the first in the country to come up with a unique millennium biotech policy in the year 2001. This provides for capitalising on available skilled scientific pool of human resources and encourages education in the

biotech field. The State Government set up the prestigious Institute of Bioinformatics and Applied Biotechnology.

In the last five years, the number of biotech companies has grown from 44 to 110. In terms of investment there has been a 300% increase. Multinationals like AstraZeneca, Novozymes, MWG, Monsanto, Aurigene etc., have also set up their operations here. The number of biotech companies entering Bangalore has seen a steady growth from one company every month to two companies a month. A biotech cluster is being planned along the lines of the IT park.

The Biotech park – Bangalore Bio-cluster, will be set up in an extent of about 100 acres of land offering world-class infrastructure for high-end research in biotechnology. Common effluent treatment plant, solid waste treatment with wastewater recycling, and various such facilities will be part of the park's amenities. The bio-park will have an institutional block with institutes dedicated to Bioinformatics and Applied Biotechnology (IBAB), Centre for Human Genetics (CHG), and library facilities, an administrative block, an incubation centre which will service biotechnology companies by helping them appraise commercial opportunities of their ideas and technology, provide information on finance and help in securing finance.

Karnataka is now completely wired and one of the first to broadband the entire state. We see a highly motivated work force that will ensure that Bangalore continues to grow in both these sectors.

*MK Shankaralinge Gowda, IAS, is Secretary, Department of Information Technology, Biotechnology, Science and Technology.*

**We used to work at lintas, mudra and contract. Then we got together and decided to get into advertising.**

A bunch of old friends running a creative boutique? Not really - we have 5 offices and close to 150 people across South India, and the Middle East.

Yet another agency aiming for top billings? No way - we like to stay away from the billings game and concentrate on advertising and brand building instead (the money has always followed, but of course!).

And that's just the way we want it to remain too. So that we get to do cutting edge work that is noticed around the world. Across all media. Seamlessly. Under one roof.

Interested? Let's talk.

699 1st Floor 7th Main HAL-2nd Stage Indiranagar Bangalore 560 038 India
Tel: +91 80 51152102 - 104 Fax: +91 80 51152106 Email: starkblr@starkgroup.net

# ING Vysya Group

Bangalore-based Vysya Bank was incorporated in 1930 and rechristened ING Vysya Bank in 2002 following an alliance with ING Group. Its major divisions are ING Vysya Bank, ING Vysya Life Insurance and ING Vysya Mutual Fund. It has a customer base of two million and has established itself as one of the biggest private sector financial institutions in the country.

ING Vysya Life Insurance Company Private Limited entered the private life insurance industry in India in September 2001. Today, it is recognised as a distinctive life insurance brand with an innovative, compelling and customer friendly product portfolio complemented with a professional advisor force. The company also distributes products in close cooperation with ING Vysya Bank through a Bancassurance model. It has over 5,000 active advisors working in 21 cities across the country.

ING Vysya Mutual Fund brings with it the vast international experience and professional expertise of the ING Group. Spread across eight cities in India, ING Vysya Mutual Fund has over Rs 1,100 crore of assets under management.
**Web** www.ingvysyalife.com

# Titan Industries

Incorporated in 1984 as a joint venture between the Tata Group and Tamil Nadu Industrial Development Corporation Ltd., Titan Industries Ltd. has been engaged in the manufacture and marketing of quartz watches since 1987. With a registered office in Hosur, just outside Bangalore, the company has, since 1995, diversified into jewellery, sold under the brand name, Tanishq. Both these divisions are brands to contend with in their respective product domains. In a further development during 2003, the watch division was divided into five business units: Titan, Sonata, Licensed Brands & Accessories, Precision Engineering and Customer Service.

Titan and Sonata products are now sold in over 2,200 cities with an exclusive retail chain, World of Titan. They command a market share of over 50% in the organised watch segment. Tanishq is India's largest and fastest growing jewellery brand with 67 boutiques in 52 cities. The range includes exquisite gold jewellery

studded with diamonds and coloured stones, jewellery in 22kt gold, exquisite platinum jewellery and designer silverware. Titan has well-established international operations; its products are sold in over 30 countries with an overseas retail value of over Rs1,000 crore.

Recognition for commitment to design innovation and marketing excellence came with national and international awards: Adjudged the most respected consumer durables company by IMRB, rated as one of Asia's top 200 companies and India's top in a survey conducted by The Far Eastern Economic Review. Titan and Tanishq were also voted the most admired watch brand at the Images Fashion Awards for three consecutive years. Tanishq was selected as a benchmark challenger organisation by Erewohn, for successful efforts in transforming the marketplace for Indian jewellery. Other awards have followed for corporate citizenship, social responsiveness and environment management.
**Web** www.titanworld.com

# Himalaya Drug Company

For over seven decades, the Himalaya Drug Company (HDC) has focused on developing safe, natural and innovative remedies, with the use of modern science. And today, over 2,00,000 doctors around the globe endorse Himalaya products and consumers in over 55 countries rely on Himalaya for their health and personal care needs. Combining ancient Ayurvedic principles with modern science and cutting edge technology, Himalaya Drugs creates pharmaceutical-grade Ayurvedic products.

Himalaya's products can broadly be categorised into pharmaceuticals, personal care, consumer health and animal health. The Ayurvedic medicinal range of products encompasses children, women's health and men's health. The company also provides well-researched and safe animal health products. Their personal care range focuses on offering natural remedies, minimising harmful side effects from the use of chemicals. Himalaya

Herbal Healthcare stores, strategically located around the city, serve as a 'one-stop-shop' for their entire range of products from therapeutic drugs to the skin and hair care products.

The medicinal range of products address ailments like liver disorders, osteoporosis, hemorrhoids and rheumatoid arthritis. Prominent among the Himalaya brands is Liv.52, a liver formulation, which is the flagship brand of the company. Himalaya has used its wealth of knowledge and research in herbal cures, to formulate a range of personal care products – Himalaya Herbals – that cater to consumers' daily needs. The products in the Himalaya Herbals range consist of products for hair, skin, body, health and oral care. Consumer Health offers a range of products that cater to the soft therapeutic needs through products like Pure Herbs, Chyavanprash, Forest Honey and Throat Drops.
**Web** www.himalayahealthcare.com

# The new face of money.

The lion has meant trust, integrity and wealth to you since it first appeared on Indian currency. Call it coincidence or good fortune, but it now reappears, with the same spirit, in a new avatar - ING Vysya.

Its face reflects 150 years of international financial expertise of ING, the world's fourth largest integrated financial services group*. Coupled with

the heritage of the 70 year old Vysya Bank, India's premier private sector bank, known for its warmth and customer-friendly solutions.

Looking for a banking partner, a mutual fund manager or a life insurance planner? Turn to one global expert, one face. Just like you always have. The lion's.

*Source : Fortune Global 500, July 2003

 ING Vysya

## BANKING | LIFE INSURANCE | MUTUAL FUNDS

Rediffusion-DY&R/Bang/INGC/BK/02/03

## Capt. GR Gopinath

# Air Deccan

India's first low-cost airline, Air Deccan is part of Deccan Aviation Pvt. Ltd., the country's largest private heli-charter company. The airline links not only large cities like Mumbai, Bangalore, Mangalore, Hyderabad and Chennai, but also smaller like Belgaum, Vijaywada, Hubli and Madurai. Launched in August 2003, Air Deccan is also expanding operations in the north.

Air Deccan is headed by Capt. GR Gopinath, ex-army man and entrepreneur farmer. It has a fleet of seven ATRs and three Airbus A320s, widely considered the most viable aircraft for regional routes.

The airline is positioning itself as the 'Udupi hotel' of airlines, a no-frills service!

Passengers have to pay for their food on board and there is only one hostess aboard each flight. You can book tickets over the phone night and day, or on the Internet. Passengers are given E-tickets for check-in at airports. The ticketing system is backed by a 24-hour call centre in regional languages linked to a central reservation system. All these factors have helped Air Deccan tickets to be upto 40 per cent cheaper than regular domestic airlines. And according to Capt. Gopinath, they are likely to fall further as the number of passengers grows!

The airline does offer a clean aircraft, reliable time schedules, 'ticketless travel', connectivity across the length and breadth of the country. It plans to offer 100 flights with a fleet of 18 aircrafts by the end of next year. Overall, Air Deccan aims to create a quality airline, accessible across India and affordable to all.
**Web** *www.airdeccan.net*

Born in Gorur, a remote village in Karnataka, with military education at the National Defence Academy in Dehradun, Capt. GR Gopinath went on to serve in the Indian Army for eight years. Having retired from service in 1978, he took over cultivating his family-owned land of 40 acres. He switched to rearing silkworms in 1985. What followed was a successful venture with spectacular results in organic farming and Capt. Gopinath was awarded the ROLEX Award for Enterprise in 1996, for his contribution to ecological silk farming.

In 1998, Capt. Gopinath teamed up with a friend to start a private sector commercial helicopter service out of Bangalore, the first of its kind in the country. Spurred by its success, he launched Air Deccan in August 2003. With a vision to make air travel affordable, Capt. Gopinath's venture has paid off with 75 flights a day operating to 118 destinations.

# Levi Strauss

With blue jeans as the cornerstone of their business, Levi Strauss & Co. has emerged as one of the is world's biggest apparel manufacturers. Levis Strauss has established itself as a premium youth brand through the years, creating new and edgy fashion trends. This 150-year old company came to India in 1995 with their subsidiary Levi Strauss (India) Pvt Ltd (LSIL) and opened the market for high quality and high fashion denim wear.

Headquartered in Bangalore, the LSIL retail network marketing their brands Levi's and Dockers spans more than 70 cities and 400 outlets in the country. It also exports the Levi's, Dockers and Slates range of products to the US, Canada, Mexico and several Asian countries. It has a significant presence in the super premium and premium denim-wear markets.

The Levi's brand offers quintessential classics as well as innovative fashion products – the classic 501 jeans, Red Tab jeans, the Red Loop range, Minus One jeans, non-denims, woven shirts, knitted tops, jackets and accessories. The Levi's Sykes range was created to offer the college-going youngster stylised clothing in denim and non-denim fabric. Their international range of Khakis and men's semi-formals, Dockers, well known for comfort, durability and style is also offered here. LSIL is known not only for its high quality apparel but for its active participation in community development programmes as well.
**Web** *www.levistrauss.com*

## Add more firepower to your marketing programs

At End To End, we're constantly creating newer and more effective ways for you to reach customers. And as one of India's leading marketing service providers, we plan and execute comprehensive marketing programs for several global leaders. Talk to us. Let us show you how our expertise will help your business.

- **Direct marketing** • **Relationship Marketing** • **Database Strategy, Implementation and Management**
- **Event Management Services** • **Creative Services** • **Marketing Program Management**

End To End Marketing Solutions Pvt. Ltd., 173, 9th Cross, Indiranagar 1st Stage, Bangalore - 560 038. India.
Tel: +91 80 25294822, 25272034. Fax: +91 80 25281471 Email: enquiry@endtoendmarketing.net **Branches:** Mumbai, Chennai, New Delhi

# Mysore Sales International

Formed in 1966, Mysore Sales International Limited (MSIL) was set up as a public sector marketing unit for various products manufactured in Karnataka. Within a decade of its inception, the company expanded its operations to managing special projects for the government and its turnover increased from an initial Rs 1.5 crores to over Rs 1,357 crores in 2004. Today, MSIL, an ISO 9001 company, has under its umbrella, self sustained paper, lottery, travel, export, hire-purchase, silk, consumer and industrial product divisions. Headquartered in Bangalore with branches in Chennai, Mumbai and New Delhi, the company today markets a host of products and manages the Bangalore Air Cargo Complex, handling import and export cargo annually.

The paper division produces an entire range of school and office stationery, including the hugely popular brands, Vidya and Lekhak, notebooks for the student community, and provides employment to over 100 small scale industries. The Lottery Division manages the Karnataka State Lottery, which is now recognised as the best managed lottery in the country.

The tours and travel division functions as an IATA approved travel agent. It promotes package tours to trade fairs and serves as a booking agent for ITDC and KSTDC tours.

Tourists visiting the state can avail services offered by the MSIL owned Information Centre in Mumbai. The centre is a single point of contact for travel related services, from hotel bookings to tour guides.

MSIL's 'hire-purchase division' manufactures consumer durables. Televisions, VCRs and refrigerators are made available throughout Karnataka in a variety of easy monthly instalment schemes for government employees. Mysore Sales International's venture into silk has been especially successful. Their silk emporiums, such as Mandara in Bangalore, stock Mysore crepe silks, georgettes and other handloom silks from Karnataka.

The MSIL brand of solar water heaters, "Hot Spring" has a wide range of products marketed through the industrial products division.

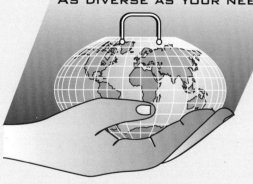

72

# BPOs and Bangalore – Sandip Sen

Sandip Sen

It's common knowledge now that information technology propelled Bangalore into becoming one of the fastest growing cities in India. In the field of IT, Bangalore saw a significant growth and attracted some of the best talent. But it did not stop there; information technology has enabled a whole new sector with business process outsourcing (BPO). Large corporate and even niche players saw outsourcing as an option with dual benefits – it reduced costs and allowed them to focus on their core business.

Customer support/technical support helpdesks, human resource and finance are three areas that are now commonly outsourced. If infrastructure problems are dealt with, Bangalore can well be the city that will serve most voice back office requirements of international corporations.

Admittedly, one of the key triggers was reduced cost. We offered the American and European market a large cost benefit. While this was an advantage they could not resist, India also offered high quality manpower that made it a lethal combination. We had a sustainable competitive advantage that gave us a head start. This is also the reason why we are ahead in the BPO race. Our schools and colleges churn out manpower that's skilled, smart and willing to learn. And the IT spurt served as a major facilitator in creating new opportunities and new markets.

'Made in India' is now a tagline to reckon with and Bangalore is a brand that is synonymous with IT, and a highly saleable one at that. Bangalore's advantages are manifold – the number of educational institutions, a cosmopolitan culture and great weather. One couldn't ask for more, except maybe infrastructure that will keep pace with this rate of growth.

The Karnataka state government's initiatives have been to decentralise and reduce the pressure on Bangalore while also exploring non-metros as possible options. IT parks in Mangalore, Hubli and Mysore have contributed favourably to this and the availability of skilled manpower in these places has reiterated Karnataka's position in the BPO industry. But Bangalore continues to be the dominant player in the BPO sector, now catering to both the international and domestic market. The domestic market also has expanded hugely – with the increase in the number of cell phone and credit card users.

For the Bangalorean who works in a BPO, this is a lucrative employment opportunity. The BPO employee also earns more than many others at the starting level. Being young, he has a higher disposable income and in an increasingly consumer-driven society, this creates a spillover effect – restaurants thrive, malls come up. The BPO has also been instrumental in creating tertiary employment opportunities, in catering, security and transport services. The down side of this is that the landscape of Bangalore has changed, from a 'Pensioners' Paradise' to a glass and chrome city. For the Bangalorean who rues this loss, the undeniable fact is that BPOs have contributed to the city's prosperity.

The industry is growing at a galloping pace and I see a growth rate of more than 25% per annum in the medium term. BPOs have helped legitimize the 'Made in India' brand. Internationally, Bangalore is an accepted brand, a name that is very familiar abroad. The market is not saturated and if infrastructure is upgraded BPOs will grow manifold. We have just tapped the tip of the iceberg. There are 15-20 large BPOs in Bangalore employing more than a thousand people each, many employ over 5,000 people. Small and medium players run into over a hundred and today, over 40-50,000 people in Bangalore work with BPOs.

Truth be told, BPO is possibly a larger phenomenon than IT ever was.

*Sandip Sen is the CEO of Customer First Services (P) Ltd. He lives in Bangalore.*

# Bangalore Beckons...

At least 2 IT companies with 100% foreign equity, moves in to Bangalore, every week.

You can outsource top-notch IT services at 70% lower cost from Bangalore.

Is the most preferred destination for investment in Customer Interaction, Tech Support and Financial Sector Back Office Processing.

Has the highest number of Engineering Colleges to a city in the world.

The UN has ranked Bangalore the 4th best 'Global Hub of Technological Innovation in the World' after
- Silicon Valley
- Boston
- London

Is the home to more than 1440 ICT companies and 110 Biotech companies.

Over 1,80,000 highly qualified IT professionals and 60,000 BPO professionals.

Over 50% of the world's SEI CMM Level 5 companies are located in the city.

Mr. William Mercer, International Consultant rated Bangalore as the world's most economical city to live in.

For the 7th consecutive year, Bangalore hosted Asia's biggest ICT event "Bangalore IT.com 2004 Tradeshow and Conferences".

Home to 103 premier R&D institutions including IISc., considered to be the 18th best University in the world.

**The Secretary**
Department of IT & Biotechnology
Govt. of Karnataka
No. 9, III Floor, UNI Building
Thimmaiah Road, Miller Tank Bed
Bangalore - 560 052, Karnataka State, India

Tel: +91-80-22280562/ 63
Fax: +91-80-22288341
Email: itsec@bangaloreit.com
    biosec@bangalorebio.com
Websites: www.bangaloreit.com
    www.bangalorebio.com

BANGALORE

THE I.T. CAPITAL OF INDIA

# Bangalore >>

## The Making Of India's
## IT Success Story

It is a story that had its genesis in 1984, when Texas Instruments set up office in Bangalore, Karnataka. A renowned centre for quality higher education, Bangalore already had the most potent resource for the knowledge industry - a vast talent-pool. The Government of Karnataka was quick to recognize the immense possibilities in the emergent tech industry.

The story unfolded over the next several years, till in 1997, began what can only be termed as an IT revolution. It was a revolution that transformed Bangalore from 'India's Garden City' into 'Asia's Silicon Valley'. The growth of homegrown companies - Wipro and Infosys - in the nineties provided the initial momentum.

To boost the state's manpower advantage, the government increased the number of engineering colleges and actively encouraged upgrading the curricula. Prestigious institutions like the Indian Institute of Science (IISc) and Indian Institute of Management (IIM) introduced specialized, IT-focused programmes. And, a state-of-the-art Indian Institute of Information Technology was established in 1997, in partnership with the corporate sector.

Karnataka was the first state to announce a comprehensive investor-friendly IT policy in 1997, which provided concessions in sales and entry tax, power tariffs and land allotments.

Today, Bangalore is ranked fourth among technology hubs in the world, after Silicon Valley, Boston and

The success of the IT sector in Bangalore has also helped promote growth of IT in other towns and cities across Karnataka. The government has set up IT parks in Hubli, earth-stations in Mysore and Mangalore, and B-SAT Certification (BPO Skill Assessment and Training), in cities like Mysore, Mangalore, Davangere, Shimoga, Belgaum, Hubli and Hassan to ensure the availability of quality manpower.

## Information Technology aiding e-Governance

The Government of Karnataka has successfully implemented e-Governance in several citizen-interface fields. Government initiatives have been using IT as a tool to simplify services like sales tax, land tax, land registration etc. These initiatives include: *Bhoomi* for computerized land

## Riding The Biotechnology Wave

Biotechnology is an extremely promising sunrise sector and Bangalore is one of the leading centres of R&D activity in this field. Clinical research, new medicines for diabetes, breakthroughs in cardiology and new vaccines can be attributed to the emergence of biotechnology. The success of Bangalore-based Biocon, has provided the impetus for the growth of the biotech sector.

The state government was the first in the country to come up with a unique millennium biotech policy in 2001, which aims at capitalizing on the available skilled pool of human resources and encourage education in the biotech field.

# The IT revolution transformed Bangalore from 'India's Garden City' into 'Asia's Silicon Valley'.

London - and, is among the most sought-after destinations for investors and professionals. Bangalore has also seen phenomenal growth in FDI - from one per week to two per week.

The rest, as they say, is history. IT exports grew from 500 million USD in 1999 to 4.2 billion USD in 2004. Estimated export revenue for 2007 from IT and IT-enabled Services are pegged at 10 billion USD. The IT industry - which includes IT-enabled Services (ITES) and Business Process Outsourcing (BPOs) - today employs about 2,40,000 people in the city. Call centres alone employ 40% of the BPO workforce.

Although Bangalore's strength continues to be in software and services, concerted efforts are being made to expand the growth in the hardware sector too. And the results are showing. The hardware industry has seen a 20% growth, and the state is going all out to attract large investments in this sector.

records in rural areas, *Nondani* for land registration, and *Mukhya Vahini* for monitoring various projects. The treasuries have been computerized and IT is now in use in the areas of education, telemedicine and rural development. *Yuva.com* is a training programme designed to bring IT education to the rural youth. The government has even introduced online transactions for trading in silk.

Bangalore and the information technology industry has inspired the entire state - as it has, the rest of the world - to reach out to greater opportunities in the new global economy.

---

Department of
IT & Biotechnology,
Govt. of Karnataka

www.bangaloreit.com
www.bangalorebio.com

BANGALORE
THE I.T. CAPITAL OF INDIA

In the last five years, the number of biotech companies has grown from 44 to 110. In terms of investment, there has been a 300% increase. Multinationals like AstraZeneca, Novozymes, MWG, Monsanto and Aurigene, have set up their operations here. The number of biotech companies entering Bangalore has seen a steady growth - from one company every month to two companies a month.

The Biotech Park, Bangalore - a bio-cluster, will offer world-class infrastructure for high-end research in biotechnology. The bio-park will have institutes dedicated to bioinformatics and applied biotechnology (IBAB) and a Centre for Human Genetics (CHG). An Incubation Centre will service biotechnology companies by helping them appraise commercial opportunities and assistance in raising funds.

# IT-enabled Health Solution: Telemedicine

Tele-consultation by Dr. Devi Shetty in Narayana Hrudayalaya

In the last few years, Bangalore has emerged as the centre for telemedicine – a method by which patients may be examined, monitored and treated via telephone, text, voice, images or even video. This allows patients in far flung locations or where there is no specialist doctor, to connect with a team of doctors and specialists, without ever leaving their location.

Bangalore has one of the largest telemedicine networks in the world. This has enabled specialists to provide specialised health care remotely, saving hundreds of lives. It is an important development in the Indian context because of the large rural population that has little or no access to treatment. Telemedicine has also made a huge difference in the lives of these people as the services are offered free of cost.

The Karnataka Telemedicine Project was inaugurated in April 2002. Since then, hospitals and health centres in remote locations have been linked via INSAT satellites with super specialty hospitals at bigger cities, helping patients connect with specialist doctors for medical consultation and treatment.

One of the forerunners of telemedicine is teleradiology where high resolution X-rays, ultrasound, CT scans, MRIs and ECGs are transferred via satellite. In Bangalore, Dr. Devi Shetty of Narayana Hrudayalaya has extended telemedicine to the field of cardiac care. Although it can be extended to any area of health care, cardiac care occupies a significant place for more reasons than one. Indians are genetically prone to heart disease and a whopping 2.4 million Indians are in need of heart operations annually. The tragedy is that only 45,000 can afford it. Telemedicine helps bring the cost down thus making treatment affordable to more.

## How it works

In order to put this into practice, you need a basic telemedicine system – a personal computer, a modem, a telephone line, a scanner and a webcam. The telemedicine system consists of customised medical software integrated with computer hardware, along with diagnostic instruments connected to the VSAT (Very Small Aperture Terminal) at each location. The Indian Space Research Organisation (ISRO) has set up an exclusive satellite for telemedicine services. This has facilitated telemedicine services by ensuring the availability of high-speed connections.

Under the circumstances where a patient requires no operation, the medical decision regarding treatment is based on the history. This can be easily obtained via good quality videoconferencing and interpretation of the images, which can be transferred with or without wire. A specialist using the technology today can treat upto 99 per cent of healthcare problems from a distance.

Using the telemedicine network, Narayana Hrudayalaya, which specialises in cardiac care, has created 22 coronary care units (CCUs) and telemedicine centres in remote parts within India and even in countries such as Nepal. These CCUs are linked to the focal centres in Bangalore and Kolkata. The specialists treat via teleconferencing and many emergencies have been handled with a high success rate. Over 12,500 patients have been treated this way, in the last three years, at no cost.

Today, 19 CCUs operate in India and 27 are being deployed across Karnataka. Narayana Hrudayalaya in Bangalore and Rabindranath Tagore International Institute of Cardiac Science in Kolkata are the main centres, linked to the CCUs. Specialists here offer their services free of cost.

Few district hospitals are equipped to deal with cardiac emergencies and the CCUs are a boon to the people here. The good news is that telemedicine has enabled cardiac care for the poor in other countries as well. The telemedicine centre at Narayana Hrudayalaya links to a clinic in Kuala Lumpur, a children's cardiac facility in Mauritius and a medical school in Germany. Plans are on to extend these to other developing countries like Bangaladesh, Tanzania, Yemen, Pakistan and Zambia.

Since its beginnings in 2001, the death rate due to cardiac ailments has seen a drop of five percent. By the year 2006, India will be the largest provider of cardiac care in the world.

## Telemedicine as the solution for the future

Most specialists are based in urban areas and telemedicine is an affordable way of reaching the patient and providing timely treatment. Dr. Shetty and his team have also brought out a Heart Care on Wheels service, where a bus equipped with state-of-the-art echocardiology, colour Doppler, a computerised treadmill and laptop computers, roam all over Karnataka. Onboard specialists communicate with the doctors in Bangalore via satellite.

As services expand, telelmedicine will find its reach extending to areas of health care as specialised as ophthalmology and mental health. The government's initiatives in this area working in collaboration with technology partners and health care professionals will go a long way in ensuring affordable health care, especially to the rural poor. In the future, telemedicine will be the norm and every large speciality hospital will have a telemedicine network with links to speciality healthcare.

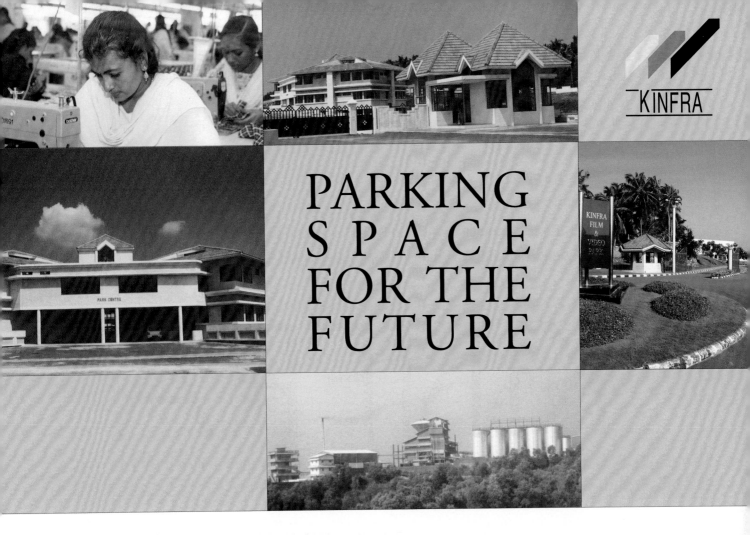

PARKING
S P A C E
FOR THE
FUTURE

## KINFRA. Providing futuristic infrastructure for emerging industries.

Kerala Industrial Infrastructure Development Corporation (KINFRA) develops state-of-the-art industrial parks and economic zones for the industries of the future. Provides world-class facilities and innovative support services like Single Window Clearance. And offers attractive incentives for expansion and diversification of businesses set up in Kinfra parks and zones.

### KINFRA Industrial Parks

KINFRA provides readymade manufacturing environment that enables easy start-ups with minimum time and cost. Self-contained industrial zones, the parks offer developed land, communication facilities, dedicated power and water supply.

### Kinfra Film & Video Park, Thiruvananthapuram

- The first infotainment industrial park in India
- A consortium of service providers in the film, video and animation industries
- Land on long lease to investors

- Equipped with common facilities like preview theatre, conference room, business centre, commercial complex etc.
- An exclusive Animation Zone with export-oriented animation production units and a world-class animation school

### Kinfra Biotechnology Parks, Thiruvananthapuram & Kochi

This proposed Park will have the following facilities:

- Technology incubation centre
- Biotech lab • Gene bank
- Computer lab • R&D facilities

### Kinfra International Apparel Park (KIAP), Thiruvananthapuram

- Provides basic infrastructure for the garment industry
- 45 acres of developed land
- Allotment nearing completion

### Other KINFRA Industrial Parks

- Kinfra Export Promotion Industrial Parks
- Kinfra Food Processing Industrial Park
- Rubber Park
- Seafood Park
- Kinfra Small Industries Park
- Kinfra IT & Electronics Park

**Kerala Industrial Infrastructure Development Corporation** (A Statutory Body of Government of Kerala)
Kinfra House 31/2312 Sasthamangalam Thiruvananthapuram 695 010 Kerala India Phone: ++91-471-2726585 www.kinfra.com

Kerala Industrial Infrastructure Development Corporation (KINFRA), the nodal agency of the Government of Kerala, enhances the growth of an industrial Kerala by identifying and developing infrastructure facilities required for industries. The Corporation is committed to developing industrial estates, parks, complexes and growth centres. Since 1993, KINFRA has been providing comprehensive support to entrepreneurs in various industrial sectors in setting up units and succeeding in their ventures.

# KINFRA

## Catalysing an industrial Kerala

KINFRA parks play a major role in building infrastructure for the industrial development of the State. In addition to this, the development work of KINFRA around its industrial parks benefits the social structure by generating more employment opportunities and enhancing infrastructure facilities of the locality.

**Dr G C Gopala Pillai,** MD, KINFRA

## KINFRA | INDUSTRIAL PARKS

KINFRA has identified a cluster of promising industries and established state-of-the-art industrial parks offering world-class infrastructure for the comprehensive development of these industries. Self-contained industrial zones, the parks provide developed land, dedicated power and water supply, unmatched communication facilities and support facilities like Single Window Clearance, round-the-clock security etc.

## KINFRA | FILM & VIDEO PARK

The first infotainment industrial park in the country, Kinfra Film & Video Park is a fully-owned subsidiary of KINFRA. Set in a scenic environment in Thiruvananthapuram, this 75-acre Park provides developed land for visual media projects. Prasad Film Laboratories Ltd has already set up their unit in the Park. And various other investments are coming up, which include projects like film post production units, media schools etc.

Realising the huge potential the animation industry has in India, KINFRA is setting up an exclusive Animation Zone in the Park. Export-oriented animation production units and a world-class animation school will be part of this Zone.

## KINFRA | FOOD PROCESSING PARKS

KINFRA, the nodal agency for the Ministry of Food Processing Industries in the State, has set up a special agency for the development of food processing industry in Kerala – ADFIK, Agency for the Development of Food Processing Industries. ADFIK initiates the formulation and implementation of State policies and guidelines for the industry. It also provides quality infrastructure and facilitates the flow of bank credit and venture funds for the industry. KINFRA has established three food processing parks in Kerala – at Kakkancherry, Mazhuvannoor and Kakkanad. Apart from the most modern quality control systems, the parks boast of storage facility for raw materials and finished goods.

## KINFRA | INTERNATIONAL APPAREL PARK

KINFRA has developed 42 acres of land in Thiruvananthapuram to provide basic infrastructure for the garment industry. Mumbai-based Leela Group has already started three manufacturing units in the Park. Realising the unmatched advantages the Park offers, more companies are in the process of setting up units here.

## OTHER PARKS SET UP BY | KINFRA

• Kinfra Export Promotion Industrial Park (KEPIP), Kochi
• Rubber Park (JV with Rubber Board), Kochi
• Seafood Park (JV with MPEDA & Seafood Exporters), Kochi
• Kinfra Small Industries Parks (KSIP) – In seven districts

## NEW VENTURES OF | KINFRA

• Hi-Tech Park (Private Partnership), Kochi
• Kinfra Biotech Parks, Kochi & Thiruvananthapuram

With all these state-of-the-art parks and pathbreaking initiatives, KINFRA is revolutionising the industrial sector of Kerala. The Corporation is taking all steps to ensure that the future of an industrial Kerala is definitely promising.

For more details log on to www.kinfra.com

# IT.com

IT.com at Palace Grounds

**B**illed as the country's largest IT show, Bangalore IT.com is hosted by the Department of IT and Biotechnology, Government of Karnataka along with the Software Technology Parks of India (STPI), Bangalore as the co-host. It has been held for a record seven years, since 1998, between the first and fifth of November in Bangalore, IT capital of the country. The objective of this event is to provide a platform for networking and facilitating business transactions between trade delegations from around the world. Technology gurus, venture capitalists, IT professionals and businessmen meet and mingle at this trade show enabling the flow of technology and ideas. The latest IT products are showcased, know how is exchanged and current and future trends in IT are analysed.

In 2003, IT.com reportedly billed $200 million worth of business and drew 1,50,000 visitors. Today, the exhibition area has increased to 20,000sqmts with specialised pavilions on animation, games, multimedia and business process outsourcing (BPO) – the single largest employment sector in Bangalore. Every year, more and more companies are attracted to this event that showcases the latest technology and allows exhibitors to reach directly to prospective customers. More than 350 companies and trade delegations from 50 nations are expected to participate in the future. Through this event the Government of Karnataka proposes to attract investments in smaller cities like Mysore, Mangalore and Hubli, where IT parks have come up.

Hardware, telecom, multimedia and BPO are expected to be the focus of IT.com in the coming years. IT.com also plans to host a career mart along with high-level conferences where IT experts discuss the latest trends in the business. Organisations like NASSCOM, TiE-Bangalore Chapter, IDC and other industry associations also lend their support to this event.

The Student Internet World has also been an integral part of the Bangalore IT.com since its inception, offering students exposure to the Internet. This event will now be taken to smaller districts around the state. Each district will receive 50 to a 100 computers with high speed Internet connectivity. The popular Rural IT Quiz is conducted in collaboration with Tata Consultancy Services (TCS). Networking dinners, award ceremonies are also part of the IT.com proceedings. Along similar lines, the Department of IT and Biotechnology also hosts Bangalore Bio.com, an annual tradeshow that brings together international delegates and experts in this field.

# Grover Vineyards

**T**he pioneering efforts of Bangalore-based wine manufacturer Grover Vineyards have been a sparkling success! The Grover brand of wines is on par with the best wines and is exported around the world.

More than a decade ago, businessman Kanwal Grover decided to extend his passion for wines by starting his own vineyard in Bangalore. Along with Georges Vesselle, former Technical Director of Champagne Mumm, Grover took on the challenge of growing French varieties of grapes for the first time in India. Bangalore with its rich, well drained soil and temperate climate was ideal for wine production. In 1988 Grover set out to grow French grapes in his vineyard at Doddaballapur, 40kms north of Bangalore. Thirty five different varieties of the Vitis Vinifera species were planted at 2,000 ft above sea level at the foot of the Nandi Hills. French oenologists lent their expertise, studying the adaptability of French grape to Indian soil and assessing the quality of the wines. Eventually nine that responded well to Indian conditions were chosen, including Shiraz, Cabernet Sauvignon and Sauvignon Blanc.

Today, over a hundred acres of land are under cultivation. They plan to produce 6,00,000 bottles in 2004 of which 1,50,000 will be exported to Britain and America. With renowned oenologist Michael Rolland coming on board as consultant and the French champagne house, Veuve Clicquot taking a stake in the vineyard, the Grover brand of wine is now accepted even in the country of its birth – Grover Vineyards has begun exporting its wines to France! Grover has also succeeded in creating a market right here in Bangalore and other Indian cities.

The company's portfolio now comprises of six varieties – Cabernet Sauvignon, Blanc de Blanc from the clairette grape, two varieties of rose, the La Reserve-red wine and the Sauvignon Blanc 2004. Cabernet Shiraz is a ruby red wine made from a blend of Cabernet Sauvignon and Shiraz vines along with the flavours of black currant and dark berries. La Reserve is their full bodied red wine that leaves a lingering spicy after taste. Sauvignon Blanc, their latest offering, is a speciality white wine. They also make Blanc de Blancs de Clairette, a white wine and a rose wine, Shiraz.

*63 Ragunathapur, Devanahalli Road,*
*Doddaballapur 560562 Tel 7622827*

# Why did Infosys move into God's Own e State?

Dusk Dawns: Technopark Park Centre

> The pro-active support we received from the Government was the final clincher.

**Nandan Nilekani**
Chief Executive Officer
Infosys

The reasons are simple ● Technopark - India's largest and finest IT park. The only CMMI Level 4 certified technology park in India ● 15 lakh sq.ft. of built-up space in a 156-acre campus ● Maximum telecom and datacom connectivity ● 60% cost advantage over other comparable destinations ● Modern infrastructure ● Fastest growing human resource pool ● Pro-enterprise government ● India's first tailor-made regulatory IT/ITES framework. All of which are fast attracting the most successful IT companies the world over. How about you? To know more, log on to www.keralaitmission.org

**technopark**
kerala
harmony at work
www.technopark.org

**kerala**
god's own e-state
www.keralaitmission.org

# Kerala

## IT'S NEW DOMAIN

A decade ago, Kerala hardly figured in the country's Information Technology map. But today, the State is riding high on the digital highway, thanks to the right kind of people at the helm and the right kind of initiatives at hand. In fact, Kerala's innovative ICT programmes and e-Governance initiatives have set new global standards of excellence and are receiving rave reviews from across the world.

Infosys, Wipro, Sify, Allianz Cornhill, McKinsey, RM plc., Ernst and Young... the list of companies that have moved into the State is impressive. And IT professionals from other States are fast making a beeline for Kerala, God's Own e-State.

# Sound Framework

Work-spaces that are world-class. The country's best telecom and datacom backbone. Most reliable and economical bandwidth. Excellent human resources. High-qualified workforce. Effortless start-ups. Single window clearances... Kerala is well-armed to take on the world.

**Technopark** India's first and only CMMI Level 4 assessed park, Technopark is Asia's largest IT Park. Nestled among green hills in Trivandrum, it has the unique advantage of having a serene working environment along with state-of-the-art IT enabling infrastructure. Which perhaps explains the country's lowest attrition rate of less than 5% that it registers.

■ 180 acres ■ 1.5 million sq.ft. spread across six blocks ■ 56 companies ■ 6000 employees ■ One-tenth of India's CMM Level 5 companies ■ 110 KV dedicated powerstation ■ 100% back up ■ OFC connected to gateway at Cochin ■ Earth Station ■ Total start-up support: ▶ Technopark Software Engineering Competency Centre ▶ Technopark Business Incubation Centre ▶ Technopark eCampus

**Infopark** Set in Cochin, the commercial capital of Kerala that is fast turning into an ITES hub, Infopark is located midway between the airport-seaport highway. Being the nearest IT park to the Cochin Digital Gateway, it enjoys singular advantages.

■ 1.1 lakh sq.ft. built-up space ■ Five-storeyed building with 4 units, each 5,500 sq.ft. ■ Another 2 lakh sq.ft. coming up ■ Smart business centre fully occupied ■ 20 MW captive substation ■ A large HR training centre within the campus ■ Area protected under the Essential Services Act

Technopark

Infopark

## Face to Face

Aruna Sundararajan
Secretary IT Government of Kerala

**From being a virtual non-entity to occupying a position in the top rung, Kerala has today come a long way. How do you view this transformation?**

It was achieved through sheer hard work. We reached here only through sustained efforts - focusing not only on matters like infrastructure development, but also on image-building exercises of Kerala, perceived as hostile to investments. Our efforts have started paying off. The last one year saw big names like Infosys, Wipro, TCS, Ernst & Young, McKinsey, Allianz Cornhill and Sify coming to the State.

**How has the growth of IT affected Kerala?**

I am happy to say that in Kerala, the use of IT is not restricted to a select few. In fact, the most effective use of IT in the State has been for the empowerment of the masses. Akshaya E-kendra, which we launched in Malappuram last year, has been extremely successful. It has changed the way Malappuram, a comparatively underdeveloped district, lived. We are now readying for a State-wide rollout of E-kendra. Apart from this, IT is also bringing the masses closer to the Government.

FRIENDS, for example is bringing about smoother citizen-to-Government interface.

**What do you think are the factors that give Kerala an edge over other IT destinations in India?**

A scenic and salubrious locale is a definitive advantage. The State's social indices are also quite impressive. On the IT front, Kerala enjoys unique advantages like having two cable submarine landings, 100% digital telephone exchanges etc. The operational costs are lower here, the quality of manpower high. Kerala is also not afflicted with problems like water scarcity and power shortages. With more IT parks coming up, we'll score high on built-up spaces too.

**What are your future plans?**

We are trying to bring in more big names to Kerala, including large global ITES companies. We'll also continue with our efforts to create better environments for attracting investments and build up enough human resources to meet requirements. e-Governance will also be given top priority. In short, we'll make sure God's Own e-State is here to stay!

# Pathbreaking Initiatives

Infrastructure development drives, ITES training programmes, ICT projects for the common man, e-Governance ventures... Kerala is the first State to make comprehensive use of IT, exploring every possibility to create a fully networked, IT savvy State.

An Akshaya E-kendra, Malappuram

FRIENDS centre

**Akshaya** The biggest ICT programme of its kind in the world envisaged to bridge the digital divide, **Akshaya E-kendras** provide functional e-literacy to one person in every family in the State and act as the front-end for Government service delivery. Thus addressing the Government's concerns of not only creating more jobs and improving governance, but also ensuring transparency in administration, facilitating empowerment of the people and fulfilling their right to information.

▎An E-kendra within 2 km of every household ▎Each caters to an average of 1000 families ▎All kendras networked together over the Internet ▎Kendras created and run by entrepreneurs ▎Tie-ups made with various organisations for service delivery, with the E-kendra playing the role of an intermediary ▎Malappuram becomes India's first 100% e-literate district

**FRIENDS** (Fast Reliable Instant Efficient Network for Disbursement of Services) An integrated utility service centre set up by the Department of IT in association with local bodies and seven Government departments, FRIENDS enables smooth and transparent C2G interface.

▎Single window service centres where all utility bills, fees and taxes pertaining to the participating departments can be remitted ▎14 centres across the 14 districts of the State ▎Each centre with 20 counters ▎Caters to an average of 12, 500 visitors per day

Bangalore has a popular café culture alongside its pub culture.

**Food & Drink**

An old world bar, Dewars is set in a British Raj style bungalow in the quaint Cantonment area of Bangalore. It's a long way from the stylish pubs of today but attracts a fair sized clientele.

The f Bar & Lounge is one of Bangalore's swankiest lounge bars and the Japanese food served here is something to rave about. Weekends are houseful with comfortable sofas and bar stools spilling over with Bangalore's hippest party crowd.

# Food & Drink

Bangalore can hold its own when it comes to places serving **gourmet** cuisine, **cool cafés**, **trendy pubs** and other indicators of the good life. The last five years have seen an explosion in **fine dining** restaurants, **ethnic eateries** and **nightclubs** that offer much more than just a table to place your drink on.

In Bangalore's balmy weather it's never too warm under a **large sunshade** and there are plenty of **open-air cafés**, **tearooms** and restaurants that let you soak in the city's sidewalk atmosphere while you grab a quick cappuccino or linger over a gourmet meal. The Café Coffee Day outlet in front of The Bombay Store overlooks the dense green of Cariappa Park while MG Road buzzes below and a cup of Mocha steams in front of you. At Sunny's, you can sit under a large beach umbrella on the third floor surrounded by lush plants and the tops of trees, while you tuck into a delicious salad created with care and served with finesse and a glass of wine.

Most restaurants and pubs are located in and around **central Bangalore**, and moving from one to another is quite easy. It's possible to rendezvous at one place, check out the 'scene' at another and end up at a pub where the food is famous. There's always a 'new' place in town and party folk are notoriously fickle, dropping last week's favourite for this week's new-kid-on-the-block without a pang.

As the sun goes down, Bangalore's **nightlife** comes alive. At last count there were over a **1,000 pubs**, **bars** and **restaurants**! From Mughlai Raan with Tandoori Roti, Neer Dosa with Pandi Curry, Wild Mushroom Stuffed Ravioli, Sushi and Miso Soup and Hummus with Pitta Bread, you can sample food from around the world. Equally significant is the dining experience: From a quick bite standing up to a leisurely sit down meal lasting seven elaborate courses, the possibilities are endless.

Other cities have discos to groove the night away, while Bangalore has pubs. Once the hangout of the party crowd, **pubs** have transformed themselves into **nightclubs** where the line between **drinking, dancing** and **socialising** mingles and merges into the early hours. The staid and stuffy pub has yielded to a modern variant with beanbags for seating, dance floors that ebb and flow depending on the size of the crowd, theme nights that drum up some excitement and even fashion shows that throw glitter and sparkle into the night.

Be warned though, that Cinderella like, all nightlife comes to a grinding halt at **11:30pm**, a **closing time** carved in stone. This is when you will be asked to place your last order, but above the din you can hear plans to shift the party to someone's house!

## Kitchen Truths

For the new age gourmand who wants the pleasures of eating without the pain of weight gain, the trend by restaurants to serve **low-cal** food is very welcome. Be pleasantly surprised to see **light salads** and **grilled food** alongside dosas dripping with ghee and Paneer Makhanwala! The use of olive oil, lemon juice and whole grains, steamed and grilled, finds many takers today. If there's nothing in print, don't succumb! Ask the chef to make a special order and sit back.

There are few things you need to **keep in mind**. For starters, there is now a grave distinction between the **Continental** food of yore and food from the Western World! Steaks, Au Gratin bakes and Roast Chicken have been joined by Italian pastas, French nouvelle cuisine, Cajun Fish, Mediterranean dips and so on. Geography lessons are in order if this is your current choice.

Keep in mind too, that **multicuisine** restaurants, once the backbone of the dining out trade, are giving way to single cuisine, speciality places. It's great for the gourmand, but terrible for large crowds of democratic eaters! However, many multicuisine restaurants hide some great stuff in their menus, and deserve a second look. A trend in the other direction may be seen in **Chinese** restaurants that have been quick to augment their tired menus with at least a few **Thai** dishes. **Japanese** food is the new rage and Bangalore's right up there with high quality Sushi and Teriyaki.

## Many Proud Cuisines

Karnataka nurtures many proud cuisines in its embrace: **Udupi, Mangalorean, Kodava** and rustic **Kannadiga** are some of the better known ones. Each relies on the fruits of the land and local spices to create distinctive dishes, relished through the centuries. So, while the speckled brown **Ragi** flour is freely adapted in the northern plains, smooth and creamy **coconut milk** is absolutely essential on the coastal belt and Kodava food uses plenty of **spices** grown on coffee plantations.

**Rice** is the most preferred grain. It is used whole, raw, parboiled, red, broken, crushed, powdered, cooked, pureed, flattened, balled up or fluffed. Teamed with lentils and vegetables and tempered with button onions, it becomes *Bisi Bele Bhath*,

a delectable 'khichdi' or porridge celebrated in Kannadiga homes. In Kodava homes, rice storms the ancient bastion of wheat – the roti! Called *Akki Roti*, it is the southern answer to a northern staple and goes very well with their chicken curries and other spicy, tart and pungent dishes.

## Legacy of Vegetarian Cooking

A small temple town off the national highway that connects Mangalore to Goa, **Udupi's** name in culinary history books is assured: It is now a byword for **vegetarian food** around the world. In fact, so powerful has the Udupi brand become that it has nearly eclipsed other southern regional cuisines! From New Delhi to New York and all around the world, Udupi is synonymous for fast or quickly served, piping hot south Indian *dosas*, *idlis* and other snacks. The abundant coconuts, perennial gourds and heavy emphasis on rice-based dishes mark the food of this eastern edge of Karnataka.

But how did Udupi food travel so well and so far beyond its local boundaries? It is believed that the practice of cooking everyday for large numbers of devotees in this **temple town** spawned a number of cooks and helpers. They were persuaded to travel with their trade by at least one entrepreneur and the rest is history. Small, functional eateries, with a limited menu and

stand-up tables encouraged those looking for a quick bite and low prices. It also appealed to the large numbers of displaced south Indians, largely vegetarian and looking for comfort food cooked in '**pure**' vegetarian kitchens.

Another revolution in vegetarian cooking has taken place right in Bangalore city. A small, high quality restaurant serving only breakfast and tiffin a few decades ago, is now the keeper of the Kannadiga faith, the pride of the Kannadiga Brahmin! Mavalli Tiffin Rooms or MTR as it is popularly known, attracts thousands despite the rushing traffic outside its doors. Diners, hungry for grandma's kitchen style of superbly cooked and traditionally served food, flock here and are never disappointed. It's the one place where even the fussiest, most conservative vegetarian, who will not touch cooked food from a non-Brahmin kitchen, is happy to take his grandmother!

## Non-vegetarian Delights – Mangalorean and Kodava Cuisine

But not all food from this state is vegetarian. A long silvery coast, fringed with coconut palms and dense forests on rain washed hills, bring a whole new perspective to the state's cooking. Mangalorean food is the name given to the food that's cooked in homes all the way down the coast. Udupi is the most popular

vegetarian one, while the region of south Kanara has Bunt cooking, Christian and Muslim as well.

The non-vegetarian food features all kinds of luscious red fish and seafood curries, cooked with freshly ground **coconut paste**, bright red *Badige* chillies and piercingly sour **tamarind** or kokum. Served with all kinds of rice dishes, they make a simple and satisfying meal. The deliciously crisp fried fish dishes have made it to the hors d'oeuvres list across India. All over the state, coconut is used extensively and is only matched by rice in its popularity.

**Kodava** cuisine has finally earned its place in the sun as a few daring Kodavas let outsiders into their culinary secrets! Hunting in the deep forests and fishing in the many streams and rivers provided enough wild pig, fowl and fish to keep home fires burning. Surrounded by **coffee estates** with **pepper** vines and **cardamom** bushes, emerald green paddy fields, coconut and banana plantations, Kodava cuisine is at once **rich** and **gracious**, leaning heavily on the fruits of the land. Expect no less than a few different meat preparations if you want to dine Kodava style. *Pandi* (pork) curry, *Kadambuttu* (rice dumplings) and *Bembla* (bamboo shoot) curry are just some of the more delectable ones.

## Bangalore's Smorgasbord!

More people than ever before are eating out in Bangalore. Couples, singles, large families, small families, friends and business associates may be seen wining and dining at all hours of the day and night! And the choices are staggering.

Most restaurants undertake **outdoor catering** and will be happy to give you the whole works, tables, tablecloths and even waiters if that is your wish. Just pick up the phone and check. The same goes for **home delivery** in white plastic tubs.

*Stark World – Bangalore & Karnataka* aims to capture the full flavour of Bangalore's many restaurants, pubs, bars and so on. This is a carefully conceived list of the nicest places in town and some of the most exclusive. We hope you **enjoy** using it as much as we enjoyed putting it together for you!

A leisurely breakfast at the India Coffee House

# KANNADIGA

## Jowar Bhakry

*Kamat Yatri Nivas, 3rd Main, 1st Cross,
Gandhinagar, Bangalore 560009*
**Tel** *2226 0088*
**Open** *12noon to 3:30pm and
7pm to 10:30pm*
**Meal for Two** *Rs 200*
**Cards** *All*
**Alcohol** *Not Served*

This down-to-earth restaurant under
the Kamat Yatri Nivas umbrella is
special – it serves the authentic fare of
north Karnataka. A many-course meal
with the region's signature jowar roti
or Bhakry is served on plantain leaves.
An assortment of curries, dry chutney
powders, raw onion, methi leaves and
cubes of butter are served as well. The
'unlimited thali' concept applies here –
you can have as many rotis as you
please and waiters stream by with
large pots of the food.
Health freaks and others take note –
the Bhakry doesn't carry a trace of oil
and is made only with water. The
traditional brinjal curry with a gravy of
sesame, peanut and jaggery is
embellished with tart gooseberry
pickle and garlic flavoured buttermilk,
all at once distinct and delicious. Rice
follows with sambar, papad and curd.
The Champakali sweet and the fruit
salad with ice cream strike a bit of a
jarring note in the otherwise strict

Kannadiga menu. Try the beeda, it's the
perfect dessert to round off the hearty
meal.
The threadbare décor is enlivened by the
view of rows of cooks making bhakris by
the dozen in deft circular movements.
(The Bhakry is fashioned by hand,
without a rolling pin.)
There is a sit-out section for more relaxed
dining. The crowds flock on weekends,
so be prepared for a long wait.

## Kadambam Iyengar Cuisine Restaurant

*4/1 Devaiah Court, 8th Main,
22nd Cross, III Block, Jayanagar,
Bangalore 560011*
**Tel** *5763 7407*
**Branch** *Dickenson Road, 2509 2055*
**Open** *7am to 10pm*
**Meal for Two** *Rs 100*
**Cards** *Not Accepted*
**Alcohol** *Not Served*

Not many people pay attention to
Kadambam's Iyengar cooking heritage,
they just appreciate the good food. The
ambience at Kadambam is in keeping
with this image – portraits of gods and
goddesses adorn the wall and classical
music plays in the background. While
the Iyengar dishes are most popular,
regular south Indian dishes like dosas
also attract many customers.

## Konkan

*3, I Floor, Coles Road, Frazer Town,
Bangalore 560005*
**Tel** *5119 1813*
**Open** *11am to 3pm and 7pm to 11pm*
**Meal for Two** *Rs 400*
**Cards** *All except American Express*
**Alcohol** *Not Served*

This is a middleclass restaurant serving
delicacies and regular fare from the
Konkan coast – the lush, green western
edge of Karanataka where the warm
waters of the Arabian Sea meet beaches
of silvery sands. Meat, fish and coconut
come together to create a distinct
cuisine, served with signature red boiled
rice or paper-thin Neer dosas. The
special of the day at Konkan is dictated

Kudla dishes out traditional Mangalorean delicacies.

by the catch, always a good sign if
you're looking for quality food. All
varieties of fish, prawns, crabs, mussels
and squids are served here in a fair
good rendition.

## Kudla

*Hotel Ramanashree,
16 Raja Ram Mohan Roy Road,
Bangalore 560025*
**Tel** *5668 4050*
**Open** *12noon to 3pm and 7pm to 11pm*
**Meal for Two** *Rs 500*
**Cards** *All*
**Alcohol** *Served*

Speciality restaurants deserve high praise
for their courage to go the whole way.
Kudla, which means Mangalore in Tulu,
the language of the Bunt community, is
such a place. Expect nothing but truly
authentic Mangalorean coastal food,
served with no shortcuts. Crabs, mussels,
prawns and fish come into their own in
this essentially homely style of cooking,
redolent with the aroma of freshly
ground and roasted spices, creamy
coconut milk and fragrant curry leaves.
Seafood lovers can savour a range of
south Kanara delicacies from Bangudde
Gassi and Yetti Fry to Anjal Masala and
Pondi with Kori Kachupu. The region's
staple cereal is rice, and it assumes many
forms as it is powdered dry or ground to
a paste, flattened or rolled and finally
cooked, fried or steamed.
All the seafood is handpicked and you
can choose the crabs from the aquarium
up front. The ambience is quintessentially
Mangalorean with an ornate décor
and stewards dressed in traditional
costume.

## MTR

*11 Lalbagh Road, Bangalore 560027*
**Tel** *2222 0022*
**Open** *Tiffin-6:30am to 11pm and
3:30pm to 7:30pm*
*Lunch-12:30pm to 2:30pm and 8pm to
9:30pm. Closed for lunch on Monday.*
**Meal for Two** *Rs 150*
**Cards** *Not Accepted*
**Alcohol** *Not Served*

A brisk morning walk in Lalbagh's lovely
gardens followed by a sizzling dosa and
coffee at MTR is the stuff old timers

lived for. Not much has changed
except the size of the crowds at MTR
that grow larger every year and the
addition of a 14-course lunch. The
lunch is a gastronome's delight and
you need an hour to get through it,
and the rest of the day to work it off!
The food is authentic Kannadiga
vegetarian cuisine with no shortcuts.
Breakfast is quickly sold out so get
there early if you want some choice in
the menu.

## Vidyarthi Bhavan

*32 Gandhi Bazaar, Bangalore 560004*
**Tel:** *2667 7588*
**Open** *6:30am to 11:30pm and
2pm to 8pm. Closed on Friday.*
**Meal for Two** *Rs 100*
**Cards** *Not Accepted*
**Alcohol** *Not Served*

Don't be misled by the non-descript
looks of this small eatery or its
middleclass location. The hotel's
clientele reads like a who's who: SM
Krishna, Girish Karnad and Anant Nag
are just some of the famous
personalities who swear by its Mysore
Masala Dosa – thick and crisp on the
outside and soft inside. It is served
with a chunk of melting butter,
traditional fresh and smooth coconut
chutney and a mashed curry of potato
and onions in just the right
proportions.
This landmark eatery has even been
featured on the BBC! Founded way
back in 1938, the hotel's old
weathered building remains
unchanged. Tucked away in the
crowded Basavanagudi suburb, the
hotel is frequented by students,
professionals and old timers.

## Woody's

*177 Commercial Street,
Bangalore 560001*
**Tel** *2558 2714, 2559 6444*
**Branch** *JP Nagar, 2649 0888*
**Open** *9am to 11pm*
**Meal for Two** *Rs 150*
**Cards** *All except American Express*
**Alcohol** *Not Served*

For years now, Woody's has
functioned as the sole restaurant on

Waiting to sample MTR's famous lunch

# Dosa Index

No south Indian snack is more popular than the Dosa – a flat pancake of fermented rice and lentils, served with chutney, a smooth paste of different condiments and sambar, a broth of vegetables and lentils. There are as many versions as there are cooks and so it is not surprising to find even Chinese and Italian pizza-style dosas on the same menu as the traditional Rava Dosa!

Plain Dosa

The most popular dosa is the regular paper thin variety roasted to a crisp on one side and soft enough to soak up the sambar on the other. But there are plenty of others – soft, crisp, spongy, sizzling with onions, coloured with green gram or ragi flour, freshly ground or fermented and finally those sprinkled with coriander, coconut or served plain.

The little bowls of sambar and chutney that are placed next to a sizzling hot dosa can raise the meal to great heights or turn it into a greasy memory. Where you choose to sample a dosa will decide it. And finally, a piping hot cup of freshly ground and roasted coffee is the best way to wash it all down.

The most famous dosa that has travelled across oceans and continents is the **Plain Dosa**. It is made from a batter of raw rice and urad dal soaked for three hours. The end result is crisp, crunchy and wafer-like. It is best eaten with coconut chutney and sambar.

It's more luxurious and filling cousin is the **Masala Dosa**, made from a combination of raw rice, urad daal, fenugreek seeds and a couple of tablespoons of rava. To achieve that prized golden brown colour, a little sugar and salt may be added. Masala dosas are served with a stuffing of boiled potatoes sautéed with onions and green chillies, seasoned with mustard and turmeric and finally garnished with fresh coriander leaves.

Paper Dosa

Masala Dosa

The holey and crunchy **Rava Dosa** is made from a batter of rava or sooji, rice flour, wheat flour, curd and salt. It is always served with an assortment of chutneys made from fresh coconut, mint or tomato.

The slightly thicker, green-hued **Green Gram Dosa** is made from rice, green gram, green chillies and fresh coriander leaves. Unlike other dosas, it comes with a vegetable saagu – a spicy curry of assorted vegetables.

The **Ragi Dosa** is a healthier alternative and features on the plate of the health conscious and those with diabetes. This nutritious dosa is made from ragi flour and buttermilk and a touch of rice flour. A traditional accompaniment is cucumber gojju – a sweet and sour paste of cucumber.

A new innovation to the dosa family is the **Vegetable Dosa** made from regular dosa batter into which mixed chopped vegetables are added. It is usually served with chutney and a pat of glistening butter.

One of the healthiest dosas is the **Sprouted Gram Dosa,** made from a batter of raw rice and an assortment of sprouted grams soaked for a couple of hours. It comes with traditional coconut chutney or sambar.

The **Methi Dosa**, made with methi seeds (fenugreek) and urad daal is given to nursing mothers, diabetics and others on a special diet.

Little known but well loved is the spongy **Set Dosa**. It boasts an unusual batter of boiled rice, flattened rice and urad daal soaked for three hours. It is served with vegetable saagu and coconut chutney.

The delicately flavoured **Coconut Dosa** is made from rice soaked and ground with coconut milk. It tastes delicious plain, but can also be eaten with any chutney.

High in proteins is the **Mixed Gram Dosa** which uses a rich batter of four lentils – toovar, urad, green gram and Bengal gram along with rice, soaked for a few hours. Both chutney and sambar are popular accompaniments.

A thick, spongy dosa sprinkled with chopped onions – the **Onion Uttappa** – makes for a satisfying meal. This popular dosa is made from a batter of rice and buttermilk. A very special dish is the **Saagu Dosa** with a thick centre filled with vegetable stuffing, but crisp and wafer-thin around the edges. It is best eaten piping hot.

Shanthi Sagar, a popular restaurant chain in the city.

Onion Uttappa

Mangalorean food's contribution to the dosa family is the **Neer Dosa**, milky white and lacy. It is made from ground rice and grated coconut. Remarkably thin and versatile, it may be eaten with a simple syrup of coconut and jaggery or a fiery red chicken curry. Bowing to popular north Indian demand is the recent **Paneer Dosa**. Grated paneer, garam masala and ginger are mixed in with regular dosa batter. Somewhere along the way, the flagship of vegetarian cuisine has accepted a meat filling and we get the **Kheema Dosa**. Aromatic mince sits well inside a crunchy dosa and is served with tomato chutney.

The Royal Afghan (See Pg 108)

Commercial Street, and no one is complaining. The service is quick, the interiors cheerful and the food is high quality south Indian vegetarian snacks and mini meals. The crisp Plain Dosa served with chutney and sambar and the filter coffee are as good as the best.

A simple no-fuss restaurant, it provides a quick food or coffee break for busy shoppers, harried parents and cosy couples. And on Sundays, when parking is possible and shopping slows down, unhurried early morning breakfasts bring back the flavour of old Bangalore. Downstairs is the self-service section where you can choose between counters and high stools (a great favourite with kids) or small tables. Upstairs is for more leisurely dining with sink-in sofas and wider tables. There are some interesting items hidden in the rather comprehensive menu. South Kanara specialities like Kadabu, Semigai with Kurma and coconut milk, Mangalore Pathrode and bajjis feature on different days through the week.

There are at least 12 kinds of dosas and rice dishes and the Mini Meal for the really hungry. The north Indian selection features the usual suspects like Channa Bhatura, Pav Bhaji, Vegetarian kababs, curries, rotis and so on. Chinese food, or rather Indianised Chinese with Gobi Manchurian and Paneer Manchurian

hold the Indo-China flag high! Besides all this, there are a variety of juices, milkshakes, beverages, sweets and ice creams.

## ANDHRA

### Eden Park
*21/1 Cunningham Road, Behind The Hindu, Bangalore 560001*
*Tel 2286 1100/4100*
**Open** *11:30am to 3:30pm and 7pm to 11pm*
**Meal for Two** *Rs 400*
**Cards** *MasterCard & Visa*
**Alcohol** *Served*

What sets Eden Park apart from the rest of the pack of Andhra food restaurants is the soothing outdoors with towering trees and lush gardens. For those seeking a quick meal there is a functional indoor seating area packed with granite topped tables laid with plantain leaves and little jars of pickles and powders. Here you get the 'unlimited' thali with plenty of everything. Meat dishes are a side order.

The outdoor restaurant with a well stocked bar is a rare jewel in the crowded commercial area. Quiet candlelit dinners and robust evenings happen simultaneously here. The children's amusement park in a corner of the property is a big draw.

### Maduri Grand
*124 D, Surya Chambers, Murugeshapalya, Airport Road, Bangalore 560017*
*Tel 2522 3939, 2522 4949*
**Open** *11:30am to 4pm and 6:30pm to 11pm*
**Meal for Two** *Rs 300*
**Cards** *All except American Express*
**Alcohol** *Served*

This is another Andhra chain restaurant serving hot and spicy food. Thalis, curries and dry meat dishes, the ubiquitous chutney powder and spicy rasam, Biryani, chicken and fish dishes are very popular. There is ample parking space.

### Nagarjuna Savoy
*45/3 Residency Cross Road, Bangalore 560025*
*Tel 2559 9775*
**Branches** *Lady Curzon Road, 2559 0777; Jayanagar, 2665 6566 Residency Road, 2559 2233*
**Open** *12:30pm to 3:30pm and 7pm to 11:30pm*
**Meal for Two** *Rs 300*
**Cards** *All*
**Alcohol** *Served*

One of the Nagarjuna chain of restaurants, Nagarjuna Savoy is the one with tablecloth, freezing airconditioning and less of the hurry and bustle of the regular Andhra eatery. The food is typical Andhra restaurant fare with an overload of green chillies. The hot and tart Fish Curry served with dosas is a favourite.

### Nandhini
*5th Main Road, West of Chord Road, Rajajinagar, Bangalore 560010*
*Tel 2335 0055, 2310 2939*
**Branches** *Minerva Circle, 2662 4444; Jayanagar, 2699 1199; Gandhinagar, 2220 3842; Indiranagar, 2521 2068; Koramangala,2563 0202; Sankey Road, 2344 8985; St.Marks Road, 5123 3333*
**Open** *11:30am to 4pm and 6:30pm to 11:30pm*
**Meal for Two** *Rs 350*
**Cards** *All except American Express*
**Alcohol** *Served*

Nandhini serves hot and spicy Andhra food with plenty of curried vegetables, aromatic daals, unique chutneys and

'unlimited' helpings, served on banana leaves in a noisy, bustling atmosphere. As in all Andhra places, the Biryani is very popular and comes in two sizes. The liberal use of red and green chillies comes as a bit of a shock to the system unless you are a regular. Non-vegetarians have a wide array of side dishes to choose from. The ambience is functional and there's a lot of seating, all quite close together. Door delivery and takeaways are a more relaxed option.

### RR
*55 Church Street, Bangalore 560001*
*Tel 5112 2323*
**Open** *12noon to 3pm and 7pm to 11:30pm*
**Meal for Two** *Rs 300*
**Cards** *All*
**Alcohol** *Served*

The first and once the only place people went for Andhra food, RR downed shutters a few years ago, (probably) went into deep introspection and has now emerged revitalised and all freshened up. The new look is bright and spacious.
The menu is the city's favourite Andhra food, unlimited thalis, spicy meat and chicken side dishes and the ever popular Biryani. The food is laced with green chillies and is definitely not for the fainthearted.

## CHETTINAD

### Annachi
*100Ft. Road, Indiranagar, Bangalore 560008*
*Tel 5126 1181*
**Open** *11:30am to 3:30pm and 7:30pm to 11pm*
**Meal for Two** *Rs 400*
**Cards** *All*
**Alcohol** *Served*

Annachi serving Chettinad food has already won the favour of foodies across the city in the few short months since opening. Food served here is tempered with pepper, cumin and ginger in a style reminiscent of the Chettinad culinary bastions of Thanjavur and Madurai in Tamil Nadu.
The restaurant has been decorated like a traditional Chettinad house with carved

Pandi curry and Kadambuttu

The journey starts here

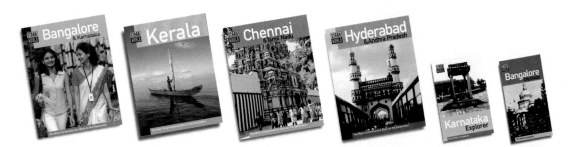

STARK WORLD

Destination books ▪ Theme guides ▪ Travel magazines ▪ Travel films ▪ Online guides ▪ Stock images ▪ Customized publishing

StarkWorld, Infinitum Publishing Pvt Ltd, 173, 9th Cross, Indiranagar 1st Stage, Bangalore - 560038. Tel: 91-80-51255036, email:response@starkworld.net

stone pillars and solid teak doors. Exotic meats feature on the menu, including Japanese quail and baby shark (goes by the name Soraputtu). The seafood on offer includes a range of crab, silver fish and prawn curries. The Vadakari, Chettinad idlis, idiappams and Vellaipoondu Kozhambu with a piquant garlic gravy are some of the traditional vegetarians dishes. Both thali meals and buffets come with a combination of rice, sambars, rasams, curries and gravies.

## KERALA

### Coconut Grove

*86 Church Street, Bangalore 560001*
*Tel 2559 6149*
*Branches Koramangala, 2550 3695;*
*Marathahalli, 2854 0603*
*Open 12:30pm to 3:30pm and*
*7pm to 11:30pm*
*Meal for Two Rs 600*
*Cards All*
*Alcohol Served*

An easy ethnic atmosphere pervades Coconut Grove with copper serving dishes, grass matting screens and waiters in traditional dress. All south Indian cuisines relying on the rich flavour of coconut are served here. So you can order from Kerala, Kodava, Chettinad, Goan and Mangalorean food. Food tourists may watch their appams fluff up on the fire right in front of them. The food is served in copper steel thalis lined with banana leaves. It's popular with the office crowd looking for a little something different.

### Dakshin

*ITC Hotel Windsor Sheraton & Towers,*
*25 Golf Course Road, Bangalore 560052*
*Tel 2226 9898*
*Open 12:30pm to 3pm and 7:30pm to*
*11:45pm*
*Meal for Two Rs 1,500*
*Cards All*
*Alcohol Served*

For a pan-southern gastronomic experience there is nothing quite like Dakshin at the Windsor Sheraton. Signature food from all the four southern states is meticulously prepared and presented here. Fresh flowers, southern artefacts and waiters in regional attire complete the picture.
Start your southern journey with Muneer, a drink of sugarcane, tender

A traditional Kerala 'sadya'

coconut, honey and the unusual and delicious flavour of sandalwood. The Mysore Rasam, hot and peppery also makes a good beginning.
Karnataka's varied cuisine is well represented with Kane Rawa Fry from Mangalore, Pandi Curry from Coorg, kootus, palyas, gojjus and others. If you choose Andhra food you can expect fiery chicken and prawn dishes, Tomato Daal and of course Gongura Chutney. Chettinad Chicken and Avial from Tamil Nadu and stew, Fish Moilee etc from Kerala are some of the others. The accompaniments like Appam, Neer Dosa, sannas, parathas, puris, Idiyappam etc give it all a truly authentic touch. The Payasam is a fine end to the meal.

### Karavalli

*Gateway Hotel on Residency Road, 66*
*Residency Road, Bangalore 560025*
*Tel 5660 4545*
*Open 12:30pm to 3:30pm and 7:30pm*
*to 11pm*
*Meal for Two Rs 1,400*
*Cards All*
*Alcohol Served*

If you have the money and the taste for top quality cooking, come straight here. Ranked one of the top ten restaurants in India, it put Bangalore on the foodie map. Karavalli, named for the lush coastal stretch along India's south-eastern edge, is a gourmet's delight: The food is sublime and so is the setting. You may choose to sit in a garden under the spreading tamarind tree or in the courtyard of a Mangalore-style house. Local spices, red chillies, coconut, peppers, fresh fish, meat and vegetables of coastal Goa, Karwar, Mangalore and Kerala, perfectly smoked Kudumpuli and toddy vinegar are cooked on wood and charcoal fires to produce a mouth watering array of fine food.
All meals are served with piping hot rasam that gets the gastric juices going! This is one place where vegetarians are treated with as much respect as the non-vegetarians.

### Padippura

*65 Jyoti Nivas College Road,*
*Koramangala, Bangalore 560095*
*Tel 2563 1999*
*Open 7:30am to 10:30am, 12noon to*
*3pm and 7pm to 11pm*
*Meal for Two Rs 300*
*Cards All except American Express*
*Alcohol Not Served*

Lovers of authentic Kerala food have good reason to celebrate at the opening of Padippura with its range of Kerala delicacies that don't often travel out of the state. Top of the list is the Kappa Biryani, a robust combination of the earthy tapioca and shredded beef or chicken. Padippura also scores some more with a delectable Prawn Biryani, and duck and quail curries. The buffet at lunchtime is a big spread and brings in the local software crowd in droves. A fried and a curried non-vegetarian dish are standard, along with a number of vegetable curries and fries, delicious date chutney and refreshing buttermilk. There are a decent number of vegetarian dishes. The special weekend menu is exciting enough to pull anyone out of bed on a lazy weekend! Festival days are heavily booked so call ahead to avoid disappointment.

### Windsor Pub

*7, 1st Main, Vasantha Nagar,*
*Bangalore 560052*
*Tel 2225 8847*
*Open 11:30am to 3pm and 6pm to 11pm*
*Meal for Two Rs 450*
*Cards MasterCard & Visa*
*Alcohol Served*

The combination of draught beer with Pandi Curry, Mangalorean prawns, Beef Fry and other robust fare is a meal in heaven. Windsor Pub has a small but satisfying selection of all the best food from the four southern states. There are no weakly flavoured curries or watery stews served here. The carefully chosen dishes are cooked to perfection and the spices, fire, flavour, colour and texture are just right.
The Pandi Curry is redolent with the aroma of black Coorg vinegar and pepper, the Mangalorean Prawn Curry is a naturally beautiful shade of red with just the right amount of coconut, ground to the right consistency. The sannas and appams are made with a light touch and the rice is perfectly sticky. The restaurant has comfortable seating and is clean and cheerful. Service is good and always ask for the special of the day or the freshest seafood on offer.

## GOAN

### Opus

*4 Off Palace Cross Road,*
*Chakravathy Layout, Bangalore*
*Tel 2344 2580*
*Open 11am to 11:30pm*
*Meal for Two Rs 500*
*Cards All except American Express*
*Alcohol Served*

Opus has swiftly stepped into the space left empty by glitzy nightclubs and stuffy restaurants. It aims to be the be the kind of place where you can hang out with your friends, strum a few chords on the guitar lying around, play a few rounds of scrabble, strike a melody on the piano or just lie back on the many beanbags and listen to the retro and jazz music playing in the background. Chess, carom and pictionary are the other temptations here. Families with kids who get to run around or scrawl on the enormous blackboard are particularly fond of the place! It's also one of the few places where you can enjoy Bangalore's famed weather – the restaurant opens into an amphitheatre of sorts with swaying coconut palms and a pebbled courtyard that can seat more than a hundred guests. This makes it a great place for private parties. The food is largely Goan with a few variations tagged along. Starters are a big hit, especially the stuffed mushrooms, fried prawns and Goan sausages. For the main course the sandwiches rate better than the Goan dishes, the latter a tad too sour. The dessert menu carries the famous Bibinca and a couple of cheesecakes and other toothsome concoctions.

### Sossegado

*1762, I Floor, Dr. Rajkumar Road,*
*Navarang Circle, Rajajinagar*
*Bangalore 560010*
*Tel 5698 6766*
*Open 12noon to 2:30pm and 7pm to*
*10:30pm*
*Meal for Two Rs 250*
*Cards All*
*Alcohol Not Served*

Sossegado is the city's first exclusively Goan restaurant serving 'essentially coastal' food, as the signboard informs. Mangalorean fare is also on the menu. No one's complaining as Bangalore's many foodies can't seem to get enough of seafood, coastal food and just good food!

The name means 'relaxed and unhurried' and reflects the chilled-out Goan way of life. The restaurant's pleasing interiors of yellow, orange and blue, the light furniture and an aquarium with bright, darting fish do just that. Stick to the rule of asking for the day's fresh catch if you're looking for seafood. For starters try the Kokum and fofos. A choice of seafood, mutton, chicken and Tandoori foods is offered for the main course. Goan specialities include the Caril de Camario, Pomfret Cladinho, Xacuti de Galinha, Chicken Cafreal and Charcoal Pomfret.

The menu also features a range of Mangalorean delicacies. The Stuffed Crab is a wonderfully fresh recipe of crabmeat, onions and coriander stirred like scrambled eggs and served in a crab shell. The Kane Rava Fry has a nice tangy masala inside and is done just right. For the main course give the regular Mangalorean Prawn Curry a miss. Instead, try the Pomfret in Green Masala. The gravy is delicately flavoured and smooth as silk, perfect with the paper thin and sticky Neer dosas.

There is the odd Bengali dish, some north Indian regulars like Kadhai Paneer, Tandoori Jhinga and so on. In fact, there is a wide array of Tandoori dishes besides the Goan and Mangalorean ones. Prices are reasonable and parking is not impossible.

## NORTH INDIAN

### Angeethi

*1 Museum Road, Off MG Road, Bangalore 560001*
*Tel 5111 3340*
*Open 12noon to 3pm and 6:45pm to 11:45pm*
*Meal for Two Rs 900*
*Cards All*
*Alcohol Served*

The rustic, roadside dhaba dishing up authentic Punjabi farmer fare, has been reinvented in the heart of the city with old movie posters, charpoys and even a paanwaala! The food is good quality and very popular. North Indian dishes rule with some seafood to widen the appeal.

### Banjara

*19/2 Kumara Krupa Road, Bangalore 560001*
*Tel 2226 2756*
*Branch Hotel Ramanashree, 2222 0247*
*Open 12noon to 3pm and 7pm to 11pm*
*Meal for Two Rs 600*
*Cards All*
*Alcohol Served*

Banjara is your regular little restaurant where good food, good service and comfortable surroundings have built up a loyal patronage. There is a variety of cuisines available under one roof –

# Darshinis: It Doesn't Get Cheaper Than This!

Imagine a restaurant where you can put aside your table manners, serve yourself and forget about tipping a waiter? Welcome to the darshini – Bangalore's chain of self-service stand-up eateries that cater strictly for those who want to eat their food with minimal fuss. These quasi-cafés dot the streets of the city, far outnumbering its pubs, gardens and software parks. Buy a coupon, gulp down the food that is ready in the time it takes you to pocket your change and be on your way. It is no wonder then that students, busy executives, morning walkers, retired pensioners and housewives with children find them convenient and acceptable.

The décor at a darshini is functional, the space limited and waiters and chairs are indulgences they do without. Despite that, you will always see crowds of people standing around cramped tables that often spillover onto the pavement, digging into Fried Rice, steaming Bonda Soup and the ubiquitous dosa.

It was almost a decade ago that the dingy coffee bar and the purist Udupi hotel fused into the cheerful darshini. These small, cramped joints sticking to the pay-first-eat-later concept, marketed the standard 'idli-vada-sambar' fare under the trendier label of 'south Indian fast food'. Branding became an important ingredient, and a string of darshinis – Upahara Darshini, Megha Darshini and Indra Darshini mushroomed across Bangalore. Over the years, darshinis have given in to the increasingly adventurous tastes of their customers by adding north Indian dishes such as rotis, naans, kulchas, curries, pulaos and even crossing the Great Wall into Chinese noodles, all strictly vegetarian! Soups, chaats, juices and even milkshakes have happily joined the menu.

Bangalore's middle class is more than happy sampling 'exotic' and once 'forbidden' dishes in the comfort of their favourite darshini. Chinese and north Indian dishes are not so much tweaked as unrecognisably altered to satisfy southern palates! The greatest attraction still remains the pricing – downright cheap. The most expensive dish never costs more than Rs 25. Auto rickshaw drivers and daily wage earners share a table with software engineers and managers. This is truly the most egalitarian eating stop!

Chinese, north Indian and Continental – which adds to the appeal. The Aaloo Channa Chaat and Jal Jeera make a great start. The salad is not very filling and the Jal Jeera gets your appetite up! Those seeking a Chinese experience may like to start with a soup – all the usual like Manchow and Tomyum or the bland cream soups like Tomato and Spinach which go down well on a cold day.

The kababs are robustly flavoured and served in generous portions. The Murgh Malai Kabab is better than average and the Macchi Tikki is quite exemplary. There are about 40 starters to choose from and if you get carried away you will not be able to do justice to the main course!

If you're looking for something spicy try the north Indian Murgh Methi Hyderabadi and others listed in the

Tandoori section. There is a selection of biryanis and an exhaustive list of Chinese dishes. Continental fare has the old time favourites like Veg Gratin and Chicken Stew, besides Pasta. There is more than one dessert depending on which country you want to end the evening with!

Banjara is a good choice when you want to take a large party out and everyone has their pet preference of dishes. It has some cosy corners that work for a small group as well.

### Biryani Merchant

*32 Castle Street, Bangalore 560025*
*Tel 5112 8081*
*Open 1pm to 3pm and 8pm to 11pm. Closed on Monday.*
*Meal for Two Rs 300*
*Cards MasterCard & Visa*
*Alcohol Not Served*

Here is a restaurant dedicated to Biryani – that combination of rice and meat that everyone has at least one favourite version of. Vegetarians won't go hungry given the wide variety and unusual combinations on offer. Thirty eight biryanis are served here including delicacies like Kolkata's Shiraz Biryani and Hyderabadi, Sindhi, and Karachi biryanis. The menu changes everyday and every biryani is served with its correct accompaniment – the Calicut Biryani cooked in dum and coconut charcoal is accompanied by pickle, papad and Suleimani Chai, while the Hyderabadi Biryani comes with Mirchi ka Salan, Dalcha and Bagare Baingan. Set Meals have a serving of Biryani accompanied by kababs, papads, pickles, two kinds of raitha, a hookah, Suleimani Chai and a choice of two desserts, all priced at Rs 300. The buffet spreads feature an extensive range of vegetarian and non-vegetarian biryanis: Calicut Fish Biryani, Awadhi Murgh Biryani Bharwan Lauki, Chettinad Biryani, Rajma and corn Biryani, Nawabi Tarkari and Sabz Kheema Biriyani are some of the highlights. Biryani Merchant offers specials for kids like the doodh and fruit Biryani! Desserts include Sheer Kurma, Shahi Tukda and Kaddu ki Kheer.

## Canopy

*II Floor, Public Utility Building,*
*MG Road, Bangalore 560001*
*Tel 2558 8542*
*Open 11am to 3pm and 7pm to 11:30pm*
*Meal for Two Rs 500*
*Cards: All*

Canopy's perched on the side terrace of Bangalore's tallest skyscraper so it has a fair view of the green surrounding MG Road. The open-air dining area, a sprawling landscaped garden including a small waterfall and the multicuisine menu have made it a popular haunt since the seventies. The lunch buffet is a favourite with the office crowd and offers great value for money – south Indian, north Indian and Chinese dishes are served along with dessert for just Rs 130.

Dinners are a fancy affair where you get to pick from Tandoori, Mughlai, Chinese and Continental cuisine. Mutton Biryani, Kabab and Gajar ka Halwa are the in-house specials. On balmy evenings, the tiled cottages set amidst green potted plants offer a quiet and cosy corner with the rush of traffic below. In winter, small charcoal braziers are strewn around for guests to toast themselves. There is also a restaurant indoors.

Canopy is a popular banquet venue where gala wedding receptions, birthday bashes, cocktail dos' and business conferences are hosted regularly. There are two well-appointed halls – Revival and Embassy – with enough room to entertain up to 2,000 people. A sumptuous buffet spread is served and part of the terrace doubles up as a dance floor. Music, decorations and entertainment are organised according to the guest's preferences like magic shows for children's parties.

Valet parking is available and the capsule elevators are a favourite with kids.

## Dum Pukht Jolly Nabobs

*ITC Hotel Windsor Sheraton & Towers,*
*25 Golf Course Road,*
*Bangalore 560052*
*Tel 2226 9898*
*Open 7pm to 11:30pm*
*Meal for Two Rs 1,600*
*Cards All*
*Alcohol Served*

True to the ITC Windsor Sheraton spirit of celebrating everything Indian, is Jolly Nabobs, the name an instant Raj reckoner. The key word is Nabob or Nawab and all manner of royal things – food and memorabilia – may be encountered here. The atmosphere is very Dak Bungalow-ish, and a step back in time.

# Dosas by the Kilo! Sambar in Litres!

Nammura is a restaurant that sells rice, idlis and dosas by the kg and sambar in litres! This unusual concept has struck a chord with plenty of harried families who appreciate the savings on bulk shopping and would like to extend it to cooked food. It's also the perfect solution for those wanting to treat a large number of people to south Indian delicacies at a low-cost.

A veritable food mart, Nammura Hotel comes as a surprise to even the most jaded restaurant hopper. Solid and liquid foods, fried or steamed, are placed on non-descript electronic weighing scales and sold wholesale. The strictly vegetarian menu features a spread of authentic Kannadiga food like Mysore Bisi Bele Bhath, Maddur Vada, Udupi Ambode, Mangalore Uddina Vada, Mavina Saru and Amtekai Tambuli. The typical south Indian curries – Padavalkai Palya, Ooty Carrot Palya or Kundapur Tondekkai Palya also feature here. A welcome addition is the host of chutneys – the Mango-Ginger Chutney and the Heerekai Chutney to name the most popular. Dosa lovers would do well to try the Davangere Open Dosa – a soft dosa sprinkled with chutney pudi, weighed down with a potato curry and topped with a generous dab of butter. A south Kanara delicacy – the elongated idli wrapped in leaves or Kotte Kadabu – is also served here. In keeping with popular demand, the odd Chinese dish like Fried Rice and the usual north Indian fare of Pulao, Daal and Roti are on offer. Prices are very economical: a kg of Lemon Rice

sells for Rs 19 and Mysore Masala dosas or Rumali rotis cost Rs 40 per kg.

A kitchen catering to individual tables is very different from one where the food is sold in large quantities. The latter must be able to dish out a turnover far exceeding table covers, and Nammura is well equipped for this. Its fully automated kitchen dishes out enormous quantities of food in record time: It takes barely six minutes to steam 400 idlis, while 50 kgs of rice is cooked in less than eight minutes.

The 9,000sqft kitchen boasts mechanised cooking equipment, ultra-violet treated water, sparkling kitchen floors, organic cleansers to remove any traces of contamination from vegetables, automatic pounding machines, mechanised potato peelers, coconut graters and a walk-in fridge. All cooks sport surgical masks, an image that adds to the overall picture of a restaurant kitchen with almost unreal standards of hygiene.

Nammura also follows a number of eco-friendly norms: No artificial colouring is used in the food and a conspicuous sign in front announces that plastic bags are banned. To overcome this contentious packaging issue, the restaurant lends out double-insulated containers to carry food and customers may also bring their own non-plastic containers.

*65, 21st A Main Road, JP Nagar II Phase, Bangalore 560079*
*Tel 2649 1188 Web www.rightcaterers.com*

Lion King

Crouching Tiger

Black Cat

Which role would you like to play?

STARK.Blr/kk/1050

Tucked inside the hotel's posh Sheraton Towers, you have to cross the Atrium Lobby with its chandeliers and mouldings before you reach the Jolly Nabobs. The food features princely delicacies like the Lucknowi Kakori, a Kabab spiced with cinnamon, cloves and the saffron and Koofthay Mayhee made of spiced Rahu fish balls, simmered in an onion gravy. The Qasar-e-Pukhtan has paneer with tomatoes and cream, always a winning combination.

## Ebony

*Hotel Ivory Tower, Barton Centre*
*84 MG Road, Bangalore 560001*
**Tel** *2558 9333/5164*
**Open** *12:30pm to 3pm and 7:30pm to 11:30pm*
**Meal for Two** *Rs 800*
**Cards** *All*
**Alcohol** *Served*

For a 180 degree view of the city, it doesn't really get better than this. Book your table by the edge as early as possible to avoid disappointment. Dining by night with city lights twinkling in all directions is a thrilling experience. When the sun is scorching at noon, it's best to choose a seat indoors. The food has many diners going into raptures: There is Indian (with a heavy accent on Parsi and Balti), European (largely French) and Thai – a twice-a-week affair that is a big draw. Parsi food is largely non-vegetarian and leans heavily on Gujarati and Maharashtrian recipes. The popular Dhansak, Patrani Machhi, Salli Boti and others bring in quite a few regulars and those searching for a new experience in 'Indian' food.
Balti cuisine is an eclectic mix of Chinese herbs and Kashmiri spices like saffron, rose petals, dried ginger, wild onion

seeds and a variety of nuts and dried fruits typical of the region. The apricot and meat combinations are interesting. Ebony is rightly famous for its exquisitely prepared and authentically sourced Thai food. The colours, textures, flavours and smells lend the evening a special international touch. The Raw Papaya Salad with crushed peanuts is a sure hit. The satays and Red and Green Curry with sticky rice has many faithfuls who will not dream of eating Thai anywhere else west of Thailand!

Terrace dining at Ebony

## Golkonda Chimney

*42/2 Airport-Whitefield Road,*
*Bangalore 560037*
**Tel** *2847 5532/6532*
**Open** *12:30pm to 3:30pm & 7:30pm to 11pm*
**Meal for Two** *Rs 500*
**Cards** *All except American Express*
**Alcohol** *Not Served*

Golkonda Chimney is set well within a large garden and offers both space and a great view. The dining area is not walled in, and the upstairs has only a thatched roof that keeps off the elements and offers a pleasing view of the surrounding plains. The food is north Indian and Mughlai and there are some Chinese dishes thrown in as well. Lots of families may be found dining here on weekends.

## Gramin

*20 Raheja Arcade, Koramangala,*
*Bangalore 560095*
**Tel** *5110 4103*
**Open** *12noon to 3:15pm and 7pm to 11pm*
**Meal for Two** *Rs 300*
**Cards** *All except Amercian Express*
**Alcohol** *Not Served*

The big crowds waiting outside this small restaurant are proof of the high quality of food served here. The lunch thalis are popular with the software crowds of Koramangala, but hungry vegetarian diners come from further away as well. The food is cooked without preservatives or added colours and the emphasis is on wholesome vegetarian cooking.

## Jamavar

*The Leela Palace, 23 Airport Road*
*Bangalore 560008*
**Tel** *2521 1234*
**Open** *12noon to 3:30pm and 7:30pm to 11pm*
**Meal for Two** *Rs 2,000*
**Cards** *All*
**Alcohol** *Served*

Jamavar restaurant at The Leela is named for the fabulous Kashmiri shawl of the same name that uses a technique dating back to the 15th century. A mark of both royalty and opulence, the restaurant aims to extend the name to include traditional recipes from royal kitchens across India.
Both south and north Indian dishes are served here, ranging from the pungent Jeera Rasam and Chicken Jehangiri to favourites like Tandoori Chicken and Biryani.
There's a tantalising selection of seafood including the Tandoori Jumbo Prawns (Jumbo Prawns marinated in lemon juice, chilli and spiced yogurt) and Silver Pomfret which is tandoor roasted whole fish. The desserts are equally exciting with the Ada Pradhaman from Kerala, made with rice and jaggery, the Khubani ka Meetha which is a cardamom flavoured apricot dessert and a selection of kulfis.

## Moksh

*The Chancery, 10/6 Lavelle Road,*
*Bangalore 560001*
**Tel** *2227 6767*
**Open** *12:30pm to 3pm and 7:30pm to 11pm*
**Meal for Two** *Rs 800*
**Cards** *All*
**Alcohol** *Served*

Moksh is an all-vegetarian restaurant with a difference. This unique concept restaurant at the upmarket Chancery serves a pan-Indian cuisine based on Ayurvedic and medicinal principles. The creation of culinary guru Jiggs Kalra and Ayurvedic expert Pushpesh Pant, the menu at Moksh is a departure from the standard Kadai Panner and Gobi Manchurian fare served at

Ramanas, an all-vegetarian restaurant

## Ramanas

*HM Geneva House, 14 Cunningham*
*Road, Bangalore 560052*
**Tel** *2226 3200, 2226 8500*
**Open** *12noon to 3:15pm and 7pm*
*to 10:30pm. Closed on Monday.*
**Meal for Two** *Rs 500*
**Cards** *All*
**Alcohol** *Not Served*

It's hard to locate a vegetarian restaurant with a tandoor that offers authentic north Indian and Chinese food. No wonder it boasts a number of devoted vegetarian patrons and followers of Ramana Maharishi.
The restaurant is spread over two levels and is bright and airy. The food is better than average and definitely less greasy. Some of the selections are rarely found in other north Indian restaurants, so order carefully to exploit this.

## Roomali with a View

*100Ft. Road, Indiranagar,*
*Bangalore 560038*
**Tel** *2520 3007*
**Open** *12noon to 3pm and 7pm to 11pm*
**Meal for Two** *Rs 500*
**Cards** *All except American Express*
**Alcohol** *Not Served*

This breezy rooftop restaurant serves a range of north Indian cuisine – food from Rajasthan, Kashmir, Punjab and Avadh. Tastefully done up with chandeliers, low seating, paintings and an indoor waterfall, it also offers a great

other vegetarian restaurants. Stewed in an assortment of herbs, the delicately flavoured food includes a range of north Indian and south Indian foods. The menu is not fixed and the adventurous get to mix and match their meal – Punjabi rotis can be had with Kerala curries! You also get to choose whether you want your food roasted, stir-fried, deep-fried or boiled. A variety of one-of-a-kind curries, kababs, daals, rice and parathas are on the menu. Some innovations include Bengali Chenna Paaturi, Bhunee Chaat, Mutterwali Tikki, Khilte Phool, Tasedy Avial, Urali Theeyal, Sabz Baoli Hundi and Kur Kure Paneer. Moksh has an exotic medley of juices, salads and desserts, including Elaichi Lassi and Sandalwood Juice! The restaurant sports a cheerful ambience with bright blue-orange walls and an open kitchen where you can watch your food being cooked. Go here for appetising food that is easy on the stomach.

## Northern Gate

*Gateway Hotel on Residency Road, 66*
*Residency Road, Bangalore 560025*
**Tel** *5660 4545*
**Open** *12:30pm to 3pm and 7:30pm to*
*12midnight*
**Meal for Two** *Rs 1,200*
**Cards** *All*
**Alcohol** *Served*

Tucked away in the fancy Gateway Hotel is Northern Gate, purportedly Bangalore's gateway to north Indian cuisine. The buffet lists 84 dishes! The silken Kakori Kabab of Lucknow that melts in your mouth is reproduced faithfully and is a great hit. A number of IT tycoons are patrons. Northern Gate is famous for its kababs and robust meat dishes, as well as its hearty vegetarian fare, all from the north of

India. The buffet lunch brings in the corporate crowd looking for a quick bite and dinners on silver bring in leisurely diners. Besides kababs and gravied dishes there are chaats, biryanis, and of course desserts.

## Poolside Barbeque

*The Taj West End, 23 Race Course*
*Road, Bangalore 560001*
**Tel** *5660 5660*
**Open** *12:30pm to 3pm and 7:30pm to*
*11pm*
**Meal for Two** *Rs 1,600*
**Cards** *All*
**Alcohol** *Served*

The Poolside Barbecue is one of the city's most popular Indian restaurants with garden and verandah seating reminiscent of the Raj. The pool and lush greenery are perfect for long leisurely meals. Tandoori food is the highlight and all varieties of delectable kababs, rolls and curries from the open hearth are served here. The chef's innovations include Dahi ke Kabab and Murgh Malai Zaffrani Kabab. Some Chettinad delicacies also feature on the menu. This restaurant is open through the day for lunch, dinner and in-betweens. Adjoining the Poolside is the Crazy Horse Bar, a private bar serving a range of cocktails and drinks.

## Queens

*7 Shrungar Shopping Centre, Church*
*Street, Bangalore 560001*
**Tel** *2559 6361*
**Open** *12noon to 3:30pm and 6:30pm*
*to 10:30pm*
**Meal for Two** *Rs 400*
**Cards** *MasterCard & Visa*
**Alcohol** *Not Served*

For that authentic Punjabi home-cooked meal, try Queen's. It's one of the few places in town where you can get fluffy

phulkas or regular chapathis and wholesome yellow daal. The non-vegetarian selection is limited, but the delicious array of vegetarian food more than makes up. The place has an ethnic Indian touch to it – from the food served in copper vessels to the rustic walls.

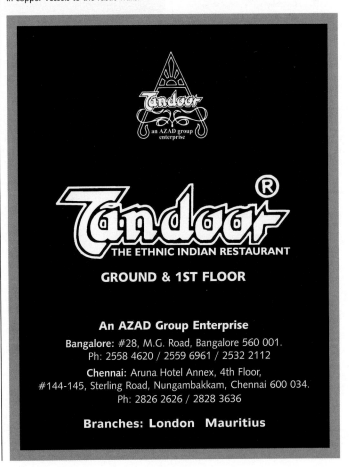

view of the skyline. Authentic north Indian food, a range of innovative mocktails, and a mobile roomali trolley that goes round to each table are some of the other attractions. The Rajasthani fare includes delicacies like the Ker Sangri, Daal Bati and Churma. A range of kababs including the famed Kakori Kabab is part of the Awadhi offering. Kashmiri specials include Tabakh Maaz or tender mutton ribs cooked in Kashmiri spices, Rista, Gushtaba, Kashmiri Rajma Masala, Kashmiri Pulao and even Kashmiri tea. Besides a la carte, the hearty buffet spread includes three varieties of roomali, four salads, starters, rice and desserts like Moong Daal Halwa and Phirni.

## Samarkhand

*Gem Plaza, 66 Infantry Road,*
*Bangalore 560001*
*Tel 5111 3366*
**Open** *12noon to 3pm and 7pm to 11pm*
**Meal for Two** *Rs 1,000*
**Cards** *All*
**Alcohol** *Served*

Rough stone floors, flame torches and a cave-like ambience set the tone for the Central Asian food served here. Afghani and Peshawari delicacies like the Sikander Raan, Mutton Biryani, Barra, Mahi Daal and Daal Afghani feature on the menu. The Chandni and Galawati kababs deserve special mention. Both vegetarian and non-vegetarian kababs are accompanied with interesting chutneys like chilly-garlic, chikoo and mint. The open kitchen and night-sky ceiling are a quaint touch. Samarkhand's Kulfi and Phirni are must-have desserts.

## Spice Gardens

*Airport Main Road, after Marathahalli*
*Bridge, Bangalore 560037*
*Tel 2847 6688*
**Open** *12:30pm to 3:30pm and 7pm to*
*12midnight*
**Meal for Two** *Rs 400*
**Cards** *All*
**Alcohol** *Not Served*

Spice Garden is well named – there are plenty of spices on the menu and a large garden around! The restaurant serves three cuisines: north Indian, Lucknowi and Chinese. Patrons include executives on weekdays and families on weekends. A well-tended garden and inviting swimming pool are great attractions. Perfect for a long swim followed by a long lunch.

## Tandoor

*28 MG Road, Bangalore 560001*
*Tel 2558 4620, 2559 6961*
**Open** *12:30pm to 3pm and 7:30pm*
*to 11:30pm*
**Meal for Two** *Rs 800*
**Cards** *All*
**Alcohol** *Served*

This upmarket restaurant is a favourite for both leisurely family dinners and corporate power lunches. The authentic Tandoori, Mughlai and Punjabi food served here is the major draw. The

interiors are opulent and the food is equally rich. Good, old fashioned north Indian fare is the highlight. The accent is on Avadhi cuisine, the richly spiced food of the Lucknow Nawabs, but lovers of Punjabi fare like Rajma and Kaali Daal will not be disappointed. The Jal Jeera, Butter Chicken, Tandoor Kabas, Mutton Balti, Bhindi Amchoorwali and Achari Ghosht come specially recommended. The restaurant is spread across two floors and ample parking space is available.

## The Royal Afghan

*ITC Hotel Windsor Sheraton & Towers,*
*25 Golf Course Road, Bangalore 560052*
*Tel 2226 9898*
**Open** *7:30pm to 11:30pm*
**Meal for Two** *Rs 1,000*
**Cards** *All*
**Alcohol** *Served*

A new client, an old love, a merry bunch of friends, the Royal Afghan celebrates any situation, under the benevolent shade of a large peepul tree. Open only in the evenings, this poolside barbecue sizzles with the aroma of charcoal and good food. Regardless of the weather, it's always packed, so book early.
A few hardy tables are set under the trees lined with damask tablecloths, gleaming silver and warm lighting. Make no mistake, this is a top class restaurant fit for special occasions.
The food is high quality – grilled delicacies superbly marinated, a maginificent tribute to the robust

flavours of the northeast frontier. The Sikandri Raan deserves special mention: A whole leg of lamb is marinated in a mixture of malt vinegar, cinnamon and black cumin and grilled to perfection in the tandoor. Other delicacies include Tandoori Pomfret and Lobster and regulars like Butter Chicken Masala. Vegetarians needn't complain as the same grilling works wonders with vegetables too. Topped with fresh spices and accompanied by soft and crisp rotis and kulchas, it's a meal fit for a king. The Tandoori Mirch is quite a hit. Round it off with a Phirni or Kesar Kheer.

## Tiger Trail

*Hotel Harsha, 11 Park Road,*
*Bangalore 560032*
*Tel 2286 5566*
**Open** *7am to 10am, 12noon to 3:30pm*
*and 7pm to 11pm*
**Meal for Two** *Rs 900*
**Cards** *All*
**Alcohol** *Served*

Built like a hunting lodge, Tiger Trail takes you back to the days of the British Raj. The cuisine of the Laat sahibs and their jungle barbeques is recreated in this open hearth restaurant, which is an adaptation of the Japanese teppanyaki. Warm fireplaces, red brick walls and mock tiger hide upholstery form the backdrop for the elaborate Mughlai and Avadhi meals served here. The buffet spread is served around the open hearth with various vegetarian and non-

vegetarian options, offered in unlimited servings. At Rs 250 per head you can have your pick of salads, appetisers, main course and dessert.
Pineapple Chaat, Macchee Do Rookhe, Du ka Tamatar and Panner Tikka Takatak are some of the the a la carte specials. The restaurant also has a Biryani counter where Avadhi Hot Matka Dum served in urns is a speciality. There is also a meaty selection of kababs and a variety of pulaos and breads listed on the menu. The vegetarians get to choose from a range of delicacies like Arbi aur Bhuttay ki Tikki from Sariska and Gobi ke Shoolay from Bandipur. Desserts include kulfi, faloodas, Khubani ka Meetha and Phirni served in a clay pot. Tiger Trail also serves a buffet breakfast between 7am to 10am.

## Aromas of China

*19 Richmond Circle, Lalbagh Road,*
*Bangalore 560027*
*Tel 5111 3355*
**Open** *12noon to 3:30pm and 7pm to*
*11:15pm*
**Meal for Two** *Rs 1,200*
**Cards** *All*
**Alcohol** *Served*

Aromas of China is a popular mid-priced Chinese eatery. The food here is good, sometimes rising to great heights. The chef is willing to experiment with your ideas so if you have a fairly good idea of Chinese spices go ahead and order. For most diners this is the closest you get to actually making the stuff yourself.

## Bamboo Shoots

*1 Museum Road, Off MG Road,*
*Bangalore 560001*
*Tel 5111 3338*
**Open** *12noon to 11:30pm*
**Meal for Two** *Rs 800*
**Cards** *All*
**Alcohol** *Served*

Bamboo Shoots specialises in Thai and Chinese cuisine and has won awards and good ratings for the same. Their Japanese Steam Boat where you can watch the food cooking in front of you is a crowd puller.

## Chinese Hut

*4105, I Floor Highpoint IV, 45, Palace Road, Bangalore 560001*
*Tel 2226 7364, 2228 1922*
**Open** *12noon to 3pm and 7pm to 12midnight*
**Meal for Two** *Rs 500*
**Cards** *All*
**Alcohol** *Served*

Here is a place where you don't have to commit yourself to only Chinese – you could opt for the north Indian as well and get to choose across 200 dishes. Young couples and young people in general, enjoy the mix'n match adventure and ladies find the atmosphere comfortable enough to hold their weekly kitty parties. The Honey Glazed Chicken ranks as one of their Chinese specialities, crisp yet juicy and a great hit with those looking for a less spicy dish. The Chinese salads come as a pleasant surprise and their light dressing of vinegar and pepper topped with crisp noodles is at once crunchy, tasty and healthy. For those on a budget, the set meal of noodles, fried

rice and a sauce of your choice is an easy option. The Indian menu boasts authentic Northwest Frontier food. The Afghan chicken is stuffed with cheese and served with green chutney. Vegetarians get to choose from 'Shakahari' and 'Gulbahaar-e-Subz'. From the Sindhi pickle – an assortment of vegetables like cauliflower, onion and carrot in vinegar and salt – to the best selling Black Daal, there are lots of exciting dishes to choose from. There is a platter of homemade sweets to round it all off.

## Mahjong Room

*ITC Hotel Windsor Sheraton & Towers, 25 Golf Course Road, Bangalore 560052*
*Tel 2226 9898*
**Open** *7:30pm to 11pm*
**Meal for Two** *Rs 1,600*
**Cards** *All*
**Alcohol** *Served*

Seaweed and carrot soup, lobster fried with red chillies... the menu at the Mahjong Room aims to attract only the discerning Chinese diner. Its elegant table settings and light Chinese food attract the upper classes looking for a taste of authentic food. Open only in the evenings, it's well suited to power dinners and important occasions.

## Mainland China

*14 Church Street, Bangalore 560001*
*Tel 2559 7722*
**Open** *12noon to 3:30pm and 7:30pm to 11:30pm*
**Meal for Two** *Rs 500*
**Cards** *All*
**Alcohol** *Served*

Mainland China can take the credit for serving good quality Chinese food outside a five-star ambience. Far removed from the gooey sauces, badly chopped veggies and lumpy meats of the average corner Chinese joint, the food at Mainland China is a big relief.

Memories of China at the Taj Residency, serves an elaborate buffet spread.

The setting is simple, elegant and spacious and the service is attentive. They are also willing to whip up the odd combination you fancy, which does not figure on their menu. The menu showcases cuisines from various Chinese provinces and vegetarians will not be disappointed. The soups are distinctive like the delicately flavoured Burnt Garlic Soup and pungent Sichuan Hot and Sour. A revamped menu boasts a range of dimsums fashioned into wontons, moneybags and rolls. These can be had with veggies or meat. The Beancurd Delight is especially recommended. The main course menu lists an array of options in seafood, poultry, lamb and vegetables. You may experiment with the sauce and meat of your choice. The Sliced Fish and Drunken Chicken with Shaoxiang Sauce and prawns in Black Bean and Butter Sauce are specialities. So is the Sesame Chicken with chillies and honey. The vegetarian Tai Ching Potatoes with the Smoked Pepper Sauce is recommended. The 'unfixed' lunch is a complete meal at Rs 175 – you get to pick a soup, main course and dessert of your choice. Date cakes, Daarsan and litchis with ice cream are the regular 'Chinese' eatery desserts served. Valet parking is available.

## Mandarin

*The Grand Ashok, Kumara Krupa High Grounds, Bangalore 560001*
*Tel 2226 9462, 2225 0202*
**Open** *12:30pm to 2:30pm and 7pm to 12midnight*
**Meal for Two** *Rs 400*
**Cards** *All*
**Alcohol** *Served*

The Mandarin has been recently renovated. It serves both Chinese and Thai cuisine and has a loyal set of patrons. Its large windows

afford a great view of the nearby golf course and of course the lush greenery of the hotel. Its brand of Chinese food including tasty inventions like the Shangai Fried Prawn and Singapore Rice Noodles are quite popular. The big attraction however, is the live band Pink Champagne, which plays anything from golden oldies to the latest in jazz and you even get to shake a leg on the dance floor.

## Memories of China

*41/3 Taj Residency, MG Road, Bangalore 560001*
*Tel 5660 4444*
**Open** *12:30pm to 3pm and 7pm to 12midnight*
**Meal for Two** *Rs 1,500*
**Alcohol** *Served*

This is another upmarket Chinese eatery with plush interiors and both Shanghai and Schezwan cuisine. Seating is comfortable and there are lots of large tables and little alcoves and even a private dining room with seating for 12 people. Diners have the choice of a buffet spread or a la carte. The buffet is quite elaborate. Look out for the salads, Chinese-style, a welcome addition to the regular sauces and fries.

## Szechwan Court

*The Oberoi, 37-39 MG Road, Bangalore 560001*
*Tel 2558 5858*
**Open** *12:30pm to 2:30pm and 7:30pm to 11:30pm*
**Meal for Two** *Rs 1,600*
**Cards** *All*
**Alcohol** *Served*

This is a high-class Chinese restaurant offering authentic Szechwan cuisine. Set

# My Top 10 – Bob Hoekstra

### Taj Kuteeram
When in the mood to relax, the best place in Bangalore to go to is Taj Kuteeram with its unique architecture and garden of abundant flowers. The food is selected by the cook and is always a great mixture of Indian and Western. The antique furniture adds to the atmosphere.
*(Kodihalli, Hesaraghatta, 560088*
**Tel** *28466332/28466347)*

### Citrus
When you have a Sunday to spend with friends, Citrus is a candidate. It is famous for its buffets. Sunday brunch has a great variety of all kinds of foods – Western, Japanese and Indian, amongst others. The (Indian) champagne and the live music

seem to come naturally with it. Plan to spend at least two to three hours here. *(See Pg 115)*

### Grasshopper
I enjoy going to the Grasshopper on weekends. The food is a blend of Western and Indian styles and is personalised. It is a small place. An avant-garde atmosphere has been created around the farmhouse which also sells designer clothes. *(See Pg 113)*

### Mainland China
I love Chinese food, it is a favourite. Fortunately Mainland China is close to my home. It has the best Chinese in town. The food comes close to original Chinese food and the selection is great. *(See Pg 109)*

### Karavalli
Fish is another one of my favourites. Karavalli gets the best fresh fish from the coast of Karnataka, the Mangalore region. It is prepared to your taste. *(See Pg 102)*

### Rim Naam
For a change of taste Thai food is a great alternative. Rim Naam has good Thai and great seafood options. The setting, outdoors in the garden of The Oberoi, is grandiose. *(See Pg 110)*

### The Only Place
When I just feel like a steak, which is fairly often, The Only Place is the first choice. It is a simple restaurant that specialises in excellent food. The steaks are unmatched and the variety is enormous. The pastas are also recommended. *(See Pg 112)*

Citrus at The Leela Palace

### Ebony
When I want to enjoy good Indian food while enjoying a view of the city, the terraces of Ebony is where I head. Bring a sweater at night, certainly in winter. Even the buckets of glowing coal do not fully chase away the cold drafts. *(See Pg 106)*

### I-t.ALIA
For real Italian food I-t.ALIA is the place I favour. This small restaurant in The Park hotel has great original Italian food. The disco next door provides a beat with the food! *(See Pg 111)*

### Koshy's
I enjoy the experience of a traditional Indian hangout such as Koshy's. It looks like an Amsterdam café and has the same lively spirit. The food is pleasantly simple and functional, like the interiors. *(See Pg 117)*

*Bob Hoekstra, acknowledged Indophile, is CEO of Philips Software Centre India. He has lived in Bangalore since 1999.*

---

in the plush environs of The Oberoi, it has two private dining rooms, which go down well with its corporate travellers. The ambience is cool, comfortable and sophisticated.

## THAI

### Civet
*Tech Park Mall, ITPL, Whitefield Road, Bangalore 560066*
*Tel 5115 6216*
*Open 12noon to 3:30pm and 7pm to 11pm. Closed on Sunday.*
*Meal for Two Rs 1,000*
*Cards All*
*Alcohol Served*

Named after a nocturnal cat, Civet is the swankiest restaurant in the city's International Tech Park. In keeping with its techie address, Civet is very modern and chic. The food is pan-Asian and goes down well with the ITPL crowd. This restaurant cum cocktail lounge serves the entire gamut of Asian cuisines, from Thai and Chinese to Burmese and Malaysian. To stop the regulars from experiencing food fatigue, the menu keeps changing and new cuisines are added all the time. Even the look is played around with – at lunch and dinner the restaurant changes its face! Specialities include the Thai Kal Phad King, the Indonesian Gulal Ikan and the Cantonese delicacy of Braised Cabbage

and Black mushrooms. Besides the a la carte menu, there are set meals with soups, salads and sandwiches. An open kitchen, a salad bar and a dessert trolley laden with goodies are other attractions that keep patrons coming back for more.

### Rim Naam
*The Oberoi, 37-39 MG Road, Bangalore 560001*
*Tel 2558 5858*
*Open 12:30pm to 2:30pm and 7pm to 11pm*
*Meal for Two Rs 1,800*
*Cards All*
*Alcohol Served*

Rim Naam is a high-class Thai restaurant set in the outdoors over a water body and surrounded by lush foliage. Food festivals are held at regular intervals throughout the year. Rim Naam plays taped jazz, pop and alternate rock music. The authentic Thai food here is a big draw. You may choose from a range of coconut milk soups and a variety of starters like the Man Thod Samros made with crisp potatoes and crushed peanuts and grilled skewers with chicken and prawn. Vegetarian and non-vegetarian stir fries and spicy green or hot red curries are served with flat wheat noodles, thin rice noodles and steamed rice. Signature desserts include the Thai Coconut Custard and the Kluay Thod where fried bananas are tossed in honey and sesame seeds.

## JAPANESE

### Dahlia
*G37 & 38 Brigade Gardens, 19 Church Street, Bangalore 560001*
*Tel 2509 1293, 2558 0958*
*Open 12noon to 2:30pm and 6:30pm to 9.30pm. Closed on Sunday.*
*Meal for Two Rs 1,000*
*Cards All*
*Alcohol Served*

An authentic Japanese restaurant, it's best to make reservations before coming.

The interiors are functional but comfortable and filled with homesick, expat Japanese executives. Sashimi, Sushi and Tempura are served twice a week. All the food is freshly prepared and high on taste.

### f Bar & Lounge
*Le Meridien, 28 Sankey Road, Bangalore 560052*
*Tel 2226 2233, 2220 8772*
*Open 5pm to 12midnight*
*Meal for Two Rs 1,000*
*Card All except Diners Club*
*Alcohol Served*

A pan-Asian spread at Civet

Busy on either side of the counter at f Bar & Lounge.

are some of its highlights. Set in a lush garden, amidst cool water lily ponds, Blue Ginger serves an authentic selection of traditional and contemporary Vietnamese foods. The restaurant is especially magical at night with hanging lanterns, mood lighting, live Vietnamese music and fire torches. An interactive 'show' kitchen and an open bar add to the effect.

Located at The Taj West End it is India's first exclusive Vietnamese restaurant. It is part of a reputed chain of international restaurants. Multifaceted Vietnamese cuisine, with its French and Chinese influences, is known for its generous use of vegetables, aromatic herbs and a minimal use of oil. The restaurant's menu has an array of delicacies like the Pho and Haricot soup, Braised Fish, steamboats, Green Papaya and Raw Mango Salad, Lotus Stem pancakes and Mung Bean Ice cream. All curries are served with French baguettes and the exotic sauces range from fish and soya-lime to bean and ginger-lime.

## ITALIAN

### i-t.ALIA
*The Park, 14/7 MG Road, Bangalore 560001*
*Tel 2559 4666*
*Open 12:30pm to 2:45pm and 7:30pm to 11pm*
*Meal for Two Rs 1,500*
*Cards All*
*Alcohol Served*

Italian food got a huge boost when i-t.ALIA opened in the city. It's not as though Bangaloreans were unaware of pastas and antipastas, but nothing like a speciality restaurant, devoted to the fervent cause of passing on a great cuisine celebrated around the world… yes, one does tend to get carried away when talking about Italian food!
To begin with, if you have the time and the taste, order a glass of wine while you mull over the menu and pick out your dishes. The dry white wine is perfect to achieve that slight astringency you need before the food descends. The bread basket goes well with a combination of the extra virgin olive oil and Balsamic vinegar filled in jars sitting invitingly on the table.

Fashion channel's FTV's offering, the f Bar draws in the city's happening crowds. Most people remember only the 'Bar' in the name and forget the 'Lounge' part. And herein they do themselves a great disservice. The f Bar is one of Bangalore's best kept secrets! The food on offer is a blend of Japanese and Korean cuisines. The Japanese food is fabulous, perfectly done, served with high quality sauces and can't be faulted on any account. The atmosphere is trendy and there is always something happening.
The f Bar shows off an edgy all-glass décor with soft multi-hued lights. There is a striking use of metal and luminous screens.
The deep, low-slung sofas in solid colours offer a lazy and welcome contrast. The f Bar & Lounge is in the shape of an 'L' and across the Bar there is an area for serious dining which is removed once the party starts to come alive at night.

### Zen
*The Leela Palace, 23 Airport Road Bangalore 560008*
*Tel 2521 1234*
*Open 12noon to 2:30pm and 7pm to 11:30pm*
*Meal for Two Rs 2,000*
*Cards All*
*Alcohol Served*

Zen is hot, new and happening on the restaurant circuit, judging by the crowds who gather to dine there everyday. One definition states that Zen is the fundamental perfection of everything existing! Well, the Zen at The Leela certainly tries very hard and you are quite certain of reaching Satori (enlightenment) if you eat here!
The finest dishes on the menu would have to be the many Sushi and Sashimi combinations, even the vegetarian version uses only the freshest ingredients. There is also a fair amount of pan-Asian cuisine served here from Thailand, Korea, Singapore and Bali. Live

counters of Tepenyaki, Yakitori, a Korean barbecue and noodle bar are the other highlights. The set menus are very popular. The set menu options are Mori (vegetarian), Kaze (meat selection) and Nagare (sea food). A typical set menu comprises of a starter, soup, salad, main course and dessert. You can opt for beef, chicken or lamb in the meat selection. Rice wines are also served here.

## VIETNAMESE

### Blue Ginger
*The Taj West End, 23 Race Course Road, Bangalore 560001*
*Tel 5660 5660*
*Open 12:30pm to 3pm and 7:30pm to 12midnight*
*Meal for Two Rs 2,000*
*Cards All*
*Alcohol Served*

Blue Ginger is as good as it gets – Vietnamese chefs and an all-oriental look

The starter of chicken wrapped in Parma Ham with a green salad on the side, is a meal in itself. The Arugula leaves are hot and mustardy, the lettuce crunchy and dry and the moist, delicately flavoured chicken has found its match. Alternatively, you could try the crumb-fried Shitake Mushrooms or Minestrone. At lunch there is a set menu that offers a choice of two or three dishes and is priced accordingly. i-t.ALIA offers a delectable range of classic Italian pastas, risottos and carnaroli. The Carbonara and the Grilled Snapper with veggies and polenta comes highly recommended here. Baked in wood fire ovens, the pizzas here come with a smoky flavour. For the main course try seafood like the Wood Roasted Lobster with Green Salsa and round off your meal with desserts like Tiramisu or Honey Semifreddo. A good selection of Italian, French and American wines are served to complement the meal. With its authentic Italian food, chic styling, pinstripe chairs and intimate environment, i-t.ALIA is perfect for special evenings as well as business lunches. It's great for vegetarians too, since Italian food pays great homage to delicious veggies.

## Little Italy

*1135 100Ft. Road, Bangalore 560038*
*Tel 2528 9126*
**Open** *11am to 3:30pm and 7pm to 11pm*
**Meal for Two** *Rs 900*
**Cards** *MasterCard & Visa*
**Alcohol** *Served*

Fine, elegant seating, livened up with delicious and authentic Italian cuisine and topped with the vegetarian only label, Little Italy brings many good things under one roof, albeit a lime green one. You can choose between outdoor seating and an air-conditioned lounge. Be warned though that prices are steep here.

The starters are varied and delicious in their own right. The Crostini is crunchy and sharply flavoured with garlic and smothered with generous helpings of sun dried tomatoes and green olives. The garlic bread is definitely one of the best served in the city. It's more of a soft bun sliced in half with plenty of butter and chopped garlic, crisp outside and softly melting inside. If you have a long evening ahead of you, try the mocktails or a glass of wine to set the mood. Alternately, you could try a soup and salad. Ask them to go a bit easy on the salt if you are particular.
The main course is spread across pastas and pizzas and a surprising addition of Mexican food. The Aglio Olio with sun dried tomatoes is highly recommended. The sweet flavour of olive oil comes through beautifully, and the dish is at once healthy, filling and delicious. The Al Funghi Porcini has a deep red sauce that clings deliciously to the furrows of the Penne Macaroni. There is plenty of sauce to go around and with a few shavings of parmesan, it makes for a robust, hearty meal. The Pesto sauce is a rich emerald green and like most Italian dishes is also helped greatly with added parmesan. There are a number of gellatos – light Italian ice creams in fresh new flavours. Tiramisu, that heavenly, scrumptious sweet concoction is very well made here.

## The Only Place

*13 Museum Road, Bangalore 560025*
*Tel 3061 8989*
**Open** *12noon to 3:30pm and 7pm to 11:30pm*
**Meal for Two** *Rs 500*
**Cards** *All*
**Alcohol** *Not Served*

Old Bangalore once dined out on the sizzling steaks and scrumptious Apple Pie at The Only Place. Many were disappointed when the restaurant downed its shutters a few years ago.

# My Top 10 – Harish Bijoor

## Tiger Bay

My top pick is Tiger Bay. The fish is as fresh as it can get, the crab cakes are divine and so is the Shrimp Popcorn. This eatery is all about seafood and Tiger Bay knows its fish for sure! The cuisine is fusion food – you can mix and match what you order. Go crazy with the south Indian fare as starters and graduate into the Continental offering. What I like best here is the rice! Restaurants are great with everything else, but rice is normally messed up. The rice here is not over cooked, not under cooked, just the right colour of white, just grainy enough and tastes great! *(See Pg 117)*

## Karavalli

Karavalli has possibly the friendliest chefs in town. And certainly one of the most competent. My favourite here is the rasam that comes piping hot, the Mangalorean fried chicken, which goes by the tongue twister, *Kozhi Kempu Bezule*. The Kane Fry is great…but insist on getting the right size of fish for the day. Not too big. Not too small. Top it all with Tender Coconut Ice cream! You can actually taste the tender coconut in this offering. *(See Pg 102)*

## Imperial

For Kerala cuisine that will leave you smacking your lips try Imperial. Known to many a die-hard Bangalorean foodie as Impies, the Chicken Kabab here is delicious! You can smell the ghee and taste batter that is very different, much copied, but never imitated to perfection! (For a while the venerable Bangalore Club had on its menu 'Impy Chicken'.) Imperial also serves Brain Fry that is delicious, I hear.
Don't be shocked when you get a bill of Rs 165 at the end of a hearty meal for two. This place is sheer value for money. *(Residency Road, Bangalore 560025 Tel 25588391)*

## Juke Box

Juke Box in Koramangala is a completely unpretentious little joint that offers you Continental, Parsi and Indian cuisine alike. Apart from the mixed cuisine, you can also get stuff that is not on the menu. Great stuff such as the Spicy Chinese Chicken Chow (a mix of rice, noodles, vegetables, chicken and whatever else) Juke Box offers good steaks and desserts such as the Chocolate Log and the Kulfi. I head here to eat one thing – the Spicy Chinese Chicken Chow! *(379 1st Main, VII Block, Koramangala, Bangalore 560095 Tel 25710032)*

## Kartik Mithai

This is my favourite Chaat shop in Bangalore. The Paapdi Chaat is divine. The Paani-puri is good as well, provided you get to the Master Paani Puri maker, who you will recognise with his adeptness at dishing out the Paani laden puris to seven folks simultaneously. *(See Pg 114)*

## RR

RR! The old one is back. Andhra food at its best, Andhra food at its spiciest. The Mutton Biryani remains the top hit out here. What masquerades as Portuguese Fried Fish (in a red masala variant) is great as well. You will need a definite dessert at the end of it all to bring you back to earth from spicy hell. *(See Pg 100)*

## Rim Naam

Rim Naam at The Oberoi is a great place for Thai food and the seating is outdoor under trellis greens. The food is absolutely authentic Thai. I rate the salad here three notches above what I have tasted in some of the best places in Bangkok. The Tom Yang Soup is superb. *(See Pg 110)*

## Unicorn

A great mix of cuisines (Mangalorean and Chinese) is dished out here. My hot favourite is the signature dish of the restaurant, Unicorn Special Prawn – spicy red batter fried prawn! The good thing is that this is not what a prawn Koliwada offers you in terms of a hard batter. Instead it is thin, wet and spicy batter and quite unique. My mouth waters even as I write this! The Chinese Boneless Chilli Chicken is good as well. The rasam and rice combination is worth a try. *(34/1, Infantry Road, Bangalore 560001 Tel 2559 1670)*

## Empire

I have never been to Empire at a decent hour! For a sumptuous meal of Kerala food at 2 in the morning, this is where you head. When five star coffee shop food is not enough to tickle your tangy taste buds, Empire it is! Kerala parathas, Ceylon parathas and Brain Fry, Chicken kababs and Ghee Rice, try it all here. The ambience is eclectic and electric as well. At three in the morning you have the scantily clad pub crowd of Bangalore heading here after all the pubs have closed. Catch a glimpse of a local celebrity here. *(12/2, Central Street, Bangalore 560001 Tel 2559 2821, 2558 7253/266; Church Street, 2559 3743/4/5; Kammanahalli, 2549 3349; Shivaji Nagar, 2286 4406)*

## Northern Gate

The Kakori Kabab at the Northern Gate at Hotel Gateway is my favourite. It melts in the mouth and feels toothpaste smooth! The mighty toothed as well as the toothless will enjoy this fare. I have demanded the Kakori Kabab in Lucknow and Hyderabad alike. None has matched what I get here right in the heart of Bangalore at Northern Gate. Now what better compliment than that?! *(See Pg 107)*

*Harish Bijoor is a foodie and a Bangalorean by desire and design. He is CEO, Harish Bijoor Consults Inc, a private label-consulting outfit in the realm of business strategy and brands, with a presence in Hong Kong, London and the Indian subcontinent. Contact him at harishbijoor@hotmail.com*

However, this Bangalore institution has opened again at a new outdoor location. The menu is largely unchanged and so is the look – charming garden benches and cheerful chequered tabletops. Set under a cool canopy, it has a laidback ambience, with green creepers and airy cane blinds. A range of seasonal juices, iced tea and fresh salads is available. Pick your own dressing – choices include Thousand Island, Viniagrette, Sour Cream and Creamy Herb. Homemade soups such as Chicken Chowder and French Onion are served, and remember to ask for the daily special.

The Only Place is well known for its sandwiches, steaks and burgers. Steak Sandwich and Pot Roast Beef with Mashed Potato Gravy are the restaurant's specialities. Fish Burger, Sloppy Joe and Beef Burger are signature American dishes listed on the menu apart from fries and Hash Browns. Priced at Rs 200, the steaks are served with potatoes, vegetables and garlic bread. Double Filet Mignon is the house special and Rising Sun Steak is a Japanese innovation. Pasta includes Lasagne, Spaghetti and Cannelloni with assorted meats and vegetable. The vegetarians have ample choice – the Babycorn Bake and Fettuccini Mediterranean are specially recommended. Stroganoff, Chicken Nuggets, Fish Sticks, Veal Cameron and Lamb kababs make up the rest of the varied menu.

### Spiga

*76/A Vittal Mallya Road,*
*Off St. Marks Road,*
*Bangalore 560001*
*Tel 5112 0077*
*Open 12:30pm to 3:30pm and*
*7:30pm to 10:30pm*
*Meal for Two Rs 600*
*Cards All except American Express*
*Alcohol Not Served*

Spiga has taken some of the most popular dishes from three famous cuisines (Mexican, Italian and Thai) and brought them under one roof. Normally, mixing cuisines is a recipe for disaster, but Spiga has turned it into their USP. A bright, cheerful ambience, good music and tasty, satisfying food bring in the crowds. There are also some home and kitchen accessories for sale.

### Sunny's

*35/2, Kasturba Cross Road,*
*Off Lavelle Road, Bangalore 560001*
*Tel 2224 3642, 2212 0496*
*Open 11am to 10:30pm*
*Meal for Two Rs 1,200*
*Cards All*
*Alcohol Beer and wine*

A meal at Sunny's is only for that select species of foodies who enjoy reading the menu as much as eating it. Run by theatre personality Arjun Sajnani and his friend Vivek Ubhayakar, Sunny's serves top quality Nouvelle cuisine in a cheerful, albeit comfortably cramped atmosphere. Beef tournedos, quiches, a variety of pastas and the famous Sunny's salad are hot favourites. The duo have a light and deft hand with their dessert

menu which features delectable pastries and cakes. There is a patisserie below that sells a variety of breads, pastries, smoked meats and cheese.

## AROUND THE WESTERN WORLD

### 100 Ft Boutique and Restaurant

*777/1 100Ft. Road, HAL II Stage,*
*Indiranagar, Bangalore 560038*
*Tel 2527 7752/8616*
*Open 11am to 3pm and 7pm to 11pm*
*Meal for Two Rs 700*
*Cards All*
*Alcohol Served*

Part restaurant, part boutique, 100 Ft will put the plate and glasses on the bill alongwith the food, if you want to buy it. You are likely to find Italian, Mediterranean and regular Continental food, decently presented and above average in taste. Opt to sit indoors at rush hour or the sound of traffic on the busy 100 Feet Road is certain to drown you out. Everything here is on sale – placemats, cutlery, furniture and knick-knacks.

### Bangalore Bistro

*214/34 Cunningham Road,*
*Bangalore 560052*
*Tel 2220 1616*
*Open 12noon to 3:30pm*
*and 7pm to 11pm.*
*Weekend Breakfast - 7:30am to 11am*
*Cards All*
*Meal for Two Rs 700*
*Alcohol Not Served*

As the name suggests, this is a Continental eatery, offering pastas, steaks, sizzlers and risottos among

others. There is an inviting salad bar with an array of different salads and the option to make your own. On weekends expect to see a live band. Breakfast on the weekend is sumptuous with many varieties of breads, pancakes, parathas and eggs.

### Casa Piccola

*Devatha Plaza, Residency Road,*
*Bangalore 560025*
*Tel 2221 2907*
*Branches Indiranagar, 2525 8823;*
*Cunningham Road, 2220 3330;*
*Koramangala, 2553 9333*
*Open 11am to 10:30pm*
*Meal for Two Rs 300*
*Cards All*
*Alcohol Not Served*

Casa's, as it's better known, is one of Bangalore's first bistros. Regulars include people of all ages who come here for their weekly take of Pasta, steaks and sandwiches. With four outlets in different corners of the city,

the restaurant is known for its pastas, sandwiches and burgers. The menu extends to Chicken Cordon Bleu, Chicken Casserole, a long list of burgers and sandwiches like Sloppy Joe, Fish Burger and the popular Casaclub Sandwich, a double decker sandwich stuffed with chicken, vegetables, fried eggs and cheese. A meal here is not complete without a pick from the desserts menu with fresh fruit pies and gooey cakes. The 'smart lunch' comes for just Rs 75 with rice, a curry, a pizza and a dessert. Round it off with the Jamaican coffee or cappuccino, rated highly here.

### Grasshopper

*45 Kalena Agrahara,*
*Bannerghatta Road,*
*Bangalore 560076*
*Tel 2659 3999, 2658 0225*
*Open 1pm to 8pm. By reservation only.*
*Meal for Two Rs 1,500*
*Cards MasterCard & Visa*
*Alcohol Served*

Fine dining and high fashion is a marriage made in heaven! A meal at Grasshopper takes you straight there. Here the clothes are good enough to eat and the food is great looking. There is a set seven-course menu that you must book a day in advance. It adds up to a lot of food, and very good too, so don't eat at least a few hours beforehand!

It's very elegant with a couple of appetisers, a salad, a starter, main course and dessert. The food styling and detailing is top class and the food tastes superb. A typical menu looks like this: Veal Roast and Veal Chops with Blue Cheese Butter, Whole Steamed Pomfret, Escapoles of Veal, Chicken Liver Plate, seasonal salads like the Baby Spinach and Arugula Salad, an excellent choice of seafood and a variety of freshly baked breads.

## Herbs and Spice
*221, 7th Cross, Indiranagar, Bangalore 560038*
***Tel** 2529 0399*
***Open** 12:30pm to 3pm and*

*7:30pm to 10:30pm. Closed on Monday.*
***Cards** All except Diners Club*
***Meal for Two** Rs 400*
***Alcohol** Not Served*

This is easily one of the best places in the city for good quality Continental food, especially desserts. Minimalist surroundings, friendly and knowledgeable service and uncluttered seating combine to create an easy, unfussy atmosphere. The blackboard menu is large enough to tempt, but it's the mouth watering, signature desserts

which leave the best impression. Walnut Meringue, Fresh Fruit Tartlets and Chocolate Roulade are just some of them.

## Jockey Club
*41/3 Taj Residency, MG Road, Bangalore 560001*
***Tel** 5660 4444*
***Open** 5pm to 12midnight*
***Meal for Two** Rs 1,600*
***Cards** All*
***Alcohol** Served*

# Something Sweet

Mysore Pak

Bangalore has a delectable spread of sweets and desserts from around the country and across the continent. Mildly sweetened Walnut Meringue, fruity sorbets and sugar rich ladoos, there is enough and more to satisfy a sweet tooth.

A multitude of Indian sweet shops spread over the city stock the best of north Indian and south Indian goodies. Bhagat Ram's is a legend. Take a trip to their cramped quarters in the bylanes of Commercial Street and you will be rewarded with piping hot jalebis and the juiciest gulab jamuns in town. The best place to pick up pure ghee Mysore Pak, Karnataka's signature sweet dish, is Sri Krishna Sweets, more an institution than a sweet mart. At their branches around the city you can also buy local delicacies like Holige.

Tewari Brother's Mithai Shoppe is best known for its saffron-soaked Petha. At Shree Mithai and Karthik Mithai variegated burfis', ladoos' and unusual sweets like the Mohan Thar and Kaju Kathli are on display.

No 'sweet' experience is complete without a visit to KC Das, the famed house of Bengali sweets. Their spongy Sandesh and tasty Rosogullas fly off the shelf in no time.

For a taste of Mumbai's mithai, head to Bombay House where delicious desserts like Kaala Khatta Gola and Falooda Rabdi as well as Bengali, Sindhi and Karachi sweets feature on the menu.

If you are seized with a sudden craving for croissants, truffle or brownies, all you have to do is head into town. Sunny's, a cosy and stylish Italian restaurant, dishes out fabulous Chocolate Ganache in a Walnut Pastry Shell. At Herbs & Spice, Sticky Toffee Pudding, apple pies and eggless chocolate cakes are lined up alongside Banana Bread and scrumptious Apple Pie. The Walnut Meringue is a firm favourite. You can order from a fine selection of German breads at Café Schorlemmer, perched on the terrace of Max Mueller Bhavan. Age-old bakeries, like the All Saints Bakery, Koshy's Bakery and Fatima are also frequented for their fresh stocks of breads, buns and sponge cakes.

A number of pastry shops dot the city. The Cake Shop of the Taj is one of the oldest and most reputed in the city. Children love their wildly designed trains and car shaped birthday cakes. Old favourites are the Rum Cake and Lemon Tart. At Sugar 'n' Spice most of the ingredients are imported: The cheese for the cheesecake and the flour for the German breads. Diabetics and those watching their sugar intake may rejoice – there are sugar free pastries available here. Another popular cake shop with a café attached is the Sweet Chariot Café, where the Black Forest Cake is the main attraction.

Bangalore's favourite indulgence remains the ice cream. The famous brand of Swiss ice creams Movenpick has a trendy café well known for its sundaes. Flavours from Gulab Jamoon to Cappucino may be sampled here. Baskin Robbins has a number of outlets across the city's suburbs. They scoop up tasty concoctions like the Fruit Overload, Coffee Almond Fudge and Waffle Cones. Free of artificial colouring and other additives, the offerings from Natural Ice-Cream come in flavours like tender coconut and watermelon. Orchard Fresh ice creams go a step further – eggs are not used and flavours range from red wine and fig to tulsi and lemon grass. Corner House is a popular ice cream parlour where innovations like the Mysore Pak Sundae and Death by Chocolate are favourites.

***Bhagat Ram's** 2558 8699*
***Sri Krishna Sweets** 2346 3582, 2527 2842*
***Tewari Bros Mithai Shoppe** 2554 9012*
***Shree Mithai** 2528 8357*
***Kartik Mithai Shoppe** 2525 8591*
***KC Das** 2555 0168*

***Sunny's** 2224 3642*
***Café Schorlemmer** 2221 4964*
***Herbs & Spice** 2529 0399*
***Cake Shop of The Taj** 2559 4349*
***Sweet Chariot Café** 2222 6923*
***Sugar 'n' Spice** 5660 4444*
***All Saint's Bakery** 2557 20916*
***Fatima** 2551 0378*
***Koshy's Bakery** 2221 1516*
***Movenpick** 2299 6855*
***Baskin Robbins** 2653 8898*
***Natural Ice-Cream** 2591 3565*
***Corner House** 2558 3262*

Bhagat Ram's

# 24-Hour Coffee Shops

If you find yourself hungry at midnight or pre-dawn, or would like breakfast at noon and lunch at 5pm, bank on the 24-hour coffee shop to see you through. Sandwiches and burgers, idlis and dosas, pizzas and pastas, thalis and curries and delectable buffet spreads feature across most menus. A toothsome variety of desserts round it off.

The most lavish spread may be found at **Citrus**, at The Leela Palace. The buffet has 10 salads including a corner where you can make your own, a few lightly cooked dishes, soups, and a delectable array of desserts. You can opt only for salad and soup if you like. The a la carte features a few rare dishes like old-fashioned pizzas burned in a wood fire. You may opt to sit indoors or take a table in the beautifully landscaped gardens.

**Le Jardin** at The Oberoi has a stylish menu that can lift the ordinary snack to great heights and a posher atmosphere than the rest of the pack. Salmon, Nasi Goreng, Appam and Stew and Khumb Palak are just some the dishes listed. This coffee shop has large bay windows overlooking The Oberoi's tropical garden and pretty pool.

**Mynt**, the all day dining restaurant at The Taj West End offers Italian, Lebanese and Indian cuisine. An open

kitchen allows customers to see Italian, Lebanese and Indian chefs cook up authentic, fresh food. On offer are Arabic grills like the Sheesh Taouk and Rubian Meshwi, chargrilled prawns marinated in traditional Lebanese spices. Various risottos and pastas like Farfalle Primavera and Gnocchi Gratinati represent Italian cuisine. Interesting main courses like Funghi Trifolati Al Vino, truffle mushroom in white wine, make sure vegetarians are not disappointed. Indian cuisine on offer varies from the Kerala-style Fish Curry to the popular Chicken Tikka. The Sunday brunch is definitely worth a try. Post-breakfast, lunch and dinner menus vary and include a range of sandwiches.

Once the only coffee shop in the hip MG Road area, **Café Mosaic** at the Taj Residency is still popular and serves a variety of food from different cuisines.

Round the corner is **Monsoon** at The Park with an informal air and an indigo décor. The 24-hour restaurant stretches into the lobby and serves up innovative, international cuisine. Midnight pizzas and the late night breakfast are a hit with those who party all night long. Exotic munchies like the Mezze Platter and Sea Tempura are ideal to snack on. The menu showcases Mediterranean, southeast Asian and Indian cuisine, with some exotic foods like Tandoori Chicken Salad with Guacamole,

Lychees in Chardonnay Jelly, Moroccan Chicken, Dum Biryani, Dakshin Kannada Prawn Masala and Kerala Appams with stew. The desserts are also equally varied, including Blueberry Pavlova, Apple Phirni, Kahlua Mousse, Passion Fruit Bavarois and its signature dessert – the chocolate mud cake. Monsoon also offers an assortment of teas and coffees.

Overlooking the lush KGA golf course is **Limelight**, a Mediterranean-theme coffee shop at the luxury hotel Royal Orchid. There is a generous buffet spread at lunch and dinner's a la carte menu includes specialities like Prawn Allepey and Calzone.

The ITC Windsor Sheraton's 24-hour coffee shop, **The Raj Pavilion** modelled along the lines of Lalbagh's Glass House, is a cheerful, happy cafe, perfect to spend a few leisurely hours. The setting is akin to a Victorian greenhouse and the food is set to match – Indian, British and some Far Eastern dishes to satsify current tastes. The result is a menu that criss-crosses continents and cultures with merry abandon.

**Potluck Café** at the Gateway Hotel on Residency Road offers continental cuisine. Their breakfast buffets are quite popular. **24/7** at The Grand Ashok, serves more than good filter coffee. Open on three sides, the coffee shop is reminiscent of old world charm and serves delicious south Indian dishes fare.

**South Parade**, the all-hour restaurant at The Chancery has the air of the British Raj with high Gothic windows, Italian marble and teakwood panelling. Here, British food takes centre stage and the authentic spread includes Steak and Kidney Pie, Irish Stew, Shepherd Pie, Cornish buttered lobster and some originals like the Lamb Cutlet Reform. Indian cuisine is not ignored either with a delectable selection of kababs and curries.

**Citrus** 2521 1234; **Le Jardin** 2558 5858; **Mynt** 5660 5660; **Café Mozaic** 5660 4444; **Monsoon** 2559 46666; **The Raj Pavilion** 2226 9898; **Limelight** 2520 5566; **24/7** 2225 0202; **Potluck Café** 5660 4545; **South Parade** 2227 6767

The Jockey Club is a cross between a bar and restaurant, with the virtues of both and vices of neither! You can expect a civilised drink in quiet, elegant surroundings and superior quality Continental food with a French accent, (Tian of Crabmeat and Prawns, Lobster Mouseline and Cacao Mousse). It is the perfect place to entertain business clients or savour a quiet moment with family and friends.

## WEST INDIAN

### Sue's Food Place
*4 Subedar Garden, Sri Krishna Temple Road, Indiranagar, Bangalore 560038*
**Tel** *2525 2494*
**Open** *12noon to 3:45pm and 7pm to 10:45pm*
**Meal for Two** *Rs 400*
**Cards** *MasterCard & Visa*
**Alcohol** *Not Served*

For authentic Carribean Indian food, it doesn't get better than Sue's Food Place. Named after its hospitable owner, the food here is fresh, delicious and has lots of interesting add-ons like the Scotch Bonnet Chilli Chutney and Cocorico. The lunch buffet is more than substantial with exciting variations like Crab Curry and Jerk Chicken. Sue's homemade confectionery and pickles make for excellent take-away.

## AMERICAN & TEX MEX

### KFC
*4 Brigade Road, Bangalore 560001*
**Tel** *2559 8782*
**Branches** *Indiranagar, 2526 0999; The Forum, 2206 7993; ITPL, 5115 8626*
**Open** *11am to 11pm*
**Meal for Two** *Rs 250*
**Cards** *Not Accepted*
**Alcohol** *Not Served*

Kentucky Fried Chicken (KFC) burst onto the Indian fastfood scene less than a decade ago. And it still manages to pull in a fair crowd that troops in to enjoy America's favourite brand of Fried Chicken, Chicken Nuggets, Zinger Burgers and fries. The crisp, crunchy fries deserve special mention. Service is efficient and friendly, but listen carefully before you agree to a few (helpfully suggested) add-ons that sometimes double the total! The true-blue American chain has adapted to the Indian palette – Pepper Rice with Paneer Tikka Wrap n' Roll is served here. An assortment of set meals feature on the menu – Family Feast, Meal Steals and Best Sellers contain varying quantities of chicken, burgers, salads, breads, fries and Pepsi. There are a number of tempting desserts such as sundaes, brownies, soft twirl ice creams and sprinkles with butterscotch crunch. In an all-out bid to woo vegetarians, KFC says it uses vegetable oil for its veggie food. So you can be assured of tallow-free fries here.

The 'Kid Meal' comes with a free toy, a choice of (less spicy) chicken or a burger and a small Pepsi.

Herbs & Spice has authentic Italian fare on its menu.

## Marrybrown Restaurant

*58 HM Towers, Brigade Road,*
*Bangalore 560025*
*Tel 5115 4444*
**Open** *11am to 11:30pm*
**Meal for Two** *Rs 200*
**Cards** *All*
**Alcohol** *Not Served*

This KFC look-alike is part of a Malaysian chain of fast food restaurants. Marrybrown sports an all-American look with bright lights and cheerful service. Nuggets and Fried Chicken dominate the menu but the burger takes centre stage with variations such as the Hot Masala, Veg Delite and Salad Burgers. There is a range of set meals with burgers, fries and coke and a Jumbo Combo meal for the entire family with burgers, fried chicken and a beverage. The Kiddy meals come with a free gift. There is also a lunch special available with rice, sauce and salad. Potato smileys, fish, chicken and vegetable nuggets and munchies make up the rest of the menu. Colourful chairs, brightly painted walls and a separate play area for kids bring in the families.

## Subway

*Mota Royal Arcade, Brigade Road,*
*Bangalore 560001*
*Tel 2509 1320, 5112 1905*
**Branch** *The Forum, 2206 7662*
**Open** *11am to 11pm*
**Meal for Two** *Rs 400*
**Cards** *Not Accepted*
**Alcohol** *Not Served*

Known for the 'biggest, meatiest, tastiest' sandwiches, American chain Subway has a slightly different take on 'fast food'. The breads include healthier options like whole wheat, honey oats, sesame parmesan, oregano etc and the fillings are not fried. There is a choice of submarine-style sandwiches or burgers and chips for those looking for a filling combo. Sandwiches for vegetarians range from the basic Veggie Delite, Cold Garden Pizza Submarine, Corn and Peas Sub, Bistro Garden Sub and a Hummus and Falafel Sub. Non-vegetarian subs use meats like turkey, ham, bacon and lamb apart from the regular chicken. Popular subs are the Italian BMT with salami, pepperoni and ham, the Subway Melt with turkey, chicken and lamb and the Meatball Sub. Chicken-based sandwiches are varied ranging from Chicken Tikka to exotic Smoked Chicken in Honey Mustard Sauce and Shredded Chicken in Teriyaki Sauce. Customers get to choose from a variety of breads and cheese as well. Subway also serves salads and is open through the day including breakfast.

## TGI Friday's

*Carlton Towers, Airport Road,*
*Bangalore 560017*
*Tel 2521 0570*
**Open** *11am to 11:30pm*
**Meal for Two** *Rs 1,000*
**Cards** *All*
**Alcohol** *Served*

If you've ever wondered what an American diner, albeit a posh one, looks like, step into TGI Friday's. Even the prices make you feel you're in dollar country! The interiors celebrate everything American and the food is nothing to write home about. However, the place has a happy buzz to it and that probably explains the young crowds surging in, especially on big sport days

The legendary Fish and Chips at Koshy's.

like a cricket match between India and Pakistan.

## MULTICUISINE

### Caesars

*Mahalaxmi Chambers, 9/1 MG Road*
*Tel 2558 4144/4699*
**Open** *12noon to 3:30pm and 7pm to 11pm*
**Meal for Two** *Rs 700*
**Cards** *All*
**Alcohol** *Served*

An old timer on the restaurant scene, Caesar's still has loyal patrons. Its location on MG Road is a great pull and the food is multicuisine – Tandoori, Chinese and Continental. The Royal Pavilion is a bar attached to the restaurant. Executive lunch packages and packed lunches are also available.

## Cosmo Village

*29 Magrath Road,*
*Bangalore 560001*
*Tel 5112 7373, 2509 1160*
**Open** *12:30pm to 3:30pm and 7:30pm to 11pm*
**Meal for Two** *Rs 1,000*
**Cards** *All*
**Alcohol** *Served*

Cosmo Village fits right into Bangalore's scheme of things. A lounge bar cum restaurant, it's small and cosy with plump sofas, plenty of cushions and fat candles lending a warm glow. The Liquor Café is located on the top and gives the feeling of a terrace home with even a diwan thrown in! The restaurant on the first and second floors follow the same pattern with floating candles, an odd assortment of furniture, sheer curtains and the colour of burnished metal all over.

# Pizzas, A Slice of America

The pizza has travelled a long way from its home in Italy. Making its way across the North American continent, this much-loved disc of flat dough and cheese is now the preferred food of hip Bangaloreans. Pizza restaurants can be found all over town – a hit with Coke-swigging teenagers and grown-ups, they are also a popular venue for kiddy parties. The city likes to have its pizzas the American way – lathered with tomato sauce and cheese. In fact, it's been further reinvented to suit Indian sensibilities. The kitsch pizza making the rounds is topped with anything from Chicken Tikka to paneer. And there are as many variants of the base as there are toppings – the thin crust pizza is for those on a diet and the stuffed crust pan pizza for those with a healthy appetite.

Cheerful and trendy, the all-American Pizza Hut has a few Indian innovations. The Chicken Supreme is topped with Spicy Tandoori Masala and Paneer Makhni. Their simpler offerings include the Veggie Supreme and Margherita. Pizza Corner is another bright and stylish pizzeria with bustling outlets throughout the city. The vegetarians can have their pick from mushrooms, sweet corn, pepperoni and black olives. The non-vegetarians get a combination of lamb pepperoni and chicken salami spread over their pizzas. The numerous outlets of Domino's Pizza are usually filled to the brim and their pizzas make for a sumptuous take-away. The speciality topping is the chicken barbecue and the curry masala with red pepper, golden corn and jalapeno. Pizza Port has been around longer than the others. Overtaken by the newer eateries, they nevertheless dish out tasty pizzas with a Mexican touch and chicken sausage toppings.

**Pizza Hut** *2532 0797*
**Pizza Corner** *2559 5393*
**Domino's** *2238 5855*
**Pizza Port** *2665 6066*

## Koshy's

*39 St. Mark's Road, Bangalore 560001*
**Tel** *2291 5840*
**Open** *9am to 11:30pm*
**Meal for Two** *Rs 600*
**Cards** *All*
**Alcohol** *Served*

A more charming café would be hard to locate. A better selection of food all under one roof would be hard to find. And a more exceptional coffee impossible to name. In other words, if you haven't been to Koshy's, you're clearly missing something. The food is the kind you can relish everyday, as indeed most regulars do. But there's also enough variety to keep the food adventurer in good humour. Sunday morning breakfasts of Appam and Stew are big-ticket items. The rest of the week there are breakfast, lunch and dinner menus to choose from.
There are in effect two Koshy's – one is the run down coffee shop variety and next door is the designer air-conditioned one. Both sides share the same kitchen. The atmosphere at the old café has artists, writers, lawyers and others firmly in its hold. The other side is almost like any other multicuisine restaurant with good food.

## Orange County

*Central Park, Manipal Centre, 47 Dickenson Road, Bangalore 560042*
**Tel** *2558 4242*
**Open** *7am to 10:30am, 12noon to 3pm and 8pm to 10:30pm*
**Meal for Two** *Rs 700*
**Cards** *All*
**Alcohol** *Served*

Orange County at the Central Park serves up an excellent selection of American and Mexican foods. A distinctly Yankee feel hangs in the air

and is supported by the cowboy duds, the light coloured furnishings and the large portions. The Mexican fajitas and enchiladas are as popular as the steaks and burgers. The restaurant's specials are baked dishes in fish and shrimp, grilled meats like the Gunslinger and a range of mini-burgers. They have an American breakfast spread, and for lunch there is a regular multicuisine buffet with Indian, Chinese and some European dishes thrown in. Live music, the all-American fare and a cheerful ambience make it an ideal family hangout.

## Tiger Bay

*99 The Bombay Store, 3ʳᵈ Floor, EGK Prestige, MG Road, Bangalore 560001*
**Tel** *2555 0888*
**Open** *12noon to3pm and 7pm to 10:45pm*
**Meal for Two** *Rs 900*
**Cards** *All*
**Alcohol** *Served*

Surprise! Surprise! There is no overhanging smell of fish in this restaurant! If you are a diverse bunch of people with a common desire to eat seafood, this is the one place most likely to satisfy everyone. Tiger Bay is an interesting concept – fish and shellfish cooked in a variety of styles ranging from Mangalorean, Kerala, Goan, Thai, Chinese, Italian, English and north Indian. Such diverse cooking styles emerging from one kitchen will not go down well with the purists, but Tiger Bay does try.
Suprisingly, vegetarians are not too badly off. The Tofu Tempura is nicely spiced with ginger and there are other attractions like Thai vegetable curry and Asparagus in Butter Sauce. Seafood lovers can choose from all manner of fish and various sizes of prawn, mussels, squid and even raw oysters

The setting is bright, airy and spacious with a lounge bar alongside. Tiger Bay overlooks MG Road and Cariappa Park, so always ask for a window seat.
There is almost no cuisine that is not listed on their menu, with more than just a couple of dishes from France, Mexico, the Mediterranean, Italy and China! Thai is the obvious favourite and has the most dishes. There is a lot of lime, garlic and basil in terms of flavours and their is a choice of prawn, squid and fish, asparagus, avocado etc. The Indian selection is quite small but rated highly – all the dishes are acknowledged as the showpieces in their state.
The dessert selection is small, but by the time you're through travelling around the culinary world, it's unlikely to sound very tempting!

## Tycoons

*83 Copper Arch, Infantry Road, Bangalore 560001*
**Tel** *2559 1356/1745*
**Open** *12noon to 3:30pm and 7pm to 12midnight*
**Alcohol** *Served*
**Meal for Two** *Rs 600*
**Cards** *All*

One of the few restaurants that made the grade in the 90s, Tycoons still attracts old patrons. A multicuisine restaurant serving north Indian and Continental food, both indoor and outdoor seating are available. The sizzlers and steaks are recommended.

## Shezan

*25/5 Maruti Complex, Lavelle Road, Bangalore 560001*
**Tel** *2224 9667*
**Branch** *Cunningham Road, 2226 2195*
**Open** *10:30am to 3:30pm & 6:30pm to 11pm*
**Meal for Two** *Rs 500*
**Cards** *All*
**Alcohol** *Not Served*

The old Shezan was surrounded by greenery, set in an old Bangalore bungalow. The new ones aren't doing too badly as far as location goes, at least the original Lavelle Road place which now operates from the first floor. The food and ambience are somewhere in between a bistro and an old fashioned multicuisine restaurant serving enough variety to keep everyone happy. The steaks are still popular.

# COFFEE & TEA BARS

## Barista

*4 St. Mark's Road, Bangalore 560001*
**Tel** *2229 7739*
**Branches** *Brigade Road, 2532 5292*
*Koramangala, 5110 4396;*
*100Ft. Road, 5115 3554;*
*MG Road, 2555 0422;*
*Walton Road, 2224 7087*
**Open** *8am to 11pm*
**Meal for Two** *Rs 300*

This is a chain of coffee shops serving a wide variety of hot and cold coffees,

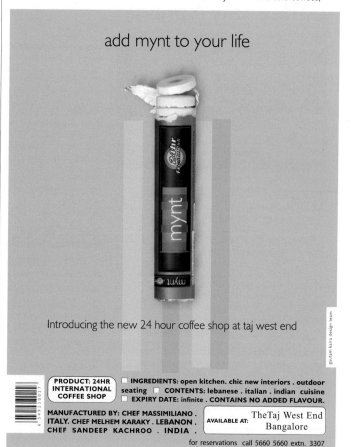

non-alcoholic drinks, sandwiches, pizzas, burgers, pastries and cookies. A guitar and board games like pictionary and scrabble are available. The atmosphere is young and friendly and you can spend hours over a cup of coffee without anyone raising an eyebrow. The St. Marks Road and Walton Road branches have great outdoor seating and are a hit with the young crowd.

## Cha Bar

*Leela Galleria, The Leela Palace, 23 Airport Road, Bangalore 560017*
*Tel 5115 5220*
**Open** *10am to 10pm*
**Meal for Two** *Rs 200*
**Cards** *All except Diners Club*

A steaming cup of tea and the company of a good book…the Cha Bar at The Leela Palace offers a taste of both. Situated alongside The Oxford Bookstore, it serves over 40 exotic tea brews and a dozen other beverages from Masala Milk to Iced Sherbet. The swanky Cha Bar flaunts a chilled-out ambience, a trendy décor and attentive service – all at an affordable price. The bookstore merges with the café and shelves lined with assorted titles run alongside the tables. You may pick and browse through any book that catches your fancy.
The range of teas is exhaustive,

stretching from classic Assam Tea to zesty Masala chas. 'Cha Hindustani' comprises a range of ginger, cardamom and cinnamon teas. Premium teas from Sikkim, Nepal and Ceylon are also listed. No tea bar is complete without Far Eastern concoctions. The Japanese and Chinese teas served here include a varied mix of green and black teas. Some other fancy world teas are the Moroccan Mint, Russian Caravan and South African Roobois. There is also a selection of esoteric Ayurvedic teas such as Brahmi, Karma, Panchadhatu and Shanty. For teas with a twist you may try Green Tea Margarita, Cha-Cha-Chino, Mint Tea Ice Crush and a few fruit flavoured ones. Coffee is not ignored with a choice of cappuccino, Mocha and Latte. The South Indian Organic Coffee served in a stainless steel glass deserves special mention.
You may also tuck into other treats like muffins, cookies, cakes, sandwiches and salads. Jellies, mugs and crockery may also be bought here.

## Café Coffee Day

*The Bombay Store, MG Road, Bangalore 560001*
*Tel 3090 2856*
**Branches** *Brigade Road, 3090 2967; MG Road, 3090 2933; Whitefield, 3090 3802; Koramangala, 3090 3012;*

*Airport Road, 3090 3798; Jayanagar, 3090 2969, 3090 2888; Basavanagudi, 3090 5104; Banashankari II Stage, 3090 2866; Lavelle Road, 3090 2889; Cunningham Road, 3090 2934; Frazer Town, 3090 2886;*

Cha Bar is a café attached to The Oxford Bookstore

*Commercial Street, 3090 2968; Sadashivanagar, 3090 2855; Indiranagar, 3090 3013; 100Ft. Road, 3090 2935*
**Open** *9am to 11pm*
**Meal for Two** *Rs 200*
**Cards** *Not Accepted*

# Coffee Day Xpress

Bangalore city has recently woken up to a whole new experience in fast food: Coffee Day Xpress is a smart, well-lit, clean and hygienic chain of mini-cafes springing up around the city, offering a wide variety of snacks and beverages for people on the go. A big improvement on the dingy roadside eatery, the Coffee Day Xpress boasts cheerful attendants and spanking premises. Pre-cooked food is heated and served in no time and these deceptively small booths are equipped with mechanised gadgets that ensure high standards of hygiene.
Coffee Day Xpress is part of the hugely popular Coffee Day brand. The 26 Xpress outlets are set in strategic locations like petrol bunks, movie theatres, offices, hospitals and colleges. The chain is pan-Indian chain and there are 82 kiosks countrywide.
What is unique to the Xpress chain is its varied menu, from subs and samosas to pasta and paneer rolls. (The names are tongue-in-cheek – Errant Currant, Strawberry Sutra, Mango Mantra shakes, Stumped Samosa and Eggy Biggy rolls are some of the specials!) Each city has its own local flavour – fish

fillings dominate Calcutta's menu and Delhi has a few extra samosas thrown in. The Coffee Day Xpress also has a few innovations up its sleeve – the thick shake made of water and icicles rather than milk is one. A more exciting menu is promised in the days to come.
The smart yet casual ambience and convenient locations of the Xpress stalls are a big draw – youngsters looking for an affordable snack, office-goers on their way to a meeting and fussy eaters who would normally not venture to eat street food, all stop here for a quick bite. The concept is not just a hit with customers but is a sound business proposition as well. Housewives, entrepreneurs and those on early retirement have eagerly taken up franchises and the returns have been rewarding. With many more outlets on the cards, Coffee Day Xpress seems to be going places.

## KIOSK LOCATIONS

**HP Hajee's Service Station** – *St. Mark's Road*

**Heartland** – *1/1 Arasikere, Bannerghatta Road*

**Sasken** – *139/25 Ring Road, Domlur*

**IBM** – *Behind Millenium Motors, Domlur; Subramanyam Arcade, Bannerghatta Road; 4th Floor, Explorer, ITPL, Whitefield; Prestige Towers, Residency Road*

**ING Vysya** – *22 MG Road*

**Transworks** – *Prestige Blue Chip, Block 9, Hosur Road; Whitefield*

**NMKRV College** – *Jayanagar III Block*

**AOL** – *7th Floor, Explorer, ITPL, Whitefield*

**ITC Infotech** – *ITC Infotech Park, Banaswadi*

**Cisco** – *Prestige Waterford; Divyashree Chambers*

**BPCL** – *Bashyam Circle, Sadashivnagar*

**Hewlett Packard** – *Wind Tunnel Road*

**MindTree Consulting** – *Banashankari*

**iGate** – *Whitefield*

**FoodMall** – *Malleswaram*

**AXA** – *Residency Road*

**TATA Elxsi** – *Whitefield*

**Hutch** – *Dairy Circle*

**Airtel** – *Bannerghatta Road*

**Progeon** – *Electronics City; Bannerghatta Road*

**Yahoo** – *MG Road*

**Philips** – *Old Madras Road*

**Sasken** – *Ring Road*

**GE Capital** – *Electronics City*

**Texas Instruments** – *CV Raman Nagar*

**Oracle** – *Thavarakere; Prestige BlueChip*

**John F Welch Technology Centre** – *Whitefield*

**Intel** – *Sarjapur Road; Airport Road*

**Accenture** – *Cunningham Road*

**Sykes** – *Airport Road*

**Khodays Contact Centre** – *Kanakpura*

**Cognizant** – *Mission Road; Basavangudi*

**C-Cubed** – *Koramangala*

**Reuters** – *Airport Road*

**Wipro** – *Electronics City*

**Msource** – *Ulsoor Road*

**Thomson Financials** – *St. Mark's Road; Commissariat Road*

**Satyam** – *Electronics City*

Java City, a popular café chain

This is a chain of young and trendy cafés selling coffee in a plethora of flavours and styles with a cheap takeaway option that brings the young crowd in droves. Burgers, sandwiches, savoury tarts, pastries and even pizzas are sold alongside. The café is comfortable and cool, and the coffee is very satisfying.

## Cottage Café

*144 MG Road, Bangalore 560001*
*Tel 2558 4083*
*Open 10am to 7pm*
*Meal for Two Rs 200*
*Cards All*

Cottage Café is a venture by the Cottage Industries Emporium, a bid to serve coffee with culture, as the caption goes. Located in the basement of the emporium its been done in style with ethnic wooden furniture, for sale if you desire. At the centre of the café is a space for meetings and discussions.
The coffee comes in many flavours – Espresso, Cappuccino, Café Amaretto, Mocha and the regular. Darjeeling whole leaf tea and a 'rejuvenation' tea from Nepal are also served. A few snacks such as pastries, samosas, pies, and chocolate are available here. Cottage Café helps young artists with display space in the corridor.

## Infinitea

*2 Shah Sultan Complex,*
*Cunningham Road, Bangalore 560056*
*Tel 5114 8810*
*Open 10am to 11pm*
*Meal for Two Rs 200*
*Cards MasterCard & Visa*

The city has a coffee culture, a pub culture and is now developing a tea culture. Reminiscent of bungalows in the tea estates during the Raj, Infinitea serves the very best Darjeeling teas and some rare, exotic ones as well. The teas are straight from the gardens and brewed right in front of you in distinctive crockery. Sand clocks help you time the brewing for that perfect cup. For a novice or non-fussy tea drinker, the sheer choice of over 50 varieties may seem a tad overwhelming but the friendly staff are there to assist. The menu includes old Bangalore favourites like the Masala Chai, Suleimani and Kadak Chai. The Peony Rosette (leaves woven like a flower) and the connoisseur's choice of the Second Flush are for those who prefer a lighter taste. Iced-tea fans should try Enigma on the Rocks at the bar counter, served in whisky glasses and topped with ice. There is a selection of excellent Continental dishes and don't miss the desserts. Tea tasting is allowed and a variety of fine teas are on sale.

## Java City

*Lavelle Road, Bangalore 560001*
*Tel 5112 0647*
*Branches Church Street, 5112 1787;*
*Brigade Road, 5112 1615*
*Open 10:30am to 9:30pm*
*Meal for Two Rs 250*
*Cards All*

Java City's airy cafés are usually bursting with youngsters, especially on weekends when live jazz music is showcased. Exotic coffees served include the Jamaican Blue Mountain, Hawaiian Kona, Mysore Filter Coffee, Irish coffee, Brazilian Santos, espressos, cappuccinos, macchiatos and coffees from Zimbabwe and Sumatra. Art by upcoming artists and caricature displays on the walls add to the café's vibrant ambience. Value meals, child specials, sandwiches, croissants, quiches, rolls, sandwiches, subs and burgers make up the menu. Indian eats include the Bombay Chutney Chicken Sandwich, Channa Chaat on Bread, Kheema Pav, Tikka Roti Roll and Chettinad, Andhra and Karnataka-style pizzas. Salads, iced teas and hot teas are also on offer.

## Qwiky's

*CMH Road, Indiranagar,*
*Bangalore 560038*
*Tel 2556 4555*
*Branches Cunningham Road*
*Open 9am to 9pm*
*Meal for Two Rs 150*
*Cards Not Accepted*

This is a quiet coffee bar on a busy thoroughfare playing soothing music. The coffee comes in 22 varieties and the seating is varied: Plush leather couches, wooden bar stools or regular glass-topped tables with shiny wooden chairs If coffee is not your drink, there are milkshakes, hot chocolate, tea and aerated drinks to choose from. An Internet browsing facility and a community message board are the other attractions.

## ICE CREAM

## Lakeview Milk Bar

*38 MG Road, Bangalore 560001*
*Tel 2559 8588, 2558 7410*
*Open 8am to 12:30am*
*Meal for Two Rs 250*
*Cards All except American Express*

There are far better ice cream parlours in Bangalore today, but Lakeview on MG Road still draws at the heart strings of old Bangaloreans! Some of their fondest memories are of a fruit salad and ice cream or Chikoo Milkshake at this ice cream bar on MG Road, where you could even drive up and eat your sundae in the car. The last is still a possibility at night as the busy shops on MG Road start winding down and fistfights over parking slots are unlikely to break out. The ice creams are sans any frills, but not cheap. The best buys are seasonal fresh fruit with a dollop of vanilla ice cream and fresh cream for the lucky ones. Strawberries and mangoes do very nicely like this. The dry fruit and ice cream combination is not a bad choice either.

## Painted Platters

*537 Robby Arcade, Indiranagar,*
*CMH Road, Bangalore 560038*
*Tel 2527 4711*
*Open 1pm to 11:30pm*
*Meals for Two Rs 250*
*Cards All except American Express*

Believing that the job of a dessert is to create a lasting impression, Painted Platters is pulling out all the stops with its range of beautifully presented mouthwatering desserts! The plates are 'painted' with swirls of chocolate sauce, polka dots of strawberry syrup and tiny curls of dark chocolate and hence rightly called 'Designer Desserts'. The fare is no less appetising: Apple Strudel, Kir Royale (flavoured with Champagne), Tiramisu, Mississippi Mud Pie, Rhum Savarain and Creme Brulee are some of the hoity toity sounding ones. The Seasonal Fruit Gratin has lightly grilled fresh fruits in warm orange liqueur flavoured custard and works very well if you're looking for a light and fruity finish to a meal. The ice creams are homemade and contain neither artificial flavouring nor egg and make a sumptuous meal when added to the desserts. Regular sundaes and Banana splits are also available. Painted Platters also doubles up as an art gallery – every fortnight a new artist is invited to place his paintings on the wall of the dessert parlour and you can pick a painting while slurping through your ice cream.

Infinitea serves a variety of Darjeeling teas.

## PUBS & BARS

### Downtown Pub
*41/42 Residency Plaza*
*Residency Road, Bangalore 560025*
***Tel** 2558 2050*
***Open** 11am to 11pm*
***Meal for Two** Rs 400*
***Cards** All*

This pub is frequented for its pool tables and pleasant slow rock music. Downtown Pub has a seating area large enough to fit big groups. They also have a small dance floor that tends to get a bit crowded.

### Dublin
*ITC Hotel Windsor Sheraton & Towers,*
*25 Golf Course Road, Bangalore 560052*
***Tel** 2226 9898*
***Open** 10am to 11:30pm*
***Meal for Two** Rs 1,200*
***Cards** All*

A regular old fashioned pub, Dublin will warm the hearts of those looking for the comfort of a watering hole without the new age frills like pounding music and strobe lights. Don't be misled though, Dublin does have its 'happening' nights when the volume is jacked up and the magic of 007 fills the air! Theme nights are very popular – Spanish nights, a Martini night where 69 kinds of martinis are served and so on.

### f Bar & Lounge
*Le Meridien, 28 Sankey Road,*
*Bangalore 560052*
***Tel** 2226 2233, 2220 8772*
***Open** 5pm to 12midnight*
***Meal for Two** Rs 1,000*
***Card** All except Diners Club*

The first f Bar in Asia, this is definitely high class and swank. The deep, low slung sofas in solid colours offer a lazy and welcome contrast. Sushi, Makis and Yakitoris are some of the hot dishes on the menu.

### Geoffrey's
*The Royal Orchid, 1 Golf Avenue,*
*Off Airport Road, Bangalore 560008*
***Tel** 2520 5566*
***Open** 11am to 11:30pm*
***Meal for Two** Rs 1,800*
***Cards** All*

Warm and plush interiors, comfortable seating and retro music – Geoffrey's has all the ingredients for a happy, convivial evening. It's English pub look comes from the stained glass windows, wood panelling and even some artefacts from 'back home' to give it that final touch. Posters of Elvis Presley, Marilyn Monroe and a Harley Davidson from across the Atlantic add a 70s feel to the place. It offers great food and beverages and the service has some of the old charm of bartenders of yore.

### Guzzlers Inn
*48 Rest House Road, Off Brigade Road,*
*Bangalore 560001*
***Tel** 2558 7336*
***Open** 11am to 11pm*
***Meal for Two** Rs 400*
***Cards** All*

Guzzlers Inn belongs to the older generation of pubs in the city. This is a good 'chill-out pub' with a mellow ambience, dim lighting and a varied choice of music. Games are regularly screened on three big screens and there is also a pool table for a round of snooker. Prices are reasonable. A variety of snacks from paneer pakoras to sandwiches are served with the beer and cocktails. Beer and snacks are also served in the pool room.

### Hibiscus Bar
*Grand Ashok, Kumara Krupa High*
*Grounds, Bangalore 560001*
***Tel** 2226 9462*
***Open** 12noon to 12midnight*
***Meal for Two** Rs 1,000*
***Cards** All*

Hibiscus is a quiet bar tucked away in the Grand Ashok. It offers a pleasant and relaxed atmosphere to unwind with friends after work. An unobtrusive ambience, impeccable service and a wide range of cocktails and drinks make it a popular stop.

### Hypnos
*G2 3 Gem Plaza, 66 Infantry Road,*
*Bangalore 560001*
***Tel** 2532 3901*
***Open** 12noon to 3pm and 6:30pm to 12midnight*
***Meal for Two** Rs 1,400*
***Cards** All*

Named after the Greek goddess of dreams, Hypnos is done up completely in white, with long flowing curtains, tall coloured glasses and old wooden benches and tables. It serves Lebanese and Mediterranean food along with 15 flavours of 'hookah' and music. Through the week the music changes from lounge music on Mondays, Tuesdays and Wednesdays, retro on Thursdays and the weekends are club nights with the latest hits and a discotheque.

### i-Bar
*The Park, 14/7 MG Road,*
*Bangalore 560001*
***Tel** 2559 4666*
***Open** 5:30pm to 11:30pm*
***Meal for Two** Rs 1,400*
***Cards** All*

Deep within the plush Park hotel is the i-Bar, named no doubt for Bangalore's IT status. Its cool neon ambience, low-floor furniture and bean bags are a hit with the partying crowd. DJ Sasha is in charge of the music and exotic cocktails dominate the menu. Indian and imported spirits, premium French, Italian and American wines are served here. Skilled bartenders create innovative cocktails like I-lychee, mojito, Mint Julep and Flaring Vodka. An array of snacks, appetisers, wraps and kababs are served to go with the drinks. Exclusive cigars, from Cohiba to Montecristo, are also offered.

### Library Bar
*The Leela Palace, 23 Airport Road,*
*Bangalore 560008*
***Tel** 2521 1234*
***Open** 11am to 12midnight*
***Meal for Two** Rs 1,000*
***Cards** All*

Here is a plush and snooty bar and cigar lounge in the equally posh Leela Palace. Expensive object d'art are scattered around and the air is quiet and elegant. The Library Bar is the perfect place for business related entertaining and lingering over a quiet drink. Attentive service and an interesting line-up of snacks complete the picture.

NASA, a space-theme pub

### NASA
*1/4 Church Street, Bangalore 560001*
***Tel** 2558 6512*
***Open** 11am to 11:30pm*
***Meal for Two** Rs 400*
***Cards** All*

The entire pub is built like a space ship, flaunting metal floors and bright blue lighting. The rest of the décor includes a Columbia-like exterior, porthole windows and table legs shaped like rockets! The cocktails are also set around the space theme – Zero Gravity is one such! The crowd puller is the laser show held everyday. The regulars come in for the reasonably priced draught beer, the long happy hours (11am to 6pm) and music from the 80s. The pub also has a separate family section.

### Oblivion
*4005 HAL II Stage, 100 Ft. Road,*
*Indiranagar, Bangalore 560008*
***Tel** 5115 3242*
***Open** 11am to 12midnight*
***Meal for Two** Rs 1,000*
***Cards** All*

Oblivion is the new club in town. Spread across four floors, it houses a glitzy basement discotheque, a trendy lounge, a gourmet restaurant and a resto-bar perched on the terrace. Mindscape is the lounge, set in the basement that houses a weekend discotheque, exotic cocktails, a liquor buffet and large television screens for the latest sporting events. It has a 'Day Long Menu' (from 12noon to 12midnight) that moves between Indian, Mexican, Chinese and American cuisine. The double whopper burgers are a big favourite and there is a range of non-alcoholic fruity drinks too. Sublime is the restaurant serving 'New World Cuisine', a blend of western Indian. Prawns on papads, Stuffed Chicken Wing and Fennel Vodka Soup are some of the highlights along with chocolate pie and cheesecake.

Dublin at ITC Hotel Windsor Sheraton & Towers

Beer City

If the Germans decide to migrate, they'd probably choose to live in Bangalore- India's beer capital. With the highest number of breweries in the country, if you're not drinking beer in Bangalore, then you're brewing some. It's no surprise then that the city also has the highest number of pubs in the country.

Bangalore is also home to one of the biggest brewers in India, the UB Group. Kingfisher (from the house of United Breweries) is the highest selling beer in India and is also an international bestseller-available in more than 52 countries.

Most people enjoy having beer with their food or vice versa (anything is fine as long as there's beer). We scoured the length and breadth of this country - from Hyderabad to Delhi and Mumbai to

Kolkata - asking chefs and food experts to recommend a light beverage that marries well with any kind of cuisine. Everyone unanimously recommended Kingfisher. It's not just the chefs' hearts that Kingfisher has won. This brand also has won several beer awards across the globe. From the best Light Lager award at Stockholm to the gold medal at the Australian International Beer awards, it has received the industry's stamp of approval.

With the beer culture running so deep in Bangalore, there seems to be a recent rise in consumption of beer at home. And with this phenomenon on a rise even in the other parts of the country; Kingfisher stepped in with its latest innovation, a 5-litre keg. Making it possible to drink draught beer at home. Which is why everyone calls it "Pub@Home".

The keg being the first of its kind in the country uses a new and unique

technology that retains the taste and freshness of Draught Beer. This compact keg contains 15 mugs of Draught Beer and can be easily stored in the refrigerator. So planning those house parties isn't so difficult anymore. The keg can be picked up at an outlet near you.

Bangaloreans also seem to be aware of the health advantages that are gained by guzzling beer, moderately.

Today, beer is supposed to work against cholesterol, heart attacks, strokes, hypertension and diabetes.

Drinking Beer is also said to improve bone density, and thus reduce the risk of fractures. Whoever said an apple a day keeps the doctor away obviously didn't drink any beer.

Cheers!

Geoffrey's, a traditional English pub at The Royal Orchid.

## Pecos

*34 Rest House Road,*
*Bangalore 560001*
*Tel 2558 6047*
**Open** *11am to 11pm*
**Meal for Two** *Rs 400*
**Cards** *All except American Express*

Regulars to this 'institution' say that the music played at Pecos hasn't changed over a decade… and no one's complaining! Pecos prides itself on its Woodstock brand of music and strict only-beer policy. This pub is spread over three tiny floors and its walls are covered with classic-rock graffiti and memorabilia. Pecos has a terrace and the spiral stairway going up is usually packed on busy nights. Try their pub lunches especially if you enjoy coastal cuisine! A free plate of snacks accompanies every pitcher of beer.

## Polo Club

*The Oberoi, 37/39 MG Road,*
*Bangalore 560001*
*Tel 2558 5858*
**Open** *11am to 1am*
**Meal for Two** *Rs 1,800*
**Cards** *All*

This English-style pub at The Oberoi boasts beautiful stained glass ceilings and windows with Tartan furnishings and pictures of legendary polo players on the walls. Seating is varied – you can choose between the bar or the cool verandah set amidst landscaped gardens. The pub meals of a salad, main course and complimentary drink are very popular, as also sandwiches and fish and chips. Besides the regular imported and Indian IMFL, there is draught beer and coffee along with soft jazz.

## Purple Haze

*17/1 Residency Road,*
*Bangalore 560025*
*Tel 2221 3758*
**Open** *10:30am to 11pm*
**Meal for Two** *Rs 600*
**Cards** *All*

One of the popular pubs in town, the music here is the biggest attraction. The hard rock and grunge is hugely popular with regulars who come to unwind after work. The dimly lit walls are adorned with pictures of Jimi Hendrix (*Purple Haze* is one of his songs), Jim Morrison and other rock greats. Music videos are played on big screens and some of them are the sing-along variety. There is a good selection of spirits and the usual variety of snacks.

## Styx

*Next to Cauvery Emporium,*
*45 MG Road, Bangalore 560001*
*Tel 2558 2259*
**Open** *11:30am to 11:30pm*
**Meal for Two** *Rs 500*
**Cards** *All*

Named after a mythological river in the netherworld, Styx is not for the faint hearted. The music gets loud and the drinks flow freely as the night wears on. This pub is mainly patronised for the heavy metal music played here. The pub's interiors are dark but pretty, with blue glass pillars, a snazzy bar counter and fish tanks. A large DVD projection screen and live performances by local bands are other attractions. Space is limited in this smallish pub that stands apart with its choice of music.

## Tavern at the Inn

*Museum Inn, 1 Museum Road,*
*Bangalore 560001*
*Tel 5111 3339*
**Open** *3pm to 11:30pm*
**Meal for Two** *Rs 600*
**Cards** *All*

Part of Museum Inn, this is a cosy pub where you can linger over your drink. The lighting is soft and there are secluded corners if you want to sit away from the noise. The DJ is obliging and plays any requests. The host of cocktails served here have been helpfully categorised into vodka-based, rum-based and whisky-based ones. Tavern's Tandoori cuisine is also a speciality.

## The Bunker

*45/3 Residency Cross Road,*
*Bangalore 560025*
*Tel 2558 1365*

**Open** *11:30am to 12midnight*
**Meal for Two** *Rs 500*
**Cards** *All*

The Bunker belongs to the newer breed of pubs with strobe lights, the latest music and a new age décor. A favourite with teenagers and executives alike, The Bunker houses three seating areas. One section has a youthful flavour with neon coloured seating and multihued lights, the others are a family section and a laidback lounge with sofas and bar stools. The DJ plays requests and a variety of snacks and kababs are served here. Cocktails range between Rs 150 to Rs 250.

## The New Night Watchman

*46/1 Church Street 560001*
*Tel 2558 8372*
**Open** *10am to 11:30pm*
**Meal for Two** *Rs 400*
**Cards** *All*

The New Nightwatchman's claim to fame is its weekly pub quiz, 'Booze & Brains', held every Thursday. No prizes for guessing what the winners get! Seating at this English-style pub is quite out of the ordinary and goes up in levels from the bar. The round up of cocktails is satisfactory and a full a la carte menu is offered for lunch and dinner. On the music front, the DJ spins a somewhat diluted medley of songs. The New Night Watchman isn't the place for those who take their music seriously.

## The Pub World

*65 Residency Road, Bangalore 560025*
*Tel 2558 5206*
**Open** *11am to 11pm*
**Meal for Two** *Rs 500*
**Cards** *All*

This was the big daddy of all pubs and one of the originals that gave Bangalore its reputation as a Pub City. The sprawling Pub World sports four different themes under one roof. The Red Lion, an English-style pub is popular with the families who hang out here over mocktails and popcorn. This roomy pub is known for its attentive service, pleasant music and good selection of beer and cocktails. The Pub World is a must-see on Bangalore's pub hopping circuit.

The Pub World

# City Of Lakes

- 3 major lakes rejuvenated
- Over 250 parks redeveloped
- More than 25,000 new trees planted

India's City Of The Future, managed by

**Bangalore Mahanagara Palike**

*Citizens First. Always.*

# Transit – The Food Lounge

Transit is the name of a sprawling food lounge at The Forum. Modelled like an airport lounge, it can seat up to 520 people at a time! Eleven types of cuisine are served here – Mughlai, Italian, Parsee, Chinese, Vietnamese, Thai, Burmese, Malaysian, American, Mexican and Indian. Buyers get to sample tacos, nachos, chaats, Falafel, Chinese noodles and a host of other interesting foods. The décor is bright, service is quick and high standards of hygiene are maintained across all counters. Plasma screens beam away while you eat.

Paramount, Beijing Bites, Salem's Kichen, Panda House, 5 Centigrade, Bay Wraps, Fry-Days, Movenpick, Shiv Sagar and Subway are the individual counters at Transit.

The wide choice of food and reasonable prices bring in droves of hungry shoppers, teenagers and entire families. There is a separate play area for kids and a stage for parties and live entertainment. A jukebox and a coffee stall are other attractions at the Transit Lounge. Establishments or individuals can hire the 'Invitation Kitchen' for a specified period of time. Salad bars, Biryani festivals etc. are regularly hosted here.

## Paramount
Paramount serves up some delectable Mughlai food – rice and biryanis, naans and parathas, grilled and `broasted' chicken, rolls and samosas. Chicken and mutton biryanis, Ceylon and Kerala parathas, Shawarma rolls and kababs fresh from the tandoor are some of the highlights. Jumbo and mini thalis are served for lunch.

## Beijing Bites
Beijing Bites is easily one of the most popular stalls at

the Transit Lounge. Their 'New Age Chinese cuisine' is a tasty departure from the regular Indianised Chinese fare. Dragon rolls, chicken lollipops, a variety of noodles and Prawn Tamporu are some of their specials. Beijing Bites serves Thai food as well. An interesting concept is the Veg and Chicken Combo meals, which come with generous helpings of noodles, rice and Schezwan sauce.

## Salem Kitchen
This is a Chettinad speciality kitchen where idlis, dosas and rice are served with piquant chicken, fish and mutton curries. Delicacies like Chicken Kolambu and Mutton Varuval feature on the menu and there is a sizeable section devoted to vegetarians as well.

## Bay Wraps
Bay Wraps serves variegated vegetarian and non-vegetarian rolls. Chicken wraps, Mutton Sheek Wraps, Hummus, Falafel and Shawarma make up the menu here.

## Fry-Days
Fry Days as the name suggests offers a range of munchies as snacks. Fries, potato wedges, corn and paneer fingers and chicken nuggets are available here.

## Panda House
An undertaking of Ebony hotel, Panda House plans to grow into a pan-Asian fast food chain. It caters to a wide palate of tastes with Italian, Thai and Vietnamese fare. Pastas, Parsi Dhansak with rice, Thai Red Curry and Satay are served here. Some exotic foods like Malaya Massaman Curry, Vietnamese Sousi Tofu and Burmese Khaoswey Chicken feature on the menu.

## Subway
This quintessential American sandwich chain serves ham, salami, lamb, pepperoni and turkey subs and hot dogs. Paneer and chicken tikka subs and other local variations also feature on the menu. Subway is also the place to go for the 'biggest, meatiest, tastiest' sandwiches. They also have a range of vegetarian picks like the Corn and Peas sub and the Hummus and Falafel sub.

## Movenpick
Head to the Movenpick outlet for ice creams, waffles, sorbets, sundaes and a range of interesting desserts. Cappuccino, apricot and apple blackberry are some of their classic flavours. Tea and south Indian filter coffee are also served here! Also available are sandwich and meal combos.

## Shivsagar
Indian `fastfood' hogs the biggest counter at Transit Lounge. The fare here is an exhaustive selection of chaats, soups, dosas, parathas, rice and juices. The parathas that stretch from aloo to mooli are served with chole, curd and pickle. The chaats are a big hit and include some originals like the Jain Pav Bhaji made without onion or garlic, Kadhai Handi Pav Bhaji and Tomato Chaat.

## 5 Centigrade
The menu lists a range of teas including jasmine, green and iced tea, milkshakes and sundaes. Tropicana juices and the usual choice of branded aerated drinks are available.

*21, II Floor, The Forum, Hosur Road, Koramangala, Bangalore 560034*
**Tel** *2206 7688*

PIZZA CORNER

PIZZA CORNER    PIZZA CORNER

PIZZA
CORNER

NESCAFÉ    NESCAFÉ    NESCAFÉ

DEENA'S

SALE SALE SALE
COOL COTTON

PIZZA
CORNER

STD
ISD
FAX

Bangalore is a great shopping destination with glitzy shopping malls, boutiques and quaint bazaars.

# Shopping

Bangalore Central is a shopping destination in the heart of the city. Both serious shoppers and window shoppers frequent such mega malls to look for the best brands and sample the latest trends.

Traditional markets with piles of fresh vegetables offer the promise of some free coriander, green chillies and a chat on the politics of the day with the vendor! Supermarkets selling packaged, cut and preserved fruits or vegetables are the new competition.

# Shopping

**M**ost visitors are surprised and incredulous that Bangalore could be considered a **shopping destination**! What exactly would you shop here for? The answer is: Just about anything. **Sandalwood** and **silk** are still the backbone of the handicraft industry, but there is much more to **browse** and **buy**. The shops have gotten bigger, hours have been extended and the merchandise available has moved from traditional to trendy.

There is a wide choice in **shopping atmospheres** as well. You could spend a quiet morning as the sole customer gazing at a Victorian chaise lounge or join eager buyers haggling with sari sellers in the cluttered and deafening **discount bazaar** of Chikpet. There are shops where you can happily break for a cup of coffee without leaving the exit! Both big malls and **bazaars** of old with lots of colour and noise are now an intrinsic part of Bangalore's shopping experience. Try them for more than just retail therapy!

Shoppers on Brigade Road

## Posh Shopping Districts

The **most favoured shopping destination** is still the central area of MG Road and all the roads that lead towards it. MG Road retains its **provincial charm** with a few remaining low-rise buildings and shop names that have stood for a half century or more. The soothing green expanse on the opposite side of the road has inviting park-style benches at regular intervals that complement the shopping experience. Products of all varieties like clothing, books, jewellery, handicrafts, gifts, crockery and services like Internet parlours, dry cleaners, taxis, hotels and photography are available on this stretch. The shopping has **extended eastwards** to Trinity junction and no one is complaining.

What makes MG Road so special is not just the **great stores**, but the presence of a variety of eating and snacking places as well. From roadside **corn-on-the-cob** sellers to swank new speciality seafood **restaurants**, **coffee bars** and regular Chinese and multicuisine places, you can spend many hours losing track of time!

Just off MG Road is **Brigade Road** where British soldiers once bought their stores, and is now the favourite hangout of the young and restless. Weekend evenings are especially crowded as thousands of young people arrive here **to see** and **be seen**. Lots of bright neon lights, **music stores**, **cafés**, **pubs** and **game arcades** let the night stay young for a long time.

A little further down is **Commercial Street**, also a British military legacy and now a hub of small and large shops packed together like sardines. But the most fascinating aspect is the **network** of **narrow lanes** that run in and out connecting 'Com' Street as it is popularly known, to the **noisy**, **bustling** and **colourful bazaars** that thrive just seconds away. Shops selling cloth stacked in bales rub shoulders with tiny jewellery and pawnshops, plastic kitchenware and rows upon rows of cheap clothing shops. Wandering in and out of the tiny lanes lets you sample some of the street food, sizzling enticingly under your nose!

## The Concept Store – Contemporary yet Classic

Streamlined trousers cut from Indian silk brocade. Khadi bustiers. Zardozi on blue jeans. Tablemats made with rolled newspapers. Jute jewellery. A computer table housed in an antique cupboard. Floor mats with zari borders. The traditional line between classic and contemporary, ethnic and modern has blurred and the result is functional and funky.

Welcome to the new fusion ware crowding Indian stores. A wide array of independent fashion, accessories, condiments, textiles, object d'art, home products and lifestyle goods are being created in a unique blend of Indo-Western styles. This creative mix may be found in Bangalore's new concept stores. Each has a definite style of its own, leaving a unique stamp on the goods they merchandise.

## Malls – Big is Best

The large shopping mall, sign of the big city, dispenser of retail therapy and store for all you ever needed and more, has come to Bangalore! A **brightly lit, air-conditioned expanse** of clothes, cosmetics, toys, gifts, crockery and more encourages plenty of window shoppers to put down good money. Some of the bigger ones have small cafés attached for those who might feel faint after a morning spent trawling through clothes, shoes, bags, CDs, etc. The perfume counters are invariably placed at the entrance, in keeping with the retail law which says that smell is a powerful draw!

For most shoppers it's a blessing to find almost everything you need under one roof. The multiple billing counters, discreet salespeople and wide variety of brands are very attractive. At festival time, malls advertise delayed closing hours to cash in on late shoppers.

## Bargain Bazaars

Old timers think nothing of making the journey to **City Market**, braving traffic and crowds, to get the best bargains. The City Market has been renamed the Krishna Rajendra Market, or **KR Market**, but has lost none of its importance from the time it was inaugurated by Sir Mirza Ismail in 1928. It is still the nerve centre of commercial and trading activity, along with neighbouring **Avenue Road** and **Chikpet**. Vegetables and clothes, electronics and saris, plastic toys and expensive white goods, jewellery and luggage – the spread is at once startling, confusing and exhilarating!

Remember the three B's of shopping in this close approximation to the bazaar of yore: **b**rowse, **b**argain and only then **b**uy.

Commercial Street is the city's shopping hub.

No study of shopping arenas would be complete without a mention of other famous markets like **Russel Market**, inaugurated in 1927 by Hajee Sir Ismail Sait and even today the most famous market for groceries in the cantonment area. **Fruits, flowers, vegetables, meats** and **seafood** arrive here early in the morning when big and small buyers and sellers gather to start the day's proceedings.

The traditional suburbs of Bangalore may be identified by their well established market areas. Malleswaram, Basavanagudi and Jayanagar residents don't find the need to venture out as everything they need is available 'down the road'. These markets brighten up when a big **festival** is in the offing. Flower sellers, their fingers busy stringing, potters with **terracota** bowls and sellers of **conical stacks** of **vermilion** move on to the sidewalk. Garlands of **jasmines** and **marigolds**, **fresh vegetables** and auspicious **banana leaves** are haggled over as money changes hands. The **Basavanagudi market** comes to life during the annual groundnut fair in November. Pavements are piled high with mounds of every kind of nut – raw, cooked, fried, roasted and dipped in sugar. As you draw closer to the Bull Temple, the groundnuts give way to flowers and *puja* articles. The covered market in **Jayanagar** is similar with rows of shops selling everything from luggage to stationery and fresh vegetables.

## Must Buys

All visitors to Karnataka are still told to bring back at least one **sandalwood product** and a **silk**! And rightly so. Sandalwood products are almost exclusive to this state and come in a variety of themes – as carvings, pendants, screens, boxes, trays, soaps, oils and incense sticks. Silk is another great attraction and anywhere you throw a stone you're likely to hit a silk shop! There is plenty to choose from – silk saris in all hues with printed, woven and embroidered designs, silk scarves, stoles, cushion covers and quilts.

The other traditional buys include **Channapatna's wooden toys** and **rosewood carvings**. Karnataka's abundant forests supply plenty of valuable wood for carving and inlay work on statues of gods, animals and furniture. There is also **Bidriware** from Bidar in north Karnataka that uses a metal alloy of zinc, copper, tin and lead and the effect is a delicate silver filigree contrasting with dark metal, appreciated around the world.

If traditional crafts are not your first choice, there are plenty of **other unique buys**. T-shirts that carry a funny message about the sights and sounds peculiar to the city make great gifts. **Terracotta jewellery** and bric-a-brac is inexpensive and trendy and the city's boutiques and design stores reflect Bangalore's unique design sensibilities.

## New Shopping Districts

The crush for space in and around MG Road, Mecca of shopping, has worked to the benefit of Lavelle Road, Ulsoor Road, Indiranagar's 100Ft. Road and major roads in Koramangala. Many **upmarket stores** have set up shop on these **quiet roads** with ample parking and none of the rush and clamour of high-octane shopping areas. These are **destinations shops** – window-shopping is rare and most buyers come with a clear demand and the knowledge that they will get what they are looking for: A dressy evening skirt with original zardozi in earth tones from Ritu Kumar, silk curtains in beige on white from Yamini and a blown glass vase to accessorise the new dining table.

*Stark World – Bangalore & Karnataka* is an unabashed tribute to the great shopping places in the city. We have tried to categorise places not just by product but by atmosphere as well – the '**concept**' store where shopping is as much about product as atmosphere. Enjoy the search!

MG Road

## OLD FURNITURE & ANTIQUES

### Alankrita

*5 Jewellers Street, Commercial Street Cross, Bangalore 560001*
*Tel 2558 9635*
*Branch Raj Bhavan Road, 2286 6686*
*Open 10am to 6:30pm.*
*Closed on Sunday.*
*Cards All*

Alankrita stocks a blend of handcrafted products and antiques from Kerala, Tamil Nadu and Andhra Pradesh. An antiquarian's delight – parrot cages, gramaphones, engraved jewel boxes, quaint masks, kerosene lamps and even battered milk cans may be found here. For the more serious collector the shop has a rare collection of Tanjore paintings, decorative brassware, glassware and old furniture in rosewood, teakwood and Burma wood. You can also order furniture.

### Almirah

*5/2 Campbell Road, Opp. Lifestyle, Bangalore 560047*
*Tel 2556 8787*
*Open 10am to 6pm.*
*Only by appointment on Sunday.*
*Cards All except American Express*

Wearing the air of a bygone era, this shop is a storehouse of carefully restored furniture sourced from old homes across India. A variety of closets, chests, chairs, dressing tables, dining tables and sofa sets in rosewood and teak are available at affordable prices.

### Dakshini

*236, 2ⁿᵈ Main, Domlur II Stage, Bangalore 560071*
*Tel 5760 0550*
*Open 9am to 8pm.*
*Only by appointment on Sunday.*
*Cards Not Accepted*

Dakshini is all about making old bric-a-brac affordable. Antiques meant for the urban home are showcased here. Tucked into every corner of the shop are quaint lamps, mirrors and decorative figurines. A wide range of ornate swings, furniture panels, marble top tables, doors, pillars, wall hangings and paintings are on display.
This family-run outfit has been in the business for the past nineteen years and also reproduces antiques. From old horse carts to bronze knick-knacks, there is something to suit everyone's budget. The decorated rosewood doors, staircases and pinewood and steel furniture are attractive buys. You may also choose from a large collection of curios – old grandfather clocks, electric fans, kitchen utensils etc.
The antiques are mainly sourced from villages and old homes across Tamil Nadu, Andhra Pradesh, Karnataka and Kerala. Prices range from Rs 50 to Rs 2 lakh.

### Krishtie Antiques

*7 Airport Road, Domlur, Bangalore 560071*
*Tel 2535 7334/3399*
*Open 10am to 7:30pm.*
*Closed on Sunday.*
*Cards All*

Krishtie deals in elegant old world furniture with a well preserved look. The store is an ideal foraging ground for grandfather clocks, Italian marble busts, intricately carved doors and stained glass partitions. The collection extends to Bohemian

furniture, Satsuma, Chinese and European vases and urns.

### Natesan's Antiqarts

*76 MG Road, Bangalore 560001*
*Tel 2558 8344/7424*
*Open 10am to 8pm.*
*Only by appointment on Sunday.*
*Cards All*

Natesan's ranks as one of the oldest 'antique' shops situated on posh MG Road. This exclusive store is run by a family of art lovers who employed master craftsmen to work on bronze, stone, silver and wood to create exquisite object d'art.

### Oriental Haveli

*47/A, IV Block, 17ᵗʰ Main, 100 Ft. Road, Koramangala, Bangalore 560034*
*Tel 2553 6239*
*Open 10:30am to 7:30pm*
*Cards All*

Oriental Haveli has a little bit of everything – usable period furniture, limited editions of Versace and Swarovski products, all set in a rustic ambience! The store also dishes out a colourful kitsch of Chinese white and blue pottery, Dresden china, Majolica vases, urns and platters, silver filigree nd carved wooden doors.

### Panchavati's Heirlooms

*126/1 Brigade Road, Opp. Brigade Towers, Bangalore 560025.*
*Tel 2555 3916*
*Open 10:30am to 6:30pm.*
*Closed on Sunday.*
*Cards All*

Cluttered with antiques and popular with locals as well as tourists, this shop on Brigade Road has been doing brisk business for the last 35 years. Old furniture, both carved and plain, art deco and colonial, in rosewood, mahogany and teakwood is on display. A variety of copper, brass, porcelain and wooden artefacts as well as Tanjore and Mysore paintings, rare lithographs and maps may also be found.

## HANDICRAFT STORES

### Andhra Handloom House

*St. Patrick's Shopping Arcade, Residency Road, Bangalore 560025*
*Tel 2532 3782*
*Branch Jayanagar, 2663 7385*
*Open 10am to 8pm*
*Cards Not Accepted*

A large collection of assorted silks and

cottons from Andhra Pradesh like the vibrant Pochampalli, the heavy Dharamavaram, light Gadwal, Kalanjali and printed silk saris are all available here. The reasonably priced ikkat material is great for kurtas. Bedspreads, dhotis and towels are also sold here.

## Asian Arts Emporium

*8 Cunningham Road,*
*Bangalore 560052*
***Tel** 2220 8963*
***Open** 9am to 9pm*
***Cards** All*

Rich hand woven carpets made from pure silk and wool, carved furniture, silver jewellery and Pashmina shawls are some of the handicrafts showcased in this emporium. Orders for custom-made carpets, washes and repairs can be placed here.

## Cauvery Arts & Crafts Emporium

*45 MG Road, KSHDC Complex,*
*Bangalore 560001*
***Tel** 2558 0317/2656/1187*
***Open** 9:30am to 8:30pm*
***Cards** All except American Express*

Cauvery represents the heart of Karnataka's handicraft industry and the shop on MG Road is a landmark of sorts. Heavy furniture inlaid with rosewood and once patronised in the royal courts of Mysore, holds pride of place in the shop. Sandalwood – the fragrance of Karnataka – takes many forms. Striking black and silver Bidriware from Bidar (the 16th century capital town of the Bahmani Sultanate) is available in the form of vases, statues and even table stationery. Bronzes inspired by Hoysala temple friezes and

lacquerware from Channapatna add colour. Targeted primarily at the tourist, there is something for everyone to carry home: Inlaid rosewood screens, Chola bronzes, sandalwood bookmarks and key chains, hair clips and beads, silk scarves, ties and evening bags. Don't be deterred by size and packing constraints, as most products can be dismantled and packaging services are available. The most popular products are the gift wrapped sandal soaps, incense sticks, sandal paste and perfumes. You may need to look carefully for that one-of-a-kind purchase, like a set of playing cards hand painted on leather, known as 'Ganjifa' painting. Cauvery also has an exhibition hall with gold, silver and semi-precious jewellery from all over the country.

## Central Cottage Industries Emporium (CCIE)

*144 MG Road, Bangalore 560001*
***Tel** 2558 4083/4084*
***Open** 10am to 7pm*
***Cards** All*

This emporium prides itself on showcasing the many different hues of India under one roof, from utilitarian artefacts to just about everything else that is classified as handicraft. Engraved brass vases, fruit bowls, carved pots, flower vases, goblets, pottery, paintings, jute and cane worked crafts, leather crafts, accessories, costume jewellery, toys, ready-to-wear fabrics, silks and saris, table linen, bedspreads, carpets, dhurries and papier-mâché artefacts can be bought here. In furniture they have an extensive range of rosewood and shesham (special wood from north India) woodcarvings and furniture with meenakari work. The CCIE is a part of

Cauvery Arts & Crafts Emporium

the Ministry of Textiles of the Government of India so you can be sure of quality handicrafts.

## Desi

*27 Patalamma Street, Near South End Circle, Basavanagudi,*
*Bangalore 560004*
***Tel** 2657 6669*
***Branch** Sita Circle, 2672 5514*
***Open** 10am to 8pm. Closed on Monday.*
***Cards** All except American Express*

This is quite a storehouse for ethnic handicrafts, sourced from rural Karnataka and the interiors of Andhra Pradesh. A variety of handmade dhurries, pottery, folders and terracotta jewellery as well as a large collection of handlooms and silks from Karur are part of the inventory here. Set in an old house replete with red oxide floors and earthen pots, the shop has a distinct rustic air.

## Ethnic Weaves

*I Floor, Safina Plaza, Infantry Road,*
*Bangalore 560001*
***Tel** 2532 0748, 2558 1837*
***Open** 10am to 9pm*
***Cards** All*

Ethnic Weaves is a world of mix 'n' match with a kaleidoscope of vibrant colours in pure cotton. Match a deep red and black mangalgiri edged with gold zari with a white salwar and maroon Pochampalli dupatta. Rows of pure cotton fabrics are neatly stacked through the entire shop – earthy reds, lime greens, bright yellows, deep blues and pinks fill the shelves. True to its name, the shop stocks only handloom dress material. Apart from the popular Kanchipuram cotton, kalamkari or vegetable dyeing from Andhra Pradesh and ikkat, a traditional tie and dye technique from Orissa are sold here. Dhurries, dupattas and saris are also available.

# Sandalwood

Sacred to all Indians, sandalwood or *chandan* grows primarily in the forests of Karnataka. The scented wood of the sandalwood tree has a variety of uses, the most common of which are beautifully carved idols, rounded prayer beads and delicately scented soaps and perfumes. Hindu cremations call for some amount of sandalwood, the Parsi community uses the wood to stoke sacred fires.

Sandalwood perfume has been described as heavenly, divine, delicate and sweet. It is very

popular in the cosmetics and soap industries. Indian women still use sandalwood paste to soften and beautify their skin. Its strong and heady fragrance is legendary and snakes are said to wrap themselves around the tree, intoxicated by its scent.

The wood's medicinal properties are extolled by many Hindu texts – a glass of cold milk scented with a drop of sandalwood oil is said to be a remedy for sunstroke, as well as an effective deterrent to skin ailments.

Karnataka grows nearly 70 per cent of the sandalwood in India, the rest is grown in Andhra Pradesh and Tamil Nadu. This tree is a root parasite – after germination the seedling finds a host tree and derives nourishment from its roots. It can grow up to 10 metres high and upto one-and-a-half metres in girth. Most trees can live for over 100 years. However, once the tree is over 30 years old, it is exploited for its wood. Among the 70-odd varieties of the species, ten are hardy and can be cultivated. The older the tree, the more the yield: A 40 to 50-year old can yield more than 250kgs of scented hardwood. Carving is done on the inner hardwood and the bark is used (after

powdering) for the manufacture of agarbathis or incense. The roots are the biggest source of oil. The production of sandalwood oil in the state began during World War I when two oil-extraction plants were set up. The 80-year old Karnataka Soaps and Detergents Limited (KSDL) is one of the largest producers of sandalwood soap in the world, with factories in Shimoga and Mysore.

There is a big market for sandalwood carvings and the Gudigar families native to the Sagar and Sorab regions of Shimoga district have been engaged in ivory and sandalwood carving for generations. Trained in the craft from childhood, their products are gender specific: Men work on figurines, idols, knick-knacks, curios, incense holders and photo frames while women make garlands and wreaths. Some of their work, on display and sale at places like the Cauvery Arts & Crafts Emporium on MG Road, is quite exquisite. The government ensures that they are supplied with wood regularly and their products are sold at licensed outlets.

The government owns all sandalwood trees. Permission is required to fell or even cut parts of the tree.

# The ultimate!

Soap with expensive
almond oil and moisturisers
in exquisite sandal oil.

Gold has the right
mix of premium
ingredients in the
right measure. That's
all you need to make
your skin glow with
beauty. So try one
today. Fix a date
with beauty.

Mysore Sandal
**Gold**
Enriched with moisturiser

Natura

Gold

Skin like never before.

# Toy Town

Channapatna, a small town off the Bangalore-Mysore road has long been popular as 'Toy Town'. A household industry, the origin of this woodcraft dates back to the rule of Tipu Sultan who encouraged the villagers to use locally available soft wood to produce toys. Chitragars or families of artists were engaged in wood-turnery and the lacquerware industry and soon Channapatna's toys were being sold on the road, in state emporiums and even exported.

Soft, cream coloured wood of the Hale tree (*Wrightia Tinctoria*) is used as raw material. The wood is extremely coarse grained, moderately hard and can be easily turned into required shapes. Lac (a resinous substance obtained from trees), vegetable dyes and paints that are non-toxic are used to embellish the woodcarvings. The wood is first turned into circular shapes by hand or using power lathes and suitable cutting tools. The turned wooden objects are then lacquered in a dry state. The lacquered piece is buffed with the leaves of the talegiri (*Pandanus Odoratissimus*) and delicate artwork applied over it.

Spinning tops, dolls and images of mythological characters are made in large numbers. With growing globalisation, Channapatna's artisans have expanded their repertoire and now make jewellery, car seats and even educational aids.

## Gurjari

*31 Pinto Towers, Residency Road,
Bangalore 560025*
*Tel 2558 3425*
**Open** *10:30am to 7:30pm*
**Cards** *All*

One of the first state emporia to combine modern day sensibilities with rustic designs, Gurjari broke the mould of fuddy duddy, badly stitched clothes, which were the norm in the eighties. Its edge has since been blunted by the wave of readymade clothes now in the market and its own limitations. However, you may still find the odd fabulous skirt, jacket and kurta if you're lucky. And prices are nothing if not reasonable. A cosy shop done up in wood, it has colourful handlooms and handicrafts stacked in every corner. An enterprise of the Gujarat State Government, it stocks an array of authentic handicrafts from the region. Embroidered wall hangings, garments and cushion covers, hand block printed furnishings, decorative boxes and bells with metal inlay work, intricately carved wood panels, furniture and sankheda jhulas, clay pots, puppets and traditionally crafted leather terracotta accessories are available at the emporium. Vibrant beadwork, woven work, bandhini fabrics and Patola saris with a distinctly Gujarati flavour are sourced from artisans across the state. Especially popular are the pure cotton, hand block printed, tie and dye dress materials, saris, bed sheets and lively knick-knacks.

## Himalayan Dowry

*72 MG Road, Bangalore 560001*
*Tel 5112 1750*
**Open** *10am to 9pm*
**Cards** *All except American Express*

The intriguing name comes from a 14th century Kashmiri tradition where Himalayan stones were exchanged as 'dowry' between the bride's and groom's families. The shop deals exclusively in Kashmiri handicrafts. Rich Pashmina shawls, pure silk and woollen carpets, sparkling diamond and ruby encrusted jewellery adorn this cramped basement shop. For those who are not looking at expensive buys there are colourful papier mâché bells, jewellery boxes, letterboxes and other quaint knick-knacks.

## Mrignayani

*31 Pinto Towers, Residency Road,
Bangalore 560025*
*Tel 2558 2495*
**Open** *10:30am to 7:30pm*
**Cards** *All*

Mrignayani has a handicraft to suit everyone's budget and taste. Don't be put off by the poor display for it hides some interesting products you're unlikely to find anywhere else. Set up by the Madhya Pradesh Laghu Udyog Nigam, the emporium displays handicrafts and handlooms exclusive to Madhya Pradesh. The varied selection of handlooms includes Chanderi, Maheshwari, Kosa and Tussar saris, scarves and batik and vegetable dyed dress materials. The collection of handicrafts is also diverse – exotic tribal art made from bell metal, iron crafts, dhurries or hand knotted carpets, decorative figures made from marble dust, wood, stone and papier mâché. A more thorough search of the emporium will reveal handmade paper stationery, tribal wall paintings, masks, bamboo and jute curios, lacquered vases and zari purses.

## National Cottage Emporium

*70 Infantry Road, Bangalore 560001*
*Tel 2558 5336*
**Open** *8:30am to 9pm*
**Cards** *All*

This is carpet town! An array of hand knotted, wool and mulberry silk carpets and tapestry rugs are exhibited. Also available are exclusive Pashmina shawls, pure woollen shawls, antiques and woodcarvings. The shop undertakes washing and mending of used carpets.

## Rajasthan Emporium and Handicrafts

*20 Public Utility Building, I Floor,
MG Road, Bangalore 560001*
*Tel 2559 6609*
**Open** *10am to 8:30pm and 10am to 1:30pm on Sunday.*
**Cards** *All*

Rajasthan Emporium offers a small peep into the state's fabulous array of handicrafts. The furniture, textiles and jewellery available here reflect a fusion of folk and Rajput-Muslim art typical to the state. A large section of the emporium is dedicated to textiles and furniture like vegetable dyed Bagru prints, saris, dress materials, camel skin chairs and brightly coloured swings. There is a also a sizeable collection of bright mojris, miniature paintings depicting the energetic Ras Leela, semi-precious jewellery with an antique finish, embroidered purses to choose from. The colourful lac bangles are available in a myriad designs but one size!

Tibetan Handicrafts

Advertising
Branding
Below The Line
Direct Marketing
Strategy Formulation
Event Management
Public Relations
Creatives
Media Buying  India and Overseas

DM Creatives | Database Generation & Fulfillment | Road Shows | Presentations | Events

699  1st Floor  7th Main  HAL-2nd Stage  Indiranagar  Bangalore 560 038  India
Tel: +91 80 51152102 - 104  Fax: +91 80 51152106  Email: starkblr@starkgroup.net

## Sudarshan Handicrafts

*United Mansions, 110 MG Road,*
*Bangalore 560001*
*Tel 2558 0738/2692*
*Open 9am to 8:30pm*
*Cards All*

Expect to find traditional gifting items here – sandalwood and rosewood fashioned into elephants, boats, huts and coffee tables. Also available at a reasonable price are terracotta wall hangings from Rajasthan, gemstone paintings, engraved wood panels and Tanjore paintings with comfortable starting prices.

## Tanjore Paintings

*Rini Kumar, Bungalow 2, House of Wills,*
*Richmond Road, Bangalore 560025*
*Tel 2557 8798*
*Open Only by appointment*
*Cards Not Accepted*

Tanjore paintings embellished with pure gold leaf foil and painted with the colours of your choice may be ordered here. Tanjore painting is an ancient art form that originated in Tamil Nadu. Mysore paintings are also available here.

## Tibetan Handicrafts

*10 St. Patrick's Shopping Arcade,*
*Residency Road, Bangalore 560025*
*Tel 2558 8573*
*Open 10:30am to 2pm and 3pm to*
*7:30pm. Closed on Sunday.*
*Cards Not Accepted*

Tibetan culture comes alive with an extensive collection of handicrafts from this beleagured country in exile. Thangka paintings, carpets, lampshades, prayer wheels, prayer beads, incense and idols of Buddha are stocked. Silver set with semi-precious stone jewellery, Tibetan music and 'Free Tibet' t-shirts make popular buys. For the more adventurous the traditional Tibetan costume 'chupa' makes for stylish wear. Books on Tibet, herbal medicine and a variety of Tibetan noodles may be bought here.
For more Tibetan goods, try the Tibetan Shopping Centre, on Rest House Road, just off Brigade Road. Here you can pick up anything from funky footwear and

bags to t-shirts, pants, scarves and lingerie. There's also a Tibetan clinic and a fast food joint that serves authentic Tibetan food like momos and Chowmein.

## Utkalika

*101 Centre Point, Residency Road,*
*Bangalore 560025*
*Tel 2558 2744*
*Open 10:30am to 7pm.*
*Closed on Sunday.*
*Cards All*

Handicrafts from the state of Orissa using the ancient craft of tarakasi or silver filigree where delicate silver strands are fashioned into ornaments, broaches, cuff links, chariots, horses, boats and even cups and spoons, are the hallmark of this store. Orissa's famed appliqué work that combines bright colours, intricate patterns and motifs of elephants, parrots and flowers, in red, blue and ochre are sewn on bed sheets, lampshades, embroidered quilts and tablecloths. The distinct tribal art of the region is seen in the small cane boxes and terracotta figures decorated with lacquer and made from insect refuse. Other unique offerings are colourful embroidered clothes from Pipli and combs, pen stands and decorative items made from horns of cows. Orissa's famous ikkat handlooms, woven into saris, bedspreads and dress materials, are also on display here. Wooden carvings and toys painted brightly from vegetable dyes and mineral colour and decorative stone carvings are usually on sale.

## Vinayaka Marble Emporium

*14/1, I Floor, Ganesha Tower,*
*Bannerghatta Main Road,*
*Bangalore 560030*
*Tel 2229 6621*
*Open 10am to 8:30pm and*
*10am to 2pm on Sunday.*
*Cards MasterCard & Visa*

This is an out and out marble emporium with busts, idols, pooja mantaps, railing and pillars carved from Rajasthani marble, Italian marble and onyx filling the shop. Traditional craftsmanship yet innovative is reflected in the intricate meenakari inlaid marble tabletops and Grecian style sculptures. Apart from marble handicrafts, stone murals and gemstone paintings, silver jewellery is also available.

## Deepam Silk International

*67 MG Road, Bangalore 560001*
*Tel 2558 6191*
*Open 10am to 9:30pm*
*Cards All*
*Web www.deepam.com*

With three decades of style and grace, Deepam has set standards in ethnic and contemporary attire, crafting dreams that inspire the wearer. Using an eclectic mix contemporary and traditional designs, it compels you to try the unchartered as well as the tried and tested.
With its very own weaving centres all over India, teams of master craftsmen artfully blend tradition and modernity into every design they weave and make sure that every woman finds just the right piece. Apart from traditional and contemporary saris, Deepam stocks a fabulous range of silk fabrics like tussars, dupions, brocades, jamevars, jamdanis and mungas.
Deepam's in-house design studio creates a range of ethnic designer wear for both men and women. Ghagra cholis, salwar kameez, chania cholis, scarves, accessories and pashmina shawls are among the popular choices for women.
The men's range includes silk shirts, sherwanis, jodhpuris, kurta pyjamas, ties, cravats, stoles and other accessories. Deepam is located at the heart of Bangalore's commercial hub, MG Road, with space of 20,000sqft spread across four floors with international shopping ambience.
In the future, Deepam will be a name to reckon with around the world, with designer ensembles and Deepam world stores, catering to those who value elegance and worship style.
Three decades of artfully blending tradition and modernity, Deepam is the presence that breathes life into endless dreams.

## Kanya

*32 Rangamandiram Cottage, 6th Main*
*Road, Malleswaram, Bangalore 560003*
*Tel 2334 5231/5710*
*Open 10am to 7:30pm*
*Cards All except American Express*
*and Diners Club*

Kanya, a store selling traditional saris, lies deep in the heart of Malleswaram, bastion of old Bangalore. Housed in an old south Indian bungalow with a massive garden, a visit here would warm the heart of any serious sari lover. Settle down comfortably on the mattress-lined floor of the shop and watch a veritable feast of classic heritage design in Kanjeevaram and other silks laid out in front of you. Co-workers of the Craft Council, Kanya aims to revive and repeat ancient designs in an effort to preserve the craft and skill of weavers. Expect to see some rare colour combinations, high quality silk and exclusive designs made by their own weavers. They also undertake special orders for exclusive designs and are willing to replicate old family heirlooms. However, they do not undertake contemporary or computer generated designs or styles.
The legendary Kanjeevaram saris are their forte but they also keep a very limited supply of upadas, paithinis, gadhwals, mangalgiris and Chettinad saris. They also stock Molakalmuru and Aarni saris, typical of Karnataka, a few printed silks, a pick of poly cottons in the daily wear segment, traditional ikkat saris from Orissa, Andhra and Gujarat as well as kantha and kasuti work on silks.

## Karishma Silks

*45 MG Road, Bangalore 560001*
*Tel 2558 1606, 2532 5314*
*Open 10am to 9pm*
*Cards All*

You get to sample the entire gamut of silk saris from the lesser known but gorgeous Tanchoi to the rich Jamevar and Benaras silks. Silk scarves, stoles and unstitched fabric are also available along with inexpensive cotton saris and cotton-silk salwar kameezes.

## Karnataka Silk Industries Corporation

*Jubilee Showroom, 44/45 Leo Complex,*
*Residency Road Cross, Bangalore 560025*
*Tel 2558 2118*
*Branches Chipket, 2226 0695;*
*KG Road, 2226 2077*
*Open 10am to 8:30pm. Closed on Sunday.*
*Cards All*

Kuberan Silks

Saris galore at Deepam Silk International

KSIC is the best place to buy the legendary Mysore silk sari. A state government undertaking, KSIC has a reputation for stocking the purest in silks as well as zari. Inheritors of the Mysore Maharaja's silk weaving factory, authentic Mysore crepe silk saris, printed silks, semi-crepe silks and georgette silk saris can be bought here. At 75g of crepe per metre, the saris have a rich drape and are also available in a splash of over 100 colours and designs. Crepe fabric, cravats, stoles, shirts, neckties and handkerchiefs in crepe and semi crepes are available.

### Kuberan Silks
*226 Chikpet, Bangalore 560053*
*Tel 2220 6514*
*Open 9:30am to 10:30pm*
*Cards All*

The seemingly inexhaustible range of saris stretch from everyday wear to wedding wear, sourced from Orissa, Surat, Kolkata, Kancheepuram and Delhi. Spread over four sections, Kuberan Silks stocks designer saris, Kuberan Silks International deals in Kanchee Co-operative Society's woven saris, Kuberan Fashions sells salwar suits and fabric and Kanchee-Co Kuberan Silks with a collection of pure silk designer saris.

A relative newcomer in the business, Kuberan makes up with over 40,000 saris on display including woven saris, south Indian silk saris, designer saris, saris with zardosi and threadwork and made-to-order saris. Today's popular buys are Kanjeevaram silks with a motif of Lord Krishna etched on the pallav and designer silk saris studded with Swarovski crystals. The 'pencil work sari' with gold threads extending from one end of the sari to the other in a zigzag pattern is another speciality. Apart from the happy mix of the old and new, an added attraction of the shop is the section where you can buy silk and cotton fabric for sari blouses.

### Mysore Saree Udyog
*294, I Floor, K Kamaraj Road, Bangalore 560042*
*Tel 2558 3255*
*Branch Jumma Masjid Road, 2221 0531*
*Open 10:30am to 8:30pm*
*Cards All*

Genuine Mysore crepe and Kanjeevaram silk saris, printed and embroidered Jamevar saris and fabric are available here. For those who are not averse to a bit of rayon blended into their silk saris, look here.

### Nalli Silk Arcade
*21/24 MG Road, Bangalore 560001*
*Tel 2558 3178/3179*
*Open 9:30am to 8pm*
*Cards All*

The famous Chennai chain, Nalli's has a wonderful range of saris – Kanchi's, Arni, Benares, Bangalore silks, Mysore silks and the list goes on. The price ranges from Rs 500 to Rs 25,000 for silks and Rs 100 to Rs 3,000 for cottons. Shoppers for weddings and special occasions will find plenty to choose from. A sizeable collection of cotton saris, dress materials and ready-to-wear salwar kameezes is also available.

### Prasiddhi Silks and Fabrics
*23/2 KH Road, Bangalore 560027*
*Tel 2223 6613*
*Branch MG Road, 2558 0433*
*Open 10am to 8:30pm*
*Cards All*

Prasiddhi made quite a splash when it opened with its stock of rare and fabulous cottons and silks. They also stock a blend of cotton and silk in traditional colours. Good buys include Gadhwal silk saris and dress materials and of course, traditional Kanjeevarams. Prasiddhi also stocks cotton-silk fabric along with dupattas that double up as formal as well as semi-formal wear.

# Mysore Crepe Silk

Deftly woven into Karnataka's heritage is the 'Queen of Textiles' – lustrous silk. With the largest number of handlooms and powerlooms in the country, Karnataka is famous for its taffetas, georgettes, crepes and printed silks. Of these, the expensive and heavy Mysore crepe silk reigns. Prized as one of the most genuine and radiant fabrics in the world, it gets its name from the Government Silk Weaving Factory at Mysore where it is produced. Mysore crepe is the legacy of the Maharaja of Mysore who set up the first silk weaving factory in 1932. It was under his patronage that crepe silk or crepe-de-chine was first produced in India.

'Crepe' is a name given to a special weave of 'highly twisted' silk. Two threads of silk yarn are doubled instead of a single yarn used to weave most other silks and the result is a very strong crepe. Delicate as well as durable, this silk has 65 to 70 grams of crepe per metre and is also crease-resistant.

Mysore crepe saris are much sought after and there is also a wide range of apparel from shirts and scarves to stoles and cravats to choose from. The saris are available in a range of colours and are priced from Rs 2,000 to Rs 25,000. Mysore crepe is available at KSIC showrooms across Bangalore.

Karnataka is also a pioneer in other varieties of silk saris such as the rustic Ilkal sari, the Molkalmuru sari that rivals the Kanjeevaram sari in its grandeur, the rayon-blended Bangalore silk sari and the semi-formal printed silk sari with innovative designs and motifs.

### Priya Simran's Silks

*G1 Prestige Meridian, 29 MG Road,*
*Bangalore 560001*
*Tel 2532 5314/5316*
**Open** *10am to 9pm*
**Cards** *All*

Delicate tissues, rich brocades and embroidered saris, all one-of-a-kind are available here. Salwar kameezes, shirts, wedding wear, party wear, men's shirts and formal women's wear are on sale.

### Shakthi Silks

*B Block, Unity Building, JC Road,*
*Bangalore 560002*
*Tel 2223 9983*
**Open** *9:30am to 9pm*
**Cards** *All*

Shakthi Silks, an outlet of Mega Silk Udyog has been in the business of selling quality silk saris for three decades. Located on bustling JC Road, the Shakthi Silks showroom is spacious, tastefully done up and fully air conditioned. A plethora of exquisite silks are part of their collection, including pure Mysore crepe silk saris and other traditional ones like Dakshinotri, Kanchivaram, Tanchoi, Valkalam and Kalam Kari. Chiffons, printed and embroidered silk saris and exclusive designer saris are on offer. Limited editions of designer Kora silk, ornate wedding saris and ghagra cholis are also available.

### Shantala Silks

*11 Public Utility Building, MG Road,*
*Bangalore 560001*
*Tel 2558 8932*
**Branch** *KG Road, 2287 2783*
**Open** *10am to 8:30pm*
**Cards** *All*

The silk salesman who knows pure zari from fake, is a cherished breed. Shantala has a few grey haired ones whose knowledge and discreet selling skills immediately put you at ease. The store showcases a wide range of silks – Kanjeevarams, Mysore silks, Bangalore silks, printed silks, Benarasi, Jamevar, Patola and Tanchoi. A few innovative fusion saris created by their own mill at Peenya are tussar silks with appliqué work, Bagalpur silks with embroidery, crepes with zardosi and Bangalore silks with kasuti embroidery. The 30-year old store has a good reputation and is a favourite stop for wedding trousseaus. A limited collection of silk dress materials, shirts, ties, stoles, ghagras and kurta pyjama sets is also available.

### Vijayalakshmi Silks & Sarees

*20J/61 Blumoon Complex, MG Road,*
*Bangalore 560001*
*Tel 2558 7937*
**Open** *10am to 8pm*
**Cards** *All*

Join a stream of celebrities, actresses and even Her Majesty Queen Elizabeth II who've shopped here! Traditional south Indian silks like the Kanjeevaram with an old temple border and the Kora silk with a pure zari border are prize buys. This is one of the oldest of the lot of silk shops Bangalore is justly proud of. Exclusive parking right outside on busy MG Road is a big help.

### Vimor

*49, 3rd Cross, Victoria Layout,*
*Bangalore 560047*
*Tel 2555 1514*
**Open** *10am to 1:30pm and 3pm to 7pm*
**Cards** *All except American Express*

Most women still treasure the memory of diving into mothers 'almirah' and unearthing the rich weaves and vibrant colours of her saris. Shopping at Vimor is a lot like that. Take a trip down memory lane as you settle on a large bed (yes, it's true!), and watch Chimmy Nanjappa and her daughter Pavithra pull out yard after yard of exquisitely woven saris in midnight blue, bright vermilion and royal aubergine from the old cupboards on the side. Feast your eyes on turmeric mustards, hot magentas and dusky greens shot with gold or thread work. This is clearly not your average sari shop or little home boutique. Each sari has a story, a heritage and an identity, a secret language that you are treated to once you step in! For almost three decades now, Vimor has been giving the customer a heritage piece at an affordable price. The mother-daughter duo de-mystify intricate antique designs for today's weavers and the result are some exquisite saris. They revived the original Puja sari by replacing the ikkat (tie and dye) with a change in the weaving pattern. Vimor has also taught weavers from Kancheepuram and Andhra Pradesh to adapt the traditional Chettinad temple sari. They now use a single shuttle instead of three, making it cost effective for both the weaver and the buyer. The handloom silk and cotton saris seen here are the last word in tradition and you can't go wrong. Timeless motifs like the Ganda Berunda or double headed eagle, the royal insignia of the court of Mysore, or a temple procession running through the pallav, are captured in their products. Vimor does not advertise. Sales are through word of mouth references. Their clientele include famous personalities like Sonia Gandhi and Shabana Azmi.

When I do find time for myself, I give my skin the pampering it deserves. With **New Himalaya Nourishing Skin Cream**. A light and non-greasy cream, it revives and rejuvenates my skin, protecting me from pollution and dry weather. Rich in natural moisturisers and nourishers like **Aloe vera, Winter Cherry** and **Indian Kino Tree** extracts, it is so gentle on my skin - just perfect for me. **New Himalaya Nourishing Skin Cream.** My luxury.

I am a wife and a mother. I deserve my little luxuries.

Nourishing Skin Cream
Refreshing and re-hydrating. All day nourishment

50ml - **Rs. 55.** 150ml - **Rs. 110.**

**Himalaya**™
HERBALS

# CLOTHING

## AND

*3 Commercial Street, Bangalore 560001*
*Tel 2555 9975, 2509 8707*
**Open** *10:30am to 8:30pm*
**Cards** *All except American Express*

The creation of designer Anita Dongri, you get a range of formals, semi-formals and casual wear in a range of cool crepes, linens and georgettes. The Tussar and cotton blended kurtas make good buys.

## Arrow

*Residency Road, Bangalore 560001*
*Tel 25584899*
**Branches** *The Forum, Hosur Road, 22067607; Kamraj Road, Commercial Street, 25596261*
**Open** *10am to 9pm*
**Cards** *All*

A premium shirt brand, Arrow entered the Indian market 10 years ago. Since then it has been voted the country's most admired shirt brand for two years in succession at the Images Fashion Awards. Offering a range of shirts, trousers, suits, accessories and sweaters, the Arrow collection is designed by the Milan-based designer Renato Grande. The range includes America's Premium which is a sophisticated and luxurious line of shirts, known for its super premium cotton and lustrous fabrics, America's Classics work wear, Urban from Arrow of international fashion and Arrow Sport casual wear. The brand also has a comprehensive range of cotton chinos, wool and poly trousers and a super premium line of suits, jackets and sweaters. Accessories including – socks, ties, cufflinks and wallets are also available. You can avail exclusive services like customised tailoring and a loyalty programme that offers special privileges. Travellers can fix an appointment and the store will take care of everything from alterations to packing.

## Color Plus

*78 Residency Road, Residency Chambers, Bangalore 560025*
*Tel 2555 9942*
**Open** *10am to 8:30pm*
**Cards** *All*

What Shyam Ahuja is to home furnishings, Color Plus is to men's clothing – exclusive, discreet, stylish and very expensive! Shirts, trousers, knits, checks, twills, shorts and vests in fine cotton and classy designs are part of the range. Their entire line is touted as wrinkle free and stain free.
The collection of cotton shirts – chequered and plain – in mint greens, cool lemon, vibrant oranges, indigos and purples, hogs the whole palette.
The range of pants includes pure linen, corduroys, chinos and denims.
Color Plus also stocks a pure formal line called Purple Club and another called Survival Gear which consists of shorts, cargos and t-shirts. The store has a section devoted to men's accessories from wallets and socks to jackets and briefcases.

## Bellaa Bella

*Bangalore Central, Residency Road, Bangalore 560025*
*Tel 5693 0000*
**Open** *10:30am to 7:30pm.*
*Closed on Monday.*
**Cards** *All except American Express*

Attention teenyboppers! Fun, funk and in your face fashion like denim jeans embroidered, embossed, sequined and mirrored, knits, blouses and shirts in daring cuts and styles, spaghetti straps, peasant blouses in lace and lycra, are all stocked here. Bags, jewellery and hair accessories are also available.

## Cotton World

*Ground Floor, 2/7 Barton Centre, MG Road, Bangalore 560001*
*Tel 2558 9443*
**Open** *10am to 8pm and 12noon to 6pm on Sunday*
**Cards** *All*

High quality, cool and trendy (Western-style) cotton clothing doesn't get any better than the products at this Mumbai-based clothing chain. The fashions are timeless, the stitching classy and the garments fabulously comfortable. Made with high quality cotton, the shorts, tops, shirts, dresses, pants and skirts are expensive but worth it. The linen selection is especially good.

## Formale – Ethnic Wear for Men

*3 Century Plaza, 294 Kamraj Road, Bangalore 560042*

*Tel 5113 0415, 2559 6090*
**Branch** *Malleswaram, 2334 6964*
**Open** *11am to 8:30pm.*
*Closed on Sunday.*
**Cards** *All*

The bridegroom gets plenty of attention here with hand embroidered kurtas, sherwanis and other essential wedding attire like churidars, pagdies, Jamevar jackets and even a self explanatory Prince Suit! Simple pathani suits, kurta sets and dhoti-kurtas may also be picked up.

## Lee

*21 Commercial Street, Bangalore 560001*
*Tel 2555 0548*
**Branches** *Safina Plaza, 2532 7333; Brigade Road, 2558 9955; The Forum, 2206 7608*
**Open** *10am to 9pm*
**Cards** *All*

The international casual wear brand Lee has a swanky outlet on Brigade Road selling trendy tees, denims, sun faded jeans, and pants. There are also new age denims and trousers such as 'anti-fits' designed for comfort and lightweight denims in 'zero gravity'. All time favourites include a collection of checked shirts. The shop has a separate ladies and kids section with a wide range of jeans, tops, casual wear, and accessories such as belts, socks, caps and shoes.

## Levi Strauss

*Mota Royal Arcade, Brigade Road, Bangalore 560001*
*Tel 5112 1649*
**Branches** *Levi's Exclusive Store, Jayanagar, 5121 0582; Levi's, The Forum, Koramangala, 2206 7628*
**Open** *10am to 9pm*
**Cards** *All except American Express and Diners Club*

The original denim brand Levi's is firmly entrenched in the fashion clothing scene in Bangalore. All the major shopping destinations – Brigade Road, Commercial Street etc, and all the malls carry these brands. The range includes classic 501 jeans, Red Tab jeans, the Red Loop range, Minus One jeans, non-denims, woven shirts, knitted tops, jackets and accessories.
The current rage are Levi's Low Rise Jeans that come in seven different fits for men and women. A recent offering is Levi's Red Loop – a range of international jeans with a red loop and linen patch instead of the characteristic Levi's leather patch. Embellished with pure copper rivets, aged Levi's buttons and a double-needle out seam, these jeans are available in several finishes. The iconic Levi's 501 was launched in April 2004.
Levi's Sykes is a line of funky street wear, very hot with teenagers. The 2-in-1 reversible jeans, 32-in-1 doublets, reversible hip huggers and tees are all part of an innovative 'Reversibles' collection. Tops and bottoms in this range can be worn in multiple ways to create different looks.

## M. Fazal & Sons

*153 Commercial Street, Bangalore 560001*
*Tel 2555 0224, 2558 8972*
**Open** *10:30am to 9pm*
**Cards** *All*

Anything a woman might need, from a simple safety pin to a wedding sari are all sold under one roof here: Different brands of clothes, lingerie, accessories and a wide range of churidars, salwar kameezes, silks, dress materials and ghagra cholis are available to choose from. A great help is the rather thorough accessories section that stocks everything from pins to scarves.

## Planet Fashion

*Devidass Building, 143 Commercial Street, Bangalore 560001*
*Tel 2558 6266*
**Branches** *Residency Road, 2558 0782; Indiranagar, 2525 3050; The Forum, 2206 7727*
**Open** *10:30am to 9pm*
**Cards** *All*

Gentlemen rejoice! Here is a store that is exclusively for the new metro male who loves to shop, demands high

The Arrow outlet on Residency Road

The Spirit of Arrow

# ARROW

>>>>>———→

EST. 1851

# Bangalore Central

Located just off MG Road, Bangalore Central is the latest addition to the city's rising mall culture. Built where the Victoria Hotel used to stand, it's spread over an area of 1,20,000sqft and is said to be the country's first 'seamless' mall, with the theme, 'Shop, Eat and Celebrate'. A host of Indian and international brands are laid out across six floors, in an organised fashion, without boundaries. A venture of Pantaloon India, Bangalore Central provides sprawling spaces and an inviting ambience along with helpful staff and multiple billing counters. Bangalore Central gives shoppers all that a mall offers in one large store, with separate sections for women, men, children, food and beverages, home appliances and furnishings.

More than 300 brands are on offer. Dedicated counters for music and books, a supermarket, speciality restaurant, pub and discotheque are some of the attractions. The mall also offers miscellaneous conveniences from travel and finance services to cinema ticket booking and insurance. There's a play area for children and a liquor store here in addition to clothing, consumer appliances, jewellery, accessories and electronic goods.

Each floor has various brands within each category starting with women's on the ground floor all the way up to the food court on the fifth. Shopping at the mall is spread over five levels. Level 1 houses the women's section featuring over 21 brands of clothing, footwear, perfumes and lingerie. The men's section on level 2 is equally extensive with over 20 brands of clothing, footwear and accessories. Level 3 is the 'Youth Section' – on sale here are denim wear, sports wear, books and stationery. Level 4 is for children while level 5 is the well stocked Food Bazaar.

Bangalore Central is interspersed with cafés and restaurants like Café Coffee Day, Bombay Blues and The Noodle Bar for the tired and hungry shopper.

Also available within the mall are services like a wedding registry, bill payment and such 'man Friday' services and a currency exchange counter. An in house jockey and radio station Radio Central, provides entertainment and various promotions and events are done through it. The Central Square is the area used for art exhibitions, music concerts and product launches.

*47-48, Residency Road, Near Mayo Hall, Bangalore 560025* **Tel** *5693 0100*

---

fashion and is willing to pay for it! Planet Fashion is a mega mens wear store, something of a one-stop-shop for men's clothing and accessories with all the big brands dancing attendance. Cufflinks, blazers, ties, belts, et al.

## Prestige – House for Men
*165 Commercial Street,*
*Bangalore 560001*
*Tel 2558 8599/8600*
*Open 10am to 8:30pm*
*Cards All*

All the big brands in male clothing ranging from office wear, Indian and western formals and casuals are sold here. A variety of brands like Zodiac, Louis Philippe, Allen Solly, Giovanni, Color Plus and Van Heusen along with retail suiting fabrics from Raymond and OCM are available.

## Rugs and Riches
*Devatha Plaza, 131 Residency Road,*
*Bangalore 560025*
*Tel 2221 4273/4481*
*Open 10am to 7:30pm.*
*Closed on Sunday.*
*Cards All*

Rugs and Riches is known for its designer saris, contemporary fabrics, scarves, shawls and semi-precious jewellery. Exclusive, yet affordable, the store has a loyal clientele that enjoys the quiet, uncluttered ambience. Trendy kurtas, tunics, shirts and enamel jewellery are also available.

## Shafali
*239 Upper Palace Orchards,*
*Sankey Road, Bangalore 560080*
*Tel 2361 2341*
*Open 10am to 7pm. Closed on Sunday*
*Cards All except Diners Club*

Shefali brings back the flavour of wooden block and silk screen printing with some fresh touches. Its signature line includes hand printed cotton household linen, salwar kameezes, saris and kaftans, created in khadi fabrics with kalamkari and ikkat prints. All the clothes have an ethnic flavour – mirror work kaftans with bright floral prints come in four thoughtful sizes from small to extra large. Salwar kameezes range from the regular prints to heavily embroidered suits with zardosi dupattas. An abundant collection of gifts and accessories is displayed – from quilted tote bags, etchings, posters by prominent artists and bedspreads to curtains, cushion covers and tablecloths made with a unique blend of woodblock and screen printing.

## Studio Akiva
*9 Gurappa Avenue, Primrose Road,*
*Bangalore 560025*
*Tel 2558 4193*
*Open 11am to 6:30pm*
*Cards All*

Akiva spins out a wholesome blend of the traditional and the modern with salwar kurtas, saris, lehengas, long skirts and trousers. You can also order clothes here.

High fashion at Balance, Cue, Evoluzione

## Tamanna
*Narayan Pillai Street, Commercial Street*
*Cross, Dispensary Road,*
*Bangalore 560001*
*Tel 2558 5483, 5698 2934*
*Open 10:30am to 9pm*
*Cards All*

An exclusive boutique with a wide range of ladies designer wear, ghagra cholis, bridal wear, short tops with pants, office wear suits and an exquisite range of designer saris with trend setting blouses. Each piece is exclusive and available at affordable rates. Orders are also accepted for customised bridal trousseau right from the mehendi ceremony to the honeymoon trip! Look out for antique embroideries.

## Terminal F
*178/5, 8th F Main,*
*III Block, Jayanagar,*
*Bangalore 560011*
*Tel 2653 9180*
*Open 10am to 9:30pm*
*Cards All*

The 'F' is for fashion and it's all directed at the metro male. A clear fashion hotspot in Jayanagar, it stocks a good collection of formals from trusted names like Arrow and Allen Solly and casuals from Color Plus, Lee, Levi's and Zodiac. There is an entire floor stacked with designer wear by Linarika and Shagufta and a range of embroidered sherwanis by

# simply everything at  BANGALORE CENTRAL

Apparels, accessories, books and music. Fashion, food, friends and fun. Everything your heart desires. And more. Over 120 brands spread over 1.25 lakh square feet. Come and shop, grab a bite or just hang out and chill!

**shop eat celebrate**

# The Forum

From Swarovski crystals to Swiss watches and Tommy Hilfiger to Khadder, The Forum, a sprawling mall on Hosur Road, offers a well-rounded shopping experience. The Forum is set along the lines of glitzy malls around the world with spanking interiors, a host of stores and a central location. A premier shopping destination, The Forum brings together the best brands, a range of restaurants and a variety of entertainment options.

United Colors of Benetton, Pepe, Jockey, Health & Glow, Mochi, Nike, William Penn, KFC, are just some of the popular brands that have set up shop here. Accessories, apparel, books, cosmetics, electronics, fitness gear, home furnishings, music, shoes and stationery are available across four levels. Clothing from popular brands like Wrangler and Weekender are available along with the latest haute couture – Mustard, Isis and The Chai Stop are the mall's hi-fashion boutiques. Jewellery from Carbon, departmental stores FabMall and Nik Nish, exclusive Italian shoes from Ffarna, handmade cosmetics from Lush and high-end audio equipment from Sonodyne are other highlights. Spread across 40,000sqft, Landmark stocks everything from books and stationery to perfumes and home furnishings.

Multiplex PVR is the major draw boasting 11 screens, stadium seating and wall-to-wall screens. Transit – The Food Lounge offers a sampling of cuisines from around the world, from Mughlai and Italian to Mexican and Vietnamese. Panda House,

Movenpick, Subway, Beijing Bites and Salem's Kitchen have their outlets here. Added attractions at the food court are flat screen televisions and a play area for toddlers. Shoppers can also sample the offerings at Café Coffee Day, Cookie Man, McDonald's and Pizza Hut. The mall also houses the Amoeba entertainment centre, a beauty salon, photo studio and ATMs.

*21 The Forum, Hosur Road,*
*Koramangala, Bangalore 560029*
**Tel** *2206 7676*

---

designer Manish Jaipuria. Accessories like belts and sunglasses are also sold here.

### The Raymond Shop
*25 Commercial Street,*
*Bangalore 560001*
**Tel** *2558 1919*
**Open** *10am to 8:30pm.*
**Cards** *All*

This store offers both readymade as well as custom made clothes. The Raymond brand – Park Avenue's ready-to-wear line of shirts, trousers, jackets, safari suits and accessories can be picked up here.

Weekender at The Forum

### Wearhouse
*CMH Road, Indiranagar II Stage,*
*Bangalore 560038*
**Tel** *2527 4719*
**Branches** *Brigade Road, 2558 4265;*
*MG Road, 2558 9489;*
*Commercial Street, 2558 3882;*
*KG Road, 2226 9049;*
*Jayanagar, 2664 2966*
**Open** *10:30am to 8:30pm*
**Cards** *All*

A chain of cheaper casuals, it sells checked shirts, sporty clothes, tops, t-shirts, jeans, cargos, wrinkle-free chinos, denims and corduroys for adults and children.

### Weekender
*393 CMH Road, Indiranagar II Stage,*
*Bangalore 560038*
**Branches** *Rajajinagar, 2357 3033;*
*Jayanagar, 2634 6689; Commercial*
*Street, 2555 0632; Residency Road,*
*2559 5893; The Forum, 2206 7626*
**Tel** *2520 4148*
**Open** *10:30am to 9pm*
**Cards** *All*

Here is a Bangalore based line of trendy clothing that has managed to hold its own against the onslaught of international brands. A smart line of casuals for men, women and children with funky pants, shirts, tops and even some party wear is available. Kids (from the ages two to 12 years) get their own line and store called Weekender Kids. There are some funky accessories like belts, caps, socks and scarves.

### Wills Lifestyle
*Brigade Road, Bangalore 560001*
**Tel** *2558 2788, 2532 1940*
**Open** *11am to 9pm*
**Cards** *All*

Wills Lifestyle is ITC's fashion retail chain with 48 branches across the country. Created from a blend of lycra, cotton, spandex and nylon, the Wills clothing line is high on style, comfort and quality. Polos, tees, stretches, linen, cashmere sweaters, stretch shirts, sports wear, safari pants and cottons are available in the latest styles and colours of the season, tailored into smart work wear, casual wear and party wear. The range of formal clothes comes in unusual blends, two-tone colours and new fabric washes. Wills

Sport has a colourful line of `relaxed wear' available in a variety of fabrics from Irish linen to Nisshinbo cotton from Japan. Spread across two storeys, the store sports a chic ambience and convenient features – you can exchange garments bought at one store at any of its other branches.

## FASHION HOT SPOTS

### Anokhi
*B-123 Leela Galleria, The Leela Palace,*
*23 Airport Road, Bangalore 560008*
**Tel** *2521 7491*
**Branch:** *Raintree, 3062 3620*
**Open** *10:30am to 7:30pm. 11pm to 6pm on Sunday*
**Cards** *All except Diners Club*

East meets west in Anokhi and the result is some pretty fabulous clothing, at home anywhere in the world. Enter, and its distinct palette of colours is striking. Clusters of jade green, indigo, rust, yellow, lilac, pink and even black and white, fill the shelves. Anokhi means unique and this comes through in its western sensibility with regard to colour and styling in combination with typical Jaipuri prints and Rajasthani embroidery. Together they create the magic of the blue sunflower, Celtic rust, olive trellis, Swedish rose and the French Provencal in clothing and soft furnishings. Not surprisingly, Anokhi is an established exporter of fine fabric and only recently

an ounce of steel
where it counts

Available at select Levi's® outlets.

Levi Strauss & Co. Original for 150 years.

501®
the original
button fly jeans

Levi's®

cazle hendricks.
olympics aspirant. athens 2004.

JWT.32148.2004

Clothing at Anokhi is a combination of ethnic fabrics and western styling.

entered the domestic market.
Stylish daywear in an Indo-western style is characteristic of their line. Basics combine with a variety of mix and match clothing and a choice of accessories, all priced reasonably. The linen section has special prints, Gudri embroidery, Rajasthani leharian, butas and mirror work with contemporary styling to create throws, table ware, quilts, bed spreads, curtains and cushions.

## Balance, Cue, Evoluzione
*Embassy Classic, 11 Vittal Mallya Road, Bangalore 560001*
*Tel 5112 1088/1089*
*Open 10:30am to 7:30pm.*
*Closed on Sunday.*
*Cards MasterCard & Visa*

Vittal Mallya Road draws all the big names in hi-fashion from around the country. At this three-in-one store there is a classy range of furniture and home accessories by Chennai-based Evoluzione, designer Rohit Bal's prêt line – Balance, Rohit Gandhi and Rahul Khanna's mens' line called H2O and a women's line - Cue.
Designer bags, soap and incense, ceramic vases and Italian lights are displayed in the Evoluzione zone. Look out for the flamboyant clothes by Malini Ramani and the more muted Varun Bahl collection.

## Bandhej
*Salarpuria Palladium, HAL II Stage, 100Ft. Road, Indiranagar, Banglore 560038*
*Tel 2520 4363/4362*
*Open 10:30am to 8pm*
*Cards All*

Bandhej is a prêt line created specially for the Indian woman. It's a very contemporary interpretation of ethnic handlooms with embellishing for ready mades that are at once exciting and elegant. From the styling to the cut and the sizing of garments, they are specifically designed to flatter the Indian figure. Similarly, colours are carefully chosen to compliment the Indian skin tone. Teenagers to women in their sixties will find something to suit their taste. The Ala label concentrates on Indo-westerns, primarily in cotton knitwear. Spaghetti straps, halter

t-shirts, kurtis and wrap around skirts make up the line in this section. Traditional clothing like the salwar kurta and trouser sets are characterised by the textured and embroidered look. The sari section is also quite special. Traditional saris are made to order in special colours and a variety of weaves. Bandhej also does contemporary saris in staple silk, Tussar, jute and other natural fibres. There is a limited men's section that stocks short and long kurtas. The black and white ikkat line should make women's head's turn!

## Be:
*50-52 Commercial Street, Bangalore 560001*
*Tel 2558 8550/8560*
*Branch The Forum, 2206 7701*
*Open 10am to 8:30pm*
*Cards All*

Be: is an essential stop on the city's fashion fraternity with hi-voltage style and the most happening names in the designer circuit. It attempts to make prêt more affordable and accessible, bringing couture designers under one umbrella alongside its own label. Launched by textile giant Raymond, there are more such stores in other metros.
Western, Indo-western and ethnic wear by famous designers are showcased here. There is an eclectic mix of office and eveningwear for both men and women. The line of bags and jewellery and a selection of belts are inspired from traditional artistry.
Most of the designers showcasing their work are picked from the Lakme India Fashion Week, a hi-fashion annual merchandising event. Aki Narula, Anshu Arora Sen, Aparna Suneja, Ashish Soni, Manish Arora, Priyadarshini Rao, Puja Nayar, Raghavendra Rathore, Krishna Mehta, Rohit Bal and Vidhi Singhania are among those who bring out a range designed just for the store.

## Cinnamon
*11 Walton Road, Bangalore 560001*
*Tel 2222 9794*
*Open 10:30am to 8:15pm*
*Cards All except Diners Club*

Cinnamon is a store that celebrates the

shopping experience and even reviewers may be forgiven for gushing over this epitome of 21st century design! Retail therapy doesn't get better than this! There is a constant blurring between store and product and most shoppers would like to pack the shop and take it home! Fabulous designer clothes are hung like exhibits in the white spaces of Cinnamon and everything is beautifully laid out with great thought and care. Hand picked and tremendously stylish products of international artistes are on sale. There is plenty to browse and yet nothing is cluttered. Quiet, timeless and distinctive, it's not surprising that the display is as attractive as the products. Surprise is a key element. As you move through the store you could chance upon anything from rolled newspaper mats and papier mâché ducks to Turkish rugs and photographs. Sequined flowers and coconut candles mingle with enamel bowls and incense sticks. A small line of crockery, cutlery and glassware is also available. Chic shoes, elegant saris, jewellery and carefully picked coffee table books make up the rest of the merchandise.
Displays change every month and products are seldom repeated. Hi-fashion designers like Abraham and Thakore, Jason Cherian hosts a series of exhibitions where young artistes and top designers of the country display work exclusively commissioned by the store.

## Ffolio
*5 Vittal Mallya Road, Bangalore 560001*
*Tel 2221 8142/8143*
*Open 10:30am to 7:30pm.*
*11am to 6pm on Sunday.*
*Cards All*

Ffolio was a pioneer of upmarket fashion in south India in the 90s. It was the first store in the city to start retailing authentic Indian designerwear. Nestled in the quiet environs of Vittal Mallya Road, it has since been joined by illustrious neighbours like Ritu Kumar and Atmosphere. The store within the store concept is unique to Ffolio. Big names like Rajesh Pratap Singh, Suneet Varma, Satya Paul and JJ Valaya have their own outlets within the store of Ffolio. The current maverick, Sabyasachi Mukherjee, also retails his line here. Handpicked others like Rohit Gandhi, and Rahul Khanna, Priyadarshini Rao,

Payal Jain and Manish Arora bring up the rest. Ffolio also stocks French and Italian labels as part of its collection.
Both men and women's clothing, in Western and ethnic silhouettes is available here. The styling is eclectic and embellishment is the buzzword. The dazzling mix of Swarovski crystal on Valaya's jacquards, the precision of Rajesh Pratap Singh, the timeless quality of Kiran Uttam Ghosh and the sensual undertones of a Suneet Varma are all seen here. Turn full circle to retro fashion from new labels like Fish Fry and Cue – trendy and hip these clothes too have a high quality finish. Accessories like bags, shoes, scarves and stoles are an integral part of the merchandise at Ffolio.

## Grasshopper
*45 Kalena Agrahara, Bannerghatta Road, Bangalore 560076*
*Tel 2659 3999, 2658 0225*
*Open 11am to 5pm and 8pm to 11pm*
*Cards MasterCard & Visa*

A visit to Grasshopper has no parallel, and is a must for fashion addicts, elegant dressers and those looking for that one single garment that will raise their wardrobe to another level.
Set in a farm, with stone buildings and trees for a setting, this is a great concept store where you can spend a few hours in the company of high quality fashion. Run by designers and foodies Sonali Sattar and Himanshu Dimri, it's a fair drive from the city, but worth every mile.
Displays range from lamps in handmade paper to glass and stoneware products. Boxes in denim and leather, utilitarian goods fashioned from recycled rubber and others make a distinct fashion statement.
The clothes are neatly laid out with each designer given a seperate stand. Western clothes for men and women hang in diagonals around the store. The look is fabric based. Textures are both natural and created. While embellishment is kept to a minimum, the clothes have fine detailing. The emphasis however is on the cut and fit of the clothes and clean sharp lines to completely bizarre silhouettes form the bases of the styling. Apart from the in-house label, the designer duo also showcase select designers from all over the country. While different

Ravina Belani is known for her Indo-western line.

# Guess who's woken up on a Restolex mattress

Wake up truly refreshed and ready for a new day... everyday. Because, the unique advantages of **R.E.S.T (Re-Energizing Sleep Technology)** - Full Body Contour Support, Breathable Design and Uniform Pressure Distribution - make a Restolex mattress the perfect place to start your day.

**R.E.S.T ADVANTAGES:** Full body contour support to help your spine retain its natural curve and prevent muscular tension. Breathable design that keeps your mattress cool in summer and warm in winter. Uniform pressure distribution to relieve pressure points and aid natural blood circulation.

## R. Restolex
### SLEEP SYSTEMS

**Sleep healthy. Start fresh.**

Mattresses • Pillows • Cushions

An ISO 9001:2000 company • Export Award Winner • Exported to the US, Europe, Australia and parts of Asia • Tel: 080-23445580/81/82

STARK.Blr./RX./1504

Colourful drapes at Blind Love

enough from each other, they work within the same concept for the Grasshopper line.

Sonali and Himanshu's line of clothes have a lot of layering and fabric techniques like heat crushing and pleating. Anshu Arora Sen works in light silks, with an interesting play in colour. She is known for her quirky detailing like embellishing the ends of a drawstring. Aparna Jaghadhari has voluminous skirts with many panels in fabrics that drape well. Sujit Mukherjee does crushing and pleating using the machine and creates an angular look. Joe Ikareth has funky retro prints on his clothes while Savio Jon has designed soft mull shirts with bees and ants! Sabyasachi uses Indian fabric creating Western silhouettes like brocade pants for women and patchwork shirts for men. Round off your visit with an excellent gourmet meal.

### Kairos

*19 Lavelle Road, Bangalore 560001*
*Tel 2227 2662, 5112 0016*
*Open 10am to 8pm. Closed on Sunday.*
*Cards All*

Kairos, owned by designer Namrata G, has a good collection of women's wear with a special focus on bridal ensembles, fusion, casual and semi-formal wear. Occasional shows are held, like a recent one on peasant tops for women. There's a separate line for men called 'Man by Nam' with all the usual suspects – wedding attire, semi-formal and formal wear, including executive ranges. Made to order and off the shelf are both available.

### Ravina Belani

*77 Ulsoor Road, Bangalore 560032*
*Tel 2559 8032*
*Open 11:30am to 6:30pm.*
*Closed on Sunday.*
*Cards Not Accepted*

The cool kurti gets even cooler with Ravina, queen of the kurti! The right mix of fabric, a touch of embroidery and the ordinary kurti or the short kurta gets a touch of pizzazz under her direction. Ravina uses a wide variety of fabrics to create elegant formals and stylish

casual wear. Chiffon, silk, crepe, cotton, denim and polyester kurtis are displayed on sweeping racks around the store. Bold prints in flowers and geometrics are picked out with embroidery and sequins. Bandhinis and leharis blaze a trail with vibrant colours while subdued tussars come alive with kantha work. Kurtis in ikkat, kanchi cotton and crushed polyesters have a more streamlined look. Parsi embroidery and zardozi, gotha work and chikan, blend with beads, spangles and mirrors.

Collars and sleeves are available in an assortment of styles and comfortable sizes. There is even a line for little girls.

### Ritu Kumar

*Embassy Chambers, 5*
*Vittal Mallya Road,*
*Bangalore 560001*
*Tel 5112 0278/0279*
*Open 10am to 7pm*
*Cards All except American Express*

Ritu Kumar is the czarina of traditional Indian design. The Ritu label is symbolic of an understanding of ancient design as well as the use of innovative craft techniques. Ritu uses them successfully to showcase India to the world. She is always the choice of Indian beauty queens participating in international pageants! Style icons like the late Princess Diana and Jemima Khan also patronise her clothes. Classy, elegant and timeless just about describes her ware.

Ritu is best known for her bridal collection. Rich silks and brocades are embellished with zardozi, kashida and dhapka. Gossamer nets, georgettes and printed crepes are worked with gold and silver to create the 'Ganga-Jamuna' effect. Saris, lehangas as well as salwar kurtas in colours ranging from saffron and terracotta to pomegranate and dusty rose may be found here.

There is a line especially tailored for working women with cotton and cotton mixes. Her signature line of printed leather and embroidered evening bags are extremely popular as well.

Ritu has recently turned her attention to designing svelte eveningwear and contemporary daywear for the younger generation. The prints are in yarn dyed ikkat and patterns created from India's tribal cultures. Geometrics in patchwork and silver dotted mukash combine with embroidery on textured and printed fabric to create original looking silhouettes. The outcome is blended into jackets, blouses, skirts and jeans.

## MEGA STORES

### Family Mart

*22, VI Phase, JP Nagar, Kanakapura Road, Bangalore 560078*
*Tel 5699 0190*
*Open 9:30am to 9:30pm*
*Cards All*

This mega mall in suburban JP Nagar has loads of shoppers streaming in, especially on weekends and holidays. It's the latest addition to the burgeoning number of all purpose stores in the city and its size – 1,00,000sqft – is a big attraction. The mart is comprehensive with a big supermarket, a departmental store, a beauty salon, photo studio, an entertainment centre and a food court. Centra the departmental store, is the heart of the mall with a large stock of clothes, bed linen, stationery, furniture and home accessories. There is something for more eclectic shoppers as well – books, fitness equipment and sports gear. The volume of merchandise laid out is quite overwhelming, but helpful signs map out separate sections, from 'infants' to 'preteens' and 'leather accessories' to 'office supplies'. Men can choose from a broad range of clothes, accessories and fabrics. The women's clothing line boasts an extensive ensemble of ethnic wear with ikkat, block print and embroidered wear along with brands like Pepe and Natalie. International brands also figure in the eyewear, watch, shoe and toy counters. A Music World outlet and a roomy Sweet Chariot Café are attached. The entertainment centre, Fun Zone, has a variety of arcade games to keep the kids busy. The vast and free parking area is a bonus.

### Globus

*Salarpuria Tower-II, Lusker-Hosur Road, Bangalore 560095*
*Tel 5667 0802*
*Branch Richmond Road, 5661 0123/ 0124*
*Open 9:30am to 9:30pm*
*Cards All*

Globus is the newest large store in town with a stock of trendy clothes and accessories for all ages but with a special eye on teenagers. Take your pick from casual clothes, formal wear, partywear, winterwear and denims. Rouched shirts, striped dupion shirts, floral shirts with lace, embroidered jeans, trousers with seam slits, club wear pants, knitted tops and crushed kurtas are favourites. There is a section for kids with a stylish collection of frocks, pants and t-shirts. With ample space, enough trial rooms and warm country music playing in the background, a visit to Globus can be a lot of fun.

### Kemp Fort

*97 Airport Road, Bangalore 560017*
*Tel 2522 6966/4977*
*Open 10am to 9:30pm*
*Cards All*

Kempfort is hard to miss for its sheer size and dramatic toy castle-like facade. Bumbling cartoon characters greet kids at the main door – a major thrill among the city's kids and their parents who come looking for clothing for the whole family, jewellery, toys and a range of accessories. There is an entire floor dedicated to games, gizmos, books, stationery and video games. The latest attraction is the Food Court on the terrace and the Shiva temple at the back.

### Lifestyle

*W-76, 1 Adarsh Opus, Campbell Road, Austin Town, Bangalore 560047*
*Tel 2556 0464/4555*
*Open 9:30am to 9:30pm*
*Cards All*

A trendy party shirt, a blown glass salad plate for tonight's dinner, shoes, music, books... Lifestyle lives up to its name! The ground floor has an extensive cosmetics and perfume section, reminiscent of Singapore malls.

Ritu Kumar, a hi-fashion boutique

Mega stores like the Family Mart are the new rage with shoppers in Bangalore.

The men's section has both formal and semi-formal clothes while the women's line has stylish skirts, colourful peasant tops, t-shirts, denims and separate sections for club wear, sportswear and ethnic Indian garments. The first floor has furniture, kitchen appliances, toys, shoes, music, books and clothes for children.

## Shoppers' Stop

*17/2 Raheja Point, Magrath Road, Ashok Nagar, Bangalore 560025*
**Tel** *2554 8224/8225/8226*
**Branch** *Bannerghatta Road 5121 5681*
**Open** *10am to 9pm*
**Cards** *All*

This is definitely one of the most shopper friendly destinations in the city. Sprawled over 30,000sqft, there is plenty of room, thousands of products and fair service. Clean and well lit, it has a spacious car park, central air conditioning, impeccably maintained restrooms and trial rooms, a play area for children, wheel chairs for the handicapped, gift wrapping and alteration services and a buyers' club. Clothes, cosmetics, jewellery, shoes, watches, toys and home furnishings are spread across two floors. There is a large and obvious presence of international brands as well as Shoppers' Stop in house label of affordable and chic ethnic and western clothes and jewellery. Theme based events are a regular feature at Shoppers' Stop.

## The Bombay Store

*99 EGK Prestige, MG Road, Bangalore 560001*
**Tel** *2532 0014*
**Open** *10:30am to 8:30pm*
**Cards** *All*

The Bombay Store is set in a swank new building on MG Road. High fashion apparel, trendy bags, jewellery and a wide range of gifts are tastefully displayed at this sprawling store spread over three floors. The collection of ethnic products is very popular with visitors from abroad as well as those looking for a little something more than what the state emporia have to offer. A counter Bagels and Bakes at the ground floor, close by the entrance offers mouth-watering cookies, home made chocolates and even herbal teas. Valet parking makes it especially attractive. There is a speciality seafood restaurant on the fourth floor and a trendy café on the sidewalk to take the edge off your appetite while shopping.

## Westside

*77 Commercial Street, Bangalore 560027*
**Tel** *2555 0861*
**Branch** *The Forum, 5667 0121*
**Open** *10:30am to 8:30pm*
**Cards** *All*

Fashionable clothes and accessories for men, women and children, well coordinated linen and home accessories are spread across three floors in what is undoubtedly an oasis of calm and comfort in busy Commercial Street. Women get a mix and match section of kurtas, pants and dupattas, men may choose from printed t-shirts with polo and V-necks, flat and pleated trousers and accessories. The selection of children's clothing is of good quality and durable cottonwear.
Westside's home store has many takers. Porcelain and melamine dinner sets, mugs, tablecloths, bedspreads, pillow packs, doormats and others are in good taste. Watch out for their annual sales where hefty bargains are for the taking.

## ACCESSORIES

### Green Hills

*159 Commercial Street, Bangalore 560001*
**Tel** *2558 7097*
**Branch** *Koramangala, 2206 7674*
**Open** *10am to 9pm*
**Cards** *All*

Bags come in different sizes and for different occasions, from the tiny lipstick bag to the bulky travelling suitcase. Top brands like VIP, Samsonite and Delsi show their range here. The shop also stocks a range of leather products that extend to handbags, briefcases and accessories like jackets and wallets.

### INC.5

*154 Commercial Street, Bangalore 560042*
**Tel** *2558 6832*
**Open** *10am to 10pm*
**Cards** *All*

Welcome to Shoe Town! Three floors of this single accessory would make anyone with a shoe fetish go weak in the knees. The misleadingly small entrance hides exclusive floors for men, women and children with a display of everyday wear, formalwear and party wear in hip colours and styles. Handbags and belts are also available.

## WATCHES

### Rodeo Drive

*101 Richmond Road, Bangalore 560025*
**Branch** *JC Road, 2227 6199*
**Tel** *2227 1977*
**Open** *10am to 8:30pm*
**Cards** *All*

You may be forgiven for thinking you've wandered into a duty free watch zone! Watches from Movado, Techno Marine, Tissot, Omega, Christian Dior and Raymond Weil, making up a collection of 23 premium watch brands for men and women, are on display at this shop. Most come with a heavy price tag but there are some reasonably priced ones as well.

### The World of Titan

*Golden Enclave, Tower A, Airport Road, Bangalore 560017*
**Tel** *5660 9028*
**Branches** *Safina Plaza, 2559 3169; Basavanagudi, 2667 5866; Brigade Road, 2559 4625; Commercial Street, 2558 7117; Jayanagar, 2634 6938; KG Road, 2226 6811; The Forum, 2206 7621; Malleswaram, 2331 8515*
**Open** *10am to 8:30pm*
**Cards** *All*

Titan's exclusive chain of showrooms, called The World of Titan, is spread across the city, offering a wide range of elegantly designed watches. The showrooms are large and comfortable. Vertical and flatbed display units make browsing extra convenient. All showrooms also have a service centre attached. You can also pick up gift vouchers, ask for special gift packaging and avail gift delivery service across the country. Titan Signet is a scheme through which repeat buyers can earn points and gifts. Titan also offers exclusive services like a five year warranty on all watches. Exchange is possible at any exclusive showroom across the country. All stores stock the various Titan sub-brands: Raga, Regalia, Steel, Nebula and Tommy Hilfiger watches and I-gear sunglasses as well.

## Bhima Jewellers

*45 Dickenson Road, Bangalore 560042*
*Tel 2506 5075, 2558 7711*
*Open 10:30am to 7:30pm*
*Cards All*

Wedding shoppers flock to Bhima for its traditionally crafted jewellery in gold, diamonds, stones and silver, fashioned into ornate and robust jewellery. An elaborate collection of finely crafted earrings, necklaces, bangles, pendants and rings spill over into two floors.

## C. Krishniah Chetty & Sons

*35 Commercial Street, Bangalore 560001*
*Tel 2558 8731/8734*
*Open 10:30am to 6:30pm.*
*Closed on Sunday.*
*Cards All*

C. Krishniah Chetty & Sons is a Bangalore institution, holding fort for the last 130 years. Historic milestones of the city are linked with them. They fashioned the silver key that was used by Sir Ismail Sait, to inaugurate Russel Market in 1927. They crafted the acclaimed 'Ganda Berunda Order' conferred on eminent citizens by the Maharaja of Mysore. This symbol is now the official seal of Karnataka. Located in the heart of Bangalore on Commercial Street, CKC (as they are often referred to), still remains the city's most exclusive jewellery establishment. You can browse through a beautiful selection in diamond, gold, platinum and the finest gemstones and pearls available. They are also well known for their wedding collection. Choose from a diamond choker necklace in a foliate pattern with a cohochon ruby in the centre to a priceless sautoir in platinum and diamond inspired by the Edwardian era. Contemporary diamond jhumkas to full ear wraps in marquise and several round brilliant cut diamonds are other fancy options.
The colour of blue sapphires, yellow sapphires, emeralds and rubies along with baguette and round diamonds are used to create many fascinating combinations of exquisite jewellery. The Estate Jewellery line from CKC is

famous. This refers to pieces that were once owned by wealthy Chettinad families of Tamil Nadu, zamindars from Andhra Pradesh and traditional Mysore families. This jewellery has a distinct cultural identity and is zealously guarded and handed down from generation to generation. The fine craftsmanship they flaunt is almost impossible to duplicate today. However, original and accurate reproductions may be found in the shop. CKC has a silver section with a segment for corporate gifts including elegant silver salvers and tea services, photo frames in varying sizes, coins and idols for festive occasions, silver bowls, tumblers, trophies and mementos. Personalised accessories are also offered.

## Ganjam Nagappa and Son Pvt. Ltd.

*148 Embassy Square, Infantry Road, Bangalore 560001*
*Tel 2226 1233/1826*
*Branch The Leela Galleria, 2520 3228*
*Open 10:30am to 6:30pm*
*Cards All*

'Worth its weight in Gold' is a saying that jewellery shops follow to the letter. Jewellery shopping is distinctly different from other shopping – it calls for large sums of money and invokes strong passions, especially amongst women. People look for quality, exclusive designs and personalised service. Ganjam Nagappa and Son, jewellers since 1889, seem to uphold the essence of all these. They were even bestowed the title – 'Jewellers to His Majesty, the Maharaja of Mysore'.
Seven generations later Ganjam still values its design and craftsmanship skills and no Ganjam piece ever has a twin! Craftsmen work over many days to cut, polish, sculpt and set precious diamonds to create exquisite handcrafted creations. Ganjam brings out three to four collections a year that are sell outs. Their Bandhan, Heritage and Ganda Berunda collections are legendary. There is a large variety to choose from: A suite from the Benares line which has a hand woven chain using flat diamonds and colour stone beads to pendants and brooches inspired from the lattice work in old palaces, the Haveli Collection. Meenakari, Kundan, and even crystals in

# Jewels & Gemstones

Indian jewellery is coveted the world over for its fine workmanship, quality metal and fabulous designs. Once regarded as a secure investment for the bride's future, jewellery is now available for simple occasions and fashionable parties as well. Gold, once the mainstay of the business, has now been joined by new age metals like platinum and white gold, brushed silver and the very latest – stainless steel!

Lightweight jewellery is the latest rage that is both trendy and affordable. Prominent jewellers like C.Krishniah Chetty have introduced a range that has the same look and feel as traditional jewellery but is not as chunky or ornate.

Most connoisseurs still have their eye on antique jewellery (45 to a 100 years old), once owned exclusively by wealthy families from Tamil Nadu, Andhra Pradesh and Mysore. This 'estate jewellery' reflects a period and a place and is preserved as a complete collection. It is very distinctive and a much sought-after collectible. C.Krishniah Chetty is famous for its range of estate jewellery and its exclusive customers.

A symbol of purity and wealth, diamonds occupy pride of place in any collection of jewellery around the world. Diamond solitaires are popular with the younger generation and are an integral part of a trousseau.

Jewellery set with gemstones is both exclusive as well as affordable. The sapphire blue to chrome green coloured tourmaline is a popular gemstone mined across Brazil, Sri Lanka, Afghanistan, East Africa and the United States.

Distinct from other white metals, silver is a soft metal which lends itself to crafting. Silver flatware and holloware are both simple and elegant and silverware is traditionally passed down from generation to generation.

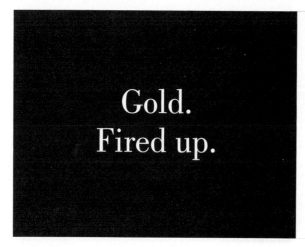

A busy evening at Ganjam Nagappa & Son

jewellery are other attractions. But Ganjam is not just traditional Indian jewellery. Their brand, Le Solitaire is strikingly modern, and they have commissioned Kazua Ogawa to do their platinum line. The Bridal Scarf and Raindrop necklaces are real eye catchers. Ganjam uses only the top one per cent of diamonds in the world, with a colour of F1 and grade purity of VVS1, among the best classifications available. Ganjam is also a partner of the International Platinum Guild.

## ORRA
### The Diamond Destination

*155 Commercial Street, Asha Centre Point, Bangalore 560001*
**Tel** *5113 0100*
**Open** *11am to 8pm*
**Cards** *All*

This is a good store for exclusive ORRA diamond jewellery, gemstones like diamond studded gold and platinum jewellery in trendy designs. The collection includes rings, pendants, bangles, chains, and necklaces, earrings, nose rings as well a range of men's jewellery. There is also an unusually named line of 'spiritual jewellery' available in 22K gold along with a host of other collections such as Nakshatra, Asmi, Couples, Career carats, Platinum and Solitaire Collections.

## Jewels de Paragon

*Rathnam's Complex, 10/5 Kasturba Road, Bangalore 560001*
**Tel** *2221 3636/1024*
**Open** *10am to7pm*
**Cards** *All*

Spread over an area of 8,500sqft, Jewels de Paragon is one of the largest showrooms in Bangalore dealing in platinum, diamond, gold and silver jewellery. A blend of classic and creative designs makes it a popular destination for jewellery shoppers.

## Oyzterbay

*145 Ground Floor, Commercial Street, Bangalore 560001*
**Tel** *2532 0823*
**Branches** *Malleswaram, 2334 8302; Jayanagar, 2653 3825*
**Open** *10:30am to 8:30pm*
**Cards** *All*

If you wished jewellery shopping was not the grave and solemn purchase its always made out to be, try Oyzterbay. The brand represents the modern shift away from heavy jewellery to understated pieces with a definite youthful flavour and Western slant. It can be used to accessorise everyday wear and Western clothes, making it especially popular with working women. Trendy jewellery in yellow, orange, pink

and white gold, silver and diamonds are presented in designs that range from bold to delicate. Especially popular are the gold pendants with semi-precious stones, delicate diamond earrings and the large collection of silver jewellery.

## Sri Krishna Jewellers

*1 Commercial Street, Bangalore 560001*
**Tel** *2532 7833/7834*
**Open** *10:30am to 8:30pm*
**Cards** *All*

Diamond, platinum, gold, gemstone and silver jewellery in the latest designs and a sizeable collection of antique jewellery are available at this spanking new store. In house designers are on stand by for custom made designs.

## Tanishq

*Dickenson Road, The Estate, Bangalore 560042*
**Tel** *2555 0907*
**Branch** *Jayanagar, 2699 1056*
**Open** *10:30am to 7:30pm*
**Cards** *All*

Tanishq made waves in the jewellery business when they first entered the market with a range intermingling traditional design and contemporary styling, created for the new Indian woman: Exquisite gold jewellery studded with diamonds, rubies, emeralds and sapphire as well as jewellery in pure 22K gold. Elegant platinum jewellery, trendy silver jewellery and designer silver are also available. The collections include FQ, Aria, Hoopla, Diva, Collection g, Lightweights and Solo Prices. Tanishq's collection of diamond jewellery is surprisingly affordable and starts at Rs 10,000.

## Trendsmith

*2017 HAL II Stage, 100Ft. Road, Indiranagar, Bangalore 560038*
**Tel** *5115 5650/5651/5652*
**Branch** *Bayleaf, 2553 5050*
**Open** *11am to 7:45pm*
**Cards** *All*

Old timers in Mumbai and Delhi lay great store by the name Tribhovandas Zaveri, its 100 years in the business

evoking deep trust and respect. Trendsmith is an offshoot with a pan-Indian collection of rings, necklaces, pendants and earrings. Eleven lines of exclusive jewellery are offered from leading brands like Ashi jewels, Asmi, Dia, Featherz, Gehna, Nakshatra, Roopa and Karishma Mehra. Trendsmith also showcases Aarzu, handcrafted jewellery from Jaipur with intricate filigree and inlay work set with the finest gems.

## CONCEPT STORES

### 100 Ft Boutique and Restaurant

*777/1 100Ft. Road, HAL II Stage, Indiranagar, Bangalore 560008*
**Tel** *2527 7752/8616*
**Open** *11am to 11pm*
**Cards** *All*

The shop and dine experience comes to Bangalore with the 100 Ft Boutique and Restaurant. This bright and airy space is packed with things you don't really need but once you see them all that will change!
Handmade paper albums, candles, chocolates and homemade jams sit along with an assortment of glass and mugs. Those who have more cash to splash can look at a clothesline as well as select pieces of designer jewellery from Ishrath Chowdhry. Cushions embroidered with butterflies and mulmul curtains with coconut ferns are part off an offbeat furnishing section. Beanbags and modern furniture bring up the rest.

### Ambara

*119 Annaswamy Mudaliar Road, near Lakeside Hospital, Bangalore 560042*
**Tel** *2557 2829*
**Open** *10:30am to 7pm*
**Cards** *All except American Express*

Gujarati block prints with Kanjeevaram borders! Mangalgiri saris with phulkari from Punjab! Tamil Nadu bronzes with Mughal florals! This is the essence of Ambara: A boutique that is a happy mélange of different styles from all over India. Four artistes came together to

Clothes, art and furnishings are showcased at Ambara.

create a bank of ideas that evolved into an art section, a furnishing section, a sari section and an Indo western clothes line for women. They are all committed to the seriously ethnic and have tried to combine different elements of Indian origin to create something modern and unique. The result is a great store with plenty to browse. The most popular is the clothesline under the OMO label. Casual and chic, the designs appeal to all age groups and are changed and updated frequently. Ambara houses a gallery where paintings, sculptures and other arty knick-knacks are on display. Ceramic pottery, leadless stonecraft vases and cheerful terracotta pots for the garden are also available. An outdoor café is attached.

## Cose Belle

*19 Shungar Shopping Complex,*
*MG Road Bangalore 560001*
*Tel 2532 1279*
*Open 10am to 8pm*
*Cards All*

As the name Cose Belle (Italian for beautiful things) suggests, this store is a melange of tasteful handcrafted wares sourced from Auroville. The international commune in Pondicherry is renowned for its ethnic line of handmade products, ranging from pottery to furniture. Cose Belle is one of the oldest shops of its kind in the city and has been around before the Raagas, Bhimas and Desis became the rage. Wind chimes, aromatherapy oils, perfumed candles, scented incense sticks, handmade paper stationery and an assortment of decorative objects are showcased here. The microwave compatible stonecraft cutlery and cookware is a good buy – these leadless pots, pans, mugs and kettles with wooden serving spoons come in shades of earthy blues and browns. Cose Belle also stocks a rather large collection of high quality leather purses, bags, wallets, briefcases, travel bags and coin purses made out of vegetable tanned soft leather. A colourful line of cotton hand knitted tops, kurtas and sweaters can be

picked up here. Lamps, candles, bookmarks and vases embellished with dried flowers are other signature Auroville products. If you browse long enough you will also find knitted hammocks, terracotta jewellery and decorative papier mache objects stashed away. Meditative music, audiotapes of discourses by Sri Aurobindo and the Mother and their books are also available here.

## Fabindia

*54, 17th Main, II Block, Koramangala,*
*Bangalore 560034*
*Tel 2553 2070*
*Branch Commercial Street, 3090 5319*
*Open 10am to 7pm*
*Cards All*

There is something special and timeless about Fabindia, a handloom institution that set the trend for all furnishing and cotton clothing stores that came later. Today there are lots of places selling cottonware, but Fabindia has held its own with great sourcing and some innovative clothing.
Everything that Fabindia sells is hand woven and handcrafted, with a clear imprint of the human hand. Furnishings, clothes for the whole family, knicks-knacks like crockery and lamps, dhurries, table, bed and bathroom linen, the list is pretty exhaustive. A small café in the store (set in a fabulously designed house) makes for a satisfying morning spent browsing among handmade products. It's an ideal place for souvenirs and gifts.

## Jute Cottage

*295/1 Sai Baba Temple Road,*
*1st Cross,Cambridge Layout, Ulsoor,*
*Bangalore 560008*
*Tel 2530 8694*
*Open 10:30am to 8pm.*
*Closed on Sunday.*
*Cards All except American Express*

Jute has struggled to shed its image of sacking cloth and shops like Jute Cottage should be lauded for their efforts in this direction. They have taken this eco friendly and biodegradable resource and fashioned it into an array of utility and decorative products. Rugs and dhurries, wall hangings and curtains, dolls and bags, jackets and shawls and lampshades and household furnishings are among the items on sale. A strong fabric with high tensile strength, its rough texture is turned into a virtue – earthy and ethnic. Hand painted jute jewellery is quite a novelty. Some are even studded with beads. The jute embroidered slippers make a fashion statement as well. Wine bags with cane handles make trendy gifts.

## Kahawa

*195/6 Kareem Towers,*
*Cunningham Road, Bangalore 560025*
*Tel 2208 8004*
*Open 11am to 8pm. Closed on Sunday.*
*Cards All*

Kahawa is a mélange of object d'art, paintings, fabric and fashion accessories. The store has an interesting and inviting display that makes for an enjoyable browsing experience. Kahawa in Sanskrit means an expression or a proverb. In the store, it translates into young artistes from all over the country being able to express themselves through their craft and work. Part of this lovely store is devoted to handmade designer jewellery. Those looking for something contemporary – kurtis in cotton, crepes and georgettes in a variety of styles and colours are available. A collection of imported bags and others embellished with beads, sequins and embroidery are also on display. You may even find saris, Pashmina shawls and designer fabric to buy.

# Sales Stop

All of Bangalore knows one address for sales – Safina Plaza. Almost everyday, a new sale opens here in its many stalls and everything from kitchen wear, clothes, linen, pottery, furniture, seconds and books is up for grabs. Big brands often hold sales here and buyers throng to buy otherwise expensive goods.
    Built around a large green square, Safina Plaza has become a landmark of sorts in Bangalore's shopping directory. It's the first choice for exhibitors and sellers and of course buyers who enjoy the bazaar atmosphere with chaat, ice cream, coffee, chocolate, Horlicks, soups and even fruits on sale at the entrance. The ample parking adds to its attraction.
    Sellers get to choose from spaces as small as 300 to 500sqft and larger ones that go up to 10,000sqft. There is a major rush for bookings during festive seasons such as Ugadi, Ganesh Chaturthi, Ramzan, Christmas and New Year and plans need to be made often eight to nine months in advance.
    Safina Plaza has a number of permanent shops as well with products ranging from designer wear, shoes, crafts, books, computers and furniture. Big brands such as Allen Solly, Scullers, Dockers, Gurlz, Titan, Lovable and others are also present.

*Infantry Road, Bangalore 560001*
*Tel 2558 1982/1989*

Safina Plaza

# City Of Tomorrow

**Bangalore**
It's great to be here!

India's City Of The Future, managed by
**Bangalore Mahanagara Palike**
*Citizens First. Always.*

- Rs. 150 crore project for water and drainage
- 100 Nirmala Bangalore toilets constructed, 200 more planned
- Swacha Bangalore - Door-to-door garbage collection implemented
- Only city in India with 2 planned landfills
- The nation's only city to declare quarterly financial results and have self-assessment of property tax

The household section has a range of ceramics, both utilitarian as well as decorative. Handmade paper lamps, perfumed candles and hand painted bamboo combs from Orissa make fun buys. They also have chattai mats edged with zari borders and other knick-knacks. The soapstone chess set from Kenya and the jewellery boxes from Thailand are real scene stealers. Kahawa hosts a series of exhibitions that are worth viewing.

## Khadder

*The Forum, 21 Hosur Road,*
*Koramangala, Bangalore 560034*
*Tel 2206 7662*
*Open 10:30am to 8:30pm*
*Cards All*

Not everything here is 'Khadi', but it's definitely handloom. Khadder stocks khadi and handloom fabric in a range of readymade clothes in vivid colours. Apart from the usual men and women's kurtas of different lengths, spaghetti strap bustiers, wrap around skirts and casual shirts for men and women are presented here. Most of the clothes have interesting detailing like wooden buttons. Khadder also keeps a stock of churidars for women and men and dupattas in an interesting combination of colours. The bright colours of India stand out here – no pastels! Some of the fabric is printed with Om inscriptions, while others have checks, stripes and polka dots in the weave. In thin and thick fabric, the styles are available in five sizes.

## Out of the Blue

*381, 13ᵗʰ Cross, Sadashivnagar,*
*Bangalore 560080*
*Tel 3061 6083, 5115 4620*
*Open 10am to 7pm. Closed on Monday.*
*Cards All*

Children's bookstore Word Play has gone and in its place has come Out of the Blue at a different location. The store has

expanded to include books for adults, aquaria, handmade gift articles like mugs and jewellery and even handpicked sterling silverware, in short a great place to browse and shop. For those interested in fish, the store provides customised aquaria. The space above the store is used to conduct activities such as story readings, Yoga classes and other creative workshops.

## Raaga

*A/14 Devatha Plaza,*
*131 Residency Road, Bangalore 560025*
*Tel 5112 0888*
*Open 10am to 9:30pm. 12:30pm to 8pm on Sunday.*
*Cards All*

Raaga has a lovely earthy and informal air to it. Earthy, because all the stuff here is handmade and informal because you can browse as long as you like across a wide range of interesting knick knacks. The products are reasonably priced and make great gifts. Wallets in pure leather, designer candles, terracotta jewellery, lampshades decorated with dry flowers and handmade stationery from Auroville are displayed in a cluttered but friendly fashion. Porcelain cups, plates, bowls, wind chimes, posters, soft toys from Kodaikanal, Rajasthani furniture and Ganesha lamps also make interesting buys. The popular Tantra t-shirts, recycled stationery, hammocks and bamboo plants for good luck may be found here. The café next door – Casa Piccola – makes a nice stop.

## Raintree

*4 Sankey Road, High Grounds,*
*Bangalore 560 052*
*Tel 3062 3251*
*Open 10am to 7pm*
*Cards All*

A beautiful old bungalow set in a sprawling garden has been converted to a

Eco-friendly products are available at Jute Cottage.

store that houses clothing, glass furniture, accessories and flowers. Facing the Windsor Sheraton on one side and the golf course on another, Raintree is perfect for an afternoon of shopping in an atmosphere reminiscent of Bangalore's trademark bungalows. Four stores have their outlets here – Anokhi with its range of ethnic chic clothing and home furnishings, Mumbai-based Verrerie's glass furniture and accessories, the Raintree brand of lifestyle products, and Ohana Fine Flowers with its unusual and breathtakingly lovely flower arrangments. Part of the bungalow has been demarcated as an exhibition hall for arts and photographs.
The final touch is a café selling excellent tea and coffee, sandwiches and desserts.

## Studio Mom

*475, 13ᵗʰ Main, Koramangala III Block,*
*Bangalore 560034*
*Tel 2553 6640*
*Open 10:30am to 6:30pm.*
*Closed on Sunday.*
*Cards Only American Express*

All those pregnant ladies eyeing high fashion garments have a store all to themselves. A wide variety of maternity clothing, both casual and formal, like tights, trousers, dresses, dungarees, shirts, t-shirts, nightwear and lingerie are available, enough to last nine months and more!

## The Candle Shop

*294 K Kamaraj Road,*
*Bangalore 560042*
*Tel 2558 2311/2312*
*Open 11am to 8:30pm*
*Cards All*

There's nothing quite like the soft, magical glow of candlelight to set the mood. The Candle Shop is all about candles for every room and every occasion. Jelly candles, water candles, floating candles and aroma candles surround you as you enter the store. Candle chandeliers, wall brackets, tee lights and innovative garden candles are also on offer. You can choose from every shape imaginable – cubes, cylinders, triangles, rectangles, hearts

# Leela Galleria

The Leela Galleria is a plush shopping arcade in The Leela Palace hotel and it's fast emerging as the city's super premium shopping destination. It's spread over 1,00,000sqft in the city's top notch luxury hotel and its luxury status is enhanced by some premium brands, Indian and international. Shoppers get to browse through an exclusive selection of clothes, accessories, art stores and more. Trendy clothes from **DAKS**, tailored suits from **Khanate**, designer wear for men from **Lokesh Ahuja**, high quality leather from **Hidesign** and the best in perfumes, books and art, all converge under one roof.

The swanky **Parco's** stocks some exclusive perfumes from Elizabeth Arden, Shiseido, Nina Ricci and Burberry's. **Anokhi** has a collection of high quality cotton clothes and accessories in contemporary designs and fabrics. Hand printed and block printed kurtas, earthy skirts and ethnic pants, salwar kameezes, saris, scarves and stoles are available here. **Mogra** has the latest in party and wedding wear from Delhi and Kolkata designers like Anju Modi and Vachi – crushed kurtis, embroidered

ghagras, saris and western wear are part of the line. There are a few handicraft stores where you can pick up Kashmiri carpets, Tibetan paintings and other valuable artefacts. The brightly lit **The Oxford Bookstore** has an impressive collection of titles from travel guides and biographies to self help books and the latest bestsellers. The bookstore also encourages browsing – you can make yourself comfortable on the couch and flip through the books without a worry. **Ganjam Jewellers** has an outlet here – finely crafted diamond, gold and platinum jewellery are their speciality. **Srishti** is another exclusive jewellery store where the latest designs in Kundan jewellery and stone jewellery from Jaipur are on display. The **Barista** and **Cha Bar** cafés offer a well deserved break from all the shopping. The Galleria also features the **Amoeba Sports Bar** a hip entertainment zone with formula racing, Air Hockey and an all night disco.

Even window shopping at the Galleria is a pleasure!

*23 Airport Road, Bangalore 560008,* **Tel 2525 3351**

and squares. Marbled and frosted, squat and tapered, they are available in every hue, encased with pearls and shells, glitter and gilt, jute and bamboo, terracotta and even ethnic fabric. Roses and even single stem flowers are moulded into candles. Festive occasion candles like Diwali diyas and X'mas Santas are hot ticket items.

The Candle Shop also stocks a variety of candle stands and jars. Candle accessories like glass pebbles and scented oils are also available. All candles are drip-less and completely burn down minimising the mess. Special orders are also undertaken.

## The Gift Room
### (Swarovski and Lladro)

*101 Prestige Meridian, Block II,*
*30 MG Road, Bangalore 560001*
**Tel** *2532 1868, 2558 9988*
**Open** *10:30am to 8pm*
**Cards** *All*

The Gift Room is a franchisee for both Swarovski and Lladro, two eminently collectible brands the world over. This is the best place to pick up something in crystal or porcelain to commemorate an important occasion in your life or to buy a gift for the same purpose.

In the Swarovski section, you can lose yourself in a crystalline world with crystals for every facet of life and fashion, from animal friends and feathered friends to flowers and foliage or the wonders of the sea. Special moments like the childhood years, classic family celebrations, memorable journeys and even hobbies are captured in crystal moments. They also have a crystal home accessories section that is very innovative.

Crystal fashion is another big section in the store. Sensual colours and many faceted stones are displayed in a striking collection of gold plated jewellery or white metal with rhodium plating. Crystal tattoos are a popular fashion accessory.

Lladro on the other hand, has fine porcelain artwork, handcrafted to the finest detail. Family affairs and events, nature, art, sculpture, spirituality or simply fantasy is the inspiration of these creations.

# Smuggled Surprises

If the aisles of foreign supermarkets are your favourite hunting ground, try Bangalore's imported goods bazaars, where everything from imported cellphones to perfumes and clothes are available with no brand warranty and often sell-by dates long past. That doesn't seem to stop the many buyers who stream in and out all day. There are six imported bazaars in all – **Hong Kong Bazaar**, **New Hong Kong Bazaar**, **Burma Bazaar**, **National Market**, **Mahaveer Plaza** and **Sukh Sagar Mall**.

Set in the crowded bylanes of the city's commercial centres, KR Market and Gandhinagar, these bazaars are a world in themselves. Rows of cramped, air-conditioned shops vie for attention with just about every kind of product, even food. The prices of these goods are much lower than at regular retail outlets anywhere else in the city. The bazaars do not operate on the concept of fixed prices and you have a free hand with bargaining.

National Market and Mahaveer Plaza shops stock a range of clothes, cosmetics, perfumes, mobiles, watches, shoes, decorative porcelain figurines and reputed brands like Nike and GAP. Burma Bazaar and New Hong Kong Bazaar sell stereos, colour television sets, camera, handy cams, suitcases and DVD and VCD players from brands like Samsung, AIWA and Sony. Look out for fakes – you might encounter brands like 'Galvin Klein' and 'Giordina' here! Crowded at all times, students and young working people flock here for the imported tag on the goods, even if some of them are fake!

The imported bazaars of Bangalore were a rage when foreign goods were not available in the regular markets. Today, with imported brands flooding the regular market, people are wary of buying electronic goods at these bazaars, where there is no guarantee on the quality of the products available. However, they are still frequented for smaller knick-knacks and consumer goods that do not need a warranty.

### The Design Store

*46 100Ft. Road, Koramangala VI Block, Bangalore 560095*
*Tel 2552 2205, 2550 2470*
**Open** *10:30am to 8pm*
**Cards** *All except American Express*

Everything at The Design Store reflects impeccable taste and the brilliant touch of simple, good design sense. The furniture, home accessories and knick-knacks are affordable and serve a purpose. Tessaract Design makes furniture in rubberwood and teak — lounge, dining and bedroom furniture. Some of the interesting pieces are a 'study in a niche', racks and other storage solutions. This stuff is generally for the urban house where space is limited.

Basket work in bright and stunning colours, natural fibres in screw pine, banana, palm leaf, korai and river grass are turned into an assortment of baskets, laundry bins, mats, bags, trays, boxes and lamps. There are even fibre floor cushions, bolsters and table linen, trimmed with Indian borders and shot with gold and silver. Some mats have recycled plastic integrated in the weave pattern. Others look really trendy with a leather trim.

The children's section features traditional toys representative of indigenous materials and cultures. Spinning tops, rattles and cars in wood, lacquer, vegetable dye, snakes and ladders, Chinese Piel, Aadu Pul Aatam and Dahdi along with interactive cloth books are also available.

### Things

*294, 1st Floor, 7th Cross, Domlur Layout, Bangalore 560071*
*Tel 2535 6678*
**Open** *10am to 7pm. 4pm to 8pm on Sunday.*
**Cards** *All except American Express*

This is the place to browse for all sorts of knick-knacks. Essentially an ethnic Indian gift shop, it showcases a variety of rural and tribal crafts of India. Banana fibre, mirror work, beads and embroidery from Bhuj to Sandur are designed in an array of travel and evening bags, jewellery and glass cases, wall hangings and cushions. Cast iron and bronze animals from Madhya Pradesh serve not only as curios but doorknobs, bottle openers and hooks! Madhubani and Warli paintings jostle for space with black and white etchings from Nepal.

Stained glass, blue pottery, handmade paper products and even herbs and herbal skin products find their way onto these shelves. Terracotta jewellery, beads and silver along with semi precious stones are hand picked items in terms of their design and finish.

There is a clothes section for women in cotton and silk that is quite popular.

### FURNITURE

### Aura

*106 Oxford Towers, 139 Airport Road, Bangalore 560017*
*Tel 2509 7777*
**Open** *10am to 7pm*
**Cards** *All except American Express*

Aura deals in imported furniture in period designs. On exhibit are ornate sofas, beds, dining tables, garden furniture, home accessories and artefacts. Each piece is exclusive and fashioned from solid teak and mahogany. One-of-a-kind carved sideboards, wall racks and antique showcases, centrepieces and corner tables are on display. There are a few unconventional couches in wood and leather as well as a range of exquisitely carved tables that fold into different shapes. Breakfast tables for two, foldable garden tables with benches, coffee tables with carved chairs, a compact nest of tables, corner tables and study tables in French and Victorian styles are some of Aura's innovations. There are also comprehensive packages on offer — complete bedroom furniture is sold for Rs 65,000 and sofas start at Rs 35,000. The curios, artefacts and knick-knacks available here have been sourced and handpicked from the Philippines, Thailand, Indonesia, Iran and Bali. Choose from carved wooden motorcycles, Iranian paintings, Mother of Pearl serving bowls, models of old ships, terracotta vases, rattan baskets, wood carvings from Bali and so on.

### Cane Boutique

*762 100Ft. Road, Indiranagar Bangalore 560038*
*Tel 2527 8017, 5115 2093*
**Open** *10am to 8pm. 2pm to 8pm on Sunday.*
**Cards** *All except American Express*

Cane is no longer confined to garden furniture. It has taken on a stylish new avatar and may now be seen inside homes as well as offices. Acknowledging this is the Cane Boutique. It uses only imported wicker and guarantees a product life of at least eight years. They also use the grooving method in weaving that involves no nails. Apart from the rattan they have also experimented with sea grass, water hyacinth, banana and natural fibres. On offer is polyurethane cane, a good choice for variable weather conditions. Largely fashioned on German designs, they offer both traditional and contemporary products in combination with wood, metal and bamboo. From headboards for beds to shutters for cupboards, wall units to laundry baskets, chaise lounges to dining tables, garden furniture to baskets, trays and lampshades, the Cane Boutique is happy to put together anything in cane.

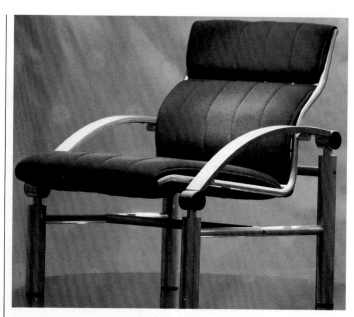

### Designo

*12 Shamrao Compound, Mission Road, Bangalore 560027*
*Tel 2224 7143, 2299 8895*
**Open** *10am to 8pm*
**Cards** *All*
**Web** *www.designosofasogood.com*

Designo has some of the best chairs on sale and a few of the city's celebrities would vouch for that. Set in a sweeping 10,000sqft showroom, Designo has finely crafted sofas, chairs and recliners made from genuine Italian leather and laid out on two floors.

Their chairs have distinctly superior seating that varies from soft and sinking to standard and firm. Sand blasted aluminium tables, Lorenzo tables and accessories like throw rugs, Tiffany lamps, art glass panels and Sahar brass artefacts are also available. Love seats, lounge chairs, three seater recliners, beanbags, bar stools, puffes, pedestals, cocktail and lamp tables, centrepieces and floor cushions make up the rest of the Designo collection. You can choose from 70 shades and five textures of Stanley Leather and custom made furniture can be ordered in mahogany, teak and rosewood. It takes four to six weeks for their leather-clad creations to be ready.

### F:Sttore

*6/2, 80Ft. Road, Koramangala VI Block, Bangalore 560034*
*Tel 5110 5488*
**Open** *10:30am to 9pm*
**Cards** *All except American Express*

Specialists in modular furniture, F:Sttore is popular with Bangalore's techies. The furniture is imported from Indonesia and China and is trendy and contemporary. Spread across three floors, the range includes sofas in leather and fabric, beds, wardrobes, dressers, side tables and centre tables. Apart from the standard fare, rocking chairs, computer tables, crockery cabinets, garden furniture, leather recliners with massage units, palm chairs, shoe racks and wine cabinets are also available.

## Furniturewalla

*756, IV Block, Koramangala Extension,*
*80Ft. Road, Bangalore 560034*
*Tel 2550 1515*
*Open 11am to 9pm*
*Cards All except American Express*

This shop will suit anyone who likes good furniture and thinks nothing of combining a 100 years of styling under one roof. A Victorian chaise lounge with a side table in glass and metal? That's possible if you shop here.
The 'Bargain Section' has modern and colonial reproductions and ethnic Indian furniture with discounted price tags. The 'International Styles Section' lets shoppers choose from the best designs across the globe. A section on colonial and ethnic styles has old world furniture in teak, mahogany and walnut wood. Finally, there is also a 'Futuristic' section with new age furniture made from a combination of fibreglass and metal.

## Good Lines

*766 HAL II Stage, 100Ft. Road,*
*Indiranagar, Bangalore 560038*
*Tel 5115 5000/5001*
*Open 10:30am to 7:30pm.*
*Closed on Sunday.*
*Cards All except American Express*

If the days of the Raj define your idea of good furniture, a visit to the Good Lines store is in order. Silk carpets, rich upholstery, layered curtains and ornate curios will blend into the stuff you find here. All the furniture is made in Burma

teak and is manufactured at in-house factories. The drawing room section offers a variety of sofas, some plump upholstered ones and some with ornate carvings. There is a large variety of centre tables, side tables, display shelves and entertainment units. Individual pieces like a plant stand or a Saxon chair make for interesting single buys.
Tables finished with mirror polish and set with gilt edged chairs sum up the dining room section. Glass tops with carved bases in various stains are also available. Bar units and sideboards reflect the same theme. If you're lucky you get to see a four poster bed, a definite conversation stopper. Tall headboards with wooden inlay work are also available.
Good Lines has mostly classical reproductions, but undertakes specific designs as well.

## Inexcezz

*227, 13th Cross, 5th Main, CMH Road,*
*Indiranagar, Bangalore 560038*
*Tel 2520 1791*
*Open 10:30am to 7:30pm*
*Cards All except American Express*

Inexcezz sells design concepts, individual pieces of furniture and decorative home accessories. Unlike standard furniture shops with custom made furniture sets, each piece of furniture here is one-of-a-kind. As a rule all displays, furniture as well as accessories, are made from natural materials like wood, stone, bamboo, slate coconut wood, paper and natural

Furniture high on comfort and style is created at Designo.

fabrics. The merchandise is arranged in a home setting to give customers a real feel.

## Kian

*99, II Floor, The Bombay Store,*
*MG Road, Bangalore 560001*
*Tel 5112 2215/2216*
*Open 10:30am to 8:30pm*
*Cards All except American Express &*
*Diners Club*

Trendy, international and chic, Kian offers a range of furniture from southeast Asia, for homes as well as cafés and food courts.
The home section carries contemporary American furniture and oriental

influences. Rubberwood combined with mild steel is a strong theme. A variety of veneers like oak, ash and cedar trace a very contemporary edge. The style varies from the very linear Scandinavian look to the heavier British colonial, expressed with its range titled 'Cameroon', in a combination of wicker and wood veneer. The leather handles used in the entire line make for an interesting detail. For those interested in ethnic design, there is the Java series that incorporates hand carving. Similarly, the Tao series has oriental overtones in the form of brass motifs. With a large variety of pieces to choose from in each style, customers enjoy the freedom to pick up the odd piece or stick to one style.

The hospitality range comes in a bold new style using a mixture of aluminum, polypropylene, wood moulding and mild steel. Funky colours like mint blue and carnation red make quite a fashion statement. One can also do a mix 'n' match from a variety of legs, bases and tabletops to reach a style goal.

With an eye to practical considerations of high usage products, Kian has introduced iso-top tables that claim to be scratch, fire and cigarette butt resistant. The entire line is also designed keeping in mind economy of space and all the tabletops and chair legs are foldable, making stacking and storing very easy.

## Maram

*57, 4th Cross, I Block, RMV II Stage,*
*Bangalore 560094*
**Tel** *2341 1427*
**Open** *Only by Appointment*
**Cards** *Not Accepted*

Old fashioned furniture has ornamental rather than functional value. If that's not how you see it, try Maram. A wooden beam (*pallang*) becomes the back of a strikingly tall chair, or the base of an easel or even the sides of a bookshelf. A *'Yarley'* (carved animal face) is the support for a shelf while a large *'urli'* (shallow cooking pot) transforms into a coffee table. You can dream up the strangest things – prayer stools as cheese platters and wooden Kerala serving dishes as magazine racks. You can even try salt and masala ducks (wooden vessels shaped like ducks used to store masala or salt) to store bric-a-brac.

Maram does not restore old furniture, but are quite happy to customise (say) damaged doors and shutters to become low benches or dining tables, to suit your needs. They prefer to deal in teak, rose and jack wood and some Australian ash. A visit to the store is by appointment only.

## Pause

*22/12 Vittal Mallya Road, Bangalore 560001*
**Tel** *5112 1025/26*
**Open** *10:30am to 7:30pm.*
*Closed on Sunday.*
**Cards** *All*

Vittal Mallya Road is the undisputed hub of Bangalore fashion and Pause is the new shop on the block. A minimalist white decor sets off the furniture, lighting, carpets and house accessories on sale. A Burma teak closet upholstered in burgundy leather, a bar cabinet with traditional inlay work and a pullout tray for mixing drinks, a teak dressing table with swivel mirrors and glass mini-drawers, a chequered table in duo-toned wood teamed with stainless steel legs, and garden benches in sal wood are complemented by Italian lights and carpets in muted shades. An eclectic collection of knick-knacks like cloth-covered notebooks and books on the tarot will make even the busiest shopper pause a while.

## Pete's Furniture

*4004 100Ft. Road, HAL II Stage,*
*Indiranagar, Bangalore 560008*
**Tel** *2520 2115*
**Open** *10am to 8pm*
**Cards** *Not Accepted*

A Victorian hat stand, a Scandinavian piano stool, an art deco table, these are a few of Peter's favourite things! Pete's Furniture is packed with period furniture, lamps, clocks and glass – an ideal hunting ground for things from a different era. Pete displays a discerning eye for detail and line. "Know an antique from a replica," stresses Pete. He says there are very few antiques left in India and the mere age of a piece does not certify it as an antique. To authenticate a piece one must trace it to the manufacturer, as well as for whom it was made. Information that is almost impossible to come by, hence the confusion over antiques in India.

Pete stocks all kinds of old furniture, which he lovingly restores to its original glory. The influences are Victorian, Colonial, Art Deco and Scandinavian. You will come across hat stands, console tables, Dutch boxes, piano stools and chaise lounges. You may even spot a portable library staircase. Cupboards and bookshelves are all part of the grand browsing experience. Pete deals in rose wood, mahogany and teak.

Kerosene and porcelain lamps, with stained glass or cut glass shades, Belgian chandeliers, lalique glass, porcelain plates, grandfather and Gothic clocks hide in every nook and cranny of his warehouse. Keep your eyes wide open – you never know what you might stumble upon.

## Quetzel Designs

*6/2 Kaikondrahalli, Sarjapur Road,*
*Carmelaram Post, Bangalore 560035*
**Tel** *2843 9685*
**Open** *9am to 6:30pm. Closed on*
*Sunday.*
**Cards** *All*

Quetzel is a line of contemporary furniture where the designers get to make the rules. The result is a line of furniture that upholds comfort, style and function. Both home and office furniture is available here.

The Q kids range deserves special mention. All the pieces have a touch of humour and warmth to them. 'Pepo' is a bed that takes inspiration from the basic shapes that a child learns. The Bud 'n' Buddy is a bed with a pullout bed below, a great space saver for siblings who share a room or for kids with frequent overnight guests. The 'Binky' table and chair grows with your child from ages two to 10, making it a very economical buy. The 'Dot' table is available in bright colours and has a laminate top making it easy to clean. Sturdy little chairs that keep good posture in mind can be picked up here. Each piece is completely child friendly.

Quetzel also has an interesting section of lamps, made in materials like textured glass, paper, plastics, foam and varied metals. They come as tabletops, pedestals and screens and there are some that may be used outdoors as well.

## Stanley Leather

*12/7, Shamarao Compound, Mission*
*Road, Bangalore 560027*
**Tel** *2222 6237*
**Branch** *100Ft. Road, 2535 7374*
**Open** *9:30am to 7pm*
**Cards** *All*
**Web** *www.stanleyseating.com*

Stanley is the city's largest stockist of finished upholstery leather from Europe. The internationally styled leather

furniture line – Stanley Ross – is created from genuine Italian leather that is both luxurious and comfortable. A range of ergonomically designed corporate chairs, lounge chairs and lobby furniture is available in over 55 colours, in high quality steel and wood.

Their brand of upholstery graces the interiors of automobiles, theatres, auditoriums and even private jets! The country's largest importer of genuine leather from Italy and Scotland, it offers customised upholstery and accessories for most leading automobile manufacturers. Five types of leather in four different fits, from tight fit and gathering fit to snug fit and designer fit, in soft, supple and natural leather are offered.

The company also markets ProGrip, Italian leather steering covers used in luxury cars like Mitsubishi Lancer, Ford Escort and Honda City. Car accessories such as steering wheels, gear lever covers etc. are also sold here. All Stanley products are made using specialised triple bonded nylon thread, high density foam and the latest German technology.

## Style Spa

*HRS Chambers, 91 Richmond Road,*
*Bangalore 560025*
**Tel** *2222 8708*
**Branch** *Rajajinagar, 2312 1555*
**Open** *10am to 8pm.*
*Closed on Sunday.*
**Cards** *All*

This is just the kind of place you need to come when you have a whole home to be outfitted with furniture or you've just signed the papers for a new office. Style Spa is the new name of Gautier furniture and it stocks both home and office pieces in fairly clean lines with a laminated finish. Box beds, two door wardrobes, dressing tables with mirrors, living room furniture like TV-audio units, corner stands and dining tables and chairs are available.

## Tangent

*Emen Arcade-1 Hosur Road,*
*Near Christ College,*
*Bangalore 560029*
**Tel** *2563 1307/1308*
**Open** *10am to 8pm*
**Cards** *All*

Furniture in a variety of styles is available at Kian.

This is the city's first furniture mall spread over 18,000sqft stocking both Indian and imported furniture. Sofas, divans, reclining chairs, dining sets, and children's furniture including study tables, bunk beds and computer desks are just some of the products on sale here. For a little harmless fun try the shoe shaped chairs, beds in the shape of flowers and enormous beach sofas! A sizeable assortment of decorative artefacts are also available.

### Thar Art Gallery

*50 Ground Floor, 100 Ft. Road, Indiranagar, Bangalore 560038*
*Tel 2527 4868, 2525 4438*
*Open 10:30am to 7:30pm and 10:30am to 1:30pm on Sunday.*
*Cards All*

Thar Art Gallery has what could be loosely termed as antiques and antique-looking reproductions with special emphasis on handcrafted wood furniture and metal goods. Suppliers to major exporters like John Lewis, Harrods and Pottery Barn, it is definitely worth a visit. Hoysala temple friezes and all the gods of heaven are carved in brass and panchaloha (a mixture of five metals). These are crafted as curios as well as hooks, bottle openers and household trivia. Thar employs master artistes so you are bound to pick up something exclusive. They also have a good sampling of art from Bastar and Chattisgarh. Tanjore paintings depicting the 800 forms of Krishna and the Nandi

Bull are popular buys. Silver jewellery made for export specifications is also worth a look. Furniture for every room in the house, jaali-fitted tables, tantra and tribal art on cupboards, canopy beds, Italian marble, tile and rollertop tables are all displayed here. Furniture with modern uses is a hot ticket. An antique looking cupboard opens up to reveal a computer room, fitted with shelves for a CPU, printer, keyboard tray, a filing cabinet along with paper and floppy storage. All furniture is in teak, rosewood and shesham. Wooden buggies, copper urns and cast iron benches are also sold here.

### Vintage Shop

*103 Oxford House, 15 Rustum Bagh Main Road, Bangalore 560017*
*Tel 2509 7777*
*Open 10am to 7pm.*
*Closed on Sunday.*
*Cards All*

Vintage is the flavour of this store: A 1931 car, Victorian piano, palm leaf manuscripts and Raja Ravi Varma imitations. Other collectibles include teakwood tiled tables, intricately carved mahogany stands, camphor chests, Chinese ceramic stools, bar units, Iranian chests, Bali wood carvings, wooden jewellery boxes and bowls, medicine stands, magazine stands, shelves, dried flowers and Bohemian handcrafted crystals. Enough to thrill the heart of anyone who likes a little bit of the past in the present.

Furniture at Quetzel Designs

The Design Store

## FURNISHINGS

### Atmosphere

*Embassy Classic, 11 Vittal Mallya Road, Bangalore 560001*
*Tel 5112 0820*
*Open 10am to 7:30pm. Closed on Sunday.*
*Cards All except Diners Club*

Himatsingka Seide, weaver and exporter of fabric extraordinaire, has done justice to its fine line of furnishing fabric with Atmosphere – the showroom is breathtakingly elegant and chic serving the double purpose of display as well as giving the customer design cues for a perfect setting. Rumour has it that Himatsingka Seide's fabrics grace Buckingham Palace and celebrity Lear jets.
Luxurious and high end, Atmosphere is clearly not for those who worry about their bank balance! Drapes and upholstery for home, office and hospitality come in silk, spun silk, cotton, linen and viscose. The line has a few pure cottons and velvets too. The sheers have double layered pockets and throw up different colour feelings.
Most of the designs are inspired by nature and the weaves are matched accordingly. The high quality finish makes the fabric reversible!

### Blind Love

*789/A, 12th Main, HAL II Stage, Indiranagar, Bangalore 560008*
*Tel 2528 5163*
*Open 10am to 6pm. Closed on Sunday.*
*Cards Not Accepted*

The humble curtain, shading the window is transformed here into a thing of beauty. Dressing up a window is no small matter when you see the options available in Blind Love. Tablecloth and dhurries, saris and dupattas, fabric and chattai's are given a new meaning under the expertise of Blind Love.
Blinds are styled with a variety of edges – some are embroidered, others shot with gold thread or affixed with beads or sequins. Striking blinds in gossamer and sheer fabrics like voile allow a lovely play of light and shade.
The popular ones are chattais with a cloth backing, plain or worked upon. The matting itself comes in bamboo, wood and cane. Some are shot with thread to create a variety of interesting patterns. Blinds can also be combined with curtains as well as interesting drapes to create the desired effect. Double blinds are an option. If you are looking for something dramatic opt for the spray painted chattai in shaded hues with a sheer organza layer.
All blinds are custom made for homes and offices.

Shopping

Gangarams Book Bureau

## Creative Living

*7 Hosur Main Road, Near Christ
College, Bangalore 560029*
**Tel** *2553 6486*
**Branch** *MG Road, 2559 1162;
St. Marks Road, 5123 3998*
**Open** *10:30am to 8:30pm*
**Cards** *All except American Express*

This is not your dingy home linen store of
yore. Instead, a lively collection of bed
sheets, bed spreads, bath mats, towels,
curtains and other home accessories are
displayed in a pleasant, contemporary
ambience. Rolls of neatly packed face
towels and hand towels from the New
York based Portico, bath towels in lime
green and indigo from Wellspun,
colourful shower curtains, bathroom
slippers and floor mats in the shape of
fish and strawberries are laid out. Bed
sheets and bed spreads from Spain in king
and queen sizes, arty drapery rods in
antique copper and matt brass, hand
embroidered cushion covers made from
satin and raw silk as well as a limited
collection of curtains are available to do
up your home. There's other interesting
pot pourri available to complete the bed
and bath experience – scented candles,
floating candles and perfumed incense
sticks that are smokeless and dripless.
Aromatherapy products from sandalwood
foot soaks and de-stress hydra eye gel to
jasmine massage oils and rose and
almond shower gels from Forest Essentials
can be bought here. Bone China cups and
saucers, Harry Potter and Winnie The
Pooh mugs for children and other kitchen
accessories from oven gloves and aprons
to salt and pepper shakers and forks are
up for sale in this 3,500sqft showroom.

## Drapes Avenue

*Ramanashree Chambers, 37
Lady Curzon Road, Bangalore 560001*
**Tel** *2559 2253*
**Open** *10am to 8pm. Closed on Sunday.*
**Cards** *All*

Drapes Avenue has a good collection of
furnishing fabrics for curtains and
upholstery, bedroom and bathroom linen
in variegated shades and textures, all
displayed in a brightly lit air-conditioned
store. Silk, satin, jacquard, polyester and
cotton fabrics are available in paisley

prints, bold checks and vibrant floral
designs. Half price sales are a regular
feature and furnishing for offices is also
available here.

## Maa House of Fabrics

*27 Safina Plaza, 84/85 Infantry Road,
Bangalore 560001*
**Tel** *2559 1376*
**Open** *10am to 8pm*
**Cards** *All except American Express*

Maa is a treasure trove of exclusive
fabrics that can be turned into anything
from clothing to upholstery. Bales of silk,
cotton and blended fabrics in muted
colours have a strictly contemporary feel.
Tussar is blended with noile, Moonga,
viscose and Matka, while lurex and lycra
combine with pure silk. Linen is available
in cotton and silk blends. Organza
streaked with velvet is another eye
catching mix. Stable silk and ghica silk
come in a variety of stripes, checks and
jacquard textures. Gossamer organzas,
net and mesh are also available in
dazzling blends to form dupattas, scarves
and stoles. Maa also stocks a limited
edition of saris in Tussar and cotton
blends. Mostly in vegetable hues they
also have funky solids like hot pink and
turquoise. The unstitched fabric comes in
44-inch yardage. Most of the fabric has
to be dry cleaned only. Many hi-fashion
designers from the city source their
fabric from Maa.

## Shyam Ahuja

*67/8 Lavelle Road, 4th Cross,
Bangalore 560001*
**Tel** *5672 9604*
**Open** *10am to 7pm*
**Cards** *All*

Shyam Ahuja brought style to the humble
Indian dhurrie. His love affair with the flat
woven rug gave him a chance to reinvent
tradition and make it a high end, must
have of the 20th century. Most westerners
see it as an Indian version of the quilt.
Trademark colours are unusual pastels –
misty blue, clear yellow and translucent
aquamarine were seen for the first time
ever in these rugs – a perfect refuge from
the clutter of urban city life. Now bold and
striking colours have added a new
dimension to these rugs.

Shyam Ahuja has also been the first to
produce dhurries in a wool weft apart
from the cotton ones. The store has
elegant furnishings in cotton and silk as
well. They also have cushion covers, bed
covers, towels and miscellaneous items
like scarves and bags.
Below the showroom there is a surplus
store in which bargain hunters get
genuine discounts. Don't miss their
annual Diwali sales in which discounts
go up to 50 per cent on the entire range
of merchandise.

## The Swadeshi Store

*31 Krishnanagar Industrial Layout,
Hosur Main Road, Bangalore 560095*
**Tel** *2553 2061*
**Open** *10am to 6:30pm. Closed on Sunday.*
**Cards** *All*

A furnishing and accessories store with
pure cotton handlooms, Swadeshi has
some loyal clientele. Everything from
bedspreads and cushion covers to table
linen and kitchen sets are available
here. The accessories are elegant, eco
friendly and easy on the pocket too.
A small selection of clothes are
pre-washed and dyed with azo-free
dyes. Fabric designs feature bold checks
and creative plaids.

## Yamini

*Arrosim Beach, 11/2 Haudin Road,
Ulsoor, Bangalore 560042*
**Tel** *5113 4781/4782/4783*
**Open** *10:30am to 7:30pm*
**Cards** *All*

Yamini's range of home decor products is
a celebration of both colour and texture.
Hand woven textiles and products
sourced from all over the country are
turned into the simplest and most usable
mats, bed covers, curtains etc.
Upholstery fabric by the metre in cotton
and silk and a line of delicate, sheer
fabrics are on offer. They have a range of
cushion covers, bedspreads, throws as
well as bath and table linen. Checked
cotton tablecloths as well as yard dyed
and richer fabrics with embroidery and
texture are available here. This includes
crisp organdy with appliqué and
embroidery as well as silks and tissues.
Interesting trivia like napkin holders,
beaded coasters, candle stands, lamps
and net sheer bags make great gifts.
Yamini has an interesting calendar of
events all year through. From tabletop
sales to cushion cover melas and the
annual X'mas fair, it is definitely worth a
visit. The store faces Ulsoor Lake and has
wonderful interiors that complement the
Yamini look.

## FRAMERS

### Lakshana Art Gallery

*29/2 Race Course Road, Bangalore 560001*
**Tel** *2220 7946/1078*
**Open** *11am to 7pm. Closed on Sunday.*
**Cards** *All*

One of Bangalore's best framers, they
have now evolved into a full fledged art

gallery. Imported prints, European
picture frames and paintings of the city's
prominent artists are up for sale here.

## Picture Perfecte

*278, 5th Main, 6th cross, I Stage,
Indiranagar, Bangalore 560038*
**Tel** *98441 18544*
**Open** *10:30am to 6pm*
**Cards** *Not Accepted*

This small, quaint store stocks a variety
of picture frames, both Indian and
imported, in a variety of sizes, shapes
and textures. The assortment has been
helpfully displayed on the wall. The
range stretches from wooden and
synthetic to antique and contemporary.
Mounting material is used innovatively
with handmade paper, self-design, raw
silk and jute as some of the options.
Picture Perfecte also stocks prints
sourced from Markham, UK. Prices range
from Rs 200 to Rs 950.

## BOOKS & STATIONERY

### Crossword

*ACR Towers, Opp. Gateway Hotel,
32 Residency Road, Bangalore 560025*
**Tel** *2558 2411*
**Open** *10:30am to 9pm*
**Cards** *All*

Crossword is a large, well-lit store
spread over two floors, with a café
attached. Expect the usual collection of
fiction, non-fiction, children's books and
magazines, neatly categorised for easy
browsing. The first floor has a collection
of CDs, board games, toys, stationery
and DVDs. Crossword also offers a Dial-
A-Book facility where you can call and
order books and avail the free home
delivery service. This should find many
takers among booklovers who don't
dare the traffic or the trek, although
parking is plentiful.

### Fountainhead

*41 Lavelle Road, Bangalore 560001*
**Tel** *2221 9777*
**Open** *10am to 8:30pm.
Closed on Monday.*
**Cards** *All*

Fountainhead is one of the well known
bookstores in the city with branches in
Chennai and Mumbai. This spacious
store has a good collection of books
across all subjects. Fountainhead's pick
of books ranges from the coffee table
variety and the classics to new Indian
English writers and sci-fi. They also
carry a wide collection of educational,
self help and children's books. Their
range of international magazines is
very impressive. There's a small
toyshop in one corner and stacks of
greeting cards.

### Gangarams Book Bureau

*72 MG Road, Bangalore 560001*
**Tel** *2558 5293*
**Open** *10am to 8pm.
Closed on Sunday.*
**Cards** *All*

One of the older bookstores in the city, the multi-storeyed Gangarams is also one of the most reputed. Spread across three floors, the busy bookstore offers lots of titles on subjects ranging from interior design to astrophysics. The usual bestsellers and pulp vie with the greeting card and stationery section. The entire third floor is dedicated to academia with a range of educational books and learning material, textbooks on management, psychology etc. The second floor houses all the bestsellers, magazines, post cards and a good selection of non-fiction books as well. Gangarams also stocks the latest DVDs and CD-ROMs, games as well as educational.

## Higginbothams

*74 MG Road, Bangalore 560001*
*Tel 2558 7359*
*Open 9am to 8pm. 10am to 8pm on Sunday.*
*Cards All*

Higginbothams has been outpaced by other bookstores but its charming edifice is still an attraction. There is a stationery store here as well.

## Landmark

*The Forum, 21 Hosur Road, Koramangala, Bangalore 560029*
*Tel 2206 7640*
*Open 9am to 9pm*
*Cards All except American Express*

Patrons of the Chennai based bookstore

will welcome the sprawling new cousin in silicon city. A worthy addition to Bangalore's list of top league bookshops, Landmark aims to be more than just a browsing nook. Spread across 45,000 sqft, it has positioned itself as a family leisure and lifestyle store. Set in the upmarket Forum mall, the store stocks books, toys, t-shirts, bags, stationery, gifts, DVDs, music and even home furnishings. A large selection of titles with 150 catalogues, neatly demarcated sections and a snazzy setting make up the Landmark package. There is an exhaustive collection of books on topics ranging from pulp and self help to philosophy and art. The store plans to organise theatre workshops, musical shows and events for kids. Landmark has a website where books and music can be bought online.

## L B Publishers

*90-91 MG Road, Bangalore 560001*
*Tel 2558 7621*
*Open 10am to 7pm. 3:30pm to 8pm on Sunday.*
*Cards All*

All the bestsellers and a few others may be found here. There is a good selection of titles for children.

## Premier Book Shop

*46/1 Church Street, Bangalore 560001*
*Tel 2558 8570*
*Open 10am to 1:30pm and 3pm to 8pm. 10am to 12:30pm on Sunday.*
*Cards All*

Premier is almost an institution in Bangalore. At the entrance sits the owner, guarding a fabulous collection of books – best sellers, pulp, literary tomes and others – placed in teetering towers. He is happy to share his encyclopaedic knowledge and quick to dish out discounts to genuine readers.

## Prism

*16, 11th Main, IV Block Jayanagar, Bangalore 560011*
*Tel 2663 7527*
*Open 10am to 9pm*
*Cards All*

This is the best known bookstore in Jayanagar. A smallish store it nonetheless stocks a good selection of titles and discounts are offered liberally.

## Sankars the book people

*15/2 Upstairs, Madras Bank Road, Off St. Mark's Road, Bangalore 560001*
*Tel 2558 6868/6867*
*Branches Airport, 2522 7418;*
*Taj Residency, 2532 5621;*
*Bangalore Central 5112 4170;*
*Le Meridien, 2220 7156;*
*Safina Plaza, 2559 5074;*
*William Penn, 2563 3161;*
*The Atria Hotel, 2225 6785*
*Rangashankara, 2649 4656*
*Open 10am to 8:30pm. 11am to 8pm on Sunday.*
*Cards All except American Express*

For many decades now, busy travellers bustling in and out of the city airport, treated themselves to a book from Sankars over a quick chat with its erudite owners. N Sankaran and Vivek Sankaran,

a father and son team, ably manage this chain of bookshops. Once known as the Airport Bookstore, Sankars now has shops spread over the city – on Madras Bank Road, in Taj Residency, Le Meriden and Safina Plaza to name a few. Their stores stock an impressive array of fiction, non fiction and coffee table books. There are usually a good selection of bestsellers and regular topics with thoughtful seating on hand! Their large outlet on Madras Bank Road is not only a storehouse of books but is a venue for book launches, poetry readings and meet-the-author sessions as well. Comfortable couches placed in the store allow for leisurely browsing.

A play corner with a slide for the kids, mural exhibits by popular artists and a mock Sistine Chapel fresco are other attractive features of this store.

## Sapna Book House

*Thunga Complex, Gandhinagar,*
*Bangalore 560009*
***Tel** 2226 6088*
***Branch** Sadashivnagar, 2344 6444;*
*Jayanagar, 5130 7322*
***Open** 10am to 2pm and 3pm to 8pm.*
*Closed on Sunday.*
***Cards** All*

Set in the busy market district, Sapna is famous for its array of educational books. Most city students browse here for textbooks and guides.

## Select Book Shop

*71 Brigade Road Cross, Bangalore 560001*
***Tel** 2558 0770*
***Open** 11am to 6:30pm. 11am to 5:30pm*
*on Sunday.*
***Cards** Not Accepted*

Both old and new books feature at the Select Book Shop. It has an interesting mix of rare books and bestsellers and a small art gallery featuring the work of local artists. Bibliophiles will be happy with a trip. The owner is willing to procure rare and out-of-print stuff.

## Strand Book Stall

*113-114 Manipal Centre,*
*47 Dickenson Road, Bangalore 560042*
***Tel** 2558 0000/2222*
***Open** 10:30am to 8pm.*
*Closed on Sunday.*
***Cards** All except American Express*

Strand rises above regular bookshops with its annual book fair, regular book readings and website. Known for

Sankars, the book people

offering sizeable discounts, the store is air-conditioned, nicely laid out and houses a varied collection of books. On the shelves are textbooks, popular fiction and some eclectic titles as well.

Strand opened its first store in Mumbai in 1948 and the Bangalore branch came more recently. Vidya Virkar, the proprietess believes in interacting closely with her customers, a tradition she has inherited from her well known father, TN Shanbag who started the original Strand in Mumbai. Strand also procures books that are not available at the store and customers are assisted with book imports for a reasonable fee.

## The Oxford Book Store

*Leela Galleria, The Leela Palace,*
*Airport Road, Bangalore 560008*
***Tel** 5115 5222*
***Open** 10am to 10pm*
***Cards** All*

The Kolkata based Oxford Book Store is the toast of Bangalore's literati. It's one of the few bookstores to boast comfortable chairs for browsers! A number of prestigious book readings are held here and autographed books are piled in a separate corner.

Of almost equal importance is the Cha Bar located alongside where book lovers presumably retire to sip a cup of delicately flavoured Darjeeling tea and peruse their buys. On sale is Oxford Book Store merchandise like 'I am a bookworm' bags. Stationery, notebooks and frames made of handmade paper and art supplies are also available here.

## William Penn

*145, 1ˢᵗ Main, V Block, Koramangala,*
*Bangalore 560095*
***Tel** 2553 7803, 5110 4428*
***Branch** The Forum, 3062 1999*
***Open** 10:30am to 8:30pm. Closed on Monday.*
***Cards** All*

High quality stationery items are available here. The shop is frequented by youngsters who drop in here to take their pick from a wide range of trendy items.

## FLORISTS

## Floral Designs

*42, Vittal Mallya Road, Bangalore 560001*
***Tel** 2299 7444*
***Open** 8am to 10pm*
***Cards** All*

Hi-fashion street's florist has gereberas, alstermarias, birds of paradise, orchids, lilies, chrysanthemums, roses and the exotic ginger lilies among others. They offer to deliver anywhere in Bangalore at a nominal charge.

## Lovely Florists

*26 Devatha Plaza, 131 Residency Road,*
*Bangalore 560025*
***Tel** 2207 5099*
***Open** 8am to 9pm*
***Cards** Not Accepted*

Orchids, lilies, chrysanthemums, carnations, roses, African daisies and even an assortment of dry flowers can be bought here. You can choose from some pre-arranged ones or try your hand at some personalised bunches.

## Ohana Fine Flowers

*23 Airport Road, The Leela Palace,*
*Leela Galleria, Bangalore 560008*
***Tel** 3090 6030*
***Open** 10am to 7pm*
***Cards** Not Accepted*

When you want to say it with flowers your choices are usually limited to an array of roses and carnations standing poker straight in wire vases, or seasonal flowers and ferns stuffed symmetrically into florist foam. Bored stiff? Try Ohana. They've single handedly raised the bar of flower styling to breathtaking and highly

original levels. Orchids and gingers, proteas and chrysanthemum, Birds of Paradise and wax flowers socialise with wild berries and eucalyptus and share a vase with tall haliconeas and rhododendrons. Branches laden with the fruit of tiny pears, lemon and even custard apple serve as fillers to the whole ensemble. Free flowing arrangements in tall glass cylinders set the mood of the store.

Ohana gets a special consignment of flowers from Australia, a fact that accounts for the rare and unusual flowers in their arrangements. They also source flowers from all over the country. The mundane and the exotic, flowers and rare foliage, are carefully assembled for maximum effect. The styling is simple and stunning. Dutch bouquets and flower boxes are also their speciality. Even if flowers are not on your list, this store is aesthetically pleasing. It deserves a visit.

## Sri Flowers

*Devatha Plaza, 131 Residency Road,*
*Bangalore 560025*
***Tel** 2227 8016*
***Open** 7:30am to 9:30pm*
***Cards** Not Accepted*

White lilies and magenta gerberas, purple and white Gladioli, orange and crimson carnations, violet Aster and the ubiquitous rose are arranged in cheerful bouquets and stiff vases.

The offer for home delivery is worth considering.

## Orchidia

*2281/B, 14ᵗʰ A Main, HAL II Stage*
*Indiranagar, Bangalore 560008*
***Tel** 2521 7118, 5116 1941*
***Open** 9am to 5:30pm*
***Cards** Not Accepted*

For some of the most unusual flowers and shrubs it is absolutely essential to seek out Orchidia, set in a non-descript house off Indiranagar's busy 100Ft. road. Fresh flowers come in everyday from their farm and greenhouses outside the city and are dispatched to other Indian metros. Lamonia, all shades of lillies, chrysantheums and gerberas are just some of the beauties on sale.

Orchidia also sells a wide variety of exotic vegetables like red and yellow bell peppers, asparagus, bokchoy, four types of salad leaves, purple cabbage, broccoli and a startling variety of fresh herbs, oregano and basil to name a few.

## SPECIALITY FOOD STORES

## All Saints

*126/2 Brigade Road, Bangalore 560025*
***Tel** 2557 2091*
***Open** 7am to 9pm. 7am to 9:30pm on*
*Sunday.*
***Cards** All*

Named after a well known church on Hosur Road, All Saints was originally a

Landmark is a bookstore that also stocks music and home furnishings.

small bakery off Brigade Road and its exciting range of breads, array of baked goodies and freshly baked pastries continue to draw in the crowds and old timers. It also stocks helpful Indian accompaniments like parathas, appams, sannas and others.

All Saints is well stocked with groceries, fresh vegetables and dairy products. Electrical fittings, floor scrubbers, soft drinks, candles and soaps are also available.

## Bamburies

*39/1 Opposite Cathedral High School, Richmond Road, Bangalore 560025*
*Tel 2530 1949*
**Open** *8:30am to 8pm. 9am to 1pm on Sunday.*
**Card** *All except American Express*

Bamburies provides you with fresh meat and fish without the chaos of the market. This is a small family run shop with a reputation for high quality that goes back 30 years. The choicest cuts of fish, meat, poultry and offal may be found here. Bamburies is well known for pre-processed and pre-cooked foods with a homemade taste. Roast beef, smoked salted beef, smoked chicken loaf, chicken pepperoni, ham made from chicken and gammon are on offer. They have a large variety of sausages, cutlets and crumb chops that are ready-to-fry. Vindaloo, Sorpatel and Tandoori Chicken are ready-to-heat foods that are extremely popular. The stuffed beef roll with bacon, onions and herbs is definitely worth sampling.

Bamburies' products are available only across the counter at their one store. They do not undertake home delivery.

## Daily Bread

*43, 4th Cross, V Block, Koramangala, Bangalore 560095*
*Tel 2563 1302/1304*
**Branches** *Chruch Street, 2559 1717; The Forum, 2206 7656*
**Open** *10am to 8:30pm*
**Cards** *Not Accepted*

This spanking new bakery has a wide selection of freshly baked breads, cookies, pastries and other speciality baked foods along with a fine selection of wines and beers. The platter of European breads includes exotic varieties like the Scandinavian Dark Rye, Russian Potato Bread and Welsh Fruit Loaf as well as healthy and wholesome multigrain breads like the Spinach Loaf. The pastry spread ranges from delectable Sacher Torte and Hamburg Harbor Harlequin to Chocolate Wrapped Berry Cheese Cake and Chocolate Praline Gateaux. A smorgasbord of gourmet sandwiches and pizzas is also served here.

# DEPARTMENTAL STORES

## Big Bazaar

*Hosur Main Road,*
*Near Madiwala Check Post,*
*Koramangala, Bangalore 560095*
*Tel 2552 0761*
**Open** *10am to 10pm*
**Cards** *All*

Generous discounts, perennial offers and a wide range of products under one roof make Big Bazaar a favourite with city shoppers. Aptly named, the roomy store covers an area of 40,000sqft. Practically every product on your shopping list from groceries to jewellery can be bought here. A division of Pantaloon Retail India, the bazaar has something for everybody. The different sections house clothes for men, women and children, furniture, cookware, footwear, accessories like bags, watches, glassware, gizmos, gifts and stationery. A sizeable section is dedicated to footwear and toys. The Food Bazaar is the highlight of the store with plenty of groceries as well as packaged food. Fresh-from-the-farm fruits and vegetables are sold with sizeable discounts. A photographer, chemist, optician, bakery and automobile accessory section complete the shopping experience!

## FabMall

*777E 100Ft. Road, Indiranagar, Bangalore 560038*
*Tel 5699 1216*
**Branches** *Airport Road, 2523 0863; St. Marks Road, 5112 0408; Koramangala, 2550 1745; Bannerghatta Road, 2648 0722*
**Open** *8:30am to 9:30pm*
**Cards** *All*

FabMall, an online shopping portal with the same name, is also a brick and mortar supermarket. A wide range of products from books, apparel, CD-ROMs, flowers, home appliances, groceries, music, jewellery and toys can be purchased here. Also available are computer products, electronic gizmos, healthcare equipment, mobile phones, paintings and portraits, handicrafts, leather items and more. Some attractive super savers are on offer.

## Food World

*MG Road, Bangalore 560001*
*Tel 5112 1561*
**Branches** *Banashankari, 2679 2684; Basavanagudi, 2650 9583; Cox Town, 2548 7380; CMH Road, 5415 3001; Jayanagar, 2634 2714; JP Nagar, 2659 7614; Koramangala, 5410 4507; Basaveshwara Nagar, 2338 2977; RT Nagar, 2353 0557; Sanjay Nagar, 2351 1365; Vijayanagar, 2350 0719; Bangalore Club, 2227 2518; BTM Layout, 2678 1845; Cunningham Road, 2228 9380; Electronics City (Infosys), 5410 2701; Jayanagar VII Block, 2653 4694; Kammanahalli, 2544 8446; Malleswaram, 5412 7561; Rajarajeswari Nagar, 860 3447; Sadashivnagar, 2361 6730; Vidyaranyapura, 2364 1447; Electronics City (Wipro), 5410 3101; Langford Town, 5414 6056; Koramangala, 51102090*
**Open** *9am to 9pm*
**Cards** *All*

Food World's well stocked aisles are replacing the friendly neighbourhood

grocery store in all corners of the city. Fresh vegetables and fruits, groceries, dairy products, kitchen utensils, toiletries, pet food and even liquor (in some places) are stocked here.

The big Food World on MG Road has a lively air with snack counters, product promos and huge crowds on weekends and evenings.

## Monday To Sunday

*Food Express Stores India Ltd., 547 Premier Court, CMH Road, Indiranagar, Bangalore 560038*
*Tel 2520 1647, 2529 5871*
**Branches** *Koramangala, 2563 0168; JP Nagar, 5121 4121*
**Open** *9am to 9:30pm*
**Cards** *All*

Working professionals and hostesses planning an exotic meal all head to Monday to Sunday (M2S), a one stop shop for convenience foods that stocks salt and salsa, tomatoes and tomyum soup paste, appams and all spices! Readymade foods, pre-cooked food, frozen food, ready-to-fry food, ready-to-heat, heat and serve fill the shelves. There are many easy and practical options to choose from: Appams and chappatis, idli/vada batter, hot dogs and hariyali tikkas allow you to whisk up a meal in no time. For the more ambitious there is Malabar vegetable curry (Avial), Khara Bhath (Bangalore vegetable upma) and so on.

M2S has a good bakery section. Bread rolls, packaged biscuits and delicious, creamy cakes as well as a variety of domestic and imported cheese and butter, and different kinds of tofu are available. For the Pasta inclined there is Penne, Rigate, Spaghetti, Spaghettini, Lasagne along with readymade Pasta sauces and green and black olives. Look for Orchard Fresh ice cream, which uses only natural flavours to make a great dessert. They have a large selection of cold meats as well. You can stock up on your fruits and veggies for the week. They even have pre-cut veggies to give you a headstart on your cooking.

Exotic fruits and vegetables at Namdhari's Fresh

## Namdhari's Fresh

*134 Doopanahalli Road, Indiranagar,*
*Bangalore 560071*
*Tel 5115 2910*
*Branches Koramangala, 5110 3777*
*Sadashivnagar, 5123 6134/35*
*Open 9am to 9pm*
*Cards All except American Express*

Namdhari's somehow gives you the feeling that you get to meet the farmer when you pick out the veggies! Regular gourds and onions sell along with exotic veggies like asparagus and an impressive line up of herbs. You don't have to make a separate visit to plan a gourmet meal. Artichokes, asparagus, sno peas, zucchini, brussel sprouts, Haricot verts and even Chinese kale and pokchoy are available along with a variety of salad leaves and sprouts, coloured peppers, pearl, cherry and salad tomatoes as well as fresh herbs like lemon grass and basil.
A certified exporter, Namdhari's Fresh is based in Bangalore with production centres all over the country. They grow over 40 different fruits and vegetables, using organic manure, bio-agents and other integrated pest management practices. They also import a large variety of fruit like Chinese apples, oranges from Brazil, Australian grapes, kiwi and passion fruit among others. Produce for the day is brought in once in the morning and is available by 11:30am. Namdhari also houses a popular salad bar – here you can sample a range of healthy salads, fresh fruit juices and some innovative sandwiches.

## Nilgiris

*171 Brigade Road, Next to Rex Theatre,*
*Bangalore 560025*
*Tel 2558 1859*
*Branch Airport Road, 2526 6956*
*Open 9:30am to 8:30pm.*
*Closed on Sunday.*
*Cards All*

For a one-stop home and kitchen shopping, try Nilgiris and you'll never want to shop anywhere else! The array of products is comprehensive and fresh and the sales staff is extremely helpful. Well known for its dairy products like milk, butter, cheese and freshly baked pastries and breads, it also stocks its own brand of spices, flour, rice and a range of frozen meat, fish products, imported foods and beverages, wines, soft drinks, cosmetics and just about anything else.
Part of a south Indian chain of supermarkets, Nilgiris has grown from a small bakery to a vast shopping network. There is a special cake section in the basement and a popular café on the mezzanine floor.

## Not Just Wine and Cheese

*132, Brigade Road, Bangalore 560001*
*Tel 5123 5642*
*Open 10am to 10pm*
*Cards All except American Express*

Finally a store that celebrates the revered tradition of wine and cheese! Imported cheese and wine are sold under the same roof here. Choose from seven varieties of cheese including Goat's cheese, Demi-sel, Petit-Suisse, Baby Hvati, Gouda and Camembert. The wines on offer are Californian Red and White, Mistral Red and White, Carlorossa Red and White and the Indian Riviera Red and White. Try some well tested combinations: Strong cheese with sweet wine, goat cheese with rose wine, hard cheese with white wine, blue cheese with red wine and soft cheese with chilled, fruity wine. Beers, cocktails and champagnes are also retailed here. Home delivery is an option.

## Supermarket

*5th Avenue, 183 Brigade Road,*
*Bangalore 560025*
*Tel 2558 1248*
*Open 9am to 8pm. Closed on Sunday.*
*Cards All*

Supermarket is a food store located smack in the middle of Brigade Road. This little shop is a food aficionado's delight. It contains virtually all the exotic food ingredients that you will ever need. From Miso paste to rice sticks and seaweed noodles to skins for samosas and spring rolls, Supermarket is a good bet. If Mexican, Thai, Chinese, Italian, Japanese and Parsi cuisine are on your regular cooking list, shop here for good quality condiments. They also have a large variety of cheeses ranging from Mascarpone, Fondue, Gouda to Brie and Emmental. Pastas as well as sauces, diet jams, Parsi pickle, vinegars, salad dressings, cookies, crackers, canned fruits, herbs, spices and other food trivia are sure to be available here. Supermarket also stocks Bombay and Gujarati short eats which are very popular: Dhokla, Khakra, Panipuri paste, Tamarind Date Chutney, Bombay Bhel and Khari biscuits.

## HEALTHCARE STORES

## Health & Glow

*21 CMH Road, Indiranagar,*
*Bangalore 560038*
*Tel 5115 3004*
*Branches Commercial Street, 2558*
*1524; Malleswaram, 5112 7566*
*RT Nagar, 5124 4106; JP Nagar, 5121*
*4001; Brigade Road, 5112 2233;*
*Koramangala, 5110 4405; Jayanagar,*
*5121 0450; Basaveshwaranagar 5128*
*7201; Airport Road, 2522 6778;*
*Basavanagudi, 5120 4537; The Forum,*
*2206 7790; Victoria Road, 3090 0677*
*Open 9am to 9pm*
*Cards All*

Is a foot cream for cracked soles a cosmetic or a pharma product? Should Ayurvedic drugs be sold alongside allopathic? Somebody somewhere discovered that customers enjoy buying drugs and cosmetics at the same time, the line somewhat blurred for many products. Enter, Health & Glow, a chain of stores that deals exclusively in healthcare products and cosmetics. Synthetic and herbal cosmetics, hot water bottles and weighing scales, stuffed toys and hair accessories are all sold under one roof. An array of international brands like Chambor, Maybelline, Marks & Spencer's and Revlon as well as Shahnaz Hussain and Himalaya Herbal Healthcare products may be found here.
There is a pharmacy counter where non-prescription drugs for diabetes, blood pressure, obesity and stress are sold as well as regular prescription ones. Clearly demarcated counters, such as personal care, baby care, men's care and aromatherapy products make shopping a pleasant affair. From basic toiletries to exclusive brands, Health & Glow has an extensive stock of merchandise with enough sales personnel and testers to go around as well. Chocolates and other small treats are also available here. A few select stores have an in-house beauty salon. Online shopping and home delivery is offered.

## Himalaya Herbal Healthcare

*24 CMH Road, Indiranagar II Stage,*
*Bangalore 560038*
*Tel 2521 9916*
*Branches Malleswaram, 2346 6678;*
*Basavanagudi, 2652 0417;*
*Basaveshwaranagar, 2358 3667;*
*Cox Town, 5125 2288;*
*Race Course Road, 3062 4028*
*Open 9am to 9pm*
*Cards All*

This is a one-stop-shop for herbal products from The Himalaya Drug Company, a path breaking synergy of traditional Ayurveda and modern technology. Not your everyday pharmacy or a stuffy Ayurvedic drug store, this cheerful chain of outlets stocks a range of pharmaceutical and personal care products. The herbal healthcare range is extensive – a variety of skin, hair and healthcare supplies as well as cosmetics like face toners, cleansers, fairness creams, soap free shampoo, slimming pills, foot care cream and hair conditioners can be picked up here. The entire store is helpfully labelled and meticulously arranged into categories. Moisturisers, dental cream, behaviour modifiers and pain relieving balm may be purchased here. Anti-stress pills, digestive capsules, memory enhancers and immune guard syrups are some of the popular products that can be bought off the shelf. Their famous innovations include the liver concoction Liv. 52, Reosto for Osteoporosis, acid neutralising agent Himcocid and stress reliever Mentat. All products are made with natural ingredients and claim to have no side effects.
There is an interesting selection of teas available including green tea, sleep tea, tea for digestion and Kof Tea to relieve chest congestion. Pure herb extracts from amalaki, tulsi, brahmi, karela and neem are sold here. A range of grooming products for animals is also on offer.

The Himalaya Herbal Healthcare store

The Taj West End, a luxury hotel in the city, is set amidst an abundance of exotic flowers and foliage.

# Accommodation

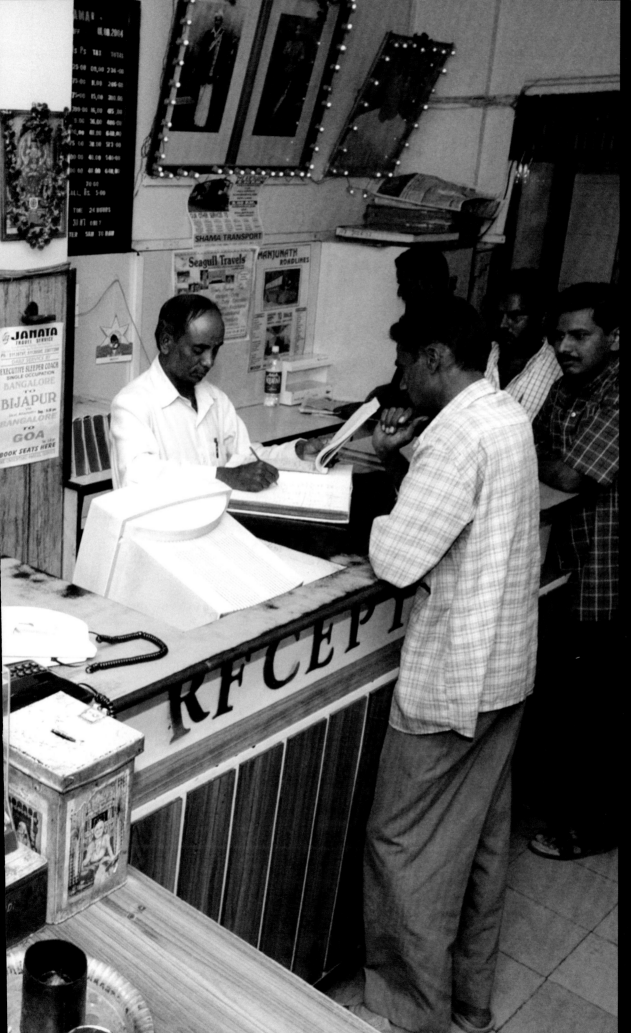

Bangalore is home to many hospitable hotels and lodges that cater to varying preferences including those on a shoestring budget. They promise a comfortable stay at a low price.

# Accommodation

Visitors to Bangalore get to choose from hotel suites with their own private gardens to no-fuss lodges, furnished apartments rented by the week, bed and breakfast rooms, palaces, old villas and an exciting array in between. Outside the city there are a host of resorts to choose from. Golfers, art enthusiasts and sports fanatics, each have a resort to call their own. Typically spread over an area of two to 20 acres, its green and uncluttered environs are a tonic for weary urbanites. For longer stays there is the serviced apartment, a home away from home. Welcome to Bangalore, where hospitality has many faces.

Many business travellers prefer the comfort of fully furnished serviced apartments.

Accommodation

## Spoilt for Choice

Starting at the top end there are many deluxe hotels located in the centre of the city. Patronised by the rich and powerful, they offer the usual amenities like 24-hour room service, laundry, choice of suites, swimming pools, health clubs and beauty salons. Speciality restaurants and nightclubs add a sparkle and the view from the rooms – of **golfing greens**, **tropical gardens** and **landscaped lawns** – more than rests the eye. Almost all of them have business centres, boardroom facilities and large halls that are popular venues for big conventions.

The **mid range hotels** score points for their choice of location – most are in and around **MG Road**, Bangalore's most famous address. Basic requirements like a travel desk, car rentals, a gym, doctor on call, banquet and conference facilities may be counted upon. Often, there is a multicuisine restaurant attached.

The backpacker or budget traveller expects **minimum fuss** at the **lowest price** and there are plenty of hotels that fit the bill. Even so, attached bathrooms and hot and cold water may be expected. You may get lucky with a television set, telephone line and sometimes even Internet connectivity. We bring you some places that are either close to the commercial part of town, or near the railway station and bus stand so that getting around is easy.

## On the Outskirts

There are over **50 resorts** on the outskirts of the city, offering a quick escape from the noise and pollution of urban life. **Sports facilities** are a big attraction as are kiddie activities like **water slides** and **amusement arcades**. If you can't find the time to exercise during the week, you can try your hand here at swimming, badminton, tennis, squash etc once you check in or sign up for the day. **Gyms** are the rage and most come with a sauna to complete the effect. Almost all of them have a children's play area, a big boon for families with small kids.

**Golfing weekends** are another option. Most golfers are only too happy to wake up to a golf course outside their bedroom window! There is the added attraction of golf coaching for those who want to start playing.

For the more adventurous there is **parasailing**, **paragliding** and visits to national parks.

The hottest resorts are the ones that offer a health benefit like Ayurvedic treatments to de-stress or holistic healing practices that promise to rejuvenate.

Corporate houses and IT companies use resorts to conduct training camps, seminars and conferences. Most resorts are adequately equipped to deal with large numbers and some even offer their own special brand of training.

## Serviced Apartments

The IT boom has brought a new kind of traveller to Bangalore – the professional on a short term visit, often with a young family in tow. Staying in a hotel for extended periods is not an attractive option and renting a house for a few months has its drawbacks. The perfect solution has emerged – the serviced apartment – checking in is as easy as in a hotel and after that there's the **comfort of a home**.

Typically, serviced apartments are furnished with a living room, bedroom, kitchenette, telephones and appliances like microwave ovens, television sets and music systems. Some of them even have gyms and a business centre attached.

Most of Bangalore's serviced apartments are **conveniently located** in the central business districts and adjoining areas. A few provide complimentary breakfast, while others have a grocery store in the apartment complex or arrange for caterers to supply lunch and dinner.

## Great Properties

A modern day palace, a **regency manor** or even a **rustic retreat** with a five star ambience, Bangalore's hotels are distinct and eclectic. The Leela Palace is built on the lines of the famous Mysore Palace with fabulously landscaped gardens and fountains in royal fashion. The ITC Hotel Windsor Sheraton's tall white columns recreate the Manor houses of London, and The Oberoi's **tropical retreat** blends beautifully into the garden city.

Villa Pottipatti brings back memories of a time when all Bangalore houses had monkey tops, plenty of fruit trees and acres of garden. Set in the traditional bastion of Malleswaram, you can stroll through colourful flower and vegetable markets nearby for the full flavour.

The old Barton's Bed and Breakfast from the 70s has given way to the penthouse Hotel Ivory Towers, an all-suite hotel with fabulous views of the city. The boarding house for British soldiers has turned into the classy West End. Chic and trendy, The Park was recently listed as one of the **top 101** hotels in the world by *Tatler* magazine.

The resorts outside the city hold their own. Eagleton is an 18-hole, 72-par US PGA course set on 500 acres while Kuteeram fills an **ethnic niche** with its rustic charm and proximity to dance village Nrityagram.

*Stark World – Bangalore & Karnataka* brings you a comprehensive list of hotels, classified as luxury, business and budget along with a list of resorts and serviced apartments in the city. Each category carries only the best known hotels and **critical information** like the address and telephone numbers, check in/out time and of course, tariffs. To further help you decide we have included **important tips** like whether it has a suite with private garden, steam and sauna facilities, Internet connectivity and so on. Enjoy your stay!

## LUXURY HOTELS

### The Leela Palace

*23 Kodihalli, Airport Road,*
*Bangalore 560008*
*Tel 2521 1234 Fax 2521 7423*
*Tariff Rs 9,000 to Rs 65,000*
*Cards All*
*Check in/out 12noon*
*Web www.theleela.com*

For sheer opulence try The Leela Palace. From the gilt edged ceiling to the international spa, the plush shopping arcade with top Indian and global brands to the fog-free mirrors in the bathrooms, this is clearly Bangalore's last word in luxury! All this comes for a hefty price, so if you're on a middleclass budget, skip the stay and settle for some serious window shopping instead!

Lavishly landscaped, The Leela Palace is the city's newest luxury hotel, close to the airport and a 20-minute drive from the International Technology Park. It's equipped with a business centre, banqueting and conferencing facilities, boardrooms, ballrooms, a sprawling commercial complex and shopping arcade, a gymnasium, a swimming pool and an exclusive spa offering Ayurvedic and Western treatments. Theme restaurants, 254 rooms and suites with handcrafted furniture, DVD players, an electronic safe, two-line telephone, high speed Internet access, luxurious bathrooms with Italian marble and fog-free mirrors and a bar

are other highlights.

The 24-hour coffee shop **Citrus** serves Mediterranean fare and has a sumptuous buffet with some interesting theme-based evenings. For serious dining there is the highly rated **Jamavar** that offers a choice of pan-Indian cuisine and **Zen** is the pan-Asian restaurant. The **Library Bar** is done up with British style interiors and has a rare collection of books.

### ITC Hotel Windsor Sheraton & Towers

*25 Golf Course Road, Bangalore 560052*
*Tel 2226 9898 Fax 2226 4941*
*Tariff Rs 6,500 to Rs 22,000*
*Cards All*
*Check in/out 12noon*
*Web www.welcomgroup.com*

The ITC Hotel Windsor Sheraton & Towers has a certain indefinable charm all its own. Overlooking the golf course, flanked by the grounds of the Bangalore Palace and posh residential areas and with major historical landmarks a stone's throw away, it attracts the patronage of the powerful. Lots of VIPs like Tony Blair, Elton John and Ranil Wickremsinghe prefer to stay here. It's been the venue for some major international events like the first SAARC meet.

Colonnaded exteriors, landscaped gardens, wood-panelled rooms and Queen Anne furniture define its Regency theme. For business guests there is a separate wing, The Towers, with an

exclusive reception area and all business related amenities, including a boardroom! It even has it's own library style tea and cocktail lounge fittingly called the **Cabinet Lounge.**

The hotel has some splendid banqueting areas, conference and meeting rooms. There is a 24-hour business centre with secretarial services, Internet access, travel desk, golf on request, swimming pool, health club, beauty parlour, men's salon, car rental, book store, a gift store, currency exchange, safe deposit lockers, doctor on call, baby sitting services and 24-hour room service and laundry.

The **Raj Pavilion** is a spacious, well-lit 24-hour restaurant with the air of a conservatory and a menu that is a throwback to the days of the Raj. The jewel in the Windsor Sheraton's crown is undoubtedly **The Royal Afghan** – a popular poolside barbecue restaurant serving cuisine from the Northwest Frontier. For upper class Chinese food there is the **Mahjong Room** and then

# The Leela Palace

Situated right on busy Airport Road, royal looking, rose-pink The Leela Palace is hard to miss. Built in the traditional palace architecture of Mysore with a little art deco thrown in, the hotel is set amidst six acres of perfectly landscaped gardens. Designed by architect Donald Fair-Weather of Wimberley, Allison Tong and Goo, a California-based firm, The Leela Palace has gone the whole hog with colonnaded hallways, grand staircases and spectacular domed roofs.

The Mysore influence is evident everywhere: At the main gate stands a pair of large brass-metal elephants with their trunks pointing upwards. The palm lined approach to the hotel leads past an exquisite black granite fountain with a medallion inlay, into a windswept lobby that overlooks lush gardens, waterfalls, lily ponds and a lazy stream. The garden boasts 300 varieties of blooms, several species of trees, most of them transplanted, three kinds of grass, exquisite waterfalls and lily ponds, 45 varieties of palms and a variety of perennials.

Inside the hotel the grandeur translates into plush hand woven carpets, copper domes, ornate ceilings, alabaster lampshades and intricate carvings on the *yalis* (stone columns carved in the shape of mythical beasts). Priceless brass antiques, fine bone china, hand picked crystals, rich silk brocaded cushions and sparkling chandeliers add to the overall effect.

*23 Kodihalli, Airport Road, Bangalore 560008*
**Tel** *2521 1234* **Web** *www.theleela.com*

there is **Dakshin**. As the name suggests, some of the best examples of food from the four southern states of India are showcased here, served in authetic south Indian style. The watering hole is **Dublin** with an Irish theme and a jolly convivial atmosphere. Hidden away in the depths of the hotel is **Dum Pukht Jolly Nabobs,** a signature restaurant serving 'royal' food gleaned from regal kitchens.

### The Taj West End

*23 Race Course Road,*
*Bangalore 560001*
**Tel** *5660 5660* **Fax** *5660 5700*
**Tariff** *Rs 7,000 to Rs 20,000*
**Cards** *All*
**Check in/out** *12noon*
**Web** *www.tajhotels.com*

A hotel in a luxurious 20-acre garden best describes The Taj West End. Bang opposite the Turf Club, the West End drips with old world charm with white colonial villas, spacious verandahs, well spaced cottages, sit-outs, four-poster beds and mahogany desks set amidst huge trees and flowering shrubs. Guests love the privacy and the comforts of a big hotel.
Rooms with a private verandah overlooking the poolside, with sit-outs or just an old world ambience are available in addition to

13 suites. The Club Lounge is a special facility with private meeting rooms, banquet facilities, a business centre, broadband wireless Internet connectivity, 24-hour room service and laundry.

The hotel has a swimming pool, fitness centre, beauty parlour, travel desk, car rental, bookshop, a floodlit tennis court, walking tracks, currency exchange services, safe deposit lockers, a doctor on

call, babysitting services, meeting rooms and laundry services.
The West End boasts a restaurant, **Poolside Barbeque,** an all-day dining restaurant, **Mynt** and a Vietnamese restaurant, **Blue Ginger**.

# Heritage Hotel

The Taj West End began its innings as a hotel a little over hundred years ago. Set up by the genteel Mrs Bronson in 1887, it was a 10-room boarding house complete with laundry, kitchen, dairy, livery, bakery, stables and magnificent sprawling gardens where Victorian ladies sipped afternoon tea on comfortable cane chairs.

As Bangalore's importance grew, Bronson's became a favourite with British officers moving to the city. The success of the inn prompted Mr Bronson to join his wife's business and soon other bungalows were added: One belonging to the Turf Club situated just across the road from the lodge, and another to the Grenadier Guards, an elite regiment that was stationed here. Parts of these blocks remain as the city's prime examples of Gothic architecture.

History lingers in all corners – in the pretty pieces of Italian tiles to the Bronson's emblem of a grenade with a flash as seen on the façade.

In 1912, business house Spencers, bought West End from the Bronson's for the princely sum of Rs 4,000. In all their extensions they took care to retain the charming tiled roofs, distinctive gables, dormers, monkey-tops and trelliswork that gave the place its country club look.

Spencer's Hotel offered its guests a taste of the good life with a large billiards table, a famous race course across the road, stables, a carriage establishment, racquet courts, a golf course within walking distance and endless costume parties and balls.

Guests who came to stay were so charmed by the place that they almost didn't leave – like the Jagirdar of Arni who stayed for a record 36 years!

In 1962, the West End played proud host to Queen Elizabeth II's entourage. Twenty years later, Spencers International Hotels Limited sold the property to Indian Hotels and it came to be called The Taj West End. Today the West End is part of the Taj Group of Hotels, Resorts and Palaces, one of India's largest and finest global hotel chains. The old cottages have been restored and new blocks of 20 rooms each were built to blend in with the existing Victorian style buildings. The Taj West End has transformed itself into a luxury hotel, offering the best in décor, service and facilities. The recently refurbished rooms sport a contemporary look, equipped with 42-inch plasma television sets, luxurious marble steam bath units, warm, classic furnishing and full butler service. The sprawling 20 acre hotel has a number of mansions, villas and two-floor cottages without elevators. The original block has been retained, with its tiled roof and characteristic monkey tops providing a pleasing contrast among the tall leafy trees. All the rooms and special suites overlook the wooded glades and ambling pathways with banks of coloured blooms. The hotel lobby is brought alive by painted fresco-like murals, the abundance of plants, balustrades and a central atrium through which the sunlight filters in giving it the air of a Victorian conservatory. Artefacts from all corners of the erstwhile British empire are showcased here. Some of the suites even have priceless British lithographs of the region. The hotel's 20-acre property has 15 acres of landscaped gardens and five acres of built-up area. Electric trolleys, called 'buggies' transport guests and luggage to far flung rooms.

Environmentalists take note: There are 45 species of butterflies, 38 species of birds and 54 varieties of trees (the oldest is a 125-year-old Rain tree) like Ashoka, Gulmohar, Indian Rubber, Tamarind, Peepul and 20 varieties of palm including four Sago palms that are more than a 100 years old.

Two new restaurants have opened at the West End – Blue Ginger is the first in the country to offer Vietnamese food and the all-day dining restaurant, Mynt, serves exotic Indian, Lebanese and Italian cuisine.

*23 Race Course Road, Bangalore 560001*
**Tel** *5660 5660* **Web** *www.tajhotels.com*

The Oberoi is one of Bangalore's top end hotels.

## The Oberoi

*37-39 MG Road, Bangalore 560001*
*Tel 2558 5858* **Fax** *2558 5960*
**Tariff** *Rs 8,000 to Rs 25,200*
**Cards** *All*
**Check in/out** *12noon*
**Web** *www.oberoihotels.com*

If you're looking for brisk service along with smart and stylish interiors, The Oberoi is the best choice. Top notch business people love to stay here, but it's not all boardrooms and fax machines. Located on bustling MG Road, barely six kms from the airport, The Oberoi boasts beautifully landscaped gardens that give it a tropical air. Designed around a 75-year old Rain Tree, it has a variety of reputed restaurants and a pretty verandah where a cup of tea or a leisurely drink will not seem out of place. The hotel has conference and banquet facilities, an executive centre, private dining and meeting rooms, a gift shop, travel desk, doctor on call, beauty salon, health club, massage parlour and a swimming pool exclusively for hotel guests. There are 149 rooms and nine suites – the executive, deluxe and the presidential suite. The emphasis is on personalised service and the concierges provide services ranging from restaurant recommendations to chartering helicopters! A 24-hour personalised butler service is available on all floors.

There is a coffee shop called **Le Jardin** that offers both Continental and Indian cuisine. The **Szechwan Court** has impeccable Chinese food and **Rim Naam** is the celebrated (covered outdoor) Thai restaurant overlooking a limpid pool that reflects the green around. **Polo Club** has the ambience of an English pub and you can try the outdoor seating in the verandah or the pergola for an informal chat.

# Business or pleasure?
# Why not both?

The Oberoi truly personifies a business hotel with a wide range of amenities aimed at the various needs of the corporate traveler. The hotel offers a wide range of facilities from exclusive business and conference infrastructure to abundant greenery aimed at relaxation and rejuvenation. A truly unique blend of hospitality that needs to be experienced to be believed.

Do call 080-2558 5858 for information.

*The Oberoi*

BANGALORE, INDIA

Origami

## The Grand Ashok

*Kumara Krupa High Grounds,*
*Bangalore 560001*
**Tel** *2226 9462, 2225 0202*
**Fax** *2225 0033*
**Tariff** *Rs 5,500 to Rs 30,000*
**Cards** *All*
**Check in/out** *12noon*
**Web** *www.bharathotels.com*

The Grand Ashok has a clear view of golfing greens, the Vidhana Soudha and other landmarks – its location scores a 10 with key government offices and commercial centres within close proximity. In the hotel's landscaped gardens is a historic landmark to mark the area where Mahatma Gandhi gave a public audience!
The hotel has 183 rooms, including 18 suites and 90 executive rooms. Facilities include conference halls, a salon, health club and swimming pool, tennis courts, a florist, travel desk, shopping arcade and a business centre. Three conference halls and a board room are available and the hotel also offers conference packages that include secretarial assistance and AV equipment.
The **Mandarin** has had a makeover and its brand of Chinese food is popular. Its big attraction however, is the live band Pink Champagne that plays anything from golden oldies to the latest in jazz and most importantly, you get to shake a leg on the dance floor! The **24/7** is a round-the-clock restaurant offering a multicuisine menu. **Baluchi** is the new speciality restaurant serving Indian and Continental cuisine. For a quiet drink head to the **Hibiscus Bar**.

## Le Meridien

*28 Sankey Road,*
*Bangalore 560052*
**Tel** *2226 2233, 2228 2828*
**Fax** *2226 7676*
**Tariff** *Rs 6,200 to Rs 16,500*
**Cards** *All*
**Check in/out** *12noon*
**Web** *www.lemeridien.com*

Le Meridien was recently refurbished and is well located with all the necessary

luxuries. Its rooms offer either an uninterrupted view of the golf course, the hotel's swimming pool or the garden. A health club with a gym, sauna, nine conference halls, a business centre with a boardroom, men's and ladies salon, shopping arcade, bookshop, gift shop, foreign exchange, travel desk, doctor on call and ramp and wheelchair access for the physically challenged are some of the highlights. There is also a lounge for Royal Club guests.
**La Brasserie** is the 24-hour coffee shop and restaurant and its buffet spread is very popular. In the hotel's premises is the **f Bar & Lounge,** Asia's first f-Bar that doubles up as restaurant serving superb and authentic Japanese food. **Insomnia** at Le Meridien is a nightclub.

## The Park

*14/7 MG Road,*
*Bangalore 560001*
**Tel** *2559 4666* **Fax** *2559 4029*
**Tariff** *Rs 6,000 to Rs 13,000*
**Cards** *All*
**Check in/out** *12noon*
**Web** *www.theparkhotels.com*

Bangalore's first boutique hotel created quite a stir when it opened with its contemporary styling, a super speciality Italian restaurant and trendy bar lounge. Designed by UK-based Conran & Partners the chic interiors rely on lots of amazing colours like iris with pale lime, bright lime, emperor red and green raw silk and splashes of ultramarine blue on saffron. The Tatler Magazine, a British publication, has rated The Park amongst the 101 best hotels in the world. The 109-room hotel is centrally located on MG Road. Facilities include a banquet hall, a gift store for luxury and contemporary designer items, 24-hour room service, indoor games, travel services, currency exchange, safe deposit lockers, doctor on call, baby sitting, library, Internet and laundry service. One of the highlights is Aquazone, a spa set below a temperature controlled pool with a range of massage options, steam and sauna.

The **Monsoon** is the 24-hour restaurant serving innovative international cuisine. The **i-bar** is the lounge bar done up in neon colours with beanbags and low furniture, and **i-t.ALIA** is the chic restaurant offering authentic Italian cuisine.

## BUSINESS

### Taj Residency

*41/3 MG Road, Bangalore 560001*
**Tel** *5660 4444* **Fax** *5661 4444*
**Tariff** *Rs 4,900 to Rs 15,000*
**Cards** *All*
**Check in/out** *12noon*
**Web** *www.tajhotels.com*

An old time favourite with business travellers, the Taj Residency was once the only big hotel on MG Road, centre of town. It's still seen as a hotel for the working visitor. The renovated guestrooms boast platform beds, ergonomically designed mobile work desks and chairs by Herman Miller.
The rooms are categorised as 'Standard' and 'Residency' and there are five executive suites. De-stress options such as individual steam units and special dual massage showerheads provide in-room relaxation. Facilities include a swimming pool, fitness centre, beauty salon for men and women, a travel desk, car rental, pastry shop, bookshop, currency exchange counter, safe deposit lockers, a doctor on call, babysitting services, banquet facilities, meeting rooms, business centre, broadband wireless Internet connectivity, 24-hour room service, express laundry service and steam rooms. The **Jockey Club** with its wood panelling, thick carpeting and smart service is the perfect venue for a quiet evening. The in-house Chinese restaurant, **Memories of China** has a popular buffet spread at lunch. **Café Mozaic** is the 24-hour coffee shop serving food from all over the world and many exciting late night specials as well.

## The Royal Orchid

*1 Golf Avenue,*
*(adjoining KGA Golf Course)*
*Bangalore 560008*
**Tel** *2520 5566* **Fax** *2520 3366*
**Tariff** *Rs 5,500 to Rs 8,000*
**Cards** *All*
**Check in/out** *12noon*
**Web** *www.baljeehotels.com*

Close to the airport and IT destinations, The Royal Orchid has another plus – it faces the Karnataka Golf Association (KGA) greens and golfer guests get to use the course. Regular rooms, serviced apartments, a travel desk, fitness centre, 24-hour room service and banquet and conferencing facilities are on offer. Two banquet halls can accommodate up to 300 persons theatre-style, and the lawns can host a 1,000 people. The 24-hour restaurant, **Limelight** serves Indian, Continental and Chinese cuisine. The pub, **Geoffrey's** is modelled along the lines of a typical British watering hole. A pan-Asian restaurant, rooftop grills, a lounge, swimming pool and spa are soon to be added

## Central Park

*47/1 Manipal Centre, Dickenson Road,*
*Bangalore 560042*
**Tel** *2558 4242* **Fax** *2558 8594*
**Tariff** *Rs 3,500 to Rs 8,000*
**Cards** *All*
**Check in/out** *12noon*
**Web** *www.baljeehotels.com*

Central Park is located off MG Road, right in the heart of town. Not surprisingly, it's popular with business travellers. There are 130 rooms including five suites and 37 Park Chamber rooms. Facilities offered include conference and banquet facilities, a business centre, safe deposit lockers, a travel desk, foreign exchange counter, shops and gymnasium. The hotel also provides Wi-Fi access.

The Park

The Grand Ashok *(See Pg 182)*

## Hotel Rama
*40/2 Lavelle Road,*
*Bangalore 560001*
*Tel 2227 3311/3314/3381/3384*
*Fax 2221 4867*
*Tariff Rs 2,099 to Rs 5,999*
*Cards All*
*Check in/out 12noon*
*Web www.ushashriramhotels.com*

A stone's throw from Cubbon Park, MG Road and Bowring Club, Hotel Rama is one of Bangalore's oldest hotels. With 55 rooms, its highlight is the roof garden. The hotel offers services like a business centre and conference hall, a travel desk and currency exchange services.
**Shilpa** is a multicuisine restaurant while **Charcoal** offers Tandoori fare.

## The Atria Hotel
*1 Palace Road, Bangalore 560001*
*Tel 2220 5205 Fax 2225 6850*
*Tariff Rs 3,700 to Rs 5,000*
*Cards All*
*Check in/out 24 Hour*
*Web www.atriahotel.com*

The Atria Hotel has a well maintained garden with 160 rooms and eight suites, two of which are based on the themes of Coorg and Feng Shui. Facilities include an in-house travel desk, a florist, 24-hour courier service, laundry and a business centre with secretarial services. The **Tijouri** serves authentic Awadhi and Hyderabadi delicacies, in an ethnic ambience. **1498 AD** is a coffee shop named to mark the landing of the Portuguese navigator Vasco da Gama in India. **Silk Winds** is a Chinese restaurant and **Trade Routes** is sundowners paradise. Sunday brunches are organised on the lawns.

## St. Mark's Hotel
*4/1 St. Marks Road,*
*Bangalore 560001*
*Tel 2227 9090 Fax: 2227 5700*
*Tariff Rs 3,200 to Rs 4,950*
*Cards All*
*Check in/out 12noon*
*Web www.stmarkshotel.com*

## The Capitol
*3 Raj Bhavan Road,*
*Bangalore 560001*
*Tel 2228 1234*
*Fax 2225 9922/9933*
*Tariff Rs 4,500 to Rs 8,000*
*Cards All*
*Check in/out 12noon*
*Web www.thecapitolhotel.com*

Walking distance from the Vidhana Soudha, The Capitol's six halls have been the venue for many seminars and conferences. A business hotel, it has 135 rooms and suites that come with a host of amenities like a convention and business centre, car rental service, travel desk, currency exchange, safe deposit lockers, doctor on call, pastry shop and Internet connectivity.
**24 Carats** is a 24-hour coffee shop that lays out a buffet for breakfast and dinner. The bar goes by the name **Upper House** and **Trivoli Garden** is a roof top restaurant that offers a spectacular green view of the city.

## The Chancery
*10/6 Lavelle Road, Bangalore 560001*
*Tel 2227 6767, 5118 8888*
*Fax 2227 6700*
*Tariff Rs 4,400 to Rs 7,400*
*Cards All*
*Check in/out 24 Hour*
*Web www.chanceryhotel.net*

Upmarket Lavelle Road has The Chancery at its top end. Gothic windows and winding stairways set the tone at this business hotel. The 140 rooms at this four-star deluxe hotel, come with a business centre, travel desk, fitness centre, doctor on call and foreign exchange bureau. There are three halls – The Walton, Lavelle Colours and

The Boardroom equipped with state-of-the-art AV equipment, projection screens and Internet connectivity. The Esquire Club is a premium business floor with a dedicated Esquire Lounge. Interestingly, The Chancery has gained a reputation as the preferred hotel among women travellers!
**South Parade** is a multicuisine restaurant, open round the clock, offering breakfast, lunch and dinner buffets and the food festivals held here are popular. There's a 24-hour coffee shop, **The Coffee Lounge**. Those who swear by vegetarian food may try **Moksh** – a pan-Indian vegetarian restaurant.

## Gateway Hotel on Residency Road
*66 Residency Road, Bangalore 560025*
*Tel 5660 4545 Fax: 5661 4542*
*Tariff Rs 5,500 to Rs 7,000*
*Cards All*
*Check in/out 24 Hour*
*Web www.tajhotels.com*

A Taj Group business hotel, Gateway scores over others in the same class with its location, heritage and famous restaurants. Business, shopping and entertainment are all within shouting distance of the hotel.
Its 98 rooms (both standard and executive) include four suites. A swimming pool, fitness centre, travel desk, car rental, currency exchange facilities, safe deposit lockers, doctor on call, business centre, banquet and laundry service are the facilities on offer.
Gateway's treasure is **Karavalli**, an ethnic restaurant set amidst gurgling streams and bright green foliage, serving authentic coastal cuisine from the Karavalli coast. It's been rated as

one of India's top restaurants, and visitors are never disappointed. The **Potluck Café** offers European and Asian cuisine in an upmarket café ambience. North Indian cuisine is laid out at the **Northern Gate**, and the **Lobby Lounge** is a busy bar and lounge.

## Infantry Court
*66 Infantry Road,*
*Bangalore 560001*
*Tel 2559 1800*
*Fax 2559 2276*
*Tariff Rs 4,000 to Rs 6,000*
*Cards All*
*Check in/out 12noon*
*Email hotelic@vsnl.com*

In close proximity to the main commercial districts, Infantry Court has 75 rooms and conference halls. A travel desk, Internet connectivity, doctor on call and an attached multicuisine restaurant are offered.

The Chancery

It's easy to spot St. Mark's Hotel – it's the only large lilac coloured hotel on St. Marks Road. A mere seven kilometres from the airport, it is in the heart of Bangalore's business, shopping and dining districts. Besides well furnished rooms and recreational facilities, it has a full-fledged business centre and banquet halls. The entire hotel is Wi-Fi enabled to suit corporate travellers. Managed by the K Raheja group of Hotels, the hotel has 78 standard rooms, 10 executive rooms and six suites. The multicuisine restaurant is called **Indian Pavilion** and the bar is **Phoenix**.

## Nalapads Hotel Bangalore International

*2A-2B Crescent Road, High Grounds, Bangalore 560001*
**Tel** *2226 8011* **Fax:** *2226 3191*
**Tariff** *Rs 2,200 to Rs 4,950*
**Cards** *All except American Express*
**Check in/out** *24 Hour*
**Web** *www.nalapad.com*

Well located, barely a kilometre from the city railway station and bus stand, this 70-room hotel has a health club with sauna, steam and massage, two banquet halls, a business centre, a men's salon, ladies beauty parlour, safe deposit lockers and currency exchange services. **Crescent Avenue** serves Indian, Chinese and Thai cuisine, while

**Height's Café** is a 24-hour coffee shop and **Great Moments Bar**, is, well, the bar.

## Hotel Monarch

*54 Brigade Road, Bangalore 560001*
**Tel** *2559 1915, 2532 7190*
**Fax** *2532 7199*
**Tariff** *Rs 2,400 to Rs 4,500*
**Cards** *All*
**Check in/out** *24 Hour*
**Web** *www.hotelmonarch.com*

One of Bangalore's more recent hotels, Monarch is right in the middle of the shopping hub of Brigade Road. Facilities include a business centre, banquet hall, convention centre, shopping arcade, car rental services, a travel desk, doctor on call and currency exchange facilities. There is a cake shop, a 24-hour coffee shop and a multicuisine restaurant attached to the hotel.

## Hotel Ramanashree

*16 Raja Ram Mohan Roy Road, Bangalore 560025*
**Tel** *5135 0000, 2222 5152*
**Fax** *5135 0007*
**Tariff** *Rs 2,495 to Rs 4,495*
**Cards** *All*
**Check in/out** *12noon*
**Web** *www.ramanashree.com*

Hotel Ramanashree overlooks the Sports Complex at Kanteerava Stadium and 24-hour room service, a travel desk, safety lockers, doctor on call, banquet and

St. Mark's Hotel is a favourite with business travellers.

conference and currency exchange facilities are available.
The **Beijing Pavilion** is a multicuisine restaurant serving buffet breakfasts and lunches and a la carte dinners. Its well kept secret is **Kudla**, a small restaurant serving authentic Mangalorean fare.

## Museum Inn Hotel

*1 Museum Road, Bangalore 560001*
**Tel** *5111 3333* **Fax** *5111 3300*
**Tariff** *Rs 2,995 to Rs 3,995*
**Cards** *All*

**Check in/out** *12noon*
**Web** *www.bjnhotels.com*

Museum Inn manages to score above the others with its location and reasonably good restaurants. It's right off MG Road – a point that always scores. Forty centrally air conditioned rooms, 24-hour room service and a travel desk are on offer here.
The north Indian restaurant **Angeethi** is a big hit with its dhaba ambience. Its pub, **Tavern at the Inn** is comfortable and the Chinese restaurant **Bamboo Shoots** serves up Thai as well.

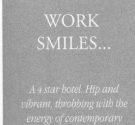

A tastefully done-up room at Villa Pottipati

## Hotel Harsha & Convention Centre

*11 Park Road, Shivajinagar,*
*Bangalore 560051*
*Tel 2286 5566/5555 Fax 2286 5943*
*Tariff Rs 2,200 to Rs 3,500*
*Cards All*
*Check in/out 12noon*
*Web www.baljeehotels.com*

One of the older hotels, Harsha is in the quieter part of Shivajinagar and famous for its open hearth restaurant **Tiger Trail**. Regular facilities such as a travel desk, currency exchange counter and a safe deposit locker, along with car rentals, a boardroom and business centre are available here. Four conference halls and one banquet hall that can take 500 people are on offer.

## Villa Pottipati

*142-New, 8th Cross, 4th Main,*
*Malleswaram, Bangalore 560003*
*Tel 5128 0832, 2336 0777*
*Fax 5128 0835*
*Tariff Rs 2,000 to Rs 3,250*
*Cards All*
*Check in/out 24 Hour*
*Web www.neemranahotels.com*

Neemrana Hotels make its first foray into Bangalore's heritage houses with Villa Pottipati, a tribute to the old world bungalows of the city. Located in Malleswaram, once a Brahmin stronghold of Bangalore, it's perfect for those who wish to experience old world living with the comforts of a hotel. The eight-room house-hotel has a giant Shivalinga tree, Gulmohar, Jacaranda, jackfruit trees, vibrant crotons and seasonal flowers. Antique furniture and long stemmed ceiling fans inside add to the charm. Each room is named after a south Indian sari – Gadwal, Anekal, Pochampalli,

Venkatagiri, Kanchipuram, Kota-Masuria, Kalamkari and Rajadurga. The rooms at Pottipati are fitted with basic hotel facilities: Air-conditioning, phones, television, Internet and computer facilities. There is a small conference room, a lounge with granite pillars and a skylight.

## The Richmond Hotel

*88/2 Richmond Road,*
*Bangalore 560025*
*Tel 2223 3666 Fax 2223 3777*
*Tariff Rs 1,900 to Rs 3,000*
*Cards All*
*Check in/out 24 Hour*
*Web www.theresidency.com*

A glass and chrome structure, The Richmond Hotel keeps the business traveller in mind.
There are 44 centrally air conditioned rooms with 24-hour room service, Internet access, a travel desk, a moneychanger and safe deposit lockers. There is also a convention hall, business centre and a gymnasium.
The **Bangalore Brasserie** is a multicuisine restaurant serving buffet breakfast, lunch and dinner while **Upper Circle** is a lounge with a bar.

## Vintage Residency

*9 Mission Road, Bangalore 560027*
*Tel 2227 4507/4509/4511*
*Fax 2227 4564*
*Tariff Rs 1,000 to Rs 3,000*
*Cards All except Diners Club*
*Check in/out 24 Hour*
*Web www.vintageresidency.com*

Just three kilometres from the railway station, the Vintage Residency is a medium-budget hotel and offers basic facilities like a doctor on call, a travel desk, safe deposit lockers and licensed moneychangers. The hotel also has

banquet and conferencing facilities and a multicuisine restaurant, **Andhra Springs**.

## Hotel Ivory Tower

*84 Barton Centre, MG Road,*
*Bangalore 560001*
*Tel 2558 9333 Fax 2558 8697*
*Tariff Rs 2,100 to Rs 2,900*
*Cards All*
*Check in/out 12noon*
*Web www.hotelivorytower.com*

An all suite hotel on the penthouse of the Barton Centre, Hotel Ivory Tower offers a spectacular view of the city, a great restaurant and a happening nightclub. The Grandmaster Suite comes with separate living and entertaining areas, while the Ivory Suite is designed for longer stays and has a separate reception and dining area. All the regular amenities are available here.
**Ebony** is a rooftop restaurant in the garden city offering an aerial view of the city along with a range of Parsee, Mughlai, Tandoori and French cuisine. A cocktail lounge, **13th Floor**, with a great view of the city is attached to the hotel.

## Nilgiri's Nest

*171 Brigade Road, Bangalore 560001*
*Tel 2558 8401/8103/8702*
*Fax 2558 2853*
*Tariff Rs 1,000 to Rs 2,800*
*Cards All*
*Check in/out 24 Hour*
*Email nilgirisnest@vsnl.net*

Nilgiri's Nest is fabulously located on Brigade Road right above the department store with the same name and next to a movie theatre! The proximity of pubs, restaurants and shops makes the hotel a popular choice. Nilgiri's Nest has a travel desk, currency exchange facilities, a safe deposit box and a car rental. In the same building are a cake shop and **Nilgiri's Café**.

## Nahar Heritage Hotel

*14 St. Marks Road,*
*Bangalore 560001*
*Tel 2227 8731/8736*
*Fax 2227 8737*
*Tariff Rs 2,000 to Rs 2,700*
*Cards All*
*Check in/out 24 Hour*
*Web www.naharhotels.com*

Here is a no-frills hotel that is conveniently located on St. Marks Road with 48 centrally air-conditioned rooms. 24-hour room service is available along with the usual facilities like a doctor on call, a safe deposit locker, a travel desk and Internet access. A business centre and three banquet halls are also available at the Nahar Heritage Hotel.
**Orchid** is a vegetarian restaurant.

## Safina Hotels

*84/85 Infantry Road, Bangalore 560001*
*Tel 2558 1982/1988*
*Fax 2558 1990*
*Tariff Rs 2,000 to Rs 2,500*
*Cards All*
*Check in/out 12noon*
*Web www.safinahotels.com*

Safina Plaza is a well known shopping arcade and its fairly recent addition of a hotel is popular with the budget crowd. Close to both Commercial Street and MG Road, it has 34 rooms with no air-conditioning. Facilities include a travel desk, safe deposit, business centre, doctor on call, Internet access and foreign currency exchange services.

## Hotel Golden Landmark

*20/21 Seshadri Road, Bangalore 560009*
*Tel 2228 4600/1182 Fax 2226 3575*
*Tariff Rs 2,150 to Rs 2,450*
*Cards All*
*Check in/out 24 Hour*
*Email golden_landmark@vsnl.com*

If you are looking for a no-fuss hotel with all the basic facilities, Hotel

Hotel Harsha & Convention Centre

# The Chancery.
## A Business CPU

India's thriving IT industry is concentrated in Bangalore - The silicon valley of India. Nestled in the heart of the city, adjoining M.G. Road, 'The Chancery' with luxurious ambience has been designed to international standards. 140 well appointed Suites, Esquire Club and Superior rooms with a choice of four Banquet halls equipped with complete range of state-of-the-art communication infrastructure provides comprehensive business support services. 24 hour check-out facilities, 24 hour eatery, 24 hour Business Centre, 'Esquire Club' - the premium business floor with a lounge along with many 24/7 facilities for jet-set business travellers, served with a choice of lip-smacking international and local cuisine, stand her out as 'Bangalore's Finest Corporate Hotel'.

THE
CHANCERY SM
BANGALORE'S FINEST CORPORATE HOTEL

**COME ENJOY THE LUXURY AND SPEED OF DOING BUSINESS**

10/6 LAVELLE ROAD, BANGALORE - 560 001 (INDIA), PH: +91-80-2227 6767 / 51188888, FAX: +91-80-2227 6700 E-MAIL: reservations@chanceryhotel.net, WEB: chanceryhotel.net

Woodlands, one of the older hotels in the city

Landmark is a good choice. It's about a kilometre from the city railway station and almost next door to the Turf Club. 54 rooms including six suites are available. The hotel also boasts a banquet hall, boardroom and party hall. There is a multicuisine restaurant **Gazebo** and a colonial style bar, **Gallops**.

## Ashraya International Hotel

*149 Infantry Road, Bangalore 560001*
**Tel** *2226 1921*
**Fax** *2226 3982*
**Tariff** *Rs 1,450 to Rs 2,250*
**Cards** *All except Diners Club*
**Check in/out** *12noon*
**Email** *ashintel@bgl.vsnl.net.in*

Bangalore's famous buildings like the Vidhana Soudha, Attara Kacheri and Cubbon Park are within walking distance of Ashraya. It's also very close to Brigade Road and Commercial Street. Ashraya has 72 air-conditioned rooms, a travel desk, money changing services, locker facilities, banquets, conferences and a multicuisine restaurant with a cocktail bar.

## Woodlands Hotel

*5 Raja Ram Mohan Roy Road, Bangalore 560025*
**Tel** *2222 5111*
**Fax** *2223 6963*
**Tariff** *Rs 900 to Rs 2,200*
**Cards** *All except American Express*
**Check in/out** *12noon*
**Email** *wood@bgl.vsnl.net.in*

Some of the older hotels in the city have the advantage of lots of lung space in the most crowded areas, like Woodlands. Located within easy reach of the shopping areas, railway station and bus stand, it's a fairly comfortable option in the medium budget class. Facilities offered are a travel desk, doctor on call, currency exchanger, safe deposit lockers, conference halls and a bookstore.
The **Sunheri** serves north Indian and Continental fare and the air-conditioned hall serves south Indian meals on plantain leaves.

## Ramee Guestline

*Plot No.1 & 2, KIADB Indl. Area, Attibele, Bangalore 562107*
**Tel** *782 0430/0434*
**Fax** *782 0435*
**Tariff** *Rs 1,195 to Rs 1,950*
**Cards** *All*
**Check in/out** *12noon*
**Email** *hgablr@vsnl.com*

Set amidst five acres of landscaped gardens and a 30-minute drive east of Bangalore, this hotel is a convenient stop for professionals headed to Electronics City and Hosur. The hotel has 96 rooms with a health club, steam, sauna, jacuzzi, Ayurvedic massage, lawn tennis, squash, badminton, table tennis, swimming pool, golf, volleyball courts, health club, shopping arcade, safe deposit, business centre, travel services and conference and banquet facilities.
There is a 24-hour coffee shop and **Time Out Bar** displaying sporting memorabilia.

## Curzon Court

*10 Brigade Road, Bangalore 560001*
**Tel** *2558 1698/2540*
**Fax** *2558 2278*
**Tariff** *Rs 1,200 to Rs 1,800*
**Cards** *All*
**Check in/out** *12noon*

Curzon Court is almost a secret hotel on Brigade Road and most visitors will miss its entrance at least once! Within easy reach of the airport, railway station and bus stand, it has a travel counter, shopping arcade and **Aathithya** serving vegetarian fare.

## Ballal Residency

*74/4, 3rd Cross, Residency Road, Bangalore 560025*
**Tel** *2559 7277* **Fax** *2559 7276*
**Tariff** *Rs 1,400 to Rs 1,750*
**Cards** *MasterCard & Visa*
**Check in/out** *24 Hour*
**Web** *www.ballalgrouphotels.com*

Pegging itself as a 'vegetarian hotel' Ballal Residency has plenty of takers for its location and price. Just off Brigade Road, it has a multicuisine restaurant **Palmgrove**, a travel desk, money exchange services and a salon.

## Pai Viceroy

*1504, 16th Cross, 9th Main, III Block, Jayanagar, Bangalore 560011*
**Tel** *2653 5400/5408*
**Fax** *2653 3701*
**Tariff** *Rs 1,400 to Rs 1,600*
**Cards** *All*
**Check in/out** *24 Hour*
**Web** *www.paihotels.com*

The only luxury hotel in south Bangalore catering to business travellers and tourists, Pai Viceroy has 42 rooms. Facilities offered are room service, laundry, Internet connection, safe deposit lockers and direct long distance dialling. There are also two banquet halls and two restaurants.
The **Royal Corner** is a multicuisine restaurant serving vegetarian food and is very popular with guests.

## BUDGET

## Adarsh Inn

*3, 1st Main Road, Gandhinagar, Bangalore 560009*
**Tel** *2238 4211* **Fax** *2238 4218*
**Tariff** *Rs 1,345 to Rs 1,995*
**Cards** *All*
**Check in/out** *24 Hour*
**Email** *adarshinn@vsnl.com*

Another popular option for the budget traveller, Adarsh Inn provides basic amenities like 24-hour room service, a doctor on call, laundry, Internet connection and a travel desk. There is a conference hall and restaurant attached.

## The Basil

*8 Sampige Road, Malleswaram, Bangalore 560003*
**Tel** *2331 5123, 2346 4353*
**Fax** *2334 3904*
**Tariff** *Rs 900 to Rs 1,850*
**Cards** *All*
**Check in/out** *24 Hour*
**Web** *www.thebasilhotel.com*

One of the few hotels in Malleswaram, The Basil is located on busy Sampige Road but double-glazed windows ensure peace and quiet. Its 35 rooms come with a banquet and conference hall and a business centre.
The hotel's highlights include an 'Oxygen Bar' and multicuisine restaurant **The Herb** that offers a choice of Indian, Tandoori and Chinese food.

## Hotel Nandhini

*14/A/37, 27th Cross (Opp. Karnataka Bank), IV Block, Jayanagar, Bangalore 560011*
**Tel** *2653 5090/1/2/3/4*
**Fax** *2634 1238*
**Branch** *St. Marks Road, 5126 6666 (Rs 1,390 to Rs 2,290)*
**Tariff** *Rs 890 to Rs 1,800*
**Cards** *All*
**Check in/out** *24 Hour*
**Web** *www.nandhini.com*

Originally a restaurant chain serving hot Andhra cuisine, they have expanded with Hotel Nandhini in south Bangalore. Standard air-conditioned and non air-conditioned rooms are available along with family rooms and suites, a business centre and banquet and conference halls. Facilities include free airport transfer, complimentary breakfast, 24-hour room service, laundry service, a travel desk and doctor on call. Sightseeing tours are also organised by the hotel. There is a multicuisine restaurant attached, but a sure bet is naturally the Andhra food.

## Hotel Chalukya

*44 Race Course Road, Bangalore 560001*
**Tel** *2226 6870* **Fax** *2225 3377*
**Tariff** *Rs 1,200 to Rs 1,700*
**Cards** *All*
**Check in/out** *24 Hour*
**Email** *hotelchalukya@cablelite.com*

Breathing the same air as the Turf Club and Golf Course is Hotel Chalukya. There are 81 rooms here and two restaurants, **Samrat**, serving vegetarian food and **Alampur**.

The Basil is set in bustling Malleswaram.

Airlines Hotel offers a low budget stay.

Centrally located at the intersection of Brigade Road and Richmond Road, the hotel is convenient with proximity to the shopping districts and pubs. The rooms come with an attached bath, hot water, telephone lines, television and room service.

### Hotel Shangrila
*182 Brigade Road, Bangalore 560001*
**Tel** *2558 8994* **Fax** *2558 2984*
**Tariff** *Rs 600 to Rs 1,200*
**Cards** *All except American Express*
**Check in/out** *24 Hour*
**Email** *lhasadolma@yahoo.com*

Originally a restaurant serving Chinese and Tibetan food on the busy Brigade Road, Shangrila now has 17 rooms with basic facilities. Backpackers love its location and price and fellow Tibetans get a discount.

### Kamat Yatrinivas
*4, 1st Cross, Gandhinagar,*
*Bangalore 560009*
**Tel** *2226 0088/3727, 2228 1068*
**Fax** *2228 1070*
**Tariff** *Rs 950 to Rs 1,100*
**Cards** *MasterCard & Visa*
**Check in/out** *24 Hour*
**Email** *kamat@bir.vsnl.net.in*

### Brindavan Hotel
*108 MG Road, Bangalore 560001*
**Tel** *2558 4000* **Fax:** *2559 6698*
**Tariff** *Rs 520 to Rs 1,650*
**Cards** *Not Accepted*
**Check in/out** *24 Hour*

Tucked away off MG Road, this is one of the city's older hotels, with a restaurant serving good vegetarian food. It's popular with backpackers and budget tourists.

### Hotel Maurya
*22/4 Race Course Road, Gandhinagar,*
*Bangalore 560009*
**Tel** *2225 4111/4119* **Fax** *2225 6685*
**Tariff** *Rs 1,050 to Rs 1,475*
**Cards** *All*
**Check in/out** *24 Hour*
**Email** *hotel_maurya@vsnl.com*

There is a great view of the racecourse from the rooms. Its pricing makes it an ideal choice for budget travellers. Two multicuisine restaurants, a full fledged bar and conference and banquet halls are the add-ons.

### Hotel Geo
*11 Devanga Hostel Road, Behind*
*Corporation Building, Bangalore 560027*
**Tel** *2222 1583*
**Fax** *2222 1993*
**Tariff** *Rs 600 to Rs 1,400*
**Cards** *All*
**Check in/out** *24 Hour*
**Email** *hotelgeoblr@rediffmail.com*

Its restaurant **Sentosa Garden** serves authentic Kerala cuisine. Two kilometres from the railway station and bus stand, it has basic facilities like a travel desk, safe deposit lockers and Internet connection.

### Sukh Sagar Hotel
*10, 3rd Main Road, Gandhinagar,*
*Bangalore 560009*
**Tel** *2220 2255/56/58*
**Fax** *2225 6730*
**Tariff** *Rs 900 to Rs 1,300*
**Cards** *All*
**Check in/out** *24 Hour*
**Email** *sukhsagar@vsnl.net*

Not too far from the city railway station, Sukh Sagar is popular with tourists and budget travellers. There are 52 rooms, a business centre, a banquet hall and a multicuisine restaurant. Facilities include a travel desk, laundry service and safe deposit lockers. **Prithvi** is the coffeeshop, popular for its chaat.

### Hotel Algate
*93 Residency Road,*
*Bangalore 560025*
**Tel** *2559 4786/4789*
**Fax** *5112 6046*
**Tariff** *Rs 850 to Rs 1,200*
**Cards** *All except American Express*
**Check in/out** *24 Hour*
**Web** *www.hotelalgate.com*

Located on busy Residency Road, Hotel Algate has 30 rooms, basement parking, safe deposit lockers, room service and **Palace Algate**, a multicuisine restaurant.

### Hotel Vellara
*126 Brigade Road, Opp. Brigade*
*Towers,*
*Bangalore 560025*
**Tel** *2536 9116/9205*
**Fax** *2536 9775*
**Tariff** *Rs 800 to Rs 1,200*
**Cards** *MasterCard & Visa*
**Check in/out** *24 Hour*

Clearly for the no-frills budget traveller, Kamat's attraction is its restaurant, **Jowar Bhakry**, serving authentic north Karnataka cuisine. There are 57 rooms with access to safe deposit lockers, car rentals, a banquet and conferencing hall and two other restaurants, **Annapoorna**, offering multicuisine fare and **Upachar**, a north Indian restaurant.

## Airlines Hotel
*4 Madras Bank Road,*
*Bangalore 560001*
*Tel 2227 3783/1602/3786,*
*Tariff Rs 375 to Rs 1,100*
*Cards All except American Express*
*Check in/out 24 Hour*

Once a sprawling, green hotel with a famous outdoor restaurant, Airlines space has been clipped by new buildings but it's still quite popular. Its tree-shaded restaurant serves some good dosas and the local ice cream shop, **Corner House** has an outlet here. No-fuss, basic rooms are available.

## Hotel Empire
*78 Central Street, Bangalore 560001*
*Tel 2558 7266*
*Fax 2559 2821*
*Branch Church Street, 2559 3743*

*(Rs 990 to Rs 1,990)*
*Tariff Rs 495 to Rs 950*
*Cards All*
*Check in/out 24 Hour*
*Web www.hotelempireinternational.com*

Stay at Hotel Empire and sample the best Biryani in Bangalore! Situated close to the business establishments and shopping areas, the hotel also has 23 rooms providing basic amenities for the backpacker.

## Nalapad Residency
*19 KG Road, Bangalore 560009*
*Tel 2226 6374/77, 5122 0012*
*Fax 2238 9209*
*Tariff Rs 750 to Rs 900*
*Cards All*
*Check in/out 24 Hour*
*Web www.nalapad.com*

Located in a busy commercial area, Nalapad Residency has 100 rooms with 24-hour room service, a business centre, conference hall, boardroom, travel desk, safe deposit lockers and a foreign exchange counter. Attached to the hotel are **Kadal**, the multicuisine restaurant and **Gossip** a 24-hour coffee shop.

Hotel Vellara

Compact's guesthouses are located across the city.

## Berrys Hotel
*46/1 Church Street,*
*Bangalore 560001*
*Tel 2558 7211/7383*
*Fax 2558 6931*
*Tariff Rs 650 to Rs 850*
*Cards All except American Express*
*Check in/out 24 Hour*

The 28 rooms and multicuisine restaurant that make up Berrys Hotel are located close to Bangalore's most famous roads and popular shopping districts.

## Hotel Mahaveer
*8/1 & 9 Tank Bund Road,*
*Near Railway Station, Subhash Nagar,*
*Bangalore 560053*
*Tel 2287 3670 Fax: 2225 3087*
*Tariff Rs 400 to Rs 750*
*Cards All except American Express*
*Check in/out 24 Hour*
*Email hotelmahaveer@rediffmail.com*

A short walk from the city railway station, Hotel Mahaveer has 45 double rooms, a travel desk and a conference hall.

## Janardhana
*6/1 Kumara Krupa Road,*
*High Grounds, Bangalore 560001*
*Tel 2225 4444 Fax: 2225 8708*
*Tariff Rs 430 to Rs 540*
*Cards Not Accepted*
*Check in/out 24 Hour*

Janardhana is reputed for its Udupi restaurant and caters to budget tourists. It has easy access to the city railway station.

## GUEST HOUSES

## Compact Guest House
*28, 3rd Main, 7th Cross, Domlur Layout,*
*Bangalore 560071*
*Tel 2535 3881/1893*
*Fax 5115 0505*
*Tariff Rs 600 to Rs 1,800*
*Cards All*
*Check in/out 24 Hour*
*Web www.compactguesthouses.com*

This is part of a chain of professionally managed guesthouses in Koramangala, Indiranagar and MG Road. The guesthouse has the feel of a home and facilities like laundry, television, the standard amenities and a host of personalised services. Facilities include a fully equipped kitchenette with a microwave, cooking range and refrigerator, laundry services, high speed Internet connections as well as food and beverages. A golf course, gymnasium, restaurant, English-style pub and a 24-hour café are some of the added attractions. The other highlights are a travel desk, currency exchange counter, electronic safe and a doctor on call.

## Anagha Guest Home
*19 Jaladarshini Layout, New BEL Road, RMV Extension II Stage,*
*Bangalore 560054*
*Tel 2360 8479/8127*
*Tariff Rs 1,650*
*Check in/out 24 Hour*
*Email karthikskanda@yahoo.com*

Located close to MS Ramaiah Hospital, Anagha has five bedrooms with attached bathrooms, a hall cum dining room, fully functional kitchen, parking space, laundry services, television, safe deposit lockers, maid services, meals on request and transportation. Shopping and medical facilities are a short walk away.

## Terrace Gardens
*15 Brunton Road Cross, Off MG Road,*
*Bangalore 560025*
*Tel 2558 4797/4987/1836*
*Fax 2559 1047*
*Tariff Rs 1,050 to Rs 1,600*
*Cards All*
*Check in/out 24 Hour*
*Email terracegarden@vsnl.net*

Located off MG Road, Terrace Gardens has all the personalised comfort of a guesthouse with a lovely terrace garden. There are 11 double rooms, all air-conditioned with attached bath and hot water. Cable television, telephone with direct dialling and south Indian and north Indian meals on request are also available. They also run a chain of serviced apartments across the city.

# SERVICED APARTMENTS

## Royal Residencies

*1 Golf Avenue, Off Airport Road,*
*Adjoining KGA Golf Course,*
*Bangalore 560008*
**Tel** *2520 5566*
**Tariff** *Rs 5,500 to Rs 8,000*
**Cards** *All*
**Check in/out** *24 Hour*
**Web** *www.baljeehotels.com*

The plush Royal Orchid was the first hotel to open serviced apartments on its premises, combining home comforts with a five star ambience. These apartments offer the standard amenities and a host of personalised services. Facilities include a fully equipped kitchenette with a microwave, cooking range and refrigerator, laundry services, high speed Internet connections as well as food and beverages. A golf course, gym, restaurant, English-style pub and a 24-hour café are some of the added attractions. The other highlights are a travel desk, currency exchange counter, electronic safe and a doctor on call.

## Halcyon

*9 Drafadilla, IV Block, Koramangala,*
*Bangalore 560034*
**Tel** *5110 2200* **Fax:** *5110 2400*
**Tariff** *Rs 2,200 to Rs 5,000*
**Cards** *All*
**Check in/out** *24 Hour*
**Email** *halcyongroup@vsnl.net*

A division of Fund Point Service Apartments, this is one of the first highly organised serviced apartments with a restaurant and pub attached! Halcyon is also one of the biggest condo-complexes in the country. Facilities include room service, doctor on call, safe deposit lockers, housekeeping with laundry facilities, Internet connection, currency exchange, a travel desk, car park, a fully equipped kitchen, in-room dining, a multicuisine restaurant, **Simply Bohemian** and an exclusive pub **Purple Panda**. For business travellers and corporates there is an attached boardroom and business centre. There is also a swimming pool, health club and billiards room in the complex.

## Homestead

*12/12, 7th Cross, Lavelle Road,*
*Bangalore 560001*
**Tel** *2222 0966* **Fax:** *2222 0967*
**Tariff** *Rs 3,100 to Rs 4,200*
**Cards** *All*
**Check in/out** *24 Hour*
**Web** *www.homesteadbangalore.com*

Homestead was Bangalore's first professionally managed facility for serviced apartments. Whether you're in the city on business or on holiday with your family, you will find Homestead a convenient and comfortable choice. Located conveniently on Lavelle Road, in the heart of the city, Homestead offers a range of services: Each apartment comes furnished with a comfortable sofa, dining table, television, music system, telephone connection and a kitchenette equipped with a fridge, microwave, coffee maker, cooking range and utensils.
There is also a gym, business centre, two party areas and a tie-up with a few restaurants for catering services. Homestead was built by Brigade Group, one of Bangalore's leading property developers and an ISO 9001-2000 certified company. And is managed by their sister-concern, Brigade Hospitality Services Pvt. Ltd.

## Stay & Work @ infantry

*145 Infantry Road, Bangalore 560001*
**Tel** *2286 4270*
**Fax** *2286 8543*
**Tariff** *Rs 2,150 to Rs 3,500*
**Cards** *All*
**Check in/out** *24 Hour*
**Web** *www.staynworkinfantry.com*

Stay & Work @ infantry has distinct apartments – 20 air-conditioned ones and two bedroom flats with attached bathrooms, well equipped kitchenettes, telephone connections, a television, music system and a visitor's area. Laundry, housekeeping services and 24-hour security is provided and a store is attached.

## Crown Plaza Hotels & Resorts

*45 Hennur Cross Road, (Opp. Little Sisters of the Poor Convent), Kalyan Nagar Post, Bangalore 560043*
**Tel** *2544 6476/3148*
**Tariff** *Rs 2,100 to Rs 3,500*
**Cards** *MasterCard & Visa*
**Check in/out** *24 Hour*
**Web** *www.crownplazagroup.com*

A fully furnished apartment at Homestead

The imposing facade of Halycon

Located on the edge of the Outer Ring Road connecting north Bangalore to major interstate routes, this property has 20 fully furnished serviced apartments with well equipped kitchenettes, cable TV, direct dial phone, daily housekeeping and laundry services. A cyber café and multicuisine restaurant are attached. Travel assistance, airport pick-up and drop and complimentary transport to the place of work is provided.

## Tristar Apartments
*1216, 100Ft. Road, Doopanahalli, Indiranagar, HAL II Stage, Bangalore 560038*
*Tel 5118 5900 Fax: 5118 5949*
*Tariff Rs 1,000 to Rs 3,500*
*Cards All*
*Check in/out 12noon*
*Web www.tristarapt.com*

Tristar's tastefully furnished serviced apartments are located in bustling Indiranagar. There are 25 serviced apartments in all – 10 are studios and the rest are deluxe and super deluxe apartments. All accommodation is air-conditioned and comes equipped with a compact kitchenette, a rooftop jacuzzi, a reading area stocked with books and magazines, a study table and a television.
Apart from these conveniences, the apartments also enjoy 24-hour Internet connectivity, an in-house restaurant, power back-up, laundry and dry cleaning services and a health club with a gymnasium. Airport pick-ups and drops,

parking space, safe deposit lockers and round-the-clock security are offered. Tristar also has a tie-up with nearby departmental stores, restaurants and clubs.

## Melange Luxury Service Apartments
*Suryamukhi Apartments, 21 Vittal Mallya Road, Bangalore 560001*
*Tel 2212 9701/9702*
*Fax 2212 9703*
*Tariff Rs 1,850 to Rs 3,200*
*Cards All*
*Check in/out 24 Hour*
*Web www.melangebangalore.com*

Melange Luxury Service Aparments on Vittal Mallya Road caters to both business travellers and families on holiday. Each apartment has state-of-the-art kitchenettes equipped with a microwave, refrigerator and utensils. Door delivery of food is also arranged through a tie-up with a few restaurants. Cable and Internet connection and an electronic safe is provided for each apartment. Other facilities and services include a business centre, a travel desk, airport and railway transport, a doctor on call, 24-hour security and laundry services.

## Craig Park Homes
*21/6 Craig Park Layout, Behind Nalli Silks, MG Road, Bangalore 560001*
*Tel 3678 5134*
*Fax 2558 1563*
*Tariff Rs1,000 to Rs 1,500*
*Cards All*
*Check in/out 24 Hour*

Located off the central MG Road, Craig Park Homes offers nine bedrooms, five of which are air-conditioned. There is a central kitchen and lobby but all rooms have a bath attached.

# RESORTS

## Golden Palms Hotel & Spa
*Golden Palms Avenue, Hobli, Tumkur Road, Bangalore 562123*
*Tel 2371 2222, 5112 6911*
*Fax 2371 0033*
*Tariff Rs 6,500 to Rs 20,000*
*Check in/out 12noon*
*Cards All*
*Web www.goldenpalmsspa.com*

Designed in Mediterranean style, the Golden Palms resort is the last word in luxury. A five star resort, it has 132 rooms and 18 deluxe suites and two presidential suites. Three restaurants and two bars offer a range of cuisines. The **Café Solaire** offers a neo tropical buffet spread and an a la carte menu. **Badsha** is the open-air poolside restaurant, open for dinner only, offering Awadhi cuisine. **Garden of Eden** is a dining cum cocktail bar with a dance floor attached. Asian and oriental cuisine is on offer here. Golden Palms offers exclusive spa packages and the Spa Bar offers post-spa refreshments. By the poolside is the **Aqua Bar** and the **Nostalgia Bar** screens popular Hollywood and Bollywood films on a large plasma screen. While here, don't miss the various spa treatments.

## Angsana Oasis Spa & Resort Bangalore
*Northwest County, Main Doddaballapur Road, Rajankunte, Bangalore 560064*
*Tel 2846 8893, 2559 1080*
*Fax 2846 8897*
*Tariff Rs 5,500 to Rs 13,000*
*Check in/out 12noon*
*Web www.angsana.com*

Located in Doddaballapur, around 24kms from MG Road, the Angsana Resort and Spa is a luxurious getaway. It offers a range of rooms like the angsana suite, two-bedroom, one bedroom suite and an executive resort room. All suites come attached with a kitchenette and large bay windows offer a great view of the landscape outside. The resort comes with a well-stocked library, aerobics centre and meditation/ Yoga room.
Facilities include an outdoor swimming pool with separate children's pool, two floodlit tennis courts, table tennis court, a glass-backed squash court, gymnasium with cardio vascular equipment, a beauty salon and a day care centre.
The Angsana Resort is also well known for its spa and spa treatments.
The group also owns resorts in Bintan, Malayasia, Great Barrier Reef, Australia and Ihuru in the Maldives.

## Taj Kuteeram
*Hessaraghatta, Opp. Nrityagram, Bangalore 560088*
*Tel 2225 2846/6326*
*Fax 2846 6347*
*Tariff Rs 4,300 to Rs 6,300*
*Cards All*
*Check in/out 24 Hour*
*Web www.tajhotels.com*

An hour's drive out of Bangalore will get you to Taj Kuteeram located next to the dance village Nrityagram. Designed by the award-winning architect Gerard da Cunha, Taj Kuteeram combines rustic charm with contemporary comforts. Red oxide flooring, rough hewn walls adorned with ancient cave art, murals and paintings mark the six rooms and three suites here. There is a lounge, a meditation hall, an Ayurveda and yoga centre, and a restaurant serving Continental and Indian cuisine. Taj Kuteeram also offers facilities like 24-hour facsimile, currency exchange, travel assistance, a doctor on call and laundry services. The added attraction here is the dance school, Nrityagram where visitors are allowed a glimpse of the gurukul system of training. Boat rides are also arranged at the Hesaraghatta lake.

## Eagleton – The Golf Village
*Bangalore-Mysore Highway, Shyanamangala Cross, Bidadi Industrial Area, Bangalore 562109*
*Tel 2676 4403, 728 7222*
*Fax 2676 2978*
*Tariff Rs 2,800 to Rs 3,800*
*Green fees Rs 500 (weekdays), Rs 1,000 (weekends)*
*Cards MasterCard & Visa*
*Check in/out 12noon*
*Web www.eagletonindia.com*

Here is a posh golf resort set on a 500-acre property adjoining Bidadi Industrial Area on the Bangalore-Mysore highway. The 18-hole, 72-par US PGA standard championship course is open all year round and has a flood-lit Golf Academy where the focus is on developing and improving your game. The academy has professional instructors and state-of-the-art training aids, including cameras and video equipment. The resort has 48 air-conditioned suites,a business centre, banquet hall, shopping arcade, health club, gymnasium and a swimming pool. For those interested in sports other than golf, there are badminton, tennis, volleyball and squash courts, a bowling alley and pool and snooker tables. Airport and station transfers are provided. There is a 24-hour coffee shop, multicuisine restaurant, bar, terrace garden grill and a rejuvenation centre. For families travelling with children, babysitting services and a play area is available.

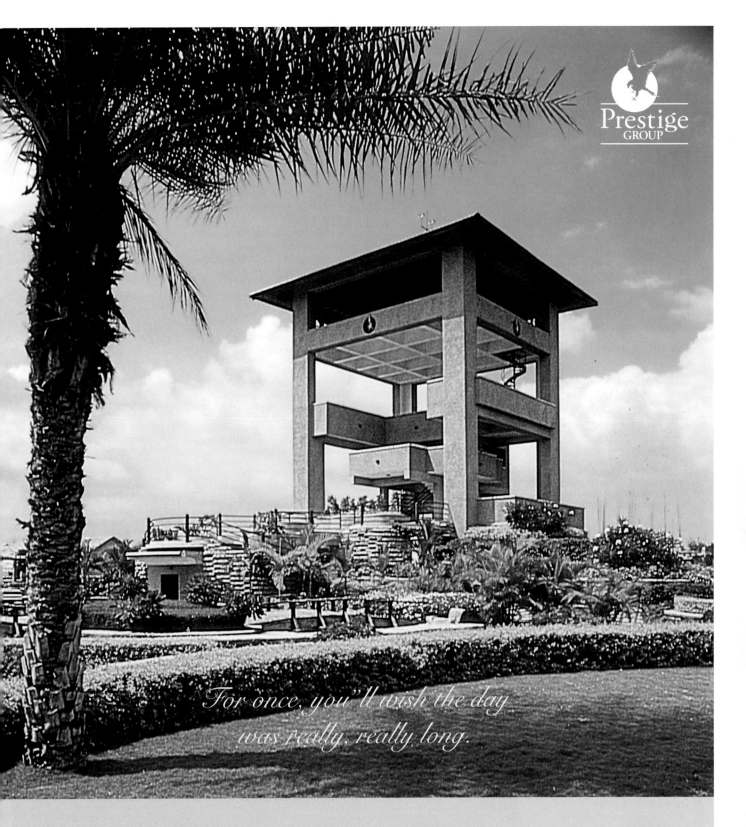

*For once, you"ll wish the day
was really, really long.*

Angana, The Country Inn

## The Village Resort

*14 Bellalu Village,*
*Chunchunkuppe Post,*
*Bangalore 562130*
*Tel 2335 9084, 2843 8241*
*Fax 2843 8444*
*Tariff Rs 2,300 to Rs 3,700*
*Cards All*
*Check in/out 12noon*
*Web www.thevillageresort.com*

Off the Mysore highway, the resort comes complete with a swimming pool, play area, table tennis, volley ball, basket ball and badminton courts, a snooker parlour, gymnasium as well as boating and travel services. The rooms are tastefully done and the resort restaurant serves an American breakfast and Indian cuisine for lunch and dinner.

## Estate Club & Resort

*Goolimangala Village, Huskur Post*
*Bangalore 560099*
*Telefax 2676 7631/1500*
*Tariff Rs 1,500 to Rs 3,500*
*Cards All*
*Check in/out 12noon*
*Web www.myestateclub.com*

A 50-acre plantation off Hosur Road, the Estate Club & Resort has 11 air-conditioned cottages and a bungalow. The resort offers the usual facilities like a swimming pool, multicuisine restaurant, bar, a conference and a party hall. There are also play areas for children, an amphitheatre and a health club.

## Sunny Holiday Village & Convention Centre

*64/1 Gottigere, Bannerghatta Road,*
*Bangalore 560083*
*Tel 2842 9620/9621*
*Fax 2842 9948*
*Tariff Rs 700 to Rs 2,850*
*Cards All*
*Check in/out 12noon*
*Email sunnyhol@vsnl.com*

Off the Bannerghatta Road overlooking a lake, this resort has 28 rooms and six cottages. Outbound training programmes for working professionals

are conducted on a regular basis here. Fitness enthusiasts can use the swimming pool, a jogging track and volleyball, badminton and basketball courts. Ideal for weekend getaways, there is also a children's play area, an Ayurvedic spa, a gym and health club. The two restaurants here are the **Riviera** with a multicuisine menu and **Jopadi** serving Chettinad food. There is a buffet spread in the restaurant **Whispering Grove**, and a poolside barbecue.

## Green Valley

*Arya Foundations Pvt. Ltd., 6, 3ʳᵈ Floor,*
*Kedia Arcade, 92 Infantry Road,*
*Bangalore 560001*
*Tel 2559 2896/3068*
*Fax 2558 5466*
*Tariff Rs 1,350 to Rs 2,840*
*Cards All*
*Check in/out 24 Hour*
*Web www.greenvalleyresorts.com*

Set within a 200-acre expanse of greenery, Green Valley is located on the Bangalore-Doddaballapur Road. About 50kms from the city, the resort has 10 single cottages, five double cottages, a multicuisine restaurant and barbecue. Guests looking for some entertainment can choose from billiards, table tennis, tennis, cricket, golf, football and basketball. There is a disco, health club, gym and conference hall. For children there is a play area, a deer park and horse riding facilities.

## Ramanashree California Club and Resort

*Ananthpura Gate, Doddaballapur Road,*
*Yelahanka, Bangalore 560 064*
*Tel 2223 5250 (City Office),*
*2846 1250/51/52/1257 (Resort)*
*Fax 2846 1254*
*Tariff Rs 2,095 to Rs 2,695*
*Cards All*
*Check in/out 12noon*
*Web www.ramanashree.com*

Popular with the weekend crowd, the resort has 34 rooms, a restaurant, **Punjabi Dhaba** that also serves Continental food and a Chinese cuisine restaurant and a theme bar, **Men at Work**. The resort has a swimming pool, manicured lawns, amphitheatre, badminton, tennis, squash, billiards, a kid's room, children's play area and health club.

## Eagle Ridge Resort

*Begur Koppa Road, Bangalore 560068*
*Tel 2532 5302 (City Office);*
*2842 9770 (Resort)*
*Fax 2558 2425, 2842 9833*
*Tariff Rs 2,600*
*Cards MasterCard & Visa*
*Check in/out 12noon or 11am*
*Web www.trailsindia.com*

Managed by Trails, Eagle Ridge is a tranquil wooded retreat with modern facilities on a 21-acre wooded area. Eagle Ridge is a 16km drive from Bangalore. It has 28 rooms and attractions like a swimming pool, horse riding, indoor and outdoor games, a play area for children, a gym and a multicuisine restaurant. The conference room with a tile and bamboo roof doubles up as a home entertainment theatre at night.

## Silver Oak Resort

*23ʳᵈ Km, Bangalore-Doddaballapur Road,*
*Rajanukunte, Bangalore 560064*
*Tel 2846 8070 Fax 2846 8265*
*Tariff Single-Rs 1,500, Double-Rs 2,000,*
*Deluxe Suite-Rs 2,600 Day package-Rs 300*
*per person inclusive of lunch*
*Cards All*
*Check in/out 12noon*
*Web www.silveroakindia.com*

Twenty three kilometres from Bangalore city is the Silver Oak Resort, a sprawling resort with 22 rooms and suites. You can make a splash in the swimming pool, go plummeting down the water slide or enjoy an exciting game of badminton, table tennis, tennis, volleyball, squash or billiards. Other facilities include a banquet hall, boardroom, cricket ground, indoor games, children's play area, health club, steam, sauna and joggers track. **Isis** is a multicuisine restaurant while **Highway** serves Indian meals and the drinks are available at the **Sphinx** bar.

## Angana, The Country Inn

*55 Pattareddy Palya, Kaggalipura, 25ᵗʰ*
*Km, Kanakpura Road, Bangalore 560062*
*Tel 2843 2888/2303*
*Fax 2657 3219*
*Tariff Rs 2,470 per day for two persons*
*(inclusive of food and taxes)*
*Cards Not Accepted*
*Check in/out 12noon*
*Web www.anganacountryinn.com*

Eagle Ridge Resort

The Grand Ashok, Bangalore

# *Go Star Trekking.*

InterContinental The Grand, Mumbai

InterContinental The Grand Palace, Srinagar

The Grand Laxmi Vilas Palace, Udaipur

The Grand Hotel presents some of the most starry destinations for you to choose from. Here, you can mix business and pleasure perfectly. Experience an altogether different level of class and beauty. Welcome to the Grand hospitality.

# THE GRAND
Hotels ÷ Palaces ÷ Resorts

InterContinental The Grand Resort, Goa

The Grand Temple View, Khajuraho

InterContinental The Grand, New Delhi

Golfing greens at Eagleton (See Pg 192)

Built in the traditional Mysore style, this is a convenient base for trips to the Art of Living Ashram (four kms away), Bannerghatta Biological Park (10kms away) and the Floriculture Farm. Five ethnic rooms, a mini amphitheatre, a conference hall, children's play area, table tennis, shuttle-badminton courts and a watchtower are on offer. The swimming pool is in the shape of a Kalyani or a temple tank with steps that lead to the pool and there is also a traditional oil bath centre. The interiors have a rugged and ancient look about them with antique telephones, tables, chairs, chandeliers, porcelain base, toggle switches, old paintings, huge teak doors and a gramophone with old LP records. Treat yourself to a massage and oil bath at the traditional oil bath centre and try the wide variety of food.

## Sun Valley Club
*21 Gollarahatti, Magadi Main Road, Vishwaneedam Post, Bangalore 560091*
*Tel 2348 0342 Fax 2348 5220*
*Tariff Rs 550 to Rs 1,500*
*Cards All*
*Check in/out 24 Hour*

Sun Valley Club offers a swimming pool, children's park and banqueting and conferencing facilities. The green lawns and poolside make it a relaxing getaway and there is also a natural rock garden.

## Emerald Isle Resort
*Kolathur Village, Kasba Hobli, Hoskote Taluk, Bangalore 561119*
*Tel 2530 2221/2223, 512 51123*
*Fax 2530 2223*
*Tariff Rs1,000 to Rs 1,500*
*Cards All except American Express*
*Check in/out 12noon*
*Email emeraldislebangalore@touchtelindia.net*

Set on six acres of land with plenty of palm trees, Emerald Isle is about 27kms from Bangalore. It has an

Outward Bound Learning Centre for team building workshops apart from the mini golf course, tennis, badminton and basketball courts and a gym. This resort makes an ideal weekend getaway, especially for those who like nothing better than sitting by a pool with a bar in close proximity. There is also a conference hall and a multicuisine restaurant.

## The Club
*7th Mile, Mysore Road, Bangalore 560039*
*Tel 2860 0665/0768*
*Fax 2860 0770*
*Tariff Rs 700 to Rs 1,500*
*Cards All*
*Check in/out 24 Hour*
*Web www.theclubbangalore.com*

Located on Mysore Road, The Club is better known for its discotheque, a big favourite with the city's youth. The Club also has a swimming pool, pool and billiard parlour, squash and tennis courts and a gym. There is also a multicuisine restaurant, bar, banquet and conference halls and an amphitheatre.

## Dharamshi Resorts
*30th Km, Bangalore- Kunigal Road, NH 48, Nelamangala*
*Tel 2558 9300 (City Office), 772 2187 (Resort)*
*Tariff Rs 1,500*
*Cards Not Accepted*
*Check in/out 9am*
*Email dharamshis@hotmail.com*

Located amidst 16 acres of greenery, it is just a 45-minute drive from the city. The resort has seven cottages, a swimming pool and a separate pool for kids and an amusement park with a toy train. Other facilities include a conference hall, an open air auditorium, health club, gymnasium, steam, sauna, indoor and outdoor games and a doctor on call. The coconut grove is an added attraction as is the vegetarian restaurant.

## MS Resort & Farms
*Moyagannahalli, Bangalore-Mysore Highway, Ramanagaram Taluk, Bangalore 571511*
*Tel 2221 0503/0554*
*Fax 2221 9300*
*Tariff Rs 700 to Rs 1,300*
*Cards Not Accepted*
*Check in/out 24 Hour*

A pleasant drive on the Bangalore-Mysore highway leads to MS Resort & Farms. (Adventure enthusiasts can head for the rocks at Ramanagaram.) The resort has an amusement park, children's play area, hanging bridge, water slides and a swimming pool. There are two air-conditioned rooms, 10 non-air-conditioned rooms and a multicuisine restaurant.

## Bindra Resorts
*35 Vajarahalli, 9th Mile, Kanakapura Road, Bangalore 560062*
*Tel 2676 323 (City Office), 2843 5457/5384 (Resort)*
*Fax 2676 3230*
*Tariff Rs 1,250*
*Cards All*
*Check in/out 12noon*
*Web www.holidayvillagebiz.com*

Bindra Resorts is located 14kms from the city and is famous for its restaurant **Baisakhi** that serves Punjabi, Tandoori and Chinese food. Guests can unwind in the pool or opt to play tennis or volleyball. There is also a discotheque and party hall.

## Woodrich Club & Resorts
*218 Woodrich Enclave, Anegatta Village, Devanahalli, Bangalore 562110*
*Tel 768 2984 Fax: 2344 0023*
*Tariff Rs 1,000*
*Cards Not Accepted*
*Check in/out 24 Hour*
*Email woodrichresorts@gardencityonline.com*

Located in Anegatta Village off the Devanahalli-Doddaballapur Road, the resort overlooks Nandi Hills. Ten cottages, a swimming pool, a children's pool and play area, a tennis court, an indoor badminton court, table tennis and billiards tables, a gymnasium with steam room, sauna and massage facilities, an artificial rain dance bay and a restaurant serving south and north Indian food are the facilities offered.

## Jade Garden
*Sadahalli Village, Devanahalli Taluk, Bangalore 562110*
*Tel 2846 7055 Fax 2846 7059*
*Tariff Rs 625*
*Cards All*
*Check in/out 6:30am to 10:30am*
*Web www.clubcabanaindia.com*

Twenty seven kilometres from Bangalore, Jade Garden makes an ideal getaway for long weekends and holidays. There's plenty to do with jogging tracks, putting greens, a bowling alley, snooker and pool table, a squash court, a skating rink and finally a steam room and sauna. A shopping arcade, amphitheatre and multipurpose hall make up the rest.
For lovers of water sports, the **Water World** at Jade Garden offers three water slides, a 10,000sqft wave pool and pool for children set within plenty of greenery and colourful cabanas. **Water Court** is a multicuisine restaurant. There is also a **Domino's** outlet and a bar, **Nautical Bar**.

Taj Kuteeram is situated next to dance village Nrityagram.

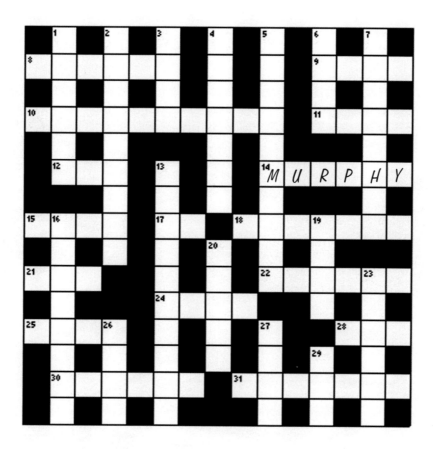

If you come across Murphy's Law lurking in
these pages, let us know.

Feel free to share your ideas, your opinions
and suggestions about this book. Simply email your feedback to
response@starkworld.net

Stark World, Infinitum Publishing Pvt. Ltd, 173, 9th Cross, Indiranagar 1st Stage, Bangalore - 560038. Tel: 91-80-51255036

Jayanagar, one of Asia's largest and Bangalore's oldest suburb.

Real Estate

A city of highrises, glass and chrome buildings dot Bangalore's skyline. Sprawling apartment complexes are springing up everyday within the city and its far flung suburbs.

Bangalore has transformed itself into a silicon city. Yet, its old world charm is still evident in colonial bungalows that lie in quiet lanes. Monkey tops, sprawling gardens, open verandahs and cool courtyards are characteristic features of these old edifices. Some of them are turning into lifestyle stores.

# Real Estate

**B**angalore, with its **leafy suburbs**, **hi-tech industry** and cosmopolitan image is the pin-up city of Indian metros. An energetic business atmosphere, **shopping malls**, **good schools**, **parks,** a variety of art, entertainment and of course its famed weather, are attractive elements. Once a sleepy cantonment city with far-flung suburbs, ethnic extensions and industrial townships on its fringes, Bangalore has now emerged as the city of the future. Everyone wants to come and live in Bangalore or at least own a square of land in what is increasingly being touted as Asia's fastest growing city.

Bangalore combines a touch of tradition with a generous helping of the modern, where the conservative meets the bohemian. There is rich and varied **art and culture** – Indian classical music evenings share the stage with lively jazz; the varied **food and drink options** – vegetarian dishes sit on the table with Japanese Sashimi! And traditional, old style houses share a wall with modern glass and chrome buildings.

One of the five big metros in India, Bangalore is well connected by air and rail to all parts of India and to major international destinations. To meet the growing demand for air services, the state government has commissioned a brand new **international airport** in Devanahalli, on the northern edge of the city.

Interest in Bangalore as a real estate destination began as far back as the 60s when it was known as a Pensioner's Paradise for the

The stream of shoppers on Brigade Road

number of retired people who chose Bangalore. It was perfect for long walks, quiet afternoons and evenings at the clubs. It also had good hospitals and was well connected to the rest of India. Within the last decade however, there has been frenzied real estate activity in the city. Prices are much lower than Mumbai and Delhi and there is plenty to choose from. You can opt to live in the heart of the city or in any one of the peripheral suburbs with mini-townships.

## Commercial Activity

The central business district of MG Road has now expanded to include peripheral roads in central Bangalore. Some IT companies with bigger needs have moved to the outskirts. Electronics City on Hosur Road and ITPL in Whitefield are designed with hi-tech companies in mind. Like attracts like and so in the last five years, the eastern stretch of land between the two is slowly being occupied by IT and IT related services and is called the **IT corridor**. **Hosur Road, Whitefield, Sarjapur** and **Bannerghatta Road** are part of

this hi-tech address.

Retailing isn't far behind. **Large shopping malls** as well as buildings with smaller shops are going up for sale all the time. And not all of them are concentrating on the central business areas but spreading into the suburbs where there is ample parking and an assured catchment area.

## Homing In

In tandem with growing commercial activity, **residential activity** has also picked up. Rising incomes, double-income families and of course, **easy financing options** are spurring more people to take the plunge and put money down on a house. There is a large variety of **budgets, locations, designs** and **facilities**. Enough to satisfy the fussiest buyer. Most of the activity is taking place in and around south and east Bangalore, in areas like **JP Nagar, HSR Layout, Indiranagar, BTM Layout, HRBR Layout, Old Madras Road, Koramangala, Sarjapur, Banashankari and Bannerghatta Road.** Competitive lending rates and quick processing have made investing in housing an attractive option.

From **independent houses** to **flats** and **sprawling farmhouses**, there is something for everyone. The current trend is towards large apartment complexes or villas with amenities like swimming pools and clubhouses.

Development of the properties has been entrusted to private builders who add their unique touch. For example, the Prestige group tries to retain some part of the old building while the Total Environment group go in for the terracotta look and ensure that terrace gardens accompany every apartment.

## Setting up Home

Nobody stops at just buying a house. Doing up **home interiors** is a specialised field today and interior designers are among the most sought after professionals. **Landscaped gardens**, plush interiors, textured walls, natural lighting, soft lighting, terrace gardens, **ethnic interiors, glass and chrome**...right down to paintings for the walls, the choice is extensive and buyers can find anything to suit their taste and interests.

One concept that is increasingly popular is **modular units** for the home, especially the kitchen. Extremely convenient, these kitchens can be done up in a few days, complete with walls, floors, cabinets, the works. Four bare walls get transformed into elegant, ready-to-use, fully equipped kitchens.

The advantages of modular units are that the material used is durable, easy-to-clean and space is efficiently used. Hundreds of combinations of colour, tiling, veneer, workspace and design are possible, so no two kitchens need look alike!

An aerial view of MG Road by night

Commercial Street, the shopping hub of Bangalore

entities with **shopping**, **schools**, **hospitals**, **malls** and so on. Others that don't make the township grade stop with **gyms**, **swimming pools**, **tennis courts** and other facilities.

Whichever way you look at it, Bangalore is the most attractive city to pensioners and young parents alike. The building and construction market is active and growing, and buyers can choose what suits them best. *Stark World – Bangalore & Karnataka* aims to inform potential buyers about the city, the essence of **suburbs** and the options of **builders** and **realtors**. Use our shopping section which carries furniture and home shopping details to compile your personal manual. And round it all off with a little advice on Vaastu or Feng Shui if you like!

The tile market has exploded with new designs and a variety of finishes to satisfy even global tastes. The finish ranges from glaze to matte and sizes are as small as your palm or as large as your cutting board. Designs vary from 10 shades of seagreen to individually designed landscapes that qualify as tile art. Individually crafted sinks are the rage and buyers are willing to put down good money for what they see as a one-time expense.

Nowhere is the change more obvious than the furniture market, where a new store opens every month. From the clean lines of Scandinavian furniture to the heavy ornamentation of Victorian styles to the new dark-finished oriental touch, the choice is really limited to how much you see! Some builders even provide **furniture** with a new flat, created to your specifications and taste and take the traditional headache of dealing with carpenters off your hands.

### Town Away from Town

To accommodate the growing demand for housing there are a number of **independent townships** springing up on the outskirts. Well beyond the ambit of old Bangaloreans, they attract the young breed of settlers who think nothing of driving an hour for the privilege of living in India's most attractive city!

These townships may have started as far flung suburbs, but as commercial and business addresses move out as well, they may soon become no more than a short drive. Almost all aim to be independent

# Indiranagar

Glitzy shops, chic restaurants and fashionable houses have replaced the dense swamp that was once Indiranagar. A few decades ago, it was called Binamangala village. Lying on the eastern edge of the city, it was known for its dense forests and bands of thieves and dacoits who roamed the area! It has since metamorphosed into a bustling commercial centre and upmarket residential layout with schools, hospitals and parks.

Three decades ago the Karnataka Housing Board constructed a few houses here, and Binamangala village became an extension of Bangalore city. At around the same time, the Chinmaya Mission Trust set up a dispensary at one end of a long, deserted road, later called the Chinmaya Mission Hospital (CMH) Road. The small dispensary has since grown into a full fledged multi-speciality hospital and CMH Road has become the nerve centre of this suburb.

Indiranagar has welcomed the IT boom and the commercialisation of the suburb has grown by leaps and bounds, as has the land value. The old KHB houses have given way to swank boutiques, malls, multicuisine restaurants and lifestyle stores. 100Ft. Road, Indiranagar's longest and widest road joins Old Madras Road to Airport Road and the junction of Ring Road leading to Koramangala. Connecting most parts of Indiranagar, 100Ft. Road showcases the best of the suburb with its palatial houses, art galleries, boutique restaurants, bookstores, hospitals and schools. Those who live in Indiranagar swear by its convenience. It's close enough to the main district (MG Road is a mere five kilometres away), yet provides everything residents need.

# Koramangala

Once a small village on the south eastern corner of the map, Koramangala is today an IT, shopping and residential hub. Koramangala is also on the route to Electronics City, so companies that needed to be close to the hub of IT, set up office here and software engineers and their families settled quickly.

Koramangala soon developed into an upmarket, cosmopolitan suburb with broad tree lined roads, well constructed apartments and an active residents association. But underneath the hi-tech surface is the story of another village transforming into a cosmopolitan suburb, a forest giving way to the IT corridor – a transition that has taken less than 30 years. Once a remote extension with badly maintained access roads, Koramanagala has benefitted hugely from the construction of the Ring Road. And it now has all the ingredients for an ideal locality.

Koramangala is vastly self-sufficient with many schools, hospitals, gyms, stores, libraries and a local club. There is hectic building activity and this suburb is likely to grow beyond its IT locality tag. Malls and plush shopping arcades like The Forum, Big Bazaar and Globus are located here.

## BUILDERS & DEVELOPERS

### Adarsh Developers
*205 House of Lords,*
*St. Marks Road, Bangalore 560001*
*Tel 2229 4727, 2227 4669*
*Web www.adarshdevelopers.com*

Adarsh Developers was started by C Jayashankar in 1988 and has developed 11 residential buildings, primarily in south Bangalore. The Bangalore Urban Arts Commission awarded their property, Adarsh Palace the 'Best Maintained Building and Garden' award. The company was recently awarded the ISO 9001 certification. One of their well known buildings is Adarsh Opus that houses the mega store Lifestyle, with a built-up area of 85,550sqft. Their latest project is off Airport Road – Adarsh Vista and it promises the best in contemporary living.

### Bhagyashree Developers
*14/529 Shakti Sri, 1ˢᵗ Floor,*
*New BEL Road, RMV II Stage,*
*Bangalore 560094*
*Tel 2351 7270/7299, 5690 8548*
*Web www.bhagyashreedevelopers.com*

With ten years experience in property development, Bhagyashree Developers aims at building comfortable and cost effective houses. Most of Bhagyashree's development is in and around the Banaswadi area, about nine kilometres from MG Road. Bhagyashree BDS Nagar has the convenience of independent homes with all amenities such as schools, supermarkets, hospitals and shopping centres in the vicinity. Parks, tree lined roads, water supply and electricity, fenced perimeter are just some of the facilities on offer here. Bhagyashree Royale is yet another development offering similar facilities. BDS Layout and BDS Garden are upcoming developments.

### Biodiversity Conservation India Limited
*609 80Ft. Peripheral Road, IV Block,*
*Koramangala, Bangalore 560034*
*Tel 2553 9300/9350/9344*
*Web www.bioconserveindia.com*

Biodiversity Conservation India Ltd. (BCIL) is one of the lesser known but discerning developers in the city. Started in the mid-1990s, BCIL has successfully brought in traditional and alternate methods to construct homes. Some of their properties are Trans Indus, TownsEnd, Tempus, T-Zed Homes, WildGrass, and Little Acre. Trans Indus is a full fledged housing development with 60 homes spread over 42 acres, offering facilities such as a swimming pool, amphitheatre, meditation centre, bar, restaurant and Internet connectivity. Plenty of greenery, a weather station and a telescope are its other highlights. The community effort includes use of indigenous varieties of trees and plants, making its own bio-fertilisers and bio-pesticides and residents have also decided that the turfed area is not to exceed 20 percent of a resident's garden – lawns being highly water-intensive. The group believes in using local materials and traditional building techniques that minimise damage to the environment. Every BCIL project is designed to address environmental, social and economic needs.
Located on Airport Road is BCIL's new age enclave, T-Zed Homes, offering 95 houses over a two hectare expanse. The T-Zed Campus will be ready in the next 12 months.

### Brigade Group
*Penthouse, Brigade Towers, 135 Brigade*
*Road, Bangalore 560025*
*Tel 2227 7017, 5137 9200*
*Web www.brigadegroup.com*

Established in 1986, Brigade Group is one of south India's first property developers to get the ISO 9001-2000 quality certification. Over the years, the group has constructed luxury apartments, self-contained enclaves, modern offices, showrooms, state-of-the-art software facilities and a multistoried industrial complex. With projects in JP Nagar, Malleswaram, Whitefield, Old Madras Road, MG Road and Mysore city, the group offers a range of projects in various stages of conception and execution.

# Flirt with five, settle for one.

Life is all about choices – the ones you make, and the ones you don't. And choosing your dream home is no different. It's about that perfect feeling, those perfect moments, in a place you call home. It's about the art of fine living. From urban sophistication to timeless elegance, from cozy apartments to luxuriant penthouses, elegant townhouses to opulent villas, we make sure you get the best of everything. With Puravankara, you never run out of choices…in fact, you're spoilt for one.

# PURVA
# RIVIERA
## ON AIRPORT ROAD

# PURVA
# PANORAMA
### ELEGANT APARTMENTS ON BANNERGHATTA ROAD

# PURVA
# CARNATION
### Premium Apartments, Cox Town

# PURVA
# PARKRIDGE
### Ultra-luxury villas & town houses
### Ring Road, near Marathahalli

TOWN HOUSES PERSPECTIVE

# PURVA
# SUNSHINE
### Exquisite apartments on Sarjapur Road.

# PURAVANKARA
## PROJECTS LIMITED

*Since 1975*

AN ISO 9001 COMPANY

SANKALP/319/04/PPL

**Bangalore:**130/1, Ulsoor Road, Bangalore – 560 042 Tel: 91-80-2559 9000 Fax: 91-80-2559 9350 E-mail: sales@puravankara.com
**Mumbai:** 227, SV Road, Bandra (West), Mumbai - 400 050 Tel: 91-22-2642 9387 Fax: 91-22-2644 1916 E-mail: purvamumbai@vsnl.com
**Dubai:** PO Box No. 5594, UAE Tel: 3527171 Fax: 3512080 E-mail: ppl@emirates.net.ae

Enjoy **'Purva Privileges'** - a unique rewards programme. Open to all Puravankara customers.  Visit us at: www.puravankara.com

DivyaSree Towers on Bannerghatta Road.

Brigade Group has progressively introduced value-enhancing features like advanced fire and security protection systems and the Integrated Building Management System (IBMS), which centrally monitors all building functions and systems. This has contributed in increasing 'building efficiency' and provides added comfort to residents. Brigade Group was one of the first to incorporate eco-friendly measures like rainwater harvesting and waste recycling systems into their projects. In the last two decades, Brigade Group has created a brand name that stands for reliability, high professional standards and long-lasting customer relationships.

## DivyaSree Developers

*DivyaSree Chambers, AV11 Langford Road, Near Hockey Stadium, Bangalore 560025*
*Tel 2224 4832, 2221 3344*
*Web www.divyasree.com*

DivyaSree properties are strategically located close to the major business hubs of Bangalore and the central business district of MG Road, the IT hub at Whitefield, the new IT corridor along the Ring Road, Bannerghatta Road and Outer Ring Road. DivyaSree Chambers on Langford Road is one of the group's prime projects. Spread over 5.5 lakh sqft. it houses top software companies. Other commercial ventures, also for IT companies, are DivyaSree Greens, adjacent to the KGA and DivyaSree Towers on Bannerghatta Road. Upcoming projects include DivyaSree Techno Park laid out on 40 acres. Another distinction has been their recent foray into neighbouring metros. DivyaSree is part of Shyamaraju & Company (India) Private Limited, a leading infrastructure developer in south India. They also provide property management services and support services like health clubs, cafeterias, air cooling solutions and dedicated optic fibre connectivity.

## Embassy Group

*Embassy Point, 150 Infantry Road, Bangalore 560001*
*Tel 2228 6868*
*Web www.embassyindia.com*

This ISO certified developer has built some of Bangalore's prime properties such as Embassy Eros, Embassy Woods and Embassy Palace. Developers of residential and commercial campuses, the Embassy group's latest projects include the Kirloskar Business Park across 26 acres of land on Bellary Road. They also offer development management and property management services.

## Ferns Builders & Developers

*1212 100Ft. Road, HAL II Stage, Indiranagar, Bangalore 560038*
*Tel 2527 0901/0905*
*Web www.fernsbuilders.com*

Ferns Builders & Developers have developed eight suburban projects in and around Bangalore and sold over a 1,000 units. There are four projects in progress offering residential plots, houses, villas, villaments, farmhouses and row houses. Each project aims for aesthetically pleasing and functional design along with high quality construction and optimum use of space.

## GESCO Corporation (South) Ltd

*21/19, Craig Park Layout, Off MG Road, Bangalore 560001*
*Tel 2532 0315/16*
*Web www.gescosouth.com*

Gesco South has developed over 1.5 million sq ft of exquiste residential and commercial developments. It is driven by the same core team that steered one property division of The Great Eastern shipping Co. Ltd. into one of India's foremost property developers.
Gesco Corporation (South) Ltd are the developers of the Gesco Lido Centre a large five star hotel, multiplex and retail complex off MG Road and stones throw

multiplex, a hotel and several retail stores under one roof. GESCO also caters to the increasing demand for large apartments. Now an ISO 9001 company, Spring Leaf is a sprawling residential complex offering just eight exclusive apartments. The Great Eastern Chalet and The Great Eastern Plaza are other up market residential properties developed by GESCO. While keeping the customer in focus, GESCO combines technology with a 'hands on' pragmatic approach.

## Gopalan Enterprises

*5 Richmond Road, Bangalore 560025*
*Tel 2227 7121*
*Web www.gopalanenterprises.com*

Founded in 1984, Gopalan Enterprises has been developing some of Bangalore's prime residential properties. Now an ISO 9001 company, most of Gopalan's activities have been in and around Indiranagar: their major projects here include Shabari, Swathi and Dwaraka. Royal Palms near Airport Road, Temple Trees at Banashankari, Gopalan Gardenia near Electronic City are upcoming residential projects. Gopalan has also shifted to commercial property development. Millenium Towers

located near Brookefields, Infotech Planet, developed on 23 acres of land near the Airport and Baroque on Hosur Road. Crossroads is another venture on Old Madras Road. This is a tech park built on a four-acre plot, with office space for IT and telecommunication ventures. Promenade is a commercial complex built on an acre near Jayanagar, and is a blessing for IT companies looking for office spaces within the city limits. Another commercial project, Milestones on Bannerghatta Road will serve as a catalyst in the development of the IT industry. Other upcoming properties include Gopalan Business Park near Brookefields, Gopalan Legacy on Mysore Road, Gopalan Baroque on Hosur Road and Gopalan Innovation on Bannerghatta Road.

## HM Constructions

*14 HM Geneva House, Cunningham Road, Bangalore 560052*
*Tel 2238 2288, 2228 9340*
*Web www.hmconstructions.com*

HM Constructions has 32 completed projects under its belt, both residential and commercial properties in prime locations of Bangalore. HM Manor was their first project on Hutchins Road. Nine apartments with exclusive penthouses in the upmarket Richmond Town were built under the name HM Avalon. In Richmond Town is HM Memphis with its 16 super deluxe apartments. HM West Park, in Malleswaram, has 18 spacious apartments.

## India Builders Corporation

*Sheriff Centre, 73/1 St. Marks Road, Bangalore 560001*
*Tel 2227 8283/1797*
*Email ibc@blr.vsnl.net.in*

India Builders Corporation (IBC) is one of the first builders of large residential properties like Golden Enclave and Diamond District on Airport Road, The Senate and Golf View Homes where the offices of Motorola, Texas Instruments, GE and Verifone are located. IBC has 30 years of experience in the industry and has worked with some of the best known architects of the city like Thomas Associates and Zachariah Consultants.

A Gopalan Enterprises property in Brookefields

Leave the stress behind...
live a greener experience

HABITAT
Splendour

Gracefully opulent, phase II is a fine tapestry of greenery and architectural elegance. In a choice of two and three bedroom and duplex homes. HABITAT SPLENDOUR is quietly prominent behind private gates, built to honour discerning buyers who yearn for nothing but the best.

A perfect complement to your lifestyle, it adds a new dimension to gracious living. And you are just a 20 min. drive from the city's nerve centre M.G. Road.

# 5, Richmond Road, Bangalore-560 025. Tel: 22277121 (6 Lines), Fax: 22212703 Website: www.gopalanenterprises.com

TWO DECADES OF ECO - FRIENDLY TRUST

# The ITPL Story

The face of Bangalore as IT city is the International Tech Park Limited or ITPL as it's popularly known. Located a half hour drive from the city, it's now almost a tourist destination. These modernistic buildings have trendy names like Discoverer, Explorer, Innovator and Creator and house some of the biggest names in the IT business the world over: Intel, Wipro, GM, AOL being just some of them. Set in Whitefield, the International Tech Park is spread over 28 hectares and boasts state-of-the-art infrastructure.

In 1992, in a meeting between the then Prime Minister of India, PV Narasimha Rao and the Singapore PM Goh Chok Tong, the idea to start the tech park germinated. The tech park was set up as a joint venture between the two countries in 1994. It was christened ITPL in 1997 when stage one was completed.

Over 9,000 employees, 102 offices of which 46 are multinational companies, a telephone exchange, dedicated power plant, a satellite dish that supports high bandwidth are just some highlights ITPL can boast of. In the last decade or so, ITPL has become one of the most preferred office spaces, with their plug-and-play facility providing more than just convenience. The Tech Park Business Centre is an ideal set-up for start-up companies with five cabins, two suites and eight workstations. In 1999, ITPL was awarded the ISO 9002.

ITPL not only offers office space but other amenities as well. The Tech Park's 12,000sqft health club runs a regular fitness programme where employees can de-stress and work out. The Tech Park Mall offers conveniences like banking and ATM facilities alongside food courts, beauty salons, supermarkets, lifestyle stores and even a medical clinic.

*International Tech Park Limited, Whitefield Road, Bangalore 560066,* **Tel** *2841 0570,* **Web** *www.intltechpark.com*

## Ittina Group of Companies
*5 Vachani Vista, IV Block, Koramangala, Bangalore 560034*
**Tel** *5110 1421/1422*
**Web** *www.ittinagroup.com*

The Ittina group comprises a number of companies that are involved with real estate development. Ittina Properties is involved in the construction of commercial complexes, sites and residential apartments. Divya Housing Pvt. Ltd. is involved in the development of layouts; their clients include the Central Silk Board and other government agencies. Ittina Housing is engaged in the construction of affordable apartments.

## Jain Housing & Constructions
*11, 1st Floor, Imperial Court, 33 Cunningham Road, Bangalore 560052*
**Tel** *2208 8287/8288*
**Web** *www.jainhousing.com*

This Chennai based group has been recognised as Bangalore's best builder by the Builder's Association of India and they have expanded their operations to Bangalore. Jains Prakriti is their first residential project here, set amidst plenty of greenery in Jayanagar.

## K Raheja Developers
*13th Floor, Raheja Towers, 26-27 MG Road, Bangalore 560001*
**Tel** *2558 9941/9945*
**Web** *www.krahejasouth.com*

One of India's leading builders and developers, the Raheja group has a presence in all leading metros. In Bangalore they have built a number of residential properties like Raheja Residency in Koramangala, Raheja Regent in Coles Park, Raheja Mansion in Milton Street and Raheja Arbor on St. John's Road. Their commercial project, Raheja Paramount is located in the busy

A property of Biodiversity Conservation India Ltd. *(See Pg 207)*

# It's a beautiful world...

and at Brigade, we continuously try to make it better.

In 18 years of operations, we have worked to make the landscape of the city a more liveable one. By creating better living and working spaces. And in the process, creating a better quality of life for the people who occupy them.

With two large enclaves slated to be launched soon—on Whitefield Road and in the Malleswaram-Rajajinagar region—we hope to take this vision further.

So whether you're looking for a home or serviced apartment, office or commercial premises, call us at 5137 9200 or visit: www.brigadegroup.com. It could change not only *where* you live or work...but *how* you live or work.

FOR A BETTER QUALITY OF LIFE

BRIGADE
GROUP

LUXURY APARTMENTS | ENCLAVES | SOFTWARE FACILITIES | OFFICES | CLUBS & RESORTS | EDUCATION

# RECOVER the INTEREST you PAY on your HOME LOAN.

India's **No.1** Solar Geyser

A 200 lt. Anu Solar Geyser can save 2400 units of power for an average home every year. That's a saving of Rs. 7560 annually! And, just one Anu Solar Geyser can provide all the hot water your home needs, instantly - even on cloudy days and at night. Plus, you can own one now for an EMI of just Rs. 395* for 24 months.

**ANU**
SOLAR SYSTEMS

*Conditions apply.

**Anu Solar Power Pvt. Ltd.** 248, 3rd Cross, 8th Main, 3rd Phase, Peenya Industrial Area, Bangalore - 58. Tel: 080-23724294/ 95/ 96. Email: info@anusolar.com **Call Toll Free: 1600 44 6001**

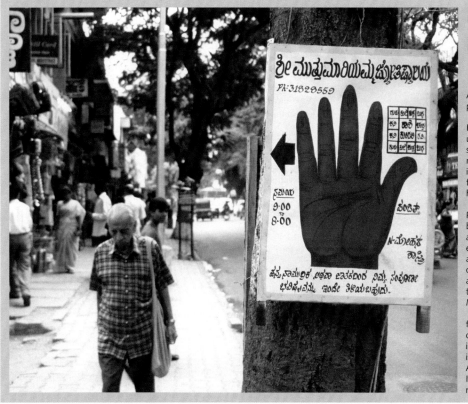

# Bangalore's Old Extensions

In the early 20th century, Bangalore gained the suburbs of Malleswaram and Basavanagudi. According to city historians, an outbreak of the plague in the late 19th century spurred this move.

These areas are regarded as the stronghold of Kannadigas and the Iyengar community. It is not unusual to find traditionally dressed women in silk saris with flowers in their hair, dhoti-clad Brahmin men and the overpowering smell of camphor and incense pervading all. A bustling vegetable and flower market along with old temples are the other highlights.

Malleswaram's Sampige Road and Margosa Road are named after the flowering trees that line its busiest roads. They are filled with shops selling anything from second hand books to prayer essentials. Hindu festivals are occasions of great activity and colour. The residential areas that were once filled with bungalows are now full of apartments, but despite of the rush of modernism, a traditional charm lingers in the bylanes of Malleswaram.

You'd know Basavanagudi if you were looking for Masala Dosa! Vidyarthi Bhavan that serves some of the best dosas in the city is a non-descript building in Basavanagudi's Gandhi Bazaar. Basavanagudi, is named after the age old Bull Temple located here. A bustling local market, regular kacheris or concerts of Indian classical music, astrologers and palmists are regular features of life here.

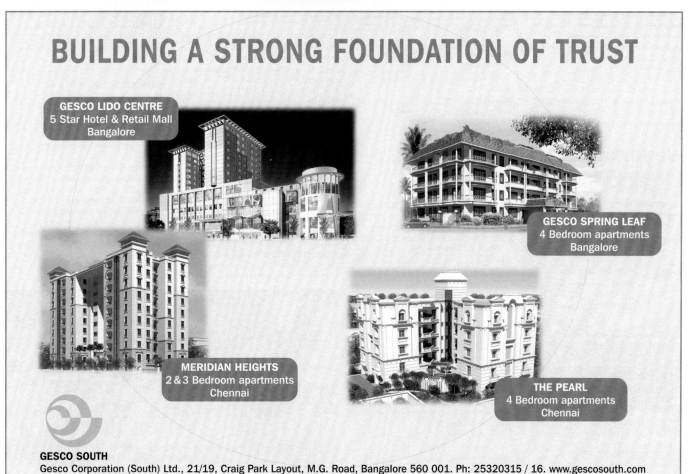

A Puravankara apartment complex

central business district of Residency Road. Jade Garden, a development on the outskirts of the city comes equipped with clubhouses, spa, villas and is set in the midst of landscaped gardens with a big pool. A bowling alley, amphitheatre and shopping mall are planned.

## Larsen & Toubro

*ECC Construction Division,*
*19 Kumara Krupa Road,*
*Sivananda Circle, Bangalore 560001*
**Tel** *2225 9675/9676/9679*
**Web** *www.ltproperties.com*

Better known as India's largest engineering and construction conglomerate, L&T has made inroads in the business of property development. Their engineering, construction and contracts division has established a reputation for timely completion, safety and reliability. South City, L&T's project in Bangalore is a township located near the Indian Institute of Management. It is south India's tallest residential building with 2,300 apartments being developed in phases.

## Mantri Developers

*The Mantri House, 41 Vittal Mallya Road, Bangalore 560001*
**Tel** *5130 0000*
**Web** *www.mantri.info*

With over 80 completed projects and over 10,000 satisfied customers, Mantri Developers has a firm hold on the Bangalore property scene. They have received the ISO 9001 certification from RWTUV, the Nirman Udyog Award, Project of the Year for Mantri Avenue II and Project of the Year 2001 for Mantri Woodlands. Most of their projects have been in Bangalore south. Commerce @ Mantri and Chambers @ Mantri are their ongoing commercial projects.

## Nagarjuna Construction Company

*301 Batavia Chambers, 8 Kumara Krupa Road, Kumara Park East, Bangalore 560001*
**Tel** *2225 8991, 2228 5669*
**Web** *www.ncclimited.com*

Nagarjuna Construction Company (NCC) is based in Andhra with branches all over the country. In 25 years the group has executed over 200 industrial and commercial projects. Asia's biggest cardiology centre, the Sri Jayadeva Institute of Cardiology was an NCC project. NCC has also developed two construction systems – cellular and modular.

## Prestige Group

*303 Copper Arch, 83 Infantry Road, Bangalore 560001*
**Tel** *2559 1080*
**Web** *www.prestigeconstructions.com*

Over the last decade, the Prestige Group has grown into one of south India's leading property developers with an impressive list of 103 completed projects, nine suburban residential layouts and upcoming projects that span over two million square feet. One of their most ambitious commercial projects is the mall that has come up in Koramangala. The Forum has multicuisine food courts, specialty restaurants and retail outlets. A 12-theatre multiplex is soon going to throw open its doors here. The group has won many accolades. The Acropolis designed with a Greek theme was named Project of the Year by Accomodation Times, Mumbai. Other impressive projects are Elgin, EGK and Sterling Square.

## Puravankara Projects

*130/1 Ulsoor Road, Bangalore 560042*
**Tel** *2559 9000*
**Web** *www.puravankara.com*

Established in 1975, the Puravankara Group has grown into one of the leading real estate developers in the country. The group began its operations in Mumbai and expanded into Bangalore in 1987. To date, they have completed over 100 projects in these two cities. The group has also extended its operations to Chennai and Cochin. In Bangalore alone, the group has developed over 10 million sqft. area, with ongoing projects measuring four million sqft and future projects in the region measuring 12 million sqft.
Backed by an in house team of engineers, architects, marketing executives, administrators and accountants, their development activities range from modern designer apartments, ultra modern bungalow complexes to plush commercial complexes. All Puravankara projects are approved by leading financial institutions like ICICI, IDBI, HDFC, LIC Housing Finance Corporation and CanFin Homes. Among

their many awards and certifications are the ISO 9001 certification since 1998, Finaliste, international Prix d' Excellence – 1998 for Purva Park, the PA 1 rating by the Credit Rating Information Services of India Limited (CRISIL) for Purva Graces and Purva Heights. Puravankara projects also come with a DA+2 CRISIL rating. This indicates an excellent track record in maintaining high quality and working within stipulated time schedules.
The group has recently launched Purva Riviera on Airport Road, Purva Parkridge on the Ring Road, Purva Panorama located on Bannerghatta Main Road, Purva Sunshine on Sarjapur Road, Purva Carnation in Cox Town, Purva Pavilion in Hebbal and Purva Fairmont in HSR layout. The company has to its credit completed projects like Purva Iris at Cox Town, Purva Heights on Bannerghatta Road, Purva Graces on Bellary Road and Purva Park in Cox Town. Among its latest commercial projects are The Pavilion on MG Road and Purva Premiere on Residency Road.

## Ranka Developers

*III Floor, 31 Ranka Chambers, Cunningham Road, Bangalore 560052*
**Tel** *2226 0426/2351*
**Web** *www.ranka.com*

The Ranka group has completed 24 projects in Bangalore, all of which are residential developments. Another five are under construction. Ranka Nagar is an upcoming township near RT Nagar that offers independent villas at affordable prices. Ranka Colony on Bannerghatta Main Road offers six residential buildings with single and two bedroom options.

## Renaissance Holding & Developers

*12, 18th Cross, 6th Main, Malleswaram, Bangalore 560055*
**Tel** *2344 2062/2063/2065*
**Web** *www.renaissanceholdings.com*

Developers of residential, commercial and plotted developments, most of the Renaissance group's development has been in the old Bangalore areas of Malleswaram and Basavanagudi. Incorporated in 1994, the group has established itself as a leading property developer. Riding the real estate wave, Renaissance's latest project, Renaissance Wings, is a township close to the upcoming international airport.

# Jayanagar

From the newest southern suburb in the 50s to the oldest suburb now, Jayanagar's identity has changed over the decades. But it is still Southeast Asia's largest suburb, spread over nine

blocks and famous for broad and well planned roads, parks and restaurants. By all standards, it is the best planned suburb in the city.
The need for a planned suburb like Jayanagar came as the thickly populated Basavanagudi began spilling over into outlying areas. And what city planner Kempe Gowda marked as the south end of the city became the beginning of Jayanagar.
In 1976, the Bangalore Development Authority set up the BDA Complex in Jayanagar's IV Block and it quickly became the epicentre of all life in Jayanagar.
Jayanagar has a definite touch of the old world and is reminiscent of the 'Pensioners Paradise' Bangalore was once called. In the busy IV Block area it's not hard to find groups of senior citizens congregating in places, catching up on news or gossip. There are plenty of old style bungalows and unlike in other parts of the city, these have yet to give way to apartments.
There are only a few restaurants but plenty of cafés and south Indian vegetarian eating places, in keeping with the rather traditional profile of the suburb.

The city boasts a number of well planned parks.

A commercial property developed by RMZ Corp

## RMZ Corp

*The Millenia*
*Tower B, Level 12-14,*
*No. 1 & 2, Murphy Road, Ulsoor,*
*Bangalore 560008*
*Tel 5111 5111*
*Web www.rmzcorp.com*

In the last two years, RMZ Corp has developed 1.8million sqft in Bangalore, Pune, Hyderabad and Chennai. One of the first projects launched by RMZ Corp was The Millenia in Bangalore with four towers overlooking the Ulsoor Lake. It houses the offices of Philips Software, Mphasis, CTS, CA, Network Associates and Nike. Other projects in the pipeline are RMZ Ecospace, offering built-to-suit campus facilities and scalability options within a secure business park, the RMZ Centennial, located in Brookefields and RMZ NXT in the Export Promotion Industrial Park zone in Whitefield. RMZ offers end-to-end solutions to its clients, from site selection, purchasing, architectural design and coordination to construction. The company ensures the availability of an experienced and creative engineering team, timely execution of projects and emphasis on tenant comfort and safety.

## Salarpuria Group of Companies

*100 Money Terrace,*
*KH Road, Bangalore 560027*
*Tel 2222 8422, 5120 6000*
*Web www.salarpuriagroup.biz*

Salarpuria started in 1985 and ranks among the top builders and developers in the city with clientele including Intel, Lucent, Pizza Corner, ICICI and HSBC. Big Bazaar on Hosur Road and the Bandhej showroom in Indiranagar are housed in Salarpuria properties. Salarpuria has also developed some of Indiranagar's swankiest residential properties like Mona Lisa, Esplanada, Salarpuria Haven and Salarpuria Residency.

## Shriram Properties

*33-44, 8th Main, 4th Cross,*
*RMV Extension, Sadashivnagar,*
*Bangalore 560080*
*Tel 5113 7966*
*Web www.shriprop.com*

Started in 1996, Shriram Properties is part of the multi-crore Shriram Group. Their residential properties like the 480 apartments Shriram White House is laid out over five acres of land in RT Nagar. Sriranjani and Shivaranjani in south Bangalore provide convenient homes for people working in and around the area. Yaletech, Shriram Properties' commercial development is located close to Electronics City.

## Sobha Developers

*368, 7th Cross, Wilson Garden,*
*Bangalore 560027*
*Tel 2229 5936, 2222 7621*
*Web www.sobhadevelopers.com*

One of the earliest ISO 9001 builders in the country, Sobha Developers was set up in 1994. Every aspect of construction is managed in-house and attention paid to details: Floor tiles, metal beading for extra reinforcement and safe wiring. Sobha Windfall, Sobha Diamond, Sobha Sapphire and Sobha Garnet are some of their projects. On the cards are Onyx, Jade, Emerald, Turquoise, Pearl, Zircon, Coral, Opal and the Sobha Alexander. The Oman Topaz was Sobha's maiden project in the city, set in Koramangala. Poised as a 'single-source multiple-services' vendor, Sobha has diversified into the areas of interior design, glazing and metalworks also.

## Sterling Developers

*401 A Wing, Queens Corner,*
*Queens Road, Bangalore 560001*
*Tel 2226 2614/3716*
*Web www.sterlingdevelopers.com*

With two decades of experience in the industry, Sterling Developers are behind landmark projects in the city. Most of their residential properties have been developed in the old Bangalore suburbs of Malleswaram, Basavanagudi and Mathikere. Their properties provide uninterrupted power and water supply and premium fixtures. Some well known Sterling buildings in the city are Sterling Park in Hebbal, Sterling Manor in Basavanagudi, Sankey Apartments and Sankey Court in Sadashivanagar.

## Total Environment

*734, 4th Main, BDA Layout, I Block,*
*HAL III Stage, Bangalore 560075*
*Tel 2521 9007, 5115 4711*
*Web www.total-environment.com*

This is a real estate organization that addresses the many facets of design and construction needs. Developers of residential and commercial property, Total Environment buildings have ivy-covered walls and terrace gardens with a lot of light and air coming in. Use of natural materials like wire-cut bricks, exposed form finished concrete and stone floors has become the trademark of Total Environment buildings. They are also one of the few builders to use the DOKA system of formwork, which translates to high quality, long lasting and more efficient construction.

A residential property developed by Sobha

# Bangalore – India's Solar Capital

Bangalore is India's Sun City, the very heart of the rapidly growing solar and sustainable energy movement. 90 per cent of the country's solar energy production is driven by Bangalore's cutting edge companies such as Anu Solar, Tata BP as well as government institutions such as Karnataka Renewable Energy Development Limited.

Rapidly depleting fossil fuel resources, heightened environmental awareness and galloping electricity tariffs have created a huge demand for solar power. More and more homes and institutions across Karnataka, especially in Bangalore, are opting for solar water heating systems as well as solar lighting.

Bangalore-based Anu Solar recognised this opportunity as early as 1979, when it began developing, manufacturing and marketing solar energy based heating systems. Today, the Rs 250 million Anu Solar, the industry leader, is leading energy conservation initiatives in India, from its headquarters at Bangalore. Its 50,000sqft state-of-the-art manufacturing and research facility is the largest of its kind in Asia. Headed by a qualified chartered accountant, TJ Joseph, Anu Solar

geysers and heating systems are making inroads into manufacturing facilities in the dairy, pharmaceutical, automobile and hospitality industries besides in villas and apartment complexes.

"Solar energy is the future. No doubt. Once you install a solar water heating or lighting system, your energy requirements are met absolutely free. In Bangalore, a home with solar geyser installation can cut their electricity bill 50%. With hot water made available 24/7, through rainy days and dark nights. Bangalore is a city of well-travelled, intelligent, discerning people and hence it is not surprising that solar energy is being rapidly accepted and adopted," says Joseph

"According to our Research Cell, an average home that uses solar water heating systems will accumulate a compounded savings of Rs 8 lakhs in 20 years. And, our products come with a warranty of 20 years though we expect them to work problem-free for a good 30-40 years," adds Joseph. No surprise that Bangalore and increasing parts of Karnataka are turning solar.

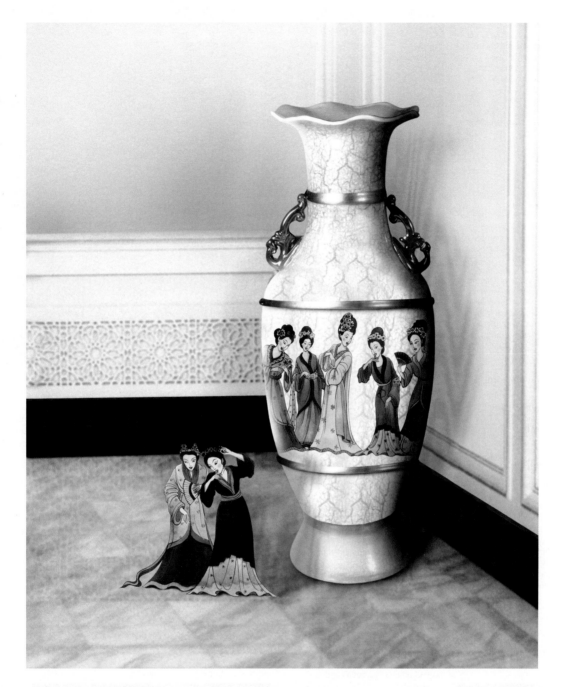

## MAYBE IT IS REVERENCE THAT MAKES PEOPLE BOW THEIR HEADS WHEN IN A SOBHA HOME.

If anything, perfection begets worship. The first thing you notice when you enter our homes is the flawless flooring. That's because we use spacers while laying floor and wall tiles to achieve perfect symmetry. Why, we even have the mason's name labeled on them to facilitate quality checks. These are only few examples of the delightful detailing that every Sobha home comes with. There are many, many more. Like we have plastic beading on wall corners for extra strength. Columns in parking lots have car fenders to ensure cars don't get dented. All these are because customer delight is an emotion that drives our every effort. It is the very focus of our architecture and construction processes. And precisely the reason why we are respected for our standards.

SOBHA

PASSION AT WORK

**BANGALORE NORTH:** SOBHA ORCHID -Off Bellary Road, SOBHA AMBER -Off Bellary Road   **BANGALORE SOUTH-EAST:** SOBHA SUNFLOWER - Off Airport Road, SOBHA ROSE - Whitefield Main Road, SOBHA IRIS - Sarjapur Outer Ring Road, SOBHA JASMINE - Sarjapur Outer Ring Road, SOBHA MAYFLOWER - Sarjapur Outer Ring Road   **BANGALORE SOUTH-WEST:** SOBHA TULIP - J.P. Nagar, 6th Phase, SOBHA MAGNOLIA - Bannerghatta Road, SOBHA ASTER - Bannerghatta Road

  SOBHA DEVELOPERS PVT. LTD., NO. 368, 7TH CROSS, WILSON GARDEN, BANGALORE - 560 027. INDIA. PH: 98801 78000, 98800 02222, 98800 03333, 98800 05555, 92431 09044 (All Days) 22295936/37/38, 22242172, 22125370 (Mon - Sat) E-mail: marketing@sobha.co.in   www.sobhadevelopers.com

Working in harmony with the elements, their projects include five completed residential blocks, with names like Reach for the Sky, Bouganvillea and The Good Earth. Footprints, Free Bird and Shine On are just three of the seven ongoing residential projects. The Ion Idea Tech Park, HAL Heritage Center and Museum and Webb India are also Total Environment buildings. Under construction are Eterna and Wings, two commercial buildings in Koramangala and central Bangalore.

## Vaswani Group

*52 Vittal Mallya Road,*
*Bangalore 560001*
*Tel 2223 0085*
*Web www.vaswanigroup.com*

Developers of both residential and commercial projects including software technology parks, the Vaswani group is also known for its plotted developments, suburban villas and townhouses. Bel Air, Villa Del Mar and God's Gift are a few popular Vaswani properties. The Bangalore Urban Arts Commission has awarded both Villa Del Mar and God's Gift for being the best maintained buildings with gardens. Vaswani Wilshire on Commissariat Road is a commercial development.

## Vakil Housing Development Corporation

*78 Koramangala Industrial Area,*
*Jyothi Nivas College Road,*
*Koramangala, VII Block,*
*Bangalore 560095*
*Tel 5119 3293*
*Web www.vakilhousing.com*

Vakil aims for international quality living spaces. Over the years, Vakil Housing Development Corporation has successfully developed many residential projects. Vakil Satellite Township is an upcoming project off the IT corridor of Sarjapur Road. Another project is Vakil Garden City on Kanakapura Road with 300 BDA approved sites. Vakil Gardenia is a completed project that comes with 36 exclusive two-bedroom houses located close to the Outer Ring Road, enroute to Whitefield, while Vakil Marina is a waterfront residential layout, overlooking the Madivala Lake. The Vakil group also owns a horse riding academy off Sarjapur Road.

# REAL ESTATE AGENTS

## Bearys Group

*40/1 Residency Road,*
*Bangalore 560025*
*Tel 2227 3124*
*Web www.bearysgroup.com*

Bearys started two decades ago as real estate agents providing comprehensive services to corporates, MNCs, government agencies and individuals. Recently, they diversified into property development and Orchard Green, a resort-style

residential property was built in Bangalore. Their other related venture includes Bearys Infrastructure Development Ltd. Their achievements include marketing almost 50 per cent of the residential units of Diamond District, Golden Enclave and ITPL.

## CB Richard Ellis

*The Hulkul, III Floor, 81/37, Lavelle Road, Bangalore 560001*
*Tel 5112 1240/49*
*Web www.cbre.com*

CB Richard Ellis' association with India began in 1994, the first international real estate services firm to establish operations in India. An integrated line of business, they offer strategic consulting, valuation advisory services, brokerage, project management and asset/facilities management. Their agency services include transaction management, services, property acquisition and disposition and rent renegotiation.

## Colliers International

*Prestige Garnet, Level II*
*201/202, 36 Ulsoor Road,*
*Bangalore 560042*
*Tel 5132 0320*
*Web www.colliers.com*

A global real estate services firm, with 7,600 employees in 51 countries, Colliers USP is their 'global breadth and local depth'. Leasing, rental and purchase of residential, commercial and industrial areas is undertaken by them. Other services include property representation, tenant representation,

corporate and investment services, development and project management and retail services.

## Cushman & Wakefield

*578 Syndicate Bank Road,*
*Indiranagar I Stage,*
*Bangalore 560038*
*Tel 2521 9756*
*Web www.cushwakeasia.com/apoffice/Bangalore.htm*

Cushman & Wakefield is a premier real estate services firm with worldwide operations and 11,000 employees. Cushman & Wakefield has been serving companies in Europe since 1820 and today provides a wide range of real estate services across North and South America, Europe, the Middle East, Africa and the Asia-Pacific region, including Bangalore. Their goal is to gain a complete understanding of how real estate fits into the business plans of their

clients. Cushman & Wakefield are involved in delivering customised services and solutions by actively advising, implementing, and managing on behalf of landlords, tenants and investors through every stage of the real estate process.

## Feroze's Estate Agency

*Cunningham Road, Opp. Westminster,*
*Bangalore 560052*
*Tel 2226 1838*
*Web www.ferozes.com*

*A* one stop shop for any property requirement at any budget. Houses, villas, apartments, office spaces and their documentation are looked into. In the business for two decades, Feroze's Estate Agency offers customised services including renting, selling, buying, lease and joint development. Microsoft, Intel, UB and HTA are some its customers. The agency also provides valuation and investment services.

Tree lined streets of Indiranagar

Aesthetics is about breathing character into form and space.

Your character.

At Total Environment, we respect that our clients are individuals with distinct tastes and lifestyles. Therefore, each of our clients has the option of customizing their living space. This is the creative space available to make their flat a home.

Interested?  Log on to www.total-environment.com to know more about us and our ongoing projects. You could also call us at 080-5115 7173/74, 98450 50833, 98450 01652 or 98800 40601.

We would love to know more about you and your needs.

www.total-environment.com

Total Environment

# Bangalore, My Favourite City – Samuel Selvakumar

Blue Ginger at The Taj West End

**B**angalore is something that is in you — the spirit of this vibrant city inspires you, energises you and gives you a sense of fulfilment. Although I am not a native of Bangalore I have spent 16 years in this city and built a large portion of my career here. I grew up in Chennai but my roots are here, in Bangalore. Wherever my job has taken me, Bangalore has always drawn me back like a magnet. I am in love with this city! And its fabulous weather spoils you!

Along with other great world cities like New York, Chicago and Mumbai, Bangalore is also a city built on migration. The result is an amazing pot pourri of diverse people and cultures – Keralites, Bengalis and Tamilians consider Bangalore home and feel a sense of pride towards it.

Bangalore is a youthful city. And the sheer variety it offers sets it apart. A plethora of eating out and entertainment options – glitzy clubs, sprawling malls, old churches, English-style pubs and speciality restaurants – all converge here. The city is a foodie's delight. I particularly enjoy the Vietnamese food at Blue Ginger, the steaks at The Only Place, the authentic Chinese fare at Memories of China, the Italian Pasta at Sunny's and Spiga...the list goes on. Bangalore also has a diverse cityscape, from the old world charm of Cox Town, the traditional flavours of Basavanagudi to the high rises of the newer suburbs. What gives Bangalore its unique edge is its people. Drawing some of the best talent from around India, its residents are an eclectic bunch of well travelled, qualified, discerning individuals.

Bangalore has displayed a sense of resilience. Its energetic entrepreneurial spirit has seen it ride the IT boom and the BPO wave. The city has outgrown its innings as a Pensioners Paradise. The Bangalore of today is a focussed city with high levels of professionalism and a sound work culture. Yet, it is not abrasive, the people here are mellow and the culture is warm. Despite the chaos of burgeoning traffic and the building pressure on infrastructure, an air of serenity pervades Bangalore. People like to hold on to this city and there is much more to it than the pleasant weather!

*Samuel Selvakumar is the CEO of Hutchison Essar South Limited, Karnataka and Andhra Pradesh. He lives in Bangalore.*

---

### Hanu Reddy Realty India
*763 100Ft. Road, HAL II Stage,*
*Bangalore 560038*
*Tel 2527 7170*
*Web www.hanureddyrealty.com*

With offices in Chennai, Bangalore and California, HRR offers professional services like selling, buying, and leasing of commercial and residential properties in prime areas in the city.

### Homing-In Realtors
*314/1, Vijay Kiran, 7th Cross, Domlur*
*Layout, Bangalore 560071*
*Tel 2535 1944/7963*
*Email girijachandran@hotmail.com,*
*girija@hammockholidays.com*

Started in1990, Homing-In is an exclusive agency offering total property management for non-resident Indians and people based outside Bangalore. The gamut of services includes identifying good bargains, taking care of all transaction formalities including legal counsel, fitting out and letting the premises for a rental return and paying property taxes.

### Jones Lang LaSalle
*Millers Boulevard, 70/2 Millers Road,*
*Bangalore 560052*
*Tel 5118 2900*
*Web www.joneslanglasalle.co.in*

Operating in India since 1998, with offices in the major metros, Jones Lang LaSalle provides transaction and advisory services, investment and asset management. Backed with a research forum, Jones Lang LaSalle provides significant value added services for investors, owners and users globally.

### Links Realty
*S&B Towers, 88 MG Road,*
*Bangalore 560001*
*Tel 2559 7606*
*Email linksrealty@vsnl.net*

Established in 1989, Links Realty caters to corporate clients. Operating within a five kilometre radius of MG Road, their clients include the Prestige Group, Embassy, Brigade Group. Links also offers car rental, residential accommodation and guesthouse services.

### Propmart
*15K, II Floor, St. Patrick's*
*Commercial Complex, Brigade Road,*
*Bangalore 560025*
*Tel 2558 2585/2586*
*Web www.propmart.com*

Propmart aims to build a customer-centric real estate service organisation with a real estate portal, a classified monthly magazine called Prop Guide, and even a help line called PropCall Centre. Property Advisors, Home Loans and even Home Loan Advising services are offered.

### Silverline Realty
*201 II Floor, Barton Centre,*
*84 MG Road, Bangalore 560001*
*Tel 2559 2881*
*Web www.silverlinerealty.com*

One of the oldest real estate agents in the city, Silverline Estates' clients include some of Bangalore's reputed property developers like Prestige, Brigade and the K Raheja group. Silverline caters to a varied market including MNCs, corporates, banks and retail markets.

---

# Bungalows

**O**ld fashioned bungalows with monkey tops, spacious front and backyards, set within tree lined avenues were once typical of Bangalore. The typical bungalow had a standard plan: Steps led up to a verandah that ran all the way around the house. The front verandah led into a spacious drawing room adorned with occasional skylights. The kitchen was removed from the main house and sometimes a passage connected the two. Typical kitchens had a small recess to hold the firewood and a chimney. Bedrooms were located in the wings, and the backyard had annexes where the household help stayed.

British architectural influence was strongly felt, and styles ranged from the simple to the elegant and even baroque. Classic Doric and Tuscan columns replaced the wooden posts and lowly thatch. Ornamental banisters were also popular.

But it is the monkey-top that was most characteristic feature of these bungalows. Named for the monkeys that regularly perched on their pointed hoods, they were built over the windows or as canopies along the front and sides of the porch. The front of the monkey tops had vertical slats, usually painted green.

The increasing demand for housing has put a squeeze on these rambling houses, but there are still a few of them that stand to remind Bangaloreans of what the city once looked like.

# City On Overdrive

India's City Of The Future, managed by

**Bangalore Mahanagara Palike**

*Citizens First. Always.*

- 106 traffic junctions redesigned
- Grade separators created
- Flyovers constructed
- 1500 kilometers of new roads laid
- Construction of multi-storied car parks in progress

# Bangalore's Heritage Buildings

Vidhana Soudha

Much of Bangalore's architectural legacy dates back to the days of the British Raj. In fact, there is a distinctly colonial air about the city, with tree-lined avenues, large parks with bandstands, army barracks, rambling bungalows and a large parade ground bang in the centre of the town. The flavour of the Cantonment lingers in suburbs with quaint names like Coles Park and Frazer Town and street names like Wood Street and Victoria Road.

Some of the British buildings stand untouched while others have been given a facelift and there are a few in dire need of restoration. A hundred years after the British made this their cantonment, the state of Karnataka's new leaders also chose from European-Classical, the Graeco-Roman, the Indo-Saracenic and Dravidian styles for the new public buildings. Today, most of these heritage buildings stand alongside gleaming glass and chrome high rises and give the city its unique mix of old and new.

## Vidhana Soudha

Built in 1956, Vidhana Soudha houses the offices of the State Secretariat and is the largest of its kind in the country. Covering an area of 50,000sqmts, this stone building is a fusion of several architectural styles, Dravidian, Rajasthani, Chola and Kannada. Fashioned out of locally quarried granite, the legislative assembly of Karnataka is decorated with frieze panels, ornamental motifs, floral carvings and geometric design. It is set amidst wide boulevards and flowering trees — the perfect setting for its intricate stonework and ornate style. Essentially Dravidian, a grand flight of steps lead to the entrance porch supported by 12 pillars alongwith Rajasthani-style 'jharokas' or balconies, landscaped gardens and two expansive quadrangles. Renowned

sculptor Shilpi Samachar has crowned the dome with the state's lion emblem. Distinctive architectural features to look out for are square and polygonal pillars with rich carvings, curved cornices, sweeping arches modelled on the Chaitya style, pillared halls, doors embellished with wood carvings and domes capping its pillars. Frieze panels borrow inspiration from the Hoysala temples at Halebid and Belur. A grand flight of steps leads to the entrance porch.

## Attara Kacheri

In the vicinity of the Vidhana Soudha is the Attara Kacheri. It translates to eighteen offices, and

housed the (18) offices of the Secretariat. Now occupied by the High Court, the Attara Kacheri is a two-storeyed structure of stone and brick built in Graeco-Roman style. The bright red of the building is offset by green wrought iron grillwork and Ionic porticos. It covers an area of 1.95 lakh sqft. A statue of Lord Cubbon seated on a horse, decorates the entrance.

## Sheshadri Iyer Memorial Hall

Sir Sheshadri Iyer was the Dewan of Mysore and a bronze statue of him graces the entrance of the Sheshadri Iyer Memorial Hall built in his honour. The State Central Library has been functioning here since 1915. The beautiful circular building in dramatic red is set around a rose garden. The striking building with lofty rooms and high windows is built in the same architectural style as the Attara Kacheri and Government Museum. The gables are outlined with floral motifs, symmetrical porches and buttressed columns.

## Government Museum

The Government Museum is located at the edge of Cubbon Park. Other state buildings like the High Court are located in the vicinity and they are all painted a characteristic Pompeian-red. The museum is adorned with Corinthian columns, decorative floral motifs and fluted pillars. The arches are decorated with heads of Greek gods. On display here are paintings, sculptures, artefacts and period paintings.

Sheshadri Iyer Memorial Hall

Mayo Hall

## Mayo Hall

This impressive brick and mortar building on MG Road catches the eye of every tourist and is held up as a sterling example of British architecture in India. It was built in the memory of Lord Mayo, Viceroy of India in 1875. The hall is open for public meetings and functions, while the adjoining block houses government offices. Gold painted Corinthian columns, a high elevation, pedimented windows, stone arches, balustrades and Greek cornices are among its attractive features.

## State Bank of India Estate

This stately two-storeyed mansion was designed in the British-Colonial style and built in 1840 for the British Resident. Set in a garden, the high-entrance porch has four Tuscan columns, covered with wooden rafters. Ionic columns, balustrades running through the verandah and a large terrace are other highlights. Original pieces of furniture have been retained including intricately carved cupboards and a stairway. A stained glass window bears the emblem of the Union Jack. The State Bank of India is now housed in this building.

## St. Mark's Cathedral

Built for the British army, the construction of this church was started in 1808 and additions were made in 1901. A High Renaissance structure, it has been modelled after St. Paul's Cathedral and other 17th century churches in England. A majestic dome, a porch with Ionic columns, moulded cornices, large windows, balustrade parapets and a circular vault on the apse are some of its special architectural features. Following a roof collapse and

fire, the church was given a facelift in 1927. Inside the church look out for beautiful stained glass in floral motifs that decorate the arches, and memorial tablets and plaques dating back to the 19th century. The church is set in a picturesque garden shaded by large rain trees, gulmohar and jacarandas.

## Puttanna Chetty Town Hall

This imposing Town Hall was built in 1935. It was named in honour of Puttanna Chetty, President of Bangalore Municipality who was known for his philanthropic interests. The Town Hall is a stone structure in European Classical style with a grand flight of steps leading to the entrance porch with Tuscan columns and twin porches on the

sides. The central part of the building houses an auditorium. A clock tower and fountain once graced the hall but have since been pulled down.

## Bangalore Palace

Built on the lines of a Tudor castle, the Bangalore Palace is one of the city's most distinctive structures. Modelled on the Windsor Castle in England, the palace of the royal Wodeyars boasts fortified towers, turrets, battlemented parapets and a beautiful manicured garden. Almost fairy-like, exquisitely carved floral motifs, mouldings, cornices, wood carvings and ceilings with painted relief work are some of its highlights. Owned by the Wodeyars, the palace is a venue for private gatherings.

BRV Theatre

## BRV Theatre

This charming stone building was originally designed as a store canteen or armoury. Now a cinema theatre, the building is almost medieval in style with striking battlements. These architectural features are shared by the Bible Society group of buildings on Kasturba Road. The battlements, steeped gables and turrets are other similarities.

Puttanna Chetty Town Hall

## Bangalore Club

Built originally as a club for British officers, the verdant and sprawling Bangalore Club has a long history. After passing through many owners since 1847, including Major General Cubbon, it was eventually sold to the Club Committee. The main structure of the Club House is a brick and mortar building, reminiscent of the White House in Washington. Cuddapah slabs have been used on the club's floors, Burma teak beams on the roof and tall Tuscan pillars, a large porch and a curved gable are its other features. The dining hall wing stands on an imposing group of pillars embellished with decorative cornices and the Brigadier Hill Annexe boasts a trellis-worked porch.

The club is an authentic period building and the British film, *A Passage To India* was shot here! Sir Winston Churchill was among the club's members. Today, it is a meeting place for the city's eminent people.

## Indian Institute of Science

The Indian Institute of Science came about in the year 1913. It is a two-storeyed grey granite building with a distinctly European-Classical look. Capped with a Mangalore-tiled sloping roof, the 160-foot high central tower is its most conspicuous feature. The tower has three levels, each bearing niches, balustraded railings and striking cupolas with moulded arches flank the tower on either side. Two soaring columns support the Ionic columned entrance. In the front stands a monument, a tribute to Jamshedji Tata one of the founders of the institute. The institution has a lush garden, one of the best in the city.

## Jumma Masjid

The oldest mosque in the city, Jumma Masjid is set in Bangalore's Cantonment area. Going by the name 'Friday Mosque', this elegant brick and mortar mosque displays intricate jali-work. Gleaming granite pillars and ornate stucco floral motifs adorn its façade. The mosque was built in the early 19th century, entirely out of razed material from Tipu's Palace from Srirangapatna. Damaged by canon balls, the mosque was renovated in 1836.

Bangalore Club

## Oriental Building

The stately Oriental Building is counted among Bangalore's best heritage buildings, lending a colonial flavour to busy MG Road. It is an aesthetically designed two-storeyed edifice built entirely in stone. Simple and elegant, balustrade railings, mouldings and cornices are its European-Classical characteristics. Stone arches framing its high windows, a diagonally placed entrance and unique window shades are among its other distinguishing features.

## Cash Pharmacy

Located at the junction of St. Marks and Residency Road, Cash Pharmacy is to date one of the best known landmarks in the city, albeit not one of the best maintained. Multiple roof planes, monkey top windows, a wooden facia, cornices and gables with trellises are its architectural highlights. The porch on the ground floor displays an attractive wooden trellis, a characteristic of the bungalow-style of architecture. A 24-hour pharmacy is housed here.

## St. Andrew's Church

This is undoubtedly one of the most eye-catching churches in Bangalore, not least because of its exteriors painted in a beautifully contrasting red and white. It is a Scottish-style Gothic church built in 1867 and its battlemented parapets, steepled turrets and tiled roof, make a striking picture. High windows, tall doors and circular ventilators have been set in white frames that contrast well with the oxide red colour of the building. Well integrated satellite buildings are set around the church.

## Gavi Gangadhareshwara Temple

This ancient cave temple in Basavanagudi dates back 500 years and is a protected monument. Renovated by Kempegowda, the temple is dedicated to Lord Shiva. The deities at this temple are set inside a cave or gavi. Legend has it that sages Gautama and Bharadwaja performed penance here. The mantapa supported by 14 pillars displays a distinct Vijayanagar style of architecture and the shikhara is built in the Chalukyan style. Shiva's trident and drum in carved granite, two monolithic pillars bearing the moon and sun discs and a stone umbrella are other features. What is unique to this temple however is that on the day of Makara-Sankranthi, celebrated in the month of January, the sun's rays fall precisely on the statue of Gangadhareswara. The temple also houses idols of Agni, Durga and Parvathi among others.

## Shankara Math

An example of modern Hindu temple architecture, the Shankara Math is an imposing structure. The temple was built in 1911 and inaugurated by Lord Harding and the Maharaja of Mysore. A good elevation, Chalukyan architectural influences and Rajasthani bay windows are the math's appealing features. A stone building, it has been made out of locally available granite and houses two storeys. Two shrines are set on the peripheries.

# Incredible India

www.incredibleindia.org

dunes have a colour here. brilliant as gold.
skies have a colour here. deeper than ink.
valour has a colour here. on the faces of men.
beauty has a colour here. in the swaying of skirts.
incredible india. infinite rainbows.

contactus@incredibleindia.org    www.incredibleindia.org

The annual Vasantahabba at Nrityagram is a nightlong festival of music and dance.

# Entertainment

Entertainment centres have mushroomed across the city. Bowling alleys, game arcades, coffee shops and restaurants now live under one roof. Some of the bigger ones like Amoeba have youngsters coming in droves.

# Entertainment

Bangalore has the reputation of a small, laid back town and not a frenzied, bustling tech city. The truth, however, lies somewhere in between. Lounge bars and laughter clubs, game arcades and glitzy malls, equine sports and exclusive clubs form the backbone of the entertainment scene here. Great weather allows for a fair amount of fun time during the day, best observed at roadside cafés.

Prices are fixed, whether it's a **cover charge** for entering or a ticket for a game and arguing won't get you anywhere. A lot of the **pubs** make you fork out a cover charge before you enter. On weekends this amount can be unusually high. However, it can usually be redeemed against the bill for food and drink. Some places sport a sign 'Entry for Members Only' but don't turn away. It's often a way of saying '**Entry Restricted**' or some such legal clause that allows the management to evict unsavoury elements.

If you're venturing out in the evening, organise your transport home beforehand or move with someone who knows the place well. The crime rate is lower than other metros, but it pays to be neither trusting nor naive. Stick to regular places of entertainment and don't go with any 'fixers'.

Whether it's **dancing**, **gaming** or chasing a ball around a table remember to check the latest entrant on the scene. You'll find it attracts the most crowds, until the next new one comes along! It's not as though Bangaloreans are incapable of loyalty, but there's nothing like a new destination to get them out of their homes.

## Pubbing & Clubbing

Remember this was once called Pub City, so pubbing is still considered a legitimate pastime. And almost every visitor has at least one pub experience to carry home. Women are welcome and may be found in fairly large numbers.

You don't have to be a beer drinker or a drinker at all to enjoy the bonhomie at such places. Good, loud music, flashing lights, smoky air and twinkling glasses are some of the attractions. All pubs serve snacks and some are pretty substantial. You can even order a full meal on a plate. For more information turn to the Food & Drink section.

The pub of yore has transformed itself into a 'club' where lots of things happen at the same time. **Drinking**, **dancing** and **DJing** may now be found under the same roof. But if you prefer to take one thing at a time, that won't be a problem either.

Bangaloreans will tell you there is a pub to suit almost every taste in **music** so just choose your style for the evening – 70s rock, hard rock, rave, jazz, pop etc – and the pub should fall into place. Some pubs have the 'young' look and some have a more genteel air. There is a rule about closing time, so work that into your schedule.

## Reel Time

Movies are a pastime that Kannadigas know best. After all, the road with a 100 cinemas on it (KG Road) runs through the heart of this city! Some of them have shut but it's still an enviable reputation. Now Bangalore finally has a multiplex with four screens and good seats. Blockbusters run simultaneously at no less than five places so you can choose a movie hall in your neighbourhood. Surround sound and DTS are mentioned on all the posters but beware! The audio is always a tad too loud.

**Hindi movie** hits enter the cantonment area and suburban localities, so a trip to the city can be avoided. **Kannada movies**, like other south Indian language films, plays in areas boasting a large population of the same kind. The most **reliable guide** to what's playing where, is the local **daily**.

However, the best film can be ruined by a humid hall, uncomfortable seats and lousy parking. To give you an inside idea of what the movie hall is really like, read our listings under movie theatres. You'll get the picture before stepping in.

**Theatre** lovers will find much to cheer about. There is a vibrant **English** and **Kannada** theatre culture in the city, and

msn india

festivals and plays are held throughout the year. Bangalore has bred many popular actors and playwrights. For more information on theatre, turn to the section on The Arts.

## Games & Amusement Parks

There are a surprising number of amusement parks scattered throughout the city. You can do everything from frying globby **space aliens** and **racing F1 cars** to splashing about in **water parks** and travelling through black holes and alien territory strapped to your seat! Work your wrists on **12 lane bowling alleys** and you could be participating in annual competitions before you know it! If you're easy with the cue and ball, there are plenty of **pool** and **snooker parlours** to slip into.

## More Entertainment

Multiple bowling lanes, an amusement arcade, a fast food joint and multicuisine restaurants at one location – all-in-one entertainment centres are the latest rage in Bangalore. Amoeba, on Church Street is one such place and entire families may be seen on weekends when the foot fall count goes up to 5,000 per day.

Eight malls are expected to spring up in the city and state-of-the-art gaming consoles, swanky restaurants and even multiplexes will be part of the deal. The Forum Mall on Hosur Road and Bangalore Central on Residency Road are a huge hit and soon, The Sigma Mall on Cunningham Road should throw open its doors. Mall rats, mall kids and mall mums may rejoice!

## The Reading Habit

Bangalore has several bookstores of note, spread mostly through the cantonment area. Academic publications and the latest fiction is available under one roof. Each store has a distinct identity – at **Premier** you'll find the proprietor is a book lover with a soft corner for any serious reader. **Gangarams Book Bureau** has all the academic publications you may need plus a variety of books under any subject, however esoteric. **Strand** has some great discounts and great books, not to mention a great ambience. From an airport bookshop, **Sankars the book people** has grown into Bangalore's biggest chain of bookstores.

At **The Oxford Bookstore** you can combine browsing with a light meal or exotic tea at the Cha Bar. In the matter of **libraries**, there are just a few, but membership is quite easy to procure.

There is a lot to do in your leisure hours in Bangalore. **Where** does it happen, **when** are opening hours and **what** are the choices?

*Stark World – Bangalore & Karnataka* brings you the full flavour of the entertainment scene in Bangalore. **Read on** to find out.

# Bangalore Habba

Fusion concerts, veena recitals, Kannada Hamlet, Ukranian dance, Yakshagana and experimental Kathak – Bangalore Habba is a stage for all this and more.

It celebrates the spirit of this vibrant city with an eclectic spread of music, dance and theatre. Held for the first time in 2003, the weeklong festival intends to be an annual gala feature on the city's cultural calendar. With a decidedly international flavour, the Habba brings together world-renowned artists like Taufiq Qureshi, Amjad Ali Khan, Karl Peters and

L Subramaniam. But the spotlight remains on indigenous folk art and regional theatre, providing a much needed fillip to artists from around the state.

Organised by the Artistes Foundation for Arts (Affa) in association with the government of Karnataka, the purpose behind the festivities is double edged: To place Bangalore on the international tourist map and build the city's cultural identity. Bangalore Habba is not for art connoisseurs alone. The entire city, strung with bright lights, wears the air of a colourful carnival. Feisty shopping, food and pub festivals are

organised. Fireworks, jugglers, film festivals, artists' walkways, live caricatures and even palm reading sessions are part of the revelry!

To make the celebrations accessible, entry to all events is free. Performances are held across the city's venues from the sprawling outdoors of the Palace Grounds and Cubbon Park, to the commodious auditoriums of Town Hall and Ravindra Kalakshetra. More has been promised in the years to come and the Bangalore Habba intends to be as grand as the Munich Festival or the Goa Carnival.

Bangalore Habba celebrations at Bangalore Palace

## MOVIE THEATRES

### Abhinay
*BVK Iyengar Road, Bangalore 560053*
**Tel** *2287 2029*
**Admission** *Balcony: Rs 45*
*Rear Stall: Rs 25*
*Front Stall: Rs 15*

Local Kannada movies regularly premier here. It has enormous, coloured cut-outs of hunky Kannada stars that grace the façade, lending the whole place local colour.

### Cauvery
*8/1 T Chowdiah Road, Bangalore 560003*
**Tel** *2336 1528*
**Admission** *Balcony: Rs 50*
*Rear Stall: Rs 40*
*Front Stall: Rs 30*

This 25 year old, air-cooled theatre is the venue for the latest Kannada, Hindi and Telugu hits.

### Innovative Multiplex
*135 Outer Ring Road,*
*Bangalore 560037*
**Tel** *2522 5944*
**Admission** *Balcony: Rs 120*
*Rear Stall: Rs 100*

This is Bangalore's first multiplex with four screens, showing the latest Hindi and English films. A good sound system and comfortable seating bring in a lot of young movie buffs.

### Plaza
*74 MG Road, Bangalore 560001*
**Tel** *2558 7682*
**Admission** *Balcony: Rs 70*
*Rear Stall: Rs 50*
*Front Stall: Rs 30*

There's nothing fancy about Plaza, unless you're looking for historical paraphernalia, like the wooden cubicle at the entrance, the old fashioned foyer and the enormous parquet dance floor upstairs. Despite its crumbling façade it manages to attract good movies and a fair crowd. Maintenance is not a priority here, the seats are hardly the last word in comfort and the screen is mid-sized. Be prepared for the balcony's steep incline.

### Rex
*12/13 Brigade Road,*
*Bangalore 560001*
**Tel** *2558 7350*
**Admission** *Balcony: Rs 100*
*Rear Stall: Rs 80*
*Front Stall: Rs 45*

This is one of Bangalore's premium movie theatres – it is well maintained with good seats and air-conditioning. A bunch of food stalls within the premises come in handy. Placed bang in the middle of Brigade Road, it's a good bet for the latest Hollywood blockbuster. A few decades ago this was a venue for concerts and bands played in front of the screen.

## Innovative Multiplex

Four theatres in one building, studio-effect interiors, screens that fill up an entire wall and central air-conditioning – the multiplex has arrived in Bangalore! Innovative Multiplex is more than just a theatre complex – it has 320-seater theatres screening English and Hindi movies, a food court, mall and game arcade, in short, plenty of entertainment. Most of the movie halls in the city are located in and around MG Road or KG Road, but Innovative Multiplex is located outside town and hopes that true film buffs will not hesitate to make the journey. Located near the Airport Road-Outer Ring Road junction, it can be easily reached from Whitefield, Old Madras Road and Hosur Road. Plans are on to set up a 90-seater in the basement that can be hired for private screenings.

*135 Outer Ring Road, Bangalore 560037*
**Tel** *2522 5944*

### Symphony
*Public Utility Building,*
*MG Road,*
*Bangalore 560001*
**Tel** *2558 5988*
**Admission** *Balcony: Rs 100*
*Rear Stall: Rs 80*
*Middle Stall: Rs 75*
*Front Stall: Rs 50*

This movie hall is the venue for hyped-up English movies and Hindi blockbusters. There is a good restaurant – Ullas Refreshments – in the foyer and plenty of parking space.

### Urvashi
*Siddaiah Road, Bangalore 560027*
**Tel** *2222 0187*

**Admission** *Balcony: Rs 80*
*Rear Stall: Rs 70*
*Front Stall: Rs 40*

The latest Hindi and Tamil potboilers arrive here first. That along with full DTS surround sound and icy-cold air-conditioning keep the crowds coming. The occasional English movie dubbed in Hindi is also screened here.

Plaza, a theatre on MG Road

## GAME ARCADES & AMUSEMENT PARKS

### Amoeba
*22 HM Leisure, Church Street,*
*Bangalore 560001*
*Tel 2559 4631/4632*
*Open 11am to 11pm*
*Admission Bowling Alley rates vary from*
*Rs 80 to Rs 100 per game on weekdays*
*and Rs 125 on weekends.*
*Cards All*
*Web www.amoebaleisurezone.com*

With 40,000sqft of assorted amusement, Amoeba is capable of enticing any game addict. The 12-lane, superbly maintained bowling alley enjoys pride of place, offering recreation for the amateur and practice for the professional. All the gear is of international quality. Huge observation windows and balconies let you in on the action. Amoeba has an array of more than 90 video game consoles gathered from all corners of the gaming globe. The noise level is very high and small children will be uncomfortable, despite the thoughtful playpen on the premises.
There is a coffee shop and snack bar on one floor and a party hall that can be hired out. Weekends are crowded and more expensive.

### Freeway 19
*Gayatri Vihar, Palace Grounds,*
*Ramana Maharishi Road,*
*Bangalore 560080*
*Tel 2361 1329*
*Open 10am to 10pm*
*Admission Rs 100 for 5 laps*
*(single seater) and Rs 150 for 5 laps*
*(double seater)*
*Cards Not Accepted*
*Web www.freeway19.com*

There is a popular 750-metre long track with double-seater go-karts for couples and specially adapted go-karts for children.

### Fun World and Water World
*Palace Grounds,*
*Opp. TV Tower, JC Nagar,*
*Bangalore 560006*
*Tel 2343 0496*
*Open 11am to 9:30pm*
*Admission Rs 150*
*Cards Not Accepted*
*Web www.funworldnresort.com*

The biggest amusement park in Bangalore, it provides hours of entertainment: Rides on stomach-churners, a 12-lane bowling alley and an array of coin-operated arcade games. The water park has 14 slides including several child-safe ones. The go-karting track is spread over an acre and has well maintained go-karts. Next to Fun World is the Star City amusement centre.

### Jaamba Jungle
*50 KH Road (Lalbagh Double Road)*
*Opp. BTS Depot,*
*Bangalore 560 027*
*Tel 2212 9020, 2299 3666*
*Open 11am to 11pm*
*Admission Free*
*Cards All*
*Web www.jaamba.com*

Jaamba Jungle is aimed at young kids – it has lots of friendly staff and plenty of coin-operated arcade games. A big attraction is the soft play station for very young children. There's a space available for birthdays and similar celebrations and a café serving fast food.

### Megabowl
*Prestige Terminal II, Airport Exit Road,*
*Bangalore 560017*
*Tel 2522 9743*
*Open 11am to 11pm*
*Admission Free*
*Cards All*

Megabowl has eight well-maintained bowling lanes and plenty of coin-operated video games. There's a separate play area for kids and a decent pub to slake your thirst and satisfy hunger. Megabowl is also open for private parties.

### Neeladri Amusement & Water Park
*15th Km, Electronic City, Hosur Road.*
*Bangalore 561229*
*Tel 2652 9370*
*Open 11am to 5:30pm*
*Admission Rs 175*
*Cards Not Accepted*
*Web www.neeladriwaterpark.com*

This water park boasts water slides, a wave-force pool, a 'lazy river' and six other games. There's also a dry games section for landlubbers where 'dashing' cars are available.

### Patel's Inn – Race Pace
*38/2/2, 15th Cross, Govindraj Garden,*
*II Block, RT Nagar, Bangalore 560032*
*Tel 2333 7575/0182*
*Open 11am to 9:30pm on weekdays.*
*11am to 10:30pm on weekends.*
*Admission Rs 100 for 8 laps*
*Cards All*
*Web www.patelsinn.com*

Patel's Inn has 15 go-karts to spin around its 400-metre track. There are special karts for kids. A small game of cricket, table tennis or basketball can be played nearby.

### Sammy's Dreamland
*NH 7, 2kms from Yelahanka Airforce*
*Station, Hosahalli Village,*
*Hunasamaranahalli Post,*
*Bangalore 562157*
*Tel 2847 8600*
*Open 10:30pm to 7:30pm*
*Admission Rs 249*
*Cards All except American Express*
*Web www.sammysdreamland.com*

This sprawling theme park promises assorted fun and games for the entire family. Set across 34 lush green acres, Sammy's Dreamland has four zones: The World Tour Area has reproductions of the world's seven wonders, the Tech Zone is a gaming arcade, the Children's Village and Lagoon Area have exciting water rides and light displays. There is also an Adventure Golf Putt and a Toon City where you can pose for photographs alongside King Kong, ghouls and cartoon characters. The amusement park is not just for kids and the virtual reality video games are a hit with adults as well. A carnival like air pervades through the park with 17 kiosks and a mini shopping mall. The Library serves continental food, the Jewel Palace is a Mughlai restaurant and the Diner and Pizzario dishes out American fastfood.

### Speed Zone
*Shantiniketan, Sadaramangal,*
*Whitefield Road, Bangalore 560048*
*Tel 3677 7908*
*Open 11am to 7:30pm on weekdays and*
*11am to 9pm on weekends.*
*Admission Rs 100 for 8 laps*
*(single seater) and Rs 150 for 8 laps*
*(double seater)*
*Cards All*

Speed Zone is spread across 60 acres and has both an amateur and pro circuit, 1.1 kms in length. A member of the International Carting Federation, it has imported racing karts, the Yamaha

Bowling alleys are a popular source of entertainment for youngsters in the city.

Pool parlours abound in Bangalore, home to World Snooker Champion, Pankaj Advani.

(16bhp) and the Rotax Max (25bhp) for the pro circuit. For those who prefer a slower pace, there is a miniature golf range next to the circuit. Spectators can get a full view of the circuit in shaded comfort and the silence is only broken by revving engines and the occasional train.

## Star City

*JC Nagar, Palace Grounds,*
*Bangalore 560006*
*Tel 2354 3291*
*Open 11am to 9:30pm*
*Admission Free*
*Cards All except American Express*

Video games and bowling are available at this amusement centre, adjacent to Fun World. There is little to do for children under the age of five, but plenty thereafter. A 15-minute drive from central MG Road, it is located inside the Bangalore Palace Grounds.

## POOL/SNOOKER/ BILLARDS

## Cue-n-Net

*650/12 BM Avenue, II Floor, Raj Kumar Road, Rajajinagar I Block,*
*Bangalore 560010*
*Tel 2352 0624*
*Open 10am to 10pm*
*Admission Rs 60 to Rs 95 per hour*

Good music and a bright ambience make this a popular hangout for students (above

18 years) and young working people. Located on the bustling Raj Kumar Road, the four year old parlour boasts nine tables – two small, three English and four French. Fizzy drinks are available.

## Greenback Snooker and Pool Association

*175/1, 1st Main, Seshadripuram,*
*Bangalore 560020*
*Open 9am to 10pm*
*Admission Rs 60 to 80 per hour*

This parlour has five tables – three small and two French – and is always crowded thanks to the 'free time' offers during the day. The blast of hip-hop and rock music brings the college crowd in droves. A number of city and state championships are held here. Light snacks like sandwiches, chaat, chips and cool drinks are served.

## Manyana Pool & Snooker Parlour

*737 B, II Floor, III Stage, III Block,*
*Basaveshwaranagar, Bangalore 560 079*
*Tel: 2322 7366*
*Open 9am to 9pm*
*Admission Rs 60 per hour*

A quaint parlour in the heart of the quiet residential area of Basaveshwaranagar, Manyana offers small-size tables. The latest Bollywood hits pound incessantly while you play. Smoking is prohibited in this cheerful parlour. Tournaments are organised every weekend. Bottled soft drinks are available.

## LIBRARIES

### Easy Library

*5, I Floor 7th Main, 80Ft. Road,*
*I Block, Koramangala, Bangalore 560034*
*Tel 2550 1499, 5110 2231*
*Open 10am to 2pm and 4pm to 8pm.*
*Closed on Wednesday.*
*Web www.easylib.com*

This is Bangalore's first online library, providing easy access to books and a great attraction for lazy book worms! Browse through the library online and choose your books which are dropped off at your address and collected once you are done reading them. Alternately, you can visit the library and borrow books. Fiction, non-fiction, magazines and children's books are available and payments can also be made online through credit card.

### Eloor Lending Library

*G9, Blue Cross Chambers,*
*Off Infantry Cross Road,*
*Bangalore 560001*
*Tel 2559 1408*
*Open 10am to 1:30pm and 3pm to 8pm*

This is a popular private library. Titles are up to date and range from popular Indian fiction to biographies, non-fiction writing, fantasy and science fiction. The 'new arrivals' section sports the latest titles almost as soon as they are out in the stores. Membership is necessary to browse and borrow.

### State Central Library

*Cubbon Park, Bangalore 560001*
*Tel 2221 2128/2229 3401*
*Open 9am to 7pm*
*Closed on Monday.*
*Web www.kar.nic.net.in/publib*

The State Central Library is a public library managed by the government and located in Cubbon Park. Borrowing of books is not allowed, only reference

and browsing. Sections range from literature and psychology to medicine, philosophy and religion. Sadly, the books suffer from a lack of maintenance and are often ragged and dog-eared with important pages missing.

### The British Council Library

*23 Prestige Takt, Kasturba Cross Road,*
*Bangalore 560001*
*Tel 2248 9220*
*Open 10:30am to 6:30pm*
*Closed on Sunday.*
*Web www.bclindia.org*

Run by the British Council, this library has British publications on information technology, science, law, engineering, medicine, economics, social sciences and just about all disciplines. The fiction section is interesting, albeit limited. You may access the Internet in the library, make use of the online information resources or use the database of journals.

## BOOKSTORES

### Crossword

*ACR Towers, Opp. Gateway Hotel,*
*32 Residency Road, Bangalore 560025*
*Tel 2558 2411*
*Open 10:30am to 9pm*
*Cards All*
*Web www.crosswordbookstores.com*

Crossword is a large, well lit store spread over two floors and with a café attached. Expect the usual collection of fiction, non-fiction, children's books and magazines, neatly categorised for easy browsing. The first floor has a collection of CDs, board games, toys, stationery and DVDs. Crossword also offers a Dial-A-Book facility where you can call and order books and avail the free home delivery service. This should find many takers among booklovers who don't dare the traffic or the trek, although parking is plentiful here.

Strand Book Stall

Entertainment

msn India

The Oxford Bookstore at Leela Galleria

## Fountainhead

*41 Lavelle Road, Bangalore 560001*
*Tel 2221 9777*
*Open 10am to 8:30pm. Closed on Monday.*
*Email fhblore@satyam.net.in*

With branches in Chennai and Mumbai, Fountainhead is one of the well known bookstores in the city. The spacious store has a good collection of books across all subjects. Fountainhead's pick of books ranges from the coffee table variety and the classics to new Indian English writers and sci-fi. They also carry wide collection educational, self help and children's books. Their range of international magazines is very impressive. There's a small toyshop in one corner and stacks of greeting cards as well.

## Gangarams Book Bureau

*72 MG Road, Bangalore 560001*
*Tel 2558 5293*
*Open 10am to 8pm. Closed on Sunday.*
*Email gangarams@vsnl.com*

One of the older bookstores in the city, the multi-storeyed Gangarams is also

one of the most reputed. Spread across three floors, the busy bookstore offers lots of titles on subjects ranging from interior design to astrophysics. The usual bestsellers and pulp vie with the greeting card and stationery section. The entire third floor is dedicated to academia with a range of educational books and learning material. The extensive text book section books from management to psychology. The second floor houses all the best sellers, magazines, post cards and a good selection of non-fiction books as well. Gangarams also stocks the latest DVDs and CD-ROMs, games as well as educational.

## Higginbothams

*74 MG Road, Bangalore 560001*
*Tel 2558 7359*
*Open 9am to 8pm;*
*10am to 8pm on Sunday.*
*Email higginbothams@vsnl.com*

Higginbothams has been outpaced by other bookstores but its charming edifice is still an attraction. There is a stationery store here as well.

## Landmark

*The Forum, 2 Hosur Road,*
*Koramangala, Bangalore 560029*
*Tel 2206 7640*
*Open 9am to 9pm*
*Web www.landmarkonthenet.com*

Patrons of the Chennai-based bookstore will welcome the sprawling new cousin in silicon city. A worthy addition to Bangalore's list of top league bookshops, Landmark aims to be more than just a browsing nook. Spread across 45,000 sqft, it has positioned itself as a family, leisure and lifestyle store. Set in the upmarket Forum mall, the store stocks books, toys, t-shirts, bags, stationery, gifts, DVDs, music and even home furnishings.
A large selection of titles with 150 catalogues, neatly demarcated sections and a snazzy setting make up the Landmark package. There is an exhaustive collection of books on topics ranging from pulp and self-help to philosophy and art. The store plans to organise theatre workshops, musical shows and events for kids. Landmark has a website where books and music can be bought online.

## L B Publishers

*90-91 MG Road, Bangalore 560001*
*Tel 2558 7621*
*Open 10am to 7pm.*
*3:30pm to 8pm on Sunday.*
*Email lbpd@touchtelindia.net*

All the bestsellers and a few others may be found here. There is a fair selection of titles for children.

## Premier Book Shop

*46/1 Church Street, Bangalore 560001*
*Tel 2558 8570*
*Open 10am to 1:30pm and 3pm to 8pm;*
*10am to 12:30pm on Sunday.*
*Email info@premierbookshop.com*

Premier is almost an institution in Bangalore. At the entrance sits the owner, TS Shanbag, guarding a fabulous collection of books – best sellers, pulp, literary tomes and others – placed in teetering towers. He is happy to share his encyclopaedic knowledge and quick to dish out discounts to genuine readers.

## Prism

*16, 11th Main, IV Block Jayanagar,*
*Bangalore 560011*
*Tel 2663 7527*
*Open 10am to 9pm*
*Web www.prismbooks.com*

This is the best known bookstore in Jayanagar. A smallish store it nonetheless stocks a good selection of titles, and discounts are offered liberally.

## Sankars the book people

*15/2 Upstairs, Madras Bank Road,*
*Off St. Mark's Road,*
*Bangalore 560001*
*Tel 2558 6868/6867*
*Branches Airport, 2522 7418;*
*Taj Residency, 2532 5621;*
*Banglaore Central, 5112 4170;*
*Le Meridien, 2220 7156;*
*Safina Plaza, 2559 5074;*
*The Atria Hotel, 2225 6785;*
*William Penn, 2563 3161*
*Rangashankara, 2649 4656*
*Open 10am to 8:30pm; 11am to*
*8pm on Sunday.*
*Web www.sankarsbooks.com*

For many decades now, busy travellers bustling in and out of the city airport, treated themselves to a book from Sankar's over a quick chat with its erudite owners. N Sankaran and Vivek Sankaran, a father and son team, ably manage this chain of bookshops. Once known as the Airport Book Store, Sankars now has shops spread over the city – on Madras Bank Road, at the Taj West End, Taj Residency, Le Meriden and Safina Plaza. Their stores stock an impressive array of fiction, non fiction and coffee table books. There are usually a good selection of bestsellers and regular topics with thoughtful seating on hand! Their large outlet on Old Madras Road is not only a storehouse of books but is a venue for book launches, poetry readings and meet-the-author sessions as well. Comfortable couches placed in the store allow for leisurely browsing.
A play corner with a slide for the kids, mural exhibits by popular artists and a mock Sistine Chapel fresco are other attractive features of this store.

## Sapna Book House

*Thunga Complex, Gandhinagar,*
*Bangalore 560009*
*Tel 2226 6088*
*Branch Sadashivnagar, 2344 6444;*
*Jayanagar, 5130 7322*
*Open 10am to 2pm and 3pm to 8pm.*
*Closed on Sunday.*
*Web www.sapnaonline.com*

Set in the busy market district, Sapna is famous for its array of educational books. Most city students browse here for textbooks and guides.

Teetering stacks of books at the Premier Book Shop.

## Select Book Shop

*71 Brigade Road Cross, Bangalore 560001*
**Tel** *2558 0770*
**Open** *11am to 6:30pm and 11am to 5:30pm on Sunday.*
**Web** *www.selectbookshop.com*

Both old and new books feature at the Select Book Shop. It has an interesting mix of rare books and bestsellers and a small art gallery featuring the work of local artists. Bibliophiles will be happy with a trip. The owner, KKS Murthy, is willing to procure rare and out-of-print stuff.

## Strand Book Stall

*113/114, Manipal Centre,*
*47 Dickenson Road,*
*Bangalore 560042*
**Tel** *2558 0000/2222*
**Open** *10:30am to 8pm.*
*Closed on Sunday.*
**Web** *www.strandbookstall.com*

Strand rises above regular bookshops with its annual book fair, regular book readings and website. Known for offering sizeable discounts, the store is air-conditioned, nicely laid out and houses a varied collection of books. On the shelves are textbooks, popular fiction and some eclectic titles as well. Strand opened its first store in Mumbai in 1948 and the Bangalore branch came more recently. Vidya Virkar, the proprietess believes in interacting closely with her customers, a tradition she has inherited from her well known father, TN Shanbag

Fountainhead

who started the original Strand in Mumbai. Strand also procures books that are not available at the store and customers can also import books for a reasonable fee.

## The Oxford Book Store

*Leela Galleria, The Leela Palace,*
*Airport Road, Bangalore 560008*
**Tel** *5115 5222*

**Open** *10am to 10pm*
**Web** *www.oxfordbookstore.com*

The Kolkata-based Oxford Book Store is the toast of Bangalore's literati. It's one of the few bookstores to provide comfortable chairs for browsers! A number of prestigious book readings are held here and autographed books are piled in a separate corner.

Of almost equal importance is the Cha Bar located alongside where book lovers presumably retire to sip a cup of delicately flavoured Darjeeling tea and peruse their buys. On sale is Oxford Book Store merchandise like 'I am a bookworm' bags. Stationery, notebooks, frames made of handmade paper and art supplies are also available.

## DJ BARS / DISCOS

### Nineteen Twelve

*40 St. Mark's Road,*
*Bangalore 560001*
**Tel** *2299 7290/7291*
**Open** *7pm to 11:30pm*
**Cards** *All except Diners Club*

Nineteen Twelve gets its name from the 1912 heritage building it's located in, at the junction of MG Road and St. Mark's Road. The décor takes you back to the turn-of-the-century when events like the sinking of the Titanic, the release of Tarzan and Robert Falcon Scott's trip to the South Pole occurred. The rest – the music, food and service – are all very contemporary. The pub is fashioned like a living room with a lounge effect, dim lighting, cosy chairs and a bar stocking a delectable choice of wines. Guests can try their hand at the piano and guitar, and there are mikes for the occasional karaoke. Food is limited to a few big dishes like Oven Roasted Chicken with Creamy =

A night out at a trendy pub in town

i-Bar, a lounge bar at The Park

and forget the 'Lounge' part too. And herein they do themselves a great disservice. The f Bar is one of Bangalore's swankiest joints! The Japanese food is fabulous, the atmosphere trendy and there is always something happening. There is a striking use of metal and luminous screens.

But the deep, low slung sofas in solid colours offer a lazy and welcome contrast. The f Bar & Lounge is in the shape of an 'L' and the across from the Bar there is an area for serious dining which is removed once the party starts coming alive at night. The first f Bar in Asia, this is definitely high class and swank. Sushi, Makis and Yakitoris are some of the hot dishes on the menu.

## Geoffrey's

*The Royal Orchid, 1 Golf Avenue,*
*Off Airport Road, Bangalore 560008*
*Tel 2520 5566*
*Open 12noon to 12midnight*
*Cards All*

Warm and plush interiors, comfortable seating and retro music – Geoffrey's has all the ingredients for a happy, convivial evening. Its English pub look comes from the stained glass windows, wood panelling and even some artefacts from 'back home' to give it that final touch. Posters of Elvis Presley, Marilyn Monroe and a Harley Davidson from across the Atlantic add a 70s feel to the place. It offers great food and beverages and the service has some of the old charm of bartenders of yore.

## i-Bar

*The Park, 14/7 MG Road, Bangalore*
*560001*
*Tel 2559 4666*
*Open 5:30pm to 11:30pm*
*Cards All*

Deep within the plush Park hotel is the i-Bar, named no doubt for Bangalore's IT

status. Its cool neon ambience, low-floor furniture and bean bags are a hit with the partying crowd. DJ Sasha is in charge of the music and exotic cocktails dominate the menu. Indian and imported spirits, premium French, Italian and American wines are served here. Skilled bartenders create innovative cocktails like I-lychee, mojito, Mint Julep and Flaring Vodka. An array of snacks, appetisers, wraps and kababs are served to go with the drinks. Exclusive cigars, from Cohiba to Montecristo, are also offered.

## Oblivion

*4005 HAL II Stage, 100Ft. Road,*
*Indiranagar, Bangalore 560008*
*Tel 5115 3242*
*Open 11am to 12midnight*
*Cards All*

Oblivion is the new club in town. Spread across four floors, it houses a glitzy basement discotheque, a trendy lounge, a gourmet restaurant and a resto-bar perched on the terrace. Mindscape is the lounge, set in the basement that houses a weekend discotheque, exotic cocktails, a Liquor Buffet and large television screens for the latest sporting events. It has a 'Day Long Menu' (from 12noon to 12midnight) that moves between Indian, Mexican, Chinese and American cuisine. There is a range of non-alcoholic fruity drinks too. Sublime is the restaurant serving 'New World cuisine'.

## Sparks

*133 Raheja Chancery, Brigade Road,*
*Bangalore 560025*
*Tel 2223 0306*
*Open 11:30am to 11pm*
*Cards All except American Express*

This is another temple of youth, patronised by the college crowd, particularly during the day. There is a special music event each weekday – rock, retro, hiphop, trance etc.

Curry, Roesti with Leek and Mushroom Ragout, Shell Roasted Lobster with Artichoke etc. The open courtyard at the back is perfect for a pub night without loud music.

## Dublin

*ITC Hotel Windsor Sheraton & Towers,*
*25 Golf Course Road*
*Bangalore 560052*
*Tel 2226 9898*
*Open 10am to 11:30pm*
*Cards All*

A regular old fashioned pub, Dublin will warm the hearts of those looking for the comfort of a watering hole without the new age frills like pounding music and strobe lights.

Don't be misled though, Dublin does have its 'happening' nights when the volume is jacked up and the magic of 007 fills the air! Theme nights are very popular – Spanish nights, a Martini night where 69 kinds of martinis are served and so on.

## f Bar & Lounge

*Le Meridien Bangalore, 28 Sankey Road,*
*Bangalore 560052*
*Tel 2220 8772, 2226 2233*
*Open 5pm to 12midnight*
*Email fbar_lounge@rediffmail.com*
*Cards All*

Does the f Bar figure only in your bar and pubbing location list? Most people remember only the 'Bar' in the name

Dublin, the Irish-style pub at ITC Hotel Windsor Sheraton & Towers

SWING IT.

STRUT IT.

STIR IT.

SHAKE IT.

## Spinn

*80, 3rd Cross, Residency Road,
Bangalore 560025*
**Tel** *2558 1555*
**Open** *7pm to 11:30pm*
**Cards** *All except Diners Club*

Spinn is clearly Bangalore's hottest nightclub. Located in an old bungalow this discothèque attempts to blend a tech atmosphere with the laid back charm of a lounge bar. There is a huge dance floor with excellent sound and light systems. Spinn has two outdoor sit-outs: A spacious veranda set with tables for eating and a terrace for those who may need a quiet moment.

## The 13th Floor

*Hotel Ivory Tower,
Barton Centre, 84 MG Road,
Bangalore 560001*
**Tel** *2558 9333/5164*
**Open** *7pm to 11:30pm*
**Cards** *All*

You get a fabulous view of the city from here. It's also one of the few places with an outdoor section.
The music is good, the crowds are happening and the food is way above average, with some Thai specialities thrown in. Both indoor and terrace seating is available. Call and reserve in advance to avoid waiting.

# Laughter Clubs

Bangalore is the city that laughs a lot: At last count, the city had a whopping 90 laughter clubs, the highest in India and the number continues to grow. Groups of men, women and children from laughter clubs across the city, gather in parks every morning and break into synchronised gales of laughter, arms outstretched towards the sky. The **boisterous belly laugh**, the **mouth wide-open laugh**, the **soundless laugh**, **laughter with humming sounds** and **'medium' laughter** are produced alternately for a period of 30 seconds. The most pleasurable of them all is **'cocktail laughter'** where hearty laughter is accompanied by jumping and clapping. The laughter is not directed at funny jokes or anything else in particular. Instead, laughter for the sake of laughter is the motto of these clubs and the Laughing Buddha is their spiritual inspiration.

Laughter is an effective medicine and research has proved that it reduces stress, relieves tension,

drives away depression and strengthens immunity. With its roots in the theory of Hasya Yoga, laughter clubs believe that you can laugh your way to a healthier and happier life. The half-hour feel good routine promotes rhythmic movement of the diaphragm, exercises abdominal muscles and increases the vitality of the lungs. The first laughter club was founded by Dr. Madan Kataria in 1995 at a park in Mumbai. But it is Bangalore that seems to have been bitten by the laughter bug and clubs have spread across the city's suburbs from Madhavan Park to Koramangala, keeping the entire city in splits. **The Romeo Laughter Club**, **Banyan Tree Laughter Club**, **Miniforest Laughter Club** and the **Basavanagudi Laughter Club** are some of most prominent clubs. Admission to the club is free and open to anyone irrespective of age and sex, the only criterion being the willingness to laugh wholeheartedly.

A typical session begins with deep breathing exercises on the lines of *pranayama*. After a warm-up the laughter begins – first as a slow murmur but soon rising to an uproarious crescendo. Simulated laughter can be difficult to produce. For the more inhibited members, maintaining eye contact with the rest of the group is recommended. Newcomers soon learn the difference between a layperson's laughter and the club's specialised forms of laughter.

Laughter clubs are a great way to socialise and make new friends. Married couples, senior citizens, teenagers and entire families flock to these clubs to spend their mornings laughing together. Laughter clubs also add a dash of humour into an otherwise stressful lifestyle. The philosophy of the laughter club is to laugh and live well as laughter is free!

**Tel** *2656 3968* **Web** *www.laughteryoga.org*

# Horse Racing

For sheer sophistication you can't beat the spectator sport of horse racing. Expensive and carefully bred animals run a short stretch while millions of rupees hang in balance. The Bangalore Turf Club (BTC) sees 65 days of top-level racing. The winter race season runs from November to February, and the summer season from May to July. Two-year olds make their debut in the winter races while three-year olds take part in the Classics. The five Indian Classics are **The 1000 Guineas, The 2000 Guineas, The Oaks, The Derbys, The St. Legers** and **The Indian Turf Invitation Cup**. Serious breeders, socialites, bookies and even auto drivers gather at BTC on Friday and Saturday afternoons during the racing season. Quick bucks for some, an enjoyable sport for others.

But Bangalore's racing world has news of a different kind. Hitting the headlines are all women syndicates – Force Ten Racing Syndicate, Prima Vera and Fiama with their horses Strombolix, Prospero and La Bella respectively. Their jockey of choice is also a woman, Sylva Storai who has already notched up one win. A deep love and understanding of horses binds the syndicate members together and their early success is spurring other women to come together and form similar groups.

India has a long tradition of equine sports like riding and polo. The British brought racing into the picture and the sport became a big favourite with the royal families. Thoroughbred breeding took off in the 19th century and stud farms mushroomed in Bangalore's salubrious climate. The BTC was formed in 1921 on land leased from the Maharaja of Mysore. The racetrack is an oval shaped, right-handed course measuring approximately 1950m with four sharp curves and pronounced gradients. Its limited space of barely 85 acres has been intelligently used to provide facilities such as stabling for over 1,000 horses, three training tracks, an equine swimming pool, training schools, walking rings, a veterinary hospital and an amateur riding school.

*57 Race Course Road, Bangalore 560001,*
**Tel** *2238 7735*

## Zero G

*10th Floor Prestige Towers, Residency Road, Bangalore 560025*
**Tel** *2207 9014*
**Open** *12noon to 12midnight*
**Cards** *All*

This new 'resto-bar' is one of the hottest nightspots in town. Modelled like a ship's top deck with multi-level translucent sail frames, white walls and wooden floors, Zero G makes for a novel experience. There is even a breeze that gusts through the terrace and enhances the cruise liner inspired open air décor! The deck aside, there is a bar with a panoramic view of the city, a sparkling blue pool – the highest in Bangalore, and a health club. The food is primarily Asian and the drinks are the usual, plus a few diet drinks for the health conscious. DJs play an eclectic selection of retro, lounge and club classics with the occasional hip-hop track.

## SOCIAL DANCING

### Chisel Reebok Aerobics Institute

*33 NR Chambers, Richmond Road, Bangalore 560025*
**Tel** *2556 7488/7489*
**Open** *Weekends 12noon to 1pm (Adults) Wednesday 4pm to 5pm (Children)*

The dance programme at Chisel is conducted by Lourd Vijay of Dance Studio Inc. Twelve hour courses in salsa, meringue, cha-cha and jiving are offered. Chisel also hosts jazz-ballet classes by fitness expert and ballet dancer Yana Lewis. A fusion of classical ballet and jazz dance, classes are for adults only. Students with a background in any dance form or just a passion for it are preferred.

### Connie and Danny Dancing School

*453, 5th Cross, 8th Main, Viveknagar, Bangalore 560047*
**Tel** *2571 4504*
**Open** *Monday to Friday 7:30am to 9pm*

This is one of Bangalore's oldest dancing schools. For the past 50 years, Max and Esther have been teaching Latin American dances, rumba, rock and roll jiving, tango, slow fox trot, quick step, waltz, cha-cha. The school is open to all. Individual as well as group lessons are offered.

### Dance Studio Inc. (DSI)

*4 Off Palace Cross Road, Chakravarthy Layout, Bangalore 560020*
**Tel** *3186 4477*
**Open** *Tuesdays and Thursdays 7:30pm to 8:30pm*

Here the purpose of teaching dance is to boost fitness and self confidence. Founded by choreographer Lourd Vijay, DSI is a performing arts academy. Students are trained in exotic dances like the salsa, meringue, rumba, waltz and tango. The speciality of the school is Latin American dance forms, hip-hop and ballroom dancing. The school is open to adults as well as children. Morning, evening and weekend batches are held at their studio and private workshops are also conducted.

### Figurine Fitness

*10 Chinnaswamy Stadium, MG Road, Bangalore 560001*
**Tel** *2286 7499*
**Branch** *Indiranagar, 2529 4019*
**Open** *12:30pm to 2:30pm and 5:30pm to 7:30pm*

Dance is taught for fitness, fun, creative expression and stress relief. Salsa, modern jive, cha-cha, meringue, free style dancing and ballroom dancing are some of the styles at Figurine Fitness. The trendy dance-fitness studio is an added attraction. The spacious 8,000sqft dance floor has suspended wooden flooring, wall to wall mirrors, soft lighting and surround sound acoustics.

### Shiamak Davar Institute for Performing Arts (SDIPA)

*C Ground Floor, 80 Casa Langford Apartments, Eagle Street, Langford Town, Bangalore 560027*
**Tel** *2299 0479/0480*
**Venue** *Chinnaswamy Stadium, MG Road; Rotary Club, Indiranagar; Platinum Bodies, Jayanagar; Indian Heritage Academy, Koramangala; RMV Club, Sanjayanagar*
**Open** *10am to 6pm*

The SDIPA is a leading dance institute with four centres in Bangalore. Classes are conducted in jazz, hip-hop, Afro-jazz, rock n' roll and salsa, for all ages. It is open to everyone including the physically and mentally challenged. The school trains students to become performers and classes are held at the elementary, intermediate and advanced levels.

### The Swingers Dance Company

*133, His Grace, 1st Main Road, HAL II Stage, Indiranagar, Bangalore 560038*
**Tel** *2520 3900*
**Branches** *Body Craft, Jayanagar; Chisel Aerobics Institute, Richmond Road*
**Open** *10am to 8pm*

The Swingers Dance Company is a progressive dance studio founded by choreographer B Murali. The school offers a number of courses in contemporary dance, jazz ballet, hip-hop and modern dance for various age groups, starting with five year olds. Students are trained at three levels – beginner, elementary, and intermediate. A 21-day crash course is held in the summer.

## CLUBS

### Bowring Institute

*19 St. Marks Road, Bangalore 560001*
**Tel** *2227 3728*
**Admission** *Members & Guests only*

The Bowring Institute was founded as a Literary and Scientific Institute in 1868. It aimed at promoting 'Intellectual and Moral Improvement in the Young Men of Bangalore'. Its beginnings were in rented premises with little more than a reading room. It was only after Lewan Botham Bowring, a British Commissioner was made its president did the club receive its present name.
The club is known for its excellent sporting facilities and enormous library.

The sprawling Bangalore Club

### The Bangalore Club
*FM Cariappa Road, Bangalore 560005*
**Tel:** *2227 1374*
**Admission:** *Members & Guests only*
**Web:** *www.bangaloreclub.com*

With over 175 years of history, The Bangalore Club is unquestionably one of the most prestigious clubs in the city. Originally a British Officers' Club, it became a private members-only club after Independence. It was earlier known as the British United Services Club and at one time the Polo Club. Like most cantonment clubs there is an unmistakable air of the British Raj about it. Tall old trees line a path curving up to colonial buildings with high ceilings, spring wooden floors and rooms adorned with priceless chandeliers, antique furnishings, weapons and trophies. The club boasts one of the best swimming pools in the city. There are tennis courts, a gym, a billiards room and other recreational equipment within its fold. A special children's play area is a big draw. A departmental store and library are the other attractions for club members.

The club's rolling green lawns turn into casual dining spaces on holidays and after dark. The food is good and costs a fraction of what it would cost outside. On weekends the club is full of families. Festival celebrations are the most zestful with the finest food. At the back there is a quiet reception area for weddings and other special functions.

### The Club
*7th Mile, Mysore Road,*
*Bangalore 560039*
**Tel** *2860 0665/0768/0769*
**Admission** *Members & Guests only*
**Web** *theclubbangalore.com*

The Club, a unit of Bangalore Resorts and Clubs Pvt. Ltd. has been in the business for 11 years. This hotel cum club with a two star classification is

### Catholic Club
*22 Museum Road, Bangalore 560025*
*Tel 2558 7593*
**Admission** *Members & Guests only*

The Catholic Club is a prominent club, popular with families interested in its sports and entertainment facilities. A popular occasion is the annual Mango Festival, a joint celebration of Mangalorean and Goan cultures, complete with dance, drink and song. The 'Rain Dances' feature Bangalore's hottest DJs and radio personalities. Older members hold regular Ladies' and Gents' get-togethers.

There's a well stocked bar and a restaurant, with moderate prices. The club has a range of sports and health facilities like a spa, a swimming pool, jacuzzi, table tennis and badminton courts. Regular tournaments are held for various sports. The summer camps are a big hit with kids.

### Century Club
*Cubbon Park, Bangalore 560001*
*Tel 2221 1633/4121*
**Admission** *Members & Guests only*

One of the low profile clubs in the city, Century Club's address must be the envy of other better-heeled ones. Enveloped in the cool, lush environs of Cubbon Park, the club offers all the regular amenities – a swimming pool, recreation centre and so on.

The industrial architect of the Mysore State, Sir M Visweswaraya established this club a hundred years ago for Indians who could not get membership to the prestigious European clubs in British-ruled Bangalore.

### Club Cabana
*Jade Garden, Sadahalli Village,*
*Devanahalli Taluk,*
*Bangalore 562110*
*Tel 2846 7055/7056*
**Admission** *Members only*

Club Cabana is an upper-end club affiliated to the International Health, Racquet and Sports Club Association and membership here automatically gets you into affiliated clubs in 50 countries.

Located on the outskirts of the city, its sprawling acres resemble a tropical

paradise. There are several facilities: a 4-lane bowling alley with AMF equipment, a water park with three slides, a lazy river and wave pool, a day spa called the Health Studio, Swedish-style sauna, jacuzzi, massage and steam rooms, a tennis court, swimming pool, squash court and billiards parlour.

There are two restaurants – Water Court and a Domino's Pizza outlet. Of the two bars, Nautica serves up spirits and Surfers caters to teetotallers. There's also an open-air amphitheatre.

Lalbagh Botanical Garden

Don't say it. Show it.
**Webcam,** another cool feature on

New
**msn** Messenger

DOWNLOAD NOW

OTHER COOL FEATURES INCLUDE INSTANT FILE SHARING, BUDDYZONE AND MORE.

## log on to msn.co.in

located on a luxurious expanse of 2.5 acres of land on the Bangalore-Mysore highway.

## GARDENS & PARKS

### Bugle Rock Park
*Bugle Rock Road, Basavanagudi, Bangalore 560004*

Located in one of Bangalore's oldest suburbs, Basavanagudi, the park has been created around an enormous rock, 3,000 million years old. It gets its name from the watchtower that stands on it. Built by the founder of Bangalore, Kempegowda, the tower was used to warn the city dwellers of intruders by sounding a bugle call. Within the park premises is the Bull Temple with a monolithic statue of the Nandi.

### Cariappa Park
*Parade Ground, FM Cariappa Road, Bangalore 560025*

Created and maintained by the army, its two artificial waterfalls are a striking feature. The 22-acre park, situated on part of Bangalore's Parade Ground is full of green lawns, lush foliage, and includes a rose enclosure, eucalyptus trees, wooden bridges, a seven foot monolithic statue of Field Marshal Cariappa and tyre swings for children to play on. Sometimes a military band plays in the park.

### Cubbon Park
*Cubbon Park, Opp. Queen's Statue, Bangalore 560001*
*Tel 2286 7440*

This 300-acre park was laid out in 1864 and named after Bangalore's longest serving commissioner, Lord Cubbon. With lush greenery, flowerbeds and shady bamboo groves, the park is popular with

joggers, morning walkers and nature lovers. The park houses a museum, an aquarium and an art gallery. Located in the vicinity are the neoclassical High Court, the Central Library and the Vidhana Soudha.

### Lalbagh Botanical Garden
*Lalbagh Main Gate, KH Road, Bangalore 560004*
*Tel 2657 9231/8184*

This 18th century botanical garden laid out by Hyder Ali is known for rare tropical and subtropical plants. Named after the profusion of red roses that bloom here, Lalbagh is home to century-old trees as well. Spread across 240 acres, the garden has a lawn-clock, a glasshouse modelled on the lines of London's Crystal Palace and the Lalbagh rock that is one of the oldest rock formations on earth. However the bi-annual flower shows are no more held here.

## MUSEUMS

### Government Museum
*Kasturba Road, Bangalore 560001*
*Tel 2286 4483*
**Open** *10am to 5pm. Closed on Monday.*
**Admission** *Rs 4 for adults and Rs 2 for children*

One of the oldest museums in India,

# International Concert Destination

**B**ryan Adams, Enrique Iglesias, The Scorpions, Roger Waters, Sir Elton John, The Rolling Stones on their LICKS tour, Deep Purple…Bangalore is without doubt a hot spot for international bands and its sometimes the only city they visit in south Asia! Some even return to perform like popstar Bryan Adams recently did. Pop and rock greats like U2 and Mark Knofler are expected to visit the city in 2004.

Most of the shows take place at the Palace Grounds. **Uriah Heep** and **Osibisa** performed here in the eighties after which there was a lull for fans of rock and pop. **Jethro Tull** was the next big group to play here and by the late nineties, the city was rocking to live performances by **No Doubt, Boyzone** and **Michael Learns to Rock**.

Some concerts attract visitors from outside the state and ticketing agents offer deals for the show with travel and a night's stay thrown in. Palace Grounds, the sprawling green lung of the city is the venue of choice. It's an open-air venue but that doesn't seem to deter fans willing to brave the elements for the chance of a lifetime!

Courtesy: DNA Entertainment

Roger Waters

Bryan Adams

it was established in 1865. The museum displays sculptures from the Hoysala and Gandhara periods. Terracotta exhibits from Mohenjodaro and Mathura may also be viewed here. The painting section has an extensive collection of miniature paintings from the Rajasthani and Pahari schools, water colour paintings and those of Bangalore's famous artist Venkatappa. There are separate sections displaying wooden sculptures and plaster of paris works.

## HAL Heritage Centre & Aerospace Museum

*HAL, Airport Varthur Road, Bangalore 560037*
**Tel** *2522 8341*
**Open** *9am to 5pm*
**Admission** *Rs 20 for adults, Rs 10 for children*

The aerospace museum is equally popular with kids and adults. Helicopters, aircraft, fighters and bombers are on display in an open garden. Inside the museum are flight simulators, audio-visual shows and a mock control tower from where aeroplanes landing and taking off from the Bangalore airport can be viewed.

## Janapada Loka

*Bangalore-Mysore Road, Ramanagaram, Bangalore 571511*
**Tel** *727 1555*
**Open** *9am to 1pm and 2:30pm to 5:30pm. Closed on Tuesday.*
**Admission** *Rs 6 for adults and Rs 3 for children*

Located in Ramanagaram, 53kms from Bangalore, this folk museum is set in a 15-acre park and showcases Karnataka's indigenous art and culture. The exhibits include folk puppets, rustic utensils, baskets, weapons and masks. Also on display are a number of photographs of remote parts of rural Karnataka and its tribes. One of the highlights of the museum is an exquisitely carved but partly damaged temple chariot. Also located in the premises is an open-air theatre, studio

and art gallery. You can spend an entire day at this museum with a north Karnataka restaurant and a lake with boat rides.

## Visveswaraya Industrial and Technological Museum

*Kasturba Road, Bangalore 560001*
**Tel** *2286 4563*
**Open** *10am to 6pm*
**Admission** *Rs 15 for adults and children above 5 years*

Named after Karanataka's dewan and famous engineer-inventor Visveswaraya, this museum displays science and technology exhibits. Spread across seven halls, exhibits range from engines, popular science, space science. The special attraction is the dinosaur's corner. The museum mixes learning with fun and is particularly enjoyable for children.

The Planet M outlet on Brigade Road

## MUSIC STORES

### Calypso

*242 Manadi Arch, 9ᵗʰ Main, III Block Jayanagar, Bangalore 560011*
**Tel** *2655 2368*
**Open** *9:30am to 9:30pm*
**Cards** *All*

Calypso has been doing brisk business since it was set up four years ago. One of the most popular music stores in Jayanagar it has a wide selection of music from techno and rave to country music and oldie-goldies. It also houses music accessories and DVDs of popular English films. Its New Age chants, pop hits and Indian classical music collection is sizeable.

### Habitat Music Shoppe

*48 Church Street, Bangalore 560001*
**Tel** *2558 6886*
**Open** *12pm to 8:30pm*
**Cards** *All*

This store on Church Street is an all time favourite with those who have an eclectic taste in music. Apart from the latest chartbusters and remixes, Habitat has an extensive hard rock collection. Some rare jazz and blues albums can be procured. However, this is an all-CD store and cassettes are not available. Habitat also lends out and sells DVDs of all the Hollywood blockbusters, classics and old Westerns.

### Music World

*174/175 Brigade Road, Bangalore 560001*
**Tel** *2558 7337*
**Branches** *Jayanagar, 2655 9399; Indiranagar, 2525 2874*
**Open** *10am to 9pm*
**Cards** *All*

It was the one of the first music stores in Bangalore to stock all genres of music under one roof. There is a comprehensive collection of rock, alternative, jazz and blues, Hindi film music anthologies, regional film music, Indian classical music available, along with a play station.
Music World has a number of chains that operate throughout the city.

### Planet M

*Curzon Complex, Brigade Road, Bangalore 560001*
**Tel** *2558 8122*
**Open** *10:30am to 9pm*
**Branches** *Jayanagar, 2634 0101; ITPL, 5762 8882; Indiranagar, 5126 9891*
**Cards** *All*

A trendy chain of music stores across Bangalore, Planet M stocks everything from devotional and regional film music to hip-hop and jazz. The latest chartbusters, anthologies, karaoke collections and new age music is what sells the most here. Also sold at the store are music books, posters, t-shirts and VCDs. Especially popular with the youngsters are the music performances by artists held in the store's premises.

River rafting on the Kali river in Dandeli, northern Karnataka

## Sports, Adventure & Fitness

Diets are out, exercise is in! Fitness is the new buzzword and a host of fashionable gyms have opened across the city in step with this fad. Workouts are not restricted to aerobics and weights alone, but stretch to Yoga, Tai Chi, jazz ballet, cycling and kickboxing. The fitness bug has bitten software engineers, housewives and teenagers alike and instructors are not complaining.

Flying clubs abound in aerospace city. A popular weekend hobby, light aircrafts are a favourite way to head into the blue yonder. The Agni Aviation Club offers microlite joyrides accompanied by trained instructors at a reasonable price.

Leading tennis player Mahesh Bhupathi hails from Bangalore.

# Sports, Adventure & Fitness

Contrary to popular opinion, pubbing is not the state sport of Karnataka! And IT professionals can play more than just video games! In fact, a national ranking of sports, fitness and adventure would put Karnataka firmly in the first five states with **international sportsmen** like Rahul Dravid, Anil Kumble, Mahesh Bhupathi, Prakash Padukone, Ashwini Nachappa, Reshma and Nisha Millet and others nurtured in the state's sporting fraternity. **Cricket**, **tennis**, **badminton** and **swimming** are played at the highest level here and there are many coaching centres that regularly turn out top level sportsmen. **Golf** enjoys a historical charm and a wide variety of greens. Yoga classes are exploding in every corner. New **gyms** open every month. Sporting adventures like **rafting**, **rappelling**, **kayaking** and **diving** find many takers on the weekend. Amateur or professional, beginner or veteran, the opportunities are immense.

Teeing off at the Karnataka Golf Association

that once famous over-arm spin on your neighbour!

All academies listed organise excellent **training programmes** that examine the techniques of **batting**, **bowling**, **fielding** and **wicket-keeping** in depth. Former and current **national-level cricketers** do much of the coaching, with occasional visits by a star from the national team.

## Racquet Sports

India's ace tennis pro, **Mahesh Bhupathi** comes from Karnataka. Bangalore city hosted the Touchtel Tennis World Doubles Championship in 2000. A growing interest in the game has come with the opening of a number of **good tennis schools**. Players can keep an eye on the **professional tennis circuit** with recent access to world-class coaching and facilities. But this is the serious stuff. If you just like to **knock a ball** around on the odd weekend, there are a number of clubs and resorts with good facilities.

## Badminton

It was Bangalore boy Prakash Padukone – **All England Champion** from '79 to '81 who put the state on the world **badminton** map. He now runs an academy for aspiring badminton players like current champion Aparna Popat. **Top class facilities** and coaching is available. Competitive badminton aside, plenty of places offer a good game. A quick round of badminton is a popular sport among the working folk in Bangalore and several resorts and clubs offer good facilities at reasonable prices.

## Swimming

Barring a few wet and cold months, **swimming** in Bangalore is an easy option. There are some **Olympic-size** pools to hone your skills and smaller ones where you can just float the afternoon away. All the big hotels have pools. Membership is expensive, and usually packaged with amenities like a gym. State-run pools are often heavily chlorinated and may need a good pair of **goggles** and a **snug cap**.

## Golf

Golfers coming to Karnataka have much to cheer about. The course at the Bangalore Golf Club is the **second oldest course** in India, the first being the one in Kolkata. Across the state, in large towns and small, up hill and down dale, there is a green to suit the mood and the weather. According to some reports, Bangalore ranks as one of just eight places around the world where you can play golf throughout the year!

For the amateur, there are plenty of **golf coaching** opportunities. For the veterans, there is no limit as major and minor **tournaments** are held throughout the year.

## Cricket

Cricket is a national obsession and Bangaloreans are no different. They can boast a long and **chequered cricketing history** dating back to the 1920s when school and college level matches were eagerly followed. In response to the interest, the Bangalore United Cricket Club came up and others followed. In due course, the Mysore State Cricket Association was formed (later 'Mysore' changed to Karnataka), and it was affiliated to the Board of Cricket Control in India in 1934.

You don't just have to be a spectator. There are a number of **cricket clubs** spread across the city. Some offer high level coaching while others let you in for that **Sunday game** where you can practice a few knocks or check

## Riding

In the erstwhile princely state of Mysore, horses, **riding** and **racing** were an intrinsic part of life. The British Cantonment added to the demand for horses and horse rearing was a lucrative profession. Over the years, while racing continued to attract patrons, riding was seen as an unaffordable pleasure. All that has changed with the arrival of **good riding schools** in and around the city. A number of young people are turning to riding as a hobby and during the season, there are friendly tournaments.

## Adventure Adrenaline

Sport with some adventure and thrill has caught the fancy of people around the world. With its great topographical diversity, Karnataka offers a range of adventure sports from the most **basic treks** to **microlite flying**. Both short-term thrill seekers and serious adventure buffs will find something to write home about. You get to choose from **mountain biking, rock climbing, trekking, canoeing, rafting, fishing, wind surfing, water skiing, scuba diving** and **snorkelling** on the long coastline, rushing rivers and hilly terrain. **Aqua sports** are concentrated around the big rivers and are best visited after the monsoons. The rapids, while exciting are not of 'extreme' standards.

As aero capital of the country, **aero sports** is a pretty important business here. There are a number of **aero clubs** in the city that cater to a serious interest in sports like **microlite flying, hang-gliding, parasailing** and **para jumping**. For adrenaline junkies there's the occasional **bungee jump** and **skydiving**. Most aero sports are centered in Bangalore, while terrestrial stuff like trekking, rock climbing etc, are organised from places like Ramanagaram, a short drive from Bangalore or near the Western Ghats that border the coast. Read the listings to get a good idea of what is available. Always check the credentials of adventure outfits before you put your life in their hands!

The forested sections around Coorg and Chikmagalur and the national parks like Bandipur, Nagarhole and the Biligiri preserve are great for **wildlife activities** and **camping**.

## Yoga & Fitness

The fitness scene has never seen so much variety. **Aerobics classes, gyms, Hatha Yoga, Ashtanga Yoga, pilates, stretch, Tai Chi**, the list gets longer every month. There are a number of well-equipped **fitness centres** to choose from. Here you can take off a few inches from that midsection or just stay fit.

**Yoga centres** help you stretch while removing those urban tangles from your mind, and you can choose from getting an instructor home or joining a class. Some Yoga classes are very strenuous, some very spiritual and some have a bit of both.

Use *Stark World – Bangalore & Karnataka* to pick and choose your regular workout or weekend adventure. All the best!

## CRICKET

### Bangalore City Cricket Club

*Sapthagiri, 63 Venkateshwara Colony,*
*New Thippasandra, HAL III Stage,*
*Bangalore 560075*
*Tel 2521 9622, 2529 1122*
*Venue NAL Grounds*
*Open 3:30pm to 6:30pm on Saturday*
*and 6:15am to 9am on Sunday*
*Admission Rs 7,500 for Academy*
*session held over weekends; Rs 3,000 for*
*the summer camp.*

This club organises cricket coaching camps for boys aged between six and 19 on a regular basis.

### Brijesh Patel Cricket Academy

*18 Lavelle Mansions, 1/2 Lavelle Road,*
*Bangalore 560001*
*Tel 2227 1359*
*Venue Palace Grounds*
*Open 3:30pm to 6:30pm on Saturday*
*and 7:30am to 10:30am on Sunday.*
*Admission Rates vary depending on level*
*of play. Rs 2,500 for a 6-8 weeks summer*
*camp.*

The session lasts from June to January and resumes in summer. Only eight year-olds and above may apply. Yoga is taught as well.

### Britannia Roger Binny Cricket Academy

*3373K, 13th A Main, HAL II Stage,*
*Bangalore 560038*
*Tel 2526 3577*
*Venue Wodeyar's Sports Centre,*
*Palace Grounds*
*Open 3pm to 6pm on Saturday and*
*7:30am to 11am on Sunday.*
*Admission Rs 4,000 for annual*
*membership; Rs 2,500 for summer camps*

Weekend coaching programmes for children and teenagers are conducted through the year. Two-month summer camps are also held.

### Imtiaz Ahmed Cricket Academy

*136 Brigade Towers, Brigade Road,*
*Richmond Town, Bangalore 560025*
*Tel 2221 2752*
*Venue Jyothi Nivas College Grounds*
*Open 3pm to 6pm on Saturday and 8am*
*to 11:30am on Sunday*
*Admission Rs 6,000 for the coaching*
*session from July to May; Rs 3,000 for the*
*session from July to January.*

Run by former Indian wicketkeeper Imtiaz Ahmed, this academy holds coaching sessions through the year and offers summer camps as well. Both morning and evening batches are held for boys above eight years of age. The academy also conducts a prestigious tournament every year that brings together cricket clubs from across the country.

### National Cricket Academy

*Chinnaswamy Stadium, MG Road,*
*Bangalore 560001*
*Tel 2286 9970/8975*
*Venue Chinnaswamy Stadium*
*Admission Selection by the Cricket Board*

Training sessions usually last four months and involve both morning and evening coaching. There are great facilities on offer – three indoor synthetic turf lanes, bowling machines, a swimming pool and health club, lecture halls and lounge rooms. Scholarships are offered to a deserving few.

## TENNIS

### The Nike-Bhupathi Tennis Village

*183/4 Tindlur Road, Vidyaranyapura*
*Post, Kodigehalli, Bangalore 560097*
*Tel 2364 1747*
*Open 6:30am to 9:30am and 3pm to 6pm;*
*Closed on Sunday afternoon and Monday.*
*Admission Rs 4,000 to Rs16,000 per month*

# The Bangalore Hash House Harriers

Not quite a sport, not just entertainment, hashing treads the fine line in between! Running and beer are the two activities. Its history can be traced to a group of British officers stationed in Kuala Lumpur in the late 30s who started a sort of running club on Monday evenings, mainly as a way to work off the weekend's Bohemian excesses! After their run the good gentlemen would hook up at the Royal Selangor Club dining hall called the Hash House. The rest is now a hoary tradition and hashers infect nearly 150 countries and more than 1,500 cities around the globe today.

Bangalore is India's Pub City so it goes without saying that hashers are very active here. The Bangalore Hash House Harriers (BH3) has participated at the Hash in Europe, Southeast Asia, South America, Australia and Africa.

On alternate Sundays there is a hash run, about 15-20kms from the heart of town. Events include the Nash (intra-national) and the Interhash, with over 5,000 participants from various nations. The game is a variant of hares and hounds in which the hares set a trail marked with paper or chalk and the hounds try to follow the trail to the holy beer grail. Understandably, there are no restrictions on membership!
*Email bangalorehash@in.msnusers.com*

Tennis lessons at The Nike-Bhupathi Tennis Village

This tennis venue boasts 12 clay courts and three synthetic ones spread over 3.5 acres. A 20-minute drive from the city, it's run by Krishna Bhupathi, father of ace tennis player Mahesh Bhupathi. Children may join at the age of five years and there are 14 professional coaches to guide them. Special focus is given to fitness and physical training.

### Garden City Tennis Clinic

*Maharaja Jayachamaraja Wodeyar Tennis Centre, Opp. Ramana Maharishi Ashram, Bellary Road, Bangalore 560003*
*Tel 98440 05588, 2346 7421*
*Open 7am to 9:30am and 3pm to 6pm*
*Admission Rs 1,500 onwards per month depending on the level of play.*

This 'clinic' has five clay courts and is open to youngsters above the age of six years. Former state champ Priyadarshi is the chief trainer.

### Karnataka State Lawn Tennis Association

*Cubbon Park, Bangalore 560001*
*Tel 2286 9797/3636*
*Venue Kanteerva Stadium*
*Open 6am to 8:30pm*
*Admission Rates vary from Rs 700 to Rs 3,000 depending on age group and frequency of sessions.*

Four synthetic courts at Cubbon Park and four clay courts at the Kanteerava

Stadium make the KSLTA the biggest tennis academy in Bangalore. Kids from the age of four are admitted. There is also a good fitness centre, a clubhouse with a bar and cafeteria. Summer camps are organised as well.

### Tennis Advantage

*Opp. St. John's Hospital, Koramangala, Bangalore 560034*
*Tel 3184 5296*
*Branch Behind Baptist Hospital, Anand Nagar*
*Open 6:30am to 9am and 3:30pm to 6pm.*
*Admission Rs 2,200 per month for six days a week; Rs 1,100 for three days in a week. (Fees vary depending on the level of play.)*

Tennis Advantage has six clay courts in Koramangala and four in Anand Nagar. Play is supervised by five qualified coaches and an assistant at each venue. Coaching programmes for children and adults are conducted here. Both individual and group coaching sessions are offered and intensive coaching is also provided with extra lessons. Tennis Academy has a tie-up with the Ranjy Mani Academy in New York – a few chosen students are sent here every year to participate in international tournaments. The academy organises state-level tournaments in Bangalore, Pondicherry and Trivandrum.

### Kims Tennis Academy

*Indian Gymkhana Club, 5 Wheeler Road, Bangalore 560005*
*Tel 98450 49405*
*Open 6am to 9:30pm and 3pm to 6:30pm*
*Admission Rs 750 per month for alternate days; Rs 1,500 per month for six days a week.*

Kims has five clay and two synthetic courts on which it conducts training programmes for a wide age group.

### Kinesis Tennis Academy

*3007, 12B Main Road, HAL II Stage, Bangalore 560008*
*Tel 2529 7083, 2522 2003*
*Open 6:30am to 9:30pm and 3:30pm to 4:30pm*
*Admission Rs 1,000 onwards depending on the level of play.*
*Web www.kinesisnet.com*

Kinesis offers year round tennis instruction for kids above the age of six. The academy has three clay courts and is spread over a lush 30,000sqft campus. Other facilities include a basketball court and a mini-gym. There are more than a 100 students across different age groups enrolled here. State-level tournaments are an annual event at the academy. A pro-shop and a tennis library are also under construction. Transportation from select locations in the city is provided.

### Malleswaram Association

*110, 7th Cross, Malleswaram, Bangalore 560003*
*Tel 2331 1924*
*Open 6am to 9:30pm and 3pm to 6pm*
*Admission Rs 300 registration fee, Rs 250 per month with a three month fee payable in advance.*

Table tennis and tennis coaching facilities are available here. There are two tennis courts and eight table tennis tables. Coaching programmes are conducted by professional trainers.

## BADMINTON

### Canara Union

*42, 8th Main Road, Malleswaram, Bangalore 560003*
*Tel 2331 7980*
*Open 6am to10am and 4pm to 7pm*
*Admission Rs 750 per month*

Coaching facilities are provided only for members and students at the three courts. Non-members can use the court for a fee.

## Karnataka Badminton Association

*4 Jasma Bhavan Road, Vasantha Nagar, Bangalore 560052*
*Tel 2225 4760*
*Open 7:30am to 9am and 7:30pm to 9pm*
*Admission Rs 1,500 for three months*

The KBA has 10 wooden courts and four national level coaches for their training programme.

## Malleswaram Association

*110, 7ᵗʰ Cross, Malleswaram, Bangalore 560003*
*Tel 2331 1924*
*Open 6:30am to 9:30am and 4pm to 7pm*
*Admission Rs 300 registration fee and Rs 250 per month.*

Badminton and tennis coaching facilities are available. There are two wooden badminton courts. Coaching programmes, conducted by professional trainers, are open for students below 16 years of age.

## Prakash Padukone Badminton Academy

*4 Jasma Bhavan Road, Vasantha Nagar, Bangalore 560052*
*Tel 2228 3747*
*Open 10am to 5pm*
*Admission Selection by the academy*

Started by Prakash Padukone, an international badminton champion, it selects students only on merit and scholarships are awarded to deserving ones. The focus is to train future champions and world class training and facilities are available. Players are encouraged to participate in tournaments and the academy sponsors toppers to play on the international circuit.

## SWIMMING

### The Grand Ashok

*Kumara Krupa High Ground, Bangalore 560001*
*Tel 2225 0202*
*Open 6am to 7pm*
*Admission Rs 2,600 per month, Rs 600 per day*
*Email bangalore@bharathotels.com*

The Grand Ashok has memberships open for its health club and pool. The pool is about 50m in length and up to14ft in depth. There is a trainer available to impart basic lessons. Members can also use the gym.

### Gateway Hotel on Residency Road

*Residency Road, Bangalore 560025*
*Tel 5660 4545*
*Open 7am to 7pm*
*Admission Single Rs 12,500 per year and couples Rs 19,200 per year. Per day charges Rs 320.*
*Email gateway.bangalore@tajhotels.com*

This 20x50ft pool is above ground level with a depth of three to five feet and there is a fitness centre attached. A team of qualified coaches and lifeguards are also present. Membership to the pool and the fitness centre is separate.

### KC Reddy Swim Centre

*Near Bhashyam Circle, Sadashivnagar, Bangalore 560080*
*Tel 2361 0774/5350*

*Open 6:30am to 11am and 12:30pm to 4:30pm. Closed on Friday.*
*Admission Rs 10*

Run by the Bangalore City Corporation, this is an Olympic-size pool, with 24-hour filtration machines. Coaching facilities by professionally trained swimmers are available. The pool measures 58m in length and its depth ranges from a foot to 15ft. There is also a lifeguard on call.

### Le Meridien

*28 Sankey Road, Bangalore 560052*
*Tel 2226 2233*
*Open 6am to 7:30pm*
*Admission Single Rs 15,000 per year and couples Rs 20,000 per year. Per day charges Rs 540.*
*Email leme@vsnl.net*

The pool is 16m long and 10ft deep and there's a lifeguard on call. Coaching is however not available and membership to the pool does not include health club membership. The health club and the pool are open to members with an annual membership costing Rs 40,000 for couples and Rs 30,000 for individuals.

### National College Swimming Pool

*National College Grounds, Basavanagudi, Bangalore 560004*
*Tel 2661 2675*
*Open 6am to 4:30pm*
*Admission Rs 250 per month or Rs 10 per visit*

This is a large pool, quite clean and well maintained. There are different timings for women, children and men. The pool is 50m in length and three feet to 16ft in depth. Qualified coaches and lifeguards are there to assist beginners. After 4:30pm, training programmes are conducted for state and national level swimmers.

### PM Swimming Centre

*III Block, Jayanagar, Bangalore 560011*
*Tel 2691 0752, 2663 0744*
*Open 6am to 4:30pm*
*Admission Rs 260 per month*

This is an Olympic-size pool here: 50m x 21m, with a depth of three to 16ft. The gardens around the pool are a little rundown. The pool has different timings for children and women. Qualified coaches conduct training programmes.

### St. Joseph's Indian High School

*2 Grant Road, Bangalore 560001*
*Tel 2221 2570*
**Open** *7am to 8am and 5pm to 6pm.*
**Admission** *Membership charges Rs 400 per month for weekday use and Rs 300 per month for weekends.*

This is a school pool open to the public during specified hours. The 25mx9ft pool is a popular venue for summer camps. Qualified coaches are available.

### The Leela Palace

*23 Kodihalli, Airport Road, Bangalore 560008*
*Tel 2521 1234*
**Open** *6am to 9pm*
**Admission** *Per day charges Rs 1,000*
**Web** *www.theleela.com*

The Leela Palace houses a large pool surrounded by lush, landscaped gardens and top class facilities. Without a doubt, it is the most luxurious option in the city. The pool is about 25m in length and four feet deep. There's a lifeguard on duty, but swimming lessons are not offered here. Membership to the pool and the fitness centre is separate.

### The Park

*14/7 Off MG Road, Bangalore 560042*
*Tel 2559 4666*

**Open** *7am to 7pm*
**Admission** *Pool & Fitness Centre: Single Rs 30,000 and couples Rs 45,000. Per day charges are Rs 250 for adults and Rs 150 for children below 12 years.*
**Email** *resv.blr@theparkhotels.com*

This pool, 25m long and 4.8ft deep, is medium sized and temperature controlled. There is a well equipped fitness centre as well, which requires a separate membership. Coaching is not provided here.

### The Taj West End

*23 Race Course Road, Bangalore 560001*
*Tel 5660 5660*
**Open** *24 Hour*
**Admission** *Adults Rs 500 and children Rs 300. Single Rs 27,000 and Couples Rs 47,000 per year. (Bi-annual, quarterly and monthly membership available.)*
**Email** *westend.bangalore@tajhotels.com*

Set amidst rolling lawns and verdant gardens, this is a luxurious pool. It's excellently maintained and all top class services are available here. This 30x60 ft pool has a depth of 14ft. Coaching services are not offered here. However there is a lifeguard present at all times. Pool members are entitled to use the gym.

## GOLF

### Bangalore Golf Club

*2 Sankey Road, High Grounds, Bangalore 560001*
*Tel 2228 1876*
**Open** *6am to 6pm*
**Admission** *Members & Guests only. Indians: Rs 250 on weekdays and Rs 450 on weekends; foreigners: $20 on weekdays and $30 on weekends.*
**Course** *Holes: 18 Par: 70 Acreage: 65 Yardage: 6703m for men and 5414m for ladies*
**Coaching** *Rs 200 per hour. Beginners train separately at the Palace Grounds, at Rs 250 per hour.*

Founded in 1876, the Bangalore Golf Club is the second oldest in the country. Along with Chennai, it shares the distinction of hosting the oldest inter-club tournament, held in 1878. Die-hard golfers once travelled as many as 300kms on horseback or in carriages to participate! The course started with browns and one of the initial hazards was not lack of water or excessive tree cover, but the pesky crow! The clever birds would scoop up the ball mistaking it for an egg. The ordinary crow now has been immortalised in the logo of the club which features a crow with a ball in its beak!
The course is spread across just 60 acres, intensifying the challenge. The lush and

Karnataka Golf Association

# Browns, Greens, Tees and Holes

Golf came to India as early as 1829. In fact, the first golf course to be set up outside the British Isles was in Kolkata at the Royal Calcutta Golf Club, still in play today.

A decade after the Kolkata course started, the Royal Bombay Golf Club sprang up followed by the Bangalore Golf Club (BGC) in 1876. The Mumbai one is now defunct, making the BGC the second-oldest course in the country! The cool climate in Bangalore afforded many hours of easy play for the British cantonment officers stationed here. Today, Bangalore belongs to a select club of eight golfing destinations in the world where the sport can be played throughout the year.

Across Karnataka, golf clubs and courses have mushroomed to cater to the growing demand for the sport. Almost all have standard to deluxe rooms attached for those looking for a golfing weekend or holiday. Whatever your handicap, if you're looking for a few games there is a wide choice of courses and locales to choose from.

The first tournament played at the Bangalore Golf Club took place more than a century ago. The year was 1892 and the event was the first Indian Amateur Championship for Men. In 1906 it was the turn of the women with the Ladies All-India Amateur Golf Championship. Together they changed the nature of golf from a sport of pleasure to a competitive one.

Indians are avid golfers and the number of courses in the country has increased dramatically in the last few years. This has eased the pressure on older clubs and thrown the sport open to new players. Even so, the waiting list of people wanting to become members of most golf clubs in India is staggering.

The Indian Golf Union (IGU) was formed in 1956. It now conducts a number of amateur and professional tournaments around the country in association with the Professional Golf Association (PGA). The armed forces still play an important role in the promotion of the sport and nearly a third of all courses belong to them.

well-manicured greens are divided with eucalyptus and flowering trees like the Gulmohar. The rocky parts of the fairway can make drives tricky, and large bunkers trap the greens.

Quite predictably there is an excellent bar and restaurant and rooms for rent. Affiliated golf club members are also allowed.

## Eagleton Golf Village

*30th Km, Bangalore-Mysore Highway, Bidadi Industrial Area, Bidadi 562109*
*Tel 2676 4403/4974*
**Open** *8am to 6pm*
**Course** *Par: 72 Holes: 18 Acreage: 168 acres Yardage: 6668m/ 6062m/5872m*
**Admission** *Rs 500 on weekdays and Rs 1,000 on weekends.*

Thirty kilometres down Mysore Road lies Eagleton, designed by Australian firm Pacific Coast Designs. It's rated among the best in India. Multiple tees are available for pros, amateurs and ladies. There is also a 24-bay floodlit academy and a whopping 2,25,000sqft clubhouse with every amenity. Deluxe rooms are also available. The greens are open to non-members at all times except during tournaments. A five-day training capsule costs Rs 5,000. Coaches here are certified members of the United States Golf Teachers' Federation and Indian Golf Teachers' Federation. Golfing equipment is provided free of cost during the course.

## Jayachamaraja Wodeyar Golf Course, Mysore

*Maharana Pratap Singhji Road, Nazarbad, Mysore 570010*
*Tel 0821-2433244, 2436409*
**Open** *6am to 6:30pm*
**Course** *Holes: 18 Par: 70 Yardage: 5446*
**Admission** *Rs 200*

Established in 1906, this golf course was redesigned in 1996 by Australian firm, Pacific Coast Design. It is laid out within and around Mysore City's racecourse on a 100-acre property. Its location in equine country puts the course off-limits during the racing season. The two major tournaments conducted here are the Maharaja's Tournament and the Addicts Golfing Society of Southern India.

## Mercara Downs Golf Club, Coorg

*Gadibeedi Village, Medikati 571201*
*Tel 08272-2223516*
**Open** *8am to 8pm*
**Course** *Par: 66 Yardage: 5443m*
**Admission** *Rs 50*

A fabulously pretty course set in the stunning Coorg countryside. Sometimes the birdie flies into the trees never to be seen again!

## Karnataka Golf Association

*1 Golf Avenue, Kodihalli, Off Airport Road, PO Box No.817, Bangalore 560008*
*Tel 2529 8845/8846/8847*
**Open** *6am to 12midnight*
**Course** *Holes: 18 Par: 72 Acreage: 124 Yardage: 6600m Championship tee - Par: 72, 6770m Men's tee: 6300m Ladies Tee: 5624m*
**Admission** *Members & Guests only. Indians: Rs 400 on weekdays and Rs 800 on weekends. Foreigners: Rs 1,000 on weekdays and Rs 1,500 on weekends.*

The sprawling 124-acre course houses a 30,000sqft clubhouse with a well-stocked bar and restaurant, swimming pool, health club including a state-of-the-art gymnasium, a pro-shop, billiards and card parlours. It was built in 1973 on the bed of the Chellagatta Tank. Peter Thomson, British Open Champ (1965) was invited to design the course. Tournaments held here include the Wills Southern Open, KGA Open Amateur Golf Championship and the All India Ladies Amateur Golf Championship. Affiliated golf club members are allowed in. Lessons cost Rs 500 per hour and golfing equipment can be hired as well.

## RIDING

## Agram Riding School

*Agram Road, Inside Command Hospital, Bangalore 560007*
*Tel 2271 6414*
**Open** *6:30am to 6pm*

Spread across 500 acres, the school has international standards. Classes in horse riding are conducted all year round.

## Bangalore Amateur Riders' Institute

*Bangalore Turf Club, Race Course Road, Bangalore 560001*
*Tel 2226 2393/2391*
**Open** *6:30am to 8:30am and 3:30pm to 4:30pm*

This is one of Bangalore's oldest horse-riding schools, situated in the Bangalore Turf Club. Both individual and group coaching lessons are conducted here.

## Equestrian Centre For Excellence

*Palace Grounds, Jayamahal Road, Ayurvedic College Campus, Bangalore 560080*
*Tel 98451 74010*
**Open** *6am to 9am and 3:30pm to 6pm. Closed on Monday.*

Retired racehorses are available for training. It is the only riding school in Bangalore where one can own a retired racehorse after learning to ride.

## The Embassy International Riding School

*149/2 and 223 Torhunse Village, Jalahobbli, Devanahalli Taluk*
*Tel 2846 8296*
**Open** *6:30am to 6:30pm. Closed on Monday.*

Located on the outskirts of Bangalore, Embassy Riding School focuses on providing world class riding facilities with highly trained personnel. Experienced instructors and well groomed horses give the school an edge. With a restaurant on the premises and an animal enclosure, the riding school is also a great place to spend the day with kids.

## The Princess Academy of Equitation

*Palace Grounds, Bellary Road, Bangalore 560080*
*Tel 2361 0695*
**Open** *6am to 9am and 3pm to 6pm.*

The riding school run by Mysore's royal family offers night riding facilities and therapeutic sessions for physically and mentally challenged children. Located within the Bangalore Palace Grounds, this 400-acre riding school offers children the chance to learn horse riding from the age of five years. Trained instructors, retired racehorses and a central location add to its appeal.

## BILLIARDS

## Karnataka State Billiards Association

*5/1 Miller Tank Bed Area, Bangalore 560052*
*Tel 2225 1223, 2226 9970*
**Admission** *Members & Guests only*
**Email** *ksba@vsnl.com*

The KSBA has 10 tables for snooker and billiards. A coaching camp is held once a year, usually during April and May. Non-members can get on the ball by paying the required fee.

Free falling – bungee jumping is a popular adventure sport.

## ADVENTURE SPORTS

### Agni Aerosports Adventure Academy

*Hanger 2, Jakkur Aerodrome, 12ᵗʰ Km, Bellary Road, Bangalore 560064*
*Tel 2856 0060/5574*
*Web www.agniaviation.net*

The Jakkur-based Agni Aviation is rated as one of the best flying clubs in the city. They offer skydiving courses and lessons that make you a licensed private pilot. Affordable microlite flying sessions are also offered – joyrides accompanied by instructors are available for different periods of time.

### Angel

*850, 13ᵗʰ Cross, 2ⁿᵈ Main, Mahalakshmi Layout, Bangalore 560086*
*Tel 2349 5789*
*Email suresh@angeladventure.com, angelsuresh@hotmail.com*

Angel conducts terrestrial and river sports in Karnataka and the Himalayas where they offer treks and skiing. All necessary safety precautions and accommodation arrangements are taken care of.

### Bangalore Aerosports

*22/2 Alfred Street, Richmond Town, Bangalore 560025*
*Tel 2363 6413, 9845 213374*
*Web www.bangaloreaerosports.com*

This is an 'aerosport village' set up in 1997 by former fighter pilot Wg Cdr Ashok Mehta. At a distance of 52kms from the city, it is sprawled across a 100-acre plantation and camping is

a treat here. They have student packages and microlite flying, parasailing, camping, obstacle training, night treks, stargazing and even some sports. Corporate clients can choose from pleasure flying packages, parasailing and 'fly-solo' programmes.

### General Thimayya National Academy of Adventures (Gethnaa)

*III Floor, State Youth Centre, Nrupathunga Road, Bangalore 560001*
*Tel 2221 0454*

Supported by the government of Karnataka, Gethnaa is involved in terrestrial, water and aero sports, at subsidised rates. An adventure holiday itinerary would include stay, food and equipment. Water sports are conducted at Mangalore, Karwar and on the rivers Cauvery, Sita, Tungabhadra and Kali.

### Jungle Lodges & Resorts

*II Floor, Shrungar Shopping Complex, MG Road, Bangalore 560001*
*Tel 2559 7021/24/25*
*Web www.junglelodges.com*

Jungle Lodges & Resorts (JLR) is a unit of Karnataka Tourism.
JLR properties have cabins, log huts and camping facilities and come ready with all modern amenities. Different resorts offer different experiences like wildlife safaris, bird watching, trekking, mahseer fishing and river rafting. JLR has properties in Kabini, Dandeli, Devbagh and on the banks of river Cauvery among others.

### Karnataka Mountaineering Association

*6 Guru Nanak Bhavan Complex, Jasma Bhavan Road, Vasantha Nagar, Bangalore 560052*
*Tel 2226 9053*
*Web www.kmaindia.org*

The Karnataka Mountaineering Association (KMA) organises several mountaineering expeditions all over the country, most of which are free. Himalayan climbing and trekking expeditions, basic and advanced mountaineering programmes, rock climbing training camps, explorative treks, cycling and motorbike trips, skiing, white water rafting in the Himalayas and desert trekking expeditions are also organised. Exclusive programmes for corporate groups are possible.

### Nataraja Gurukula Adventure Academy

*Somanahalli Post, Bangalore 560062*
*Tel 2843 2496*
*Email gurufreddy@hotmail.com*

Day or weeklong camps with trekking, cave exploration, river crossing, rappelling, rock climbing (both basic and advanced), bird watching and obstacle courses are offered.

### Ozone

*4, 9ᵗʰ A Cross, XII Block, Kumara Park West, Bangalore 560020*
*Tel 2356 1871/1872*
*Web www.ozoneindia.com*

Ozone is best known for its bungee jumping events but backpacking, camping, trekking, rock climbing, paragliding, white water rafting and kayaking events are part of its operations. Outward-bound training programmes for corporates can be organised.

### SAHAS

*20 Ganesh Prasad, Kirloskar Colony I Stage, Bangalore 560079*
*Tel 2323 1970*
*Email pareshdodiedo@hotmail.com*

Parasailing on Hoskote lake is offered along with wildlife camps in Karnataka and bird watching tours.

### SPARK (Society for Propagation and Activation of Rock Klimbing)

*Corporation Station Complex, Jayanagar, Bangalore 560011*
*Tel 2553 2146*

One of the older organisations, SPARK still conducts occasional trekking and rock climbing camps.

### Sports Promotion Team

*830, 17 F Main, VI Block, Koramangala, Bangalore 560095*
*Tel 2552 6296*
*Web www.sptindia.com*

Activities here include adventure camps, treks, rock climbing, river crossing, microlite flying and parasailing. Team building exercises like outbound training and personality development programmes for corporates are organised. Activities for children include summer camps in aerosports at the Bangalore Aerosports Club.

# Biking in Karnataka
## – Bob Hoekstra

Bob Hoekstra at Nandi Hills

**You need...**

A sturdy bicycle offers an unmatched experience of Karnataka's countryside. It combines the pleasure of exercise with great scenery and an authentic, quiet view of rural life.

Hilly terrain needs a good machine with at least eighteen gears. A mountain bicycle with Indian tyres that have a heavy tread is a good choice. Indian roads are a challenge for tyres and the freshly chipped granite gravel has surprisingly knife sharp edges. You may want to replace the brake shoes with imported ones as the braking function is vital and indigenous ones wear out very fast. It's also a good idea to replace the fancy multi-layer tyres of foreign bikes with Indian ones to reduce the occurrence of flats – always an unpleasant experience but especially so at high speeds downhill.

A good cycling helmet is an essential part of all journeys, I would recommend real helmets instead of the rubbers strap type.

A car or knowledge of a bus service to get you to your cycling spots is a good idea. Essential equipment also includes a cooler with beer for the end of your journey!

**Watch out for...**

Riding on highways is not a good idea, as traffic tends to pass very close and forget your presence once you are out of sight. That leaves the tail-end of a large vehicle dangerously close sometimes. Buses will overtake a slow truck and come straight at you, blinking furiously to get out of the way. Don't wait to argue, dive for the ditch!

In rural areas there is very little traffic, and cycling is fun. Occasionally an old Ambassador may puff up a hill leaving a black cloud of exhaust in its wake. But mostly there is the healthy smell of flowers, Eucalyptus trees and manure.

**I recommend...**

My favourite biking destination is **Nandi Hills** – a hill station north of Bangalore with a good road to the top. It's a 10kms road from the base to the top at 1,400m. The first five kilometres are relatively easy, but the second five are fairly steep and I need to switch to a low gear. The road has 41 curves, many of which are steep hairpins especially near the top.

The views of the farmland surrounding Nandi Hills are spectacular – palm trees, banana plantations, water tanks and paddy fields. Curve Number 35 is a great Kodak spot, with views of many hills forming a backdrop. Plenty of young couples would agree with that! Groups of monkeys try to balance their curiosity with their fear as they watch you pass.

At the bus stop just below the summit I prefer to walk to the top as two wheelers are not allowed further. It's time to turn around now. The wind in my face cools me as I descend, and is a great reward for the sweaty one-hour climb.

Halfway down, ladies selling fresh coconuts with a straw to slurp up the water, beckon. Take this moment to look up at the vertical rocks of Tipu drop – the steep side of Nandi Hills where the Tiger of Mysore, Tipu Sultan took his English prisoners a couple of centuries ago and – hold your breath – pushed them over the edge!

The descent from here onwards has mild curves, not very steep and you get a speed thrill without braking. The rustic scenery comes closer and closer almost like a plane touching down! Watch out for the odd silent cows or grazing goats around a blind curve. Cars are not a danger as they honk continuously!

It's possible to make a tour around Nandi Hills – turn right towards the village seen on the descent and take the mud road into the village, heading back for the hill. It climbs to a saddle pass between Nandi and a neighbouring hill. A tough rocky climb, it makes for great mountain bike terrain. It descends to a small Nandi temple where the dirt road turns to tar once again.

The other option is to turn left instead, in Nandi Hills village at the old temple, and cycle on to Chikballapur. It lies a few kilometers down a narrow road with light traffic, so once again you need to make timely escapes plunging off the road! You can conclude the tour sitting on the edge of the dam overlooking a huge tank surrounded by hills.

**Ramanagaram** to the south west of Bangalore is another good biking destination, unique for its many trails through mango groves and odd shaped monolithic rocks. The best approach is to physically climb a hill, take in the landmarks and plan a route. The trails can be narrow and may pass through creek beds, so a car following behind is not an option. This applies to the west of the road, for on the east there is a road passing pleasant villages to the dam and the water reservoir, all very scenic. From the reservoir I sometimes continue to the Big Banyan Tree, not easy to find but villagers will help with directions.

**Devarayanadurga** is a little known hill destination. It has a road to the top where a temple nests picturesquely in a rock. The climb is short – a little more then half an hour – but it's quite tough, very steep at the base and easier in the winding hairpins at the top. I warm up by starting a few kilometres from the base of the climb. Halfway to the top, is a village and on festival days throngs of people climb the steep footpath from the main temple to the small one on top. The road ends at a parking area. From here it is a hundred or so steep steps to reach the temple, well worth it. From the top there is a great view of the valley, the village, hills and forest. The descent is marvellous despite the poor road. Watch out for buses that are as wide as the road! The rice and ragi fields surrounding the village are a joy on a mountain bike and the small trails into the forest, made by cattle, are ideal to spend a last burst of energy.

**Other Great Cycling Tours...**

**Chamundi Hills** in Mysore, can be easily reached from the Lalitha Mahal Palace Hotel and has a road going to its top. The journey takes less than 45 minutes. On the way down explore a little dead-end road to the left to visit the Nandi.

**Bannerghatta**, outside Bangalore city, has some good cycling on the west of the national park. Venture into the fields but watch out for elephants.

The forest near the **Cauvery Fishing Camp** provides great cycling opportunities.

**My Wish List...**

The area around **Shravanabelagola** with its scenic hills with the thousand-year-old Jain statue. The scenery surrounding the vast paddy fields in this well irrigated area is impressive.

**Kolar** Gold field area. The gold fields have been abandoned, but the boulder-strewn hills are appealing. **Coastal Karnataka**, around Manipal, in the hills close to the sea, but only in winter when it is cool there.

A few days around **Hampi**, with its ruins of the Vijayanagar period, just after the Middle Ages.

*Bob Hoekstra is CEO of Philips Software Centre India. He has lived in Bangalore since 1999.*

---

### The Adventurers, A Wilderness School

*142, 69th Cross, V Block, Rajajinagar, Bangalore 560010*
*Tel 2330 5508, 2340 9712*
*Email honnemardu@satyam.net.in*

The Adventurers conduct trekking, rock climbing, cycling, camping, canoeing, kayaking and windsurfing activities. Most of their treks and tours take place in the Western Ghats.

### The Wild

*42-40/1 3rd Main, VII Block Jayanagar, Bangalore 560082*
*Tel 2634 7639*
*Email thewld_india@yahoo.com*

A minimum of six people in a camp is required for them to conduct trekking and wildlife camps within the state. Home stays can be put on the itinerary.

### Le Wild

*75, III Floor, Farah Commercial Complex, JC Road, Bangalore 560002*
*Tel 2227 6299*
*Web www.lewild.com*

Le Wild offers adventure and wildlife activities, corporate and outbound training programmes. Their camps in Karwar, Dandeli and on the Cauvery are very popular. Le Wild also makes high quality adventure sports equipment.

### Woody Adventure

*12/A, III Floor, Yamuna Bai Road, Madhavnagar, Bangalore 560001*
*Tel 2225 9159*
*Email woodyadventures@mailcity.com*

Trekking, camping, cave exploration, jungle treks, fort exploration, microlite flying, parasailing and white water rafting on the river Sita are offered here. They also organise jeep safaris and skiing in the Himalayas. Mountain biking is planned.

## World Wide Fund for Nature, India

*143 Kamala Mansion, Infantry Road, Bangalore 560001*
*Tel 2286 6685/3206*
*Email wwfkso@vsnl.com*

Set up in 1969, WWF-India is the country's largest voluntary organisation in the field of conservation. They organise camps that are meant to expose people to the intricate balance of nature and wildlife. Camps require a minimum of 20-25 people. Called 'nature clubs', their objective is to sensitise participants about nature conservation and promote environmental education.

## Youth Hostels Association of India (YHAI)

*6 Guru Nanak Bhavan Complex,*
*Vasantha Nagar,*
*Bangalore 560052*
*Tel 2235 0906*
*Web www.yhaindia.org*

The YHAI is actively involved in various adventure activities like trekking, rock climbing, mountaineering and even socio-cultural activities at various locations in Karnataka and Kulu-Manali. They have a vast network of affiliated organisations and provide a platform for adventure activities.

## BIRD WATCHING

### Bird Watchers Field Club of Bangalore

*13, 7th Cross, 2nd A Main,*
*KSRTC Layout, JP Nagar II Phase,*
*Bangalore 560078*
*Tel 2658 9818*

This is an informal group of bird watchers and open to new members.

Meetings occur on the second and fourth Sunday of every month, the former at the Lalbagh Botanical Garden and the latter (in association with the World Wildlife Fund) usually at the Valley School campus on Kanakapura Road.

## Institute for Natural Resources, Conservation, Education, Research & Training

*10 Sirur Park B Street,*
*Seshadripuram, Bangalore 560020*
*Tel 2336 4682*
*Email navbharat@blr.vsnl.net.in*

This institute will put a trusty pair of binoculars in your right hand and the latest Bird Watcher's Guide in the other! Frequent ornithological camps in and around Bangalore to study and observe feathered creatures are organised. Anyone is welcome. A bi-monthly newsletter with details of their activities and interests is available.

## YOGA

### Atma Darshan Yoga Ashram

*Dayananda Sagar College Road,*
*Kumaraswamy Layout,*
*Bangalore 560078*
*Tel 2666 4016, 2666 7369*
*Web www.atmadarshan.org*

Classes are open to all. Discourses and programmes on health management are also held. Special courses for specific health problems are conducted. Asanas, pranayama, Yoganidra, ajata jaap, antar maun, chakra sadhana, kriya and meditation receive special emphasis. Beginners are charged Rs 400 and advanced learners pay Rs 800. Residential courses are offered for an additional fee of Rs 200 per day, inclusive of food.

### Bharat Thakur's Yoga Classes

*Platinum Bodies, Jayanagar; Indian Heritage Studio, Koramangala; Malleswaram Club*
*Tel 2508 9493*
*Web www.bharatthakur.com*

Bharat Thakur's style focuses on body sculpting, weight loss, relaxation and stress management. Pranayama, Yoganidra and meditation are part of Yoga sessions. Training in 'artistic Yoga', created by Bharat Thakur, is also provided. This is an experimental form of Yoga where ancient yogic techniques have been adapted to suit the needs of a contemporary lifestyle. Classes are conducted across four studios in Bangalore and are open to children above the age of 13. Yoga sessions can be complemented by meditation workshops. Techniques from Zen Buddhism, Sufism and Yoga are incorporated in a unique two-day workshop called 'Tapasya'.

### Foundation of Pathanjala Yoga Kendra

*4, 3rd B Main Road, 9th Cross, Sarakki, JP Nagar I Phase, Bangalore 560078*
*Tel 2665 0382*
*Email yogivishwa@yahoo.com*

Yoga classes, ashtanga (Mysore style), pranayama and other practices are taught here. More than 30 years old, this Yoga Kendra also provides certified training to teachers in this field. Their course includes yogasana, pranayama, mudra mantra and japa, yogic philosophy, psychology and lifestyle teaching techniques and methodology. Classes cost Rs 4,000 per month and Rs 2,000 per month for three classes a week.

### Javed's Yoga Classes

*17 Imperial Court, Cunningham Road, Bangalore 560052*
*Tel 2351 2239*
*Branch Figurine Fitness, Indiranagar*
*Email javed@kayavyuha.com*

Javed trains his students in the ancient art of Hatha Yoga, the Yoga of the physical body. The one-hour classes fuse physical exercise with meditation and breathing techniques. Classes are held throughout the week for adults and workshops for children are held during summer. Special batches in the morning are held for pregnant women. Javed writes a regular column for *The Economic Times* titled, 'Yoga and Disorder'.

### Siddha Samadhi Yoga

*176, 31st Cross, 11th Main,*
*IV Block East, Jayanagar,*
*Bangalore 560011*
*Tel 2663 1909*
*Email rsvkssybangalore@yahoo.com*

The 17-day course combines the Art of Living programme with courses on food habits and meditation. The last three days in the sylvan setting of the Maralawadi Ashram near Kanakapura are worth looking forward to. There are special courses for people suffering from diabetes, blood pressure, asthma, etc. They also have a residential school, Rishi Gurukulum, with traditional-style classes that attract students from all over the world.

# The New Yoga

The science of Yoga dates back 5,000 years and offers healing for both the mind and the body. According to Yoga, mental, psychosomatic and physical diseases are created by wrong thinking, eating and living. Yoga uses a series of physical poses called asanas, and once there were only a handful of teachers who knew its nuances, spiritual significance and arduous physical technique.

Today all that has changed. There is a Yoga guru to be found at every corner, some genuine some not. The cloak of spiritual mysticism that once covered Yoga completely, has almost vanished. In its place, is a quiet acceptance of the physiological benefits it has to offer. Yoga purists are however unhappy at the manner in which Yoga is being propagated around the world – with emphasis only on the physical aspect. It is now touted as the modern day stress buster and has burst onto the fitness scene in all corners of the world. Yoga is practiced not just in specific Yoga centres but also in aerobics classes, gyms, living rooms and lawns. Young and old, lean and fat, are using Yoga to stretch, relax and meditate. Done correctly, it stretches muscles and improves their flexibility, recharges and revitalises, putting people back in control of their own bodies.

# When you walk in, you've already exercised 45 muscles

Inside, we'll help you tone up the other 595 too

The human body has over 640 muscles. At Figurine Fitness – the complete fitness centre – you can feel the difference of workouts that help tone the entire body. And refresh the mind too. The programmes include weight loss and body sculpting (inch loss) workout modules.

From a conventional gym to aerobic exercises that include elements of folk dance, kick boxing, Kalaripayattu, yoga, Tai Chi... Even Bhangra and Jazz fusion!

Come, step in and experience the difference.

**Figurine Fitness**
Oxygen'eration

• 3167, Service Road, HAL II Stage, Bangalore 560008. Tel: 2529 4019. • Gate 10, KSCA Stadium, MG Road, Bangalore 560012. Tel: 2286 7499. Open: 6am – 10pm

## Swami Vivekananda Yoga Anusandhanam Samsthana

*Prashanti Kuteeram Campus,*
*Jigani, Bangalore District*
**Tel** *2652 8822*
**Web** *www.vyasa.org*

Svyasa offers one month residential Yoga courses for therapeutic purposes, stress management and a sense of holistic well being. An integrated Yoga Therapy is applied to the treatment of psychosomatic and psychiatric problems. Specialised programmes are conducted for the corporate sector, advanced Yoga techniques are taught for those who want to expand their consciousness and certified courses for instructors and therapists are available after the completion of the foundation course.
A 12-month diploma in yoga and naturopathy is also offered here.

## NATURAL HEALING

### Prithvi Natural Healing & Yoga

*841, 10ᵗʰ Main, 5ᵗʰ Cross, Indiranagar*
*II Stage, Bangalore 560038*
**Tel** *5116 1666, 9845162225*
**Branch** *JP Nagar I Phase,*
*2634 9007*
**Web** *www.naturalhealingdoctors.org*

Dr. Bhanu offers customised 'holistic lifestyle solutions', incorporating Ayurveda, aromatherapy, Yoga, naturopathy and traditional Chinese medicine at his centre, Prithvi Natural Healing and Yoga.

A range of healing systems like acupressure, acupuncture, aromatherapy, reflexology, mud, herbal and Swedish massage therapy are used to restore mind-body equilibrium and enhance physical as well as emotional growth. The centre's focus is on the areas of fitness, weight reduction, nutrition, healthcare, beauty treatment and counselling. All age groups are welcome and there is even a growth enhancing programme for children and emotional healthcare for adolescents, as well as detoxification and stress management for adults and rejuvenating therapies for the elderly. The speciality of the centre is a seasonal diet regimen, body massages and therapies like the Panchakarma. Classes in Hatha Yoga are held here. The Yoga workout is targeted at heightening relaxation, enhancing immunity, overcoming stress, managing diabetes, hypertension and other chronic muscular afflictions. Pranayama, Yoga nidra and meditation are also incorporated into the session. Classes are tailored to suit the individual requirements of temperament and flexibility. Lessons in Swara Yoga, Ashtanga Yoga and Shatkarma are offered to advanced learners.
Physical ailments from varicose veins, asthma, acidity and arthritis to spondylitis, insomnia and migraine are treated through a combination of various therapies, exercise, diet and counselling. Head-to-toe beauty packages are also available, including skin and hair treatments, facial massages and herbal body wraps.
The doctors here are trained medical practitioners and consultation is by appointment only.

Figurine Fitness is equipped with a state-of-the-art gymnasium.

## KARATE

### National Institute of Korean Martial Arts

*419, 6ᵗʰ Main, 6ᵗʰ Cross,*
*MSR Nagar, Bangalore 560054*
**Tel** *2360 0541/0558*
**Admission** *Rs 1,500 for eight weeks*
**Email** *ddutta5@rediffmail.com*

The school from the Chang Mok Kwan Taekwondo family focuses on the traditional aspect of Taekwondo. They also have short term self defence classes lasting eight to 10 weeks. Classes are held at 10 schools in Bangalore and are quite popular with women seeking to learn self defence.

### Young Men's Indian Association (YMIA)

*5 Assayee Road, near Ulsoor Road,*
*Bangalore 560042*
**Tel** *2571 5649, 94484 20082*
**Open** *6:30am to 7:30am*
*on Tuesday, Thursday, Saturday*
*and 5pm to 6pm on Monday,*
*Wednesday, Friday.*
**Admission** *Rs 150 per month*
**Web** *www.kyokushinbangalore.com*

Sensei Ravi Carvalho has mastered the famed Kyokushin Karate and he is the branch chief in Karnataka, with the headquarters in Japan. He promises a black belt after a rigorous training of 64 months.

# Figurine Fitness

Figurine Fitness is one of the trailblazers on Bangalore's fitness circuit. Set up in 1987, this aerobics and gym centre is known to be the biggest and the best in the city. It's a one-stop-shop for fitness with suspended wooden flooring, wall-to-wall mirrors and surround sound acoustics across three centres. Engineer and now dancer and fitness guru Santosh Kumar is the driving force behind the centre and is the city's most well known fitness expert. Armed with a degree and a gold medal in fitness, physiology and sports injuries, his clientele lists cricketers, beauty queens, techies and housewives alike.

The aerobics regimen here is not run of the mill – elements of dance, Yoga, Kalari, Tai Chi and kick boxing have been incorporated into the sessions. Creativity and variation are part of every workout and innovations include bhangra aerobics and high intensity jazz aerobics with bits of Indian folk dance thrown in. The workouts are comprehensive and include cardio dance, Tae-Bao steps, bands, tubes and pilates. A rigorous Yoga programme is offered to tune into the body's natural rhythms.

Figurine Fitness offers dance as a medium of exercise for the mind, body and spirit. A variety of dance forms from freestyle to ballroom dancing, are taught for fitness, fun, stress relief and creative expression. Students learn to salsa, jive, meringue and cha-cha at the chic dance studio.It has a state-of-the-art gymnasium with a unique circuit slimming programme – a combination of aerobics and gym training. Apart from traditional weight training gear, the gym is equipped with treadmills, low impact climbers, rowing machines, a cardio theatre and recumbent bikes. Qualified trainers ease clients into customised programmes designed to suit age, weight and medical history. Consultations on weight management and diet are also part of the package. A massage parlour and steam and sauna room are the de-stress options at this fitness centre.

*3167 Service Road, Hal II Stage, Indiranagar, Bangalore 560008,* **Tel** *2529 4019*
*Gate 10, KSCA Stadium, MG Road,* **Tel** *2286 7499* **Web** *www.figurinefitness.com*

Santosh Kumar leading a workout session at Figurine Fitness

## FITNESS

### Chisel

*36 NR Chambers,*
*Opp. Cathedral School, Richmond Road,*
*Bangalore 560025*
*Tel 2556 7488*
*Open 6am to 10pm on weekdays.*
*6am to 9pm on Saturday and*
*6am to 3pm on Sunday.*
*Admission Rs 1,425 per month for the*
*gym and Rs 990 per month for aerobics*
*Web www.chiselindia.com*

Stop here for international quality equipment tested for safety and efficiency and overseen by a number of fitness instructors. Chisel also has an aerobics section in collaboration with Reebok and is the first certified aerobics studio in south India.

### Creative Body Works

*15 Cotton Complex, Residency Road,*
*Bangalore 560025*
*Tel 2221 7997, 2224 4361*
*Open 6am to 9pm. Closed on Sunday.*
*Admission Rs 700 per month for*
*6 days a week or Rs 400 per month for*
*alternate days.*

A well equipped modern gymnasium, they offer services in bodybuilding, aerobics and fitness training under the guidance of qualified in-house trainers. Dance classes are also conducted.

### Figurine Fitness

*3167 Service Road, Hal II Stage,*
*Indiranagar, Bangalore 560008*
*Tel 2529 4019*
*Branch MG Road, 2286 7499*
*Open 6am to 10pm*
*Admission Rs 1,000 per month for the*
*gym and Rs 1,000 per month for aerobics*
*Web www.figurinefitness.com*

There's plenty of hi-tech equipment and a general air of freshness. Summer camps for children are conducted each year in dancing and exercises. There is also a good aerobics section. Yoga classes are conducted by well known instructors Javed and SN Omkar. Classes are designed to work across skill levels from beginner to advanced courses.

### Figure It Out

*Next to Shoppers' Stop, Magrath Road,*
*Northern Stand, Football Stadium,*
*Bangalore 560025*
*Tel 2536 8076*
*Open 6am to 10am and 4:30pm*
*to 9:30pm*
*Admission Rs 750 per month for the gym*
*and Rs 800 per month for aerobics*

This centre offers a variety of pro-grammes at a reasonable price. Located in the city's football stadium, Figure It Out has a fully equipped gymnasium. Highlights include the aerobics and kick boxing classes that are held in flexible batches. Apart from regular workout sessions you can also enrol for a range of programmes from weight gain to weight loss and body conditioning to spot reduction. Weight management and diet plans are also provided.

### Fitness World

*2350 Benaka Krupa,16ᵗʰ B Main,*
*2ⁿᵈ Cross, HAL II Stage, Indiranagar,*
*Bangalore 560038*
*Tel 2529 2939*
*Open 5:30am to 10am and 4pm to 9pm.*
*Admission Rs 300 per month*

Body building, weight training, massage and weight reduction programmes are available. Gym facilities come at a reasonable price with discounts on yearly payments. Aerobic classes and massages are on the menu.

### Fosette Slim Gym

*Chaitra Complex, 39ᵗʰ Cross,*
*28ᵗʰ Main, Jayanagar IX Block,*
*Bangalore 560069*
*Tel 2634 4116*
*Open 9:30am to 8pm*
*Admission Rs 700 per month*

This gym is exclusively for women and offers aerobic classes as well. There is a beauty parlour attached.

### Steve's Gym

*23 Wheeler Road, Cox Town,*
*Bangalore 560005*
*Tel 2548 6099*
*Branch Airport Road, 2535 3323*

**Open** *6am to 9pm*
**Admission** *Rs 3,000 for three months*
**Web** *www.stevesgym.com*

Fitness, weight loss, weight gain, body-building, aerobics and dance classes are some of the activities offered. They have several fitness programmes including some for children and those over 40 years and an exclusive batch for women.

## Talwalkars Fitness Planet

*27/1, III Floor, Batra Centre,*
*Ulsoor Road, Bangalore 560042*
**Tel** *2506 5020, 2559 5817*
**Open** *5:30am to 9pm on Monday to*
*Saturday and 7am to 1pm on Sunday.*
**Admission** *Rs 6,000 for three months for*
*the gym*
**Web** *www.talwalkarsgym.com*

A fully equipped gymnasium, steam and sauna, aerobics and customised weight loss programmes are available. It's part of a chain of 18 centres around the country. Their programmes for weight loss and maintenance are very popular. A personal trainer and beauty clinic services are also available. Other packages include body shaping, aerobic workouts, Yoga, meditation and one for senior citizens.

## SPORTING EQUIPMENT

## Billiard's Point

*263 K Kamaraj Road, Bangalore 560042*
**Tel** *2556 7416*
**Open** *9:30am to 6pm*

Billiards and snooker tables are manufactured and sold here.

## Get Off Your Ass

*472 Srikrishna Temple Road,*
*Indiranagar I Stage,*
*Bangalore 560038*
**Tel** *5116 1600*
**Open** *10:30pm to 8pm*
**Cards** *All*

Go here if you are planning to trek, canoe or do anything adventurous. Aptly named, this is an unusual adventure store that stocks all the essentials, from tents to backpacks, geared bicycles, Swiss Army knives, powerful torches and other survival gear. Camping equipment and sleeping bags can be rented as well as bought. Jackets, vests, a climbing wall for children, skateboards, shoes and head torches make for innovative gifts.
To complete the package, the owner of the store is an adventure consultant who organises treks, eco-tours, nature appreciation camps and weekend getaways, for children as well as adults.

## Golfware India

*16/7A Binny Crescent, Benson Town,*
*Bangalore 560046*
**Tel** *2333 6355*
**Open** *9:30am to 6pm*

Golf gear and equipment can be bought or hired.

## Hatrick Sports

*2 Church Street, Bangalore 560001*
**Tel** *2558 6833*
**Open** *10:30am to 8pm*

The store is frequented for sports equipment and gear for cricket, track and field, shuttle, tennis, football and badminton.

## Hole-in-One Golf Shop

*582 KGA Road, Kodihalli,*
*Off Airport Road, Bangalore 560008*
**Tel** *2527 5657*
**Open** *7am to 9pm*

Golf gear and equipment are up for sale and hire. Hire charges start from Rs 200 per hour.

## Hoysala Sports

*78/A Sapthagiri Complex, Magadi Road*
*Circle, Bangalore 560010*
**Tel** *2330 5302*
**Open** *9:30am to 9pm*

This shop is well stocked with sports equipment and gear for cricket, shuttle, tennis, football and badminton.

## Kadamba Sports

*49/2, Near Kanti Sweets, 5th Main,*
*Ganganagar, Bangalore 560032*
**Tel** *2592 9300*
**Open** *10:30am to 8pm.*
*Closed on Sunday.*

A comprehensive range of sports gear is available here.

## Lal Rakhra Agencies

*15/39 Cambridge Road,*
*Ulsoor, Bangalore 560008*
**Tel** *2555 5684*
**Open** *10:30am to 8pm*

Sports equipment and gear for cricket, badminton, tennis, football, track and field can be purchased at this store.

Dilip Mistry at Figurine Fitness

# Working Out!

A software executive who's traded his laptop for a pair of gym shoes! The result: A 20kg weight loss in one and a half years, a calmer frame of mind and a healthier lifestyle. Meet Dilip Mistry, Director (Developer Relations) at Microsoft India. This 36 year old Londoner resides in Bangalore, the Silicon Valley of the East. His high profile job takes him around the world, managing a dynamic team of techies and diverse clients. Inhabiting a world of 24-hour connectivity and blurred time zones, Mistry's work keeps him on his toes for up to 12 hours a day, six days a week.

But there is another side to this work driven achiever – his passion for fitness. Mistry begins his day at the gym, no matter how busy his schedule. His workouts last for an hour and a half every morning! His preferred form of exercise is a cardio vascular routine with equal portions of aerobics, running and weight training. Essentially a team player, Mistry prefers working out in a group, enjoying the fun, competition and camaraderie that comes with it. Although Mistry enjoyed an interest in sports all his life, he got into the fitness groove only after he moved to Bangalore. The need to break away from his sedentary work routine and the desire to be a more participatory father, pushed him to start working out seriously. The desire to feel energised, motivated him to stick with the programme.

Exercise, Mistry says, infuses him with a daily quota of feel good endorphins. It also calms him down, acting as energiser and stress buster. "I'm not the best person to be around unless I've worked out in the morning", is how he puts it. Adding that fitness is not only about working out, but also about adopting a simpler, healthier lifestyle: He follows a healthy diet, avoids heavy meals and prefers to walk to the gym and to work. Clearly, he does not belong to the tribe of fitness freaks who jump into their cars and ride up the elevator, only to sweat it out in the gym! Mistry's message to other techies is clear – an active and healthy lifestyle goes hand in hand with a successful career. He further emphasises that fitness and fun are as essential as work. And exercise, is a crucial ingredient of self development.

He doesn't leave the city without a reservation in a hotel with a well-equipped gym and his fitness gear! Clearly then, as Mistry shows, good health and a demanding job can go together.

## Olympics Sportswear and Equipment

*59/1 NS Palya, Bannerghatta Road, Bangalore 560076*
**Tel** *2668 9830*
**Open** *8am to 4:30pm*

They specialise in track and field gear and table tennis equipment.

## Olympic Toys & Sports Wear

*84 KH Road, Bangalore 560027*
**Tel** *2227 0879, 2224 4303*
**Open** *10:30am to 8pm Closed on Sunday.*

They stock indoor and outdoor sport equipment, medals, cups, trophies, swimwear, golf gear, hiking gear, carom boards and just about anything else in this department. Bulk purchases are also possible.

## Padukone Pro-Sports

*4/1, 4th Main, Between 8th & 9th Cross, Malleswaram, Bangalore 560003*
**Tel** *2346 2014*
**Open** *9:45am to 6:30pm. Closed on Sunday.*

The store stocks all badminton related equipment.

## Rakhra Sports

*6 Commercial Street, Bangalore 560001*
**Tel** *2558 8776*
**Open** *9:30am to 1:30pm and 4pm to 8pm. Closed on Sunday.*

Sports gear, gym gear and sports wear are available here.

## Sports Shoppe

*Ranka Park, Lalbagh Road, Near Richmond Circle, Bangalore 560027*
**Tel** *2222 7223*
**Open** *10am to 7pm. Closed on Sunday.*

Sports equipment and gear for cricket, track and field, shuttle, tennis, football and badminton can be bought here.

## Wildcraft India

*121, 8th Main, III Block, Jayanagar, Bangalore 560011*
**Tel** *2664 7036*
**Open** *10:30am to 8:30pm*

You can choose from a range of camping and rock climbing equipment including sleeping bags, backpacks and jackets.

## SPORTING RESORTS

## Angsana Oasis Spa & Resort

*Doddaballapur Road, Ateebishwanathapuram Village, Rajanakunte, Bangalore 560064*
**Tel** *2559 1080/8892/8896*
**Admission** *Rs 5,000 per couple per night (includes the rental, lunch, dinner and use of facilities.)*
**Facilities** *Tennis, squash, swimming and table tennis.*
**Web** *www.angsana.com*

Part of a southeast Asian chain of speciality spa resorts, their fitness centre meets international standards. Angsana has a variety of luxury rooms to suit different budgets and a multicuisine restaurant with a bar attached.

## Eagleton – The Golf Village

*30th Km, Bangalore-Mysore Highway, Shanamangala Cross, Bidadi Industrial Area, Bangalore 562109*
**Tel** *2676 4403/4974*
**Admission** *Open to all.*
**Facilities** *Swimming, health club, badminton, table tennis, squash, pool.*
**Web** *www.eagletonindia.com*

Recreational packages are available at their sprawling clubhouse along with the standard bar and restaurant facilities.

## Emerald Isle Resort & Club

*NH 4, Old Madras Road, Kolathur Village, Hoskote Taluk, Rural District, Bangalore*
**Tel** *2530 2221/2223*
**Admission** *Entry Rs 50 and Snooker Rs 100 per hour.*

**Facilities** *Swimming, snooker, mini golf, tennis, badminton, table tennis and basketball.*
**Email** *emeraldislebangalore@yahoo.com*

The entry fee covers tennis, swimming, table tennis and badminton facilities. Double rooms and individual villas are available along with a multicuisine restaurant and bar.

## Golden Palms Hotel & Spa

*31-32 Nagarur Village, Off Tumkur Road, Bangalore 562123*
**Tel** *2371 2222*
**Admission** *The 'Day Out' package is priced at Rs 750 per person and includes use of the sports complex, swimming pool and a buffet lunch.*
**Facilities** *Racquetball, squash, swimming, tennis, billiards, snooker, table tennis, fitness centre, massage and spa.*
**Web** *www.goldenpalmsspa.com*

This sprawling five star resort is justly famous for its modern fitness and massage centres and spa. There is a bar, restaurant and rooms for rent.

## Green Acres & Fantasy Golf Resort

*Yelahanka - Devanhalli Road, NH 7 Doddajala Post, Bangalore 562157*
**Tel** *2847 7450/7451*
**Fax** *2847 7450*
**Admission** *Members only*

A 30-minute drive from Bangalore gets you to this rustic retreat on the road to Nandi Hills. The property's 18 acres boasts an 18-hole miniature golf course, a tennis court and billiards tables. Other facilities include a banquet and convention hall, a poolside barbeque, a well stocked bar and a dance floor.

## Patel's Inn Club Resort

*38/2 15th Cross, II Block, Govindaraj Garden, RT Nagar, Bangalore 560032*
**Tel** *2333 7575/0182*
**Admission** *Go-karting: Rs 100 for 8 laps. Swimming Rs 60 per hour. Other facilities open for members only.*

**Facilities** *Swimming, basketball, table tennis, indoor badminton, lawn tennis and go-karting.*
**Web** *www.patelsinn.com*

Only the swimming pool and go-karting are open to non-members. The rest of the facilities are exclusively for members. There is a clubhouse attached.

## Silver Oak Resorts & Hotels

*23rd Km, Bangalore-Doddaballapur Highway, Rajankunte Post, Bangalore 560064*
**Tel** *2846 8070/880*
**Admission** *Swimming Rs 120 for adults per hour and Rs 100 per hour for lawn tennis and table tennis.*
**Facilities** *Swimming, health club, gym, lawn tennis and table tennis.*
**Web** *www.silveroakindia.com*

The weekends promise quite a crowd with their special weekend package of Rs 350 per person which includes lunch and evening tea as well as use of the pool.

## Sunny Holiday Village

*64/1 Gottigere, Bannerghatta Road, Bangalore 560083*
**Tel** *2842 9620/9640/41*
**Admission** *Swimming Rs 50 per hour and Snooker Rs 100 per hour.*
**Facilities** *Swimming pool, snooker and volleyball.*

A choice of standard and deluxe rooms is available. The Sunny Holiday Village has a multicuisine restaurant and cottages for hire.

## The Club

*Mysore Road, Bangalore 560039*
**Tel** *2860 0665*
**Admission** *Entry charge Rs 10, Rs 60 per hour for pool and billiards, range of Rs 30-40 per hour for the other sports.*
**Facilities** *Pool, health club, billiards, squash, badminton, tennis & basketball.*
**Web** *www.theclubbangalore.com*

Membership and 'pay and play' options are available. There is also a bar and restaurant facility.

Golden Palms Hotel & Spa boasts a well equipped gym and fitness centre.

# Karnataka: A Cricketing Powerhouse – Ramachandra Guha

Ramachandra Guha

Rahul Dravid

Anil Kumble

For a cricket-mad boy growing up, as I did, in the nineteen sixties, there was no television and no one-day cricket either. India played, on the average, three or four Test matches a year. Now, there is a surfeit of international cricket, but back then one had to make do most of the time with the Ranji Trophy. This competition then exercised ferocious interest and promoted deeply partisan loyalties.

I grew up, naturally, supporting my home state, Mysore. My first heroes were all cricketers from Mysore – such as the brilliant attacking batsmen B Frank and Budhi Kunderan, and the great spin duo of Erapalli Prasanna and Bhagwat Chandrasekhar. And the cricketers I hated all came from Bombay. For Mysore often played Bombay in the knock-out rounds of the Ranji Trophy. The script was wearingly familiar, and it always ended the same way. We scored two or three hundred in our first innings; in reply, Ajit Wadekar would get that many off his own bat. There were, when I was coming of age, three or four such matches, of which I heard on the radio or read about in the newspapers. But there came a day, in January 1974, when I went in person to see Mysore, now Karnataka, play Bombay – not yet Mumbai – in the then half-built Chinnaswamy Stadium. We batted first, and the great GR Viswanath who was out plumb l.b.w first ball but not given out. My side went on to score in excess of four hundred, with Vishy and Brijesh Patel both making centuries. In reply, Bombay lost Sunil Gavaskar early, but Wadekar came in and looked good from the start. Then he slipped, and was run out. Prasanna and Chandrasekhar went through the rest of the Bombay batting, and Karnataka won on first innings, thus ending the island city's fifteen-year-reign as Ranji champions.

Years later, I met Wadekar, and reminded him about the incident. 'New shoes', he said, enigmatically. I still believe that had he not slipped Bombay would yet be Ranji champions. Nor would Karnataka have won had the (Bengali) umpire given Vishy out first ball. This man took the train back to Howrah, and from the station proceeded straight to the Eden Gardens. There he told the Bengali cricketers: 'I have done what you chaps couldn't do all these years – make sure Bombay does not win the Ranji Trophy'.

Syed Kirmani

Brijesh Patel

In a cricket-filled life I have seen, live, at the ground, Kapil Dev and Viv Richards hit their first Test hundreds; seen Indian spinners win Test matches and Indian batsmen lose them; and watched, breathless, India play Pakistan in a World Cup match in icy cold Manchester, this while the two countries were engaged in battle in an even colder Kargil. But without question, the happiest moment of my career as a cricket spectator was to watch Karnataka beat Bombay for the first time.

You only live twice, said Ian Fleming. I have had two lives as a cricket fan, and luxuriantly happy ones too. First, in the seventies, Karnataka replaced Bombay as the finest cricket side in India. They won the Ranji Trophy three times, and had six members in the Indian Test team: the batsmen Viswanath and Patel, the bowlers Prasanna and Chandrasekhar, the wicket-keeper Syed Kirmani, and the all rounder Roger Binny.

Javagal Srinath          GR Vishwanath

My second life was granted to me in early middle age. For once again, in the nineteen nineties, Karnataka came to dominate the cricketing landscape of India. Leading the challenge were those marvellous bowlers Javagal Srinath and Anil Kumble, and the stylish and massively accomplished batsman, Rahul Dravid. Behind these three stars, or superstars, were the honest craftsmen: The all-rounders Sunil Joshi and Vijay Bhardwaj, and the fast bowlers Venkatesh Prasad, Dodda Ganesh and David Johnson. In this decade Karnataka won the Ranji Trophy three times and contributed as many as eight men to the Indian side.

One reason that Karnataka has emerged as a cricketing powerhouse is the weather. The climate is moderate all year round. In May, Delhi is boiling, or in July, when Bombay is deluged by rain, one can still play cricket in Bangalore.

A second reason is the capacious cosmopolitanism of Karnataka's capital city. The Kannadiga is a reluctant chauvinist; despite his being a minority in Bangalore, there has not yet

been, nor is there ever likely to be, a mass popular movement directed against the 'outsider'. People from other states have been welcomed in the sphere of business, science, and the arts. And on the cricket field too. As I write, the Secretary of the Karnataka State Cricket Association is a Gujarati. The manager of the state cricket side is a Muslim, and its captain originally came from Maharashtra. At other times, Parsis, Tamils, Bengalis, and Hindiwallas have played cricket for the state alongside home-grown Kannadigas.

Whatever language they speak, the cricketers of Karnataka speak it with tact and refinement. They are all gentlemen. Whether it be Vishy or Chandra of an earlier generation, or Srinath and Kumble now, no cricketer from the state has been known to swear on the field, dispute a decision, or intrigue in the dressing-room. In a game driven with discord and corruption their reputations are close to lily-white. Talk of match-fixing and betting, or talk of anything else underhand, and you will find that there is not a whiff of scandal about the name of any cricketer from Karnataka.

The quality of their cricket, and the decency of their character – that is why I supported the Karnataka cricketers when I was eight years old, and that is why I support them now, when I am forty-five. As a final tribute, let me then select this all-time Karnataka eleven, a team that, in my not wholly unbiased opinion, would comfortably outplay the all-time eleven of any other Ranji Trophy side – yes, even Bombay:

**All-time Karnataka eleven (in batting order)**
1. BK Kunderan
2. B Frank
3. GR Viswanath
4. R Dravid
5. BP Patel
6. SMH Kirmani
7. RMH Binny
8. A Kumble
9. EAS Prasanna
10. J Srinath
11. BS Chandrasekhar

*Ramachandra Guha is a historian, biographer, and cricket writer. His works include 'Environmentalism: A Global History' and 'A Corner of a Foreign Field', which won the Daily Telegraph/Cricket Society Award for the best cricket book of 2002. Guha has been described in the New York Times as 'perhaps the best among India's non-fiction writers'.*

The Art of Living Ashram on the outskirts of Bangalore

**Spiritual Matters**

The sacred temples of Udupi and Dharmasthala are proud owners of a troupe of elephants. In Udupi, a trained elephant makes daily rounds through the city accepting bananas and coins from pilgrims. When there are temple celebrations, bedecked elephants are taken out in a procession around town with much fanfare.

Bangalore is home to a large community of Muslims. On festival days, a large congregation gathers at sprawling prayer grounds like the Eidgah Khuddus Saheb to offer special prayers.

# Spiritual Matters

India has always been the **source** of **spirituality**. We bring forth gurus, sants and sages with astonishing regularity! Some live on for centuries, others last a season. Some show the path to enlightenment while others stop at adding an alphabet to your name. Some insist on abstinence while others promise integration into normal life. For today's spiritual refugee, the choices are many.

This outpouring of free thought can be traced to our rich religious tradition. Diverse dogmas like Hinduism, Islam, Buddhism, Christianity, Jainism and others have always flourished and prospered in India's secular atmosphere. It is also the reason why **new age spiritualism** has its roots firmly embedded in the Indian diaspora, always searching for a new meaning to life, a more fulfilling existence. Whether you choose the beaten track or stay off it, you'll find that Bangalore has both a spirit and a soul.

and revered as spiritual masters. They possessed knowledge of the ancient texts and were able to deflect criticism from priests and bearers of organised religion. The **Buddha** is such an example. Regarded as a saint in the 6th century BC, his asceticism and criticism of the caste system led him to found a new religious order – Buddhism. **Sufi saints** similarly struck a new path in medieval India and Basava's teachings find many takers in the modern day.

## Spiritual Masters

In the last 50 years, there has been a resurgence of these masters of the spirit, a **spiritual renaissance** of sorts. Along the way, some have dropped the austere lifestyle but continue with the preaching and meditation. They offer a new look at strict and orthodox religious interpretations. Some insist on not being deified while others unabashedly claim to be **reincarnations** of **God**.

Simultaneously, there has been a globalisation of these saints and they have both followers and centres to propagate their teachings spread around the world. Chief among the early ones are J Krishnamurthi, Maharishi Mahesh Yogi, Osho Rajneesh, Shirdi Sai Baba and Satya Sai Baba.

## Sathya Sai Baba

One of the most popular and powerful spiritual leaders of the 20th century is undoubtedly Sai Baba, estimated to have a following of half a million or more, spread around the world. Dressed in saffron robes

## Ancient Religions

Well before secularism was officially recognised, Karnataka's ancient temple sites showed the way. The 1,500 year old ruins at **Aihole**, known as the cradle of Hindu temple architecture are a case in point. Secure within the limits of the **Muslim** capital of Bijapur, Aihole boasts temples of not just **Hindu** deities but **Jain** and **Buddhist** ones as well. In fact, one temple even bears a Muslim name!

Karnataka also deserves special mention for housing some of the oldest monuments of religious significance worshipped even today. Ancient Hindu temples built centuries ago are still adorned daily with fresh flowers and offerings. **Shravanabelagola**, a three-hour drive from Bangalore and the site of a 1,000 year-old soaring statue of Gomateshwara, son of the first Jain tirthankara, is a fine example of living history. Jainism's most important festival, the Mahamastakabhisheka (head anointing ceremony) has been held here for centuries. During the festival, precious liquids – water, ghee, milk, coconut water, turmeric paste, honey and vermilion powder – are poured over the statue's head from a temporary scaffolding. There are also plenty of Jain structures in **Mudabidri** (also known as **Jain Varanasi**) and Karkala which has a giant monolithic statue, pointing to Jainism's firm footing in the state. The **Jami Masjid** in Bijapur built over 500 years ago attracts a 2,000 strong crowd of worshippers every Friday. And the famous **Bull Temple** in Bangalore city entertains a stream of visitors five centuries after it came into being.

The **British** erected a number of **churches** for their worship. These may be found in garrison towns and cantonments scattered through the state, especially in Bangalore. The western coast from Goa to Kerala through Mangalore also witnessed a great influx of Christian missionaries and preachers, resulting in a large Roman Catholic population and many churches bearing Portuguese influences.

## Holymen

From ancient times, India has been home to **rishis**, **munis**, **sants** and **sages** who led simple, austere lives and were respected

Many a miracle has been attributed to the Infant Jesus in Viveknagar.

with a black curly crop of hair surrounding his head like a halo, he has followers from among heads of state, scientists, bureaucrats and other eminent personalities.

Sai Baba began life as Satyanarayana Raju in an obscure village in **Puttaparti**, in neighbouring Andhra Pradesh. He quickly rose to fame as a saint who could work miracles: Assorted gifts like diamond rings, watches and other trinkets were regularly produced out of thin air, always covered in holy ash and passed on to his visitors and devotees.

Over the years, Sai Baba's profile has changed from **miracleman** to

Spiritual guru Sri Sri Ravishankar is world renowned for his movement, The Art of Living.

**philanthropist**. The once obscure village of Puttaparthi has been completely transformed by a school, university and medical college. His 50-acre **Whitefield ashram** campus houses an enormous meditation hall, the free Sathya Sai Hospital, Sathya Sai University, Baba's private residence and the ashram living quarters.

At the ashram, time is set aside for meditation after the **morning meeting**, an important highlight of Baba's teaching. His ability to work miracles – producing gifts and trinkets for visitors – has won him devotees who insist his magical powers extend to all matters. A few decades ago there was a movement by rationalists and sceptics to denounce and prove him nothing more than a magician, but nothing came of it.

## Art of Living

The most recent address in spirituality is the Art of Living led by its charismatic guru, **Sri Sri Ravishankar**, once a close and trusted lieutenant of the transcendental guru Maharishi Mahesh Yogi. From early childhood he showed an inclination for the scriptures, reciting the Bhagawad Gita effortlessly. He went on to complete a traditional study of the various scriptures and acquire a degree in science.

In 1982, Sri Sri Ravishankar or 'Guruji' as he is fondly called, started teaching the **Sudarshan Kriya**, a powerful **meditation technique** that is known to eliminate stress. It is supposed to oxygenate and rejuvenate cells and remove all toxins from the body. His Art of Living course is pegged as a programme of **breathing**, **meditation** and **Yoga**.

He now travels to 40 countries to spread his message. His Bangalore International Centre has philanthropic schemes on education, child health and vocational training for women.

## Mata Amritanandamayi

The daughter of an impoverished fisherman, 'Amma' 'as the Mata is popularly called, has nothing more than a loving hug to offer her followers. But going by the multitudes that gather around her, that's enough and more. Called the '**hugging saint**', she neither believes in preaching sermons nor performing miracles, instead she offers a warm hug and a big smile to her 'children' as she refers to her devotees.

Her organisation has set up a hospital in Mysore, an engineering college in Bangalore and is involved in housing for the homeless.

**Bangalore** has something to offer people of **all faiths** and **spiritual conviction**s. Temples, churches and mosques are liberally distributed around the city, offering believers a place to worship and reflect. There are some unusual experiences to be had by those wishing to tread the road less travelled. *Stark World – Bangalore & Karnataka* helps you access the minor details of **soul searching**! Enjoy the journey.

## TEMPLES

### Baidhanmai and Cawasji Dadhabhai Dar-E-Meher

*Near Indian Express, Queens Road, Bangalore 560052*
**Open** *9am to 7pm*
**Admission** *Parsis only*

The unique feature of this Parsi temple, built in 1926, is the presence of the sacred fire that represents the infinite light of Ahura Mazda. The rows of bulls sculpted on the temple's pillars make a striking picture. The temple is open to Parsis only.

### Banashankari Temple

*Banashankari, Kanakpura Road, Bangalore 560078*
**Open** *6am to12:30pm and 4:30am to 8:30pm*
**Festivals** *Birthday of Banashankari Devi, Dasara*

Dedicated to Goddess Banashankari this temple lights up thrice a week on Tuesdays, Thursdays and Fridays. Hundreds of lamps made of halved lemons are offered to the goddess by a sea of devotees seeking fulfillment of their prayers.
It was an ardent devotee, Somana Shetty, who brought the idol of Banashankari all the way from Badami district in Bijapur to Bangalore and built the temple in 1915.
There are three major celebrations during the year – the birthday of Banashankari Devi on September 13th, the Dasara celebrations and the temple's anniversary held between December and January. During these times, the entire Banashankari area wears a festive look and a colourful fair is held right outside the temple premises.

### Bull Temple

*Bull Temple Road, Basavanagudi, Bangalore 560004*
**Open** *6am to1pm and 4pm to 9pm*
**Festivals** *Kadalekai Parishe*

Lending its name to one of the oldest residential localities in Bangalore, is 'Basavana Gudi' or Bull Temple, one of the most famous landmarks in the city. Built during the time of Kempegowda I, this large monolithic idol of black stone is usually the first stop for most tourists. The story of how the Bull Temple came into being is an interesting one. A bull, clubbed by a groundnut farmer, turned to stone. The farmer then decided to build a temple for the bull, which kept growing until it reached its present impressive stature. The groundnut farmers decided to make an offering of their first crop to the bull and that was how the legendary groundnut fair or 'kadelekai parishe' held in November every year, was born. The 20-feet stone

pillar outside the temple with carved figurines at its base is worth some study too. The river Vrishabhavati is said to begin at the temple premises.

### Deenabandhu Ashram

*CMH Road, Indiranagar, Bangalore 560038*
**Tel** *2528 2207*
**Open** *6am to 12noon and 4:30pm to 8pm*
**Festivals** *Gokulashtami and other Hindu festivals*

The devasthanam is also called the 'Temple of the Healer' and is dedicated to Deenabandhu Krishna or the Lord of Compassion. The idol of Krishna dancing over the seven-hooded serpent Kalinga is a tourist attraction.
Swami Chinmayananda, founder of the Chinmaya Mission and one of the pioneers of the holistic health

The Shiva Temple on Airport Road. *(See Pg 285)*

movement, built this Devasthanam in a mix of north and south Indian temple architecture. The five gopurams represent the five mahayagnas and the crown of the temple depicts the dasavatharas in their full glory, flanked by the mythical Garuda and Hanuman. The main entrance or 'mahadwara' is in the form of an 'agnijwala' or roaring fire. This fire is said to purify the devotee who surrenders his ego to become worthy of the Deenabandhu's blessings.

### Dharmaraya Temple

*Nagarthpet, Bangalore 560002*
**Open** *6:30am to 9pm*
**Festivals** *Hoovina Karaga*

In April every year, the Dharamaraya temple is the site of a colourful festival 'karaga', a form of shakthi worship celebrating woman power. Dedicated to Dharmaraja or Yudhishtira and Lord Krishna of the epic Mahabharata, the temple hosts the 'hoovina karaga' procession. The 'karaga', a jasmine bedecked pot symbolising Draupadi as a manifestation of Shakthi, is carried in a ceremonial procession through Bangalore in celebration of the Pandavas winning Draupadi's hand in marriage. The festivities at the temple continue for nine days during which the Deepaarathi Utsav, Hasi Karaga, Pongalu Seve, Hoovina-Karaga, Vasanthostava and Gaavu Seve are performed. This grand visual spectacle culminates on the full moon day of Chaitra Poornima in April. On this day, the priest wearing the 'karaga' on his head dances through the streets of City Market followed by hundreds of sword-wielding devotees.

### Dodda Ganesha Temple

*Bull Temple, Basavanagudi, Bangalore 560004*
**Open** *6:30am to 12:30pm and 5pm to 8:30pm*
**Festivals** *Benne Alankara*

Through the years, 'Dodda Ganesha' has endeared himself to the people of Bangalore as the 'Satya Ganapati' or the 'Shakthi Ganapati'. Kempegowda I, the founder of Bangalore, built and renovated many temples dedicated to him like the Dodda Ganesha. Kempegowda is believed to have chanced upon an etching of a Ganesha on a rock near the Bull Temple.
His sculptors soon turned the etching into a massive stone sculpture, 18ft high and 16ft wide.

The Shankara Math is an example of modern temple architecture.

But this was a temple with only a thatched roof until 1971 when the Shankaracharya of Sringeri had a large structure built around the monolithic Ganesha. The decoration of the idol with butter, betel leaves, flowers and turmeric takes place on a special day.

## Gavi Gangadhareshwara Temple

*Gavipuram Guttahalli, Srinagar, Bangalore 560050*
**Open** *7:30am to 12noon and 5pm to 8:30pm*
**Festivals** *Makara Sankranti*

Mentioned in the travelogues of the British as early as 1792, the 'gavi' or cave temple is located in the nook of a small hill called Harirayanagudda. Dedicated to the celestial couple Shiva and Parvati, this temple is also the site where sage Gouthama performed penance and hence the name 'Gouthama Kshetra'.
Kempegowda I, the founder of Bangalore, renovated the temple and the tall, monolithic structures such as the disc-shaped suryapana, the trident, the 'damaru', Shiva's musical instrument and a parasol were all etched during his time.
On the day of Makara Sankranti, the sun's rays fall directly on the presiding deity of Gangadhareshwara Swamy, an event designed by architects over two centuries ago!

## International Society for Krishna Consciousness (Iskcon)

*Hare Krishna Hill, West of Chord Road, Rajajinagar, Bangalore 560010*
*Tel 2332 1956, 2347 1956*
**Open** *7am to 1pm and 4:15pm to 8:30pm*
**Festivals** *Gokulashtami*
**Web** *www.iskconbangalore.org*

The Krishna temple at Bangalore matches the grandeur of other Iskcon temples worldwide. One of the biggest temples in recent times, it was built to commemorate the birth centenary of its founder Sri Prabhupada. The seven-acre temple combines neo-classical architecture with traditional elements of temple architecture, and hi-tech facilities. Ornamental arches and illuminated cascades of water lead to the elaborate rajagopuram with a backdrop of four gopurams connected by a glazed canopy. The lofty ceiling of the temple has paintings of Lord Krishna. Other features of the temple include a vedic museum, an open theatre for concerts, a massive 10,000sqft hall and landscaped gardens.

## Kadu Mallikarjunaswamy Temple

*Sampige Road, Malleswaram, Bangalore 560003*
**Open** *6:30am to 12noon and 6:30am to 9pm*
**Festivals** *Bramharathotsava*

In the midst of bustling Malleswaram lies the Kadu Malleswara temple, a peaceful oasis with large parijatha, bilwa and peepul trees dotting the temple courtyard. Its origins date back to 350 years when it was built around a 'swayambhu' or spontaneously manifested Shivalinga discovered by Venkoji, a stepbrother of Shivaji, the great Maratha warrior.
It earned the prefix of 'kadu' or 'jungle temple' as Bangalore was more wilderness than city when the temple was consecrated in 1669. Renovated in 1889, recent additions to its façade are the idols of Ardhanareeshwara, Shiva-Parvati and Ganesha. An Anjaneya temple, the Basavatheertha Kalyani and the Narasimha temple complete the pantheon of gods present here.

This historically significant temple has been declared a protected monument. The Bramharathotsava is celebrated every year on Shivarathri, and thousands of devotees come to pay obeisance.

## Prasanna Veeranjanaya Swamy Trust

*Mahalaxmi Layout, Bangalore 560086*
**Open** *6am to 8:30pm*
**Festivals** *Hanuman Jayanthi*

The outstanding feature of this sprawling 13-acre temple complex is the 22ft tall idol of Lord Anjaneya, carved out of a monolithic rock. During the sixties, early settlers in the area painted an image of Anjaneya holding up the Sanjeevani hill, on a rock on the hillock. In 1975, the painting was sculpted into the towering idol we see today.
The Benne Alankara ceremony is celebrated every year in August when priests cover the monolithic idol of Anjaneya with 420kgs of butter, bought with the donations of over 18,000 devotees.
The temple has a large meditation hall surrounded by lush greenery, called the 'Dhyanamandira' where those seeking a few quiet hours may retire.

## Someshwara Temple

*Ulsoor, Bangalore 560008*
**Open** *5:30am to 12noon and 5:30pm to 9pm*
**Festivals** *Karthika Poornima, Ugadi*

The pillars of this temple hide a secret – the sound of a strumming guitar emanates when tapped! One of the most ancient temples in Bangalore, it was built by a king of the Chola dynasty. It is the only place where the trinity of Brahma, Vishnu and Shiva are worshipped together. Architecturally, the temple has some beautiful features: An ornate rajagopuram and intricately carved pillars bear the stamp of the Chola period, while the towering 'dwajasthamba' was built later by Kempegowda.
Although the temple is dedicated to Lord Shiva, it is also home to the Goddess Kamakshamma, and the gods Arunachaleshwara, Bhimeshwara, Nanjundeswara and Panchalingeswara. Special pujas are held on Ugadi and Karthik Poornima. When the ceremonial procession of Sri Someswaraya in a floral palanquin moves out, thousands of devotees gather to watch.

## Shankara Math

*Shankara Math, Basavanagudi Road, Bangalore 560004*
**Open** *6am to 12noon and 5:30pm to 9pm*

It is considered one of the more modern examples of Hindu temple architecture. The temple's idols, Adi Shankaracharya and Goddess Sharada date back to the Vijayanagar empire and were brought to Bangalore only in 1935.
The Shankara Math was inaugurated by Lord Harding and the Maharaja of Mysore in 1911.

Iskcon, Bangalore

Gavi Gangadhareshwara temple

## Shiva Temple

*Kemp Fort, Airport Road,*
*Bangalore 560017*
***Open*** *10am to 8pm*
***Festivals*** *Shivarathri*

The well-lit 65ft tall statue of Lord Shiva in Padmasana (the lotus pose), with river Ganga flowing out of his matted locks, catches the eye of visitors flying into Bangalore airport. The Shiva Temple is a recently built open-air temple, located next to the palatial Kemp Fort store. Devotees may also undertake a simulated 'Amarnath Yatra' around a cement cave with 12 replicas of jyotirlingams. This is a popular destination on Shivarathri and the experience is enhanced by the ceaseless chants of 'Om Namah Shivaya' and a wishing pool.

## Sri Digambara Mahavir Jain Sangha

*DK Lane, Chikpet, Bangalore 560053*
*Tel 2226 4549*
***Open*** *9:30am to 5pm*

One of the prominent Jain temples in the city, it is situated in the busy Chikpet area. Housing the idol of Bhagawan Mahavir, the temple was constructed as early as 1878 AD and has undergone many renovations since. The idols of Bhagawan Parshwanatha, Bahubali, Vimalanatha, Ananathanatha and Brahma Yaksha are worshipped here. A dharmashala offering accommodation to pilgrims and a well stocked library with books on Jainism are also set within the temple premises.

## Srinivasa Prasanna Venkataramanaswamy Temple

*Albert Victor Road, City Market ,*
*Bangalore 560002*
***Open*** *6am to 8:30pm*
***Festivals*** *Hanuman Jayanthi*

Chikkadevaraja Wodeyar built this temple 300 years ago and it later came to share a wall with Tipu Sultan's summer palace in City Market. Originally built in a forest, the temple now lies in the heart of the city! A tall, octagonal Garuda pillar marks the beginning of the temple. A mukha mantapa supported by carved pillars with lion brackets and carved images of Vishnu, Brahma and Shiva astride their 'vahanas' or vehicles on the temple walls, are examples of Dravidian architecture at its ornate best. Recent renovations have added a rajagopuram and a vaikuntadwara to the temple.

## Sri Rajarajeshwari Plagueamma Temple

*2ⁿᵈ Main Road, II Block,*
*Thyagarajanagar, Bangalore 560028*
***Open*** *6:30am to 10:30am and*
*5pm to 8:30pm*
***Festivals*** *Navarathri,*
*Varshikothsava (Annual Festival of Rajeshwari)*

Nestled in the narrow lanes of Thyagarajanagar is the Rajarajeshwari temple dedicated to Plagueamma. When the dreaded plague struck a 100 years ago, terrified residents deified two stones and that is the location of this temple. The idol of Rajarajeshwari is a recent addition and was installed only 20 years ago. Tuesdays and Fridays are special days and offerings of 'lemon lamps' are made to the goddess. The Navarathri festivities in October and the Varshikotsava or annual festival of Rarajeshwari in December attract large numbers.

## Sri Guru Singh Sabha

*Opp. Ulsoor Lake Kensington Road,*
*Bangalore 560008*
*Tel 2555 3461*
***Open*** *4am to 9:30pm*
***Festivals*** *Guru Nanak's Birthday*

On the banks of the picturesque Ulsoor Lake stands the large gurudwara, painted in white with pristine marble floors to match. Built in April 1946, it is the main Sikh centre of worship in Bangalore. Special prayers are offered every Sunday, after which free meals are served to all. The gurudwara also offers accommodation to tourists for a day.

## All Saints Church

*Hosur Road-Richmond Road Junction,*
*Bangalore 560025*
***Open*** *6am to 8pm*

This small but picturesque church is set in a large garden with a high stonewall and is often mistaken for an elegant bungalow with its exposed stonework, Gothic architecture, steep bagels and tall pointed windows.

## Holy Trinity Church

*MG Road, Bangalore 560001*
***Open*** *9am to 6:30pm*

The commercial complexes and high rises that surround the Holy Trinity Church today have not dimmed its beauty or diminished its grandness. A dramatic landmark at the east end of MG Road, this renaissance-style church was built in 1851. It is said to be the largest military church in south India with enough rooms to house at least 700 people at a time. It is famous for its wood panelling, stained glass windows and an expansive garden.

## Hudson Memorial Church

*Nrupatunga Road, Narasimharaja*
*Square, Bangalore 560001*
***Open*** *8am to 6:30pm*

With its gabled entrance, rose-tinted windows, large bell and western tower, the Hudson Memorial Church catches the eye of passers-by, especially those waiting for the traffic lights to turn green at the Narasimharaja Square where it is located! A harmonic blend

Devotees at the Guru Singh gurudwara, a striking edifice on the banks of Ulsoor Lake.

Spiritual Matters

of Gothic and classic architecture, this charming edifice built in 1904 is evocative of a medieval church. The traditional church furniture and the intricate designs that embellish the pulpit along with other architectural features transform the Hudson Memorial Church into a heritage building.

## Infant Jesus Shrine

*Viveknagar, Bangalore 560047*
**Tel** *2530 1206*
**Open** *5:45am to 11:15am and 4pm to 7:30pm on Sunday.*
**Admission** *Free*
**Web** *www.infantjesusshrine.org*

Established in 1979 by Rev. Dr. Lourduswamy then Archbishop of Bangalore, the church sees huge crowds on Thursday, the day dedicated to Infant Jesus. The church draws devotees from all religious faiths.

## St. Andrew's Church

*27 Cubbon Road, Bangalore 560001*
**Open** *8:15am to 6:15pm*

A Gothic-style classic Scottish 'kirk' built in 1867, St. Andrew's Church has an imposing visage with a low-slung cast-iron gate, battlement parapets, steeple turrets and a tiled roof. The church draws attention to its dramatically painted exteriors – where circular ventilators framed by rusticated white slabs contrast with the red oxide paint of the entire building.

## St. Francis Xavier's Cathedral

*St. John's Church Road, Frazer Town, Bangalore 560005*
**Open** *6am to 7:30pm*

The cathedral's large dome is its most outstanding feature. Built by Father Chevalier, the first Parish priest of St. Francis Xavier, in 1851, it was redesigned by architect-priest Father Visaac in 1932. Twin Tuscan pillars, a granite cross and tall belfries give the church an imposing facade.

## St. Joseph's Church

*Briand Square, Mysore Road, Bangalore 560002*
**Open:** *6am to 6:30pm*

Here is the only church in Bangalore to possess a crypt as it was built as early as 1852. The underground vault with life size statues of St. Joseph, Jesus and Mary are a major draw.

## St. Luke's Church

*Pampa Mahakavi Road, Chamarajpet, Bangalore 560018*
**Open** *8:30am to 6:30pm*

St. Luke's Church is reminiscent of an English county church and has a large picture of Jesus at the Last Supper. Built in 1935 with brick and stone, it has tall, rectangular windows, circular ventilators, semi-circular arches and a well maintained garden.

St. Mark's Cathedral

# Two Altars, Many Faiths

Miracles happen on Earth! Or so visitors who flock to the **Infant Jesus Church** and **St. Mary's Basilica** fervently believe. Setting aside individual religious beliefs and caste/class considerations, millions of people flock to these shrines to seek forgiveness, request miracles and promise lifelong devotion.

Thursday is a busy day at the church of Infant Jesus when believers of all kinds gather to light a candle to fulfill their prayers. The day's papers carry many insertions with the message 'Thanks for Favours Granted', as man's faith in the power of prayer is noted. On Saturdays, the scene is repeated at the busy St. Mary's Basilica where Mother Mary, also called 'Our Lady of Health', is sought for her legendary healing powers. For nine days in September, all roads leading to the Basilica are filled with a sea of devotees dressed in orange who come to pay grateful homage to the Virgin Mary.

The story of St. Mary's Basilica goes back more than a hundred years, to 1882 when Rev. LE Kleiner remodelled a humble 60-year old chapel into an ornate Gothic-style church in an area once called 'Blackpalli', now known as Shivajinagar. The church came to be credited with a number of incredible 'healings': Legs recommended for amputations healed miraculously with prayer and St. Mary is said to have even quelled a plague epidemic in the 19th century, earning her the title 'Plagueamma'. Equally fantastic legends surround the idol of the Virgin Mary at the Basilica. According to local lore, a mob that stoned the procession of the Virgin Mary was struck down by cholera. Another remarkable story tells of how the wooden idol of Mary remained intact while the whole church burnt down and how the idol could not be physically moved when church authorities wanted to shift it to another location!

The Infant Jesus Church in Viveknagar enjoys equal adoration, expressed in the nine-week novena or intensive prayer undertaken by its many believers. Star-crossed lovers, worried parents and sick people may all be found here.

It all began quite literally, in a rose garden. Three decades ago, parish priest Fr. Paul Kinatukara was drawn to a well tended rose garden in an area known as Somanahalli (now Viveknagar). A series of miracles all occurring on Thursdays, led to it being declared 'Infant Jesus Day'. The miracles included the building of a small church in the rose garden despite innumerable setbacks. Today, belief in Infant Jesus' miraculous powers has only increased and transcends religious and economic boundaries.

The innumerable healings that have taken place and the countless prayers that have been answered have hoisted these two churches into the league of those places of worship where miracles lie within reach.

The elegant facade of Jamia Masjid

mosque is spread across two floors and adjacent to it is a separate prayer area for women.

### Jamia Masjid

*Silver Jubilee Park Road,*
*KR Market, Bangalore 560002*

The Jamia Masjid is a majestic five-storied mosque, its interiors made of pure white marble from Rajasthan. The sprawling mosque can accommodate a staggering 10,000 worshippers at a time. The masjid was built in 1940 and is located in the heart of City Market.

### Jumma Masjid

*Old Poorhouse Road, Shivajinagar,*
*Bangalore 560025*

The 'Jumma Masjid' or 'Friday mosque', is among the oldest mosques in the city. Built by Abdul Quddus in the early 19th century, it is an imposing structure with tall ornamental granite pillars and an elevated prayer hall. Scores of devout Muslims visit the masjid during big festivals. Damaged by cannon fire during the Mysore war, the mosque was renovated in 1836 AD.

### Maaroof Mosque

*Old Poorhouse Road, Shivajinagar,*
*Bangalore 560025*
**Open** *11am to 2pm and 4:30pm*

This beautiful mosque is characterised by gleaming black pillars, ornamental motifs sculpted across its brick-red façade and spanking clean interiors. It also goes by the name 'Lal Masjid'. This mosque was built as early as 1845 with leftover materials from Tipu Sultan's palace in Srirangapatna. Maaroof Mosque is situated in Bangalore's old Cantonment area, on the same street as the older Jumma Masjid.

### St. Mark's Cathedral

*MG Road, Bangalore 560001*
*Tel 2221 3633*
**Open** *5am to 9pm*

The cathedral's majestic dome lends a grand touch to the city's skyline. Modelled on the lines of St. Paul's Cathedral and other 17th century churches of England, this has the look of a Renaissance church. Built for the British army posted in Bangalore in 1808, it was renovated following a fire in 1924. The cathedral is the venue for many choir services and is on the itinerary of international as well as Indian dignitaries.

### St. Mary's Basilica

*Shivajinagar, Opp Russel Market,*
*Bangalore 560001*
*Tel 2286 5434*
**Open** *5am to 7:30pm*
**Festivals** *St. Mary's Feast*

The chaos of busy Shivajinagar hides the quiet calm of this legendary church where the patron saint, Mary, is said to excercise miraculous powers. Built as a small chapel in 1818 by Abby Dubois, St. Mary's Basilica stands as a Gothic example of Bangalore's many ecclesiastical edifices. In 1874, Rev. LF Kleiner transformed the church from a small chapel to the baroque edifice it is today. The interiors of the church reveal stately arches vaulting towards the ceiling, rich Corinthian capitals of moulded bunches of grapes and artistic stained glass windows from Paris. The annual feast of St. Mary starts on the eighth of September and continues over the next eight days. Thousands of believers drawn from different faiths come dressed in the customary orange to pay obeisance.

### St. Patrick's Church

*Brigade Road, Bangalore 560025*
**Open** *5am to 12noon and 4pm to 8pm*

St. Patrick's Church was built for the Irish soldiers posted in the British Cantonment of Bangalore in the year 1844. Originally built by a military chaplain, the church was renovated in 1898. It now boasts fluted pedestals, circular ventilators with floral grazing and dormer windows on a sloping Mangalore-tiled roof. But its most arresting features are the tall twin belfries set in Corinthian plaster that stand out from a distance.

## MOSQUES & DARGAHS

### Charminar Masjid

*Shivajinagar, Bangalore 560051*

Set in bustling Russel Market, this is one of the old mosques in Bangalore. The

The Mahabodhi Society is a prominent Buddhist centre in the city.

### The Art of Living International Ashram

*21st Km, Kanakapura Road, Udayapura, Bangalore 560062*
**Tel** *2843 2274*
**Open** *9am to 9pm*
**Festivals** *Sri Sri Ravishankar's Birthday*
**Web** *www.artofliving.org*

The Art of Living ashram lies off Kanakapura Road, one of the busier roads leading out of the city. This is the home of 'Sudarshan Kriya', Sri Sri Ravishankar's internationally renowned breathing technique and his Art of Living course that has attracted people from all around the world. The campus is spread over 24 acres with lush green hills and even a sparkling lake. Residential courses to enhance mental, physical, emotional and spiritual health are conducted here. Visitors may choose to stay at the small *kutirs* (homes) that dot the landscape of the ashram.

### Bahá'í Bhavan

*Spencer House, 82 Coles Road, Frazer Town, Bangalore 560005*
**Tel** *2536 7707*
**Open** *9:30am to 1:30pm*
**Web** *www.bcca.org*

The Bahá'í Faith is a widespread religion, established in 235 countries throughout the world. At the heart of Bahá'í faith is the conviction that humanity is a single people with a common destiny.
The Bahá'í centre in Bangalore hosts regular 'firesides' or discussions among small groups on the teachings of the Bahá'í Faith along with prayer meetings

### Masjid e Askeri

*Richmond Road, Bangalore 560025*

This elegant mosque is distinguished by its simple whitewashed exterior and classic lines. Situated in the heart of the crowded Richmond Road, Masjid e Askeri was built nearly 90 years ago by Ali Asker, a relative of Sir Mirza, the Dewan of Mysore. It has recently been renovated.

### Masjid e Azam

*Old Poorhouse Road, Shivajinagar, Bangalore 560025*

Another mosque hidden in the quaint Old Poorhouse Road is the Majid e Azam. This small but attractive mosque is replete with colourful floral motifs carved on its walls and cornices.

### Sangeen Jamia Masjid

*Kumbarpet, Bangalore 560002*

The oldest masjid in Bangalore, Sangeen Jamia Masjid in Taramandalpet, was built by the Mughals between 1687 and 1690. The roof of the mosque was damaged by stray cannon balls during the Third Mysore War. It has since been renovated.

### Tawakkal Mastan Dargah

*OTC Road, Cottonpet, Bangalore 560053*

The most well known dargah or shrine in the city is dedicated to the Sufi saint Hazrat Tawakkal Mastan Shah Suharawandi. This dargah typifies the city's secular traditions – the karaga procession from the Dharmaraya temple stops here every year. According to a legend, the saint from Arabia rushed to catch a glimpse of the colourful karaga procession and was knocked down by the crowd. Revived by priests and healed with holy kumkum powder, the saint then wished that the procession stop at the door of his shrine every year. This tradition has carried on.

This striking green and white dargah boasts ornate minarets and is set against a backdrop of tall palm trees. Other aesthetically appealing features of the shrine are its coloured floor tiles and tinted glass lamps strung from the ceiling. Jasmine and rose garlands decorated with tinsel moons are special offerings that are placed on the tomb. This dargah also houses a school and wedding hall.

# Military Guru, Warrior Hermit

Freddy Rene Marie van der Borght was a Belgian engineer when he met Nataraja Guru on a tour of Europe. Nataraja Guru was a follower of Narayan Guru, a 19th century social reformer from Kerala. The meeting set off a chain of events that led to Freddy moving to India, adopting Indian citizenship and finally setting up the Nataraja Gurukul in Somanahalli near Bangalore. But this is where any similarity to other ardent followers of countless gurus ends. Instead, Guru Freddy, as he is popularly known, has broken the mould and runs an institute offering multiple skills in survival training, mountaineering, adventure sports and self-defence. Spread over 15 acres, his courses attract candidates from the army's many regiments, various police academies and the National Cadet Corps.

His ashram is a home for like-minded people and those interested in eco-friendly living, social forestry and wasteland regeneration. An energetic 63-year old, Guru Freddy shies away from any deification and encourages people around him to find their own personal formula for spirituality that must tie in with everyday living.

Guru Freddy started his first ashram in 1969 in Erimala near Kannur in Kerala. Unfortunately, the land was taken over by the Kerala government to start a naval academy. Unfazed, Freddy found a barren stretch of land an hour's drive from Bangalore. Denuded and ravaged by granite felling, he and his disciples worked hard to bring it to its present fertile and lush state, generously sprinkled with fruit trees. The gurukula also has a kitchen garden, dairy, nursery, homoeopathic clinic and Guru Freddy doubles up as resident mechanic for the villagers around him.

*Somanahalli, Bangalore 560062* **Tel** *2843 2496*

# Meditation

Once considered the technique of ancient Indian mystics and holymen, meditation has experienced a revival this century with a less mystical, more mainstream approach. The simple technique of watching your breath come and go, or focussing on a sound, is now universally acknowledged to benefit both the mind and the body in strange but measurable ways.

Science has offered grudging respect. The positive (and everyone agrees there are only positive) effects of meditation are being recommended by physicians the world over for slowing or at least controlling the pain of chronic ailments. It is also credited with restoring the balance of psychological disturbances. Most importantly, there is seen to be a direct correlation between meditation and stress – the more you meditate the less stress you experience. Immune systems are boosted and brains amazingly rewired to reduce stress. In other words, you may no longer feel acute irritation to the point of rage at a telemarketer, if you begin to spend time meditating everyday!

Hinduism is the acknowledged spearhead of meditation, the first descriptions in Vedic texts dating back to 3000 BC! But other ancient religions were not far behind. By the 2nd century AD Christian monks found that meditation brought them closer to God. A 1,000 years later there are records of Jewish mysticism and meditation. And about the same time, Muslim Sufi saints were incorporating meditation into their daily rituals.

## How to Meditate

### Find your retreat

Find a quiet place where you can meditate. If possible, meditate here everyday. The minute you step into your retreat, you will relax on cue. Darken the room and do not answer the phone.

### Travel Inward

Close your eyes to keep out any incoming sensory information. Shut yourself to the world outside and look within.

### Pick a Mantra

Find a word or phrase that means something to you. Or pick a meaningless sound that has a calming effect.

### Chant the Mantra

Repeat the mantra you have chosen soundlessly as you inhale and exhale. Whenever your mind gets distracted by thoughts, the mantra will pull you back gently into the meditation.

### Let go

Don't concentrate. Relax, and let the meditation take you to a quiet inner place.

and study groups. This is also the administrative headquarters and secretariat of all Bahá'í activities in Karnataka.

## Brindavan

*Whitefield, Kadugodi, Bangalore 560067*
*Tel 2845 2622, 2845 2233*
*Open 7:30am to 5:30pm*
*Festivals Sai Baba's Birthday, Guru Poornima*

Sathya Sai Baba divides his time between his ashrams in Bangalore, Puttaparti and Kodaikanal. This is the Bangalore home of Sathya Sai Baba, a popular spiritual guru once known for pulling trinkets out of thin air. His ashram was established in the outlying suburb of Whitefield in 1964 and is called Brindavan. Set in 50 acres of land, the focal point of the ashram is the Trayee Brindavan, Sai Baba's residence and the Sai Ramesh Darshan Hall where he gives darshan. The ashram is surrounded by Baba's philanthropic gestures like the Sri Sathya Sai Institute of Higher Learning and the Sri Sathya Sai Hospital where treatment is free.

## Mahabodhi Society

*14 Kalidasa Road, Gandhinagar, Bangalore 560009*
*Tel 2225 0684*
*Open 10am to1pm and 2pm to 8pm*
*Festivals Buddha Poornima*
*Web www.geocities.com/ mahabodhibangalore.com*

The Mahabodhi Society is replete with a stupa, monastery and a Bodhi tree which arrests the eye. The Bodhi tree spreads across the campus and is said to have grown from a sapling of the tree below which Gautama Buddha received enlightenment. Established in 1956 by Acharya Buddharakkhita Maha Thera to propagate the teachings of Buddha, the society attempts to put his teachings into practice through spiritual, social and educational activities.

The Vishwa Maitri Stupa is an imposing granite structure inscribed with the basic tenets of the Buddha. Other structures include a meditation hall and the Sangharama or Bhikku Training Centre. Weekly discourses on Buddhism and meditation retreats are organised by the Mahabodhi Society. It is a resource centre for the detailed study of Buddhism and facilitates research in Buddhology. The library is home to over 2,000 books including ancient Buddhist texts. Buddha Poornima is celebrated for a week every year in the month of May.

## Ramakrishna Math & Mission

*Bull Temple Road, Basavanagudi, Bangalore 560004*
*Tel 2667 5351*
*Open 9am to 12noon and 4pm to 6:30pm*

Dedicated to the order of the renowned guru, Sri Ramakrishna Paramahansa, the math is an island of peace in the midst of the busy Basavanagudi locality. Swami Ramakrishnananda, often called the other Vivekananda, set up this serene math in 1909. The math attracts disciples and passers-by looking for a few moments of calm. The Ramakrishna Mission campus includes a bookstore, large meditation hall and a well tended garden.

Devotees at a Sai Baba temple

# Health & Wellness

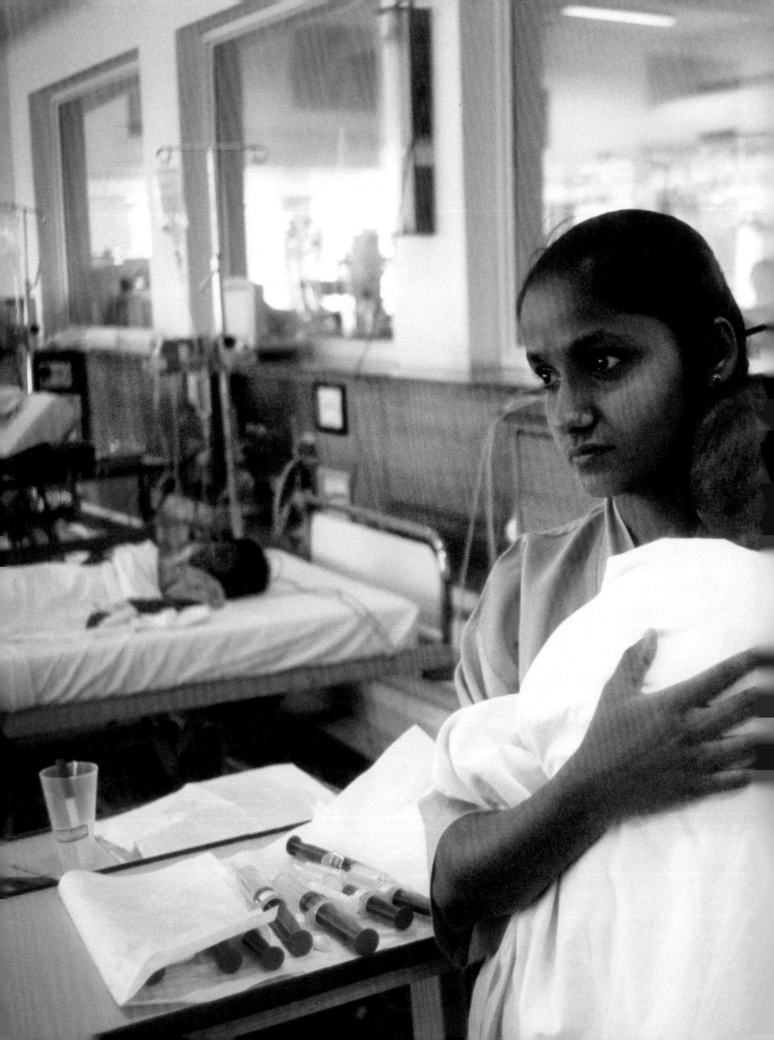

Narayana Hrudayalaya is a leading cardiac care hospital in Bangalore. Set up by renowned cardiac surgeon Dr. Devi Shetty, the hospital is known for quality medical care as well as its philanthropic work. A major proportion of surgeries performed here is on children below 12 years of age. Narayana Hrudayalaya's specialised paediatric cardiology department performs critical heart procedures on children from countries like Pakistan, Bangladesh, Sri Lanka and Africa.

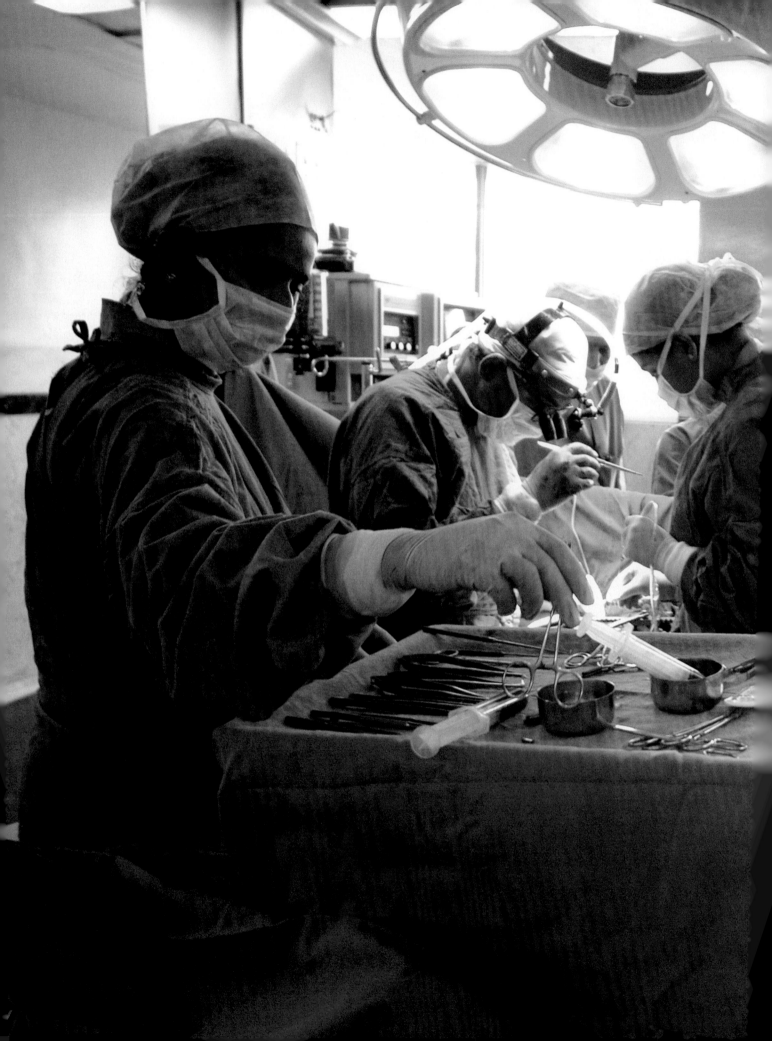

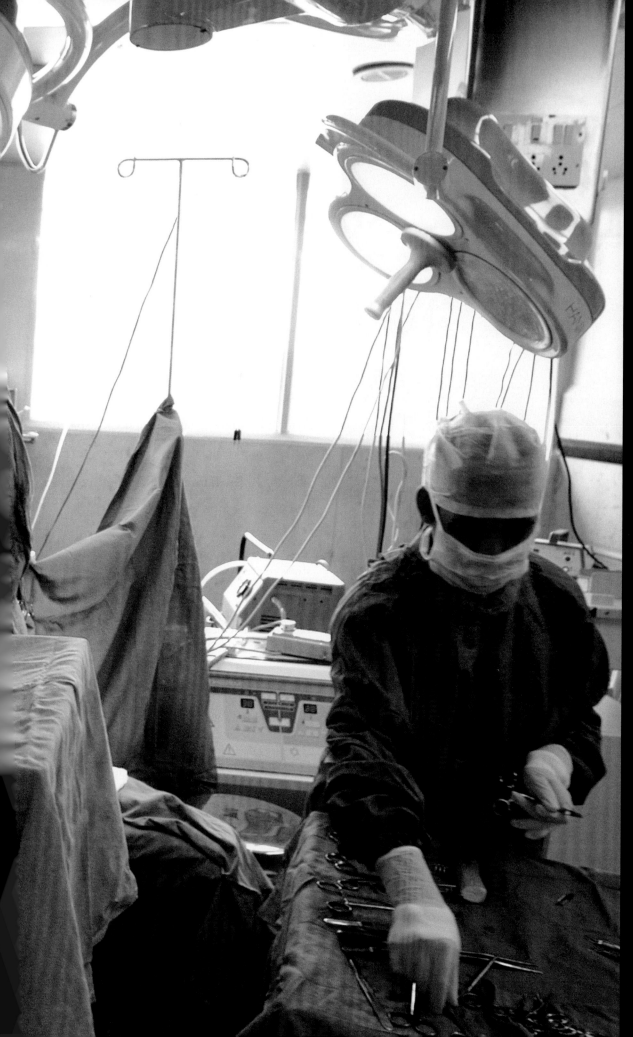

Bangalore is now a premier destination for health tourism. Equipped with the latest technology, state-of-the-art facilities and highly skilled doctors, its hospitals attract medical tourists from around the world. The Manipal Hospital is one of the city's best known multi-speciality hospitals with expertise in areas ranging from cardiology to paediatrics.

# Health & Wellness

From the most modern and hi-tech scientific care to the oldest recorded holistic healing cures, Bangalore has it all. **Speciality hospitals, Ayurvedic therapy centres** and even **spas** have taken firm root in and around the city, earning it the title '**Asian Capital of the Health Services Industry**'. Complex heart surgeries, joint replacements, niggling backaches and urban stress-related diseases find the right cure in the many healing centres located in salubrious Bangalore. Medical services extend to **heli-ambulances** that take off at very short notice, and a swift-response **dial-an-ambulance** telephone number linking all the ambulances available within the city. Blood banks and diagnostic centres sport high quality machines and trained technicians.

For patients arriving from other cities, Bangalore **airport** connects major cities in India and abroad. A wide range of **hotels** and well-established hire services like **taxis**, lend valuable support to the city's healthcare infrastructure.

## Choose Your Medicine

The world over, constraints of modern medicine are drawing more and more people towards ancient proven healing methods, also termed 'traditional' and 'alternative' medicine. In this field, Bangalore is far and away the top destination with a number of health resorts and spas dotting the outskirts of the city. The **Institute of Naturopathy & Yogic Sciences** in Bangalore was one of the first alternative healing centres to open in India. It attracted and continues to attract a number of people seeking long-term natural cures for chronic diseases, at a very modest price. To meet the growing demand for such places, Ayurvedic centres, holistic healing homes and international standard **spas** boasting ancient remedies as well as modern therapies have sprung up.

As a cantonment city, Bangalore inherited a number of good **missionary hospitals** such as the Bowring Hospital, Philomena's Hospital and St. Martha's Hospital. Prime among these is St. John's Medical College & Hospital, a leading medical college as well as hospital in the state. Over the years **corporate** and **speciality hospitals** have sprung up to cater to the growing demand for top quality healthcare.

## Speciality Hospitals

Bangalore's reputation for speciality hospitals is well founded. There are **nine hospitals** specialising in just cardiac care – the **Wockhardt Hospital & Heart Institute, Bhagwan Mahaveer Jain Heart Centre, Narayana Hrudayalaya, Manipal Heart Foundation,** Jayadeva Institute of Cardiology, **Sagar Apollo, BMJ Heart Centre, Mallya Hospital,** and **St. John's Medical College & Hospital.** More significantly, the cost of cardiac treatment in Bangalore is almost 20 to 30 per cent lower than other Indian cities like Delhi and Mumbai.

Most of the hospitals in Bangalore offer state-of-the-art facilities. For example, Manipal Hospital recently launched a **heli-ambulance service** for its comprehensive **trauma consortium** with a field of operation of a 100kms radius around Bangalore. Similarly, Wockhardt has a tie up with Harvard International – the overseas arm of the Harvard Medical Centre – giving it access to the latest research and treatment methods. Wockhardt plans to start another heart hospital as well as a brain and spine hospital and a bone and joint hospital in a three-acre campus on Bannerghatta Road.

Sports related injuries, organ surgery, joint replacement, neuro-surgery and neo natal care are some of the other specialities offered here. Paediatric care is gaining attention as hundreds of children seeking high quality care flock to the city.

A leading psychiatric and neurological treatment centre in Asia – the National Institute of Mental Health and Neuro Sciences (**Nimhans**) is based in Bangalore and attracts people from all over. Other speciality hospitals include the cancer

Cardiac surgeon, Dr. Devi Shetty

(at last count) 75 patients. **West Asia** and even **Africa** are putting little children into the highly specialised care of Bangalore's paediatric doctors.

While cardiac surgery always enjoys the spotlight, equally serious work in **kidney, eye, ear, nose, throat** and

The Institute of Naturopathy & Yogic Sciences is India's leading naturopathy centre.

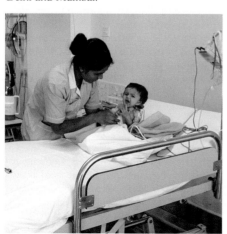

hospital – **Kidwai Memorial Institute of Oncology** – and **Sri Satya Sai Baba** super-speciality hospital where treatment is free.

## Paediatric Centre

The story of **Noor Fatima**, the toddler from Pakistan who came all the way to Bangalore for critical heart surgery, brought attention to the city's vital role in paediatric care. In fact, the number of children from **South Asia** who have chosen Bangalore for heart surgery runs into many hundreds, Pakistan alone has been sending

**brain surgery** is being undertaken across the city. At Manipal Hospital, critical and complicated airway surgeries on newborns and toddlers from outside the city are routinely performed. Another leading hospital, St. John's, has a well known paediatric nephrology unit that is witnessing an influx of referral cases.

There are at least **two hospitals** only for **children** – the Bangalore Children's Hospital and the KR Hospital. Most others have departments headed by highly qualified paediatricians willing to undertake complicated cases.

## Alternative Medicine – Therapy Capital

Bangalore is home to a number of **alternative medicine** centres that offer **Ayurveda**, **Homoeopathy**, **Unani** and other ancient systems of medicine. Long stay as well as consultation options are available. The **AyurvedaGram** offers the full range of Ayurvedic treatment for ailments as varied as back problems and diabetes. Sanjivini Heart Care Foundation combines Sanjivini treatment methods with a holistic approach to diet and exercise to help heart patients. Many homoeopathic doctors tackle serious conditions like cancer and asthma. The most notable being Dr. Isaac Mathai and his centre, **Soukya**, which offers a range of holistic healing therapies.

The alternative healthcare market attracts a number of **overseas patients**. AyurvedaGram for example, has a number of Europeans, especially Germans flying down for treatment lasting up to a month or more. Similarly, Soukya, whose most famous patient was Sarah Ferguson, the Duchess of York, is very popular with people of all nationalities.

## Spas

Bangalore is the city with the **most number of spas** that have emerged as the next level of places to retreat and recharge. The Indian concept of wellness and therapy so far restricted to Ayurveda, has received a shot in the arm with the coming of spas. They are seen as comfortable, protected, soothing retreats with all the virtues of wellness. In short, a perfect **vacation spot** for those who think nothing of taking time off to focus on their health.

## Health Tourism

Apart from meeting local needs, Bangalore's hospitals draw patients from **around the world**. A large number of people from neighbouring countries like Pakistan, Bangladesh, Sri Lanka, Africa and West Asia, make their way to Bangalore to get world-class treatment at a **fraction of the price**.

Recently, the government of Karnataka began talks with the United Kingdom's National Health Service (NHS) to treat British patients in need of urgent intervention, since waiting lists in UK hospitals are very long. A person slotted for heart surgery under the NHS, usually has to wait six months. Considering that heart surgery in Bangalore costs one-fifth what it would in the UK, it also makes economic sense to fly here for treatment.

The state government is trying to boost Bangalore's reputation as a health destination. It is setting up a **Bangalore International Health City Corporation** that will formulate and execute plans to expand the city's healthcare infrastructure.

The Karnataka State Tourism Department plans to offer health packages to tourists which will include both regular as well as alternative treatments. Currently, the biggest influx of health tourists is from West Asia, Africa, Bangladesh and neighbouring Asian countries and most recently, with the easing of visa norms, Pakistan.

Today, Bangalore accounts for almost **five per cent** of India's healthcare services market which McKinsey estimates at Rs 86,000 crore per annum. It is well connected to all major aiports and cities around the world and flying in and out is not a problem. The healthcare services industry is expected to touch a staggering Rs 2,00,000 crore by the year 2012, according to a CII-McKinsey report, and Bangalore is poised to grab at least 10 per cent of it. Clearly then, its reputation for world-class treatment is set to match its reputation in world-class IT companies!

*Stark World – Bangalore & Karnataka* takes a fresh look at **Health & Wellness**. Conventional hospitals and diagnostic centres are listed along with spas, acknowledged cures for modern day maladies. A brief history of Ayurveda and alternative therapies fills in the gaps.

Courtesy: AyurvedaGram

AyurvedaGram has been created by supplanting heritage homes from Kerala.

## HOSPITALS

### Bangalore Hospital

*202 RV Road, Bangalore 560004*
**Tel** *2656 2753, 5118 7600*
**Web** *www.bangalorehospital.com*

The Bangalore Hospital provides expert consultation, diagnosis, treatment and surgical facilities. They also specialise in cancer care, cardiac care, vision care, gastroenterology, dialysis and renal transplants. The Bangalore Hospital has a 24-hour lab and X-Ray centre, trauma and emergencies services and an ICU.

### Bhagwan Mahaveer Jain Hospital

*Miller Road, Vasantha Nagar, Bangalore 560052*
**Tel** *2220 7640, 5110 0550*
**Email** *bmjainhospital@vsnl.net*

Located in the heart of the city, Bhagwan Mahaveer Jain Hospital is a 200-bed multi modality, speciality hospital. With 30 speciality areas, the hospital is equipped with a state-of-the-art ICU, 24-hour casualty and a blood bank. The hospital provides treatment at subsidised costs to economically backward sections and offers free plastic surgery camps and polio limb correction camps.

### Hosmat (Hospital for Orthopaedics, Sports-Medicine, Arthritis, Neuro & Accident-Trauma)

*45 Magrath Road, Off Richmond Road, Bangalore 560025*
**Tel** *2559 3796*
**Web** *www.hosmatnet.com*

This is the first hospital in India specialising in orthopaedics, sports medicine, arthritis, accident related trauma and neurosciences. Hosmat has earned its reputation with high quality care in the field of orthopaedics and comprehensive neurosurgical care. It has a well known Joint Replacement and MRI Centre. It is currently undergoing an expansion to accommodate 250 beds.

### Kidwai Memorial Institute of Oncology

*Dr. MH Marigowda Road, Bangalore 560029*
**Tel** *2656 0708*
**Web** *www.kar.nic.in/kidwai*

Established in 1973, Kidwai has been accorded the status of a Regional Cancer Centre. The institute offers all modalities of cancer treatment including cancer surgery, chemotherapy, blood transfusion and palliative care. The institute has a wide range of sophisticated diagnostic and research equipment, as well as a new operation theatre consisting of five modern fully equipped operation rooms with a critical care unit. Its 430 beds include accommodation for ambulatory cancer patients along with their attendants. Shantidhama, a rehabilitation and

# Ayurveda Brief

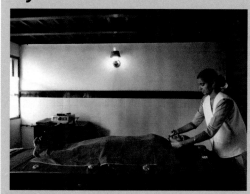

The word Ayurveda is derived from two words: Ayush meaning life and Veda meaning knowledge or science. Life, in Ayurvedic terms, is a union of body, senses, mind and soul. Man is considered a combination of five primary elements – space, air, fire, water, earth and three doshas or humors. Vata, a combination of air and ether, governs the principle of movement and is the force directing circulation, respiration and elimination. Fire and water are the elements that combine to form the Pitta dosha that transforms or metabolises the assimilation of nutrients. Finally, water and earth elements combine to form the Kapha dosha, responsible for growth and protection.

The system of Ayurveda holds that humans are made up of unique proportions of Vata, Pitta and Kapha. Ill health is the absence of a balanced state, caused by dietary indiscrimination, bad habits, insufficient exercise and general incompatibility of body and mind. An Ayurvedic doctor's diagnosis is always done on the person as a whole – taking into consideration physiological characteristics, mental disposition, daily routine, dietary habits and general environmental situation. Ayurveda offers lifestyle and nutritional guidelines to correct any imbalances and herbal supplements to aid the healing process. It also offers specific treatments, some of which are outlined below, that may be tried once or repeated over time to overcome the problem.

## Therapies for Today's Lifestyle
### Abhyanga
This treatment is particularly useful in weight reduction and is a rejuvenative therapy. Refined and developed by generations of practitioners, it involves a synchronised massage by two trained therapists. Carefully synchronised strokes are used with variations in pressure, sequence and oils to treat different ailments.

### Sirodhara
Herbal oil, medicated milk or buttermilk-based concoctions are poured on the forehead and head in a steady stream. Sirodhara is an oil based therapy recommended for paralysis, neurological problems, memory improvement, stress relief and rejuvenation. Thakradhara is yoghurt based and known to have a calming influence. Dhayamladhara uses medicated rice and is generally prescribed for arthritis, rheumatism and gout. It is also used to alleviate psychiatric and psychosomatic diseases, insomnia and general debility.

### Nethratharpanam
Specially prepared herbal oils and herbs are used to revitalise the eyes. This therapy is especially effective in soothing the nerves around the eyes, relieving eye strain and improving eyesight. It is particularly recommended for those who work long hours in front of a computer.

### Greevavasthi
In this therapy, medicated oil is poured within a ring made from a natural paste on the back of the neck. Greevasthi is

effective in combating cervical spondylosis and neck pain that is a result of a sedentary lifestyle.

## Traditional Ayurvedic Therapies
### Pancha Karma
Pancha Karma therapy is an overall wellness therapy and is the cornerstone of the Ayurvedic management of disease. It aims to correct the essential balance of mind, body, and emotions so as to increase the efficiency of medicines, foods and rasayanas (tonics). It also enhances natural immunity and restricts toxins from accumulating in the mind and body. There are several eliminative processes in Pancha Karma: Vamana promotes elimination from the stomach and thoracic cavity; Virechana promotes elimination from the small intestine, Vasti works on the colon to eliminate toxins and strengthens tissues and finally Nasya cleanse toxins from the head and sinuses.

### Pizhichil
This is a rejuvenation therapy to prevent ageing, scales and wrinkles, to cure rheumatism, arthritis and spastic muscular disorders. Medicated warm oil is poured on the body for an everyday or for a period of three, five, seven or 14 days.

### Sirovasthi
In this procedure medicated oil is poured into a cap-like fitting around the head and is retained for about an hour. This is an effective treatment for facial palsy and diseases of the head and neck.

### Njavarakkizhi
This is the process to correct neurological disorders, rheumatism, arthritis, under nourishment of limbs and sports injuries. A hot medicinal pudding tied up in cloth pouches is applied on the whole body or affected parts. This treatment is restorative and nourishing.

### Herbal Steam Bath
This exudation process uses medicated steam to reduce high blood pressure, stiffness, pain and swelling. During this steam bath, herbal oils are absorbed, and impurities are released through sweat glands, kidneys and the liver.

### Marma Kizhi
This is a massage with cloth bags filled with herbal powder and used in the treatment of backache, joint pain, sprains, nerve problems and rheumatic ailments. It works on the 107 sensitive points called marmas in Ayurveda. It is recommended for patients with musculo-skeletal ailments resulting from trauma and accidents.

### Sveda Karma
Medicated steam baths remove impurities from the body, improve the tone and complexion of the skin, reduce weight and help ease rheumatic pain.

### Shastika Pinda Sveda
Hot medicated, cooked rice in cloth pouches applied rhythmically, a form of massage for neurological, rheumatic and stress related problems.

### Elakizhi
This herbal treatment is used to alleviate stiffness and body pain, arthritis and paralysis. Fried herbal leaves are dipped in medicated warm oil and then massaged all over the body.

### Kadeevasthi
In this treatment, highly medicated oil is poured within a ring made from a natural paste on the back. This procedure is effective in treating spondylosis, lower backache and sciatica. It also energises the body and has a rejuvenative effect.

The Manipal Hospital is a reputed super-speciality hospital.

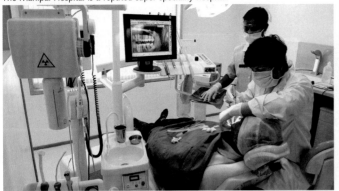

continuing care centre, offers all diagnostic and treatment services. Psychological and spiritual counselling and occupational therapy services are also provided. In collaboration with NGOs and the Rotary Club, Kidwai conducts cancer awareness and detection camps in rural and urban areas.

## Lakeside Hospital

*33/4 Meanee Avenue, Ulsoor,*
*Bangalore 560042*
*Tel 2556 6738, 2536 0823/6723*
*Email dr_paramesh1@yahoo.com*

This is a teaching institute with specialities in gastroenterology, endoscopic surgery, plastic surgery, ENT, non-invasive cardiology, dentistry, obstetrics and gynaecology. The hospital has 150 beds and four fully equipped operation theatres.

## Mallige Medical Centre

*31/32 Crescent Road, Bangalore 560001*
*Tel 2226 1135*
*Web www.mallige.com*

Established in 1978, this multi-speciality medical centre with 75 beds offers prompt attention, preventive advice, screening protocols and prophylactic care. Mallige is also part of the Comprehensive Trauma Consortium that provides emergency and critical care for accident victims. There is a wide choice of rooms available here, from the general ward to special suites.

## Mallya Hospital

*2 Vittal Mallya Road, Bangalore 560001*
*Tel 2227 7979/7997*
*Web www.mallyahospital.net*

Mallya Hospital is a multi-speciality medical centre with a team of specialists of repute. Round-the-clock health care is available with 24-hour emergency services, laboratories, a radiology department, CT Scan, ambulances and a pharmacy.

## Manipal Hospital

*98 Rustom Bagh, Airport Road,*
*Bangalore 560017*
*Tel 2526 8901/6441/4408*
*Web www.manipalhospitals.org*

The Manipal Hospital is a multi-speciality health destination managed by Asia's largest hospital management group. It is a premier destination in Bangalore for quality healthcare. A tertiary care hospital, certified with ISO9001, with state-of-the-art technology and 650-bed strength, Manipal Hospital renders some of the most sophisticated and specialised medical services at affordable costs in 40 different specialities. The hospital is spanking clean with a team of dedicated doctors and nurses.

Manipal Hospital's Heart Foundation is one of Bangalore's best. It comprises four operation theatres where upto 15 heart surgeries per day can be performed. The Manipal Institute for Neurological Disorders is arguably the largest and most advanced unit of its kind in India. The Manipal Institute for Nephrology and Urology has performed over 300 kidney transplants and has a state-of-the-art dialysis centre. The hospital specialises in plastic surgery, paediatric surgery and paediatric cardiology as well. The Department of Oncology offers comprehensive cancer care with the latest surgical, medical and radiation facilities. The hospital has a reputed dental medicine centre equipped with 16 'ultra-modern' suites and facilities for basic dental treatment as well as aesthetic and cosmetic dentistry. The key orthopaedic programmes run here include joint replacement, spine surgeries and total hip replacement procedures. Manipal Hospital is equipped with all the requisite diagnostic facilities from Ultrasound and Doppler to CT and MRI centres. The hospital runs an all-hour, automated laboratory with the largest blood bank in the state. Comprehensive emergency services are rendered round-the-clock and under one roof.

## MS Ramaiah Hospital

*MSR Nagar, MSRIT Post,*
*New BEL Road, Bangalore 560054*
*Tel 2360 6545/8888*
*Email msrhospital@vsnl.com*

This is a general hospital, well established in the areas of general surgery, cardiology, neurology, psychiatry, dermatology and gynaecology. It offers a range of clinical services, modern diagnostic facilities and all other amenities.

## Narayana Hrudayalaya

*258 /A Bommasandra Industrial Area,*
*Anekal, Bangalore 560099.*
*Tel 783 5000/5018*
*Web www.hrudayalaya.com*

Narayana Hrudayalaya is a 280-bed cardiac hospital with 10 operating rooms and the facility to perform 25 heart operations a day. Cardiology and cardiac surgery for all types of heart diseases is the hospital's main speciality. Other specialties include dialysis, heart valve bank, telemedicine and endoscopy. Founded by the renowned cardiac surgeon Dr. Devi Shetty, the hospital has been in the news for its philanthropic work and for treating children from as far as Bangladesh and Pakistan. Spread over 12 acres, it offers special concession for the economically backward. Air-conditioned suites and deluxe rooms are also available.

## Nimhans
## (National Institute for Mental Health & Neuro Sciences)

*Hosur Main Road, Bangalore 560029*
*Tel 2699 5000*
*Web www.nimhans.kar.nic.in*

Nimhans is the most reputed multi disciplinary institute and hospital in the area of mental health and neurosciences in India. Clinical services offered here include psychiatry, neurology, casualty and emergency services. The hospital has a rehabilitation centre, Community Health Programme and a National Mental Health Programme. It is also a premier teaching and research institute with state-of-the-art technology for diagnosis and surgical care. It is also a custodian of the nation's first brain bank.

## Sagar Apollo Hospital

*44/54 Tilaknagar Main Road,*
*Bangalore 560041*
*Tel 2653 6700*
*Web www.sagarapollo.com*

Sagar Apollo provides comprehensive healthcare with nephrology and cardiology receiving special focus along with neurology and orthopaedics. The hospital has seven operation theatres equipped with sophisticated technology and a 250-bed multi-speciality tertiary care centre.

## St. John's Medical College & Hospital

*Sarjapur Road, Koramangala,*
*Bangalore 560034*
*Tel 2206 5000*
*Web www.stjohns.org.in*

One of the top five medical colleges in the country, St. John's was set up by Catholic Bishops in 1963 and functions as a leading general hospital with specialities ranging from cardiology and ophthalmology to plastic surgery. There are a total of 779 beds with private, semi-private, suite rooms and general wards.

## St. Martha's Hospital

*Nrupathunga Road, Bangalore 560001*
*Tel 2227 5081*
*Email stmarthas@vsnl.net*

Set up in 1886 by a Catholic missionary, the hospital now has 600 beds and five operating theatres. The hospital offers speciality treatment in 16 different areas from general surgery to cardiology along with 24-hour laboratories, X-ray, ECG facilities and a pharmacy. Centres for speech and hearing, physiotherapy and prosthetics have also been introduced. St. Martha's is known for excellent nursing services and specialised neonatal care.

## Wockhardt Hospital & Heart Institute

*14 Cunningham Road, Bangalore 560052*
*Tel 2226 8367, 5113 1333*
*Web www.whhi.com*

Wockhardt specialises in the treatment of heart diseases. Its centre for cardiology ranks among the best for diagnostic and therapeutic treatments in interventional cardiology. More than 500 angioplasties and 2,500 cardiac interventions including paediatric catheterisations are carried out every year. Other services include Congenital Surgery, Valve Surgery and Coronary Artery Surgery. Wockhardt also works in the area of preventive medicine with the government and private sectors to reduce the occurrence of heart problems.

# Noor – Bangalore's Ambassador

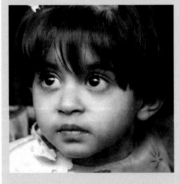

She came, she saw, she conquered...The story of little Noor Fatima who travelled thousands of miles from Lahore, Pakistan to Bangalore in search of her heart surgeon, has touched millions of people in both countries. Only two years old, she won diplomatic laurels for the Indian side, achieving in a matter of days what Indian and Pakistani diplomats could not achieve in years!

Noor's heart was in the care of cardiac specialists at the Narayana Hrudayalaya. A spanking new hospital on the outskirts of Bangalore, it has already received accolades for its comprehensive range of cardiac care and surgery and the rush of international patients.

Bangalore's response to Noor was overwhelming – a steady stream of children from a number of schools in the city visited her and an anonymous benefactor offered to foot her bill. Daily updates on her treatment and recovery were carried on the front pages of local papers!

# MANIPAL
# HOSPITAL-ITY

STARK.Blr/mh/0104

There are two simple reasons why people from across the world choose Manipal Hospital.

One: Being a part of Asia's Largest Hospital Management Group, the medical systems and practices (by internationally trained and certified doctors and nurses) are the latest and the most comprehensive for true quality care.

Two: The Hospital will also help you with visa and travel arrangements. And, of course, language translators should one need one. It's just another way of showing how far we'll go to ensure the most friendly care for our patients.

The fact that one does not pay international prices for international quality services may, perhaps, cross the mind. Okay, make that three reasons to opt for Manipal Hospital.

**Manipal**

INSPIRED BY LIFE

98, Airport Road, Bangalore - 560 017,
Karnataka, India.
Tel: 91-80-25268901, 25266441.
Fax: 91-80-25266757.
Email: info@manipalhospital.org
Website: www.manipalhospital.org

■ Manipal Heart Foundation ■ Manipal Institute of Neurological Disorders ■ Manipal Institute of Diabetes, Endocrinology & Metabolism ■ Manipal Comprehensive Cancer Centre ■ Manipal Hospital Diagnostics Services ■ Manipal Institute of Nephrology & Urology

# Integrative Medicine Fact File

## Siddha

Siddha is recognised as one of the oldest systems of medicine with roots in the southern part of India and followers in Sri Lanka, Malaysia and Singapore. The word Siddha comes from Siddhi, which in Sanskrit means achievement or perfection. Its principles are similar to that of Ayurveda in which the body is a replica of the Universe and so are food and drugs, irrespective of their origin. This system aims at **healthy living** and the **elimination of disease**. It is also called the Agasthyar system after its famous exponent, Sage Agasthya.

Siddha is based on body humors and other characteristics similar to those in Ayurveda. According to the Siddha system, the universe consists of **five elements** or *Bhootas*: earth, water, fire, air and ether. A suitable mix proportion of these five produces a healthy person. Siddha medicine has an interesting view on drugs – they are categorised as friends or enemies!

## Unani

Unani is a system of healing that originated in Greece and ancient healer Hippocrates gave it the status of a science. It has its origins in the Mediterranean world and was developed further in West Asia, from where it came to India around the 10th century AD.

According to the basic principles of Unani, a perfect balance of elements, humours and temperament are vital for a healthy body. The cardinal humours are blood, mucus, yellow bile and black bile. A mutual **equilibrium of humours** creates health. A body's equilibrium may be affected by climate, age, profession and customs that cause a dominance of one of the humours. **Diet** plays an important role in Unani medicine. The stress is more on fruits and vegetables and non-vegetarian food is taboo.

Simple diseases are treated only with dietary restrictions, but complex disorders are treated with drugs of plant origin and a few of animal and mineral origin as well.

The strengths of Unani lie in the treatment of sinus, pulmonary disorders, bronchial asthma, gastro-intestinal disorders, ulcers, diabetes, joint disorders, arthritis and skin problems.

## Homoeopathy

Dissatisfied with the common medical practices of the time, Dr Samuel Hahnemann sought to create a system of **gentle healing**. He found a therapy using plants, minerals and animal substances and combined them into energetic compounds that

he used to stimulate and encourage the body's **natural healing forces**.

The word 'Homoeopathy' is derived from two Greek words, Homoeo meaning similar, and pathos, meaning suffering. It is based on the natural law of 'like is cured by like'. It treats diseases with remedies prescribed in minute doses that produce symptoms similar to the disease when taken by a healthy person.

Homoeopathy says symptoms are the body's natural reaction to fighting illness, and seeks to simulate the symptoms rather than suppress them. Homoeopathy is concerned with the **treatment of the whole person** as an individual, rather than the disease alone. Homoeopathy came to India in 1839 with Dr. John Martin Honiberger.

## Tibetan Medicine

Two thousand years ago the indigenous people of Tibet had a traditional medical system closely connected to their native spiritual beliefs. It is based on an ancient form of medicine known as 'Gso-wa Rig-Pa' or the knowledge of healing, believed to integrate the teachings of the Buddha.

Tibetan medicine believes that illness is caused by attachment, anger and ignorance, known as the **'three interior poisons'** and the imbalance of wind, bile and phlegm. Tibetan medicine is a **holistic tradition** and a lasting cure can only take place within the whole psychosocial environment. Tibetan medicine is increasingly gaining recognition as an effective system of medicine for paralysis, gallstones, mental illness and arthritis.

## Naturopathy

The nature cure movement that originated in Germany, gained momentum in India with Mahatma Gandhi, a prominent believer. Naturopathy believes that nature is the greatest healer and the body has the capacity to prevent disease and perpetuate good health. The practice of nature cure is based on the three principles: the accumulation of morbid matter, abnormal composition of blood and lymph and lowered vitality. Naturopathy does not believe that the cause of disease is bacteria. It takes into account the totality of factors responsible for diseases such as eating, sleeping and general habits. Nature cure advocates the practice of drugless therapies like electrotherapy, acupressure, acupuncture, physiotherapy, massage and magnetotherapy.

## Aromatherapy

Aromatherapy has been around for over 6,000 years. Ancient civilisations used fragrance to purify the air, like *agarbattis* or incense sticks, in use even today. The modern era of aromatherapy dawned in 1930 when the French chemist Rene Maurice Gattefosse coined the term 'Aromatherapy' for the use of essential oils that possess **psychotherapeutic benefits.** For instance, lavender oil can heal burnt skin.

Our sense of smell works on a subconscious level, affecting and regulating our moods, emotions, memory and learning. Some oils are relaxing, some soothing and some are pain relieving. Aromatherapy is particularly effective for stress, depression, anxiety, psychosomatic problems.

## Gem Therapy

Gem therapists believe that crystals, gems, minerals are solidified reflections of properties already existing within our bodies. Gems and precious metals are used to balance **planetary influences** and have the capacity to dispel negative energies and this may be experienced by wearing them or having them close to the body.

Gems to be used for healing need to be purified by immersion in salt water. They are most effective when they weigh more than two carats and should preferably be

set in gold. Topaz is said to help overcome fear, while yellow Sapphire enhances energy and vitality.

## Pranic Healing

Pranic Healing uses the catalyst of Prana to accelerate healing. Prana is a vital life force and Pranic healing is a non-touch, non-invasive process. This system of medicine believes that all living beings have two selves, the physical self and the energy that forms the exterior cover. Healers cure diseases by clearing or **cleansing the energy system**, comprised of 11 major chakras. The healers use their hands to detect malfunctioning in the body and clean the diseased energy with their hands. This system may be used to alleviate a large number of ailments from brain tumors and skin diseases to mental diseases like schizophrenia and depression.

## Reiki

Allowing energy to flow through people harmoniously and diverting the flow of excessive energy is the essence of Reiki. 'Re' means **universal** and 'ki' means **vital life force**. According to Reiki, disease is caused by an energy imbalance, depletion or congestion. Reiki is similar to Pranic healing, but in this system, the healer is the channel of energy and he/she draws the Prana energy through his or her own crown chakra and allows the energy to flow through the hands or the chakras.

## Chakra Therapy

Chakras are centres of **psychic energy** located at points on the spinal chord. They are also associated with the five elements of earth, water, wind, fire and ether. Each *chakra* corresponds to a specific mantra or sound and a specific geometric pattern or yantra. Through **meditation,** mastery can be gained over our bodies and each corresponding element.

## Herbalism

Herbalism uses plants to restore health. This system of medicine believes in the curative qualities of plants, flowers and **herbs** that stimulate the healing system.

## Allopathy

Considered a modern system of medicine, allopathy was developed in the West. Here diseases are treated with **drugs** that act against existing symptoms.

## Meditation

Meditation is a **scientifically proven technique** to relieve stress. It is also believed to strengthen a person's mental make up and improve memory as well as concentration if practiced on as regular basis.

# 30 minutes*
## to the Spa of your dreams

The Spa at the Golden Palms is an oasis for rejuvenation, restoring harmony in all 3 dimensions of our existence; physical, emotional & spiritual.

**contemporary European and
exotic East Asian treatments,
traditional ayurvedic therapies,
hydrotherapy . exfoliation . body wraps
skin care . beauty salon . reflexology
yoga . meditation**

→  State-of-the-art Fitness Centre & Health Club
→  130 metre free-shaped Swimming Pool
→  Squash, Tennis, Billiards, Ping Pong &
   Virtual Games for Kids
→  Spa Rooms

**Packages ranging from Spa Day Escapes and short breaks to time-bound therapeutic programs.**

To Know more, please call **080 2371 0001**
or mail us at **spa@goldenpalmsspa.com**
w w w . g o l d e n p a l m s s p a . c o m

## GOLDEN PALMS
### HOTEL & SPA

Golden Palms Avenue, Off Tumkur Road, Bangalore 562 123
Tel: +91 80 23712222  Fax: +91 80 23710022

✳  from Bangalore city centre

# Holistic Health & Medicine – Dr. Issac Mathai

Holism is more than a medical method, it is a philosophy of life that relates to the whole rather than to the parts. Currently both medical practitioners and the public are moving towards a holistic view of health and illness which believes that any drastic intervention or action in one system affects other systems.

The mind-body-spirit connection is very important for good health. In holistic health we recognise that our bodies have remarkable power to heal themselves and fight diseases. Medicine's role is to help the healing process rather than control the entire system. Mark Twain once quipped that "nature heals and the doctor sends the bill". Throughout history, cultures world wide have provided us with incontrovertible evidence that under certain circumstances the body heals itself and the mind has great influence over the body's health. Western trained physicians are sceptical about the role of the mind in medicine, but this scepticism is gradually eroding in the face of overwhelming evidence. Scientists have already discovered definite links between the mind and the central and autonomic nervous system, the endocrine system and the immune system. Psycho-neuro immunology and the other mind-body-sciences are rediscovering the connections between feelings, thoughts, personality and health.

Many people are also making a connection between spirit and healing. Over the last century we have largely turned healing over to science. With its emphasis on physical causes and physical cures of disease, we have compartmentalised our culture, assigning spirit and religion to one side and health and healing to another. Hippocrates, the father of medicine urged physicians to study not the diseases but the whole patient including the environment, emotions and spiritual life. "Observe the nature of each country" he wrote. "The diet customs, the age of the patient, speech, manners, fashion, even his silence, his thoughts, sleep, dreams…one has to study all these signs and to analyse what they portend."

Physicians in the east, mainly India and China always see health as a balance of natural forces within the body. They also believe in the life force, called 'prana' by the Indians and 'chi' by the Chinese. Without giving proper importance for all these very essential principles of health and healing, the western attempt is to focus only on more high-tech investigations rather than knowing the patient. Modern development in medicine is very advanced and essential but it also needs to be humanistic and holistic.

Dr. Issac Mathai

Twenty first century medicine will become really scientific only when physicians and their patients have learnt to manage the forces of the body, mind and spirit that operate in accordance with the healing power of nature.

The term 'holistic', derived from ancient Greek 'holos' meaning whole, was revived in the early 1970s. The idea of holism and the word itself were first introduced by the south African statesmen and biologist, Jan Christian Smuts. Holism was a way of viewing and describing living things as entities greater than and different from the sum of their parts.

It is also an antidote to a scientific approach that attempts to understand all phenomena including human beings, by reducing them to their most basic biological processes. There are a great many people who feel that the focus of modern Western medicine is too impersonal and narrow, that many doctors tend to view their patients as biological machines rather than human beings.

Holistic medicine is an alternative to this type of medical approach. It does not ignore the need for swift and sophisticated medical or surgical action, but does emphasise health promotion and patient education. In doing so, it respects the capacity people have for healing themselves and regards them as active partners in health care, rather than passive recipients. In addition to including the use of modern technology and medicines, holistic medicine welcomes all the techniques that have been developed in other cultures and at other times, thus including a variety of therapeutic approaches. These approaches have sometimes been described as 'alternative' or 'complementary' medicine (Eg. Homoeopathy, Ayurveda, acupuncture etc.)

Holism has always been vital to healing and some of history's most gifted physicians have embraced holistic beliefs. The ancient Greek physician Hippocrates, writing in the 5th century BC emphasised the environmental causes, the importance of emotional factors and nutrition in health and disease.

Holistic medicine can be described as a marriage of the art of healing so vital to medicine throughout history and the scientific precision of modern medicine. It may well represent a significant advance not only in the health care but in the way we live and think and feel about ourselves.

A holistic physician is someone who is concerned with promoting wellness through educational means and encouraging self care as well as with testing illness with a holistic approach.

Integrated medicine is a comprehensive form of medical care delivered by physicians who are dually trained in eastern and western medicine and who are able to integrate concepts from both systems. Early recognition and treatment of subtle signs of dysfunction start with the safest and most effective approach and only move to more invasive interventions if necessary.

Integrated medicine is the methodology of integrating different systems of medicines from different parts of the world, it is provided by the qualified expert in each system of medicine who is working together with the experts of other systems of medicines to help a person for curative, preventive or health improvement purpose. It is not the simplistic concept of a doctor of one system of medicine practising other systems of medicine and incorporating one or two therapies. Instead, an ideal integrated doctor is an expert in one system of medicine with awareness in the benefits of other systems of medicine, and one who has an attitude of openness for accepting and respecting the benefits of other systems of medicines. Thus each system of medicine is able to complement the other. The focus is on health and healing, not just disease and treatment, bringing together body, mind and spirit so that healthcare encompasses the whole person.

The distinctive features of integrated medicine is its application of science to prevent or treat disease by healing the person who is sick, rather than just treating the disease. An integrated holistic approach has a much wider understanding about the person. It is more health oriented than disease oriented.

*Dr. Issac Mathai is a world-renowned holistic doctor. An MD in Homeopathy and an MRCH from London, he has worked as a physician in Europe's first and largest holistic health clinic, the 101 Clinic. His healing centre Soukya is located on the outskirts of Bangalore. Dr. Mathai can be contacted at info@soukya.com.*

SOUKYA™

# Energize the body.
# Refresh the mind.
# Invigorate the spirit.

STARK.Blr/skya/0104

## t SOUKYA - The International Holistic Health Centre.

t on a serene 30-acre organic farm just minutes from the heart of Bangalore City, SOUKYA is first-of-its-kind centre. Offering a holistic medical approach to healing the body, mind and irit. The centre integrates diverse systems of medicine and complementary therapies to provide rsonalized treatment programmes that are constantly monitored by resident physicians.

All while you immerse yourself in the soothing splendor of nature and traditional architecture th aromatic gardens, open-air showers and outdoor dining.

**eatments:** Ayurveda ▪ Yoga ▪ Homeopathy ▪ Naturopathy **Programmes:** Stress Management ▪ Weight duction ▪ Rejuvenation ▪ De-toxification ▪ Medical Conditions

ukya Road, Samethanahalli, Whitefield, Bangalore - 560 067, Karnataka, India. Tel: 91-80-7945001 /2 /3 /4. Fax: 91-80-7945010. Email: info@soukya.com  Website: www.soukya.com

# Suit your Spa

## Angsana Oasis Spa & Resort

Here is an out and out luxury spa, offering an extravagant and lavish experience. Part of the southeast Asian chain of speciality spa resorts, Angsana boasts international standards and unarguably the best traditional Thai massages. Spa treatments include eight kinds of massages including the Ayuthaya Massage and Maui Massage, five kinds of body wraps, including the Thai Herbal and Tangerine wraps, a choice of four facials and three kinds of body scrubs of which the Aroma Salt is recommended. Ayurvedic packages are also offered here which include Yoga sessions, a wholesome vegetarian diet and consultations with an in-house doctor.

Angsana is located 45 minutes from Bangalore towards Doddaballapur. There are different packages to suit individual requirements that go by exotic names like 'Contentment in Paradise', 'Satisfy your Soul' and 'Taste of Heaven'!

The resort also provides a lush setting for conferences, seminars and relaxing retreats. Exclusive air-conditioned rooms and suites, which open onto spacious patios and tropical gardens, are available. The Angsana suites and executive resort rooms are equipped with a living and dining area, along with a kitchenette and luxury bathrooms. The sprawling resort also offers a host of recreational facilities, from a well-stocked library, aerobics centre and meditation room to squash and tennis courts. The resort serves both food and alcohol.

*Northwest County, Main Doddaballapur Road, Rajankunte Bangalore 560064* **Tel** *2846 8893* **Web** *www.angsanaspa.com*

Angsana Oasis Spa & Resort

## AyurvedaGram

This Ayurvedic spa village has been created by transplanting heritage homes from Kerala. The result is an aesthetically pleasing, calming and professional environment for some fabulous Ayurvedic treatment. An amphitheatre, Ayurvedic library and authentic Kerala restaurant are part of the package. Steam baths, treatment with medicated oils and synchronised massages where two therapists work on you simultaneously, are some of AyurvedaGram's special features. Customised Ayurvedic treatment and rejuvenation packages are on offer, including the popular Panchakarma therapy. Stress management courses and weekend packages are also available but if time is a constraint, you can opt for a single day's tour which includes a massage and steam bath, consultation with an Ayurvedic doctor and lunch or dinner.

AyurvedaGram is a short drive from Bangalore. Rooms are available from Rs1,550 to Rs 3,500, categorised as Standard, Deluxe, Luxury and Suite. The Treatment & Health Centre or Pulinkunnu Mana is a typical house built of timber and tile. It has eight treatment rooms, four herbal baths and a well-equipped facility with modern diagnostic equipment. Ootupura is the restaurant serving vegetarian Keralite and south Indian cuisine. Predictably, smoking and drinking are not allowed.

*AyurvedaGram Heritage Wellness Centre Bangalore 560067* **Tel** *794 5430/5433,* **Web** *www.ayurvedagram.com*

AyurvedaGram

## Golden Palms Hotel & Spa

Indian actor-director Sanjay Khan has built a luxury spa with a spectacular range of baths, body treatments and massages. It also offers yoga and meditation programmes and is equipped with a state of the art gymnasium. A Life Rejuvenation Centre has different therapies, Ayurvedic treatments, weight management programmes, preventive cardiology and image enhancement treatment. The resort boasts a huge swimming pool, theme restaurants, bars and a dance floor. Golden Palms is a 35-minute drive from Bangalore and the room rates vary from Rs 7,500 to Rs 25,000.

*Nagarur, Dasanpura, Hobli, Tumkur Road, Bangalore 562123* **Tel** *2371 2222* **Web** *www.goldenpalmsspa.com*

## Institute Of Naturopathy & Yogic Sciences (INYS)

Many decades before naturopathy, Ayurveda and Yoga caught the fancy of the world and the Indian urban elite, the Jindal institute on the outskirts of Bangalore city was the first stop for those seeking the natural option to good health. This famous charitable health centre attracted people from all over.

INYS uses powerful curative tools of naturopathy and Yoga to help fight diseases and strengthen mental and emotional health. Some of its specialised therapies include the asthma bath, mud bath, jet massage and acupuncture treatment. Single rooms, double rooms, cottages and free wards are available.

*Institute Of Naturopathy & Yogic Sciences, Jindalnagar, Tumkur Road, Bangalore 560073* **Tel** *2371 7777*

## Soukya

Soukya is a spa that stresses on its medical treatments rather than its luxurious environs. It boasts visitors like Sarah Fergusson and Deepak Chopra. Soukya claims to be the world's only holistic medical spa that integrates Indian and international therapies, Hawaiian stones with Ayurvedic oils. The therapeutic treatments are a fusion of Yoga, Ayurveda, Siddha and Unani with western Homoeopathy and Naturopathy. Soukya is a comfortable drive from Bangalore, located just 24kms from the city. Facilities include a swimming pool and pool table. Non-vegetarian food, smoking and drinking are not on the menu.

*International Holistic Health Centre, Soukya Road, Samethanahalli PO, Whitefield, Bangalore 560067* **Tel** *794 5001-3* **Web** *www.holisticmedic.com*

Soukya

## The Spa, The Leela Palace

Located in the heart of the city, The Spa at The Leela Palace is of international standards. The Spa has special packages such as the 'Executives Package' with intensive back massages, the `Back to Nature' package with a rose, vetiver and jasmine body polish and the 'Top to Toe Day Spa Experience' where you are pampered with the Vedic Aromatic Body Scrub and the Orange Blossom Bathing Ritual for an entire day. The 'Precious Stones' treatment uses special ESPA herbal oils and hot volcanic stones. This luxury spa is also the sole distributor for ESPA's high quality herbal products in India.

*The Leela Palace, 23 Airport Road, Bangalore 560008* **Tel** *2521 2222* **Web** *www.theleela.com*

# If Health Is Wealth...
## Welcome To The Richest Place On Earth.

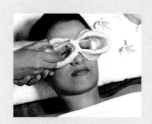

Experience the healing touch of pure Ayurveda at AyurvedaGram. Holistic preventive therapies and authentic treatments for specific ailments...

Amid centuries-old traditional architecture from Kerala... recreated brick by brick, woodwork and all. Set in a herbal garden just minutes away from the heart of Bangalore City.

**Ay rvedaGram**™
HERITAGE WELLNESS CENTRE | BANGALORE

Whitefield, Bangalore - 560 067.
Ph: 91 80 51161195. Mobile: 98450 71990
Email: response@ayurvedagram.com
www.ayurvedagram.com

• Rejuvenation packages • Stress management • Weight reduction therapies • Body purification treatments...

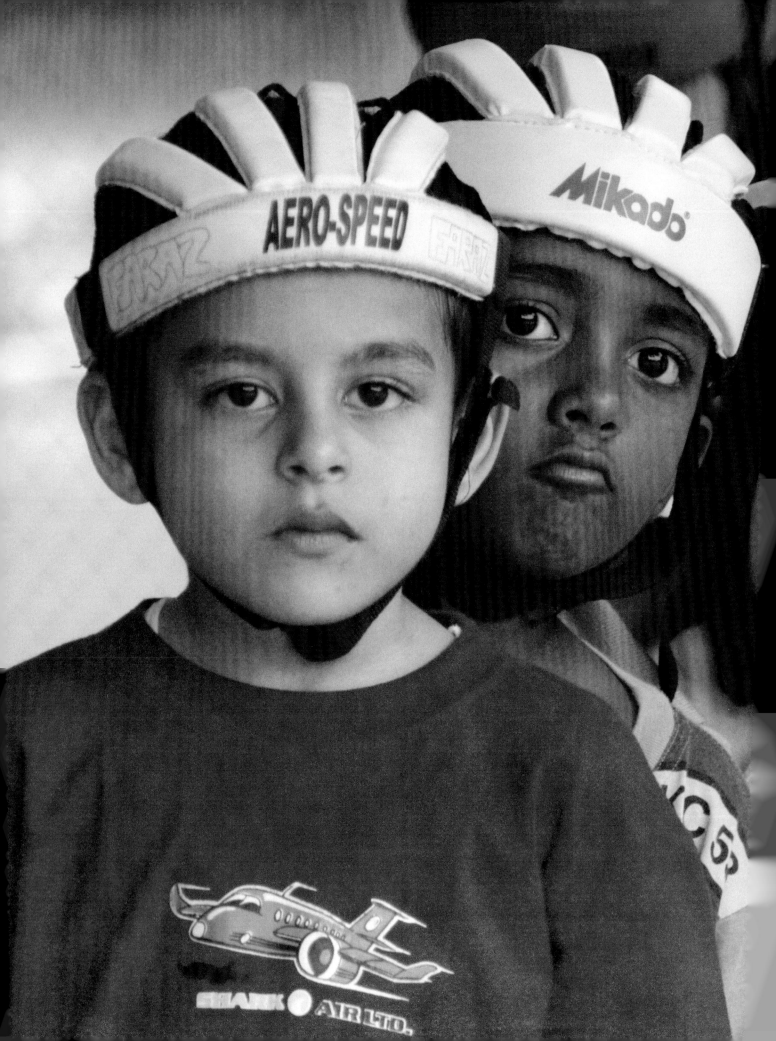

Children

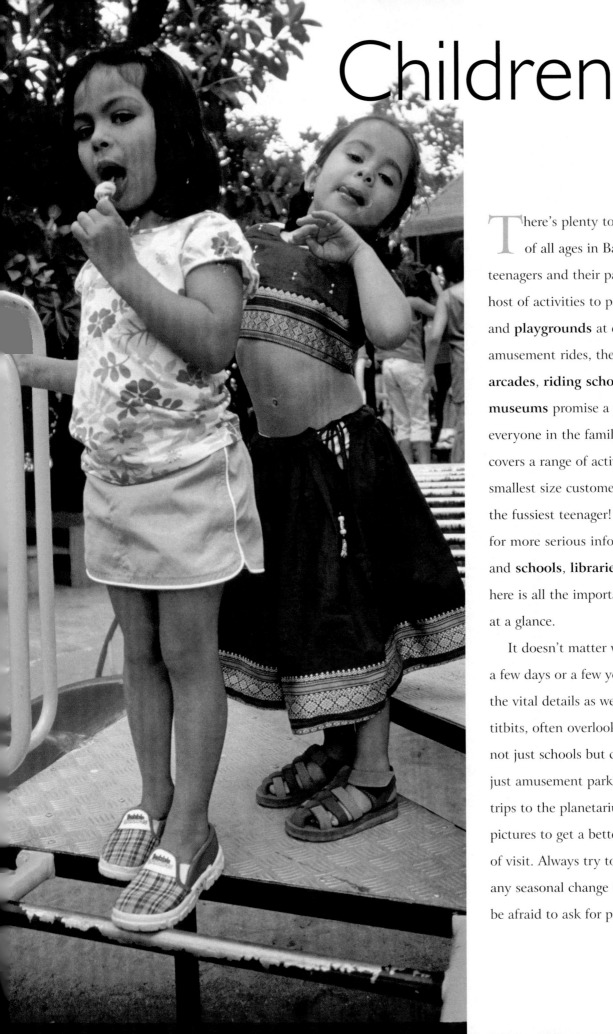

# Children

There's plenty to do for children of all ages in Bangalore. Toddlers to teenagers and their parents will find a host of activities to pass the time. **Parks** and **playgrounds** at every corner, amusement rides, the **planetarium**, **arcades**, **riding schools**, malls and **museums** promise a good time for everyone in the family. This section covers a range of activities that suit the smallest size customer to the fussiest teenager! For those looking for more serious information like **crèches** and **schools**, **libraries** and **hospitals**, here is all the important information at a glance.

It doesn't matter whether your visit is a few days or a few years. You will find all the vital details as well as some little titbits, often overlooked. So, we've listed not just schools but crèches too, and not just amusement parks, but educational trips to the planetarium as well. Use the pictures to get a better grip on your places of visit. Always try to call and check for any seasonal change in timings and don't be afraid to ask for prices and rates.

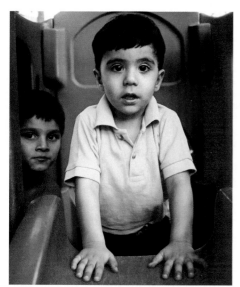

## Parks & Planetarium

The most popular places are undoubtedly the parks – **Cubbon Park** and **Lalbagh**. Parents of toddlers happily let them have a free run of the place, under the leafy shade of the many trees. For older children, the wealth of green information serves as a lesson in botany! Lots of families bring picnic meals and spend the whole day in the shadow of the blossoming giants.

Bangalore's **Bal Bhavan**, dedicated to kids, is located within Cubbon Park. Check the timings and you can promise your kids a variety of recreational activities such as rides on the toy train, boating, film shows, nature camps and a library.

An hour's drive south of the city will bring you to **Bannerghatta Biological Park** with a zoo in its premises. Spread over 25,000 acres it boasts of panthers, lions, tigers and a large collection of reptiles and fauna. Tiger safaris, trekking locations and a children's corner make it an ideal destination for children and adults alike.

Right within the city, set in a large campus, is the **Jawaharlal Nehru Planetarium**. The schedule here changes quite often but there are some standard shows that go down very well with children of all ages. There are also talks and movies on science-related topics such as astronomy and astrophysics. The science museum nearby offers hobby classes, quizzes and painting competitions.

## Arcades

Sheer fun and games places also exist side by side with arcades like **Amoeba**, **Jaamba Jungle** and **Megabowl**. There is always a festive atmosphere at such places and the incessant music and chatter all around act like a tonic for bored kids!

For the more adventurous, there are a number of water parks, go-karting arenas and carnivals in the city. Turn to the **Entertainment** section to locate the fun.

## Arts & Crafts

Karnataka's premier art institute, **Karnataka Chitrakala Parishath**, conducts weekend art classes for children and holds exhibitions throughout the year profiling art and crafts from across the country. There is much to learn just by visiting the place, although those arriving with very small kids must steer clear of the sculpture section with its tottering creations.

There are a number of small schools, often in the teacher's house, offering classes and courses across a wide range of hobbies. **Dance, drama, ikebana flower arrangements, papier-mâché, puppet making** and the entire orchestra of **instruments** and **voice training** are available in each area. There is something for children of all ages and all interests. The community hall or club in your area is a good place to check.

The **Hippocampus Experience Centre** offers everything from a library to weekend activities, a great boon for the city's parents and children.

## Riding

For those who prefer the outdoors, Bangalore's fabulous weather and its long history as a British Cantonment make **horse riding** a viable option. This is reflected in the number of riding schools in the city. Notable among them are the **Embassy Riding School** and the **Princess Academy of Equitation**. Children attending these riding academies are encouraged to take part in competitions. Some riding schools have neat canteens and sit-outs and many Bangaloreans prefer to while away their weekend here, while their kids go riding.

## Schools

For those looking at a long term stay, information on schooling is vital. As one of the most cosmopolitan cities in the country, Karnataka's schools rank among the best in India. The best systems are represented here – the ICSE, IGSCE, HSC and IB. The State Board is also popular among some schools. Bishop Cotton Boys School, one of the oldest and most reputed, has consistently been ranked among the top ten schools in India. It offers a wide range of extracurricular activities for all-round development.

Alternative schooling has come into its own in Bangalore. Some of the best schools are alternative, or getting there. Lured by the open-mindedness of the local population and the space available on the outskirts of the city, many educationists have opened schools. The city's rapidly growing population has put pressure on school admissions and any more supply is welcome!

## Shopping

Finally, shopping for children in the capital city of Karnataka rivals any other big metro. All the big brands of children's clothing and shoes are easily available and some smaller ones as well. The regular toyshops have the usual array of inviting goodies, but there are others if you wish your purchase to be educational as well. All the big bookstores have large kiddie sections as well.

Whichever way you look at it, Bangalore is a happy and happening place for children and their parents. There's something for everyone. And you can cheerfully promise a family holiday to both a toddler as well as teenager. We hope *Stark World – Bangalore & Karnataka* answers all your questions.

Hippocampus Experience Centre

# ENTERTAINMENT

## Amoeba

*22 HM Leisure, Church Street, Bangalore 560001*
*Tel 2559 4631/4632*
*Open 11am to 11pm*

Just a few seconds from Brigade Road (Bangalore's haven for shop trawlers), Amoeba is ideally located. It boasts an amusement complex that promises fun for kids of all ages with bowling, arcade games, a toddler section and a restaurant. The latter serves Chinese and a bit of north Indian food and thus goes by the name: Three Quarter Chinese. Good food, music and general merrymaking have turned Amoeba into a great entertainer.

## Bannerghatta Biological Park

*Anekal Road, Bangalore 560083*
*Tel 782 8540*
*Open 9:30am to 5:30pm. Closed on Tuesday.*

Only 20 kilometres from Bangalore, Bannerghatta's forests are filled with lions, tigers, elephants and other wildlife. Its zoo boasts a snake park, crocodile farm and a wide variety of birds and reptiles. Children love the safari and get to learn about animals and their habits. A visit to the national park is not just fun but informative and educative as well.

## Fun World

*Palace Grounds, JC Nagar, Opp. TV Tower, Bangalore 560006*
*Tel 2343 0496*
*Open 11am to 9:30pm*

Fun World offers something that Bangalore is quickly running out of – space in the heart of the city. Around five kilometres from MG Road and located on the sprawling Bangalore Palace Grounds, it offers a full day's fun for children – with rides, games and other amusements including water rides. There are two restaurants and an ice-cream stall so there's no need to pack

refreshments. Next to Fun World is the Star City amusement centre.

## Speed Zone

*Shantiniketan, Sadaramangal, Whitefield Road, Bangalore 560048*
*Tel 3677 7908*
*Open 11am to 7:30pm. Open till 9pm on weekends.*

Although a bit out of town, this is one of the best places for go-karting. There are bigger cars for older children and smaller ones for younger kids. Snacks and drinks are sold at the Speed Zone and there is a restaurant next door.

## Hippocampus Experience Centre

*25, 16th Main, III Block, Kormangala, Bangalore 560034*
*Tel 2563 0206*
*Open 10:30am to 7:30pm. Closed on Monday.*
*Web www.thehippocampus.com*

There is something for every child, that's what Hippocampus wants you to know. It has everything from a library and play area to clubs and summer camps. There are over 7,000 children's books, a home theatre, computers, games like chess and lots of fun and games on weekends.

## Jaamba Jungle

*50 KH Road (Lalbagh Double Road), Opp. BTS Bus Depot, Bangalore 560027*
*Tel 2212 9020, 2299 3666*
*Open 11am to 11pm*

This is a great place to take children who are under eight years of age. It has pinball machines, arcade games, mini-basketball court and an area for toddlers. The food court offers child-friendly snacks, food and drinks and there is even a shop selling toys on the premises. You can book the place for parties and special games are organised.

## Jawahar Bal Bhavan

*Cubbon Park, Bangalore 560001*
*Tel 2286 4189/1423*
*Open 10:30am to 5:30pm. Closed on Monday.*

The most attractive activity in this recreational park located within Cubbon Park is the toy train, loved by children of all ages. Boat rides on little coracles add to the fun. Bal Bhavan also has a centre that screens movies, a library and nature camps. There is ample space for picnics and plenty of play equipment like slides, jungle gyms and swings. Altogether, it's a very popular destination for kids.

## Jungle Lodges & Resorts

*II Floor, Shrungar Shopping Centre, MG Road, Bangalore 560001*
*Tel 2559 7021/7024/7025*
*Open 10am to 5:30pm*

This is the place to book wildlife holidays around Karnataka and you can also use their expertise to plan a nature holiday for kids. Safaris at the Kabini River Lodge, fishing at Cauvery Fishing Camp and white water rafting at Dandeli are some of the options you may choose from.

## Lalbagh Botanical Garden

*Lalbagh Main Gate, KH Road, Bangalore 560004*
*Tel 2657 9231*
*Open 8am to 5:30pm*

This sprawling 240-acre park is arguably the most beautiful garden in Bangalore with exotic flowers, plants and trees. Lalbagh is the ideal place to spend a day or have a picnic. In season, the glasshouses are a riot of colour and the pleasantly shaded walks provide children with a wonderful and safe place to run wild.

## Megabowl

*Prestige Terminal 2, Airport Exit Road, Bangalore 560017*
*Tel 2522 9743/6071*
*Open 11am to 11pm*

Situated on Airport Road, Megabowl offers an opportunity for bowling and playing arcade games. There is a snack bar and a facility to host parties. Younger kids can zoom around in little toy cars. A toddler-friendly section allows you to keep the babies down.

## Sammy's Dreamland

*Hosahalli Village, NH 7, Hunasamaranahalli Post, Bangalore 562157*
*Tel 2847 8600*
*Open 12noon to 7:30pm*

This sprawling theme park promises assorted fun and games for the entire family. Set across 34 lush green acres, Sammy's Dreamland has four zones: The World Tour Area has reproductions of the world's seven wonders, the Tech Zone is a gaming arcade, the Children's Village and Lagoon Area have exciting water rides and light displays. There is also an Adventure Golf Putt and a Toon City where you can pose for photographs alongside King Kong, ghouls and cartoon characters. The amusement park is not just for kids and the virtual reality video games are a hit

with adults as well. A carnival-like air pervades through the park with 17 kiosks and a mini shopping mall. The Library serves Continental food, the Jewel Palace is a Mughlai restaurant and the Diner and Pizzeria dishes out American fastfood.

## Sportz Village

*55/11B, 24th Main, HSR II Sector, Opp. KEB Substation, Bangalore 560034*
*Tel 98455 13529*
*Open 6am to 11:30pm*
*Web www.sportzvillage.com*

Sportz Village is a unique programme that offers kids a chance to get their physical exercise and have fun doing it. It's a multi-sport facility and open to children from the ages of five to 15 years. Team sports are given special emphasis here, since they build both physical strength and social skills. There are facilities to play soccer, cricket, handball, badminton, tennis, volleyball and basketball. Only members are allowed to play and each child gets a chance at all games over a period of three months. Other activities include outdoor adventure sports such as rock climbing, trekking, nature walks and wall climbing. Sportz Village offers a safe and well equipped environment for kids and one that is likely to keep them busy all year long!

Children at the Sportz Village

## Star City

*JC Nagar, Palace Grounds, Bangalore 560006*
*Tel 2354 3291*
*Open 11am to 9:30pm*

Video games and bowling are available at this amusement centre, adjacent to Fun World. There is little to do for children under the age of five, but plenty thereafter. A 15-minute drive from central MG Road, it is located inside the Bangalore Palace Grounds.

## MUSEUMS

### Government Aquarium

*Cubbon Park, Opp. Queen's Statue,
Kasturba Road, Bangalore 560001*
*Tel 2286 7440*
*Open 10am to 5:30pm. Closed on public
holidays, Mondays and second Tuesdays
of every month.*
*Admission Rs 5 for adults and Rs 2 for
children above five years*

Located within Cubbon Park, the
aquarium is a great attraction for
children of all ages. Run by the
government, it has a number of local
and imported varieties of fish. To whet
a different kind of appetite, there is
even a fish canteen located on the
same premises!

### Government Museum

*Kasturba Road, Bangalore 560001*
*Tel 2286 4483*
*Open 10am to 5pm. Closed on Mondays
and public holidays.*
*Admission Rs 4 for adults and
Rs 2 for children*

One of the main attractions of this
museum is a full dinosaur skeleton
that may be mechanically operated
to chomp its jaws. The museum is a
good place to bring kids of five
years and older. A natural history
section, galleries showcasing art,
ethnography and archaeology make
up the package.

### HAL Heritage Centre &
### Aerospace Museum

*HAL, Airport Varthur Road,
Bangalore 560037*
*Tel 2522 8341*
*Open 9am to 5pm*
*Admission Rs 20 for adults and
Rs 10 for children*

The HAL Aerospace Museum is a sure
fire hit with children. It has a number of
aircraft and helicopters parked outside
and children are thrilled to be within
touching distance of mighty fighters
and bombers. Inside the museum there
are simulators, audio-visual shows and
a viewing gallery with a mock control
tower to view aeroplanes taking off and
landing at the Bangalore airport, which
is just across the road. Talks on aviation
and aircraft are of interest for older
children.

### Janapada Loka

*Bangalore-Mysore Road, Ramanagaram,
Bangalore 571511*
*Tel 727 1555*
*Open 9am to 1pm and 2:30pm to
5:30pm. Closed on Tuesday.*
*Admission Rs 6 for adults and Rs 3 for
children*

Although Janapada Loka is situated 50
kilometres from the centre of
Bangalore, it's worth a visit. It has a
museum displaying folk art and music
and a wide range of masks and other
artefacts. Its library of audio and
videocassettes showcase the state's folk

# Hippocampus – Big Fun for Small People!

Bangalore's parents and children are cheering the
opening of Hippocampus, a one-of-its-kind library and
experience centre, open to children of all ages. It has a large,
well-lit library with book-lined shelves, child-friendly
furniture, a home theatre room, computers, a sand pit and
lots of space to play. There's always plenty to do at
Hippocampus – read books, sketch, conduct science
experiments, watch movies, play with other kids, listen to
stories, go cycling and much more.

Weekends are chock-a-block with activities like, puppet
shows, games and club sessions. The clubs were started to
provide for kids with an interest in a particular area. At present,
there are clubs for Adventure, Cooking and Journalism. Each
club has a mentor and the sessions are informal and geared
towards making learning fun. The younger kids get to dabble
in art, cooking, science workshops.

Behind all the fun is a serious purpose – to cultivate the
reading habit, in danger in the digital age. Over 8,000 books
may be found here along with magazines, movies and
CD-ROMs. From graded reading to old favourites like Enid
Blyton, comics to classics, it's hard to stay away from them.
New releases each month ensure a steady supply.

Hippocampus also organises an annual summer camp
for kids, and a carnival, Hoophoria, with 2004 being the
debut year.

*25, 16th Main, III Block, Kormangala, Bangalore 560034*
*Tel 2563 0206 Web www.thehippocampus.com*

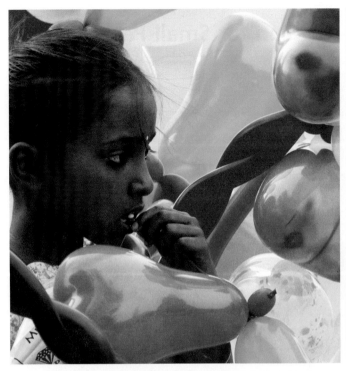

music and dances. This museum is ideal for kids between the ages of seven and 12 years.

## Jawaharlal Nehru Planetarium

*T Chowdiah Road, High Grounds, Bangalore 560001*
*Tel 2220 3234*
*Open 10am to 5:30pm. Closed on Monday and second Tuesdays.*
*Show in Kannada at 3pm,*
*Show in English at 4:30pm*
*Admission Rs 25*

Many a budding scientist has had their imagination fuelled by a visit to the local planetarium! It's a sure draw for children over the age of six years. Younger children may find the place a little too esoteric for their tastes, but the outside is strewn with scientific paraphernalia, presented in a fun way and even the smallest visitor will not be disappointed. There are talks and movies on science-related topics such as astronomy and astrophysics everyday and the schedule frequently changes. Kids are encouraged to ask questions and peer through the telescopes used for sighting the universe. This is definitely a must-see for kids.

## Visvesvaraya Industrial and Technological Museum

*Kasturba Road, Bangalore 560001*
*Tel 2286 4563*
*Open 10am to 6pm*
*Admission Rs 15 for adults and children above five years.*

Most adults can draw a connection between science and technology. This museum initiates the process for kids, preferably over the age of six years. It showcases the interface between science and technology and guides children. It opens a window on how scientific

research helps technological advancement. There are also talks, quizzes and painting competitions held throughout the year.

## Karnataka Chitrakala Parishath

*Art Complex, Kumara Krupa Road, Bangalore 560001*
*Tel 2226 1816*
*Open: 10am to 5:30pm. Closed on Sunday.*

The Chitrakala Parishath is a great place for painting and art workshops for children. It also holds folk art, toy and puppet exhibitions through the year and these provide urban children a chance to view ancient folk Indian toys and games.

## RIDING SCHOOLS

### Bangalore Amateur Riders' Institute

*Bangalore Turf Club, Race Course Road, Bangalore 560001*
*Tel 2226 2393/2391*
*Open 6:30am to 8:30am and 3:30pm to 4:30pm*

One of Bangalore's oldest horse riding schools, it dispenses both individual as well as group coaching on seasoned horses. Situated inside the Bangalore Turf Club grounds, it has a great atmosphere of horses and racing. There's a long waiting list to sign up.

### The Embassy International Riding School

*149/2 and 223 Torhunse Village, Jala Hobli, Devanahalli Taluk*
*Tel 2846 8296*
*Open 6:30am to 12:30pm and 2:30pm to 6:30pm. Closed on Monday.*

Located on the outskirts of Bangalore, Embassy Riding School focusses on providing world class riding facilities with highly trained personnel at higher than average rates. The riding instruction is excellent, the horses look happy and there's even a nice restaurant at the school. This is a great place to spend the day. Kids love the other pet animals housed here along with the horses.

### The Princess Academy of Equitation

*Palace Grounds, Bellary Road, Bangalore 560080*
*Tel 2361 0695*
*Open 6am to 9pm and 3pm to 6pm.*

Located within the Bangalore Palace Grounds, this riding school offers children the chance to learn horse riding from the age of five. Trained instructors and retired racehorses teach riding to both children as well as adults. It's centrally located and this adds to its attraction.

## BOOKSHOPS & LIBRARIES

### Butterfly Books

*Tel 2212 8191, 98451 83730*

Watch out for Butterfly Books' regular exhibitions to stock your home library. They have more than a 1,000 titles of imported books for children, infants and teens. Informative and visually appealing, they use innovative teaching aids like pop-ups, puppets, touch and feel and magnetic devices to hold the attention of the reader. Old fairytales have been repackaged and there is a variety of encyclopaedia, atlas and history books. Cookery, craft, health, astrology and gardening make up the rest. The Mumbai based Butterfly Books does not have a retail outlet in Bangalore but holds regular exhibition and sales in Safina Plaza. Most books are priced reasonably between Rs 50 and Rs 500.

### Crossword

*ACR Towers, 32 Residency Road, Bangalore 560025*
*Tel 2558 2411*
*Open 10:30am to 9pm*
*Cards All*
*Web www.crosswordbookstores.com*

A well-stocked children's section is one of the biggest attractions of Crossword bookstore. Popular children's titles and multimedia are categorised neatly and customers can browse comfortably for hours on end. The first floor has toys, board games, a limited collection of music titles and stationery. The store offers options such as dial-a-book, fax-a-book and email-a-book. For those interested, their website (crosswordbookstores.com) has a bestseller list for children.

### Eloor Lending Library

*Blue Cross Chambers, Off Infantry Cross Road, Bangalore 560001*
*Tel 2559 1408*
*Open 10am to 1:30pm and 3pm to 8pm.*

Here is a lending library with an entire section devoted to children's books. Going by the well thumbed, dog-eared look of most books, it's also very popular! Eloor has the usual ticket Enid Blytons, red hot Harry Potters, ancient Tintins, horrors and mysteries and all of Roald Dahl's delicious selection. Only members are allowed to browse and borrow, but the process of becoming one is relatively simple.

### Fountainhead

*41 Lavelle Road, Bangalore 560001*
*Tel 2222 9759*
*Open 10am to 8:30pm. Closed on Monday.*
*Cards All*
*Email fhblore@satyam.net.in*

Fountainhead stocks a wide array of children's books, soft toys and games. It's a good place to pick up presents for kids.

Sankars the book people

## Gangarams Book Bureau

*72 MG Road, Bangalore 560001*
*Tel 2558 5293*
**Open** *10am to 8pm. Closed on Sunday.*
**Cards** *All*
**Email** *gangarams@vsnl.com*

Touted as the biggest bookshop in Bangalore, Gangarams has a huge selection of books, CD-ROMs and audio as well as videocassettes for children. This is the first stop for schoolbooks and stationery requirements. Stickers, poster paper, art material, pens and other accessories are all available here.

## Landmark

*The Forum, 2 Hosur Road, Koramangala, Bangalore 560029*
*Tel 2206 7640*
**Open** *9am to 9pm*
**Cards** *All except American Express*
**Web** *www.landmarkonthenet.com*

This sprawling bookstore has a sizeable children's section. The mezzanine floor of the 45,000sqft shop is devoted entirely to gifts, toys and stationery for children. The book section stocks an extensive selection of encyclopaedia, educational books and storybooks. Landmark houses an exclusive reading zone just for kids where you can browse through Enid Blytons and Judy Blumes in a cosy carpeted room.

## Sankars
## the book people

*15/2 Madras Bank Road, Bangalore 560001*
*Tel 2558 6867/68*
**Branches** *Airport, 2522 7418; Taj Residency, 2532 5621; Bangalore Central 5112 4170; Le Meridien, 2220 7156; Safina Plaza, 2559 5074, The Atria Hotel, 2225 6785, William Penn, 2563 3161, Rangashankara, 2649 4656*
**Open** *10am to 8:30pm and 11am to 8pm on Sunday.*
**Cards** *All except American Express*
**Web** *www.sankarsbooks.com*

Just off St. Mark's Road, Sankars has a wide selection of children's books, games and colouring books. Run by a father and son team (N Sankaran and Vivek Sankaran), this bookstore has a chain of outlets across the city. An impressive pick of children's books is available here from comics to general knowledge tomes. A lot of hard-to-find titles can be found here. Their collection of CD ROMs is well chosen and satisfies both educational and entertainment parameters. There is also a separate play corner for kids.

## Strand Book Stall

*113-114 Manipal Centre,*
*47 Dickenson Road, Bangalore 560042*
*Tel 2558 0000/2222*
**Open** *10:30am to 8pm. Closed on Sunday.*
**Cards** *All except American Express*
**Web** *www.strandbookstall.com*

Just off MG Road, the Strand Book Stall is a branch of the famous Strand in Mumbai. It has a great selection of books for babies, toddlers and children. What makes this place special is that kids can pick up books and go through them before buying. Books are stacked at a level conducive to browsing by small citizens. There is also a good CD-ROM collection.

## The British Library

*Prestige Takt, 23 Kasturba Cross Road, Bangalore 560001*
*Tel 2248 9220*
**Open** *10:30am to 6:30pm. Closed on Sunday.*
**Web** *www.bclindia.org*

This library, run by the British Council, has a well stocked children's section with over 2,000 children's books. There are videos and CDs to choose from. You have to become a member to browse and there are facilities to photocopy material, use the Internet as well as programmes dealing with different topics for members.

## The Oxford Bookstore

*Leela Galleria, The Leela Palace, Airport Road, Bangalore 560008*
*Tel 5115 5222*
**Open** *10am to 10pm*
**Cards** *All except Diners Club*
**Web** *www.oxfordbookstore.com*

The Oxford Bookstore's kids' section is quite a treat for children. Low tables and chairs in bright colours, surrounded by all the favourite titles with cakes and scones from the adjacent Cha Bar make the store a perfect outing. Look out for their annual sale offering huge discounts.

## TOY STORES

### Big Kids Kemp

*Ramanashree Arcade, 18 MG Road, Bangalore 560001*
*Tel 2558 6666*
**Open** *9am to 9pm*
**Cards** *All*

All the stores under this label share big, brightly lit facades and cartoon characters who leap out at customers at the entrance. Located on MG Road, it's hard to miss and even harder not to go in if you're passing by with kids! There is a general party air throughout the store with freebies and attentive sales people.

### Kemp Fort

*97 Airport Road, Bangalore 560017*
*Tel 2522 6966/4977*
**Open** *10am to 9:30pm*
**Cards** *All*

This is one toy store that's difficult to miss because of its sheer size, colourful facade and loud presence. There are a host of cartoon characters dressed in costume at the entrance to welcome and entice small people. Built on the lines of a castle, Kemp Fort boasts one of largest toy stores in the country, with a huge range of toys, video games, DVDs and CD-ROMs on its second floor. The store has a distinct carnival air with freebies like juice and popcorn and loud music. A food court upstairs lets you make a longer stay than planned.

### Lifestyle

*W-76 Adarsh Opus, Campbell Road, Austin Town, Bangalore 560047*
*Tel 2556 0464/4555*
**Open** *9:30am to 9:30pm*
**Cards** *All*

A complete shopping mall, Lifestyle's first floor contains a wide range of toys, clothes, CD-ROMs and books for children. There are also lots of toy equipment like slides, and garden toys on display. You can shop for strollers, nappies, baby clothes and other infant needs here.

### Sapphire Toy Shop

*6 Brigade Road, Bangalore 560001*
*Tel 2558 7255*
**Branch** *Jayanagar, 5130 7220*
**Open** *9:30am to 8:30pm*
**Cards** *All*

Located right in the middle of the city's busiest shopping area, Sapphire has a wide range of toys, imported as well as Indian. The shop's two floors are filled to the roof with children's products such as plates and cutlery, party decorations and colourful stationery. Big toy cars and swimming pools are also stocked here. They arrange to pack 'return gifts' for guests at kids' parties, normally a big headache for parents!

## Shoppers' Stop

*17/2 Raheja Point, Magrath Road,*
*Ashok Nagar, Bangalore 560025*
**Tel** *2554 8224*
**Branch** *Bannerghatta Road, 5121 5681*
**Open** *10am to 9pm*
**Cards** *All*

This is a great place for kid's shopping because you can take them along and they will be entertained nearby in an area specially designated for them. Clothes, toys and accessories are in plenty and you sometimes get good bargains. Most of the top clothing and toy brands are stocked here.

## Sutradhar

*599, 7th Main, 17 A Cross, Indiranagar*
*II Stage, Bangalore 560038*
**Tel** *2528 8545*
**Open** *10:30am to 5pm. Closed on*
*Sunday & Monday.*
**Cards** *All*

Sutradhar is not just a toy store, it's the thinking toy store! Located just off CMH Road in Indiranagar, it lies outside the main shopping hubs. It's a little difficult to find among the many bylanes, but once there you get to see toys that don't feature anywhere else. Wooden toys, a wide range of educational aids and books for children in English, Hindi and regional languages are stocked here.

## The Bombay Store

*99 EGK Prestige, MG Road,*
*Bangalore 560001*
**Tel** *2532 0014*
**Open** *10:30am to 8:30pm*
**Cards** *All*

Spread across three floors, this store has only a small collection of toys, books and clothing for children. If your shopping focus is on home stuff and adult clothing, with the odd child's demand thrown in, this store measures up.

## Toys Kemp

*5 Commercial Street, Bangalore 560001*
**Tel** *2559 2688, 2509 8709*
**Open** *9:30am to 9pm*
**Cards** *All*

A branch of Kemp Fort, Toys Kemp is smaller but carries similar toys as its parent. The dancing characters at the entrance and the big signboard in front maintain the character of the chain.

## Toyworld/Babyworld

*44 Commercial Street, Bangalore 560001*
**Tel** *2558 9760*
**Open** *10:30am to 9pm*
**Cards** *All except American Express*

The store has a wide range of toys, CD-ROMs and stationery for babies, toddlers and children. Toyworld is actually much larger than it looks and has two floors stacked with almost everything other toy stores have.

## Toys 'N' Toys
## The Baby Shop

*238, 7th Cross, Off CMH Road,*
*Indiranagar I Stage, Bangalore 560038*
**Tel** *5126 9426/36/46*
**Open** *10:30am to 8pm*
**Cards** *All except Diners Club*

This is a dedicated toy store and baby shop, spread across three floors. Clothing, playthings and other essentials from feeding bottles to strollers for newborns and toddlers are available here. A range of toys for kids of all ages makes up the rest of the store. Games, action figures, dolls, books, stationery, cycles, tricycles and CD-ROMs are stocked across 5,000sqft. A range of sports gear, from badminton racquets to basketballs, for the older kids and fitness equipment for teenagers are other highlights at Toys 'N' Toys. The sizeable selection of board games finds many takers among grown-ups as well.

## Vellara Junction

*Opp. Brigade Tower, Bangalore 560001*
**Tel** *2530 1147*
**Open** *9:30am to 2pm and 4pm to 9pm*
**Cards** *All except American Express*

Centrally located at the Richmond Road-Brigade Road junction, Vellara has a wide range of toys, stationery and games. Parking can be difficult as it is located in a busy area.

## APPAREL

## Always New

*181 Commercial Street,*
*Bangalore 560001*
**Tel** *2558 8754*
**Open** *10:30am to 8:30pm*
**Cards** *All except American Express*

One of the oldest and most established children's stores in the city, Always New has a range of clothing and lingerie for adults as well. Babies and children's clothing, underwear, accessories, toys, nappies and play equipment are sold here. Service is attentive and helpful.

## Baby Shop

*7/1 Ulsoor Road, Bangalore 560042*
**Tel** *2559 6104*
**Open** *10:30am to 8pm. Closed on Sunday.*
**Cards** *All except American Express*

This is one of the city's best stores dedicated to newborn babies and children. All types of baby gear – from cribs to strollers to bouncers and sterilizers and soft toys, Lego and Fisher Price toys may be found here. Clothes come in all sizes and for all seasons. There is a wide variety of shoes as well. Mums-to-be are not neglected and they will find a range of products from lotions to nightwear and nursing gear. The Baby Shop also makes cribs, playpens and clothes to order.

## Gini & Jony

*B/2 Residency Chambers,*
*78/2 Residency Road,*
*Bangalore 560025*
**Tel** *2559 1667*
**Open** *10am to 9pm*
**Cards** *All except American Express*

This store stocks clothes for boys and girls over four years under the Gini & Jony label. This is a premium brand and prices are a little higher than other stores. However, the quality is good and there is a wide choice.

## Just Born

*Mota Chambers, 9 Millers Road,*
*Bangalore 560052*
**Tel** *2225 8294*
**Open** *10am to 9pm and 10:30am to*
*8:30pm on Sunday. Closed on Friday.*
**Cards** *All*

This store is aimed at babies and children up to the age of four. Clothes and accessories, toys, nappies and other kiddie paraphernalia are available here. Situated just off Cunningham Road, parking can be tough.

## Mother's Choice

*28 Shrungar Shopping Centre,*
*MG Road, Bangalore 560001*
**Tel** *2559 4268*
**Open** *10:45am to 8:30pm*
**Cards** *All except American Express*

This store is a branch of the big Always New at Commercial Street and is aimed almost solely at babies and toddlers. You can get everything a baby would need: Strollers, toys, nappies, clothes and personal care products.
You also get a small range of clothing and undergarments for children up to four years of age.

## Shoppers' Stop

*17/2 Raheja Point, Magrath Road,*
*Ashok Nagar, Bangalore 560025*
**Tel** *2554 8224*
**Branch** *Bannerghatta Road, 5121 5681*
**Open** *10am to 9pm*
**Cards** *All*

This is a good place to hunt for kids' clothing, accessories and toys as it has a well developed children's section. And since you can shop for the rest of the family here it becomes a one-stop-shop.

## Weekender Kids

*180 Commercial Street,*
*Bangalore 560001*
*Tel 2555 0694*
*Branches Residency Road, 2559 5893;*
*Jayanagar, 2634 6689;*
*Marathahalli, 2522 6243;*
*Indiranagar, 2520 4148*
*Open 10:30am to 9pm*
*Cards All*

This is a good place to buy clothes for children over four years. There is a wide range of clothes for both boys and girls, all sold under the Weekender Kids label. They often have sales where you get great bargains.

## Westside

*77 Commercial Street,*
*Bangalore 560001*
*Tel 2555 0861*
*Branch The Forum, 5667 0121*
*Open 10:30am to 8:30pm*
*Cards All*

A wide choice of clothing for babies, toddlers and children is available here. The store's regular sales offer good bargains. Westside also has fun plates, cups and cutlery for children in bright colours and designs. Furnishings for children's rooms are also available here.

## HOSPITALS

### Bangalore Children's Hospital and Research Centre

*6 Chitrapur Complex, 8th Main,*
*15th Cross, Malleswaram,*
*Bangalore 560055*
*Tel 2334 2035*

### Hosmat

*45 Magrath Road,*
*Off Richmond Road,*
*Bangalore 560025*
*Tel 2559 3796*

### Mallya Hospital

*2 Vittal Mallya Road,*
*Bangalore 560001*
*Tel 2227 7979/7997*

### Manipal Hospital

*98 Rustam Bagh, Airport Road,*
*Bangalore 560017*
*Tel 2526 6646/6441*

### St. John's Medical College & Hospital

*Sarjapur Road, Bangalore 560034*
*Tel 2553 0724, 2206 5000*

## PRESCHOOLS & CRÈCHES

### Akshara

*15 Thamarai Kannan Street, Ulsoor,*
*Murphy Town, Bangalore 560008*
*Tel 2554 8280, 2536 3312*
*Open 9am to 3pm. Closed on Saturday & Sunday.*

One of the oldest play schools in Bangalore, Akshara follows the Montessori system of teaching. Children are taken in after they turn two and a half years. They also conduct summer camps and other activities for children.

### Casa Dei Bambino

*'Forever', 584 Syndicate Bank Road,*
*Indiranagar, Bangalore 560038*
*Tel 2528 2880*
*Open 8:30am to 4:30pm. Closed on Saturday & Sunday.*

This school also follows the Montessori system of teaching and children may join only after they turn two and a half years. There are over 70 children here and four teachers. The school has special counsellors who come in for children with learning disabilities.

### Cherry Tree

*19 Cunningham Road, Bangalore 560052*
*Tel 2226 0753*
*Open 9am to 12noon. Closed on Saturday & Sunday.*

Children start at the age of two years in this smallish playschool with only 50 children, a garden and playground equipment. It has a lovely atmosphere as it's situated behind an old Bangalore bungalow with trees, a lawn and lots of space for kids to run around.

### First Step

*12 Cunningham Crescent Road, Bangalore 560052*
*Tel: 2225 8109*
*Open: 9am to 3pm. Closed on Saturday & Sunday.*

Situated in the compound of one of Bangalore's few remaining large bungalows, First Step's best feature is its location. The school has a nice play area, a lovely garden, pet animals and chicken and geese racing around. Kids here start at the age of two years and there are about 200 students who come in shifts: 9am to 12noon and 12noon to 3pm. Each class has two teachers and a helper.

### Golden Bead

*157 Richmond Road,*
*Bangalore 560025*
*Tel: 2555 0126*
*Open: 9am to 3:30pm.*
*Closed on Saturday & Sunday.*

Golden Bead is a very child-friendly Montessori school and parents are encouraged to participate. The pre-school has over 60 students, six teachers and two helpers. The compound is small but fascinating for children with a tree house, play equipment and a sand pit. The Montessori instruction continues into the primary school.

### Gokulam Crèche

*20/2 Ali Asghar Road,*
*Bangalore 560052*
*Tel: 2228 4807*
*Open: 9am to 6pm on weekdays and 9am to 12noon on Saturday. Closed on Sunday.*

Gokulam takes in children after they turn one year old. Situated in a beautiful house, Gokulam offers excellent facilities including a garden with play equipment, a toy house and toys. The crèche actively involves the children in a range of activities including singing, dancing, craft and reading.

### Head Start Educational Trust

*32 P, 16th Main, IV Block, Koramangala,*
*Bangalore 560034*
*Tel 2553 7025*
*Open 9am to 5pm. Closed on Saturday & Sunday.*

This school has around 250 children and is reputed to be one of the best Montessori schools in the city. There are around 20 teachers and the school prides itself on paying individual attention to each student.

### Imperial Mothercare

*32 Cunningham Road,*
*Bangalore 560052*
*Tel 2208 8156*
*Open Nursery: 9am to 12noon from Monday to Saturday.*
*Day Care 9am to 6pm on weekdays and 9am to 1pm on Saturday. Closed on Sunday.*

One of the older crèches in the city, Imperial Mothercare is centrally located on Cunningham Road. It has well trained staff that look after children as young as eight months old. Lunch and snacks are provided and the children have plenty of space to run around.

### Kangaroo Kids

*34, 3rd Cross, RMV II Stage, Khodays Colony, Bangalore 560094*
*Tel 2351 3822/3826*
*Branch Indiranagar, 5115 4677*
*Open 9am to 2pm. Closed on Saturday & Sunday.*

A branch of Kangaroo Kids, Mumbai, this playschool takes children from the age of two years. It has a low teacher-

student ratio and encourages parents to come along with the kids to ease settling in problems. More branches are planned in the future.

## Lumbini

*5/1 Museum Road, Bangalore 560001*
*Tel 2558 7289*
*Open 9am to 12:30pm.*
*Closed on Saturday & Sunday.*

Lumbini is a small preschool with around 30 students. The school has a nice garden, play equipment and a sand pit. It's located in the heart of the commercial area.

## Prayag Montessori

*59, 5th Main Road, Kadernahalli,*
*I Stage, Padmanabhanagar,*
*Bangalore 560055*
*Tel 2223 0641*
*Open 9:30am to 12:30pm.*
*Closed on Saturday & Sunday.*

With a staff to child ratio of 1:10 children, Prayag offers children a cheerful environment to learn and play in. Teachers are qualified and trained under the Indian Montessori Association and all equipment is specially designed for Montessori purposes. An extensive curriculum that covers the entire gamut from math and science to language, art and music

complemented with state-of-the-art audio-visual equipment and computers is provided. A courtyard and garden allows children to spend time outdoors. Prayag also encourages parents to be involved in the Montessori training of their children.

## Shishya Nursery

*3 Sankey Road, Opp. the CM's residence,*
*Bangalore 560052*
*Tel 2226 6690, 2220 5504*
*Open 9am to 12noon. Closed on Sunday.*

Kids here start at the age of two years. There is a playground and the school offers transport in autorickshaws and vans. On the larger side – 120 students – each class has three teachers. The school has spacious grounds and a nice garden and play area.

Play time at the Shishu Griha Montessori and High School.

## Small World

*1079, 13th A Main, HAL II Stage,*
*Bangalore 560038*
*Tel 2527 1686*
*Open 9am to 12noon. Closed on Saturday & Sunday.*

This is one of the oldest and largest play schools in the suburbs of Indiranagar. It takes in children at the age of two and a half and has transport facilities as well.

## Vidya Sagar

*9, 3rd Cross, Bhupasandra Main Road,*
*Raj Mahal Vilas II Stage,*
*Bangalore 560094*
*Tel 2341 8997*
*Open 8:45am to 4pm. Closed on Sunday.*

This is a large pre-school with over 200 students. Each class has 35 students and a teacher and a helper. The students wear uniforms and there are two shifts: 9am to 12noon and 12noon to 3pm. The buildings and gardens are huge and well maintained. Students start at the age of two years and automatically get admission into Vidya Niketan and Vidya Shilp.

## SCHOOLS

## Baldwin Boys High School

*14 Hosur Road, Richmond Town,*
*Bangalore 560025*
*Tel 2221 1981/3720*
*Open 8:15am to 4pm*

An old Bangalore school, Baldwin Boys follows the ICSE syllabus. The school has boarding facilities. It's a large place with over 2,500 children 50 students to a class. There is a range of facilities available including computers, basketball courts and science labs.

## Baldwin Girls High School

*90 Richmond Road,*
*Bangalore 560025*
*Tel 2221 1743/4125/1413*
*Open 8:30am to 4pm*

A sister school of Baldwin Boys, this all-girls school follows the ICSE curriculum. A boarding school, it also offers computers and sports facilities including a swimming pool.

## Bangalore International School

*Geddalahalli, Hennur*
*Bagalur Road, Kothanur Post,*
*Bangalore 560077*
*Tel 2846 5059/5060*
*Open 8:30am to 3:30pm*

This school focusses on keeping the student-teacher ratio low. Bangalore

International offers the IGSCE syllabus and plans to introduce the ICSE curriculum. Children are taken in from the age of three. This is a co-ed school with 160 students and it offers a number of sports and extra curricular activities to its pupils.

## Bishop Cotton Boys School

*1 St. Mark's Road,*
*Bangalore 560001*
*Tel 2221 3835/3608*
*Open 8:30am to 3:30pm*

Bishop Cotton Boys has consistently been rated one of the top schools in India. This all-boys school offers both the ICSE as well as the ISC syllabus. It has large playing grounds and a swimming pool. It recently acquired a huge, state-of-the-art auditorium. The school has turned out some of the best athletes and scholars in the city.

Boarding facilities are available. The school is very large with over 5,000 children and more than 60 students to a class.

## Bishop Cotton Girls School

*71 St. Mark's Road,*
*Bangalore 560001*
*Tel 2221 0268, 2227 9660*
*Open 8:30am to 3:30pm*

A sister concern of Bishop Cotton Boys, this all-girls school offers the ICSE and ISC curriculum. The school strength is around 3,000 students and with 60 students to a class. The school has playgrounds, an auditorium and computer facilities.

## Clarence High School

*Richards Town,*
*Bangalore 560005*
*Tel 2547 0868*
*Open 8:35am to 3:45pm*

A traditional ICSE and ISC school, Clarence prides itself on its students' academic performance. A co-educational establishment, Clarence focuses on imparting Christian religious instruction to pupils, which is compulsory. The school has playing fields and offers extracurricular activities like music to students.

## Frank Anthony Public School

*13 Cambridge Road, Ulsoor,*
*Bangalore 560008*
*Tel 2554 0973*
*Open 8:30am to 3pm*

Frank Anthony's has been in the news for its good academic and sports records. It offers both the ICSE and ISC syllabus and has around 2,500 students and 100 teachers. Facilities include an auditorium, playing fields and computers.

## Mallya Aditi International School

*PO Box 6427 Yehalanka,*
*Opp. Escort Factory, Bangalore 560064*
*Tel 2846 2506/2508*
*Open: 8:30am to 3pm*

This 25-year old school prides itself on its student friendly attitude. There are around 490 students and the class strength is approximately 35. The school offers both the IGSCE as well as the ICSE and ISC curriculum. Mallya Aditi encourages its pupils to take part in extracurricular activities.

## National Academy For Learning

*3rd Cross, III Stage, III Block,*
*Basaveshwaranagar, Bangalore 560079*
*Tel 2323 9281*
*Open 8:30am to 3:30pm. Closed on Saturday.*

This school offers the IGCSE, CBSE and ICSE curriculum. NAFL is aimed at children who have had to shift schools regularly due to their parents' transfers. With only 300 students, the teacher-student ratio is low. Focus is on all round development rather than just academics.

## National Public School

*12th A Main, HAL II Stage,*
*Bangalore 560008*
*Tel 2528 0611*
*Branches Rajajinagar, 2320 5016;*
*Koramangala, 2570 5171*
*Open 8:30am to 3pm*

This co-educational school offers the CBSE syllabus and is focussed on churning out toppers. There are around 1,500 students and 100 teachers. Facilities include a playground, computers, a gym and auditorium.

## Prakriya Green Wisdom School

*70 Chikkanayakanahalli Road, Off Doddakanelli, Sarjapur Road,*
*Bangalore 560035*
*Tel 2333 3001*
*Open 8:30pm to 3:45pm*

This school believes in imparting education within a community setting. The ICSE syllabus is followed through primary, middle and high school. Along with a strong academic education, the school focusses on experiential learning and expression of creativity. Along with academic training, physical exercise, dance, karate and music lessons are also incorporated into the syllabus. Special emphasis is given to computer and environmental education. Mock apprenticeships and 'earn while you learn' projects are organised under the guidance of teachers. Prakriya has a separate nursery school in Koramangala.

## Shishu Griha Montessori and High School

*3 New Thippasandra, HAL III Stage,*
*Bangalore 560075*
*Tel 2521 3940/3941*
*Open 8:30am to 3:30pm*

This school offers the ICSE syllabus. There are over 800 students and 55 teachers and the focus is on teaching according to the Montessori method as far as possible. The school's facilities include a playground, computers, basketball and volleyball courts as well as other extra curricular activities. Shishu Griha also has a preschool with a large play area.

## Sophia's High School

*70 Palace Road, Bangalore 560001*
*Tel 2226 6825*
*Open 8am to 3:15pm*

This is probably Bangalore's best known girls school. Run by Catholic nuns, the school follows the ICSE syllabus. The school is huge with a strength of 3,000 students and each class has over 60 children. The school offers extracurricular activities such as sport, theatre and music.

## St. Joseph's Boys High School

*PB 25003 Museum Road,*
*Bangalore 560025*
*Tel 2221 4416*
*Open 8:30am to 3:30pm*

This all-boys school is one of Bangalore's oldest and is known for its all rounders who also turn in good academic performances. St. Joseph's (which starts at the I Standard) also has a history of turning out top-notch sportsmen, like its historic rival – Bishop Cotton Boys. The school has a good swimming pool and big play grounds for around 1,200 students and 30 teachers. The school offers the ICSE syllabus and plans to introduce the ISC curriculum soon.

## The International School, Bangalore

*NAFL Valley, Whitefield-Sarjapur Road,*
*Bangalore 562125*
*Tel 782 2393/2550*
*Open 8:30am to 3:30pm*

This sprawling school set on 36 acres of landscaped gardens has around 600 students. Its facilities include a 25-metre swimming pool, a 400-metre athletic track, separate cricket and soccer playing fields, a billiards room and basketball courts. TISB offers three syllabi – the ICSE, the International Baccalaureate and the IGCSE. Boarding facilities are available.

## The Valley School

*17th Km, Kanakapura Road,*
*Tataguni Post, Bangalore 560062*
*Tel 2843 5240/5241*
*Open 9am to 3pm*

The school offers the ICSE and ISC curriculum and follows the precepts of philosopher, J Krishnamurthi. Set on 100 acres of woodland, the school has 330 students and 50 teachers. The art village and science centre are particularly good. The school offers boarding facilities and is strictly vegetarian.

## Vidyaniketan School

*30 Kempapura, Hebbal,*
*Bangalore 560024*
*Tel 3233 1531, 2353 1338*
*Open 8am to 3:10pm*

This school offers the ICSE syllabus and is focused on keeping its student-teacher ratio low. Each class has around 35 students and the total school strength is less than a thousand. The school offers a range of facilities, has a large playground, a well stocked library and computers.

Trumpeter Denzil Bentley plays for a nine member band, the Jazz Revival in Bangalore.

**The Arts**

Karnataka boasts a rich veena tradition, nurtured since the time of the royal Wodeyars. Considered the original veena, the Mysore Veena holds a prominent place in Carnatic music. Upholding the tradition of an illustrious line of veena maestros including the late Doraiswamy Iyengar, Veena Seshanna and RK Suryanarayana are artistes like Dr. Suma Sudhindra who also runs a school.

A premier fine arts institution, Chitrakala Parishath works to revive dying art forms like puppetry and traditional Mysore paintings. The Parishath houses five art galleries that showcase contemporary and traditional art. Workshops and artist camps are held here as well.

The Double Helix by Yusuf Arakkal stands on MG Road.

Karnataka has a rich history of art and culture and its many indigenous forms are popular even today. Interestingly, there is almost nothing in common between art in Bangalore and art in Karnataka! Fusion thrives in Bangalore while it's folk art for the rest of the state. A resident of Bangalore is likely to know more about Kathak or Kalaripayettu than Yakshagana, Karnataka's tradition of dance dramas! Similarly, jazz bands and chamber music strike more chords than Kunita.

# The Arts

Bangalore has woken up to a vibrant cultural scenario. On any given weekend, there are new releases in the movie halls, plays, dances, art exhibitions, book signings, concerts or just groups of people getting together to jam. This section is devoted to the arts and artists. Art galleries, music schools, dance schools and theatre groups are described briefly. The section on Entertainment carries details about venues and movie theatres.

Yusuf Arakkal

# Painting & Sculpture

Contemporary art is the rage all over the country and Bangalore is no different. There are a number of art galleries here and a large number of local artists that keep them supplied. The few state-run galleries like the Venkatappa Art Gallery and those at the art school Karnataka Chitrakala Parishath are a boon to the young, impoverished artist. Even some private galleries have benevolent sponsors. From simple etchings to grandly framed originals, copies of great masters and fine works of sculpture are available in the city. There are many Bangalore-based artists that are appreciated in wider circles like the late KK Hebbar, Yusuf Arakkal, Sheela Gowda, JMS Mani, SG Vasudev, Balan Nambiar,

John Devraj and Sudesh Mahan.

Yusuf Arakkal acquired his diploma at the city's premier fine arts institute, Karnataka Chitrakala Parishath. Today, his work has won him not just the National Award but international acclaim as well. Hailed as the artistic voice for the unsung, his concern for social issues is evident in his work. Arakkal is also an accomplished sculptor and his experiments with texture extend to this medium as well. Yusuf Arakkal won the silver medal at the prestigious Florence International Biennale, 2003.

Winner of the 1998 Sotheby award, Sheela Gowda studied painting at the Ken School of Art. Her work has evolved from

painting to sculptural works to installations using varied materials like cow dung, kumkum, thread and needles and most recently, incense.

Celebrated sculptor and researcher Balan Nambiar is equally well known for his enamel paintings. Some of this National Award winner's sculptures have gone as public art and may be seen at major intersections in the city.

SG Vasudev, another National Award winner, studied in Chennai. While there, he also went on to set up the Cholamandalam Art Village, a co-operative society that generated income through the arts. Vasudev works with oils on canvas, murals, copper reliefs and tapestry.

Winner of Karnataka Lalith Kala Akademi Award, JMS Mani's paintings have a strong Dravidian theme. Once a

*Immortal Stranger* by Sudesh Mahan

student of the Ken School of Art, he now heads it. Mani's famous 'Badami People Series' is perhaps the most representative of his work, with a rural ambience portrayed in bright colours.

Sudesh Mahan is counted among the city's upcoming painters. Having dabbled in theatre, sculpture and film, Mangalore born Mahan is best known for his paintings, characterised by energetic lines, stimulating colours and fluid forms.

John Devraj hides his social worker persona under a sculptor's mantle. He is known for his 'Brown Aesthetics' movement to 'rid' society of 'Western influences'. One of his important contributions to Bangalore has been his active support for the Born Free School in Bangalore, an association that he has symbolised with his famous sculpture of a girl with her arms open wide to the sky.

SG Vasudev

# Karnataka Chitrakala Parishath

An exhibition at CKP

Karnataka Chitrakala Parishath is an eclectic art complex and one of Karnataka's premier art institutes. Set in a sprawling campus in Bangalore, Chitrakala Parishath has become a cultural landmark in the city and plays an active role in the promotion of various art forms.

Established in 1960, the Parishath is home to five permanent galleries and is a veritable storehouse of traditional as well as contemporary paintings. Exhibitions of well known artists from around the world are frequently held here. There is a strong emphasis on providing space for the display of contemporary Indian art.

Of the many galleries, the Roerich Gallery holds pride of place. Dr. Svetoslav Roerich, one of the centre's benefactors, donated a sizeable collection of his paintings to the Parishath, now housed in two exclusive floors. The works of graphic artist, Dr. Krishna Reddy and renowned painter SS Kukke also feature among the Parishath's permanent displays.

A big draw is the Chitra Santhe, an art bazaar replete with painters, cartoonists and art connoisseurs. This is an annual event with more than 600 artists from around the country converging at the Parishath to participate in the day-long fair. The bazaar spills over into the streets and showcases affordable art.

The open-air theatre at the Parishath hosts performing arts like folk dance and street theatre. A fully equipped graphic workshop and a sculpture studio are housed here as well. The Parishath also organises artist camps and workshops on a regular basis. It works with organisations like UNESCO to provide patronage to traditional forms of art in Karnataka. It is actively involved in preserving indigenous art forms like leather puppetry.

Chitrakala Parishath is known for its College of Fine Arts. Established in 1964, it is rated among the best art institutes in the country. Bachelor programmes in Fine Arts are offered in painting, sculpture, art history and print-making.
**Web** www.chitrakalaparishath.org

Crimson has the distinction of being the oldest surviving gallery in the city – it's been around since 1989. The gallery's monsoon sale held in July throws up some good work from new artists at attractive prices. Crimson hosts almost eight exhibitions a year and among the artists who have exhibited here are Anwar Khan and Yusuf Arakkal.

## Fluid Space
*S 105 Manipal Centre, Dickenson Road, Bangalore 560042*
**Tel** *2509 2305*
**Open** *11am to 6pm*
**Web** *www.fluidspace.org*

Fluid Space tries to go beyond the common perception of art as painting or sculpture, trying instead for work that is cross-cultural and inter-disciplinary. It has invited corporate sponsors and currently the ING Vysya group is paying the bill for a year so that upcoming artists can exhibit their work without financial angst. Big names as well as young, often sidelined artists show here. The gallery is tastefully done up in steel and glass, the perfect setting for exhibits.

## Gallery Sumukha
*24/10 BTS Depot Road, Wilson Garden, Bangalore 560027*
**Tel** *2229 2230*
**Open** *10am to 6pm. Closed on Sunday.*
**Web** *www.sumukha.com*

This gallery offers 2,500sqft of space to exhibit paintings, sculpture and installations as well as conduct workshops or discussions. Built like a warehouse, it features a mezzanine floor for displaying smaller works. There are numerous options within the spacious interiors and artists can use the space in their own distinctive fashion. The focus is, again, contemporary Indian art; SG Vasudev, Akbar Padamsee and Ajit Dubey have exhibited here.

## gallery g
*38 Maini Sadan, 7th Cross, Lavelle Road, Bangalore 560001*
**Tel** *2221 9275*
**Open** *11am to 7pm. Closed on Sunday except during exhibitions.*
**Web** *www.gallerygbangalore.com*

artmantram

# bangalore
# international
# art festival

In a city that has produced some great artists, here's a festival that will celebrate the vibrant culture of art - The Bangalore International Art Festival. This annual event - to be held every October - will be a potpourri of art and culture, with art camps, art seminars, art exhibitions, art tours, dance, pottery, film festivals and fashion shows. The festival will be the stage where art comes alive. And becomes an inevitable part of everyday life.

**Mantram Art Foundation Bangalore**
Phone: 080-57635602, 25263268
Telefax: 080-22081033
Email:info@bangaloreartfest.net
**www.bangaloreartfest.net**

# Gallerie Sara Arakkal

Gallerie Sara Arakkal is situated in picturesque Brookefields on the outskirts of Bangalore. This sprawling gallery provides a space for artists from across the country, especially those from the south. The creation of art connoisseur Sara Arakkal, the gallery promotes young and fresh talent. Artists are aided through the entire process, from the creation of a portfolio to the exhibition itself. A division of Arts in Crafts, this gallery showcases contemporary Indian art. Affordability is an important focus here.

A collage of exhibits from well known Indian painters and sculptors are displayed across 1,500sqft. The aesthetic and minimalistic setting of the gallery complements the art displays. The works of eminent artists like Yusuf Arakkal, SG Vasudev, Laxma Goud, Balan Nambiar, Basuki Dasgupta, Anuradha Nalapat, Babu Namboodri, Jatin Das and Surekha have been featured here. Available at the gallery are limited editions of acclaimed paintings that have been reproduced in different media. Gallerie Sara Arakkal also houses an art museum and an exclusive art bookstore is in the pipeline. Exhibitions are held once in three months.

*156, 4th Main Road, BEML Layout*
*ITPL Road, Bangalore 560066*
**Tel** *5116 2622*
**Web** *www.artincrafts.com*

One of Bangalore's newest art galleries, this gallery showcases lesser known artists and relatively affordable art. It's not just paintings and sculptures that find their way here but antiques, handicrafts and furniture as well. The gallery is naturally lit and offers 1,800sqft of space, all centrally air-conditioned.

## Masters Gallery

*1209 100Ft. Road, Indiranagar,*
*HAL II Stage, Bangalore 560038*
**Tel** *2520 3535*
**Open** *9:30am to 9:30pm*
**Email** *masters-gallery@eth.net*

A fairly new gallery, Masters made plenty of news when it opened in January 2003 under the guidance of Swami Viswambhar Isaiah Streisand. Both original works and reproductions by Western artists are exhibited here. Masters also sells exquisite handcrafted wooden frames, imported from Europe and the US, in styles ranging from antique to contemporary. Also available is an excellent selection of mirror frames. Indian contemporary art may also find a forum here but upcoming artists may have to wait a while longer. Devotional art by PG Sharma (mainly images of Lord Krishna) is also available.

## Renaissance Gallery

*104 Westminster,*
*13 Cunningham Road,*
*Bangalore 560052*
**Tel** *2220 2232*
**Open** *10:30am to 7pm.*
*Closed on Sunday.*
**Email** *renaissancegallerie@hotmail.com*

Sudeep Roy, Milind Nayak and Suresh Jayaram are some of the leading artists who have exhibited here. The gallery is committed to showcasing at least one or two new artists every year. An average of six exhibitions are held per annum. Renaissance sells art in the range of Rs 1,500 to Rs 1,00,000.

## Time and Space

*55 Lavelle Road, Bangalore 560001*
**Tel** *2207 5163*
**Open** *11am to 6pm and 11am to 2:30pm*
*on Saturday. Closed on Sunday.*
**Email** *timeandspace@lycos.com*

Time and Space opened at its present address, around the corner from the old one, in August 2003. Around six exhibitions are held each year featuring both upcoming artists and seasoned professionals in contemporary art. Dhiraj Chaudhury, Yuriko Lochan and Mohan Singh are few of the artists who have exhibited here. On display are also a few antiques. Founder Renu George is focussed on making art affordable and there are seldom very expensive pieces on sale here.

## Venkatappa Art Gallery

*Kasturba Road,*
*Bangalore 560001*
**Tel** *2286 4483*
**Open** *10am to 5pm. Closed on Monday.*

The government-owned Venkatappa Art Gallery is set in spacious grounds bordering Cubbon Park and you have to cross a moat to enter! The entire first floor of this spacious gallery is devoted to the paintings of the artist after whom it was named: K Venkatappa was a famous artist of the 20th century. He belonged to a family of court painters and in his time, received patronage from the Mysore royal family. Artists can hire the first floor for as little as Rs 300 per day, for a minimum of five days. Its fabulous location and low cost makes it ideal for student artists. On the first floor is the permanent exhibit of wood sculptures by Major Rajaram, in whose name a scholarship is offered for students of art. The second floor exhibits the work of the late KK Hebbar including some of his excellent line drawings.

# Svetoslav Roerich

Russian-born artist of international repute and Indophile, Svetoslav Roerich had a close relationship with Karnataka. This was his home for the last few decades of his life and he lived on a sprawling estate outside the city. He was a patron of the Karnataka Chitrakala Parishath (CKP) and donated many of his valuable paintings that hang in a permanent gallery in his honour.

Roerich was born on October 23rd, 1904. The second son of celebrated artist Nikolas Roerich, young Roerich displayed an exceptional talent for the arts at a young age. A student of architecture at Columbia University, New York and later Harvard, he soon found his calling in painting.

In the 20s, the whole family left the US for India. For young Roerich it was the beginning of a lifelong love affair with this country. He was exposed to traditional art forms of the east and he mastered the art of Indian miniatures and Tibetan icon paintings. The family eventually settled in the Kulu valley where they set up the Himalayan Research Institute.

An active supporter of the Indian Independence struggle, Svetoslav Roerich's paintings titled *Where mankind goes, Liberation, We are building prisons for ourselves*, reflect social concerns. He married Indian actress Devika Rani in 1945 and the couple settled in Bangalore where he forged a close association with the Chitrakala Parishath. The Roerich Institute of Fine Arts, also at the CKP, has been named after him and imparts training at the foundation level for students of fine arts.

Roerich Gallery at Chitrakala Parishath

*Courtesy: Karnataka Chitrakala Parishath*

The journey starts here

# Music

Pandit Basavaraj Rajguru

Pandit Mallikarjun Mansur

Pandit Bhimsen Joshi

Dr. Gangubai Hangal

Dharwad, a small town in northern Karnataka is considered the cradle of Hindustani music. Great singers like Bhimsen Joshi, Gangubai Hangal, Basavaraj Rajguru and Mallikarjun Mansur emerged from here.

Pandit Bhimsen Joshi, one of the renowned Hindustani vocalists today, hails from the town of Gadag, near Dharwad. A master in the Kirana Gharana, the octogenarian has endeared himself to the masses and continues to enjoy critical acclaim. Pandit Mallikarjun Mansur (1901-1992), another legendary singer from Dharwad, was known for his tremendous range of voice and a repertoire that encompassed the genres of khayal and bhajan. Born into a family of classical singers, Dr. Gangubai Hangal has been wooing audiences with her sonorous voice and purist renditions of traditional Hindustani music. With her roots in Hangal, a small village in north Karnataka, her illustrious singing career spans more than five decades. Pandit Basavaraj Mahantaswamy Rajguru (1917-1991) was another great exponent of Hindustani classical music from this region. Born in the village of Yeliwal, he was initiated into classical music from the tender age of seven. Pandit Kumara Gandharva (1924-1992) adds to the ensemble of classical singers from Dharwad. The child prodigy, who began performing at the age of ten, was best known for his experimentation with ragas and his unique style of rendition. He enjoyed a prolific career as a composer as well.

But in all other classical respects, Karnataka is a significant part of south India and shares its heritage of south Indian Carnatic music. There are schools at every corner in big towns and small, that offer voice and instrument training in the Carnatic style.

Further south in Bangalore, it's fusion that gives the city its unique musical identity. It's serious business with the likes of Dr. L Subramaniam who has collaborated with legends like Yehudi Menuhin and jazz greats like Stephane Grapelli, Joe Sample and Herbie Hancock. Local musicians of repute include Konarak Reddy, ace guitarist with a background in Western Classical and Hindustani music and Amit Heri, the face of jazz in India.

Bangalore's ease and comfort with Western music lies in its history as a Cantonment city where live bands were a permanent fixture on the social scene. Several musicians started their careers in Bangalore before moving to other parts of the country. Today's local rock and pop bands carry the legacy left behind by Bangalorean legends like Freddie Hitchcock, Eddie Saldanha aka Dizzy Sal, Hal and Eddy Greene. Weekend gigs feature local names like Thermal and a Quarter, Angeldust, Cryptic and Kryptos.

## MUSIC SCHOOLS

### Bangalore School Of Music
*32 Netaji Road, Frazer Town, Bangalore 560005*
*Tel 2548 4064/3409*
*Web www.bsm.org*

The Bangalore School of Music (BSM), started by Aruna Sunderlal, is a premier institution for the study of Western Classical music in Bangalore. The school offers courses in piano, violin and classical guitar among others, with around 300 students. The BSM, in collaboration with the Royal College of Music in Sweden, plans to conduct various exchange programmes for teachers and students. The school also provides Bangalore with an exciting concert schedule throughout the year, with as many as 20 concerts featuring both talented students as well as local and international artistes. Its collaboration with Indian musicians throws up the East West Music Encounter, held every two years.

### Guruskool
*1 Abishek Complex, 17th Cross, Sampige Road, Malleswaram, Bangalore 560003*
*Tel 2334 0309*
*Web www.guruskoolmusic.com*

Located on three acres of lush greenery on the outskirts of Bangalore, Guruskool was started by Gopal and Geeta Navale. Workshops, regular classes and crash courses are held here. With residential facilities, an amphitheatre, a rehearsal studio with instruments and a library on offer, artists from all over the world come to visit, stay and collaborate. The Navale couple are part of Esperanto, a world music band working towards music for global appeal. At Guruskool, they arrange teachers for any form of Indian Classical music, provide accommodation for students of music as well as arrange recordings and concerts.

### Karnataka College of Percussion
*15/1 Lakshminilaya, Kodandarampuram, Next to Corporation School, Bangalore 560003*
*Tel 2344 1515*
*Email ramamani50@hotmail.com*

Started by famous mridangam player TAS Mani and Ramamani, the Karnataka College of Percussion (KCP) has achieved significant international recognition. Its vibrant fusion ensemble, Tala Tarangini, has performed within India and abroad. The KCP uses only Carnatic percussion instruments like the mridangam, ghatam, kanjira and morsing and also incorporates konnakol, the art of uttering percussive syllables articulately, sometimes at impossible speeds. The sheer variety and complexity of their rhythmic structures have fascinated musicians from the West, especially those interested in jazz.

Several students are trained each year in the rigorous percussive disciplines of this tradition. The best make it to the troupe. As part of the training, periodic concerts are arranged to encourage talented youngsters.

### Konarak Reddy Music School
*58 St. Marks Road, Bangalore 560001*
*Tel 2558 5395*

Konarak Reddy is a leading guitarist, trained in Western Classical music, Hindustani music and jazz composition. The guitar is the exclusive focus of his music school. Lessons are offered in Western Classical, contemporary and jazz music genres. Students may choose between basic or advanced batches according to their level of comfort and proficiency with the instrument. Classes are open to those above the age of 12.

### Saraswati Sangeet Vidyalaya
*114 'Swarsatkar', Nehru Circle, Sheshadripuram, Bangalore 560020*
*Tel 2344 3900*

The Saraswati Sangeet Vidyalaya was started in 1931 by Pandit GV Bhave and Lakshmi G Bhave as a centre to impart quality training in both Carnatic and Hindustani music. Present guru Shyamala Bhave follows the ancient gurukul system of education. Students of the Hindustani tradition may learn the tabla, dholak, bansuri (flute), violin, harmonium, guitar and mandolin, among others. The Carnatic wing teaches veena, violin, flute, mridangam, ghatam, khanjira (percussion) and harmonium.

## MUSIC LIBRARY

### Ananya
*91/2, 4th Main, Malleswaram, Bangalore 560003*
*Tel 2344 0409*

Bangalore's unique music culture has finally thrown up a music library. Housed in Malleswaram, it boasts 5,000 hours of eclectic music including Iranian, West African and Egyptian music, but the accent is mainly on Indian Classical music including some rarely heard concerts dating back to the 1920s. You can also look up books, journals, dictionaries, and old manuscripts on music here. Ananya is actively involved in spreading awareness about Indian classical music. Carnatic music concerts by well known musicians are regularly organised at venues across the city. Ananya also conducts music programmes for school children.

# Dance

Karnataka and Bangalore share different sensibilities in the matter of dance. Yakshagana, the vibrant folk dance-drama performed in harvested paddy fields, sometimes all night, is unique to Karnataka. Bangalore, on the other hand has a metro approach to dance with many classical and other styles being practiced and performed here and even dance therapy hitting the headlines. The south Indian classical dance style, Bharatanatyam is a favourite and is taught in both living rooms and big schools across the city. Kalaripayettu, the martial art form of Kerala and the north Indian classical dance style Kathak, have made their mark on the city's cultural scene. Odissi came into the spotlight with the arrival of Nrityagram, the dance village on the outskirts of the city.

The Natya Institute of Kathak and Choreography (NKIC), established by Maya Rao, Kathak danseuse and choreographer, is widely known. Its Bachelors degree in choreography and post-graduate diplomas in Kathak and choreography, have found many

takers. Her daughter Madhu Natraj Heri's dance group, called Stem (Space, time, energy and movement) is one of Bangalore's contemporary dance groups blending Kathak, Kalaripayettu, Thaang Ta and even Yoga. A professional performing unit, it is also a training centre for contemporary dance.

The Attakkalari Centre for Movement Arts (Acma) was formed in 1992, in Bangalore. Artists from different disciplines came together to develop a 'South Asian' dance idiom. Attakkalari is also engaged in enquiries in the fields of pictorial, plastic and electronic arts, stagecraft and theoretical discourses on performance.

Treading off the beaten path is teacher, therapist, choreographer Tripura Kashyap who has introduced Dance Movement Therapy (DMT). A trained classical dancer and martial arts expert, she founded the Apoorva Dance Theatre. Her DMT is based on Indian folk and classical dance and is accepted as a non-medical treatment for a range of disabilities, from mental retardation to visual and aural impairments.

Stem Dance Theatre

The Arts

Dansuese Surupa Sen, Artistic Director of Nrityagram

she teaches Bharatanatyam to a select group of young dancers.

## Stem Dance Theatre

*62, 4th Main, 18th Cross,*
*Malleswaram, Bangalore 560055*
**Tel** *2334 8645*
**Web** *www.stemdance.org*

Stem (space, time, energy and movement) is a contemporary dance group, fusing traditional dance forms with newer ones. The dancers here are trained in modern dance techniques, Yoga, classical dance, martial arts and mime. Founded by dancer and choreographer Madhu Nataraj Heri, the group believes in experimentation and creating a vocabulary for contemporary Indian dance. Their performances have been showcased in India as well as abroad.

## Sri Padmavati Kala Niketan

*65 Bhargavi, Charles Campbell*
*Road, Cox Town, Bangalore 560005*
**Tel** *2548 5773, 2337 9968*

One of the few schools in Bangalore to teach Kuchipudi, the classical dance from Andhra Pradesh, Kala Niketan is run by Manju Bhargavi, an award winning dancer. Plans are underway to set up a Kuchipudi Research Centre at the school. The school has organised two dance festivals in Bangalore.

# Nrityagram

Odissi dancer Protima Gauri Bedi started Nrityagram in 1989 as an experiment to preserve and propagate the seven Indian classical dance forms and two martial art forms. Styled after the ancient gurukul system, Nrityagram was envisaged as a residential school where only the most committed artists would engage in the long-term study of classical dance and its allied subjects – choreography, music, mythology, philosophy and painting.

Today, Nrityagram continues to be a one-of-its-kind venture and an important dance school. Its founder is no more, lost in a tragic Himalayan avalanche, but under managing trustee Lynne Fernandes and Artistic Director Surupa Sen, the school continues to flourish. The Nrityagram dance ensemble has received rave reviews from around the globe.

The dance village aims to offer a separate gurukul for each classical dance form, at present the Bharatanatyam and

Odissi ones are functioning. It has recently extended its services by launching a series of classes within the city. There are day scholar programmes and an outreach programme that takes classical dances to the villages nearby.

Nrityagram's biggest attraction is undoubtedly its annual Vasantahabba or Spring Festival. Celebrated on the first Saturday in February to mark the traditional arrival of spring, Vasantahabba is a nightlong musical and dance extravaganza flagged off by the rhythmic sounds of drums of the Dollu Kunita dancers. Starting with an audience of 3,000 in 1990 to over 40,000 now, the outdoor festival draws a mixed audience, from villagers to hip youngsters, software engineers to serious musicians, tourists and families.

*Hessaraghatta, Bangalore 560088*
**Tel** *2846 6313/6314* **Web** *www.nrityagram.org*

## Prasiddha Foundation

*33 Palace Orchard Apartments,*
*III Floor, 9th Main Road,*
*RMV Extension, Bangalore 560080*
**Tel** *2361 5055/3073*

Bharatanatyam and Kuchipudi dancer Pratibha Prahlad heads the Prasiddha foundation. The school offers regular classes in Bharatanatyam and organises workshops and interactive sessions with leading dance gurus and other artists. The objective of the cultural foundation is also to encourage new artists by giving them a platform to showcase their

art. The foundation organises three festivals of music and dance every year – Sharad Vaibhava is a three-day dance festival held in Bangalore, Eka-Aneka is an all night dance festival held at a national level and Vijayotsav is a cultural programme held in Hampi every year.

## Sanchari

*458 HMT Layout, Anand Nagar,*
*Bangalore 560024*
**Tel** *2333 3993*

Sanchari is run by Bharatanatyam dancer, Vani Ganapathy. Trained under Guru Kalyana Sundaram in Bombay,

A theatre festival in the city

A Black Coffee theatre workshop in progress

# Theatre

The origins of Kannada theatre go back over a century. Probably the best known of the earlier theatre groups is the Gubbi Theatre, started by Gubbi Veeranna in the late 19th century. Many legendary theatre personalities like Dr. Rajkumar, BV Karanth, Varadachar and GV Iyer cut their teeth with Gubbi Theatre.

In the early 20th century, a group called the Amateur Dramatic Association (ADA) was set up. Deviating from traditional forms of theatre, the ADA pioneered and popularised contemporary theatre instead. It is believed that even Nobel Laureate Rabindranath Tagore attended their performances. Theatre members included TP Kailasam and Sriranga who are now accorded the status of legends in Kannada theatre. This legacy is being kept alive with groups like Ranga Sampadha, Vedike, Samudaya and Abhinaya Taranga. Rangayana, the Karnataka government's theatre repertory in Mysore and Ninasam in Shimoga district are other important centres for theatre in Karnataka.

The seventies were the period of renaissance for Kannada theatre. Many great artistes were born and plays ranging from Greek tragedies to absurdist theatre rang out to packed houses.

English theatre more than holds its own with the cosmopolitan Bangalorean as its audience. Small and intense productions, big budget musicals, even experimental theatre is performed here and theatre festivals

keep actors busy. Playwrights like Girish Karnad and more recently Mahesh Dattani have provided a much needed momentum with original scripts to stage.

Set to provide a culture boost to the city is Ranga Shankara, the brainchild of Arundhati Nag and the late actor Shankar Nag. Readying to open in 2004, it aims to be more than just an amphitheatre. Besides staging plays six days a week, Ranga Shankara is also committed to holding dance, music and folk art festivals. Workshops on acting, writing, lighting, sound, mime and theatre appreciation will also be conducted here. Art and theatre buffs will find plenty to do from hanging out at the café to browsing through the bookstore and art gallery.

The most popular performance venues are Chowdiah Hall and Ravindra Kalakshetra. Built to commemorate the birth centenary of Rabindranath Tagore, the Ravindra Kalakshetra on JC Road is a cultural hub that also houses the offices of the Kannada and Culture ministry. It can seat about 1,500 people and most Kannada plays are staged here. Big budget performances favour the Chowdiah Memorial Hall, named after the famous violinist, T Chowdiah. Built in the shape of a violin, it's known for its acoustics and can seat over 2,000 people. ADA Theatre on JC Road, Alliance Francaise and HN Kalamandira in Jayanagar are other cultural centres in the city.

## THEATRE GROUPS

### Artists Repertory Theatre
*Tel 2847 5373*
*Email theart@vsnl.com*

The Artist's Repertory Theatre (ART) is one of Bangalore's most experienced theatre groups with almost 40 productions to its name. Jagadish and Arundathi Raja, founders of ART, are ranked among the pioneers of English theatre in Bangalore. ART has partnered with the British Council and also works with Samuel French (producer of plays) as his Indian agent. The group is Bangalore's representative at the Trinity College for Drama and Speech. The Questor's Theatre in London played host to ART in 1998 in the first ever English performance by an Indian theatre company there. ART has produced Shakespeare's *A Midsummer Night's Dream*, PG Wodehouse's *Wilmot in Hollywood*, as well as numerous other adaptations.

The youth wing, ART Youth, offers school and college students theatre workshops and drama training.

### Bangalore Little Theatre
*Tel 2223 6890*

The oldest English theatre group in the city, the Bangalore Little Theatre (BLT) has been around since 1960. Scott and Margaret Tod started it along with a handful of other expatriates and Bangaloreans and their first production was a reading of Oscar Wilde's *The Importance of Being Earnest*, followed by Moliere's *The Prodigious Snob*. In 1962, BLT produced its first Indian play in English, an original adaptation of

Professor B Chandrasekhara's *Mrichakatika*. Since then, BLT has produced Indian plays, translations, adaptations and original scripts. The Summer Project on Theatre (SPOT) was started in the mid-1970s, and is a regular training event. Their annual Festival of Short Plays (SHORTS) is held in October.

### Black Coffee
*Tel 2553 4021*
*Email blackcoffee@rediffmail.com*

The founder of Black Coffee, Preetam Koilpillai is a major force in Bangalore's theatre and music circuit. He is busy through the year with old and new productions. Martin Sherman's *Bent*, Irvine Welsh's *Filth*, Bill Manhoff's *The Owl and the Pussycat*, Edward Albee's *Zoo Story* and Yasmin Reza's *Art* have been some of the group's hugely popular productions. Black Coffee's performances are almost always staged in intimate spaces providing a heightened interaction between actors and the audience. 2004 saw Black Coffee showcase original and unstaged scripts for Bangalore's theatre goers.

### The Script
*Tel 2668 0628*
*Web www.theatrecapital.com*

Playback theatre has a select audience in urban Bangalore. In a playback performance, actors react to responses from the audience spontaneously. Monitored by the International Playback Theatre Network (IPTN), Playback Theatre is a worldwide movement prevalent in 30 countries. In India, Playback theatre is propagated

Naseeruddin Shah in a play staged at Chowdiah Memorial Hall.

# Ninasam

KV Subbanna

boasts a publishing house, Akshara Prakashana, a full-fledged auditorium with a seating capacity of 750, a film society, a residential drama school, the Ninasam Theatre Institute and a theatre troupe called Ninasam Tirugata. Film appreciation courses, four productions each season – one Indian, one international, one Kannada and one children's play, Ninasam has done much to promote theatre and films in rural areas.

Accolades came after decades with the Ramon

Magsaysay Award for KV Subbanna and financing from the Ford Foundation to promote theatre and film culture in rural areas. For the villagers of Heggodu, Ray, Kurosawa, Bergman, Brecht and Chinua Achebe are familiar names thanks to a cultural revolution called Ninasam that has successfully bridged the gap between urban and rural, elitist and commoner.

*Heggodu, Shimoga* **Tel** *08183-265 646*

Yakshagana has for long been the traditional folk form in Heggodu village, Shimoga district. In 1949, Ninasam, an acronym for Nilakanteshwara Natya Seva Sangha was started by KV Subbanna and his friends. Moving beyond tradition, the idea was to provide a forum to stage modern plays. Passionate about theatre, films and literature, Subbanna adapted some of the best known Western plays for Heggodu's audience.

In the last five decades, Ninasam has grown from its beginnings in a thatched hut into a multi-faceted cultural organisation. Today, Ninasam

by a Bangalore-based group, The Script and is licensed to train people in this genre. They hold monthly workshops for people of in the age group of 14 to 80 years.

## Vedike
**Tel** *2672 4373*
**Email** *vedike@hotmail.com*

Vedike is an amateur theatre group committed to Kannada theatre. Their repertoire stretches from light comedies like *Maduve Maduve* to serious Shakespearean tragedy. They encourage crossover productions as well. For example, their play *Bhairavi* has a healthy dose of Bharatanatyam. Formed in 1983 by well-known actor and director CR Simha and his wife Sharada Simha, some of their productions include *Typical TP Kailasam, Meese Bandooru, Karna, Rasarishi,* and *Bhairavi.* The group usually performs on first and third Saturdays and the venue is the HN Kalakshetra in Jayanagar's National College campus.

A Kannada play in progress at Ravindra Kalakshetra

Advertising
Branding
Below The Line
Direct Marketing
Strategy Formulation
Event Management
Public Relations
Creatives
Media Buying - India and Overseas

PR Campaigns | Press Conference | Media Familiarisation Tours | House Magazines

699  1st Floor  7th Main  HAL-2nd Stage  Indiranagar  Bangalore 560 038  India
Tel: +91 80 51152102 - 104  Fax: +91 80 51152106  Email: starkblr@starkgroup.net

■ Bangalore ■ Chennai ■ Kochi ■ Trivandrum ■ Dubai ■ www.starkgroup.net    S T A R K

# Film

Dr. Rajkumar

MS Sathyu

Girish Kasaravalli

The birth of the Kannada film industry is traced to the year 1934 when the first movie *Sati Sulochana* was released. The Kannada film scene is well established with many greats like Nagathihalli Chandrashekhar, Girish Kasaravalli, TS Nagabharana and MS Sathyu. Films like Kasaravalli's *Dweepa*, *Ghata Shraddha*, Chandrashekhar's *America, America*, Nagabharana's *Singaravva* and Kavita Lankesh's *Deveeri* have won critical

acclaim with numerous state and national awards. An all-time great in Kannada film history is Puttanna Kanagal, credited with making a string of memorable films during the sixties and seventies like *Bellimoda, Gejje Pooje* and *Nagara Havu*.

The best known face in Kannada cinema is matinee idol and living legend, Dr. Rajkumar, who has acted in over 200 films since his debut in *Bedara Kannappa* in 1954. He is a recipient of the Dada Saheb Phalke and Padma Bhushan awards and enjoys a massive fan following throughout Karnataka. The actor-brothers Ananth Nag and the late Shankar Nag also enjoyed prolific careers in the Kannada film industry. Shankar Nag, a successful actor and producer, was equally known for his directorial ventures including *Accident*, the television series *Malgudi Days* and other commercial successes like *Ondu Muthina Kathe*. Anant Nag is a household name with over three decades in the film industry. He has acted in runaway hits like *Ganeshana Maduve, Hamsa Geethe, Beladingala Bale* as well as critically acclaimed films like *Ankur* and *Stumped*.

Bangalore's multilingual profile is best reflected in its cinema options – there is at any point in time, at least one Hindi, Tamil, Telugu and English film running in its many theatres.

In recent years there has been an effort towards making English films and cinema is finally beginning to speak the language of the contemporary Bangalorean. The recent National Award winning film *Stumble*, directed by Prakash Belawadi, explored the insecurities brought on by the IT slump. An extremely low-budget film called *20-Plus*, by three young Bangloreans, *Freaky Chakra*, the work of six young ad filmmakers and *Mango Souffle*, playwright Mahesh Dattani's debut as filmmaker, seem to mark the beginning of a new genre of films.

## Bangalore's Film Societies

From Russian masterpieces to off beat Indian classics, Bangalore's movie buffs are treated to a rare variety of films. The city's many film societies showcase the best of world cinema. Films cutting across various countries, genres and times find their way into the auditoriums of the Bangalore Film Club, Suchitra Film Society and Collective Chaos. These clubs are popular with a diverse group of members, from serious filmmakers to students, the equaliser being a love for meaningful cinema.

The Bangalore Film Society, set up in 1977 promotes aesthetic cinema. Films are screened and then discussed, encouraging viewers to understand the medium of cinema. The society hosts biennial film festivals and regular screenings of a spate of international films, from Iranian to German, are held here.

The Suchitra Film Society views cinema as a social catalyst. Dating back to 1971, the society promotes film appreciation and holds courses in the same. Monthly screenings of a few handpicked Indian and foreign films are held for members and greats like Pedro Almodovar and Laurence Von Daniken feature regularly on the itinerary. Suchitra also has a film club for children. Weekend screenings of regional cinema is open to public.

The youngest film club in the city Collective Chaos is a non-profit forum of young filmmakers and enthusiasts. Spreading aesthetic cinema consciousness, the group has brought a series of award winning documentaries like *Bowling For Columbine* to Bangalore's audiences. With 300 members in its fold, Collective Chaos plans to open its own studio and bring out an e-zine for film lovers.

*Bangalore Film Society* **Tel** *2549 2781*
*Suchitra Film Society* **Tel** *2671 1785*
*Collective Chaos* **Tel** *2520 3932*

Feel free to share your opinions, your suggestions
and other inputs regarding this book. Simply email your
feedback to response@starkworld.net

Stark World, Infinitum Publishing Pvt. Ltd, 173, 9th Cross, Indiranagar 1st Stage, Bangalore - 560038. Tel: 91-80-51255036

# Literature

Mahesh Dattani

**B**oth Kannada and English literature find expression in Bangalore as some of the big writers live here. Story readings, book releases and poetry workshops are regularly held at the city's many bookshops. Kuvempu, Shivarama Karanth, TP Kailasam, Prof. UR Ananthamurthy, Girish Karnad, Shashi Deshpande and Kamala Markandeya are the backbone of the literary scene. But there is plenty of new talent that has done Bangalore proud. Ramachandra Guha, Anita Nair and Mahesh Dattani are some of the more famous names, recognised across the country.

Some of the writers who have passed on include Kuvempu, DR Bendre, Shivarama Karanth, P Lankesh and Gopalakrishna Adiga.

No piece on Indian literature would be complete without a tribute to one of the first Indians writing in English, RK Narayan. Raja Rao is another writer, whose *Kanthapura* is set in Mysore district and the language evokes colloquial sounds and mannerisms. Stalwart of post-Independence Indian writing, UR Ananthamurthy was deeply influenced by the Left. His best-known work is *Samskara*, written in Kannada and translated into English by AK Ramanujam. He has also written several volumes of short stories, literary criticisms and the novels *Awasthe* and *Surya Nambudire*.

Ramachandra Guha's *A Corner of a Foreign Field* has won rave reviews. Guha lives in Bangalore and has authored a number of essays and books on the environmental movement and

Ramachandra Guha

his other passion, cricket. He is rated as one of the best non-fiction writers the country has ever produced. Sahitya Akademi winner Shashi Deshpande is another Bangalorean. Deshpande is attuned to women's issues and her characters, usually women, seek to explore themselves more

Shashi Deshpande

deeply, shorn of roles as mother or wife. *That Long Silence*, *Matter of Time* and *That Binding Vine* are some of her popular novels. Anita Nair, who dabbled in journalism and advertising turned to writing fiction. Her works include *The Better Man*, *Ladies Coupe* and *Malabar Mind* and have been translated into twenty languages.

Anita Nair

# Doyens of Kannada Literature

**T**he Jnanpith award is the highest literary award in India, given for the best creative writing in Indian languages. Karnataka has the proud distinction of being home to seven of these awardees.

**Kuppalli Venkatappa Puttappa** or Kuvempu is the grand old man of Kannada literature. Hailed as the greatest Kannada poet of the 20th century, he was awarded the Jnanpith award in 1967 for his magnum opus *Sri Ramayana Darshanam*. A prolific writer, his works include the famous debut novel, *Kanooru Heggadathi* (The Mistress of the House of Kanoor) and an equally famous second novel *Malegalalli Madulagalu* (A Bride Among the Hills).

**Dattatreya Ramachandra Bendre** was the second Kannadiga to be awarded the Jnanpith award, in 1973 for *Nakutanti*. Bendre's poems have been hard hitting with his *Narabali* (Human Sacrifice) even leading to

imprisonment. His style is quite unsurpassed with the use of traditional poetic elements like vachanas and kirthanas, imagery and colloquialisms. *Nada Lila* (The Play of Sounds) is perhaps the most remarkable of his poems and displays his reformatory zeal mingled with a strong sense of patriotism.

**Dr. Kota Shivarama Karanth** was awarded the Jnanpith in 1977 for *Mukajjiya Kanasugalu*. Inspired by Mahatma Gandhi, Karanth also took part in the country's

freedom struggle. A multifaceted writer, his expertise extended to areas like environmental studies, lexicography and the folk art of Yakshagana. *Marali Mannige* (Back to the Soil) is one of his best known works.

The next Jnanpith award for a Kannada writer came in 1983 for **Masti Venkatesha Iyengar**. Poet, dramatist and critic, he is regarded as the father of Kannada short story. His first published work *Kelavu*

*Sanna Kathegalu* (A Few Short Stories) is a noted work in the history of modern Kannada short stories. *Subbanna* based on the life of a musician has been translated into several Indian and foreign languages.

# The Storyteller from Mysore

Literary genius, celebrated author, architect of Malgudi, friend of Graham Greene, RK Narayan set the tone for what is today known as 'Indian Writing in English'. Narayan held India under a literary spell for more than six decades with scores of novels, essays, short stories, travelogues and a biography. Author of such memorable books like, *Malgudi Days*, *The Guide* and *The English Teacher*, Narayan's prolific writing career began in 1935 with the much loved novel *Swami and Friends* and

continued over the next five decades. RK Narayan was honoured by the Indian government with a Padma Vibhushan and by the Royal Society of Literature with the AC Benson award. He was also nominated to the Rajya Sabha for his remarkable contributions to world literature.

Born in 1906 into a middle class Brahmin family, Narayan graduated from Maharaja's College in Mysore. He turned away from the more 'respectable' jobs of schoolmaster and railway officer and instead chose to be a writer. Success eluded him until the manuscript of his first novel *Swami and Friends* fell into the hands of novelist Graham Greene who had it published in 1935. Later he would be hailed as one of the finest writers by renowned peers like EM Forster and Somerset Maugham. Graham Greene would become his close friend and declare that Malgudi seemed 'more familiar than England's Battersea or Euston Road'.

Considered to be one of India's greatest storytellers, Narayan wrote equally delightful essays and colourful vignettes about everyday life, laced with his characteristic brand of humour. He wrote about any sundry subject that caught his fancy – umbrellas, cats, south Indian coffee, the caste system, cultural ambiguities and so on. Shorn of political rhetoric, dark violence or belaboured profundity, Narayan wrote about a world he knew best – a semi-urban British colony trying to break into the New World, and later, an independent

India grappling with its new identity.

Writing from his serene home in Yadavgiri, in the quiet city of Mysore, his literary genius transcended geographical boundaries. Yet, it was Mysore that stoked the writer's imagination and canonised him as the 'Storyteller from Mysore'. Narayan described it as a place "with beautiful sunsets, colourful skies, dark mountains edged with lightning, canopies of Gulmohur trees and unexplored caves". He also wrote a travelogue on Mysore, *The Emerald Route*. Bewildered by the English language as a child, Narayan went on to transform English in such a way that made it an idiom to express Indian thoughts and experiences, and 'Indian writing in English' – where the language matched the authenticity of the experience – was born. Through deceptively simple prose, tragic-comic characters, the enchanting Malgudi and universal themes, Narayan captured the true spirit of India. He died at the age of 94 in the year 2001.

But Iyengar's best known works remain his historic novels, *Channabasava Nayaka* and *Chikkaveera Rajendra*. Iyengar also penned quite a number of poems and has written and translated several important plays. He has authored several works in English and edited a monthly journal *Jeevana* from 1944-1965, of considerable significance in Kannada journalism.

**VK Gokak** was a prominent academician. His writing career began in English and with encouragement from DR Bendre, he embarked on what turned out to be a prolific life as a writer. He wrote many poems, plays and criticisms. His best known work remains the epic

poem *Bharatha Sindhu Rashmi* for which he was awarded the Jnanpith in 1990. It is said to be the longest epic written in an Indian language in the 20th century.

Among the modern writers, the most prominent is **UR Ananthamurthy** who was awarded the Jnanpith in 1994. With early education in Sanskrit and a PhD in English and Comparative Literature from the UK, Ananthamurthy has penned many stories, poems, essays and novels in Kannada and English. His best known work is the novel *Samskara* which has also been made into a movie. His most recent works include a novel, *Divya* and a collection of essays, *Literature and Culture*, in English.

An actor, director and playwright, **Girish Karnad** is one of the most respected figures in Indian theatre. *Yayati* was his first play, written in the early sixties. It chronicled the adventures of characters from the Mahabharata. But it was *Tughlaq*, his second and most popular play that established Karnad as a master playwright. In typical Karnad style, it draws from the life of Muhammed bin Tughlaq, erstwhile ruler of Delhi and surrounding areas. The play was an undeniable allegory to Jawaharlal Nehru's rule in India. The last four decades have seen Karnad at his best with critically acclaimed plays like *Nagamandala*, *Hayavadhana*, *Agni mattu Male*, *Taledanda* and *The Dreams of Tipu Sultan*. As with *Yayati*, these plays were written originally in Kannada and translated into English by the playwright himself.

# Indigenous Art Forms

Yakshagana, a form of dance-drama indigenous to Karnataka

## Kavi Art

Found only in the coastal regions of Karnataka, Kavi is a form of wall art or murals. It gets its name from the local term for a red pigment, the only colour used in these murals. The murals are etched on the walls built from laterite, found in abundance here. The process is quite painstaking – first the wall is covered with white lime (made from seashells, jaggery and sand) followed by a mixture of lime and the red pigment. It is left to dry for an hour after which etching begins, using steel bodkins of different sizes. A careful curing process ensures their lasting value.

Most of the murals are based on mythological themes. Three-dimensional perspectives are often added and geometrically precise shapes adorn corners and borders. Often, the mural will use a window or ventilator as part of the picture. Identical designs are not easily found. Kavi art is remarkable in several ways but a lack of recognition and patronage leave it in danger. The Sirsi Marikamba temle and the Mahalsa Narayani temple in Kumta display intricate Kavi art.

## Kunita

The fascinating ritualistic dances of Karnataka come under the generic term Kunita. Known for their vibrancy, elaborate and colourful costumes and make-up, the Kunita is very popular in rural Karnataka. Dollu Kunita is a drum-driven group dance, performed by men of the Kuruba community. Powerful, energetic drumming, acrobatic movements (often involving building human pyramids) and synchronised formations are characteristic of this dance.

Variants of the Kunita are Puja Kunita where a wooden structure with a deity is carried on dancers' heads. Devare Thatte Kunita, and Suggi Kunita take their names from the deity, the symbol or the instruments that are balanced on the head or held by the dancer. The Patada Kunita (where men carry tall bamboo poles decorated with coloured ribbons and crowned with a tiny silver or brass umbrella), the Gorava Kunita (performed by men in a black rug-like costume with fur caps, carrying percussion instruments and flutes) and the Kamsale (originally a religious dance, performed by men with cymbals) are other common ritualistic dances.

## Bhoota Aradhane

Intrinsic to the coastal regions that make up Tulu Nadu is the Bhoota Aradhane or spirit worship. Departed souls, natural phenomena and animals are worshipped through the Bhoota Aradhane. Wearing resounding anklets, a dancer whirls in front of the idol representing the bhoota, accompanied by music that varies from region to region. Every spirit has its own narrative folk prayer. It is not uncommon to find the dancer in a trance-like state, often performing the role of an oracle. Their costumes and make-up heighten the effect and make for a truly fascinating spectacle.

## Yakshagana

The Vaishnava Bhakti movement, an 11th century school of religion sought to reach the common people for whom the formalised Vedic system was beyond reach. It was a form of mass media and adapted local folk and classical forms to spread the new message. Yakshagana is a form of dance-drama that traces its roots to this period.

It evolved mostly in the coastal districts of Karnataka and continues to be a medium of both entertainment and dissemination of Hindu philosophy. Colloquially, it is often referred to as Bayalata (open-air play) or simply Ata.

Yakshagana performances usually begin late at night and continue till dawn. Costumes and make-up are elaborate and colourful. Characters are usually drawn from the Ramayana and the Mahabharata. Through the ages, men have always portrayed the female roles but now, there is a move to involve women.

As a tradition, Yakshagana is intensely alive with over 30 professional troupes, over 200 amateur ones and as many as 10,000 performances each year!

## Gombe Ata

Gombe Ata or puppet play is an art form practiced by the nomadic tribes of Karnataka. A rectangular stage is set up using bamboo and blankets with a white semi-transparent cloth as the backdrop and a simple oil lamp to provide the lighting. After an invocation to Lord Ganesha and Goddess Saraswati, the performance begins typically with an introductory routine featuring a couple of clowns. The stories used in these plays are drawn from the epics. It's not uncommon to see an entire family of puppeteers working on various aspects of the performance, providing voices and music (harmonium and percussion). Sometimes, Gombe Ata performances are held for special reasons like invoking the rain god, praying for a good harvest or at weddings.

A window displaying Kavi Art

Devbagh, a beach resort along the Karavali coast.

## Around Karnataka

Talacauvery is the birthplace of the sacred river Cauvery, revered as one of the seven holy rivers in India. Tula Sankramana is an important festival for the Kodavas. On this auspicious occasion, thousands of pilgrims visit Talacauvery to witness the river water gushing out from its source. It is believed that Goddess Cauvery appears in the form of a spring at Talacauvery, causing the upsurge.

The mighty Hoysala kings built a number of temples in and around Halebid, Belur, Somnathpur, Javagal and Belawadi. Characterised by their use of soft soap stone, the Hoysala temples bear exquisite carvings and are raised on a star shaped platform. The Chennakesava temples at Belur and Somnathpur and the Hoysaleswara temple at Halebid are considered the finest examples of Hoysala architecture.

Karnataka is a prominent centre of Jainism, and has been for the last 2,000 years. A number of basadis or temples dot its landscape and Shravanabelagola is Karnataka's most sacred Jain site. A trek through the Indragiri Hill leads to a colossal statue of Gomateshwara. Scores of devotees from across the country come to witness the spectacular *Mahamastakabhisheka* or head anointing ceremony held every 12 years.

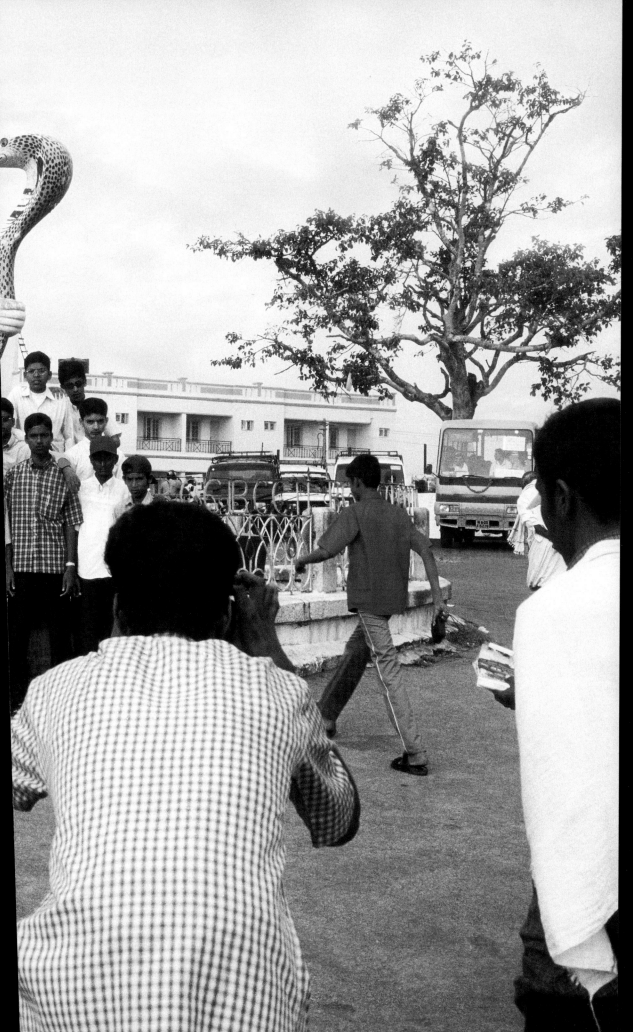

Perched on Chamundi Hills, just outside Mysore city, is the 12th century temple dedicated to Goddess Chamundeswari. A towering statue of Mahishasura and a black granite Nandi are other attractions.

The ghostly ruins of Hampi, the ancient capital of the Vijayanagar kingdom, come alive during the Hampi Festival held every November. Christened the Vijay Utsav, the festival recreates the erstwhile grandeur of this fabled city with a cultural extravaganza of dance, music, drama and spectacular fireworks. Organised by the Government of Karnataka, renowned artists from around the country travel to Hampi to participate in the celebrations.

# Around Karnataka

For the first time traveller to Karnataka as well as those who may have lived here all their lives, the state has a wide array of tourist options to choose from. Ancient history by way of temples, forts and palaces, extreme topographies of stunning waterfalls and placid beaches, dry plains and lush jungles broadly describe Karnataka's many attractions. White water rafting in Dandeli, coffee picking in Coorg and Chikmagalur, wildlife sightings in Nagarhole, pristine beaches, heritage sites, the royal flavours of Mysore and the colonial air of Bangalore are just some of the unique attractions of the state.

The colossal monolith of Gomateshwara at Shravanabelagola

In the following pages we bring you the big tourist attractions as well as the lesser-known destinations. Hampi, Bijapur, Shravanabelagola, Halebid, Bandipur, Talacauvery, Mangalore and Chikmagalur are some of the big names that draw the crowds. Kalasa, Bhadra Widllife Sanctuary, Mahakuta, Bhatkal and Kurmagad are usually off the regular tourist map but well worth a visit. A series of special features focus on art village Hastha Shilpa, Home Stays in Kodagu, Divine Karnataka, the JLR story, Karnataka's Waterfalls, Dandeli, Yana, Tibetan Settlements and others give you the full flavour.

We have listed a number of circuits around a specific theme – Heritage, Coastal and Wildlife. You can take a few days or a few weeks to cover each, depending on the level of interest and time. The section on Mysore and Bangalore offers not just fabulous sights but quick and exciting getaways as well. Information on both day excursions and overnight trips is provided, from the Kokkrebellur Pelicanry near Mysore to the hilltop temples of Devarayanadurga close to Bangalore. The Mysore section also lists places to shop, eat and stay. All important information like how to get there, places to stay and travel tips may be found at the end of each section.

We have appended an exhaustive compilation of maps on Karnataka. Detailed maps of north, south and west Karnataka have been included along with Mysore and Bangalore city maps. Maps of getaways from Bangalore and Mysore are also provided.

Whether this information guides you towards a lifelong dream of studying ancient, carved pillars or sends you for a blissful weekend on the beach, we hope the journey is as rewarding as the destination.

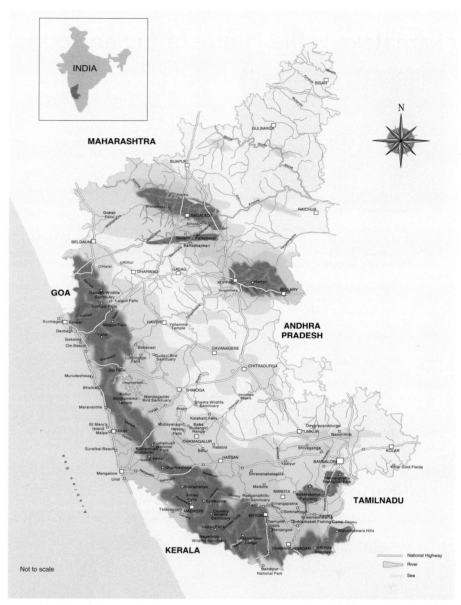

Melkote

# Karnataka is the Future of Indian Tourism – Dr. CS Kedar, IAS

I have been to many parts of the world, but the wonders of Karnataka never cease to amaze me. Many leading tourist destinations of the world are uni-dimensional, centred around one or two major destinations.

Karnataka is a world of attractions, the essence of India… with something for everyone. The gods have blessed Karnataka with innumerable attractions from the natural riches of the Western Ghats to the picturesque hills of Kodagu. From the virgin beaches of Ullal to Karwar, to the abundant wildlife in our nature reserves and game sanctuaries. Man has added to these gifts with splendours such as the World Heritage sites of Hampi and Pattadakal to the innumerable forts and palaces. Indeed there is no place like Karnataka.

It is no surprise that Karnataka is among India's top tourist destinations, attracting over 12 million domestic tourists and about 2,63,000 foreign tourists. We are also a global brand, setting the pace in the world of IT, BT and business. Tourism is the new frontier.

Today the growth of tourism has made it virtually impossible to get a hotel room in Bangalore even during what is considered off season. Even furnished apartments and home stays are full up. This creates huge opportunity for investors in the hospitality, tourism and entertainment industries. Immense opportunities are opening up… and the government itself is dis-investing in its properties that are with Karnataka Tourism Development Corporation. Some of the leading global hospitality groups are entering Karnataka. The Government is considering tourism zones, on the lines of business parks, to provide 'single-window' approvals for speedy start-up of hotels, resorts, convention centres, entertainment parks etc…

Government is looking at partnering with private enterprise to develop specific attractions and facilities such as Nandi Hills, Brindavan Gardens, etc… A theme village, with comprehensive infrastructure, is being considered at Hampi. There is immense scope for developing water sports and theme parks.

Already the adventure tourism capital of India, Karnataka is renowned for white water rafting, rock climbing, trekking, parasailing, diving etc…there is much that an investor can gain by developing on these.

Interestingly, India's first no-frills airline is headquartered in Karnataka, and a second is poised to gain wing. This has already started opening up far-flung destinations of the state. Many leading airlines have started operations into Karnataka: Lufthansa, Singapore Airlines, Thai, Malaysian… Many others are waiting in the wings. The new airport at Devanahalli is gaining shape and will come up fast.

I am bullish on Karnataka. I see Karnataka as India's single most important tourist destination in the near future. There are innumerable opportunities for investors and I will not be surprised if tourism emerges as Karnataka's most important economic activity.

*Dr. CS Kedar, IAS, is Secretary, Information, Tourism & Youth Services, Govt. of Karnataka.*

Hampi

# Helitourism

Courtesy: Deccan Aviation

If you want to travel from Bangalore to Hampi, be prepared for a 10-hour journey by train covering 365kms. And a tour of the ancient temples of Belur and Halebid would take the better half of the day. But for those with little time on their hands, helitourism is an exciting travel option that cuts travel time and does away the fatigue of a long journey.

Offered by Deccan Aviation in Bangalore, most of the tours cater to small groups of six or nine people. The Grand Karnataka Heli-Tour, for instance, is an overnight package with the first day spent in the south – Shravanabelagola, Belur and Halebid, lunch in Coorg and dinner in Hassan. The second day is spent exploring the ruins of Hampi and the cave temples of Badami. The return flight to Bangalore is over the impressive Jog Falls and hills of the Western Ghats.

Deccan Aviation offers chartered tours to quite a few places. Within Karnataka, helicopter tours are offered to Mysore, Kabini River Lodge, Cauvery Fishing Camp, Biligiri Rangaswamy Wildlife Sanctuary and Shravanabelagola. A combined package offers travel to the heritage spots in the south or the Upper Karnataka Experience to Hampi. Travellers may choose from pilgrimage, leisure and honeymoon packages (which includes having a flower-bedecked copter!). Popular destinations are Ooty, Coorg, Kochi and Kodaikanal. Pilgrimage packages are available to Tirupati, Puttaparti and Vaishnodevi. The more adventurous get to choose from the jungles of Corbett National Park and Sariska, the caves of Ajanta and Ellora etc. If you wish to spend a weekend teeing off, try the Ooty Golf Package. Popular tourist spots like Goa, Hampi, Ajanta and Ellora are also on Air Deccan's itinerary.

# Presenting three of India's best kept secrets.

*Behold the timeless beauty of the Taj.*

It's not just another journey when you board

a Deccan Aviation chopper

on one of our heli-holidays.

It's a voyage of discovery. From taking off to landing at the

exotic destination of your choice,

*Absorb the ancient history of Hampi.*

we showcase the delights that it has to offer.

From a different perspective.

To know more about our heli-packages to

Hampi, Cauvery Fishing Camp and

the Taj Mahal (Agra),

please call any of the numbers listed below.

*Escape to the banks of the river Cauvery.*

# North Karnataka
## Heritage Circuit

Badami, Aihole, Pattadakal, Banashankari,
Mahakuta, Hampi, Bijapur

North Karnataka is a treasure of ancient temples and important ruins. **Sculpted caves, exquisite carvings** of mighty kings and legends stand testimony to a fusion of north and south Indian temple architecture.

Begin your journey at the **Chalukyan** capital of **Badami** where you can choose from many small, yet comfortable hotels. The road from Badami leads straight into the sacred temple complex of **Pattadakal**. Further downstream along the river **Malaprabha** lies the dusty town of **Aihole**, cradle of south Indian temple architecture. From here it is only a matter of short detours to the temple towns of **Banashankari** and **Mahakuta**. Further north lies **Bijapur**, a storehouse of elegant Muslim architecture. Complete your journey through Karnataka's northern heritage sites with a visit to **Hampi**, legendary capital of the mighty **Vijayanagar** Empire. Altogether you gain an insider's view into the fascinating history of northern Karnataka.

The dramatic boulder strewn landscape of Hampi

The ancient Chalukyan capital Badami is poised between soaring cliffs and Agasthya Lake.

Not to scale

## Badami

*A*n overnight bus journey from Bangalore will bring you to the town of Badami, ancient capital of the Chalukyan Empire from 540 to 753 AD. Rock cut cave temples, a ruined fortress and an emerald green lake make for an exciting itinerary. The caves remain open from sunrise to sunset and guides usually charge Rs 150 for a tour of the cave and twice the amount for the entire site. Enjoy a night out in the Badami village – walk through the busy bazaar, scattered ruins, winding bylanes and quaint houses with a hoard of farm animals, eager children and curious villagers for company! If you want to cover Badami as well as Mahakuta in a single day, the bus would be too ambitious a means of transport. Instead hire a car for a comfortably paced journey.

Badami or Vatapi was built towards the turn of the 6th century by the wise and benevolent king Pulikeshin I, as a capital city for his kingdom. Spread around a hill, the city is also built into it and indeed excavated from it. It is picturesquely situated at the mouth of a ravine between two red sandstone cliffs overlooking the cool green waters of Agasthya Lake. Atop the sandstone cliffs lie the legendary **cave temples** of Badami. The north cliff has ruins of the fort while the southern cliff has the famous decorative rock-cut cave temples. The caves are best seen at sunset when the evening sun captures the rust-red tints of the sandstone. You need to clamber up a steep flight of steps to reach the four rock-cut caves replete with carved pillars and bracket figures, all hewn out of red sandstone located at varying heights and connected on the precipice of a hill. The rest of the city is a complex of flat-roofed houses extending from one side of a huge lake. The

mountains, which make Badami a natural fortress, close in on the lake's other sides.

The south fort has four rock-cut caves (Cave 1, 2, 3 and 4) where robust sculptures contrast with delicate friezes, gods and goddesses share space with amorous demigods and the ceilings of caves are embellished with elaborate flowers and foliage. The interiors of the caves are luxuriously carved in contrast to the spartan exteriors. Beware of the bands of monkeys lurking around.

Dedicated to Lord Shiva, the first and oldest 6th century cave's walls are adorned with captivating figures of the 18-armed Nataraja striking 81 dance poses and the imposing figure of Ardhanareeshwara. Shiva

assumes the male as well as the female form in this sculpture – the right half is characterised by Shiva's matted, flowing hair and third eye, while the left half takes on the features of Goddess Parvati.

Walk through a courtyard to enter the second cave temple flanked by celestial guardians and pot bellied dwarves. Dedicated to Lord Vishnu, the work here is marginally less elaborate than the first. Four ornate pillars with carvings of the mythical lion *yali* support this temple. There are other mythical creatures carved into Cave 2 – the boar-headed creature Varaha, the coiled serpent Naga and Vishnu astride the legendary bird Garuda. The ceiling is dotted with images

An imposing statue of Vishnu in a columned hallway graces the entrance of Cave 3.

The cave temples in Badami are hewn out of red sandstone.

of soaring celestial couples and the lotus motif encircled by fish and symbols of the swastika.

Bearing the richest traces of painting, the third cave is the largest and some say the most spectacular of the four caves. The grand figure of Lord Vishnu seated on a coiled snake is accompanied by smaller carved images of Indra on his elephant, Brahma on a swan and Shiva riding the bull, on the ceiling.

The fourth and the most recent of the cave temples is right at the top of the cliff. An eighth century cave dedicated to Jainism, its walls are covered with standing and seated tirthankaras and the sanctum holds a large sculpture of Mahavira.

Beyond the caves, past the jade green Agasthasyatheertha Lake stands the archaeological museum with unusual exhibits and a Buddhist cave temple. A dramatic climb through the path behind the museum brings you to a sandstone chasm with fortified gateways and finally to the ruins of the north fort: A treasury, granary, watchtower and the upper Shivalaya temple. The exploration of Badami's temples ends at the Bhuthanatha temple on the lakeside, best seen in the light of the setting sun. If you are game, take a dip in the lake, said to have healing powers.

## Aihole

*O*n the banks of the parched but beautiful river Malaprabha, stands the ancient temple site of Aihole. Two hours on the dusty road from Badami brings you to this solitary town teeming with Hindu and Jain rock cut caves and temples.

*In the centre of the village are a couple of enclosures, fenced off by the ASI, that house beautiful temples. Aihole's museum displays fine specimens of Chalukyan sculpture. Entry for foreigners costs five dollars. Exploring Aihole is simplified if you lay your hands on the guidebook, Glorious Aihole, which provides helpful maps and all necessary information about the temples.*

The ancient commercial city of the Chalukyas, there is an interesting story to the name. It is said that Parasurama, after avenging the death of his father, came to the Malaprabha river to wash his bloody axe. The profusion of Kshatriya blood turned the river red and the village belles who had come to fill their pots with water exclaimed: *Ai* (oh dear) *hole*! (the river).

Aihole, also called Ayyavole or Aryapura, was the stronghold of the Rashtrakutas as well. Most importantly, it is the birthplace of Dravidian temple architecture. Dedicated to Vishnu and Jain divinities, you can witness the beginnings of Hindu temple architecture in the simple shrines, the ancient Ladh Khan temple and the more recent temple complexes like the Meguti temple. Aihole was a veritable laboratory where Chalukyan artisans and architects created and tested new forms of architecture. Their brave experiments are displayed in 140 odd temples spread across the rocky outcrops and fields.

Don't let the sheer number of the temples at Aihole daunt you! Start your sojourn with the most impressive Durga temple. The unusual temple shaped like a horseshoe, with a semi-circular apse is reminiscent of a Buddhist chaitya and keeps you going around in circles! Elevated on a lofty plinth, the temple's elaborate friezes are resplendent with sensuous angels or gandharvas, narratives from the epic Ramayana and unusual depictions of the boar-headed incarnation of Vishnu and goddess Lakshmi. The sculptural masterpiece is a niche with the fierce multi-armed Mahishasuramardini slaying a buffalo demon. Filling the niches are rows of pot bellied comical dwarves or *ganas* that stand in merry contrast to the larger awe-inspiring deities. The name 'Durga Temple' is in fact a misnomer and came from '*durgagudi*' meaning 'temple within the fort'.

The exquisite temples of Aihole display the beginnings of Dravidian temple architecture.

# /səˈrenəti/

Green Cove Resort & Spa.

By the deep blue sea. On a lush green hillock.

Where you can experience pronounced serenity.

Where the fragrant breeze will wipe away your worries.

And where rejuvenative Ayurveda and a Tropical Spa will give you a new life.

● Beach-backwater resort ● Hillside cottages ● Floating cottages

## Green Cove Resort & Spa *Kovalam*

G.V. Raja Vattapara Road Kovalam-695 027 Trivandrum Kerala India
Tel: (91-471) 2487733 Fax: (91-471) 2487744 E-mail: greencove.kovalam@tajhotels.com www.tajhotels.com

A Muthoot Pappachan Group Concern

Banashankari temple, a sacred pilgrimage site

The Ladh Khan temple nearby, is one of the earliest temples and was originally a royal assembly and marriage hall, and later the abode of a Muslim mendicant. It has a projecting porch with carvings of loving couples on its decorative pillars.

A path to the right of Durga temple leads to the Huchimalli temple with a north Indian style tower and a larger than life statue of Vishnu seated atop a cobra. Nearby lies the rock cut Ravalaphadi Cave that celebrates the many forms of Shiva and Vishnu – a spirited dancing Shiva, the duo of Shiva and river goddess Ganga and Harihara.

If this has only whet your appetite for more, walk to the quartet of temples at the more recent Konti Complex. A climb up the hill southeast of Aihole, takes you the oldest Jain Meguti temple – a richly decorated Dravidian temple ensconced with Lord Mahavira. En route you also pass a two-storied Buddhist temple with a smiling Buddha seated under the Bodhi tree.

## Banashankari

*A short drive northwest of Badami leads to Banashankari, a pilgrimage town where you can recoup from the Chalukyan temples before you make your way to Pattadakal.*

This is a small but sacred temple town dedicated to Goddess Banashankari. It draws devotees from all across Karnataka. The crowded temple showcases the powerful eight-armed idol of Goddess Banashankari seated on a lion and trampling a hapless demon with her foot. The hallowed Harida Teertha Tank across the road, enclosed by stone mantapas and colonnades is worth a quick visit.

After a heavy diet of temples and history, wander through the village markets with stalls selling everything from colourful toys and utensils to woodcarvings and other keepsakes from the temple. If you visit during the temple's annual festivities, you get to watch elaborate pujas and take part in a vibrant fair.

## Pattadakal

*Less than an hour's journey from Badami is Pattadakal, coronation city and World Heritage Site. It is well connected to Badami and Aihole with state as well as private buses doing the rounds. There are no full-fledged restaurants in Pattadakal, so stock up on food and water. Pattadakal is open from 6am to 6pm.*

It is said that this town was once known as Kisuvolal or red town because of the reddish colour of the local sandstone from which the temples were constructed. What we see today is an isolated cluster of rust-tinged golden sandstone temples that go by the name Pattadakal or 'coronation stone', built from the 6th century up to the 9th century.

Along the river Malaprabha, set amidst landscaped gardens, these delightful 8th century temples carry on the artistic legacy of the Chalukyan kings. They are a blend of northern and southern or Nagara and Dravidian styles.

Pattadakal is easier to explore than Aihole. All the temples here are located around a main temple complex. Stepping into the temple complex, the partly damaged Kadasiddheshwara and Jambulinga temples in the north Indian

The imposing sculptures and friezes of Pattadakal draw inspiration from mythology.

**celebrate**
the sun sets gracefully
the surf washes the
beach and there is music
in the air

The 7th century temples of Mahakuta are set around a large spring-fed tank.

## Mahakuta

*There are only a few buses to the next pilgrimage site of Mahakuta, so it's best to hire a tempo or car. If you are in the mood for a little adventure take the ancient 'paved pilgrim trail'. Arm yourself with an umbrella, sun block and plenty of water to beat the scorching Deccan heat. There are only a couple of teashops and a few basic rooms, so carry both food and water.*

You need to pass through the rocky hills of Badami to reach the pilgrimage centre of Mahakuta. Mahakuta is said to have been the abode of sage Agasthya and the temples here are dedicated to Lord Shiva. Nestled among hills, this beautiful Chalukyan temple complex was built in the 7th century and is a confluence of north and south Indian styles of architecture. The old gateway of the temple complex is flanked by the figures of Bhairava and Chamunda and a large Nandi greets you at the entrance.

Inside a large walled courtyard are the two central temples of Mahakuta, on either side of a spring-fed tank. The older Mahakuteshwara temple built in the Dravidian style displays delicate scrollwork, a statue of Ardhanareershwara and scenes from the epics. The Mallikarjuna temple is on the other side of the tank with finely chiselled carvings of mithuna couples and Hindu deities. Both temples have a dome-like tower and tiers with miniature shrines.

Near the Sangameshwara temple stands a gigantic stone-wheeled chariot, which is still in use for religious ceremonies held in the month of May. Scattered around the complex are at least two dozen restored Shiva temples. Shaivite Hindus consider Mahakuta to be a Dakshina Kashi because of its religious sanctity.

style with characteristic nagaras present themselves. The theme of fusion continues with the grand Papanatha temple with an elaborately carved 16-pillared main hall. The north Indian style temples end with the Kashi Vishwanatha temple to the west of the complex.

Across the lawns, past the older and simpler temples, are the more complex south Indian vimana temples with their stepped pyramidal formation. Sangameshwara, the oldest temple in the complex, is dedicated to Lord Shiva. The largest and most opulent temples of Pattadakal, the Virupaksha and Mallikarjuna temples, were erected by two sister-queens commemorating the Chalukyan victory over the Pallavas.

The deep-green stone figure of Nandi at the entrance of the Virupaksha temple, covered in a red floral cape, set against pink-tinged sandstone shows an early use of colour. The Chalukyan love of imagery is reflected in the magnificent friezes of the temple with mythological stories and tricky sculptures that look like a bull and an elephant at the same time! The columned hall leads to the inner sanctum, which houses a Shiva linga that is worshipped even today. The smaller Mallikarjuna temple matches the grandeur of other ornate Chalukyan temples. Finely depicted on its walls are unusual fables from the Panchatantra. For those who want to venture further than the temple complex, there is a Jain temple in the village built by the Rashtrakutas.

The Virupaksha temple in Pattadakal is flanked by statue of Nandi.

## GETTING THERE

### Badami

- Aihole-46kms
- Hubli-130kms
- Bijapur-150kms
- Bangalore-420kms

- Hubli-130kms
- Bijapur-150kms
- Gadag-70kms

- Dabolim (Goa)-290km

### Pattadakal

- Aihole-24kms
- Badami-29kms
- Bangalore-480kms
- Badami-29kms

- Dabolim (Goa)-319kms

### Aihole

- Badami-46kms
- Bijapur-129kms
- Bangalore-460kms
- Badami-46kms
- Hubli-128kms

- Dabolim (Goa)-336kms

## WHERE TO STAY

### Badami

**Hotel Badami Court**
17/1 Station Road,
Badami,
Bagalkot District 587201
**Tel** 08357-220 231-33
**Email** rafiqmht@blr.vsnl.net.in
**Tariff** Rs 1,480 to Rs 2,500

**Hotel Anand Deluxe**
Near Bus Stand, Badami,
Bagalkot District 587201
**Tel** 08357-220 074/904
**Tariff** Rs 150 to Rs 1,200

**Hotel Mookambika Deluxe**
Station Road,
Opposite KSRTC Bus Stand,
Bagalkot 587201
**Tel** 08357-220 067/637
**Fax** 08357-220 106
**Tariff** Rs 250 to Rs 950

**KSTDC Mayura Chalukya**
Ramdurg Road, Badami,
Bagalkot 587201
**Tel** 08357-220 046
**Tariff** Rs 160 to Rs 500

**Shri Laxmi Vilas Hotel**
Tonga Stand Station Main Road,
Badami 587201
**Tel** 08357-220 077
**Tariff** Rs 150

### Aihole

**Tourist Home**
**Tel** 08351-284 541
**Tariff** Rs 100 to Rs 200

### Travel Tips

Badami is connected by road to Bijapur, Hubli and Bangalore. Trains link Badami to Gadag, Guntakal, Hubli and Bijapur. From Gadag, it is easy to get a connecting train to Hospet or Hubli. The railway station is about four kilometres from Badami and buses, tongas and autos are available to reach the town. Buses are available from Badami to Pattadakal and Aihole, though the services are not very frequent. To save time and cover more places, engage a taxi (Rs 700) for a day trip covering Aihole, Pattadakal, Mahakuta and Banashankari. It is best to stay at Badami, to cover these places. Carry food and water when you visit the neighbouring places as there are no decent restaurants except small eateries there. If you are adventurous,

you can explore the closer sites of Mahakuta as well as the temple village of Banashankari by hiring a cycle.

For tourist information, contact:
Tourist Office, New Wing of KSTDC
Hotel Mayura Chalukya,
Ramdurg Road, Badami,
Bagalkot 587201
**Tel** 08357-220 414
**Open** 10am to 5:30pm.
Closed on Sunday.

# Ten Must See Destinations in Karnataka – Mahendra Jain, IAS

**H**ampi has an absolutely magical effect on me. The rugged landscape, miles and miles of ruins and monuments amidst huge boulders, the meandering river all make for an incredibly surreal experience; a step back into history and time. It helps that modern development has not marred the ancient and mesmerising landscape of the area.

**Nagarhole** with its incomparable forest sounds, sights and smells and the varied wildlife that you encounter never ceases to surprise and refresh me.

**Dandeli** has a secret: I have sighted more tigers and panthers just driving around the area than in the biggest of reserves! River rafting is, no doubt, a thrilling experience and so is bird watching. The evergreen Western Ghats present unparalleled bio-diversity.

**St. Mary's Isle** is just a half hour ferry ride from Udupi, the land of idlis and dosas. The rock-cut crystal formation, glowing white sand and fabulous views of the Arabian Sea make it an idyllic setting straight out of a picture postcard.

**Bangalore** is young at heart and you thank your stars everyday for being a Bangalorean. The weather is great and the city has a unique cosmopolitan culture. Definitely, India's finest global city. There are countless little things than one can do here. This is a city for those who enjoy le bon vie!

**Madikeri** has a picturesque beauty amidst the rolling hills and coffee plantations. I especially love the place during the monsoons. You can watch the unabated fury of the rain-gods from the cozy confines of the planters bungalow, with steaming cups of coffee and your favourite book.

**Shravanabelagola** has immense emotional significance for me. The grandeur of the majestic idol and its benign expression humbles you and brings you in communion with the sublime. The Mahamastakabhiksheka, when the statue changes colours as thousands and thousands of gallons of milk, saffron milk, sandalwood water and flower petals are poured is an awesome sight

**Chikmagalur** has numerous trekking trails and adventure options. The green hills of the Western Ghats paint some spectacular sunsets and sunrises. It has some exciting home stay options and resorts.

**Mysore** has a unique heritage grandeur, especially the amazing Mysore Palace and the regal Dasara celebrations. The city is also close to so many interesting places like the Ranganathittu Bird Sanctuary, Tipu's Palace in Srirangapatna, the forests of Bandipur and more.

**Chitradurga**, I feel, is the most underrated fort in the country and definitely one of the largest and historically significant. Carved out of huge stone boulders, I love its raw beauty and unique ambience. It's also surprisingly well preserved for a fort of such antiquity! An ideal stopover on the way to Hampi!

*Mahendra Jain, IAS, is the Commissioner of Tourism, Govt. of Karnataka and Managing Director, KSTDC.*

Shravanabelagola

# Hampi

Hampi is just a five hour drive from the Chalukyan capital Badami and 13 kms from the sleepy town of Hospet in Bellary district. Most of the structures and ruins in Hampi are located in two areas, generally referred to as the Royal Centre and the Sacred Centre. Before heading out to the main sites, stop at the Kamalapur Archaeological Museum which displays sculptures and artefacts unearthed from excavations. The scale model of Hampi exhibited here helps the visitor get a better picture of the ruins, otherwise a confusing maze! The museum is open from 10am to 5pm and closed on Friday. You can explore Hampi by bicycle, bus or car, the more leisurely, the better. The months from October to March are ideal if you want to explore the ruins by foot. Avoid the summer months when the mercury soars to 45 degrees.

World Heritage Site Hampi was the capital of the mighty Vijayanagar empire

Hampi lies on the banks of the mighty Tungabhadra, a ghost town, set amidst a desolate landscape strewn with boulders. It is hard to imagine a time when Hampi was a bustling metropolis and world famous bazaar! Trade in spices, jewels, silks, cottons, diamonds and horses were mentioned extensively in the travelogues of visiting Arabs and Persians. The 200-year-old seat of the Vijayanagar empire was said to be larger than Rome and its palaces were said to be grander than those of Lisbon!

Hampi rose to glorious heights under the benevolent and mighty king, Krishnadevaraya. The seemingly impregnable hill fortress of this 'City of Victory' was finally invaded and destroyed by the Sultans of the Deccan region. Today, the magical ruins of Hampi have been accorded the status of a World Heritage Site.

With the museum as your first stop, proceed to the Queen's Bath, a graceful structure with an arched corridor and lotus-shaped fountains that were once filled with perfumed water. It is said that in the earlier days musicians played from the projecting balconies and the ladies of the court watched the pomp and ceremony of the queen taking a bath!

The Royal Centre (as part of the ruins in Hampi are referred to) is a miniature city within Hampi, housing palaces, pavilions, royal stables and temples. The King's Palace is the largest enclosure in all of Hampi with an underground chamber that served as a treasury and private audience hall.

Further away is the Hazara Rama temple, or the temple of a thousand Ramas. It was meant strictly for the use of royalty. To the north of the King's palace is the Zenana – a palace built for queens. The Lotus Mahal, an elegant two-storied palace, gets its name from the beautiful recessed archways arranged like the petals of a flower. It reflects the fusion of both Hindu and Muslim styles of architecture. To the east of the Zenana area lie the Elephant's Stables with domed ceilings, labyrinthine doorways, caves and chambers.

The Sacred Centre is a complex of four gigantic stone-carved gods. The most imposing of these is the figure of Lakshminarasimha seated on the coils of a seven-hooded snake with a fierce, fixed stare. The Virupaksha temple, the only temple in active worship, is dedicated to Lord Shiva and his consort Pampa Devi and has its own resident elephant. The idols are set within an ornate mantapa and decorative paintings cover the ceiling.

An ideal place to end the day would be the Vitthala temple, one of the most splendid monuments at the World Heritage Site. With open pillared halls, carved columns, towering gateways and an elaborate miniscule stone ratha it is easily one of the most exquisite monuments at Hampi. The richly decorated pillars are musical and produce an entire scale of musical notes when tapped! A beautiful stone chariot stands proudly in the temple courtyard. One of three such sculptured chariots in India, it has been delicately carved from seven pieces of rock. The chariot also reflects superb engineering skills – the wheels could actually turn once!

The Hampi Bazaar is a colourful place to explore – once a world famous marketplace, today it bustles with souvenir shops, hawkers, small restaurants and handicraft stores.

Once you have had your fill of these ruins and temples, take a coracle and drift down the placid Tungabhadra river. You pass Sugriva's Cave where it is said that Sita's jewels were dropped as she was abducted by the demon Ravana. The King's Balance and the fortress town Anegundi across the Tungabhadra river also merit a visit. The Mahanavami Dibba and the Achutaraya temple are other notable monuments here.

The towering monolith of Narasimha

## GETTING THERE

There are several private buses plying from Goa and Bangalore to Hampi. But you will have to go to Hospet, to catch your bus out. There are regular buses every hour from Hampi Bazaar to Hospet or an auto can be hired. From Hospet there are bus services to Bijapur, Gadag, Badami and Gokarna. Hubli is also connected by rail to Hospet. But to get to Badami and Bijapur, board a Hubli train, alight at Gadag from where onward connections will be available. There is only one direct train to Bangalore. There are trains from Margao, Goa on Tuesdays and Saturdays to Hospet (8 1/2 hours).

 Hospet-13kms
Bangalore-365kms

 Hospet-13kms

✈ Dabolim (Goa)-300kms

### KSTDC's Special Air Package to Hampi

Departure 8am from Bangalore Airport, arrival at 6:30pm
**Fixed Wing Aircraft (5 seater)**
Bangalore-Hampi-Bangalore.
One-day package-Rs 74,500
($ 1,700)
**Helicopter (6 seater)**
Bangalore-Hampi-Bangalore. One-day package-Rs 1,79,000 ($ 3,900)
Package includes a local guided tour by taxi and is inclusive of breakfast, lunch, and high tea at Hampi.

For bookings, contact:
### KSTDC, Badami House
Opp. City Corporation Office,
NR Square, Bangalore 560002
Tel 080-2227 5869/5883,
2221 2098
Fax 080-2223 8016

## WHERE TO STAY

If you're looking for basic accommodation with creature comforts, Hampi would be a better place to stay than Hospet, with several guesthouses in the vicinity of Hampi Bazaar. Don't be surprised if you are solicited by the owners offering rooms in their houses. There are many eateries catering to the Western palate. Other restaurants serve standard Indian thali meals or food. During the peak season from December end to February mid week, the rent doubles, so book in advance. Hospet has a better choice of accommodation but you'll miss the atmosphere of Hampi. Meat and alcohol are not served in Hampi because of the site's religious importance. But alcohol is available in KSTDC's Mayura Bhuvaneswari at Kamalapura.

### Hotel Malligi
PB 1, 6/143 JN Road, Hospet,
Bellary 583201
Tel 08394-228 101-08
Fax 08394-227 038
Web www.hotelmalligi.com
Tariff Rs 300 to Rs 2,500

### Kishkinda Heritage Resort
Near Broken Stone Bridge Cross,
Sanapur, Gangavathi Taluk,
Koppal 583231
Tel 08533-287 034/035
Email kishkindavillage@usa.net
Tariff Rs 1,200 to Rs 1,700

### Shanbhag Towers International
Shanbhag Circle,
College Road, Hospet,
Bellary 583201
Tel 08394-225 910-17
Fax 08394-225 919
Tariff Rs 400 to Rs 1,200

### Hotel Karthik Boarding & Lodging
4th Ward, SP Road, Hospet,
Bellary 583201
Tel 08394-226 643/639/938/038
Fax 08394-220 028
Tariff Rs 100 to Rs 1,000

### KSTDC Mayura Bhuvaneshwari
Kamalapura (Hampi), Bellary 583221
Tel 08394-241 574
Fax 08394-228 537
Tariff Rs 250 to Rs 950

### Hotel Priyadarshini
5/45A, Station Road, Hospet,
Bellary 583201
Tel 08394-228 838/096/139,
227 313
Fax 08394-224 709
Tariff Rs 250 to Rs 1,000 (Foreigners);
Rs 150 to Rs 700 (Indians)

### Wonder Valley Holiday Resort
Narihalla Dam, Sandur
Tel 08395-260 378, 261 393, 261 299
Fax 08395-260 448
Email kmws_lad@indiatimes.com

### KSTDC's Hotel Mayura Vijayanagara
Via Hospet, Tungabhadra Dam,
Bellary 583225
Tel 08394-239 270
Fax 08394-228 537
Tariff Rs 200 to Rs 450

## Travel Tips

If you want to enjoy Hampi at its best, October to March is ideal when the days are pleasant to allow long forays on foot through the ruins. Avoid summer months when the mercury soars to 45 degrees and the monsoon months which bring in swarms of mosquitoes.

The best time for sightseeing and photography is from early morning to 11am and 4pm to 6:30pm. The ruins are very secluded and lonely after sunset and it's not advisable to move around alone, especially with valuables like an expensive camera. Tourists are required to register themselves with the tourism police in the main Hampi Bazaar.

You can make Hospet your base for exploring Hampi. The other options are Kamalapura village and Hampi Bazaar where most of the hotels, eateries and ruins are situated. Make the best use of your time by hiring a guide (through the government tourist office) to provide you with basic information, as well as to guide you through roads. If you are fit, you can walk or cycle around Hampi. Otherwise hire an auto or cab. Be prepared to walk to reach some of the monuments.

For tourist information, contact:
**Regional Tourist Office**
Taluk Office Premises, Old Fire Force Buildings, Hospet, Bellary 583201 **Tel** 08394-228 537 **Fax** 08394-228 537

The walls of Mahanavami Dibba depict lively friezes.

Incredible India

a monument to love. an ode in white.
a caravan of colours. bathed in light.
a river of passion. a timeless tide.
the colours of india. an incredible sight.

contactus@incredibleindia.org   www.incredibleindia.org

# Bijapur

Bijapur houses some marvellous examples of south Indian Islamic architecture with clear Hindu influences. The biggest unsupported dome and the inspiration for the Taj Mahal lie in this sleepy town. Even Mughal Emperor Aurangazeb's hand stretched all the way here!

There are direct buses that ply regularly from Hospet and Badami to Bijapur. The town itself can be explored by auto, bicycle and horse carriage. Gol Gumbaz is open from 6am to 6pm but the museum at its entrance opens an hour later and shuts at 5pm. All tourist sites are closed on Friday. You need more than one day to do justice to the many beautiful and elegant architectural monuments.

The massive Gol Gumbaz houses the tomb of Mohammed Adil Shahi.

Bijapur, the fortified citadel of the Sultans of the Deccan has an understated elegance and classic sense of aesthetics reflected in the profusion of mausoleums, mosques, forts and palaces. Bijapur was once the powerful capital of the Adil Shahi dynasty that ruled in the 16th and 17th centuries. It flourished under the benevolent and tolerant patronage of its Turkish rulers until it was finally conquered by the Mughals. Every street of Bijapur greets you with graceful minarets, stately monuments, symmetrical gateways and scattered ruins steeped in history.

The massive dome of the Gol Gumbaz towers high above the city's skyline. The Gol Gumbaz is an enormous cubical structure of stone and masonry, capped by a gigantic dome. In the centre of the hall set on a plinth, are the gravestones of Muhammed Adil Shahi along with those of his wife, daughter, grandson and favourite courtesan, Rambha. The Whispering Gallery is an acoustic and architectural wonder. If you stand in the gallery and murmur you can hear the distinct echoes of what you say. It is best to visit early in the morning before the busloads of tourists and school children come visiting. The dome has a 126ft diametre at its base and is the fourth largest in the world.

There is an Archaeological Museum in the gatehouse of the Gol Gumbaz with an excellent collection of Chinese porcelain, paintings, armoury, miniatures and stone sculpture, including carvings from Chalukyan temples.

The Ibrahim Roza, a palatial mosque and tomb in Bijapur is said to have been the inspiration for the Taj Mahal in Agra. The tomb of Ibrahim Adil Shah II and his family,

Ibrahim Roza, an elegant mausoleum, flaunts walls with striking geometric designs.

is noted for its striking symmetry, elaborately decorated walls, slender minarets, and cornices. The carved panels are decorated with crosses, lotuses, wheels and calligraphic inscriptions, reflecting the religious tolerance of the Adil Shahi dynasty.

Another architectural wonder is the Jami Masjid, set in a sprawling ground covering 1,16,300sqft. With its graceful arches, aisles, halls, intricate designs and a large crowning onion dome, it is said to be the jewel of Adil Shahi architecture. Mughal Emperor Aurangzeb added a sprawling prayer hall laid out in squares of different colours to house more than 2,000 worshippers. What makes the masjid even more interesting are the carefully preserved verses of the Quran beautifully inscribed in gold.

The Malik-e-Maidan or Lord of the Plateau is reputedly the largest medieval cannon in the world. Fourteen feet long and weighing 55 tonnes it was hauled to its location by 400 bullocks, 10 elephants and an army of men. The head of the cannon is fashioned in the shape of a lion whose jaws are set to devour an elephant. The accompanying sound made by the firing cannon was so explosive that gunners would dive into a special water tank or risk going deaf! The cannon has other powers – legend has it that if you touch the gun and make a wish it will come true!

Mehtar Mahal, Gagan Mahal, Taj Bawdi and Jod Gumbaz are some of the other important sites.

# Travel Information

## GETTING THERE

 Aihole-129kms

Pattadakal-130kms

Badami-132kms

Bangalore-580kms

 Bijapur

 Hyderabad-375kms

## WHERE TO STAY

**Hotel Kanishka International**
Next to Hotel Samrat,
Station Road,
Bijapur 586101
**Tel** 08352-223 788/789, 255 506
**Fax** 08352-243131
**Tariff** Rs 450 to Rs 1,250

**Hotel Madhuvan International**
Station Road, Bijapur 586104
**Tel** 08352-253 254, 255 571/573
**Fax** 08352-256 201
**Tariff** Rs 450 to Rs 800

**Hotel Samrat**
Station Road, Bijapur 586104
**Tel** 08352- 251 620, 250 512
**Tariff** Rs 150 to Rs 540

**Hotel Sagar Deluxe**
Near Basaveshwara Chowk,
Bijapur 586101
**Tel** 08352-251 121,
259 234/36
**Tariff** Rs 200 to Rs 750

**Hotel Sanman**
Station Road, Opp. Gol Gumbaz,
Bijapur 586104
**Tel** 08352-251 866, 253 977
**Tariff** Rs 150 to Rs 500

**Hotel Meghraj**
Station Road, Bijapur 586101
**Tel** 08352-251 458, 254 458
**Tariff** Rs 150 to Rs 500

**KSTDC Mayura Adil Shahi Annexe**
Station Road, Near Ambedkar
Stadium, Bijapur 586010
**Tel** 08352-250 401/934
**Tariff** Rs 450 to Rs 500

**Shree Godavari Lakshmi Hotels**
Athani Road, Near Sainik School,
Bijapur 586101
**Tel** 08352-272 556/169
**Tariff** Rs 150 to Rs 350

## Travel Tips
Buses and trains are available from Badami to Bijapur. From Bangalore, you can take a train to Gadag and change to a train to Bijapur. Alternately you can take the bus. KSRTC buses ply every evening from the City Bus Stand.

HuTch

# Enact your wildest fantasy

With its unique geographical features, Karnataka provides adventure lovers with every kind of terrain except snow-clad mountains. Thrill seekers and environmentalists can indulge in a host of outdoor activities on land, water, and sky. Karnataka's jagged coastline, the Western Ghats with their beckoning peaks, incredible craggy formations, expansive water bodies, and the many rivers that crisscross the state make it a haven for adventure sports and other outdoor activities.

Hang Gliding

Experience the thrills of white water rafting on some unpredictable stretches of the Kali river at Dandeli - an experience so far unavailable this side of the Ganga. Kemphole is another popular destination for white water enthusiasts. Sitanadi (near Agumbe) and Netravati are also favourite white water rafting spots.

Honnemaradu, along the Sharavati backwaters in the Western Ghats, is an ideal place for watersports like coracle rafting, canoeing and windsurfing. The azure waters of the Cauvery also provide for some great opportunities for river rafting and sport fishing.

With its lush tropical forests, hills and dales, caves and cascades, roaring rivers and gurgling streams, and flora and fauna, Karnataka is a trekker's paradise. Trekking trails are mostly located in the Ghat districts of Uttara and Dakshina Kannada, Shimoga, Chikmagalur, Hassan and Kodagu. Over 200 trails have been marked for trekkers in the Western Ghats, while rock climbers will find Ramnagar on the Bangalore-Mysore highway an exciting challenge. Trekkers can explore the coastline on foot via the enchanting Golden Trek from Karwar to Gokarna.

White water rafting at River Kali

KARNATAKA
Theatre of Inspiration

# Release your wild spirit

Tiger at Bandipur National Park

Karnataka enjoys some of the largest and most diverse tracts of unspoiled ecosystems South of the Vindhyas. From dense tropical rainforests of the Western Ghats to the scrub forests of the plains, there are over 21 nature reserves in the state offering breathtaking, up-close and personal encounters with numerous species. The state's wildlife sanctuaries have the highest density of tigers in the country is found here, as are a quarter of the world's population of Asiatic elephants. Once the private hunting ground of royalty, the Bandipur National Park is among the best-known wildlife reserves in the country today. Part of the Nilgiri Biosphere Reserve, Nagarhole (Kannada for Snake River) has an astonishing abundance of wildlife. A unique blend of hill resort and wildlife sanctuary, BR Hills has the ancient Champak tree which is believed to be over 2000 years old. Some of the other wildlife spots around the state are Bannerghatta National Park, Kokkrebellur Pelicanry, Ranganathittu Bird Sanctuary, Dandeli Wildlife Sanctuary, Anshi National Park and Bhadra Wildlife Sanctuary

# Idle on eternal sands

Kaup Beach

Flanked by the soaring Western Ghats in the east and caressed by the blue waters of the Arabian Sea in the west, Karnataka has a 320km long golden coastline dotted with unspoilt beaches and scores of temples. Gokarna, with its narrow streets, traditional houses, and temples, has become a favourite with pilgrims, Sanskrit scholars and beach buffs. Kaup has a lovely beach, a ruined fort and an old 100ft. high lighthouse. Marawanthe has the Arabian Sea on one side, and the picturesque Kodachadri Hills forming a backdrop to the Sauparnika river on the other. The gentle waves, miles of golden sand, tranquil ambience and acres of emerald foliage at Karwar is said to have inspired Rabindranath Tagore to pen his first play.

# Amaze yourself in shopper's paradise

Shopping Malls at Bangalore

Karnataka is a great place to shop. A unique blend of the traditional and the modern, the trendier face of Karnataka is most evident in cities like Bangalore which have some of India's largest shopping malls and entertainment centres. Here nights come alive at pubs and nightclubs while horse racing and golf add zest to the days. In stores across the State, sandalwood, carved sandalwood artefacts and sandalwood oil are favourite buys. Mysore is a major silk centre in India. Bidriware is a unique craft of the Bidar district in Karnataka and the Lambadi tribal jewellery is a much sought after item in the State.

# Trace your way back in time.

Hemakuta Hill, Hampi

Nowhere else in India can you find such a profusion of monuments as in Karnataka. No wonder, then, that Karnataka has been called the "Cradle of Stone Architecture." The magnificent World Heritage Sites at Hampi and Pattadakal, the exquisite temples at Belur, Halebid, and Somnathpur, the cave temples of Badami and Aihole and the stately forts, domes and minarets of Bijapur resurrect the state's history and cultural affluence. These peerless wonders are eloquent reminders of a rich heritage.

Hampi was the capital city of the powerful South Indian Vijayanagar Empire. Founded in 1336, it fell to the rulers of Northern India in 1565, and subsequently lapsed into decline and abandonment. The ruins of these historical monuments have stood the ravages of man and time and still evoke memories of the grandeur of a bygone era.

In Karnataka history mixes freely with legend at places like Anegundi, once part of the mythical kingdom of Kishkinda across the Tungabhadra River from Hampi. The fortress town, in fact, pre-dates the Vijayanagar Empire and its headquarters. Pattadakal - a World Heritage Site on the banks of the Malaprabha river - with beautifully chiselled cluster of temples, each displaying interesting architectural features, bears testimony to the richness of Chalukyan architecture. Pattadakal reached its pinnacle of glory under the Chalukyas and was the ceremonial coronation centre for their kings. The star-shaped Chennakesava Temple on the banks of the Yagachi river in Belur is a perfect example of the Hoysala architecture. At Halebid, the ancient capital of Hoysalas, the Hoysaleswara Temple complex with its walls richly carved with an endless variety of Hindu deities, sages and friezes, has a museum which houses idols, statues and sculptures excavated by the archeological department.

Shravanabelagola is home to Asia's largest monolithic statue of Lord Gomadeshwara which stands 58 feet tall. Every 12 years, Jain pilgrims gather here to participate in the colourful Maha Mastakabhisheka of the statue.

# Mahendra Jain
## Commissioner of Tourism, Karnataka
# speaks...

As far as destinations with inherent attractions for tourists go, Karnataka is right on top. There is something for everyone. There are hills, forests, beaches, heritage sites and more. But tourism is not limited to sprucing up places of interest. It's about giving the tourist access to reliable information at every point of contact, offering a satisfying experience with adequate travel and stay options, easy reservation and streamlined tour arrangements.

On this count, we have created extremely relevant maps and brochures, which are available at all our offices, at airports and at railway stations and at travel agencies. We are also in the process of making existing counters more user-friendly and creating special tourist reception centres at the airport.

Another project on the anvil is a Tourism Complex - a one-stop-shop for travellers. The first one, which will come up soon, will offer comprehensive information on specific destinations and have dedicated travel counters. Travellers can book tour packages or reserve rooms across a wide spectrum of resorts, economy hotels and homestays from the Complex. There will even be a moneychanger and an ATM.

We have concrete plans to improve connectivity to tourism hotspots like Hampi, Mysore, Gulbarga and Hassan. There will soon be an airport at Hampi, and one in Mysore in about a year. This will shorten travel times, improve local economies and increase employment opportunities.

The establishment of high profile resorts, we believe, will have a 'trickle down' effect that is, it will spur the growth of more hotels, even budget hotels. Just one luxury hotel or resort at a destination can encourage smaller establishments. This pattern been observed in other states.

Health Tourism is another area with high growth potential where Karnataka already has a lead. We have state-of-art hospitals, excellent medical professionals and salubrious climate. Karnataka also has adequate infrastructure in a wide variety of medical systems. In fact, a number of internationally acclaimed wellness centres offering traditional and alternative therapies have already been set up around Bangalore and Mysore.

Karnataka easily has all the potential to become South Asia's premier tourist destination. Our endeavour is to help develop and realise that potential.

# At times, you need a consultant to help you do nothing.

For holidays anywhere in the world, consult The Great India Tour Company, the total leisure management

company with an experience of over 25 years in managing holidays. GITC has an impressive range of leisure

services including tours in India and abroad, health and wellness holidays and cruises. With GITC, make

sure your next holiday will be a more enriching experience.

**Great India Holidays:** Beach Holidays, Backwaters Holidays, Ayurveda Retreat, North Indian Splendour, Best of South India, Kerala Greenery, Splendours of India, Hindu Pilgrimage Tour.

**Dream Holidays:** Far East, Middle East, Europe, Star Cruises, Special Tailor-made Packages, Weddings and Honeymoons, Monsoon Holidays. **Events & Special Packages:** Conferences, Conventions, Special Events, Cultural Programmes, Educational Packages, Silver Screen Packages for Film Units.

Corporate Office: 1 Floor, New Corporation Building, Palayam, Trivandrum 695 033, Kerala, India
Tel: 91 471 2334512, 2334513 Fax: 0471 2320710 e-mail: contracting@gitctour.com www.greatindiatourcompany.com

Branches: Bangalore, Tel: 080 25307804 New Delhi, Mumbai, Chennai, Coimbatore, Mangalore, Kozhikode, Kochi.
Overseas Representatives: Milan, Hong Kong.

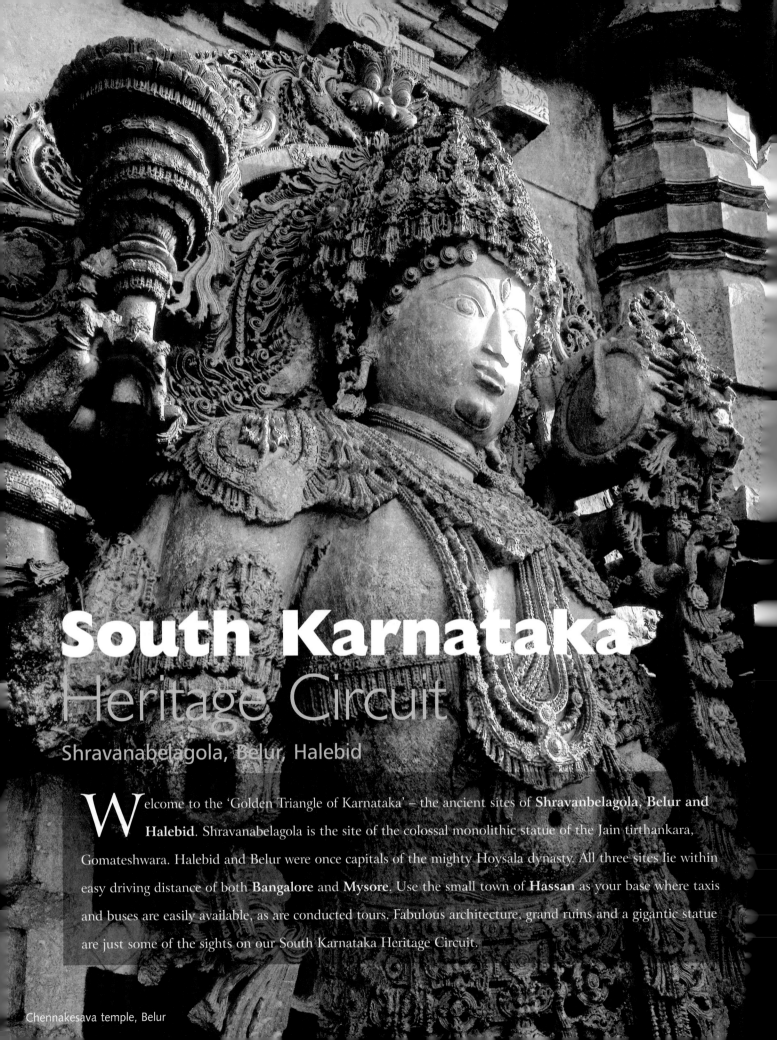

# South Karnataka
## Heritage Circuit
### Shravanabelagola, Belur, Halebid

**W**elcome to the 'Golden Triangle of Karnataka' – the ancient sites of **Shravanbelagola, Belur and Halebid**. Shravanabelagola is the site of the colossal monolithic statue of the Jain tirthankara, Gomateshwara. Halebid and Belur were once capitals of the mighty Hoysala dynasty. All three sites lie within easy driving distance of both **Bangalore** and **Mysore**. Use the small town of **Hassan** as your base where taxis and buses are easily available, as are conducted tours. Fabulous architecture, grand ruins and a gigantic statue are just some of the sights on our South Karnataka Heritage Circuit.

Chennakesava temple, Belur

Friezes of mythological figures and ornamental motifs are characteristics of Hoysala architecture.

Not to scale

## Shravanabelagola

*H*assan is a fairly big town with hotels to suit all budgets. The Karnataka State Tourism Development Corporation (KSTDC) runs package tours covering Shravanabelagola, Halebid and Belur from Bangalore and Mysore. They depart at 7:30am and return at 10pm. Private agencies in Mysore and Bangalore also run similar tours.

*A two-hour drive along the Bangalore-Hassan highway gets you to Shravanabelagola which translates as 'White Pond of the Monks'. The drive is extremely pleasant for the road cuts through the picturesque countryside, sugarcane and paddy fields. Channarayapatna is a good stop for a*

*traditional south Indian breakfast of idlis, vadas and filter coffee. You know you have arrived when you see the sign 'Welcome to Shravanabelagola' and rows of shops selling souvenirs!*

Dawn is the ideal time to climb the Indragiri Hill to catch a glimpse of sunrise over the sugarcane fields and rocky escarpments dotting the surrounding plains. The **Indragiri Hill** (or Vindyagiri) has 612 steps cut into the hillside leading to the temple at the summit. You can visit Shravanabelagola through the day but it's advisable to get there in the cooler early morning hours to avoid the blistering heat.

## Mahamastakabhisheka

*O*nce in every 12 years, the Mahamastakabhisheka or head anointing ceremony takes place to commemorate the consecration of the statue. The first one was held in 1396 and the occasion continues to draw huge crowds. Jain monks, priests and pilgrims make their way here for the ceremony. The ceremony is a truly fascinating display where 1,008 brass pots of holy water are poured over the statue accompanied by the sound of bugles, drums and trumpets. This is followed by curd, milk, honey, vermilion, rice powder, coconut water, turmeric paste and sandalwood! Precious metals like gold and silver also find their way down, along with flowers as devotees pay homage to Bahubali. The next Mahamastakabhisheka will be held in 2005.

Carry a pair of socks to save your feet getting scorched by the hot, paved stones. Dholis (cane chairs tied between two poles carried by four strongmen) are available for Rs 150. At the base of the hill is a long row of shops selling mostly tourist junk from fluorescent images of Lord Bahubali to plastic toys. It's worth carrying home some of the stone carvings. There is an entry fee of Rs 5 for the site.

The temple dedicated to Adinatha, the first tirthankara, is the first of many shrines on the way up. Most of the shrines like the **Odeagal Basadi**, **Akhanda Bagilu** and **Siddhara Basadi** were built in the 12th century. At the summit is the statue of Gomateshwara. Fifty eight feet tall, it is believed to have been erected between 980 and 983 AD by Chavundaraya, a minister of the Ganga kings. Bahubali, son of Adinatha, fought a fierce battle with his brother Bharata, over the throne. Despite winning the battle Bahubali gave up his right to the throne and renounced the world to go in search of truth. After spending years in deep meditation, he attained enlightenment and acquired the name Bahubali. The statue at Shravanabelagola depicts Bahubali, removed from worldly life, standing naked and in deep meditation oblivious to the anthill below and creepers growing over his arms and legs.

Across the Indragiri is the smaller **Chandragiri Hill** with 14 shrines dedicated to Jain tirthankaras. The most remarkable of them all is the Parashwanatha Basadi with a 15ft statue of Parashwanatha, a tirthankara. The famous

Hoysaleshwara temple, Halebid

Mauryan emperor, Chandragupta, a staunch follower of Jainism is believed to have been buried here. The **Bhadrabahu cave**, the **Bhandari Basadi** and the **Akkana Basadi** containing images of all 24 Jain tirthankaras are worth a visit. The Jain Math here displays beautiful mural paintings.

## Belur

*An hour's drive from Shravanabelagola gets you to Belur. If architecture and history interest you, there's much to see in the temples of Belur. The best way to do it is to engage a government-approved guide. They usually charge Rs 60 per hour. For a small fee, you can get a spotlight turned on to see the carvings and bracket figures on the walls and ceiling.*

On the banks of the river Yagachi lies Belur. The Hoysala rulers made this their first capital. Prime among the sites is the **Chennakesava temple**, hailed as the 'Taj of south India'. Its study can keep you busy for hours, perhaps even days.

Built in 116 AD to commemorate the victory of the Hoysalas over the Cholas in the battle of Talakad, this temple took more than a hundred years to complete. The first thing that arrests your attention is the towering ornamental gopuram and the winged figure of Garuda, Lord Vishnu's carrier at the entrance. Friezes of marching elephants, mythological figures, battlefields, dancers, musicians and decorative motifs line the walls along with scenes from the Mahabharatha and Ramayana. The bracket figures depicting 38 madanikas or celestial nymphs, with intricate carvings as seen in their makeup, jewellery, and coiffures, are exclusive to Belur. The stunning sculpture of the Darpanasundari (lady with a mirror) almost steals the show.

No two pillars are alike, and the Narasimha pillar in the centre was built to rotate on its base. The Chennakesava temple is still active and draws huge crowds for the daily prayers.

## Halebid

*A mere 16kms drive from Belur is Halebid, the second capital of the Hoysalas originally known as 'Dwarasamudra'. The temple complex has a museum maintained by the Archaeological Survey of India. Twelfth and 13th century sculptures, woodcarvings, idols, coins and inscriptions, excavated by the department are displayed here. The museum is open from 10am to 5pm and closed on Fridays. Photography is not allowed inside the premises.*

Halebid, meaning ruined village was so named because it was destroyed in the 14th century by a Muslim invasion! You can see the remnants of the nine kilometre walls and earth ramparts on both sides of the main road that connect Belur and Hassan. There are two temples at Halebid, the famous **Kedareshwara** and **Hoysaleswara** temples built in the 12th century. The Hoysaleswara temple is set on a twin star-shaped base, typical of the Hoysala style of temple architecture. Depictions of Hindu deities, sages, animals and birds portray life in the time of the Hoysala kings. The temple, dedicated to Shiva was designed by a Vaishnavite follower and has images of Vishnu in his various incarnations. Frescoes of elephants, lions, a battlefield with horsemen, mythical animals and peacocks fill the walls. However, the most striking scenes are those of dance and music performances.

Just outside Halebid is **Bastihalli** the site of the 12th century Jain basadis. The exteriors of these temples seem spartan in comparison with the ornamentation outside the Hoysaleshwara temple. But their interiors with lathe-turned columns, carvings and ceiling friezes are definitely worth a look.

Darpanasundari at Belur

# Travel Information

Shettyhalli Church, Hassan

## GETTING THERE

### Shravanabelagola

Halebid-32kms
Belur-40kms
Hassan-52kms
Bangalore-148kms

Hassan-52kms

Bangalore-148kms

### Belur

Hassan-38kms
Bangalore-220kms

Hassan-38kms

Bangalore-220kms
Mangalore-154kms

### Halebid

Belur-17kms
Hassan-31kms
Bangalore-220kms

Hassan-31kms

Mangalore-148kms
Bangalore-220kms

## WHERE TO STAY

### Shravanabelagola

There are dharamsalas, guesthouses and a Yatri Nivas run by the Shravanabelagola Digambara Jain Managing Committee.
Tel 08176-572 258
Tariff Rs 100 to Rs 500

### Belur

**Vishnu Regency Deluxe Boarding & Lodging**
Sakleshpur Road, Belur, Hassan 573115
Tel 08177-223 011-13, 223 490

Fax 08177-230 310
Tariff Rs 400 to Rs 500

**Hotel Mayura Velapuri**
Temple Road, Belur 573115
Tel 08177-222 209
Tariff: Rs 200

### Halebid
**KSTDC Mayura Shantala**
Halebid, Hassan 573121
Tel 08177-273 224
Tariff Rs 150 to Rs 275

### Hassan
**Hoysala Village Resort**
Handinkere, Belur Road, Hassan 573201
Tel 08172-256 764/792/793
080- 2532 5302 (Bangalore)
Fax 2558 2425
Web www.trailsindia.com
Tariff Rs 3,700 to Rs 4,200

**Hotel Hassan Ashok**
PB 121 Bangalore-Mangalore Road, Hassan 573201
Tel 08172-268 731-36
Fax 08172-267 154
Email hsnashok@yahoo.com
Tariff Rs 700 to Rs 2,990

**Southern Star Hassan**
Bangalore-Mangalore Highway, Hassan 573201
Tel 08172-251 816/817/595/596
Fax 08172-268 916
Email sshassan@sancharnet.in
Tariff Rs 995 to Rs 1,595

**Hotel Gurudev International**
Bangalore-Mangalore Road, NH 48, Hassan 573201
Tel 08172-261 051/052, 269 525
Fax 08172-269 528
Email gurudev_hotel@rediffmail.com
Tariff Rs 395 to Rs 850

**Hotel Suvarna Regency**
PB 97 Bangalore-Mangalore Road, City Point, Hassan 573201
Tel 08172-266 774, 264 006/279
Fax 08172-263 822
Tariff Rs 275 to Rs 847

**Hotel Sri Krishna**
Bangalore-Mangalore Road, NH 48, Hassan 573201
Tel 08172-263 240/243
Fax 08172-233 904
Tariff Rs 250 to Rs 700

*For Tour Bookings, contact*
**KSTDC, Bangalore**
Tel 080-2227 5869/5883
Fax 2223 8016

**Mayura KSTDC Hoysala**
JLB Road, Mysore 570005
Tel 0821-242 5349/5597/6160

For Tourist Information, contact:
**Assistant Director**
Regional Tourist Office
Yatri Nivas Building, Near Bus Stand, Hassan 573201
Tel 08172-268 862

## Travel Tips

KSTDC organises tours from Bangalore and Mysore. They depart at 7:30am and return at 10pm. If you are not taking one of these tours, your best but slightly cumbersome option is to take a bus from Hassan to Channarayapatna and a connecting bus from there to Shravanabelagola. Taxis are available from Hassan to Belur, Halebid and Shravanabelagola. Fix the rate before you start your journey.

Shoes must be removed at the temple but the stone floor can get unbearably hot, so carry a pair of thick socks. It's advisable to carry your own water. For more information on KSTDC tours call 080-2227 5883(Bangalore) or 0821-242 3652 (Mysore).

# Hoysala Village Resort

Hassan, land of the sunflower, is the location for a cosy, ethnic hideout, Hoysala Village Resort, christened after the famed 12th century Hindu dynasty. A three hour drive from Bangalore through the pastoral countryside and quaint hamlets gets you to this charming location. The cheerful tiled cottages form a relaxing backdrop to explore the temples of Halebid and Belur – the twin Hoysala capitals – just 15kms away.

Modelled along the lines of a local village, the resort has a lush garden lined with a thicket of trees, shrubs and a profusion of flowers. Crisscrossing flagstone pathways lead into a maze of cottages with inviting hammocks and private gardens. The cottages are in earthy terracotta colours with large, airy rooms.

Happily, there is nothing rustic about the facilities! And you may expect hot running water and cable television among other amenities. Belur is the multicuisine restaurant at the resort and the fare features Tandoori and Continental cuisine with a fair share of local delicacies.

There are many activities you can enjoy at the resort – a relaxing swim in the pool, an Ayurvedic massage in deft hands, cycling through the many pathways, a quiet board game or a bullock cart ride through surrounding villages. The green countryside can be explored on foot and is perfect for long walks.

The temples of Halebid and Belur, the gigantic Gomateshwara statue at Shravanabelagola and the ruins of an ancient church at Shettyhalli are short excursions from the resort. The resort is managed by Trails and their trademark warm service is evident here.

*Handikere, Belur Road, Hassan 573201,* **Tel** 08172-256 764
**Web** www.trailsindia.com

# Divine Karnataka

Legends mingle with history in the temples and shrines of Karnataka, and there is a wealth of sights to see here. Karnataka has a rich spiritual heritage, boasting ancient temples, Jain basadis, churches and mosques. These sacred monuments stand testimony to its secular history.

Melkote is an important temple town for Hindus, especially the followers of Saint Ramanuja. According to a legend, Ramanuja set up the temple dedicated to Lord Krishna at Melkote. However, the idol was taken away by the Muslim king of Delhi who gave it to his daughter. When Ramanuja went to retrieve it he found that the princess had fallen in love with the idol and was loath to part with it. She followed Ramanuja on horseback. As she reached out to touch the idol at Melkote, it disappeared never to be seen again. One version has it that the princess merged with the idol and there is even a statue dedicated to her known as Bibi Nachiyar that is worshipped along with the main deity. The Vairamudi festival that takes place in March-April every year is one of the main festivities when Selvapillai or Krishna is adorned with a diamond-studded crown and taken out in procession.

The temple of Ranganatha at BR Hills near Mysore is another must-see on the itineraries of most Hindus. Built in Dravidian style, the temple is looked after by the Soliga tribes who live in these hills. The annual Rathotsavam and Kalyana Uthsavam are festive occasions that attract many devotees.

The Ranganatha temple built in the 9th century AD in Srirangapatna was patronised by Tipu Sultan. Created in both Hoysala and Vijayanagar styles, the main deity here is Ranganatha reclining on Adisesha, the snake.

Chamundeswari or Durga is the presiding deity of the Chamundeswari temple located on the Chamundi Hills in Mysore. Said to be the guardian goddess of

the kings of Mysore, the temple received the patronage of the Wodeyar rulers. Nanjangud, also near Mysore has the famous Nanjundeswara temple dedicated to Shiva.

Talakad, known for its sand dunes once had over 30 temples. It is now famous for the Vaidyeshwara temple dedicated to Shiva, built in Dravidian style and the Kirtinarayana, a Hoysala monument.

The seven muktisthalas of Karnataka, so called because they are built on land reclaimed from the sea by Parashurama (an incarnation of Vishnu), lie on the

St. Aloysius Church, Mangalore

west coast at Kollur, Udupi, Gokarna, Subramanhya, Kumbasi, Kodeshwara and Sankaranarayana.

On the outskirts of Bangalore, at the foot of Nandi Hills is the Bhoganandeeshwara temple that dates back to the 9th century AD, the time of the Banas. Up the hill is the Yoganandeeshwara temple built by the Cholas of Tamil Nadu.

The home of dharma or righteousness, Dharmasthala is another important pilgrimage centre for Shaivites, Madhawas and Jains. The temple has a shrine dedicated to Shiva, under the trusteeship of a

A sacred grove in Iruppu

Jain family and prayers conducted by Madhava priests. There is also a statue of Gomateshwara at Dharmasthala.

**Udupi** is a celebrated Vaishanvite temple situated north of Mangalore. Saint Madhavacharya installed the idol here as early as the 14th century.

Jainism came to Karnataka in the pre-Christian times and some of the important Jain pilgrimage centers are Shravanabelagola, Halebid, Badami, Karkala, Koppal and Mudabidri. The Parashwanath and Padmavathi temple at Humeha, Shimoga district attracts thousands of devotees each year. Karkala nearby, has a towering Gomateshwara monolith and the Chaturmukha Basadi.

**Koodalasangama**, a revered pilgrimage centre, lies at the confluence of the Krishna and Malaprabha rivers. Situated in Bagalkot district, Koodalasangama houses the famous Chalukyan Sangameshwara temple. The great 12th century poet-reformer Basaveshwara, is said to have attained nirvana at this sacred centre. Thirty kilometres from Koodalasangama is Basavana Bagewadi, a well known pilgrimage centre and the birth place of Basaveshwara.

The Mughal rulers brought Islam to northern Karnataka as may be seen in the regions of **Bijapur, Gulbarga** and Bidar. One of the many saints who lived here was Mouneshwara, now known as Karnataka's Kabir. Born in the 16th century in Sagarnad to Hindu parents, Mouneshwara is considered as the reincarnation of Khwaja Aminuddin. He sought to bridge the gap between Hindus and Muslims and was revered by the then ruler of Bijapur.

Solah Masjid or the 16-pillared mosque in **Bidar** is among the largest prayer halls in India. The Jumma Masjid in Gulbarga is said to be one of the oldest mosques in India. It was built in 1367 by Muhammed Bahmanshah. Gulbarga district has been a significant centre for Islam in Karnataka and home to a number of Sufi saints, Khwaja Bande Nawaz being one of them. Bidar was the second capital of Bahmani rulers and houses the famed Gavan's Madrasa and a number of beautiful forts and tombs.

Kanakana Kindi at the revered Krishna temple in Udupi

Jami Masjid, Bijapur

Locked into the densely forested hills of the Western Ghats, lies lush green Coorg or Kodagu. Stroll through the countryside, picnic in the vast plantations, hike through the rolling **Western Ghats** or go on fishing trips in the river **Cauvery**. Its temperate climate, densely forested slopes and vast tracts of coffee and spice plantations make it an ideal getaway for a laidback holiday. Misty mountains, charming hamlets and fresh air scented with coffee and cardamom makes the heat and the crowds of other south Indian cities fade away.

Begin your journey at the attractive hill town of **Madikeri**, the 'capital' city with plenty of hotels to suit all budgets. It's a convenient base from where the rest of Kodagu may be explored. Most tourists start with a trip to the religious site of **Talacauvery** where the mighty river Cauvery was 'born'. The Abbey falls, Kodagu's highest peak **Tadiyendamol**, the honey farms in Kakkabe and the Valnoor Fishing Camp are other attractions accessible from here. A few hours away is the nature resort **Cauvery Nisargadhama** and the Tibetan settlement **Bylekuppe**.

# Nature & Wildlife Trail
## Kodagu (Coorg)

Lush Kodagu is flanked by the Western Ghats and river Cauvery.

Talacauvery, the birthplace of river Cauvery

## Travelling to Kodagu

Kodagu lies 240kms southeast of Bangalore. The only way to get there is by road, as there are no air or rail services available beyond Mysore (128kms away). Regular express buses ply between Bangalore, Mysore, Coimbatore and Kodagu. The road meanders through lovely wooded hills, paddy fields, picturesque towns and a wildlife sanctuary. Hiring a taxi is the best proposition for those who prefer to travel at their own pace. Choose a base in the well-connected city of Madikeri from where the rest of Kodagu can be reached by car. Madikeri's roads dip and rise unexpectedly and are perfect for walking. Kodagu enjoys a pleasant climate through the year, especially the months from September to May. The wet monsoon months are best faced with umbrellas and raincoats! But even the torrential rains slamming through the wet earth are a sight to behold.

## History

The earliest references to the Kodavas are found in Tamil Sangam literature dating back to the 2nd century AD. Many dynasties ruled the region, accounting for its unique culture and heritage, distinctly different from its neighbours. The Haleri Lingayat Rajas set up an independent 'Kodagu' kingdom in the 11th century.

For a brief but significant period in the 18th century, it was wrested from them by the Tiger of Mysore, Tipu Sultan. The British helped the determined Lingayat Rajas regain their hold. Finally, in 1834, Kodagu was colonised by the British and its ruler, King Chikkaveerarajendra, sent into exile. It gained independence along with the rest of India in 1947 and was declared a separate state only to merge with Karnataka in the year 1956. But the brief imperial rule left behind a legacy that is the source of Kodagu's identity and income – the cultivation of coffee and spices.

## Talacauvery

Begin your journey through Kodagu with a spiritual sojourn to the sacred site of Talacauvery, 45kms southwest of Madikeri. Source of the mighty river Cauvery, it is one of the seven sacred rivers of India. Set amidst the lush-green **Brahmagiri Hills**, 4186ft above sea level, Talacauvery is a site of great religious significance for the people of Karnataka. Legend has it that Cauvery, wife of sage Agasthya, transformed herself into a river to serve the people. She submerged herself into the ground after which she rose up again as a forceful river. At this site a small shrine was built signifying the birth of the river. According to the story, when sage Agasthya tried to stop his wife from becoming a river the pleats of her sari were pushed back and to this day Kodava women wear their sari with pleats at the back!

Another legend has it that the Goddess Cauvery appears every year on a specific day in October. She manifests herself as a sudden upsurge of water in a small tank. A large number of devotees gather to witness this bubbling spring and coconuts adorned with flowers are floated down the river as part of a special prayer. The water is especially potent on this occasion and is said to possess healing powers.

At **Bhagamandala**, 36kms from Madikeri, river Cauvery merges with two of its tributaries, Kanike and Sujyothi. A cluster of three temples has been built at this confluence. The temples in this region display exquisite woodwork. You may pick up some good quality honey at the Bhagamandala Honey Cooperative Society.

If you've packed a picnic lunch, head towards the beautiful **Abbey Falls**, a steep descent through a private coffee estate and splash around in its pristine waters.

Mangalore · Chikmagalur · Bangalore
Talacauvery · Madikeri · Mysore
Nagarhole · Bandipur
Wildlife Sanctuary · National Park
Not to scale

Alternately, you could trek here from Madikeri, an eight-kilometre walk through verdant scenery and coffee plantations.

## Madikeri

Madikeri, the erstwhile capital of the Lingayat Rajas is located in the heart of the Kodagu district. Sitting pretty at 4,921ft above sea level, the tiny outpost is hemmed by craggy hills, charming cottages, colourful bougainvillea gardens and bustling bazaars. Madikeri, also known as Mercara, is a tourist destination in its own right. With rolling coffee and orange plantations and secluded picnic spots, it has been called the **'Scotland of India'**. A walk through the streets affords panoramic views, twisting roads, crowded bazaars and the delightful old-world charm of a village nestling in the

Tea plantations in coffee country

The verdant coffee plantations of Kodagu

countryside. Coffee, cardamom, green and black pepper, bamboo shoot pickle and honey make some of the best buys from the region. Check for the 'Agmark' sign before you settle.

To get a panoramic view of the town, head for the **Raja's Seat**. Frequented by the kings of Kodagu, the Raja's Seat gives a sweeping view of the entire city of Madikeri, the distant mountain ranges, meandering roads, the green valleys, paddy fields and the little hamlets. Sunsets are particularly beautiful.

In and around Madikeri are plenty of sightseeing opportunities. The **Mercara Fort** is one such spot that lies within the city. Its numerous edifices still stand as testimony to the illustrious rule of the Lingayat kings. Built in 1812, the fort is replete with winding corridors and secret passageways. The fort also holds the simple and unassuming palace of the Lingayat rulers along with a church, museum, temple and prison. It has been converted into the District collector's office quarters.

The **English Protestant Church** with colourful stained glass windows and marble engraved memorials is well worth a visit. The church was built 100 years ago to honour the British soldiers who died in battle here. Now it houses a museum. Outside the fort, there is a more recent memorial of the gallant sons of Kodagu who died fighting in the First World War.

The **Omkareshwara Shiva temple** built by Linga Raja in 1820, is situated in the east of the fort. Dedicated to Lord Shiva and Vishnu, the temple complex is surrounded by a lake built in a distinctly Indo-Saracenic style. On the outskirts of Madikeri are other noteworthy monuments such as the Royal Tombs of the Lingayat Kings. In keeping with the secular atmosphere within the fort, the Hindu tombs display a marked Islamic influence reflected in the large domes, elegant minarets and trelliswork.

If you are attracted by heights, head to the highest peak in Kodagu – **Tadiyendamol**. On a clear evening you may see the orange sun as it sinks into the distant Arabian Sea. Under the Tadiyendamol peak is the Nalakunad Palace that was originally used as a hunting lodge, today a camping site. The Padi Igutappa temple and the honey farms in

Kakkabe are worth a visit. The **Valnoor Fishing Camp** is great for anglers. Stroll along the banks of the Cauvery and you can fish for the elusive mahseer. Fishing permits can be obtained from the Coorg Wildlife Society. The fishing camp is also a haven for birdwatchers with over 300 species of birds flying in and out.

On the Madikeri-Mysore highway, next to the commercial town of Kushalnagar is **Bylekuppe**, the largest Tibetan settlement in south India. The only mode of transport from the main highway of Kushalnagar to Bylekuppe are auto rickshaws. The Karnataka Government gifted 3,000 acres of land to the uprooted Tibetan refugees who have converted the area into a mini Tibet with monasteries, monks in maroon robes, prayer wheels, butter tea and prayer flags. The Namdroling Monastery has a 40ft high idol of the Buddha. Handicrafts, carpets and jewellery are sold at Bylekuppe's regular shops and at the weekly bazaar. The tiny Tibetan restaurants serve up some good momos and noodles.

A few hours out of Kodagu is the serene forest retreat **Cauvery Nisargadhama**, a picturesque forest with the river Cauvery coursing through it. Nisargadhama is 27kms from Madikeri and two kilometres from Kushalnagar, off the Mysore-Madikeri

highway. This is really an emerald green riverine island in the middle of the Cauvery. The sprawling 64-acre nature resort has luxuriant bamboo groves, rosewood and teak trees. Cosy bamboo cottages have been built by the Forest Department. A deer park, orchidarium and elephant rides are some of the attractions.

Kushalnagar is just two kilometres from Cauvery Nisargadhama. From Kushalnagar head 15kms south and you'll reach the village of **Dubare** where Jungle Lodges & 7 Resorts has started an **Elephant Camp**. Visitors get to watch elephants having a scrub in the river and being trained and tamed by mahouts. You can offer ragi dumplings prepared at the camp, coconut, jaggery, sugarcane, and plantains to the pachyderms. Elephant rides into the Dubare forest are a big attraction.

Kodagu comes alive during the monsoons.

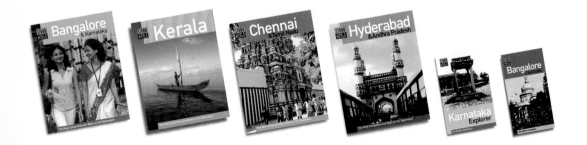

## GETTING THERE

### Madikeri

Mysore-120kms
Mangalore-136kms
Bangalore-260kms

Mysore-120kms

Mangalore-136kms

## WHERE TO STAY

### Orange County Resort
Karadigodu Post, Siddapur,
Kodagu 571253
Tel 08274-258 481,
2532 5302 (Bangalore)
Fax 2558 2425
Web www.trailsindia.com
Tariff Rs 6,500 to Rs 13,500

### Misty Woods
Kakkabe, Coorg, Karnataka
Tel 08272-238 561/351
Web www.coorgmisty.com
Tariff Rs 2,000 to Rs 3,500

### Hotel Coorg International
Convent Road,
Madikeri 571201
Tel 08272-229 390, 228 071/72
Fax 08272-228 073
Web www.coorghotels.com
Tariff Rs 1,400 to Rs 2,200

### Hotel Rajdarshan
8/13 MG Road, Madikeri,
Kodagu 571201
Tel 08272-229 142, 228 823
Fax 0827-228 367
Email hrdraj@sancharnet.in
Tariff Rs 850 to Rs 1,350

### Veerabhoomi Tourist Village
Kudige Road, Kushalnagar, Kodagu
Tel 08276-278 113/213
Tariff Rs 700 to Rs 3,000

### Capitol Village
5th Cross, Chettahalli,
Siddapur Road, Madikeri,
Kodagu 571201
Tel 08272-225 929/975
Fax 08272-228 455
Tariff Rs 750

### Kannika International
4-12 IB Road, Kushalnagar,
North Kodagu 571234
Tel 08276-274 728, 273 401-403
Fax 08276-273 318
Web www.coorgtourism.net
Tariff Rs 550 to Rs 650

### Hotel Cauvery
School Road, Madikeri
Tel 08272-225 492,
Fax 08272-229 455
Tariff Rs 200 to Rs 500

### East End Hotel
General Thimayya Road, Madikeri
Tel 08272-229 996, 225 749
Tariff Rs 500 to Rs 650

### KSTDC Mayura Valley View
Raja's Seat, Madikeri 571301
Tel 08272-228 387
Fax 08272-224 430
Tariff Rs 275 to Rs 500

### Hill Town Hotel
Daswal Road, Madikeri
Tel 08272-223 801-05, 229 479
Fax 08272-223 805
Email hilltown@rediffmail.com
Tariff Rs 250 to Rs 750

### Travel Tips

There are no air or rail connections to
Madikeri or any part of Kodagu. The
nearest airport is Mangalore, 136kms away.
Bangalore is a more convenient point of
access, 260kms away. While at Coorg,
watch out for the thick fog that suddenly
descends in the hills and reduces visibility.
It's also advised to carry a torch, especially if
you are going out on long walks.

## Orange County

If you desire a holiday in scenic Kodagu (Coorg) with the luxury of a Tudor style cottage, Ayurvedic massage treatments and lazy afternoons lounging on a hammock, try Orange County, the resort that made Kodagu a popular destination. It's well located, comfortable with understated elegance, welcomes families as well as singles, and has a wide range of activities from spice tours to bird watching.

Named for the orange trees that grew here a few decades ago, Orange County was started in 1994 by the Ramapuram family. The Ramapurams have since expanded to make this an award winning resort with an ISO 9001:2000 certification to boot. Orange County was awarded the Gold Crown Award RCI's (Resort Condominiums International) highest accolade for surpassing international standards of excellence in resort quality and hospitality for four consecutive years. The forty eight thatched cottages have bright airy rooms with a fireplace, a kitchenette and a balcony.

The Camp is the latest addition to the resort, offering air-conditioned luxury tents. Ten tents with an exclusive restaurant and an 'infinity' pool jutting into the lake, offer the experience of the outdoors in a serene setting. A splendid view of the lake combined with the famed Orange County hospitality makes The Camp a great holiday option.

Located 900m above sea level, Orange County has more to offer than a quiet holiday in an upmarket resort in the hills. The Dubare Forest Reserve begins next door and the Kodavas' cherished Cauvery river flanks the resort on the other side. Guests can choose from plenty of nature-related activities. Coracle rides, rafting and safaris are possible at the Dubare Reserve. You can also go trekking or fishing at Valnur Fishing Camp. The less adventurous can choose from bird watching, boat rides or nature walks through hills and coffee plantations.

Granary is a multicuisine restaurant attached to the resort and Peppercorn is the speciality grill restaurant at The Camp. There is also a bar, the Hunters Lodge and conferencing facilities for corporates. In addition to the Ayurvedic centre, there is a gym and swimming pool for fitness enthusiasts. The resort is managed by Trails, known for their warm and friendly service.

*Karadigodu Post, Siddapur, Kodagu 571253*
**Tel** 08274-258 481 **Web** www.trailsindia.com

SHARE MOMENTS AS HEADY
AS FRESHLY BREWED COORG COFFEE.

Trails, Second Floor, St. Patrick's Business Complex,
21, Museum Road, Bangalore - 560 025, Karnataka, India.
Ph: ++91 80 25325302, 25582525, 51126013.
Fax: ++91 80 25582425.
Email: info@trailsindia.com  www.trailsindia.com

Welcome to Orange County in Coorg - a land once described by the British as the 'Scotland of India'. And, experience nature, adventure and romance like nowhere else.

Soak in the serenity of the cool slopes of the Western Ghats. Revel in the world-class hospitality. Experience the rejuvenative powers of Ayurveda. Set off on an elephant safari. Battle it out with the mighty Mahseer on a fishing expedition. Or, just laze out.

# Home Stays in Kodagu

**B**ed and breakfast home stays have sprung up throughout Kodagu, giving tourists a chance to experience the legendary Kodava hospitality. Enterprising coffee plantation owners have opened their wooden beamed bungalows set in rolling plantations to visitors, providing them with an authentic flavour of Kodagu, its customs, cuisine and traditions.

Home stays are ideal for tourists who want to sample the delicious Kodava cuisine, enjoy the warm hospitality of knowledgeable hosts and a tailor-made itinerary. Some places organise a range of activities such as birdwatching, trekking, cycling through the estates, plantation tours, angling and picnicking. But if you are looking for five-star comforts, home stays is not an option.

### Hillyside Estate
Hardoor Post via Suntikoppa, Kodagu
**Tel** 08276-262 666, 080-2299 0364 (Bangalore)
**Tariff** Rs 1,000 to Rs 3,000

### Sand Banks
PB 30 Polaycad Estate, Ammathi Post, Kodagu 571201
**Tel** 08272-252 130, 264 130
**Email** kalaps@sancharnet.in
**Tariff** Rs 1,500 to Rs 2,000 per couple, inclusive of breakfast

### Rain Forest Retreat
Mojo Plantation, Kaloor Road, Near Galibeedu Village, Madikeri, Kodagu 571201
**Tel** 08272-265 636/638
**Fax** 08272-265 636
**Web** www.rainforestours.com
**Tariff** Rs 1,000 to Rs 2,000 per person, inclusive of meals

### Pearl Garden
PB 60 Kutta, Kodagu 571250
**Tel** 08272-244 233
**Tariff** Rs 1,600 per couple, inclusive of two meals and breakfast

### Coorg Dale Home Stay
Valnoor Post, via Kushalnagar, North Kodagu
**Tel** 08276-297 496
**Email** geoffrey_muthanna@yahoo.co.in
**Tariff** Rs 1,500, inclusive of food

### Vana Arathi
Nanchi Estate, Near Nagarhole Game Sanctuary, South Kodagu
**Tel** 08274-244 228/888
**Tariff** Rs 1,500, inclusive of non-vegetarian meals or Rs 1,250, inclusive of vegetarian meals.

### Ananda Estate
Arapattu, Kodagu 571212
**Tel** 08274-269 345
**Tariff** Rs 1,000 to Rs 1,500, inclusive of breakfast

### Alath-Cad Estate Bungalow
PB 7 Amathi, Kodagu 571211
**Tel** 08274-252 190, 9845445519
**Fax** 08274-452 589
**Web** www.alathcadcoorg.com
**Tariff** Rs 1,000 per couple, inclusive of breakfast

### Honey Valley Estate
Yavakapady Village, Kodagu 571212
**Tel** 08272-238 339
**Email** honeyvalley_2000@yahoo.com
**Tariff** Rs 150 to Rs 900

### The Last Resort Home Stay
Hosapatna, Kushalnagar, Kodagu
**Tel** 08276-297 540, 080-2548 5705 (Bangalore)
**Web** www.iciti.info/thelastresort
**Tariff** Rs 1,000 inclusive of food or Rs 650 to Rs 750 excluding food.

### Sylvan Cottage, Muthar Mudi Village
Muthar Mudi Village Murnud Post, Kodagu 571252
**Tel** 08272-232 283
**Tariff** Rs 650

### Chilligiri Estate
PB 167, Manchally Village, Kutta, Kodagu 571 250
**Tel** 08274-244 265
**Tariff** Rs 500, inclusive of vegetarian meals or Rs 600, inclusive of non-vegetarian meals.

Sera Jhe Monastery, Bylekuppe

# Tibetans in Karnataka

**T**housands of miles from the Himalayan plateau, a mini Tibet may be found in Bylekuppe, Hunsur, Mundgod and Kollegal! These are the locations for the five Tibetan settlements in Karnataka. Women in chupas with their prayer wheels, momos and thukpas at street stalls, reincarnate lamas, monasteries and many aspects of traditional Tibetan life may be seen here.

Karnataka has been home to Tibetans for the last 40 years, following the Chinese invasion of Tibet in 1959 when tens of thousands of them left Tibet for India, along with the Dalai Lama, their spiritual and political head. Prime Minister Jawaharlal Nehru was quick to offer asylum and house them in Dharamsala in the Himalayas and later in Karnataka. The settlements here have some of the important monasteries imparting knowledge of Tibetan Buddhism like the **Sera Jhe**, **Namdroling** and **Tashi Lhunpo** monasteries in Bylekuppe, and the **Ganden** and **Drepung** monasteries in Mundgod.

Tibetan settlements encourage their national art and culture. Thangkas or scroll paintings depicting Buddhist divinities, embellished with gold and set in a brocade frame and carpets woven with typical designs are made and sold in these settlements. Tibetan medicine dates back 2,000 years and is based predominantly on the use of herbs. It has found many takers among the locals.

**Losar** or the Tibetan New Year is celebrated in the months of February and March with great fervour and from time to time the Dalai Lama graces the settlements with his presence.

For information on Tibetans and the settlements, contact: *The Office of the Chief Representative Cum Central Tibetan Relief Committee, No 7, Sampangiramaiah Garden Srinivagalu Tank, Viveknagar Post , Bangalore 560047 Tel 2550 6842*

W <

> E

# PIONEER
# TRAVELS

(Your ultimate travel partner in South India)

AT PIONEER TRAVELS we have one holy writ: Attention to detail. Which is why we will never offer you any of the usual package tours. To us, you are an individual, whether you are travelling alone or with company. You tell us what you want and the way you want it. We will customise your tour package exactly, down to the last detail. Across Kerala, Karnataka, Tamil Nadu and Goa.

We will go that extra mile for you with our own fleet of luxury, chauffeured vehicles and our round-the-clock hotline connection. All to make sure that your holiday remains uniquely unforgettable.

**PIONEER**

• Package Tours • Own Vehicular Fleet • Hotel Reservations • Conference and Incentives Planning • Honeymoon Packages • Air/Rail Ticketing

PIONEER TRAVELS: Pioneer House, Willingdon Island, Cochin 682003. Kerala, India  Tel: 91-484-2666148,  2669148  Fax: 91-484-2668490
E-mail: pioneer@pner.com **Chennai Branch:** Office No 10, City Centre, T Nagar, Chennai. Tel 044 28158393, 52125127. email : pioneertt@satyam.net.in www.pioneertravels.com

Courtesy: Orange County

# The Kodavas

The origin of the Kodava people remains a mystery and there are a number of interesting theories about their origin. One traces their racial origins to the Kurds of Iraq and Iran. Another popular theory gives them a Greek lineage. The story goes that a group of soldiers from the army of Alexander the Great went missing and were believed to have wandered past the Vindhya mountains into south India as far back as 327 BC. Tired of the fighting, they stayed back in the tranquil Western Ghats and their descendants are believed to be the Kodavas. The traditional kupya costume worn by the men resembles the Greek toga and their fair complexions and aquiline features are said to resemble Greek people. But some historians believe that they migrated instead from West Asia and the kupya costume resembles the kuffia worn by Arabs.

The Kodavas have a distinct ethnic identity they have zealously safeguarded over the centuries. They have their own unique customs and traditions, including a separate language. The modern Kodava is as urbane as his neighbour but still remains deeply connected to his roots. Every household possesses a picture of the Talacauvery and a heavy brass lamp is lit every evening to honour ancestors. Ancestors are revered at all times and religious functions are held in the traditional **ainmane** or family home.

The Kodava attire is especially striking and an integral part of their heritage. Men dress in traditional **kupyas** or long black coats tied at the waist with a red and gold sash and an ornamental dagger tucked into its folds. The women dress in rich silk saris worn with pleats at the back and complemented by colourful headscarves.

Kodava ceremonies of birth, marriage and death are very different from the rituals and traditions practiced by Hindus in south India. Marriage ceremonies are not solemnised by a priest but by family elders. Their wedding ceremonies are lively affairs. The bridegroom dressed as a warrior slashes a banana stump with a single deft stroke of his sword, symbolising the winning over of the bride. Family disputes are not taken to a court of law but settled by elders of the community instead.

Festivals are special events when the entire community comes together. The **Keilpodhu** is one such and celebrated with great gusto – after an elaborate lunch the men show off their shooting prowess by splitting open coconuts tied to the highest tree. **Huthri** is a harvest festival held in November that is celebrated by the ceremonial cutting of the paddy crop on a full moon night.

The exotic and differently flavoured Kodava cuisine is predominantly non-vegetarian. Their signature dish is the unusual **Pandi** or pork curry served with **Kadumbuttu** or rice dumplings. Succulent koli or chicken curry, **Nool Puttu** or rice noodles and **Bembla** or bamboo shoot curry are other unusual Kodava dishes.

## The Kodava Military Tradition

The Kodavas are proud of their martial origins and many of them sign up for India's military. Many distinguished generals, like the late Field Marshal Cariappa, the late General Thimayya, and General BC Nanda hail from here. The Kodavas consider it an honour for at least one member of a family to serve in the nation's army or defence services. The national costume of the men – the white turbans, the long black coats with the ornamental daggers reflect their warrior heritage.

Kodavas are the only community that enjoys the privilege of owning guns. Under the Indian Arms Act, they can carry firearms without a license. This privilege was granted to them by the British in 1861, since the gun is as much an emblem of religion to the Kodavas as the Kirpan is to the Sikhs. Even before the advent of telephones and telegrams, gunshots were used as a means of communication between estates to announce births and deaths. A single shot fired into the air heralded the birth of a boy and two announced a death in the family.

Pandi curry and Kadumbuttu, a Kodava delicacy

# Set sail on the Kerala Coast

## with ABAD

Innovations

# Nature & Wildlife Trail
## Chikmagalur

Chikmagalur, Bhadra Wildlife Sanctuary, Kemmangundi, Mullayanagiri, Baba Budangiri, Kalasa, Kudremukh

This circuit hides a wealth of natural beauty undiscovered by the regular tourist. Stumble upon an invigorating climate, a rare wildlife sanctuary, tall mountains with exciting trekking trails, ancient temples and forts and above all the fragrance of coffee and spices. If this is your idea of a perfect holiday, welcome to Chikmagalur district in southwestern Karnataka's Malnad region.

Chikmagalur is home to wildlife sanctuaries, coffee plantations and cool mountains.

## Chikmagalur District

*Legend has it that the district takes its name from the main town Chikmagalur or 'younger daughter's town'. You travel due west to Hassan and then move north to Chikmagalur, a six hour drive from Bangalore. Alternately, you could board a train from either Bangalore or Mysore and alight at Kadur, the closest railway station from where it's a short and pleasant hill drive to Chikmagalur town. Taxis and buses ply frequently between Chikmagalur and all major towns. There are quite a few resorts and hotels at Chikmagalur, if you choose to stay.*

With the town as your base the rest of the district's highlights are an easy drive. The **Bhadra Wildlife Sanctuary** offers not just animals but great scenery too. The mountain ranges of **Mullayanagiri** and **Baba Budangiri** have plenty of trekking trails. Kemmangundi, a popular hill station in the Malnad region is easily accessible from here. Stop at the sacred hamlet of **Kalasa** considered one of the pancha-kshetras on the banks of river Bhadra. Twenty kilometres from Kalasa is **Kudremukh**, home to a small mining township, a national park and more trekking trails. Hoysala temples are set in Belawadi and Amritpura in the Chikmagalur District. Heritage enthusiasts will also be happy to note that Chikmagalur is only a few hours from the ancient temples of Belur and Halebid.

## Bhadra Wildlife Sanctuary

*An hour's journey from Chikmagalur town, past bamboo thickets and coffee plantations, lies Bhadra Wildlife Sanctuary, only recently identified as a tiger reserve.* Originally called the Jagara Game Area, this was a popular hunting ground of the British and landed aristocracy. The sanctuary takes its name from its lifeline, the Bhadra river. If you are lucky, you might sight the pride of the sanctuary, the tiger. Look out for the gaur, the striped hyena and the rare flying lizard while driving through these dense forests. The **Jagara Giant**, a 300-year old teak tree with a 5.21m girth is a big draw.

## Mullayanagiri and Baba Budangiri

The Mullayanagiri range, 6,317ft above sea level, boasts the tallest peak in Karnataka. Located six kilometres from Chikmagalur, Mullayanagiri is a huge favourite with avid trekkers. A 15km trek through dense teak forests will get you to the Seethalayanagiri range. It offers a great view of the **Chandra Drona Hill** in the Baba Budangiri range.

The range is named after Baba Budan or Hazrat Dada Hayat Mir Kalander, a famous Muslim saint who made these hills his home. He was the first to introduce coffee cultivation in the country. The story goes that while returning from Mecca in 1650, the saint picked up a few coffee berries from the famous port of Mocha. He planted them on the high ridges of these mountains and India's first coffee plantation took root.

A laterite cave at the peak – the **Inam Dattatreya Peetha** – is the site where Hindu saint Dattareya Swami and Baba Budan lived. Now venerated by both Hindus and Muslims, the annual jatra or urus is a time of great festivity.

## Kemmangundi

Kemmangundi is a beautiful hill station, an hour's drive from Chikmagalur. Surrounded by thick, evergreen forests and coffee estates, it was once the summer camp of the Maharaja of Mysore, Krishnarajendra Wodeyar IV and is also known as **KR Hills**. Sights worth visiting include the **Hebbe Falls** and **Kalhatti Falls**.

At Hebbe, water rushes down from a height of 250ft in two stages to form Dodda Hebbe (Big Falls) and Chikka Hebbe (Small Falls). The falls start at the top of the Chandra Drona Hill and crash 45m below.

## Kalasa

Eighty four kilometres southwest of Chikmagalur lies Kalasa, an old *agrahara* settlement on the banks of the river Bhadra. It is believed that Shiva appeared before the sage Vashishta here. Kalasa looks like an island with the Bhadra encircling it. The *pancha theerthas* or the five sacred ponds: Koditeertha, Rudrateertha, Ambateertha, Nagateertha and Vasishthateertha are also found here.

The **Kalaseshwara temple** (dedicated to Lord Shiva) is believed to be over a 1,000 years old. It is situated on a hillock. Not far from it are the Kshetrapala shrine made of soapstone and the Girijamba temple built in honour of Girijamba who came down from Varanasi to marry Kalaseshwara. If you are in Kalasa during the month of Karthika (just after Diwali), you can witness the spectacular Girija Kalyanotsava or the wedding of Shiva and Girija.

This region has several pilgrimage spots such as **Sringeri**, famous for its Vidyashankara temple and **Horanadu**, known for the Annapoorneswari temple. The Vidyashankara temple is an architectural marvel. Twelve sculpted pillars, each representing a sign of the zodiac, are placed such that the sun's rays fall on each in the order of the solar months.

## Kudremukh

Southwest of Chikmagalur town lies Kudremukh or the 'Horse Face Range' at a distance of 95kms. The broad hills overlook the Arabian Sea and are connected by deep valleys and steep precipices. Off the regular tourist itinerary, Kudremukh is a trekker's paradise, with lush forests, gushing rivers, grassy slopes and waterfalls. A ruined fort (the **Jamalabad fort** built by Tipu Sultan in 1794), a dilapidated church, tiny hamlets and the famous **Lobo's House** (a conveniently located guesthouse), lie on the regular trekking route.

Kudremukh is also the location of the Kudremukh Iron Ore Company Limited (KIOCL) and its township. The **Lakya Dam** located near KIOCL is worth a visit. Ten kilometres from the township is the **Kudremukh National Park**. The moist, deciduous and evergreen forest is great for bird watching and to spot many species of butterflies. These forests are also home to the leopard and the Malabar giant squirrel. **Ganga Moola** where the rivers Tunga, Bhadra and Netravathi originate and the **Hanuman Gundi waterfalls** are must-see places here.

Coffee cultivation in India first began in Chikmagalur.

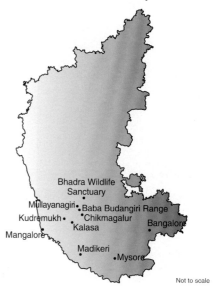
Bhadra Wildlife Sanctuary
Mullayanagiri • Baba Budangiri Range
Kudremukh • • Chikmagalur
Kalasa Bangalore
Mangalore •
Madikeri
• Mysore

Not to scale

## GETTING THERE

### Bhadra Wildlife Sanctuary

 Bangalore-265 kms
Chikmagalur-30kms

 Kadur-40kms

 Bangalore-265kms
Mangalore-180kms

### Kemmangundi

 Chikmagalur-53kms
Bangalore-210kms
Tarikere-35kms
Kadur-80kms

 Mangalore-180kms

 Mangalore-180kms

### Kudremukh

 Kalasa-20kms
Karkala-50kms
Mudigere-75kms
Mangalore-130kms
Bangalore-350kms

Mangalore-130kms

Mangalore-130kms

### Kalasa

Bangalore-310kms
Hassan-128kms
Karkala-70kms
Udupi-120kms

Mangalore-132kms
Udupi-120kms

Mangalore-132kms

### Chikmagalur

 Kalasa-20kms
Karkala-50kms
Mudigere-75kms
Mangalore-137kms
Bangalore-251kms

## WHERE TO STAY

### Bhadra Wildlife Santuary

**Muthodi Nature Camp**
Deputy Conservator of Forests,
Bhadra Wildlife Division,
Chikmagalur 577101
**Tel** 08262-234 904 **Fax** 08262-228 026
**Email** dcfbadra@blr.vsnl.net.in
**Tariff** Rs 250 (Indians),
Rs 500 (Foreigners),
8-bed dormitory, Rs 400

### Kemmangundi

**Horticulture Department Guest Houses**
Special Officer, Kemmangundi Post,
Chikmagalur District 577141
**Tel** 08261-237 126
Director of Horticulture, Lalbagh,
Bangalore 560004
**Tel** 080-2657 1925

## Kudremukh

**Seethanadi Nature Camp**
Kudremukh Wildlife Division,
Seethanadi, Hebri Village, Karkala
Taluk, Udupi 574104
**Telefax** 08258-231 183
**Email** dcfwlkarkala@rediffmail.com
**Tariff** Deluxe rooms, Rs 400
(Indians), Rs 800 (Foreigners),
Tent, Rs 200 (Indians),
Rs 300 (Foreigners)

**Silent Valley Corporate Resorts**
Thodlu, Kalasa, Kudremukh Road,
Chikmagalur 577124
**Tel** 08263-274 801
**Email** enquiry@silentvalley.net
**Tariff** Rs 2,400 (Couple)
For bookings, contact:
080-2334 2525, 2334 2521 (Bangalore)

## Chikmagalur

**The Taj Garden Retreat**
KM Road, Jyothinagar,
Chikmagalur 577102
**Tel** 08262-220 202/404
**Fax** 08262-220 222
**Email** tgrresv.chk@tajhotels.com
**Tariff** Rs 2,600 to Rs 3,300

**Nature Nirvana, A Plantation Getaway**
Bynekhan & Eldorado Plantations,
Baba Budangiri, Chikmagalur
**Tel** 0824-525 9152, 98452 15152,
98440 42152
**Web** www.naturenirvana.com
**Tariff** Rs 600 to Rs 2,000

## Texwoods
Sheegekhan Estate,
Next to Muthodi
Wildlife Sanctuary,
via Mallandur, Chikmagalur
**Tel** 08262-259 026
**Web** www.texresorts.com
**Tariff** Rs 1,600

### River Woods
Avanthy Estate, Magundi Post,
Chikmagalur 577160
**Tel** 08266-248 054
**Fax** 08266-248 044
**Tariff** Rs 800 to Rs 1,250
For bookings, contact:
98862 99889

### The Planter's Court Hotel
PB 109, KM Road,
Chikmagalur 577101
**Tel** 08262-235 881-85
**Fax** 08262-231 169
**Tariff** Rs 300 to Rs 1,210

### Hotel Malnad Paradise
Indira Gandhi Road,
Chikmagalur 577101
**Tel** 08262-234 531/532, 232 218
**Tariff** Rs 250 to Rs 800

### Hotel Mount Palace
Indira Gandhi Road,
Chikmagalur 577101
**Tel** 08262-237 050
**Tariff** Rs 300 to Rs 650

### Travel Tips
Carry a packed lunch if you plan to spend a day out. If you are travelling from Bangalore, you can break the journey by stopping at Shravanabelagola, Belur and Halebid.

# Jog Falls

The Jog Falls are the highest waterfalls in Asia, tumbling a spectacular 253m as river Sharavathi drops. The roar is audible as you approach the thick forests of its setting. There are four distinctive cascades that take shape with the curious names, **Raja, Rani, Rover** and **Rocket**. Of these, Raja has the longest drop.

When the sluice gates of the **Lingamakki Dam** are closed, you can trek right down to the bottom of the gorge. The Inspection Bungalow perched on the top of the falls affords a great view. The nearby town of Kumta has a beach, temples and a popular sandalwood handicrafts bazaar.

## GETTING THERE

Getting to and from Jog falls by public transport is difficult. It takes two hours to Udupi and eight hours to Karwar. But there are innumerable private buses plying to Shimoga and Sagar from where you can get onward connections to Jog Falls.

 Sagar-45kms
Honnavar-56kms
Shimoga-113kms
Bangalore-390kms

 Shimoga-113kms

Mangalore-180kms

## WHERE TO STAY

**KSTDC Mayura Gerusoppa**
Jog Falls, Sagar Taluk,
Shimoga 577435
**Tel** 08186-244 732
**Tariff** Rs 200 to Rs 400

**Youth Hostels Association of India**
Jog Falls, Shimoga
**Tel** 08186-244 251/375
**Tariff** Rs 15 and Rs 10
for school children.

**Forest Guest Houses**
For details, contact:
DCF, Shimoga Wildlife Division,
DC Compound,
Shimoga 577201
**Tel** 08182-222 983

# Karnataka's Waterfalls

Shivasamudram Falls

Three major rivers flow through Karnataka's high mountain ranges, dropping thousands of feet down rocky gorges before they empty into the sea. They traverse a variety of terrain on their journey – rugged hills, dense forests and unspoilt beaches, producing some spectacular waterfalls in their wake. Most of the rivers originate in the hilly Western Ghats and most of the falls lie in the district of Kodagu and Uttara Kannada.

Some of the falls are well known and attract visitors from far. Many of the falls come alive in the rainy season as the rivers swell and turn even the smallest outpouring into a cascade of great majesty, often accompanied by loud drumming sounds. Uttara Kannada is called the land of waterfalls. Westward flowing rivers gush through thick forests breaking into small streams before plunging hundreds of feet into the sea. The most famous is the **Jog Falls**

of the Sharavathi river, known locally as the Gerusoppa. Located at the border of Shimoga and Uttara Kannada districts, the waters of the Sharavathi hurtle down a dark precipice of 810ft in four distinct cascades known locally as Raja, Rani, Rover and Rocket. The **Unchalli Falls** (also known as Lushington Falls) is set amidst the dense jungles of Uttara Kannada district and is known for its deafening roar, 'Keppa Joga' in local parlance. In the midst of thick forests, close to Yellapur, in Uttara Kannada district, are the **Sathodi Falls** and **Lalguli Falls**. **Magod Falls** (located 80kms from Karwar) are worth a look as the Bedthi river plunges 180m down a rocky valley in three distinct leaps. Deep inside the Kudremukh forest is the **Hanuman Gundi Falls**, best seen after the monsoon. To the south, along the Cauvery and her tributaries, lie some magnificent falls. The **Abbey Falls**, set in a private coffee plantation near Madikeri is notable among them. Another exotic locale is the **Iruppu Falls**, nestling just outside the Rajiv Gandhi National Park, which starts in the Brahmagiri Range and then plunges 170ft. The picturesque hill station of Kemmangundi has the **Kalhatti Falls**, which hurtles from the top of the Chandra Drona Hill and the sprightly **Hebbe Falls**, which plunges in two stages to form Dodda Hebbe (Big falls) and Chikka Hebbe (Small falls). Sixty five kilometres east of Mysore, in Malavalli Taluk of Mandya district, is the island of Shivasamudram. It is encircled by two arms of the Cauvery which plummet from a height of 75m into a deep, rocky gorge with a deafening roar to form two picturesque falls – **Barachukki** and **Gaganachukki**.

Equally impressive are the horseshoe shaped Balamuri Falls and the Shimsha Falls in Mandya District. For those who don't want to travel out of Bangalore, there is the **Pearl Valley** formed by thin jets of water hurtling down a height of 90m on Bangalore's outskirts.

# Nature & Wildlife Trail
## Bandipur, BR Hills, Nagarhole

The three wildlife parks at Bandipur, BR Hills and Nagarhole offer an exciting glimpse into Karnataka's wildlife: Herds of elephants, deer, gaur, exotic birds and even the big cats. Ride on elephant back or opt for the jeep safari, but the view from a watchtower placed above watering holes is still considered the best option. Start your wildlife tour with Bandipur forest, home of wild elephants. Move onto sloth bears, sambar and gaur at the BR Hills sanctuary. Save the best for the last – the Nagarhole National Park with coracle boat rides and campfire dinners and of course, plenty of animals to sight.

Nagarhole National Park

Kabini River Lodge in Nagarhole is ideal to spot a variety of wildlife.

## Nagarhole National Park (Rajiv Gandhi National Park)

*The most well known forest in Karnataka is undoubtedly Nagarhole National Park with the Brahmagiri mountains as its backdrop. It lies southwest of Mysore district, a 50km drive from there. Nagarhole rests in the foothills of the Western Ghats with gentle slopes and shallow valleys. The park gets its name from the Nagarhole river or 'snake stream' for the manner in which it snakes through the forest. The sprawling forests stretch across 641sqkms with the turbulent Kabini descending from its upper reaches. Nagarhole was once the hunting ground of the Maharajas and it became a national park in 1975. The ancient tribe Kurumbas, inhabit the park and take care of its elephants. The park is accessible by both road and river. Jeeps, vans and guides from the Forest Department are available on hire. One-hour coach rides offer a brief tour of the park. Coracle rides, jeep rides, wildlife sightings and boating are some of the options.*

The forest is a mix of deciduous trees, swamps, rushing streams, tall bamboo groves and priceless rosewood trees. Jeeps safaris take you into the jungles where wild elephants, spotted and barking deer, sambar, wild cats, four-horned antelope, monkeys, sloth bears, flying squirrel and gaur can be sighted. Tigers and leopards are rarely spotted. A boat ride along the river shows up large crocodiles and waterfowls. The park is a birdwatchers delight – the rare Malabar trojon, great black woodpecker, Indian pitta, pied hornbill and green imperial pigeon build their nests here.

In the monsoon months the Iruppu Falls in nearby Kodagu are a magnificent sight. Mastigudi at Nagarhole National Park was also the place where the Maharaja's annual elephant round up or khedda took place.

## Bandipur National Park

*B*andipur National Park is a comfortable five hour drive from Bangalore on the smooth Mysore-Ooty highway. Private cars are not allowed into this protected reserve but regular jeeps and vans will take you into the forest on a wildlife safari. One-hour coach rides give you a quick tour of the forest but are not recommended as noisy tourists on the bus manage to scare away most of the wildlife! The most exciting way to spot wildlife is from machans or watchtowers located near watering holes. The best time to visit the park is between November and May when the animals come out in full strength.

Once the exclusive hunting ground of the Maharaja of Mysore, Bandipur is a combination of subtropical, deciduous forest and scrubland, home to Karnataka's wild elephants. Set against the backdrop of the mist covered Niligiri mountain range, Bandipur's abundant wildlife can be observed and photographed from fairly close quarters. A jeep safari is recommended.

Wandering herds of elephants may be spotted anywhere. Deer, gaur, peacocks, flying squirrels and the four-horned antelope are easily sighted. The langur and bonnet macaques with their piercing 'alarm-cries', flocks of birds (330 species in all) and a rich reptilian population make up the rest. Unfortunately, the number of tigers in the reserve has dwindled over the years and tiger and leopard sightings are rare. (In 1973, the area was brought under Project Tiger.)

## BR Hills Sanctuary

*N*estling 3,500ft above sea level, 85kms southeast of Mysore lies BR Hills off the popular tourist map. The two-hour drive from Bandipur to BR Hills takes the visitor through the countryside of Chamarajanagar, past a fabulous temple at Nanjangud. The sanctuary may be explored by jeep; safaris are conducted twice a day. For permits to enter the forest, contact the Forest Department. The best time for a visit is between November and May when plenty of wildlife present themselves. The K Gudi (Kyathadevaraya Gudi) camp housed in the Maharaja's Lodge, offers a package of a night's stay, a jeep safari, a buffet lunch and campfire dinner. Both tented cottages and log huts are available.

A blend of hill resort and wildlife sanctuary, Biligiri Rangaswamy Hills or BR Hills is a moist deciduous and semi-evergreen forest interspersed with grassland. Gaur, elephants, spotted deer, sambar, wild boar, barking deer, porcupine and 250 species of birds may be seen here. Some exotic birds such as the blue jay, Malabar whistling thrush, hill mynah, racquet tailed drongo and the paradise flycatcher may also be sighted.

A rather difficult trek gets you to a Champak tree (*Dodda Sampige Mara*), said to be 2,000 years. The tree, with an incredible girth of over 10m and a height of 30m, is revered by the Soliga tribes of the region and worshipped on Mondays and Fridays. The three branches of the tree are supposed to represent the trinity of Brahma, Maheshwara and Vishnu and the 100 small stones lying near the base are believed to be Shiva lingas. A rivulet of cool water that flows nearby is perfect for soaking tired feet.

The hills take their name from the age-old Ranganatha temple dedicated to Goddess Mahalaksmi. The temple is perched dramatically on the edge of a granite precipice. For those who are not scared of heights, there is a 1000ft drop right here that offers a spectacular view at sunset. Coffee estates and tribal hamlets dot the landscape. The Vivekananada Girijana Kalayana Kendra located beyond the temple displays information about local tribes and the biodiversity of the region. There are a number of trekking trails converging here – one of them leads up to Honnamati, the highest point on the range of BR Hills.

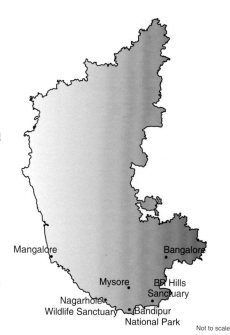

Mangalore

Bangalore

Mysore

BR Hills
Sanctuary

Nagarhole
Wildlife Sanctuary

Bandipur
National Park

Not to scale

# Travel Information

## GETTING THERE

### Bandipur National Park

 Mysore-80kms

    Ooty-80kms

    Bangalore-220kms

 Mysore-80kms

 Bangalore-220kms

### BR Hills Sanctuary

BR Hills is 85kms from Mysore City via Nanjangud and Chamarajanagar. Bangalore is 220kms away and the recommended route is Mysore, Chamarajanagar, K Gudi. Buses ply from Bangalore and Mysore though not regularly.

 Mysore-110kms

    Bangalore-260kms

 Mysore-110kms

 Bangalore-260kms

### Nagarhole National Park

 Mysore-96kms

    Bangalore-230kms

 Mysore-96kms

 Bangalore-230kms

## WHERE TO STAY

### Bandipur National Park

**Bandipur Safari Lodge
(Jungle Lodges & Resorts)**
Hangala Post, Melkamanahalli, Near Bandipur, Gundulpet Taluk, Chamarajanagar 571126
**Tel** 08229-233 001,
080-2559 7021/24/25 (Bangalore),
**Web** www.junglelodges.com
**Tariff** Rs 1,500 per person, inclusive of food and safari.

**Tusker Trails**
Mangala Village, Gundulpet Taluk, Chamarajanagar 571126
**Tel** 080-2361 8024 (Bangalore)
**Email** rajsafaris@hotmail.com
**Tariff** Rs 1,700 to Rs 1,900

---

**Forest Department Cottages**
Tiger Division, Bandipur, Gundulpet Taluk, Chamarajanagar 571111
**Tel** 08229-236 043
**Tariff** Rs 340 to Rs 490 (Indians), Rs 500 to Rs 800 (Foreigners)

### BR Hill Sanctuary

**K Gudi Wilderness Camp
(Jungle Lodges & Resorts)**
PO Kyathadevaraya Gudi, Mysore, Chamarajanagar 571313
**Tel** 08226-706086
**Web** www.junglelodges.com
**Tariff** Rs 1,500 (Indians), $ 50 and $ 45 (Foreigners)

**Forest Department Guest House**
For bookings, contact: Deputy Conservator of Forests, Wildlife Division, Chamarajanagar
**Tel** 08226-222 059
**Tariff** Rs 400 per head and Rs 750 for couples (Indians), Rs 1,500 (Foreigners)

### Nagarhole National Park

**Kabini River Lodge
(Jungle Lodges & Resorts)**

---

Karapur
**Tel** 08228-264 402/403 (Resort)
**Email** junglelodges@vsnl.com
**Tariff** Rooms, (Indians), Rs 2,300 (weekend) and Rs 2,070 (weekday); River Side Cottages, Rs 2,000 (weekend) and Rs 1,800 (weekday); Rooms, (Foreigners), $ 110 (weekend) and $ 100 (weekday); River Side Cottages, $ 100 (weekend) and $ 90 (weekday)

**The King's Sanctuary**
Nagerhole
Sales office: 210 Barton Centre, 84 MG Road, Bangalore 560001
**Tel** 080-5112 2661
**Telefax** 080-5112 2662
**Web** www.vivekhotels.com
**Tariff** Cottage, Rs 3,500 (Indians) and $ 140 (Foreigners); Suite, Rs 3,000 (Indians) and $ 110 (Foreigners); Single Supplement, Rs 1,000 (Indians) and $ 50 (Foreigners)

**Jungle Inn**
Veeranahosalli, Hunsur, Murkal-Nagarhole Road, Hejjur Post, Hunsur Taluk, Mysore 570011
**Tel** 0821-247 061,
080-2573 5289 (Bangalore)
**Email** jungle_inn123@rediffmail.com
**Tariff** Rs 2,000 (Indians), $ 75 (Foreigners)

---

**Forest Department Cottages**
For bookings, contact:
Conservator of Forests, Kodagu Circle, Aranya Bhavan, Madikeri 571201
**Tel** 08272-225 708, 228 305
**Telefax** 08272-228 439
**Tariff** Rs 650

### Travel Tips

In most of the wildlife sanctuaries like Bandipur and Nagarhole, the safaris organised by the Forest Department take place between 6am to 9am and 3pm to 6pm daily. Each year, Bandipur and Nagarhole parks are closed for the summer on account of forest fires. Keep in mind that monsoon months are not good for animal sightings. Sometimes the safaris are cancelled during heavy rains. However, if you are here during the monsoons, watch out for leeches.

Treks on designated routes are permitted with prior permission from the Forest Department. Contact the Forest Department located in the town for permits to enter the forest. The charges include an armed guide who accompanies you.

If you are taking the public transport, all buses from Mysore headed to Ooty stop at Bandipur. Avoid coming here on weekends as it gets very crowded. There are direct buses to Nagarhole from Mysore. Entry of private vehicles is restricted to between 6pm and 6am.

# My Perfect Holiday – GB Kumar

Bheemeshwari

**M**y preferred holiday would be in the forests and mountains and Karnataka offers both in abundance. **Kabini** is an easy drive from Bangalore and I like staying at the JLR camp. You get to see plenty of wildlife there and both the food and stay are simple and comfortable.

The **Chikmagalur** belt is another favourite. I usually stay at the Taj Garden Retreat and make day trips to Baba Budangiri and Mullayanagiri. The drive up the hills is very exciting and slightly risky as the road slopes into the valley. I especially like to visit the Inam Dattatreya Peeth in the Baba Budangiri range — an excellent example of cultural integration.

**Kodagu** is outstanding as a holiday destination combining both the Western Ghats and coffee plantations. It is rich in tradition and the people are hospitable. I usually stay at Orange County and enjoy trekking and cycling in these parts. A day trip to **Talacauvery** is always on the agenda.

**Murudeshwar** has an amazing beach, good seafood and plenty of water sports. It's also safe for swimming. If you are a temple buff, this is a good base to visit some fabulous examples along the coast.

My roots are in **Gokarna** and Om Beach is fantastic and in my opinion, even better than Goa. I usually return through Sirsi, Hubli and stop at Yana for a couple of days.

For a purely cultural holiday, I recommend **Hampi**. The weather is not very comfortable but Hampi and **Chitradurga Fort** are outstanding.

Talacauvery

A quick weekend getaway from Bangalore would be to Amblee Holiday Resort at Srirangapatna. The first half of the day is spent visiting the temple at **Melkote**. The authentic Iyengar Puliyogre here is excellent. Post lunch, we make our way to **Talakad**.

Another favourite weekend getaway is to **Bheemeshwari**. I enjoy going here because it's just an hour's drive from Bangalore, the angling is good and an added plus is **BR Hills** which is about 120 kms from there. If you like trekking, both these places offer good trails.

*GB Kumar is Director-Sales (South Asia), Intel Technology (India) Pvt. Ltd. He lives in Bangalore.*

# The JLR Story

Twenty five years ago, Karnataka's Tourism Minister, the (late) Gundu Rao, visited Tiger Tops in Chitwan National Park, Nepal. Greatly impressed with the concept of ecologically sound wildlife tourism, he decided to try it in the state of Karnataka. In 1980, Jungle Lodges & Resorts (JLR) was formed as a joint venture between Tiger Tops, Nepal and the Government of Karnataka. (JLR is now owned and managed exclusively by the Karnataka government, after Tiger Tops pulled out in 1987.) The objective of JLR is to sensitively develop wildlife tourism while respecting and protecting the environment. Consequently, it has developed a range of back to nature holidays, exciting outdoor and adventure tours in different wildlife sanctuaries and places of natural beauty that have been explored by thousands of visitors across the state.

JLR's properties are located in close proximity to the state's wildlife zones. In many cases, they are the only access a tourist has to visit these places. From a single camp enterprise in Karapur village, JLR now has eleven wildlife resorts spread across the state.

The Indian-born European, Colonel John Wakefield, also known as 'Papa' has played an important role in JLR's success. He is also credited with the selection of sites for tourist accommodation and facilities. This octogenarian has been the Resident Director of Kabini since 1986 and is now involved in planning the new resorts. A hunter turned conservationist, he is considered a walking encyclopaedia on the region's wildlife.

JLR's resorts are: The **Kabini River Lodge**, 80kms from Mysore, **Cauvery Fishing Camp** at Bheemeshwari, Galibore and Doddamakali fishing camps, 100kms from Bangalore, **K Gudi Wilderness Camp at BR Hills**, 86kms from Mysore, **Bandipur Safari Lodge**, 220kms from Bangalore, **Kali Adventure Resort** at Dandeli 95kms from Belgaum, **Devbagh Beach Resort**, accessible by boat from Karwar, **Bannerghatta Nature Camp** 20kms from Bangalore and the **Dubare Elephant Camp**, 15kms from Kushalnagar.

Kabini River Lodge

Colonel John Wakefield

Dubare Elephant Camp

Depending on where you are, the camps offer wildlife safaris in open jeeps, elephant safaris, coracle boat rides, parasailing, snorkelling, river rafting, angling, trekking and so on. None of the resorts cater to more than 50 guests at a time. There is no room service except coffee and tea and no television either. Air-conditioning and a la carte menus are out of the question! JLR won the National Eco Tourism Award in 1997-98 and other accolades since then. Upcoming projects include the property of the erstwhile Wodeyar dynasty – Hotel Metropole in Mysore and a three-storeyed hotel at Krishnaraja Sagar Dam overlooking the Brindavan Gardens and a new project in Bhadra.

## Kabini River Lodge

Kabini River Lodge is set near the famed Nagarahole National Park. Once the hunting lodge of the Mysore Maharaja, Kabini still retains much of its grandeur. Rated as one of the **top five resorts of the world** by *Tatler* magazine, the resort houses a cluster of colonial bungalows, cosy cottages and comfortable tents. In the middle of a garden of flame-red Gulmohar trees is the open-to-sides gazebo or the 'Gol Ghar', with a campfire site.

Apart from a spectacular view of the river and a fair share of wildlife, you can expect elephant rides, nature walks, coracle boat rides and motorboat rides. Naturalists will lead guests on nature walks and jeep drives to explore the diverse flora and fauna of the jungle. *(Refer Pg 408 for information on tariffs)*

## Bandipur Safari Lodge

This elegant safari lodge is adjacent to the Bandipur Tiger Reserve and stands against the backdrop of the Nilgiris. Set in the erstwhile hunting grounds of the Maharaja of Mysore, the lodge boasts elegant rooms with all modern amenities and a

spacious bath. There is a gazebo or Gol Ghar where cosy campfire buffet dinners are organised. There is also a restaurant called 'Pugmark' that is open to guests and highway travellers. Open jeep safaris at sundown and trekking inside the park are the main attractions. The months between March and May are best for wildlife sightings and bird watching. *(Refer Pg 408 for information on tariffs)*

## K Gudi Wilderness Camp

This camp nestles in the popular Biligiri Ranganna (BR) Hills, 3375ft above sea level. Open jeep safaris through the BRT Wildlife Sanctuary, treks through the forest and elephant rides are some of the activities offered. Hordes of elephant, panther, tiger, wild boars, barking deer, sloth bear and a variety of rare birds can be spotted here. Furnished tented cottages, ethnic huts on stilts and spacious rooms at the Maharaja's bungalow give you a back to nature experience. *(Refer Pg 408 for information on tariffs)*

## Kali Adventure Resort

Just outside the town of Dandeli and on the banks of river Kali, lies the Kali Adventure Resort. White-water rafting on Kali, hikes through the hilly trails and safaris through the Dandeli Wildlife Sanctuary make up the itinerary. Crocodile sightings, coracle boat rides and bird watching are also possible here. Furnished rooms and tented cottages are the staying options. *(Refer Pg 427 for information on tariffs)*

## Bannerghatta Nature Camp

Located in the vast expanse of the preserved Bannerghatta National Park, this camp is ideal for an overnight getaway from the city of Bangalore. Visits to the sprawling zoo, a lion and tiger safari, screening of wildlife films and campfire dinners are part of the itinerary. Treks through the Herbivore Safari enclosure will get you up close and personal with deer, gaur, sambar, black bucks and barking deer, birds and crocodiles. Accommodation is offered in Swiss tents and the backpacker's dormitory. *(Refer Pg 457 for information on tariffs)*

## Cauvery Fishing Camp

Located in picturesque Bheemeshwari, this camp is set on the banks of river Cauvery and offers a tranquil holiday experience less than three hours from Bangalore. A haven for anglers, the much sought after mahseer can be found here. Coracle boat rides, camping, trekking, river rafting and bird watching are the other activities organised. Ethnic log huts and spacious tented cottages overlooking the river make for an interesting stay. *(Refer Pg 457 for information on tariffs)*

Courtesy: Jungle Lodges & Resorts

The mahseer is a prized catch in river Cauvery

## Galibore Fishing & Nature Camp

The Galibore Camp is also set on the banks of river Cauvery, about 6kms downstream of Bheemeshwari. This fishing camp is located in the middle of thick forests and is flanked by hills. The main attraction here is the mahseer fish. You can also spot wildlife, from tuskers to the Indian mud turtle. Rustic but comfortable, spacious tented cottages are available to camp in. This eco-friendly nature camp uses solar energy to run the fans, heat the water and light the lamps.

## Doddamakali Nature Camp

Exuding an unspoilt charm, this getaway is located further upstream from Cauvery Fishing Camp. At this nature camp, you can take coracle boat rides on the Cauvery, fish for the mahseer or go on a safari through the wilderness. Tented cottages strung with hammocks, winding pathways and pretty sunsets make it a great place to unwind.

## Devbagh Beach Resort

Devbagh is a pristine beach with cool casuarina groves and the Arabian Sea on three sides. This serene getaway is an eco-friendly resort without any frills.

A peaceful holiday spot with unspoiled sand and surf, para-sailing, speed boat rides and snorkelling are some of the activities offered here. Watch out for sprightly dolphins diving around. For those craving adventure, the vibrant underwater is a veritable rainbow of colourful fish and aquatic plants, perfect for snorkelling. The resort houses tents and furnished huts on stilts and is a great place to laze in the sun by day and watch ships sink into the distant horizon as night falls. *(Refer Pg 425 for information on tariffs)*

## Dubare Elephant Camp

The Dubare Elephant Camp in Kodagu is a novel concept where tourists have an 'intimate' experience with elephants. Located within the Dubare Forest Reserve, the gentle pachyderms may be observed in their natural habitat. Campers can feed them, watch them being groomed and perform mock logging operations. In keeping with the eco tourism theme, talks on elephant ecology and conservation are organised. Watch out for the one-hour joy rides on elephant back to forest waterholes. Bird watching, nature walks and visits to neighbouring tribal hamlets are other highlights. The camp is located on the banks

of Cauvery and river rafting is organised during the monsoon months. Homestays near the camp offer comfortable accommodation options.

## Om Beach Ayurvedic Resort

A few kilometres from the popular Om Beach in Gokarna, is the Om Beach Resort, set atop a hill and offering some breathtaking views of the sea beyond. Jointly run by JLR and Kairali, Om Beach Ayurvedic Resort is a quiet getaway offering 12 spacious, English villa rooms. JLR has joined hands with Kairali, a renowned Ayurvedic resorts company in Kerala, to offer traditional Ayurvedic massages and treatments by trained professionals. Water sports such as para-sailing, banana boat rides and speed boat rides are other highlights at this tranquil resort. *(Refer Pg 425 for information on tariffs)*

**Jungle Lodges & Resorts**
*Shrungar Shopping Centre, II Floor, MG Road, Bangalore 560001* **Tel** *2559 7021/7024/7025*
**Web** *www.junglelodges.com*
**Email** *info@junglelodges.com*

A log hut in K Gudi

# Give In To The Call Of The Wild.

**At India's finest chain of eco-tourism resorts - Jungle Lodges & Resorts.**

It's the best way to explore Karnataka's rich natural treasures, which include some of the last remaining 'Bio-diversity Hotspots' in the world.

Jungle safaris with a naturalist guide. Long nature walks. Bird watching. Elephant rides. Wildlife photography. Treks to panoramic hilltops. And, the adventure continues with White-water rafting. Snorkelling...

ST ARK.Blr/JLR/0104

**Ten pristine settings:** • Bandipur Safari Lodge • Galibore Nature & Fishing Camp • Bannerghatta Nature Camp • Devbagh Beach Resort, Karwar • Kabini River Lodge, Nagarhole • Dubare Elephant Camp, Coorg • Kali Adventure & Wilderness Camp, Dandeli • B.R. Hills Nature and Adventure Resort • Cauvery Fishing Camp, Bheemeshwari • Doddamakali Nature & Fishing Camp • K Gudi Wilderness Camp, B R Hills

**Jungle Lodges & Resorts Ltd.** 2nd Floor, Shrungar Shopping Complex, MG Road, Bangalore - 560 001. Tel: 91 80 2559 7021/ 24/ 25. Fax: 91 80 2558 6163. Email: sales@junglelodges.com, info@junglelodges.com

www.junglelodges.com

# **Coastal** Circuit

Mangalore, Ullal, Udupi, Agumbe, Malpe,
St. Mary's Isles, Maravanthe, Bhatkal,
Murudeshwar, Gokarna, Karwar, Kurmagad

Karnataka's Karavali coast is India's beach and temple country. From Karwar in the north to Mangalore in the south, a journey of 320kms, verdant green mountains reach down to silver beaches. The effect is dramatic: Miles of golden sand, emerald beaches, sweeping paddy fields, breathtaking sunsets, winding roads, lush forests, temple towns and the roar of the deep blue sea. Start with the temples, move to unspoilt beaches, try your hand at white water rafting and explore Portuguese ruins. Anything is possible on the Sapphire Route.

## Mangalore

*The bustling port city of Mangalore is the best place to start your journey of coastal Karnataka. You can spend a few days soaking in its charms – ancient churches, old temples, fabulous food and the warm Arabian Sea. The Portuguese influence may be felt in the architecture as well as the family names like Albuquerque, D'mello, Moraes and Da Cunha that grace the name boards of colonial bungalows.*

*There are a variety of hotels to choose from in and around the city. Autos get you around efficiently, albeit not very cheaply. Locals speak either Tulu or Konkani, but you can try English just as well.*

A maritime city with a busy port, Mangalore has a languid charm all its own. Large sects of Catholic Christians, Hindus and Muslims give the city a cosmopolitan air. Narrow, winding streets lined with coconut palms, quaint houses with terracotta-tiled roofs, attractive beaches, old temples and even older churches – there are many tourist treasures to be found here.

Mangalore port carried out trade in the 6th century with Arabia and Persia, and the kingdom was fought over by the Portuguese and the indigenous rulers. In the 18th century it was a key port and shipbuilding centre under Hyder Ali. In the 18th century it was a key port and shipbuilding centre under Hyder Ali and Tipu Sultan left a bastion, the Sultan's Battery here.

The city takes its name from Mangala Devi who is the presiding deity at the 10th century temple. She was a princess, revered as an incarnation of Goddess Durga. With three silver doorways framing the inner sanctum, the temple has expanded under different rulers through the centuries. It is believed that the princess was a follower of Sadhu Matsyendranath, leader of a sect, the Natha Pantha.

Start your sightseeing tour with the **Sultan's Battery** a remnant of Tipu Sultan's fort. Meant to guard his naval station, it shows off pretty turrets built in laterite stone. The **Seemanthi Bai Memorial Government**

**Museum** at Kadre makes for a worthwhile browse with an impressive collection of object d'art, archaeological and ethnological exhibits and porcelain and wooden carvings.

Southeast of the city is the **Kadri Manjunatha temple** which enshrines a small but exquisite bronze idol of Lokeshwara created more than a 1,000 years ago. Cobra statuettes and a majestic sculpture of the seven-headed serpent Adisesha accompany it. The temple houses a dramatic dwajasthamba at the entrance and nine tanks with curative waters flow to the temple.

A multitude of churches reflect Mangalore's strong Christian heritage which can be traced back to Portuguese invaders. One of the most impressive is the **Rosario Cathedral**, modelled on the lines of St. Peter's Basilica in Rome. Other famous churches are the **Milgres Church**, **Church of the Most Holy Rosary**, the **Shanthi Cathedral of the Basel Mission** and the **St. Aloysius College Chapel** with striking Biblical frescoes across the ceiling and walls. Its private museum, **Aloyseum**, is worth a peek. On display are priceless antiques, artefacts and zoological exhibits. Rare exhibits include an ivory cross, a statue of Mother Mary with Tipu Sultan, volumes of the Imperial Gazetteer of India and a vintage De Dion.

Mangalore boasts a few historic mosques as well: The **Jumma Masjid** was built by Arabs and the **Idgah Mosque** that followed in the 18th century by Mysore's ruler Tipu Sultan. The **Pilkula Nisargadhama** is a sprawling 300-acre park 12kms out of Mangalore with boat rides, wildlife safaris, a science centre, aquarium and arboretum.

## Ullal Beach, Suratkal & Kaup

*Ullal has the perfect ingredients for a leisurely holiday: A large beach, historical ruins and a Shiva temple. The 19th century dargah of an Arab saint is also located at Ullal. Remember to cover your head and wash your feet before you enter. A natural spring is located an hour from Ullal and a dip in this tank is said to be rejuvenating. Suratkal and Kaup can be covered on the way to Udupi. Laidback and lazy,*

*they are perfect for building sandcastles on the beach.*

The secluded **Ullal Beach** is lined with casuarinas. It lies on the south bank of the Netravati river and is just eight kilometres from Mangalore. Ruins of the brave Queen Abbakka's citadel from where she repulsed a Portuguese attack in 1618 may still be seen. A number of resorts are set along Ullal's picturesque beach.

The 19th century tomb of Arab saint, **Syed Mohammed Shareeful Madani** is located here. It is said that he came to Ullal 400 years ago from Madina, floating across the stormy seas on just a flimsy piece of cloth! A few kilometres away is **Someshwara Beach** with a **Shiva temple** overlooking the rocky promontory. Drive through rolling hills and thick forests to reach **Bendre Teertha**, a well-known natural water spring with healing powers, 65kms south of Mangalore.

The town of Suratkal has an expansive beach, a new lighthouse and the **Sadashiva temple** as tourist sights. On NH 17 you may stop at seaside Kaup with its long beach, ruined fort, ancient **Jain basadis**, a soaring lighthouse and a couple of temples.

Seaside getaway, Kaup

Dandeli Wildlife
Sanctuary
Kurmagad
Karwar
Gokarna
Murudeshwar
Bhatkal
Maravanthe
St. Mary's Isles
Udupi
Malpe
Agumbe
Mangalore
Bangalore
Ullal
Mysore

Not to scale

## Udupi

*The holy town of Udupi lies an hour north of Mangalore. An important Hindu destination, Udupi is also famous for its pure vegetarian Brahmin cuisine that is now famous in Udupi Tiffin Rooms across the world. The town also makes a convenient base for visiting Malpe, Manipal and St. Mary's Isles.*

Saint Madhavacharya, revered by Vaishnavite Hindus, lived in the small town of Udupi, home to eight holy maths or monasteries. It is also one of the seven sacred sites in coastal Karnataka and is of great religious significance.

Car Street, in the heart of town, houses the **Sri Krishna temple** along with **eight maths** or monasteries set around a big tank – **Madhava Sarovar** – where Ganga is believed to flow once in a decade. The main attractions of the temple are the beautiful bejewelled idol of Lord Krishna and the **Kanakana Kindi** a small window through which Krishna is believed to have revealed himself to his ardent devotee, Kanakadasa.

The **Sri Ananthasana temple** in the centre of the temple complex is another sacred site where Madhavacharya preached. The math buildings are important religious centres and are also architecturally appealing with wide arches, large temple squares and wooden temple chariots. Trained elephants circle the temple at dusk and 'bless' devotees with their trunk. They also accept coins and bananas from them. It all adds up to quite a spectacle especially for children.

Udupi plays host to several colourful festivals but the biennial **Paryaya** festival where officiating priests hand over responsibilities to other pontiffs, attracts thousands from all over the country when elephants, temple chariot processions and noisy fireworks fill the streets.

Udupi's famed vegetarian food (where even onions and garlic are shunned) is said to have originated at the Krishna temple.

## Agumbe

*Regular buses ply between Mangalore and Agumbe. Located in the southwestern part of Shimoga district, Agumbe is situated at an altitude of 826kms. The best time to visit is from December to March. Serious trekkers need to obtain permission from the Forest Department. Contact The DFO, Shimoga Division or Range Forest Officer, Megaravalli, Agumbe Range.*

The scenic mountains of the **Western Ghats** are best explored with Agumbe as your base. Famous for its rains – it receives the highest rainfall in the country after Cherrapunji – and a view of the sunset, Agumbe is a quaint town nestling in the ranges of the Western Ghats. There are a number of trekking routes from here, passing through the forests of the Ghats. Places of interest are the **Gopalakrishna temple**, said to be over 800 years old, the **Barkana Falls** and a hillock, **Nishani Gudda**. There's a co-operative movement in the town – their greeting cards make for interesting souvenirs.

## Malpe-St. Mary's Isles

*Malpe is a mere four kilometres from Udupi and St. Mary's Isles, six kilometres off its coast. A 30-minute boat ride from Malpe's harbour leads into St. Mary's Isles. The islands may be visited throughout the year except during peak monsoon when the seas are rough. Boats to the island can be hired from the Malpe Development Committee. It's best to give Malpe a miss on Sundays when there is a big rush.*

Malpe is an important fishing centre with a picturesque beach and natural harbour. Across the bay lies the island of **Darya Bahadurgarh** with the **Balrama temple** and Malpe's oldest **tile factory** set up by the Basel Mission.

St. Mary's Isles, a group of rocky outcrops lie off the coast of Malpe. A **National Geological Monument**, it bears the cross that **Vasco da Gama** placed when he landed in 1498. The isle, 300m long and 100m wide is composed of striking hexagonal basalt rock formations in varying shades of red and black that rise majestically out of the Arabian Sea.

## Maravanthe-Ottinane-Bhatkal

*An hour's drive north of Udupi leads to the small coastal towns of Maravanthe and Bhatkal. Together they offer a substantial taste of the idyllic beauty of the coast. The road leading up to Maravanthe lies strategically between two stretches of water – the Arabian Sea and river Suparnika on either side and the rolling Kodachadri Hills looming in the distance. The sunset viewpoint Ottinane is off the highway as you head out of Maravanthe. Before you travel to Murudeshwar, the next important stop on the coastal itinerary, Bhatkal makes for an interesting visit. Just 16kms before Murudeshwar, it is dotted with interesting temples.*

Maravanthe is great to drive through – the road passes rivers, sprawling cashew and coconut plantations and jackfruit and mango orchards. Located off the highway, beyond Baindoor, is the lush viewpoint of **Ottinane**, atop a hillock. Here you can witness the confluence of **Baindoor river** with the sea. Ottinane is especially appealing after the

A store selling puja essentials in temple town Udupi.

## IT'S ONLY *Natural!*

*Tree house in Vythiri, Wayanad*

## WEEKEND VITALISERS
### IN GOD'S OWN COUNTRY

## *Wayanad*

**Bangalore - Wayanad**
**Accessibility:** Only by road
**Distance by road:** 350 km
**Duration of journey:** 7 hours
**Tourist season:** August to May
**Tourist information office:**
04936 - 202134, 255207

### *Don't miss*

- Horse riding ▪ Boating
- Camping ▪ Rock climbing
- River rafting at Kabini

### *Best stays*

- **Green Magic Nature Resort**
  (Rs. 8000) Ph: 0495-2744948
- **Vythiri Resort**
  (Rs. 3000-4250) Ph: 04936-255366
- **Jungle Park Resorts**
  (Rs. 3000-4500) Ph: 0495-2744948
- **Rain Country Resorts**
  (Rs. 2000-2500) Ph: 04936-255287
- **Royal Palm Holiday Home**
  (Rs. 1800-2000) Ph: 04936-206096
- **Green Gates Hotel**
  (Rs. 900-2800) Ph: 04936-202001
- **Pachyderm Palace**
  (Rs. 1500) Ph: 0484-2371761

*A weekend with wild, virgin Wayanad famed for its arresting beauty. Tucked away in the striking greenery of this land are picturesque hill stations, sprawling spice plantations and luxuriant forests. All marked with a pristine beauty that is the hallmark of this beautiful district. Discovering Wayanad is discovering nature, its many hues, its hidden treasures.*

You can start from Mananthavady, a 125 km drive from Mysore along the State Highway. 20 km east of Mananthavady lies the **Tholpetty Wildlife Sanctuary.** A floating population of 900 elephants is Tholpetty's own and the chances of having a close encounter with them is higher here than in nearby Nagarhole.

From Tholpetty, it is only a 20 km drive to **Thirunelly Temple.** Behold the architectural beauty of this temple, surrounded by the hills, Kambamala, Karimala and Varadiga and guarded by 30 majestic granite columns. With the crystal clear waters of River Papanashini gurgling downhill, enchantment will be close at hand.

The more adventurous can take a 17 km detour from Tholpetty to **Kuruvadweep**, on the eastward bound Kabini River. This 950-acre uninhabited island can be reached only by wading across the 70 m wide river!

From Mananthavady, it is a 40 km drive to lush and picturesque **Vythiri.** 5 km from here is **Lakkidi,** referred to as the gateway to Wayanad. Lofty peaks, gurgling streams and luxuriant forests will add magic to your journey to this hill station situated 2297 ft. above sea level.

A short 3 km drive from Lakkidi is **Pookot Lake,** a hotspot for picnicking. Nestled among wooded hills and punctuated with lotuses, the lake is the only one of its kind in the State. The best way to drink in its beauty is to go boating; the Park has ample facilities for it.

A 22 km drive from Pookot Lake will take you to the base camp of **Chembra Peak**, the highest point in the Wayanad Hills at 6860 ft. It takes a whole day to trek to the top from Meppadi, near Kalpetta. Temporary camps have been set up here and the District Tourism Promotion Council (DTPC) provides guides, sleeping bags, canvas huts and trekking implements on hire.

25 km from here is the **Edakkal Caves** - twin natural caves with New Stone Age pictorial writings on its walls - that talk volumes about the civilisation that existed in the region during pre-historic times. Located at an impressive 1000 m of height, the caves can be viewed best during the morning hours.

Round off your rendezvous with Wayanad with a stay at the famous tree houses, erected atop huge trees in the rainforests of Vythiri. Play Tarzan and live your childhood dream.

Theyyam, the ritual artform of Kerala

Muzhappilangad beach

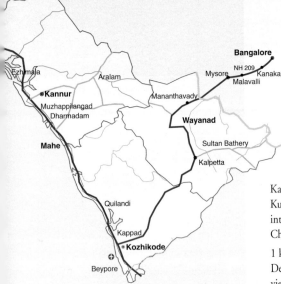

# Kannur

**Wayanad - Kannur**
**Accessibility:** By road and rail
**Distance by road:** 100 km
**Duration of journey:** 2 1/2 hours
**Tourist season:** September to May
**Tourist information office:**
0497 - 2706336

*A weekend with colourful, magical Kannur that proudly flaunts exotic folk art forms like Theyyam, along with a prized natural collection of beaches, hills and lush countrysides. This district, with a rich history has been a key contributor to the State's cultural, religious, political and industrial heritage.*

Kannur is 97 km away from Mananthavady and can be accessed through Mananthavady-Nedumpoil-Kuthuparamba route. 2 km from Kannur is **Payyambalam**, a lovely beach that has flat laterite cliffs jutting into the sea. Incredibly beautiful with well-laid gardens and a massive landscaped sculpture of 'Mother and Child', the beach is an ideal place for picnics and quiet evenings.

1 km from here is **Fort St. Angelo**, constructed in 1505 AD by the first Portuguese Viceroy Don Francisco De Almedia. A protected monument under the Archaeological Survey of India, remember to take in fascinating views of Mappila bay fishing harbour from here.

A totally different experience awaits you 16 km from Kannur town - at **Pappinisserry,** famous for a snake park. About 150 varieties of the slithery species can be seen here including the Spectacled Cobra, King Cobra, Russell Viper, Krait and Pit Viper. Demonstrations that are held every hour will help you discover more about them.

3 km from here is **Parassinikadavu Sri Muthappan Temple** situated on the banks of Valapattanam River. *Muthappan Theyyams* are performed here every morning and evening.

Go where the sea and the sands are of a different hue. Go to **Ezhimala,** 55 km from Kannur town. A combination of high hills and sandy beaches makes this place a lovely picnic spot. Watch dolphins at play at the Ettikulam bay.

About 3 km from Thalassery lies the beautiful 5 acre island of **Dharmadam**, covered with coconut palms and green bushes. Permission is required to enter this privately owned island.

A walking distance away is **Muzhappilangad Beach** (5 km from Thalassery). This is the only drive-in beach in India where you can drive the entire length of 4 km.

In the heart of the Thalassery is the **Thalassery Fort**, built by Tipu Sultan and a British military centre turned historical monument. The Jagannatha temple and the Thiruvangad Sree Rama Swami temple are two attractions nearby.

To discover artistic Kannur, visit the **Malayala Kalagramam** (MAKAM) at New Mahe, 7 km from Thalassery. This centre conducts courses in painting, sculpture, music, dance and pottery.

# WEEKEND VITALISERS
## IN GOD'S OWN COUNTRY

### Best stays

**The Pearl View Regency, Thalassery**
(Rs. 700-1400) Ph: 0490-2326702

**Mascot Beach Resort, Kannur**
(Rs. 350-2000) Ph: 0497-2708445

**Parassini Tourist Home, Parassinikkadavu**
(Rs. 150-350) Ph: 0497-2780545

**Omars Inn, Kannur**
(Rs. 150-690) Ph: 0497-2706313

**Royal Omars**
(Rs. 650-2000) Ph: 0497-2769091

*Explore the backwaters of Calicut in a houseboat.*

*Kalaripayattu, Kerala's martial art form*

*A weekend with charismatic, culture-rich Calicut (now Kozhikode), breathing the spicy scent of a vibrant history. Once the capital of the powerful Zamorins and the most important region of Malabar, Calicut was a prominent trade and commerce centre of yore and had close ties with the Arab world. The district still retains the glory of the past.*

# Calicut

**Bangalore - Calicut**
**Accessibility:** By road, rail and air
**Distance by road:** 350 km
**Duration of journey:** 9-10 hours
**Tourist season:** September to May
**Tourist information office:**
0495 - 2701234, 2712762

## Don't miss

- Shopping at SM (Sweet Meat) Street
- A leisurely cruise in Kalipoika
- A visit to the Krishna Menon Museum, dedicated to the late V K Krishna Menon, renowned statesman.
- Houseboat cruises
- Ayurvedic rejuvenation treatment
- Traditional Mappilah cuisine

## Best stays

- **Taj Residency**
  (Rs. 2200-3300) Ph: 0495-2765354
- **Fortune Hotel**
  (Rs. 1700-2500) Ph: 0495-2768888
- **Hotel Beach Heritage Inn**
  (Rs. 1200-1400) Ph: 0495-2762055
- **Kadavu Resorts**
  (Rs. 2450-2800) Ph: 0483-2830570
- **Riverside Retreat**
  (Rs. 750-1500) Ph: 0495-2766313

*Hotel rates as on September 2004.
*For bookings, please contact the hotels directly.*

Calicut can be reached via Mysore-Muthanga-Kalpetta-Thamarassery route. Synonymous with this district is **Kappad Beach**, 16 km away. This is the historic place where the world's favourite explorer, Vasco da Gama, landed on 27th May 1498. One of the most interesting features of this beach is a sprawling rock that protrudes into the sea, with a 800-year old temple perched on it.

Calicut's strong aura of history also permeates at the **Lokanarkkavu Temple** (50 km), associated with folk heroes like Thacholi Othenan, whose exploits are celebrated in Malabar's famed ballads, the *vadakkanpattukal*.

Vadagara, 2 km away is Othenan's birthplace. Once a flourishing trade and commerce centre, Vadagara boasts of a great tradition of **Kalaripayattu**. The *kalari* (gymnasium) of Othenan, Thacholi Manikkoth, is worth paying a visit.

For an authentic taste of Calicut, go to **Beypore**, a prominent port and fishing centre of ancient Kerala. Famous for its ship-building industry, the boat building yard here constructs *Uru*s (Arabian trading vessels) even today - a tradition that is almost 1500 years old! Beypore is 10 km from Calicut.

50 km from Calicut is a definitely-not-to-be-missed spot - **Velliyamkallu**, that shelters a massive rock, once much dreaded by navigators. The Thikkoti Lighthouse which overlooks Velliyamkallu was built after a shipwreck, the remains of which can still be seen here.

A favourite spot of sunset viewing is **Kozhikode Beach**, about 2 km from the city heart. The beach, lined with a long stretch of trees is popular with the local people because of a Lion's Club Park, a lighthouse and two piers.

Offering more leisure options is **Kuttiyadi**. This picturesque village, 78 km from Calicut, is a much sought-after picnic spot, thanks to the scenic surroundings that include a beautiful garden. Kuttiyadi also houses a hydro-electric power project.

Equally enchanting places are **Thusaragiri waterfalls** (50 km), where land and water have struck an extraordinary kinship, and the **Kadalundi Bird Sanctuary** (25 km), a haven for migratory birds.

*God's Own Country*

For more details contact,
**Kerala Tourism** Park View
Trivandrum 695 033 Kerala
Phone: 0471 2321132 Fax: 2322279
Email: info@keralatourism.org
Toll free infoline: 1-600-444-747
**www.keralatourism.org**

monsoon when the hills are carpeted with a multitude of wild flowers.

**Bhatkal**, a predominantly Muslim town, was the trading port of the Vijayanagar kingdom in the 16th century and frequented by Jain and Arab merchants. It boasts two attractive temples, 42 mosques, a beach and a small fishing wharf. The two prominent temples are the **Jain Chandranatha Basadi** with stone tiles and a 17th century **Vijayanagar temple** with characteristic animal carvings. The busy bazaar has lots of local delicacies like date halwa, salted roti and biryani to offer. The Khetpai Narayana temple at Mudbhatkal has interesting engravings of everyday life carved on its walls.

## Murudeshwar

*Murudeshwar is a 14kms drive from Bhatkal on the Mangalore-Karwar highway. Its picturesque beaches are a popular choice for low-budget holidays.*

With plenty of sun and sand, Murudeshwar is famous for its expansive beaches where turquoise waters offset the white sands and a balmy breeze blows through the day. The town is a sacred site with its famous **Shiva temple** built on a hillock overlooking the sea. The large temple was renovated recently in keeping with its earlier classical style.

There is an ancient legend associated with Murudeshwar – the demon Ravana was transporting a sacred Atma linga. During his sojourn through Gokarna, he threw the sacred cloth covering the linga in a fit of anger. A Shiva linga materialised out of the cloth which was then named Mrideshwara or Murudeshwara.

The uninhabited **Netrani Island** is just a boat ride away. Also called Netra Hill or Pigeon Island, it is set atop a hillock and worthy of leisurely exploration. A rather arduous trek to the top of the hillock takes you to an old temple which offers a stunning view of the sea below.

## Gokarna

*The drive up the winding path that leads to Gokarna is an enchanting one, dotted with rocky cliffs on one side and the Arabian Sea on the other. The town itself is charming, with temples, a wide expanse of beach, two principal streets and clusters of traditional tile-roofed brick houses alongside quaint Udupi eateries, souvenir shops and cyber cafes. Gokarna is also a sacred site and foreigners are not allowed into its temples. The adventurous can explore the coastline on foot. If you can't withstand the strenuous trek to the four beaches around Gokarna, opt for the boats that leave Gokarna every hour. The rates are usually Rs 100 or thereabouts. There are lots of food stalls on the beach and local families run comfortable guesthouses for long haul tourists.*

Gokarna is a perfect foil to the crowded beaches of Goa. A quaint mix of backpackers, beach bums and devout Hindu pilgrims frequent its fabulous beaches! The name 'Gokarna' is born out of a legend where Lord Shiva emerged from a cow's ear. Like Udupi, this too is an ancient pilgrimage centre and an important seat of Sanskrit education. The sleepy streets are lined with traditional wooden houses; Brahmin priests reciting Sanskrit *slokas* in temple courtyards and pilgrims taking a hurried dip in the temple tank are common sights. Gokarna is home to the ancient temple of **Mahabaleshwara** with the mythical **Atma linga** that Ravana was outwitted into leaving here by the clever

*Malpe's picturesque beach*

Ganesha. The **Venkataramana temple**, **Ganapathi temple** and the **Koti Teertha Temple Tank** lie in close proximity. Two enormous temple chariots are housed nearby. They are taken out during the **Shivaratri** celebrations held with great fanfare in February.

Four beautiful beaches wedged between cliffs, surround the town of Gokarna. The closest of these is the **Kudle Beach**. Further down, through numerous alleys and 'Way to Beach' signs, lies the **Om Beach** where a promontory breaks from the coastline, dividing the beach into two semi-circular halves resembling the letter 'Om'. The more isolated **Half Moon** and **Paradise** beaches further south are 30-minute and 60-minute walks from Gokarna.

## Karwar

*You could trek from Gokarna to Karwar. This route has earned the sobriquet of 'Golden Trek', taking you through quaint fishing hamlets, the seaside and a long river crossing. Karwar has some lovely stretches of beach and sand flanked by soaring hills on one side and the Arabian Sea on the other. Surrounded by five islands, the port town is located on the banks of the Kali river. A large naval base, Project Seabird is under construction. Some parts of Karwar's beaches are thus off limits. Entry is prohibited to the Anjediva Island near Karwar due to the naval presence.*

This sleepy coastal town was once a vibrant trading outpost where the Arabs, Dutch, Portuguese, French and British did business. Karwar's beauty is inspiring. The famous poet Rabindranath Tagore is said to have penned a poem here and one of its beaches has been named in his honour.

The Karwar Bay is packed with a large harbour, **Tagore Beach** and the more secluded **Binaga** and **Arga beaches**. The **Sadashivgad Hill Fort** with a **Durga temple** at its summit, a unique octagonal Catholic church in the nearby Kadwad Village and the 300-year old **Venkatarama temple** with rare ochre Kavi paintings are all must-sees. The **Naganatha**

Shiva temple, Murudeshwar

<sup>99</sup> Could you move that cloud a
little to the right please? <sub>99</sub>

When you're on holiday, it's the finer details that matter. Which is why we
don't just connect destinations. We take care of everything in between. Be
it rooms with a view, tours that suit your taste, shopping expeditions or just
star gazing, we'll work it all out. Just the way you want it. Anywhere in India.
Or the world. We'll move the earth to ensure that you are on cloud nine.

Hammock
LEISURE HOLIDAYS
—— PVT LTD ——

designed just for you

HAMMOCK LEISURE HOLIDAYS PVT. LTD. 314/1, Vijay Kiran, 1st Floor, 7th Cross, Domlur Layout, Bangalore 560 071
Tel: 5126 2220, 2535 1444, 2535 1555 Telefax: 2535 4222 Email: hammock@vsnl.net www.hammockholidays.com

Because the best of the world lies in the

## Less is more.　　smallest and the most inconspicuous.

Because luxury lies in simplicity.

Because reality is more enchanting than fantasy.

Because magic lies in what you already have.

Bangaram Island

—

Brunton Boatyard

—

Casino Hotel

—

Coconut Lagoon

—

Kalari Kovilakom

—

Marari Beach

—

Spice Village

—

Spice Coast Cruises

experience hotels

www.cghearth.com

contact@cghearth.com
+91-484-2668221

Devbagh Beach Resort offers a range of adventure activities, like banana boat rides.

temple where an anthill is worshipped and the famous dargah of Peer Shan Shamsuddin Kharobat, a saint from Baghdad are other quaint attractions. The islands around Karwar can be reached by boat. Of these, a prominent island is **Anjediva**. It is said that Vasco da Gama came calling here in 1498. The Portuguese later built a fort. The island has also served as a Goan penal colony. From Karwar, Devbagh Beach Resort is a short boat ride away.

## Kurmagad

*A 20-minute motorboat ride from Kodibagh brings you to the island of Kurmagad where fishing trips, nature walks, swimming, snorkelling and dolphin watching happen at the same time. The tableland offers some memorable views of the sea and clusters of neighbouring islands.*

Encircled by the Arabian Sea, this secluded tortoise-shaped island is an ideal getaway. There is an eco-friendly rustic resort by the sea with quaint huts and tents for accommodation. Kurmagad possesses an isolated beach in the shape of a crescent moon. A flight of rather steep steps descends into this stunning beach flanked by the craggy coastline on both sides. A guided exploration of the island reveals the remains of a fort. An old canon and ruins of a rampart are the remainders of the war fought by Basalinga Nayak of Sonda with the British in 1705. There is also an intriguing cave on the island that opens into the **Narasimha temple** perched on a hillock. An annual fair or jatra held in January brings hoards of devotees to its helm. The nearby islands of **Madalingagad or Sanyasi Island, Devagada or Oyster Rock Island** are just a boat ride away. The latter has an operational lighthouse that is more than 140 years old.

Om beach, Gokarna

### Mangalore

Mangalore is well connected by rail, road and air. Hamapankatta is the traffic hub of the city from where you can catch city buses to most destinations. It is a major crossroads for tourists heading along the Konkan coast between Goa and Kerala, and between Mysore and the coast.

Bangalore-357kms
Karwar-285kms
Hassan-172kms

Bangalore-357kms

Bajpe-20kms

### Udupi

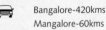

Bangalore-420kms
Mangalore-60kms
Malpe-6kms

Mangalore-60kms

Mangalore-60kms

### Murudeshwar

Bhatkal-16kms
Karwar-126kms
Mangalore-160kms
Bangalore-520kms
(via Shimoga)

Murudeshwar (Main station on Konkan Rail)
Bhatkal-16kms
Bangalore-520kms

Mangalore-160kms

### Gokarna

Karwar-60kms
Bangalore-470kms

Kumta-32kms

Dabolim (Goa) 185kms

### Karwar

South Goa border-10kms
Panaji-135kms
Mumbai-500kms
Bangalore-530kms

Karwar-7kms, main station on the Konkan Railway.

Dabolim (Goa)-90kms

424

## WHERE TO STAY

### Mangalore

**Taj Manjarun**
Old Port Road, Opp. DC Office,
Mangalore 575001
**Tel** 0824-242 0420
**Fax** 0824-242 0585
**Web** www.tajhotels.com
**Tariff** Rs 1,300 to Rs 4,400

**Summer Sands Beach Resort**
Chotamangalore, Ullal,
Mangalore 575020
**Tel** 0824-246 7690-92
**Fax** 0824-246 7693
**Tariff** Rs 645 to Rs 3,800
**Web** www.summer-sands.com

**Hotel Poonja International**
KS Rao Road, Hampanakatta,
Mangalore 575001
**Tel** 0824-244 0168/0183
**Fax** 0824-244 1081
**Web** www.hotelpoonjainternational.com
**Tariff** Rs 550 to Rs 2,200

**Hotel Moti Mahal**
Falnir Road, Mangalore 575001
**Tel** 0824-244 1411/1412
**Fax** 0824-244 1011
**Email** motimahal@vasnet.co.in
**Tariff** Rs 950 to Rs 2,100

**Hotel Pentagon**
Kankanady, Mahaveer Circle,
Mangalore 575002
**Tel** 0824-224 9203-08
**Fax** 0824-224 6700
**Tariff** Rs 430 to Rs 1,500

**Hotel Mangalore International**
Ayesha Towers, KS Rao Road,
Mangalore 575001
**Tel** 0824-244 4860-64
**Fax** 0824-244 4859
**Tariff** Rs 530 to Rs 1,390

### Udupi

If you are scouting for cheap accommodation, try the temple guesthouses around the Central Square. Normally they are reserved by pilgrims. There are several Udupi Brahmin vegetarian restaurants available.

**Karavali Hotels**
NH 17, Adi Udupi, Udupi 576103
**Tel** 0820-252 2860-64, 252 2851
**Fax** 0820-252 2862
**Email** karavalihotel@hotmail.com,
karavali@satyam.net.in
**Tariff** Rs 265 to Rs 4,500

**Paradise Isle Beach Resort**
PB 21, Malpe Beach, Udupi 576108
**Tel** 0820-253 7791/7300
**Web** www.theparadiseisle.com
**Tariff** Sea facing rooms, Rs 4,250 and non-sea facing rooms, Rs 3,750

**Hotel Sri Ram Residency**
Opposite Head Post Office,
Udupi 576101
**Tel** 0820-253 0761/0762
**Tariff** Rs 300 to Rs 1,000

**Palm Grove Beach Resort**
Fisheries Road, Yermalbada,
Udupi 574119
**Tel** 0820-2577 115, 2555 823
**Tariff** Rs 1,000 to Rs 1,200

**Hotel Swadesh Heritage**
Maruti Veethika Road, Udupi 576101
**Tel** 0820-2529 605/705/805/305
**Fax** 0820-2520 205
**Web** www.hotelswadesh.com
**Tariff** Rs 250 to Rs 1,050

**Hotel Sharada International**
NH17, Adi Udupi Bypass,
Udupi 576103
**Tel** 0820-252 2912-20, 252 1968
**Tariff** Rs 295 to Rs 1,000

**Sai Vishram Baindoor Beach Resort**
Dombe Village, Paduvari, Baindoor,
Udupi 576214
**Telefax** 08254-253 935
For bookings: 080-2559 5175/77/79,
3678 5134 (Bangalore)
**Fax** 080-2558 1563
**Email** natventure@yahoo.com
**Tariff** Rs1,200 to Rs 3,000

**Aane Jhari Nature Camp**
Mookambika Wildlife Sanctuary,
Kollur, Udupi
**Tel** 080-25597021/24/25, 5695 5044,
98454 07672 (Bangalore)
**Web** www.adreno.org
**Tariff** Rs 330 to Rs 750

### Murudeshwar

**RNS Yatrinivas**
Off NH17, Murudeshwar, Bhatkal
Taluk, Uttara Kannada 581350
**Tel** 08385-260 060, 268 900-03
**Fax** 08385-268 990
**Tariff** Rs 600

**Naveen Beach Resort**
Off NH17, Murudeshwar, Bhatkal
Taluk, Uttara Kannada 581350
**Tel** 08385-260 415/428
**Fax** 08385-260 427
**Tariff** Rs 1,200 to Rs 2,000

**Murudeshwar Guest House**
RN Shetty Trust, Bhatkal Taluk,
Murudeshwar,
Uttara Kannada 581350
**Tel** 08385-268 860, 260 424
**Fax** 08385-268 990
**Tariff** Rs 375 to Rs 1,000

**Benzy Intercontinental**
Village Mavalli Post Murudeshwar,
Uttara Kannada 581350
**Tel** 08385-260 565/988/977/999
**Tariff** Rs 400 to Rs 600

**Murudeshwar Boarding & Lodging**
Temple Road, Murudeshwar, Bhatkal
Taluk, Uttara Kannada 581350
**Tel** 08385-260 479/480
**Tariff** Rs 250 to Rs 350

### Gokarna

**Om Beach Resort (Jungle Lodges & Resorts)**
Om Beach Road, Bungle Gudde
Gokarna PO, Kumta Taluk,
Karwar 581326
**Tel** 08386-257 052
**Tariff** Rs 1,500 to Rs 2,300

**Opening Mar'05: CGH Earth property at Gokarna**
Donibail, Gokarna Village,
Kumta Taluk
**Tel** 08386-257 131/133
Sales Office 0484-266 8221
**Web** www.cghearth.com

**Hotel Gokarna International**
Main Road, Kumta Taluk, Gokarna,
Uttara Kannada 581326
**Tel** 08386-257 368, 256 622
**Fax** 08386-256 848
**Tariff** Rs 195 to Rs 700

**Om Lodge**
Ganjigadde, Gokarna, Kumta Taluk,
Uttara Kannada 581326
**Tel** 08386-256 445/244
**Tariff** Rs 150 to Rs 700

**Nimmu House**
Mani Bhadra Road, Gokarna, Uttara
Kannada 581326
**Tel** 08386-256 730/712
**Email** nimmuhouse@yahoo.com
**Tariff** Rs 150 to Rs 200

**Hotel New Prasad Nilaya**
Near New Bus Stand, Ganjigadde,
Gokarna, Kumta Taluk,
Uttara Kannada 581326
**Tel** 08386-256 250/675, 257 135
**Tariff** Rs 100 to Rs 300

**Hotel Samudra**
Gokarna, Kumta Taluk,
Uttara Kannada 581326
**Tel** 08386-256 236
**Tariff** Rs 135, Rs 50 for extra bed.

### Karwar

**Devbagh Beach Resort (Jungle Lodges & Resorts)**
Opposite Bhadra Hotel, Kodibagh,
Karwar, Uttara Kannada 581301
**Tel** 08382-226 596
**Web** www.junglelodges.com
**Tariff** Rs 1,500 (Log Huts & Rooms at Sadhashivgad), Rs 1,000(tents)

**Riveredge Paradise Resort**
Hankon Village, Karwar Taluk
**Tel** 080-2010 5015 (Bangalore)
**Web** www.paradiseadventureresorts.com
**Tariff** Rs 3,300 (Log Cabin), Rs 2,200 (Luxury Tent), all meals included and one hour of water sports per day.

**The Great Outdoors**
Vanashree Building, NH-17,
Sadashivgad, Karwar,
Uttara Kannada 581301
**Tel** 08382-220 265, 98452 15152
**Web** www.thegreatoutdoorsindia.com
**Tariff** Rs 1,250 to Rs 1,450
(Closed in June, July and August)

**Hotel Bhadra**
NH17, Kodibagh, Near Kali Bridge,
Karwar, Uttara Kannada 581303
**Tel** 08382-225 212/213
**Fax** 08382-227 147
**Tariff** Rs 250 to Rs 1,250

**Hotel Subhadra**
Kaiga Road, Mallapur,
Uttara Kannada 581400
**Tel** 08382-254 883-85
**Fax** 08382-255 454
**Tariff** Rs 350 to Rs 800

**Hotel Sadanand**
Chendia, Uttara Kannada 581324
**Tel** 08382-273 182/183/033
**Fax** 08382-273 184
**Tariff** Rs 450 to Rs 1,000
**Web** www.hotel-sadanand.com

### Travel Tips

The best takeaways would be cashew or coffee, both of which are traded extensively here. Buses ply frequently between Udupi and Mangalore. Within Udupi, bicycles can be hired to move around.

# On the Jain Trail

Once the citadel of Jainism in the south, Karnataka hides a wealth of Jain temples and monuments. Unknown to most tourists, the abundant Jain heritage sites across the coast are home to some of the grandest monuments and temples created under royal patronage several centuries ago. In fact, Jainism was Karnataka's state religion for a long period of time and the contribution of Jain artists, poets and saints to Karnataka's architecture, language and literature has been immense.

About 180 basadis (as the Jain temples are called), dot southern Karnataka. The towns of Mudabidri and Karkala alone boast 18 temples each. The first one is at **Dharmasthala**, 75kms east of Mangalore. This lively temple town is home to a number of Jains and Hindus and both Jain tirthankaras and the resident Hindu god Lord Manjunatha are worshipped without incident. Interestingly, Lord Shiva or Manjunatha is worshipped by Vaishnavite priests, while the Manjunatha temple is run by a Jain family!

An important festival is the legendary Laksha Deepotsava when the temple is lit with a 100,000 lamps. Religion and charity are a way of life and it is said that no one leaves Dharmasthala hungry – 10,000 pilgrims, irrespective of their religious identity are given a free lunch at the Manjunatha temple everyday. Apart from the Jain basadis, catch a glimpse of the 39ft tall monolith statue of Bahubali that was brought here in 1882.

On your way out of Dharmasthala take a detour to the **Car Museum** where custom-built cars created for the Maharaja of Mysore, vintage cars from the Chevrolet Impala to the Jaguar are on display. Another interesting stop is the **Manjusha Museum** that showcases a variety of old artefacts from ancient scriptures on palm leaves, bells and jewellery to old sewing machines, typewriters and cameras.

The evergreen town of **Venur**, another renowned centre of Jainism, is reached by travelling 40kms out of Dharmasthala. It has eight famed Jain basadis and the ruins of a temple dedicated to Shantinatha, marked by profuse decorative carvings of the tirthankaras. An 11m high **Bahubali statue**, dating back to 1604, stands on the southern bank of the Gurupur river. The statue was commissioned by the Jain ruler Veera Thimmana IV Ajila in 1604.

The trail continues through **Mudabidri**, otherwise known as the Jain Varanasi of south India. Near Karkala, it is a celebrated Jain centre with 18 Jain basadis, the oldest of which is the 15th Century **Chandranatha temple**. One of the most magnificent Jain shrines, the **'Thousand-pillared Basadi of Mudabidri'** is located here. Built by a group of Jain merchants as far back as 1430, the temple is a three-storey granite structure with a conspicuous gabled roof. Over 500 years old, the roofs of this temple rise above one another in a curious fashion. The wealth of decorative relief work carved on the pillars are striking. The pillars themselves are massive and soar to a height of 12ft. The monolithic pillar at the entrance and the jewel-encrusted metal sculptures of the tirthankaras are other sights to watch out for. The Jain Math near the temple entrance is also worth a visit – the library preserves rare palm leaf manuscripts dating back to the 12th and 13th centuries. In the vicinity is the 17th century **Chowta Palace** displaying beautifully carved wooden pillars and ceilings.

A 45-minute drive down a meandering road from Mudabidri is the famous coastal town of **Karkala**. A 42ft tall **monolith of Gomateshwara** is the highlight here. The enormous statue set amongst granite outcrops attracted pilgrims from all over India in 2002 when the Mahamastakabhisheka ceremony was performed. The **Chaturmukha Basadi,** another attraction of Karkala dating back to 1586 AD has four identical Jain tirthankara images facing different directions. There are also life-size statues of three prominent Jain tirthankaras, smaller idols of 24 tirthankaras and a rare sculpture of Padmavathi Yaksha. The Jain equivalent of the dwajasthamba found in Hindu temples is the manasthamba. The 600-year old **Neminatha Basadi** has the tallest manasthamba in India.

The basadis preserve the ancient Jain faith and the temples stand testimony to the refined aesthetic sensibilities and craftsmanship achieved in medieval south India.

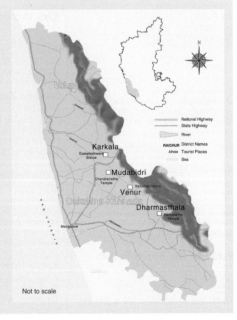

Not to scale

# Dandeli

Dandeli is home to Karnataka's second largest sanctuary. Clear streams, thick bamboo groves, diverse wildlife and umpteen pathways to trek through make Dandeli an exciting and enjoyable destination. The pitch-dark Kavle caves are best explored with a powerful torch and a guide in tow to get you through the maze of openings.

The **Dandeli Wildlife Sanctuary** is spread across 834sqkms, on the banks of river Kali with its gushing tributaries Kaneri and Nagajhari flowing through it. The moist deciduous and semi-evergreen forests hide the graceful **Virnoli Rapids**, the majestic **Supa Dam** and the **Nagajhari Viewpoint** within them. The river is an excellent vantage point to observe the animals as they gather to drink at the water holes. The sanctuary is home to the elusive black panther, elephants, gaur, sambar, sloth bear, wild boars, wild dogs, jackals, langur and a few tigers. Among birds, the golden-backed woodpecker, crested serpent eagle and the Malabar pied hornbill inhabit the forests. Large crocodiles and snakes can also be spotted along the rivers. In the heart of the forest, is the formidable **Syntheri Rock**, a monolithic granite structure covered with honey combs. The **Sykes Point** provides spectacular views of the forested slopes and valleys, rivers Nagajhari and Kali and colourful sunsets. This spot has been named after a British engineer, who worked here.

For those who are game, a 40-minute jeep ride followed by a trek through narrow pathways and a climb up 350 steps takes you to the mysterious **Kavle Caves**. The exertion is worthwhile – the caves are replete with ancient limestone formations, labyrinthine passages and impressive stalactite and stalagmite structures. As you proceed through the caves the openings get smaller and you may have to crawl through some of them. The heart of the caves hold a gigantic stalactite in the shape of a Shiva linga.

The **Kulgi Nature Camp** is situated 12kms from the Kavle Caves. Here you can stay in pitched tents amidst sylvan surroundings. Alternately, you can stay at the **Kali Adventure Resort** and try your hand at white water rafting in the unpredictable rapids of Kali or trek through the forested hills. Canoe tours through the uninhabited islands on the shores of the Supa reservoir and coracle rides down the river to spot crocodiles and aquatic birds are possible. The Kulgi and Kali nature camps within the sanctuary offer accommodation.

# Travel Information

## GETTING THERE

There are buses to Dandeli from Hubli, Dharwad and Karwar. If you are travelling by rail from Bangalore or Mumbai, alight at Londa or the Dharwad/Hubli railway station and proceed by road. A 90-minute journey will take you to Dandeli.

    Dharwad-57kms

    Hubli-72kms

    Belgaum-109kms

    Goa-145kms

    Bangalore-480kms

    Londa-25kms,

    Dharwad-57kms

    Hubli-72kms

    Dabolim (Goa)-145kms

## WHERE TO STAY

### Kali Wilderness and Adventure Camp
**(Jungle Lodges & Resorts)**
Kogilban, Dandeli, Haliyal Taluk,
Uttara Kannada 581325
**Tel** 08284-230 266 (Resort)

080-2559 7021/7024/7025
(Bangalore)
**Web** www.junglelodges.com
**Tariff** Rs 1,500
Outdoor activities, Rs 1,200

The package includes a coracle ride down Kali river, a jungle safari, a camp-fire buffet dinner. A trek to the Kavle Caves and a visit to the Syntheri Rock is usually arranged. White water rafting is offered at extra cost.

### The Old Magazine House Forest Camp
**(Jungle Lodges & Resorts)**
Ganeshgudi,
Londa-Dandeli Road
**Tel** 08284-234 380, 233 360
**Email** jpollard46@hotmail.com
**Tariff** Rs 1,200 (per person)
For bookings, contact:
080-2557 9021 (Bangalore)
or Kali Wilderness Camp,
Dandeli, 08284-230 266

### Bison River Resort
Karwar Belgaum Highway,Village
Ambeli, Ganeshgudi Post, Joida Taluk,
Uttara Kannada 581365
**Tel** 08383-246 539
**Fax** 08383-246 539
**Email** iawr@vsnl.com
**Tariff** Rs 1,100 to Rs 3,500

### Kulgi Nature Camp
Kulgi Village, Haliyal Taluk,
Dandeli Wildlife Division, Dandeli,
Uttara Kannada 581325
**Tel** 08284-231 585
**Fax** 08284-231 585
**Tariff** Rs 200 to Rs 400 (Tent)
For bookings, contact:
Deputy Conservator of Forests,
Wildlife Division,
Uttara Kannada 581325

### Anashi Nature Camp
Near Anashi Village,
Anashi Ulvi Road,
Uttara Kannada District
For bookings, contact:
Deputy Conservator of
Forests,Wildlife Division, Dandeli,
Uttara Kannada
**Telefax** 08284-231 585
**Tariff** Rs 50 to Rs 200
(per person)

Kayaking in Dandeli

# Hastha Shilpa Heritage Village

Take a trip back in time at the Hasta Shilpa Heritage Village, a unique museum that brings together coastal Karnataka's history, architecture and precious artefacts. More than 20 traditional homes which have been reconstructed from ruins and artfully restored, now live on in this heritage village.

Kunjur Chowkimane is an Udupi home from the early 19th century. Some of the oldest homes include the 400-year old Barkur Olaginamane, a quintessential Bunt household and the 700-year old Jungama Mutt. The three-century-old Sringeri House has been built according to Vedic traditions and the Vidyamandira was the residence of the pontiff of Ramachandrapura Math in Shimoga. Other restored homes including the Deccani Nawab Mahal, Mangalore Christian House, Bhatkal Muslim House and the Mudhol Palace Durbar Hall are now restored to their former glory.

A rare collection of utensils, carved wooden doors, elaborate period furniture, decorative cast iron grills, quaint puja articles, clusters of folk idols and terracotta artefacts are showcased here. There is a 280-year old vessel of bell metal where curd or buttermilk stays fresh for a week and containers where rice stays fresh for five years!

Established seven years ago with aid from the Norwegian Government, the Hasta Shilpa Trust aims to preserve the rich legacy of Dakshina Kannada or southern coastal Karnataka. Rare houses and structures of heritage value with priceless antiques that were near ruin or on the verge of being demolished were acquired by the trust. They have been carefully rehabilitated and transplanted into the complex. The chief architect of Hastha Shilpa is Vijaynatha Shenoy a bank employee by profession, whose love of traditional homes and antiques has taken this shape. Anyone with slightest interest in history will find the visit more than worthwhile.

*Hastha Shilpa, Ananth Nagar II Stage, Manipal 576119* **Tel** *0820-2572061*

# My Perfect Holiday – Anita Nair

I enjoy travelling at my own pace, with no particular destination in mind. My most memorable journeys through Karnataka are the road trips I have taken along with my husband and son. Driving is a great way to experience Karnataka's dramatic landscape – vast expanses of wilderness dotted with huge boulders. And the well maintained roads make this kind of travel easy. My car trips include those to Kodagu, Bandipur and the coast.

My favourite holiday destination is **Karwar**, set on the northern most tip of Karnataka's coastline. The drive from Bangalore to Karwar is an interesting one that takes you through the lush Karavali coast, the road rising and dipping along with the Western Ghats. With cliffs on one side and the sea on the other, Karwar reminds me of the coast in Greece. Its beaches are pristine and don't have the feverish frenzy of Goa. The Binaga and Arga beaches are particularly beautiful and Rabindranath Tagore is said to have penned a poem here. I have made numerous trips to Karwar and like everything about it – miles of sand, limestone formations and of course, the seafood. December is a good time to visit here.

I also enjoyed my stay in **Chikmagalur**, with forests, hiking trails and empty roads. The landscape lends itself to long, aimless walks, something you cannot do in a city like Bangalore. Down south, the temples of **Halebid** and **Belur** have a desolate beauty that appeal to me. I would love to visit Hampi, the Gol Gumbaz in Bijapur and Mudhol.

*Anita Nair is a writer based in Bangalore and her novels include The Better Man and Ladies Coupe. Her works have been translated into twenty languages.*

**Surf Rider**

**Which role would you like to play?**

**Water Babe**

**Beach Bum**

**KARNATAKA**
Theatre of Inspiration

Outplay the surf at Marawanthe. Discover the virgin Ullal beach. Tan in solitary splendour at Karwar. Tuck into a tender coconut at Kaup. Ride out in a catamaran from Malpe. Settle for a hammock at Om. Or just whip up your own script. On this stage, it's easy to find your place in the sun.

Karnataka Tourism  #49  Second Floor  Khanija Bhavan  Race Course Road  Bangalore - 560 001  Fax: ++91 80 2235 2626  Email: discoverkarnataka@vsnl.net  www.karnatakatourism.org

STARK.Blr/kk/1050

# My Perfect Holiday – Omer Bin Jung

Karnataka has some great routes to drive through and here are a few that I recommend.

## 1. One night and two days covering the wildlife and jungle circuit

Day 1: Depart from Bangalore in the morning. Drive to Kanakapura and onto Sathnur. This route takes you to Malavalli, continue driving till you turn left into Shivasamudram.

You can break for lunch at the Cauvery Falls. Post lunch, drive on to Kollegal. Continue till you pass Yadanur and Chamarajnagar. Your halt for the night is the K Gudi Wildlife Camp or BR Hills Wildlife Sanctuary.

Day 2: You can go on a safari in the morning and after breakfast, leave for Mysore via the Kollegal route. Around Mysore is the Ranganathittu Bird Sanctuary and the erstwhile capital, Srirangapatna. The drive back to Bangalore is through Mandya, Maddur and Channapatna.

## 2. Two nights and three days along the coast

Day 1: Depart from Bangalore early morning. Drive on the road to Nelamangala and head for Tumkur. The road goes through Gubbi, Tiptur, Arsikere, Kadur onto Shimoga from where you can drive through Sagar and Talaguppa to Jog Falls. You can stay at Jog Falls for the night.

Day 2: Visit Siddapur and the Lushington Falls. Your next stop is Honnavar on the coast. Follow the coast along Kumta, Ankola and Karwar. There are quite a few resorts to check into for the night.

Day 3: Head for Hubli and south to Haveri and Ranibennur. The blackbuck sanctuary is worth a visit. From here, drive to Chitradurga, which has an outstanding fort.

Return to Bangalore from Tumkur, via Hiriyur and Sira.

## 3. Three nights and four days covering the heritage sites

Day 1: Depart from Bangalore early morning and drive to Tumkur onto Chitradurga.

Once you leave Chitradurga, take a right to the road going to Jagalur and Kudligi. Keep driving till you reach Hospet.

This is a good base to visit Hampi and the bear sanctuary near Hampi.

From Hospet drive four kilometres onto the Amigudi Road and take a right and drive 11kms to the Boulders Resort which is a comfortable place to check into.

Day 2: Drive to Koppal and the Tungabhadra Dam. There are cottages available for rent and you can spend the night here.

Day 3: Drive through Gadag to Badami and Aihole. Both these places have a wealth of heritage. From here, drive to Bijapur, via Bagalkot and Gaddankeri. You can stay at Bijapur overnight.

Day 4: Sightseeing in Bijapur and from here, drive through Hungund, Kushtagi to Hospet and back to Bangalore via Chitradurga and Tumkur.

Alternately, you can take a night train from Bangalore to Hospet and have a car meet you at the station. The same route can be followed from Bijapur to Hospet and back by train from there.

## 4. Two nights and three days in the 'Scotland of India' (Kodagu)

Day 1: Start from Bangalore and drive up to Mysore early morning. Drive to Elivala. Enroute, take a detour to visit the Tibetan settlement. The route is Bilikere-Hunsur-Periyapatna-Siddapura. Stay overnight at Siddapura.

Day 2: Post breakfast drive to Madikeri and onto Jambur, Somvarpet and Sanisvarsante.

At Sanisvarsante take a left into Bisle Ghats and drive to Kukke Subramanya.

Break here to visit the temple. Drive back to Kurubathur onto Sakleshpur. Stay at Hassan or Sakleshpur for the night.

Day 3: Visit Belur and Halebid. From Halebid, you can also drive down to Javagal and Banavar. Drive back to Bangalore through Arsikere, Tiptur and Tumkur.

*Omer Bin Jung is the Managing Director of Prestige Leisure Resorts. He lives in Bangalore.*

Srirangapatna

# Yana – Rocked By Nature

On the rim of north Karnataka's coastline lie a cluster of dramatic rock formations that collectively go by the name Yana. Sharp edged cliffs made of black crystalline rock stand out in contrast to the evergreen Sahyadri Hills and the blue of river Chandika.

Once off the beaten track of travellers, today Yana bustles with film crews who like to shoot song and dance sequences in its picturesque locales.

A short drive from the sleepy coastal towns of Sirsi and Kumta, the crystalline rock formations of Yana begin to take shape. A 16km trek off the highway in the cool green hills gets you to the foot of Yana's most impressive peaks: The twin shikharas of **Jagamohini** and **Bhairaveshwara** stand tall at 120m and 90m respectively. At the foot of the two peaks, named after the incarnations of Lord Shiva and Vishnu, is a large **cave temple** dedicated to Lord Bhairaveshwara. The three-metre cave also holds a Shiva linga. Water from a nearby spring flows on its façade and devotees liken this to the descent of river Ganga from heaven. Adjacent caves house bronze icons of Chandika, an incarnation of Goddess Durga.

There is a legend around Yana and its cliffs. It is said that the evil demon Bhasmasura possessed the power to turn anyone into ashes with the mere touch of his hand. He tried to vanquish Lord Shiva with his newfound powers, but Shiva took refuge in the caves of Yana. Meanwhile, Lord Vishnu assumed the incarnation of a seductive dancer, Jagamohini and challenged the demon to outdo her in a dance performance. During the demon's dance she lured him into placing his hand on his own head. The demon turned to ashes and Lord Shiva was the supreme ruler once again. Even today, the faithful believe that the white-ash like substance found in and around Yana is the remains of demon Bhasmasura.

An annual festival held in Yana attracts a large gathering of devotees. A dip in the lake **Danditirtha** is followed by worship to the Shiva linga. The holy water from Yana travels to another coastal temple town Gokarna. Here the water is used to perform theMahamastakabhisheka of Lord Mahabaleshwara. Take care not to disturb the wild bees that have made their home in the rock shelters as they are considered guardians of the cave temples.

Tourists to Yana can also stop at Banavasi, located by the banks of river Varada. Once an important centre for learning, Banavasi is also the erstwhile capital of Karnataka. The **Madhukeshwara temple** is representative of Kadamba architecture but parts of the temple were built during the reign of the Chalukyas in the 12th century. If you are travelling in December, don't miss the Kadambothsav, a large-scale cultural festival that draws artists from all over south India. Banavasi is also an important centre for Yakshagana.

## GETTING THERE

Sirsi is the closest town and buses ply everyday from Bangalore to Sirsi. The most convenient transport would be a deluxe bus that leaves at night and reaches Sirsi in the morning. A number of hotels are available at Sirsi. From here, Yana is about 50kms. Camping is also possible at Yana.

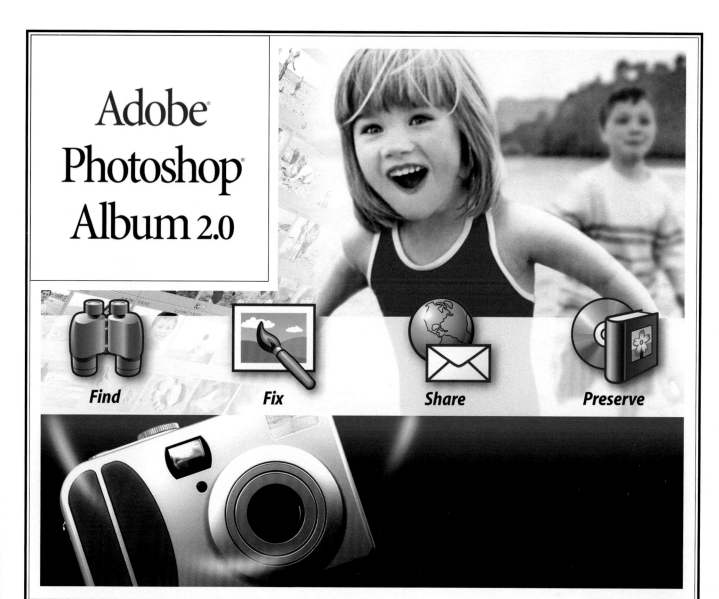
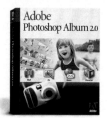

# The Royal City of **Mysore**

For many centuries Mysore was the richest, most lavishly built, powerful state in the region. Former capital of the illustrious Wodeyar kings, it still maintains some of its grandeur. The city's royal heritage is carefully preserved in 10 magnificent palaces, a 100 heritage buildings, beautifully laid out gardens, broad avenues, boulevards and sacred temples.

The rest of Mysore city has an old world charm that lingers in its quiet residential areas and bustling markets. Apart from the regular tourist itinerary, there is plenty to see in the long tradition of music and dance, art and literature, scholarship and time-honoured crafts. Traditionally, the biggest event in Mysore is the 10-day long Dasara festival, where the erstwhile king is once again in the public eye.

Mysore's many attractions can hold a visitor's attention for days. It's also a great base to explore the surrounding areas filled with wildlife sanctuaries, temple towns, hill stations and coffee plantations.

The illuminated Mysore Palace

The golden throne at the Mysore Palace

### Mysore Palace

**Open** *10am to 5:30pm*
**Admission** *Rs 5, free for children below 10 years. (Shoes and cameras must be left at the cloakroom.)*

All roads in Mysore lead to the palace, also known as the Amba Vilas Palace. Designed by British architect Henry Irwin, it was built on the site of an earlier structure destroyed in a fire. Created in the Indo-Saracenic style, it has brass-plated domes, turrets, arches, and colonnades.

The palace houses a treasure of exquisite carvings and works of art gathered from all over the world. Twelve temples surround the palace along with six gates and entry is from the southern side only. Inside the walled area reside a museum of art, more temples and shrines, including the Shwetha Varahaswamy temple. The entire palace is illuminated on Sundays and public holidays and people come from miles to witness this sight.

Visitors enter through the Doll's Pavilion – once a showcase for the dolls featured in the Dasara celebrations and now a gallery of European and Indian sculpture and ceremonial objects. The main attraction of the palace is the majestic Durbar Hall with an ornate ceiling and many sculpted pillars. Intricately carved doors open into luxuriously furnished rooms. The octagonal Marriage Pavilion is adorned with glazed tile flooring, cast-iron pillars from Glasgow and Bohemian chandeliers. The Belgian stained glass used in the domed ceiling is arranged in a graceful peacock design and the walls display exquisite paintings.

The magnificent jewel-studded gold throne, the pride of the Wodeyars and the symbol of their sovereignty, is displayed here during the Dasara festival in October.

A line of souvenir shops leads to a small museum run by the royal family which displays paintings from the Tanjavur and Mysore schools, some inlaid with precious stones and gold leaf.

### Mysore Zoo

**Open** *8.30am to 5:30pm. Closed on Tuesday.*
**Admission** *Rs 15 for adults and Rs 5 for children*

On the eastern edge of the city lies a sprawling zoo that mimics the animals' natural environment with plenty of trees and lush green foliage. It was set up with royal patronage in the 19th century and houses some rare and exotic species like the white tiger. Other attractions are the swamp deer, chimpanzee, gaur, giraffe, baboon, zebra, Asiatic elephant, tapir, lion-tailed macaque, sloth bear and others. The zoo doubles up as an exotic garden with a 110 species of plants and trees from other countries.

### St. Philomena's Church

**Open** *5am to 8pm*
**Admission** *Free*

A miniature reproduction of the Cologne Cathedral, this imposing neo-Gothic structure was finished in 1941. It has beautiful stained glass windows, Corinthian pillars, an underground crypt and lofty twin spires that can be seen for miles. Designed by French architects, it was built under the patronage of Krishnaraja Wodeyar IV.

The stained glass windows depict Biblical scenes like the Last Supper and the birth of Christ. Below the altar is a reclining statue of St. Philomena, visited by devotees from all over. During the feast of Philomena held in August, the statue of the saint is taken in a procession through the city.

St. Philomena's Church

### Sri Jayachamarajendra Art Gallery

**Open** *8am to 5pm. Closed on Sunday.*
**Admission** *Rs 10 for adults and Rs 5 for children*

The Jagan Mohan Palace was built in 1902 to mark the coronation ceremony of Krishnaraja Wodeyar III. It now houses an art gallery that boasts an excellent collection of exquisite pieces of metal, ceramics, sandalwood, ivory, stone, antique furniture, ingenious indoor games and ancient musical instruments.

On display are priceless paintings of reputed artists like Ravi Varma (a separate gallery is devoted to his works) and Roerich, as well as the traditional Mysore gold leaf paintings. A series of faded black and white photographs of ceremonial state occasions share space with elaborate clocks including a French musical calendar clock.

Other interesting exhibits include a cluster of

Mysore Zoo

musical instruments, chief among them a brass jaltarang set, a glass xylophone, harmonicas and a clarinet played by Krishnaraja Wodeyar.

## Folklore Museum

*Folklore Museum, Janapada Museums, Manasagangotri, Mysore 570006*
**Open** *10am to 1:30pm and 2:30 to 5:30pm. Closed on Sunday.*
**Admission** *Free*

The Folklore Museum is located in the imposing Jayalakshmi Vilas Mansion, set in the Mysore University Campus at Manasagangotri. The University of Mysore and Infosys Foundation joined hands to convert the mansion into the largest university museum in the country, with 6,500 folklore articles on display. Among the exhibits lies an intriguing collection of carved wooden figures from Karnataka's villages: Rural costumes, utensils, ornaments, metal ware, implements and tools used in village settings. Models of temples, houses, decorative masks and ceremonial headwear share space with a display of leather shadow puppets and a sandalwood oil soap used by Mahatma Gandhi during his visit to Karnataka in 1930! A 300 year old temple car, from Thirthahalli in Shimoga district is a rare heritage piece.

## Rail Museum

**Open** *10am to 5:30pm*
**Admission** *Rs 2*

Close to the Mysore Railway Station is the little known but impressive Rail Museum.

Priceless ancient locomotives and royally upholstered coaches, along with a collection of paintings and photographs narrate the story of the railways in India.
On display is a converted four-wheel goods brake van manufactured in 1923 by Stable Ford and Company, England and the Austin Rail Motor built in 1925 with the body of an Austin car and four locomotive wheels! The prize exhibit of the museum is the Maharani's Saloon of 1899 vintage and a kitchen-dining car built in Mysore in 1914.

## Oriental Research Library

*Tel 0821-2423 136*
**Open** *10:30am to 5: 30pm. Closed on Sunday.*

The Oriental Research Library is rightly housed in a100-year old heritage building with impressive Roman architecture. Earlier known as the Oriental Research Institute, it preserves some rare and ancient manuscripts dating back to the 11th century.
The manuscripts deal with different subjects like astronomy, astrology, botany, mathematics and applied sciences. The 2,300 year old *Arthashastra* of Kautilya was first published from the manuscript preserved here.Some of the ancient and rare manuscripts have been conserved with microfilming. The Kannada and Persian manuscripts have been transferred to the Kuvempu Institute of Kannada Studies and the Arabic College.

## Chamundi Hills

**Open** *All day*

Overlooking the royal city of Mysore is a beautiful temple atop Chamundi Hills. It affords a stunning view of the city, especially at night. Chamundi Hills lies at an altitude of 3,489ft and is only a short drive from the city, through a dense forest.
Halfway up the hill is the 16ft monolith of Nandi the bull, Shiva's chosen carrier with a magnificent pendant bell around its neck. Visitors to the temple may either drive up or climb the 1,000 stone steps. The temple at the top has a colossal pyramidal gopuram dedicated to Goddess Chamundeswari, the patron saint of the royal Wodeyars, who is said to have delivered the people of the area from the buffalo-headed demon Mahishasura. Legend has it that after she killed him she took

The Raja Ravi Verma collection at the Jayachamarajendra Art Gallery

# My Perfect Holiday – Sankalp Saxena

If I had to pick my favourite places in Karnataka, the first choice would be **Hampi**. The history attached to this place is mind boggling. This age-old temple still functions. The food is quite surprising – besides Indian and the ubiquitous Chinese, you can even get Israeli food here! I recommend renting a cycle and biking along this old city.

**Kodagu** during the rains is breathtakingly beautiful. The entire place is green and acres and acres of plantation are a sight to behold. This is a great place for walks and you are bound to run into honeymooners here. Kodava cuisine is a must try, so don't give that a miss. Good buys are bamboo shoot pickle, honey and some homemade wine.

**Mysore** is just two and a half hours from Bangalore. Its royal past makes it a very interesting city. Mysore is also a good base to visit most of southern Karnataka's places of interest. If you can, try and make it during Dasara, when the whole city celebrates for nine days. It's easy to get around in Mysore and there are plenty of options for staying and eating out.

For some of the country's best beaches, head for **Mangalore**. The stretch extends from the Kerala coast in the south to Goa in the north but is less crowded.

It goes without saying that the seafood here is excellent. The coast has some age-old temples and churches that are well worth a visit but if it's a quiet holiday you want, there are quite a few beaches to laze on.

One of my favourite getaways is to **Kabini** in the jungles of Karnataka. The safaris are exciting and naturalists here are knowledgeable and friendly.

*Sankalp Saxena is Managing Director, i2 Technologies. He lives in Bangalore.*

Mysore Dasara festivities

Chamundi Hills

## Rangayana
*Vinobha Bhave Road, Mysore 570005*
*Tel 0821-2512 639, 2415 905*
**Admission** *Free*
**Open:** *10am to 5pm*

Launched in 1988, Rangayana is the only theatre repertory that stages quality weekend plays on a regular basis. The cultural hub of the city, Rangayana promotes varied indigenous art forms. Folk dance and music performances are a staple and local artists showcase their art works here. Rangayana has an open-air theatre Vana Ranga, where a national level theatre festival is held every year. Workshops in acting, music, direction and theatre are conducted from time to time. It is also a popular venue for book launches, photography and painting exhibitions.

# AMUSEMENT PARKS

## GRS Fantasy Park
*KRS Road, Metagalli, Mysore 570016*
*Tel 0821-2582 781*
**Open** *10:30am to 6pm (weekdays),*
*10:30am to 7:30pm (Sundays and holidays)*
**Admission** *Adults Rs 239*

Set across 30 sprawling acres on the outskirts of Mysore, this amusement and water park has amazing rides, souvenir stores and a restaurant.

## Planet X-Amusement Park
*Maharana Prathap Singh Road, Near Horse Park,*
*Nazarbad, Mysore 570010*
*Tel 0821-3090 300*
**Open:** *4pm to 11pm*

This amusement centre is famous for its go-karting track. Located in Nazarbad, the park has attractions like a bowling alley, video game arcade, a restaurant and a weekend discotheque.

up residence on the hill. Inhabitants of the city below named it Mysore after the demon himself.

## Regional Museum Of Natural History (RMNH)
**Open** *10am to 5pm*
**Admission** *Free*

Located on the banks of Karanji Lake with Chamundi Hills in the background, lies the Regional Museum of Natural History (RMNH). The Museum provides a unique opportunity to explore the natural world, understand the story of life, the diversity of plants and animals and the importance of conservation of natural resources.
There is an impressive collection of exhibits ranging from fossils of the Mesozoic and the pre-Cambrian era, to the skeletal remains of creatures from contemporary times. Life size representations of various habitats found in south India and the story of evolution of life on earth, find their expression here. Exhibits include specimens, models, translites, audio-visual aids, presentation of natural habitats in the form of dioramas, thematic exhibits, interactive and participatory exhibits. There is a temporary exhibition hall and a Discovery Centre. The Biological Diversity Gallery depicts the biodiversity of the region while the section on tropical rainforests showcases the enormous wealth of rainforests.

## Brindavan Gardens
**Open** *8am to 8pm (weekdays), 8am to 9pm (weekends)*
**Admission** *Rs 10. Free for children below 5 years.*

These famous gardens, located at the Krishnaraja Sagar Dam come alive at dusk when musical fountains bathed in coloured lights rise and fall in time to music. Brindavan is a fine example of a garden where architecture, horticulture, engineering and aesthetics come together.
The adjoining dam is Karnataka's earliest and was built across the river Cauvery using stone, mortar and no cement. Brindavan Garden was laid out under the rule of Krishnaraja Wodeyar and the dam was built by the brilliant engineer, Sir M Visveswaraya. In a niche on the western wall of the dam is an image of river Goddess Cauvery holding an inverted pitcher from which water gushes – a symbol of prosperity.

The musical fountains at Brindavan Gardens

## GRS Fantasy Park

GRS Fantasy Park

Sprawled across 34 acres, GRS Fantasy Park is an amusement and water park set amidst lush greenery. It boasts a host of exciting water games and amusement rides along with a variety of shops and restaurants. The water park is the high point of GRS, with multilane racing slides, dry slides, a beach with a wave pool and a warm pool, the Lazy River. An interactive water based game, the Multipurpose Play System, has been designed specially for kids. Other child-safe water rides include the Mini Aqua Bowl and smaller ramp slides. Music, lights and water surround the 4,500sqft Aqua Dance Floor. The amusement area has a number of fun rides for the entire family, from dashing cars and carousels to toy trains and the ferris wheel. The Dragon's Den takes you back to the Jurassic Age of super predators and fire breathing dragons, with an ambience of the pre-historic era. Spread over 60,000sqft, this award-winning ride is hugely popular across age groups. The latest attraction is the Red Indian Falls with 72,000 litres of water being discharged from a height of 80ft each minute. A Red Indian village with tepees, totem poles and Red Indian figures completes the picture. There is a large shopping area – the souvenir stores stock curios, artefacts, toys and other knick-knacks.There's a choice of two restaurants serving a range of multicuisine food. A number of food kiosks dot the poolside as well. Facilities include public telephones, a large parking area and a first aid centre. Lifeguards are employed across the park and wheel chair access is provided throughout the park for the disabled. Groups of thirty people and more can also avail special discounts.

*KRS Road, Metagalli, Mysore 570016*
**Tel** *0821-2582 781* **Web** *www.grsfantasypark.com*

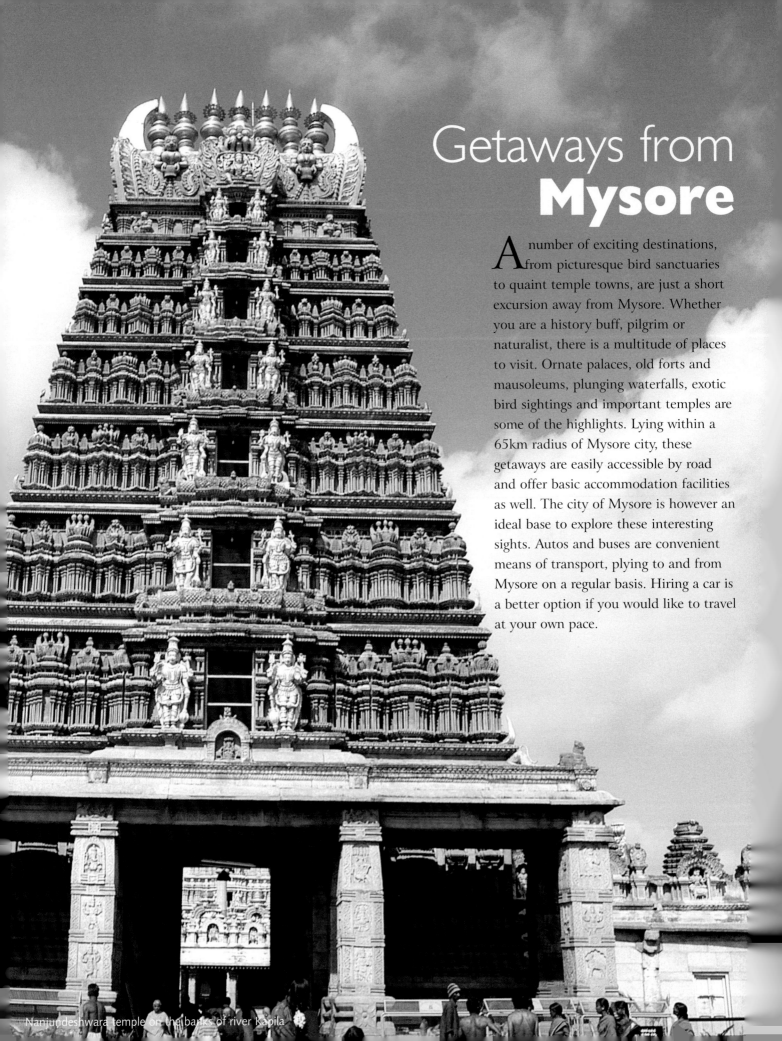

# Getaways from
# **Mysore**

A number of exciting destinations, from picturesque bird sanctuaries to quaint temple towns, are just a short excursion away from Mysore. Whether you are a history buff, pilgrim or naturalist, there is a multitude of places to visit. Ornate palaces, old forts and mausoleums, plunging waterfalls, exotic bird sightings and important temples are some of the highlights. Lying within a 65km radius of Mysore city, these getaways are easily accessible by road and offer basic accommodation facilities as well. The city of Mysore is however an ideal base to explore these interesting sights. Autos and buses are convenient means of transport, plying to and from Mysore on a regular basis. Hiring a car is a better option if you would like to travel at your own pace.

Nanjundeshwara temple on the banks of river Kapila

## Srirangapatna

*An island on the Cauvery river*
**Open** *Museum, 1pm to 5pm, Closed on Friday. Temple, 5am to 1pm and 4pm to 8pm.*
**Admission** *Rs 5*
**Approximate distance from Mysore** *16kms*

Srirangapatna is the site of the island fortress of warrior king Tipu Sultan – the Tiger of Mysore. Don't miss the mosque with twin minarets, the Ranganatha Swamy temple with the colossal reclining image of Vishnu, the Wellesley Bridge and the dungeons where chained British officers were allegedly tortured. Stroll over to Tipu's Summer Palace (known as the Daria Daulat Bagh), set amidst a lovely garden, now converted into a museum. The interior of the palace is adorned with gilded wall-panels, carved ornate arches and floral decorations. The building houses Tipu's memorabilia in the form of his weapons, a map of his fort, an assorted collection of old paintings, coins, European paintings, Persian manuscripts on handmade paper, a model of Srirangapatna, 18th century coloured frescoes and murals depicting his armies and the splendour of his kingdom.

The ornate white-domed Gumbaz is a grand mausoleum of Tipu and his father Hyder Ali. This is an imposing structure with ivory inlaid rosewood doors, lacquered with Tipu's tiger-striped emblem. It leads to the tombs of Hyder Ali and Tipu Sultan and an Urdu tablet here records Tipu's martyrdom.

Srirangapatna is situated 16kms from Mysore. Regular buses and trains from Mysore and Bangalore stop here. It is advisable to hire an auto or a tonga (horse drawn carriage). Bicycling is also possible.

## WHERE TO STAY

### Fort View Resorts
*Near Check Post, Bangalore-Mysore Highway, Srirangapatna, Mandya 571438*
**Tel** *08236-2521 777, 2522 777*
**Fax** *08236-653 877*
**Email** *chairman@fortviewresorts.com*
**Tariff** *Rs 700 to Rs 950*

Tipu's Summer Palace, Srirangapatna

### Amblee Holiday Resort
*PB 17, Srirangapatna, Mandya 571438*
**Tel** *08236-252 326-28*
**Fax** *08236-252 357*
**Web** *www.ambleeresort.com*
**Tariff** *Rs 1,200 to Rs 1,800*

### KSTDC Mayura River View
*Srirangapatna, Mandya 571438*
**Tel** *08236-252 115*
**Tariff** *Rs 450 to Rs 750*

## Somnathpur

*10kms from T Narasipur in Mysore district.*
**Open** *9:30am to 5:30pm*
**Admission** *Rs 10 (Indians), $ 2 (Foreigners)*
**Approximate distance from Mysore** *35kms*

A small detour off the road to Mysore leads to the modest village of Somnathpur where the Chennakesava temple is the site of some of the finest representations of Hoysala architecture. Built in 1268 AD by Somnatha, a general of King Narasimha III, the temple stands on an elevated platform. Visitors enter the temple from the east where a slab records Somnatha's generous donations. Miniature shrines flank the entrance steps.

The temple's sanctum sanctora are shaped like stars. Its triple towers are surmounted by pyramidal vimanas (shrines). Intricately carved friezes on its outer walls show rows of caprisoned elephants, charging horsemen and mythological birds and beasts executed perfectly and delicately in the Hoysala style. Sculpted images of gods, goddesses and scenes from the epics, as well as the remarkably ornate ceilings in the pillared hall are breathtaking.

To reach Somnathpur, find a bus going to T Narasipur from the private bus stand in Mysore. Regular buses ply every hour from T Narasipur to Somnathpur.

## Ranganathittu Bird Sanctuary

*Set around a handful of tiny islands in the Cauvery river*
**Open** *8am to 6pm*
**Admission** *Rs 10 (Indians),*
*Rs 150 (Foreigners)*
**Approximate distance from Mysore** *19kms*

Ranganathittu Bird Sanctuary

A few kilometres upstream of Srirangapatna, the Cauvery river meanders around a string of tiny islets, home to many species of birds. An early morning boat ride will also reveal some marsh crocodiles lazing open-mouthed on the rocks along the riverside! At dawn, this picturesque preserve of water birds turns into a mosaic of colours as cormorants, spoonbills, river terns, plovers, open-billed storks, white ibises, egrets, darters and herons foray into the water.

The winged residents can be seen building nests or plunging into the water to catch fish for their young. At dusk, lucky visitors might spot flying foxes roosting on tall trees and in bamboo clumps.

To reach the sanctuary, take a regular bus to Srirangapatna and then hire an auto.

## Kokkrebellur Pelicanry

*12kms from Maddur in Mandya district*
**Open** *Best to be there early in the morning or evenings.*
**Admission** *Free*
**Approximate distance from Mysore** *44kms*

If you are visiting the area in December set aside time for this unusual sight. Birdwatchers and nature enthusiasts from all over make a beeline to a tiny hamlet deep in the sugarcane rich Mandya district where spot billed pelicans and painted storks congregate in hundreds to build nests in the trees dotting the village! Brightly adorned in breeding plumage, they build and guard their nests, incubate the eggs and nurse and feed their young ones. This little village is the chosen site where the birds live in perfect harmony with the villagers, and enjoy their protection.

The best season to visit Kokkrebellur is between the months of December and April. Take any regular bus from Mysore and alight at Maddur. From there you can charter an auto.

## WHERE TO STAY

### Hari Priya Hotel
*Bangalore-Mysore Highway, Mandya 571401*
**Tel** *0823-2226 112/117*
**Tariff** *Rs 250 to Rs 1,250*

### Shivasamudram Falls
*Malavalli Taluk, Mandya district*
**Open** *From morning till evening*
**Admission** *Free*
**Approximate distance from Mysore** *65kms*

Shivasamudram Falls

A short drive from Mysore through forested hills and lush green valleys, the mighty Cauvery river hurtles down a height of 75m into a deep, rocky gorge with a deafening roar. The result is two picturesque falls: Barachukki and Gaganachukki, most spectacular during the monsoons when the Cauvery is in spate. You can get close enough to feel the spray as it thunders down.

Around the corner from Shivasamudram is Bluff, Asia's first hydroelectric project established by Sheshadri Iyer in 1902 to harness the natural fall and speed of the waters. Other sights in the area are the Ranganatha and Someshwara temples.

This makes an ideal day trip during the wet season, but there are few restaurants in sight so carry a picnic hamper. The falls are at their best during the monsoon. Buses ply between Mysore and Malavalli. If you are driving, take the Bangalore-Mysore Road. At Maddur, take a left at Maddur circle and proceed 47kms, past KM Doddi and Malavalli.

## Talakad

*Lies to the south east of Mysore*
**Open** *All day*
**Admission** *Free*
**Approximate distance from Mysore** *45kms*

"I curse the spires with creepy sands.... May a cruel whirlpool scourge death by the Malangi....And the kings of Mysore suffer the pangs of childlessness ..."
Thus spake Alamelamma as she plunged into the lap of the swirling Cauvery, and a legend was born! A princess who had been insulted by a Wodeyar king, her curse turned Talakad into a barren expanse of shifting sand dunes, and the royal family of Wodeyars into a clan without a continuous line of succession. Incredible as it may sound, the curse has held for centuries!
Talakad was once the capital of the Western Ganga kings. It was subsequently captured by the invading Cholas who renamed it Rajarajapura. Next came the Hoysalas followed by the rulers of the Vijayanagar Empire and finally it fell into the hands of the Wodeyars. There is a Dravidian style temple of Lord Vaidyesvara, worshipped as the main deity among the Panchalinga (five symbols of Lord Shiva) that stands intact. Nearby is the Kirtinarayana temple where the 10ft high image of Vishnu is worshipped even today. Every 12 years, this sleepy town is roused by festivities when thousands of devotees throng to Talakad for the Panchlinga darshan.
Talakad can be visited all year round. There are no government run buses to Talakad. However private buses ply between Mysore and Talakad.

## Melkote

*Located north of Mysore, in Mandya district*
**Open** *All day*
**Admission** *Free*
**Approximate distance from Mysore** *50kms*

Melkote is the quintessential south Indian town of magnificent temples and the famous Iyengar Puliyogre. The Academy of Sanskrit Research is located here.
The 12th century Cheluvarayaswami temple has a rose coloured gopuram and lion heads facing the north, south, east and west. Wander around the temple and gaze upon ornately carved pillars. Legend has it that Vaishnavite saint

Ramanuja, recovered the idol of the main deity and so Ramanuja is also worshipped along with Vishnu in the Narayana temple. On another hill is the small Narasimha shrine, overlooking the Kalyani Tank. The spectacular Vairamudi festival, held between March and April, is Melkote's annual fair when the deity is adorned with the legendary diamond crown and other jewels belonging to the former Maharajas of Mysore and paraded through the town. KSRTC buses leave thrice a day from Mysore to Melkote.

## Nanjangud

*On the banks of the Kapila river*
**Open** *The temple is open from 6am to 1:30pm and 4pm to 9pm. 6pm to 10pm on Sunday.*
**Admission** *Free*
**Approximate distance from Mysore** *23kms*

Nanjangud takes its name from the Nanjundeswara temple on the banks of river Kapila. Built in the Dravidian style, this massive temple has an imposing rajagopuram sculpted into mythological scenes and supported by 147 columns. It is believed that this temple enjoyed the patronage of the Mysore Maharajas as well as Tipu Sultan who believed that his elephant was cured of a disease by the grace of the presiding deity of this temple.
This somnolent town brings back memories of the erstwhile Nanjangud Tooth Powder Express – a steam engine train that once chugged into the narrow gauge railway station. While in Nanjangud you can pay a visit to the famed Sadvaidyashala, the first Ayurvedic centre in Karnataka. Don't forget to sample the rasabale, the famed bananas of Nanjangud! Regular buses ply from Mysore to Nanjangud.

# Dasara

The Hindu festival of Dasara, held in the months of October and November, transforms Mysore and brings back all the pomp and pageantry of royal times. The palace is a showstopper, strung with twinkling lights that light up every evening. The whole city wears a festive look – there are cultural evenings of music, dance and theatre, craft fairs, film festivals and traditional wrestling matches.

The festival celebrates the victory of the Goddess Chamundi over the demon Mahishasura. Millions of tourists descend on the city to catch a glimpse of the idol of the Goddess Chamundeswari seated on a golden howdah and carried in a procession led by caparisoned elephants on the 10th day. She is followed by decorated horses, folk dancers, colourful floats and soldiers in ceremonial dress, wending their way from the palace gates through the streets to end at the Banni Mantap. Here a magnificent torchlight parade and a display of equestrian skills of the Mounted Police mark the finale.

# Mounted Police

Few are aware that Mysore has a rich equestrian heritage, best showcased by the city's flamboyant Mounted Police. On the way to Chamundi Hills at the stately building of the Karnataka Armed Reserve Police (KARP), resides a heritage unit of the erstwhile Palace Guards where policemen on horses are a regular sight. A horseshoe shaped arch leads to a sprawling ground with 55 stables, a horseshoe-making workshop and a horseshoe shaped waterhole for horses to quench their thirst! A visit to the museum and the Saddle Stores shows different kinds of saddles like the sawar saddle used for regular riding, the jumping saddle, dressage saddle and monogrammed lances and swords used in ceremonies.

The Mounted Police is also famous for its music. During the Dasara festival, visitors entering the courtyard are privileged to hear popular melodies, classical hits and even Carnatic music numbers! More than 350 uniformed men dressed in dazzling colours, perform against the backdrop of the illuminated Mysore Palace.

Shimmering silks, fragrant sandalwood and extravagant rosewood carvings are just some of the wares found in Mysore's many shops. Inlay work and wooden toys along with perfumed incense sticks are other purchases that figure on visitor's shopping lists.

Mysore paintings with their bright vegetable-dye colours and lustrous gold leaves are much sought after by connoisseurs of art.

To get a feel of the marketplace, wander around areas such as Ashoka Road, Sayyaji Rao and Devaraj Urs Road which are lined with souvenir stores spilling over with sandalwood wares. Be warned though, that touts abound!

# Shopping in **Mysore**

# Devaraja Market

One of the liveliest and oldest bazaars in the country, the city's famous Devaraja Market is located on the western side of Dhanwanthri Road. Built by Tipu Sultan to encourage local commerce, the market begins buzzing with life early in the morning and business goes on till late at night. Its crowded alleys bustle with vegetable sellers, fruit sellers and food stalls. Incense sticks, essential oils, fragrant herbs and sandalwood products are other characteristic wares of this market. The air is thick with smell of spices and the fragrance of a thousand heaped flowers, especially the famed Mysore Mallige. A short stroll through a maze of narrow lanes leads to stalls bursting with Nanjangud rasabales (bananas), mangoes, spices, betel nut, blocks of jaggery, antiques and conical heaps of kumkum powder. Bargaining is de riguer. Scores of tourists frequent the market to get a full flavour of local life. The Mysore Area Heritage Task Force plans to restore the Devaraja Market to its former glory.

## Badsha Textiles

*75 D Devaraj Urs Road,*
*Mysore 570001*
**Tel** *0821-2422 997*
**Open** *10am to 9pm. Closed on Sunday.*
**Cards** *All*

A wide range of silk sarees, dress materials, silk scarves, shawls and ghagra cholis are sold here and tailoring orders are undertaken.

## Cauvery Arts & Crafts

*Sayyaji Rao Road, Mysore 570001*
**Tel** *0821-2521 258*
**Fax** *0821-2434 265*
**Open** *10am to 7:30pm*
**Cards** *All*

This is the best stop for traditional as well as modern object d'art of Karnataka. Sandalwood carvings, soaps, perfumes, powder and oil, inlay work, incense, Bidriware, lacquerware, bronzeware, brassware, jewellery, silk saris, scarves, ties and wooden toys are some of the popular products on sale. They all make great gifts and the emporium will arrange for packing and transport to any part of India or the world. You may also order handicrafts in a style or design of your choice.

## KSIC Factory

*HD Kote Road, Mysore 570008*
**Tel** *0821-2481 803*
**Open** *9:30am to 6:30pm. Closed on Sunday.*
**Cards** *All*

You need prior permission to visit the factory. It's worth it if you are buying large numbers and want a small bill. The KSIC showroom at KSTDC Yatri Nivas may do for the not so adventurous.

## Mysore Sandalwood Oil Factory

*Manandavady Road, Mysore 570008*
**Tel** *0821-2483 651*
**Open** *9am to 5:30pm. Closed on Sunday.*
**Cards** *All*

Sandal powder, sandalwood oil and perfumed incense sticks are sold at this quaint old building set in a quiet area. Be warned though, genuine sandalwood oil is very expensive.

## Mysore Silk Emporium, Netra Arts & Crafts Emporium

*3 Netra Nivas, Nazarbad Main Road,*
*Mysore 570010*
**Tel** *0821-2521 247*
**Open** *8:30am to 9:30pm*
**Cards** *All*

This is the place for pure silks, handlooms, crepes, georgettes and chiffons. Sandalwood and rosewood artefacts, wall plates, artificial jewellery and semi precious stones are the other attractions.

## Ramsons Arts & Crafts

*1160 Ramsons House,*
*Opp. Mysore Zoo,*
*Mysore 570010*
**Tel** *0821-2443 669*
**Open** *9:30am to 7pm*
**Cards** *All*

Spread over 15,000sqft and three floors, Ramsons is a 30 year-old treasure house of handicrafts. For those who want a little more, trips to view artisans at work can be arranged. Custom-made wooden artefacts and furniture are available here.

A handicrafts store inside the Jaganmohan Palace

# Eating Out in
# **Mysore**

For a long time, the Mysorean's idea of a good meal began and ended with a trip to Dasaprakash, bastion of good vegetarian food. There he could indulge in his favourite Four M's: Masala Dosa, Mallige Idli, Mysore Pak and Mysore filter coffee!

A lot has changed in the last decade and today's Mysorean has shed his reservations and is ready to sample the food of the world. Ethnic Indian to exotic European, this *idli-dosa* town has a new treat everyday.

The legendary Mysore Pak

## Guru Sweet Mart

*67/2 New Sayyaji Rao Road, Devaraja Urs Market Building, Mysore 570001*
**Tel** *0821-2443 495*
**Open** *7am to 11pm.*
*Closed on Tuesday afternoon.*
**Cards** *Not Accepted*

This highly recommended sweet mart is famous for its legendary Mysore pak, a rich sweet made from ghee and gram flour. The wide variety of sweets can be complemented with the salty snacks available here. The halwas come in many varieties – carrot, paneer and pumpkin. Do remember to place an order in advance if you want large quantities of Mysore pak, priced at Rs 140 per kilogram.

## Hotel Dasapraksh Paradise

*104 Vivekananda Road, Yadavagiri, Mysore 570020*
**Tel** *0821-2410 366, 2515 655*
**Open** *7am to 11pm*
**Cards** *All*

Part of an impressive chain of restaurants throughout south India, it is known for its superlative vegetarian food and sumptuous breakfasts. The hotel is also rumoured to make the most authentic Bisi Bele Bhath and coconut rice in the city.

## Hotel Quality Inn Southern Star

*13, 13/1, 14 Vinobha Road, Mysore 570001*
**Tel** *0821-2426 426/7427*
**Open** *Gardenia, 6:30am to 10am, 12pm to 3pm, 7pm to 11:30pm; Charcoals, 7:30pm to 11:30pm; Derby Bar, 11:30am to 11:30pm*
**Cards** *All except Diners Card*

Gardenia is a multicuisine restaurant that doubles up as a coffee shop.

There are a host of cuisines served under one roof – Charcoals, a Northwest Frontier restaurant serves delectable kababs and the Derby Bar is a cocktail lounge with an equine theme – the restaurant has horse head shaped menus, saddle bar stools and miniature fodder containers to serve snacks!

## Hotel RRR

*Gandhi Square, Mysore 570001*
**Tel** *0821- 2441 979*
**Open** *11:30am to 4:30pm and 6:30pm to 11:30pm.*
**Cards** *Not Accepted*

Andhra style non-vegetarian food is served on banana leaves here. It's centrally located and tends to get crowded at lunch and on weekends. The spicy chicken, Mutton Biryani and fried fish are very popular. The vegetarian meals are equally tasty.

## Indira Bhavan

*Dhanwantri Road, Mysore 570001*
**Tel** *0821-2423 933*
**Open** *6:15am to 10:30pm*
**Cards** *All*

Come here for a taste of north Indian food in the land of idli-dosa, which is incidentally available at breakfast only. Excellent vegetarian thali meals, north Indian as well as south Indian are available at meal times.

## Lalitha Mahal Palace Restaurant

*Lalitha Mahal Road, Mysore 570011*
**Tel** *0821-2470 473/474/472*
**Open** *12:30pm to 2:45pm and 8pm to 10:45pm*
**Cards** *All*

You can wine and dine in style at this gourmet restaurant that was once a ballroom. The large stained glass domes and the Durbar-like ambience form the ideal setting to savour the exclusive 'Mysore Silver Thali' available here. This royal meal consists of a large silver platter filled with an array of delicately flavoured signature dishes from Mysore. If you are looking for a snack visit the Tea Lounge.

## Le Olive Garden

*Chanappaji Road, Opp. Horse Park, Nazarbad, Mysore 570010*
**Tel** *0821-2448 762*
**Open** *11:30am to 11:30pm*
**Cards** *MasterCard & Visa*

The restaurant is set amidst lush green foliage with a gurgling stream and an artificial waterfall. Far from the hustle and bustle of the city, added attractions for children are the rabbits and geese.

## Mysore Memories

*Kings Kourt, Jhansi Laxmi Bai Road, Mysore 510004*
**Tel** *0821-2421 142*
**Open** *10:30am to 3:30pm and 6:30pm to 11pm*
**Cards** *All*

The restaurant has a reputation for impeccable service and tasty food. The Indian cuisine is the high point of the restaurant – sizzlers and idlis with Naatu Koli Curry are some exotic foods that can be ordered at dinner.

## Nalpak Restaurant

*131 D Devaraja Urs Road, Mysore 570001*
**Tel** *0821-2410 833*
**Open** *7:30am to 9pm.*
*Closed on Friday.*
**Cards** *Not Accepted*

Go here to sample Karnataka's national dish – Bisi Bele Bhath and ragi and akki rotis. Besides that, all manner of south Indian vegetarian fare, Chinese and north Indian *thalis* are also served.

## Om Shanthi Restaurant

*Hotel Siddharta, 73/1 Guest House Road, Mysore 570010*
**Tel** *0821-2522 999/888*
**Open** *12noon to 3pm and 7pm to 10:30pm*
**Cards** *All*

This multicuisine restaurant dishes out the usual Chinese, Continental, north Indian and south Indian fare. The north Indian curries, vegetable Kolhapuri and vegetable Jaipuri in particular, are the restaurant's specialities. Thali meals are equally popular at this restaurant.

## Park Lane Hotel

*2720 Harsha Road, Mysore 570001*
**Tel** *0821-2430 400*
**Open** *10:30am to 3:30pm and 6:30pm to 11:30pm*
**Cards** *All*

Set under the open sky this versatile restaurant cum bar serves anything from Tandoori Chicken and chopsuey to sandwiches and beer. Nightly concerts of live classical instrumental music are held in the open courtyard under a leafy canopy. A favourite with foreign tourists, Continental food is served at breakfast, while dinner is a multicuisine affair. Drop in over the weekends for pleasant barbecue nights.

## Ramya Drive-In Restaurant

*995/1 Radhakrishna Avenue, Mysore 570005*
**Tel** *0821-2424 811*
**Open** *7:30am to 11:30am and 3:30pm to 8pm. Closed on Tuesday.*
**Cards** *Not Accepted*

Patronised by politicians and cine stars, they stop to pick up packed breakfasts, savouries and sweets. Ramya's regulars also stop by for a scalding hot filter coffee after a morning stroll. Idlis, vadas, sambar, set dosas, curd vadas, masala dosas, Badam Halwa, Gulab Jamun and Basundi are rated highly here.

## Southern Spice

*Hotel President, 2723/A Near Harding Circle, Mysore 570001*
**Tel** *0821-5269 001*
**Open** *12noon to 3:30pm and 7pm to 11:30pm*
**Cards** *MasterCard &Visa*

The authentic cuisine of old Mysore and other exotic foods from Chettinad, Andhra Pradesh and Malabar find their way into the menu of Southern Spice. For the more adventurous gourmets, the coffee shop serves Mexican, Italian and Chinese foods over candlelight dinners. 'Executive Thali' meals are also served at lunchtime.

## Vinayaka Mylari

*769 Nazarbad Main Road, Mysore 570010*
**Tel** *0821-2430 372*
**Open** *7:30am to 11:30am and 4pm to 8pm*
**Cards** *Not Accepted*

This is a small, four decade old eatery, off the regular tourist map but very popular with the locals. Trust their taste and try the luxuriantly soft Mysore idlis with fragrant Coconut Chutney and Sagu, Butter Masala Dosa and aromatic filter coffee. Get here early to avoid standing in a queue.

# Staying In **Mysore**

**O**nce considered a small university town, almost a quiet extension of Bangalore, Mysore has come into its own with magnificent palace hotels, Ayurvedic resorts and luxury hotels that offer global cuisine. Business travellers are not ignored and conferencing facilities are offered by all top-end and most mid-range hotels. Since Mysore is often the base to explore southern Karnataka, most of these hotels provide travel assistance.

Lalitha Mahal Palace

Hotel Metropole

Courtesy: Baljee Group

### Lalitha Mahal Palace

*Lalitha Mahal Road, Mysore 570011*
*Tel 0821-2470 473/474/472*
*Fax 0821-2470 555*
*Web www.lalithamahalpalace.com*
*Cards All except Diners Club*
*Tariff Rs 5,500 to Rs 6,000*

Many a Bollywood film has been shot in this palatial hotel built by the Maharaja of Mysore. It still retains the grandeur it had in 1921 when the Viceroy of India came calling. The lavish interiors, chandeliered ceilings, Belgian glass domes, Venetian marble floors, rich carpets and priceless rosewood furniture create an ambience of opulence and pageantry. The walls of the stately Central Hall are adorned with larger than life portraits of Mysore's royal family and lithographs of Tipu Sultan battling the British. The Maharani's suite is fit for royalty and even the bathtub here is a priceless antique! This heritage hotel houses 54 luxury suites and a multicuisine restaurant. Built to capture the mood of a bygone era, the hotel is equally well equipped with modern facilities.

### Hotel Metropole

*5 Jhansi Lakshmibai Road, Mysore 570005*
*Tel 0821-525 5566*
*Fax 0821-525 5555*
*Web www.baljeehotels.com*
*Cards All*
*Tariff Rs 4,000 to Rs 6,000*

Built by the Maharaja of Mysore, Krishnaraja Wodeyar IV during the 20s to accommodate his British guests, Hotel Metropole shut down for a few years. Now open under the management of

heritage hotel has regained some of former elegance. The hotel houses 30 exclusive rooms done up with antiques and expensive objects d' art. It is centrally located and all modern amenities like tea/coffee maker, mini bar, electronic safe, high speed Internet access, a swimming pool and spa are provided.
Guests may choose from a variety of entertainment options including vintage car tours, readings by astrologers, Ayurvedic massages and Yoga lessons. In keeping with its royal heritage, shows by magicians, court jesters, snake charmers, dancers and musicians are staged at the Banquet Hall. Tours to nearby tourist destinations like Bandipur National Park, Coorg, Ooty and Coonoor and day trips to Ranganathittu Bird Sanctuary, Edakkal Caves and the Cauvery Fishing Camp are easily organised. Indian, Chinese and Continental cuisine is served at the restaurant and the lounge bar has the regular range of spirits and cocktails.

### Indus Valley Ayurvedic Centre

*PB 3, Ittgegud, Lalithadripura Road, Mysore 570010*
*Tel 0821-2473 437/263/266*
*Fax 0821-2473 590*
*Web www.ayurindus.com*
*Cards MasterCard, Visa & Cancard*
*Tariff Rs 1,000 to Rs 5,400*

Nestled at the foot of the Chamundi Hills, this new-age Ayurvedic resort specialises in rejuvenation and therapeutic cure. Thirty two kinds of Ayurvedic treatments are offered here. The aesthetically built resort, designed according to the principles of Vaastu, has the effect of soothing and relaxing visitors. The food, strictly

vegetarian, is made according to Ayurvedic traditions with organically grown fruits and vegetables. The resort also houses tennis courts, a Yoga centre, a herbal products store and a gift shop.

### The Green Hotel

*2270 Vinoba Road,*
*Next to BM Hospital, Jayalakshmipuram, Mysore 570012*
*Tel 0821-2512 536, 5255 000/001*
*Fax 0821-2516 139*
*Web www.greenhotelindia.com*
*Cards MasterCard & Visa*
*Tariff Rs 1,100 to Rs 4,750*

Built for the royal Wodeyar princesses, the Chittaranjan Palace has been transformed into a luxury hotel. Winner of many awards, the hotel is lined with trees, shaded by pergolas and carpeted by lush green lawns. The eco-friendly hotel uses solar lamps and candles and

televisions, air-conditioning and generators are shunned. Part of the profits made are contributed towards charitable causes and environmental projects.

### Hotel Quality Inn Southern Star

*13/14 Vinobha Road, Mysore 570005*
*Tel 0821-2426 426, 2427 427*
*Fax 0821-2421 689*
*Web www.ushashriramhotels.com*
*Cards All except Diners Club*
*Tariff Rs 2,700 to Rs 4,325*

This luxury hotel with tastefully decorated rooms and central air-conditioning, is eco-friendly as well. Mysore's Quality Inn boasts of a large swimming pool, a well equipped health club, beauty parlour, men's saloon, poolside barbeque, bookstore, jewellery store and an Ayurvedic massage centre. You get to sample a variety of cuisines – Charcoals specialises in Northwest Frontier food, **The Derby** is a theme-based cocktail lounge and **Gardenia** gives you a taste of cuisines from around the world. The well stocked pastry shop in the hotel completes the Southern Star experience.

### Kings Kourt

*Jhansi Laxmibai Road, Mysore 510004*
*Tel 0821-2421 142, 2425 350/159*
*Fax 0821-2422 384*
*Web www.kingskourt.com*
*Cards All*
*Tariff Rs 1,800 to Rs 4,000*

Frequented by film stars, celebrities, politicians and foreign tourists, Kings Kourt has maintained excellent standards of service over the last 25 years. Located in the heart of the city, the hotel has 56 rooms, a fitness centre, swimming pool, barbecue, multicuisine restaurant, conference room, bookshop, gift shop and a travel desk. **Cocktail Circuit**, the hotel's bar is a good place to unwind.

Kings Kourt

## Hotel Ramanashree

*BN Road, Hardinge Circle,*
*Mysore 570001*
*Tel 0821-2522 202/265*
*Fax 0821-2565 781*
*Web www.ramanashree.com*
*Cards All*
*Tariff Rs 1,695 to Rs 3,995*

The hotel offers all the facilities for a comfortable stay. Part of the Ramanashree group of hotels, the hotel has air-conditioned rooms, two banquet halls and an Ayurvedic health centre. **Darpan** is the multicuisine restaurant.

## Nalapad Residency

*Dr. Nelson Mandela Road, New Bannimantap Extension, Mysore 570015*
*Tel 0821-2491 117/984, 2492 978*
*Fax 0821-2495 663*
*Web www.nalapad.com*
*Cards All*
*Tariff Rs 800 to Rs 3,000*

With 40 well-furnished rooms, a banquet hall, conference room, travel desk, business centre, safe deposit locker, foreign exchange counter and a doctor available on call, this hotel is one of the most convenient places to stay in. Guests can choose from three restaurants at the hotel – **Nalapad Kadal** is the multicuisine restaurant, **Gossip** is a 24-hour coffee shop, while **Kamat** serves purely vegetarian fare.

## Hotel Dasaprakash Paradise

*104 Vivekananda Road, Yadavagiri, Mysore 570020*
*Tel 0821-2410 366, 2515 655*
*Fax 0821-2514 400*
*Email hotelparadise@sancharnet.in*
*Cards All*
*Tariff Rs 950 to Rs 2,750*

This hotel reflects the old world charm of Mysore with rooms built around a large central courtyard. Part of 90-year old chain of south Indian hotels, it is known for its excellent vegetarian restaurant where 'unlimited' south Indian thalis are dished out. Other facilities include a coffee shop, shopping arcade, beauty parlour, conference room and business centre.

## Hotel President

*2723/A, Near Hardinge Circle, Bangalore-Nilgris Road, Mysore 570001*
*Tel 0821-5269 001, 2425 111*
*Fax 0821-2441 672*
*Email hotel_president@sancharnet.in*
*Cards All*
*Tariff Rs 1,495 to Rs 2,695*

Mostly patronised by those in business circles, guests here enjoy facilities like 24-hour Internet connectivity and a well appointed business centre. Entertainment facilities include the shopping arcade, beauty parlour, coffee lounge, health club and a south Indian speciality restaurant.

## The Viceroy

*Sri Harsha Road, Mysore 570001*
*Tel 0821-2424 001/8001, 2434 687*
*Fax 0821-2433 391*
*Web www.viceroymysore.com*
*Cards All*
*Tariff Rs 875 to Rs 2,300*

The appeal of the hotel is its location – in the vicinity of the palace, other tourist spots and commercial centres in Mysore. It also provides luxury rooms with a range of facilities. The open-air garden restaurant, 'Rooftop', affords a stunning view of the Mysore palace.

## Kadur Inns

*Mysore Mercara Road, Hinkal, Mysore 570017*
*Tel 0821-2402 840/841/210*
*Fax 0821-2402 209*
*Email kadurinns@hotmail.com*
*Cards All*
*Tariff Rs 900 to Rs 1,500*

The hotel provides all the customary facilities of banquet hall, swimming pool and multicuisine restaurant. What sets it apart is the balmy poolside restaurant, **Tandoor**, and a cocktail lounge aptly named **Booze Bay!**

## Hotel Palace Plaza

*2716 Sri Harsha Road, Mysore 570001*
*Tel 0821-2430 034, 2420 424, 2417 592 Fax 0821-2421 070*
*Web www.hotelpalaceplaza.com*
*Cards All*
*Tariff Rs 575 to Rs 1,400*

This is a hotel with tastefully furnished rooms and all the modern amenities. A variety of rooms are available to suit different budgets.

## Hotel Siddharta

*73/1 Guest House Road, Mysore 570010*
*Tel 0821-2522 999/888*
*Fax 0821-2520 692*
*Email siddhartahotel@hotmail.com*
*Cards All*
*Tariff Rs 760 to Rs 1,160*

This commodious hotel has 75 well-furnished rooms, air-conditioned as well as non air-conditioned and a spacious family room.

## Hotel Darshan Palace

*Lokaranjan Mahal Road, (Opp. Regency Theatre), Nazarbad, Mysore 570010*
*Tel 0821-2520 794, 5566 055*
*Fax 0821-2564 083*
*Web www.hoteldarshanpalace.com*
*Cards All*
*Tariff Rs 400 to Rs 1,000*

Away from the bustle of the city, Hotel Darshan Palace is in close proximity to tourist attractions like the Mysore Zoo, the Race Course, Karanji Lake and Chamundi Hills. The hotel has 30 elegantly furnished rooms with 24-hour room service, a travel desk and a doctor on call. The restaurant serves wholesome vegetarian as well as non-vegetarian food.

## Ganesh Palace Inn

*L-1 Chandragupta Road, Mysore 570001*
*Tel 0821-2428 985, 5266 020*
*Cards Not Accepted*
*Tariff Rs 200 to Rs 850*

This hotel is ideal for a mid-range budget and is just a 10-minute walk from the city's central bus stand. It has a multicuisine restaurant with an attached bar.

## KSTDC Mayura Hoysala

*2 Jhansi Laxmi Bai Road, Mysore 570005*
*Tel 0821-2425 349/597, 2426 160*
*Web www.kstdc.nic.in*
*Cards Not Accepted*
*Tariff Rs 400 to Rs 800*

The quaint Indo-Saracenic structure of the Mayura Hoysala stands out amidst the teeming commercial complexes in the heart of the city. Most sightseeing trips begin at this architectural landmark built way back in 1914. The **Bamboo Grove**, a tastefully done up bar-cum-restaurant is a good place to chill out.

## Hotel Roopa

*2724/C, Bangalore-Nilgiri Road, Mysore 570001*
*Tel 0821-2443 770, 2440 044*
*Fax 0821-2443 755*
*Web www.hotel-roopa.com*
*Cards Visa*
*Tariff Rs 400 to Rs 750*

This is a budget hotel with comfortable rooms and hot running water, located strategically between the Central Bus Stand and railway station. All the regular facilities of travel desk, gift shop, boardroom and multicuisine restaurant are available here.

## Hotel Prakash Deluxe

*Sayyaji Rao Road, Mysore 570021*
*Tel 0821- 2521 676, 5260 552*
*Telefax 0821-5260 551*
*Email alevurhotels@yahoo.com*
*Cards Not Accepted*
*Tariff Rs 390 to Rs 750*

This hotel is conveniently close to the shopping centres and prominent tourist spots in the city. South Indian thalis in unlimited portions can be sampled at the hotel's restaurant, **Venkatesh Bhavan**. The hotel also has a multicuisine restaurant, **Vybhav**.

## Hotel Dashrath

*Opp. Zoo Main Gate, Mysore 570010*
*Tel 0821-2449 121*
*Fax 0821-2563 602*
*Email ramsonsarts@sify.com*
*Cards Not Accepted*
*Tariff Rs 200 to Rs 750*

Comfortable rooms with all the standard amenities are available at a reasonable price.

## Hotel Indra Bhavan

*Dhanvantri Road, Mysore 570001*
*Tel 0821-2423 933/755/833*
*Fax 0821-2422 290*
*Email hotelindrabhavan@rediffmail.com*
*Cards All*
*Tariff Rs 170 to Rs 400*

Hotel Indra Bhavan is ideal for an inexpensive stay. Apart from the facilities it offers, the hotel is known for its unlimited thali meals. The restaurant **Samrat** serves north Indian, Chinese and Continental food.

# Lalitha Mahal Palace – Royal Hotel

Set on a gentle slope overlooking the royal city of Mysore and visible for miles around, is the Lalitha Mahal Palace – one of India's most magnificent palace hotels. Grand and opulent with Italian marble floors, chandeliers, priceless carpets, antique furniture, a 500-year old carved rosewood table and lithographs from the period of Tipu Sultan, it is guaranteed to take the visitor back a few centuries.

In the year 1920, Krishnaraja Wodeyar, Maharaja of Mysore commissioned EW Fritchley to design a special palace to accommodate his royal guests, a plan that took a decade to complete. The erstwhile Maharaja had his most important guest – the Viceroy of India – in mind when he planned it. Lalitha Mahal Palace remained the official guesthouse of the Mysore State till 1960. It was transferred to ITDC's Ashok Group of Hotels in 1974.

A superb marble staircase sweeps up to the stately upper floors where the guest rooms and suites in the old palace wing are of princely proportions. Cool, airy and high-ceilinged, it is furnished with genuine old palace furniture like king-sized four poster beds with scalloped diaphanous canopies, carved and lacquered cupboards, velvet-covered armchairs and gilt-framed Belgian mirrors.

The bathroom is bigger than an average room! It's fitted with an interesting and antiquated bathtub and a washbasin cast in marble. The bathtub was imported from Shanks & Co. UK for the visiting Viceroy and Vicerina. It is maintained as an antique piece in working condition. Another antique is an old-fashioned wooden carriage lift with a huge cushioned seat on one side.

The palatial Banquet Room of the Lalitha Mahal is now a gourmet restaurant where you can wine and dine under glowing stained glass domes. A speciality of the Palace kitchens is the thali – a large silver platter that brings together in several small bowls the finest array of delicately spiced dishes typical of India's southern cuisine. The dining room even has a spring-loaded dance floor!

Lalitha Mahal Road, Mysore 570011
**Tel** 0821-2470 473 **Web** www.lalithamahalpalace.com

# My Perfect Holiday – Rahul Dravid

It's really hard to choose from the many beautiful places in Karnataka. One of my favourite cities in the world is **Bangalore**. That's why I live here! What I like about Bangalore is that it's both young and old, and there's a nice balance between the conventional and the contemporary. A vibrant city, it has plenty to offer everyone – cutting edge technology, exotic cuisine and history. The weather's a big plus. Bangalore has a wealth of greenery and I especially like the gardens and parks.

I enjoy visiting **Mysore**. The palace with its royal splendour, Chamundi Hills, and the proximity to Srirangapatna, which was once the capital of Mysore State are huge attractions. Packed with history, Mysore also has a rich tradition of music and theatre. The people are warm and friendly and it's a pleasure to visit.

**Kabini** is one of the most beautiful spots in the world. It's a place I go to as often as I can. There's plenty to do here, and you can choose between a laidback holiday or a jungle safari.

**Kodagu** natural beauty and lovely people are two of its biggest attractions. I like going for long walks along the jungle trails.

I've been to **Hampi** when I was very young and it's a place I would definitely love to visit again.

There's so much I've heard about this World Heritage Site and its wealth of history.

The beaches along **Mangalore's** coast are a perfect getaway. I have pleasant memories of holidaying there with my family. These are just some of my favourite places and I'm sure I'll discover more once I have the time.

*Rahul Dravid is vice captain of the Indian cricket team and brand ambassador for Karnataka Tourism. He lives in Bangalore.*

Kabini Reservoir

# Indus Valley Ayurvedic Centre

The Indus Valley Ayurvedic Centre (IVAC) is a traditional Ayurvedic health centre set in Mysore, overlooking the palatial Lalitha Mahal Palace. Here the ancient science of Ayurveda is practiced in its traditional form. This health resort specialises in providing authentic Ayurvedic treatments like the Panchakarma, the Ayurveda-detox, Shirodhara, Abhyanga and Ayurvedic oil baths and massages. There are also specially formulated packages offered for rejuvenation, stress management and weight loss. A team of qualified doctors and experienced Ayurvedic physicians take guests through the therapies, starting with a detailed case history and medical examination.

IVAC offers a variety of treatments, for rejuvenative purposes and for chronic health problems, from neurological disorders to degenerative illnesses. Rejuvenation therapies at IVAC are designed to revitalise body tissues, improve circulation and remove accumulated stress and toxins. Shorter rejuvenative therapies include Abhyanga and the Shirodhara, which help achieve a deep state of body-mind relaxation. The Panchakarma, an amalgam of five cleansing therapies, is one of the most sought after rejuvenative therapies here. Curative treatments are offered for obesity, anxiety, depression, hypertension, strokes, diabetes, lower back and neck trouble and chronic pain. Treatments at IVAC also include advanced massage therapies and detoxification treatments. Ayurvedic beauty treatments from herbal facials to pedicures are offered at 'Shringar', the herbal beauty parlour, using pure herbs, natural ingredients and Ayurvedic techniques. The health centre also offers courses in Ayurveda, Vaastu and Ayurvedic cooking.

Managed by Trails, the Indus Valley Ayurvedic Centre boasts a warm and friendly ambience and is designed according to Vaastu and Feng Shui principles. Accommodation includes luxurious suites and private rooms, equipped with all the modern amenities. Wholesome vegetarian fare cooked in the Ayurvedic tradition with organic vegetables and fruits, is served at the in-house restaurant. IVAC also conducts workshops on aromatherapy, astrology, herbal therapies, Vaastu and gem therapy.

**Tel** 0821-2473 437/263,
**Web** www.ayurindus.com, www.trailsindia.com

# Bangalore Sights

**B**angalore is a few hundred years old and for the tourist there is a wealth of sights to see and places to visit. For a slice of religious history try the ancient temples and churches that attract followers from far away. Heritage buffs get to see the summer palaces of the Wodeyars and Tipu Sultan, erstwhile monarchs of Mysore. Nature enthusiasts have much to cheer about: Lalbagh and Cubbon Park were laid a long time ago and are mini-forests now with ancient bamboo groves, rare flowering trees and walking pathways. On the outskirts of the city lies Bannerghatta Biological Park, a naturalist's delight with a small zoo thrown in. The city has a number of picturesque lakes, some of which have boating facilities. A plethora of museums, galleries and even a planetarium for the astronomically inclined, are located around central Bangalore. If you have the time, take a day trip to see ancient temples, historic sites and scenic spots.

Except for a few summer months, the rest of the year presents great weather for sightseeing. There are many means of transport to suit your budget.

The stately Vidhana Soudha is a blend of four architectural styles.

Cubbon Park

## Vidhana Soudha

*Vidhana Soudha, Bangalore 560001*
**Open** *The exterior may be viewed anytime.*
**Admission** *Restricted to members and civil servants.*

The Vidhana Soudha is the House of the State Legislature and the Government Secretariat of Karnataka. Built in 1956, the birth year of the state of Karnataka, it was executed under the stewardship of Kengal Hanumanthaiah, then Chief Minister of Mysore State.
It took four years of work by 5,000 labourers and 1,500 craftsmen to finish this magnificent structure, a fusion of at least four architectural styles – Dravidian, Rajasthani, Chola and Kannadiga. It has an imposing granite edifice with gleaming white onion domes, 12 massive pillars, archways and a wide flight of steps leading up to its entrance. Frieze panels, geometric designs and ornamental motifs embellish the walls and a sandalwood door graces the entrance to the cabinet room.
The Indian national symbol lies atop the biggest dome, ornamented by Bangalore's reputed sculptor Shilpi Samachar. The sprawling lawns are open to public but permission is necessary to view the interior. The entire edifice is lit up every Sunday and on public holidays.

## Attara Kacheri

*Vidhana Veedhi (opposite the Vidhana Soudha), Bangalore 560001*
**Open** *The exterior may be viewed anytime.*
**Admission** *Exteriors free, but entry is restricted inside.*

Facing the Vidhana Soudha is the red brick and stone Attara Kacheri, designed by Colonel Sankey in the Graeco-Roman style of architecture. When the British shifted governance of the state from Mysore to Bangalore they needed a building to house the Public Offices and Commissioner Lewin

Bowring, oversaw the construction. The oldest public building in Bangalore, Attara Kacheri literally means 18 offices or courts and it now houses the state High Court. The Annexe was built in 1991 and replicated in the same style.

## Bangalore Palace

*Sankey Road, Bangalore 560080*
**Open** *Entry restricted*
**Admission** *Call 23360818 for permission to visit.*

Set in 400 acres of the Palace Grounds, the Bangalore Palace is modelled on the lines of the Windsor Castle in England. It was built in 1880 in the Tudor style. It boasts turreted parapets, battlements, fortified towers and arches set amidst sprawling gardens.

## Lalbagh Botanical Garden

*Lalbagh Main Gate, KH Road, Bangalore 560004*
**Tel** *2657 9231/8184*
**Open** *8am to 5:30pm*
**Admission** *Rs 5*

This is 240-acre famous botanical garden was laid out by Hyder Ali, the ruler of Mysore in 1760. Modelled on the lines of a Mughal garden he saw in Sira, Hyder Ali imported plants from Delhi, Lahore, Multan and even London. Lalbagh houses India's largest collection of rare tropical and sub-tropical plants, as well as many century-old trees. In the Centenary Rose Garden you can witness hundreds of roses bloom simultaneously. A mango grove, a glass hothouse, a lotus pond, deer park and a floral clock are some of its other attractions. There is also a topiary park, an aquarium and a charming wooden bandstand. A 20-million year old tree fossil, donated by the National Fossil Park in Tiruvakkarai, Tamil Nadu is a big attraction. A pair of mango trees planted by Tipu Sultan, add to its historical charm. The lake, spreads over 30 hectares, is a haven for birdwatchers. At the main entrance to Lalbagh lies a watchtower built by Bangalore chieftain

Kempegowda, part of a series of four built by him. It is located atop a rocky outcrop dating back 3,000 million years and is today a national geological monument. This park is best visited during the day and is not considered safe after dark.

## Cubbon Park

*Cubbon Park, Bangalore 560001*
**Tel** *2286 7440*
**Open** *8am to 8pm*
**Admission** *Free*

Filled with exotic and indigenous flowering trees and bamboo groves, the 300-acre Cubbon Park is a quiet, green getaway right in the heart of the city. It is named after Sir Mark Cubbon, a former British Commissioner who placed a statue of the reigning Queen Victoria at the entrance. Nature lovers, walkers and joggers use the park especially during the early mornings when it is declared a silent zone. Only light vehicles are allowed to ply at other times.
A number of important structures like the State Central Library (an impressive, red Gothic structure), Bal Bhavan and the government aquarium may be found within its precincts. During the Raj, military bands played at the bandstand here.

## Visveswaraya Industrial and Technological Museum

*Kasturba Road, Bangalore 560001*
**Tel** *2286 4009/5823*
**Open** *10am to 6pm*
**Admission** *Rs 15 for adults and children above 5 years*

This museum showcases a brief history of technological development in the country. It is dedicated to the memory of Sir M Visveswaraya, the architect of modern Karnataka. The Engine Hall, Electronic Technology Gallery, Popular Science and Children's Science Gallery make it a comprehensive and educational trip.

Bangalore Palace

Lalbagh Botanical Garden (See Pg 453)

## Government Museum

*Kasturba Road, Bangalore 560001*
*Tel 2286 4438*
*Open 10am to 5pm. Closed on Monday.*
*Admission Rs 10*

This museum features a stunning collection of archaeological and geological objects, some dating back to the Indus Valley civilisation. Stone carvings, pottery, weapons, paintings, coins, textiles, sculptures, inscriptions, antique jewellery and musical instruments belonging to bygone eras may be seen here.

## HAL Heritage Centre & Aerospace Museum

*HAL, Airport-Varthur Road, Bangalore 560017*
*Tel 2522 8341*
*Open 9am to 5pm. Closed on Monday.*
*Admission Rs 20 for adults and Rs 10 for children*

India's rich aviation heritage is celebrated here with real aircraft models and a breathtaking collection of photographs, at this first and only Indian aero museum. There are a number of planes and helicopters lined up outside. For the aerospace buff, there are aircraft simulators, a mock air traffic control tower and an aero modelling club.

## Venkatappa Art Gallery

*Kasturba Road, Bangalore 560001*
*Tel 2286 4483*
*Open 10am to 5pm. Closed on Monday.*
*Admission Rs 4 for adults and Rs 2 for children.*

Venkatappa was a famous court painter of the Wodeyars. This gallery houses his work and art materials as well as those of other renowned artists. Other exhibits include 20th century landscapes and abstract wood sculptures. Contemporary art shows are often held here.

## Jawaharlal Nehru Planetarium

*T Chowdiah Road, High Grounds, Bangalore 560001*
*Open 10am to 5:30pm. Closed on Monday. Show in Kannada at 3pm, Show in English at 4:30pm.*
*Admission Rs 15 for adults and Rs 10 for children*

The planetarium houses a permanent exhibition on space and astronomy. A regular schedule of programmes and shows on different aspects of the universe and space are shown here.

## Indira Gandhi Musical Fountain

*Raj Bhavan Road, Bangalore 560001*
*Open 6pm to 6:30pm on weekdays and 6pm to 8pm on Sunday. Closed on Monday and second Tuesday of the month.*
*Admission Rs 10 for adults and Rs 5 for children.*

This is a popular family spot to watch the swirling, gushing fountains dance in tune to various Indian and Western musical themes.

## Sankey Boat Club

*Sankey Tank, Bangalore 560080*
*Open: 9am to 4pm*
*Admission: Rs 10*

Lazy boat rides and leisurely strolls on breezy evenings are possible at Sankey Tank.

## Tipu's Palace

*Albert Victor Road, City Market, Bangalore 560002*
*Open 8am to 5:30pm*
*Admission Rs 5*

This was initially a mud fort, built in 1537. Two centuries later, Tipu Sultan, the then ruler of Mysore, rebuilt it and turned it into his summer retreat.
The palace is an ornate wooden structure with fluted pillars, cusped arches and balconies and ceilings painted in brilliant colours with beautiful carvings. Similar to the Daria Daulat Bagh in Srirangapatna,

Tipu named it 'Rash-e-Jannat' or 'the Abode of Peace'. Inscriptions carved on the wooden banisters may be seen.
Tipu's father, Hyder Ali laid the foundation for the palace, which was completed during Tipu's reign. It has been turned into a museum of objects relating to their regime. Close to the palace is a rare monument called Hyder Ali Armoury and a fort of their reign. Cells where the British were imprisoned can also be seen. There is a white stone plate which says that Lord Cornwallis barged through the breach here.

## Karnataka Chitrakala Parishath

*Art Complex, Kumara Krupa Road, Bangalore 560001*
*Tel 2226 1816/3424*
*Open 10am to 5:30pm. Closed on Sunday.*
*Admission Rs 5 for adults and Rs 2 for children.*

This is the state's premier institution offering courses in painting, sculpture, graphic art, applied art and art history. Regular workshops, artists' camps and demonstrations, dance performances, folk theatre, photography exhibitions, puppet shows and musical recitals are held through the year. Courses in traditional Mysore paintings and leather puppetry are offered. There is a permanent exhibition of eminent artists like Roerich on display here. Recent additions include the Folk Art Gallery, an International Paintings Gallery and the Karnataka Gallery.

## Bull Temple

*Bull Temple Road, Basavanagudi, Bangalore 560004*
*Open 6am to 1pm and 4pm to 9pm*
*Admission Free*

Reminiscent of 16th century Dravidian architecture, this temple was built by the early chieftain of Bangalore, Kempegowda. It has a huge granite monolith of Nandi, made of grey granite and polished with a traditional mixture of groundnut oil and charcoal. At the time of the groundnut festival Kadalekai Parishe, worshippers arrive with groundnut garlands for the bull!
Just below Bull Temple is the Dodda (huge) Ganesha Temple with a monolith Ganesha idol 18ft high and 16ft wide. An inscription at the base of the left foot of the idol indicates the origin of the Vrishabhavati river. The idol is decorated with a 100kgs of butter on certain days of the week!

HAL Heritage Centre & Aerospace Museum

Attara Kacheri, (See Pg 453)

It was established over 500 years ago and built in the Chola style by Kempegowda. The central shrine is dedicated to Someshwara and the adjoining one to his consort Kamakshi, with her vehicle, the lion. Devotees often line up before the bronze Nandi in front of the sanctum sanctorum to whisper a wish. An imposing gopuram (gateway tower), a pyramidal brick tower built in the Vijayanagar style and multiple reflections of the image of Lord Shiva placed on a swing, are other attractions.

### Infant Jesus Church

*Viveknagar, Bangalore 560047*
**Open** *5:45am to 11:15am and 4pm to 7:30pm on Sunday.*
**Admission** *Free*

Established in 1979 by Rev. Dr. Lourduswamy, then Archbishop of Bangalore, the church sees huge crowds on Thursday, the day dedicated to Infant Jesus. The church draws devotees from all religious faiths.

### St. Mary's Basilica

*Shivajinagar, Bangalore 560001*
**Open** *5am to 7:30pm*
**Admission** *Free*

The only church in the state to be elevated to the status of a Basilica, this imposing Gothic structure was built in 1875. Its stained glass windows, multiple columns and stately arches are remarkable. The tall spires surmounted by a cross, towers above the rest of the buildings in the crowded Shivajinagar area.
Saturday is a busy day as thousands of devotees congregate to seek blessings. In September the Virgin Mary's festival is celebrated with gusto.

## Gavi Gangadhareshwara Temple

*Gavipuram Guttahalli, Srinagar, Bangalore 560050*
**Open** *7:30am to 12noon and 5pm to 8:30pm*
**Admission** *Free*

Expanded during the chieftain of Bangalore Kempegowda's reign, this unique 1000-year old cave temple contains a remarkably well-preserved granite moon, sun-disc monoliths, an enormous stone umbrella, a Shiva Linga and three cave passages. Crawling through them is an experience!
During the festival of Makara Sankranthi this cave temple witnesses a strange phenomenon – a ray of light passes precisely through the horns of the stone bull sitting in front of the Shiva Linga and illuminates the inside of the cave.

## International Society for Krishna Consciousness (Iskcon)

*Hare Krishna Hill, West of Chord Road, Rajajinagar, Bangalore 560010*
**Tel** *2347 1956*
**Open** *7am to 1pm and 4pm to 8:30pm*
**Admission** *Free*

Built by the International Society for Krishna Consciousness, the Iskcon temple is a blend of modern and traditional temple styles. The huge cultural complex surrounding it enshrines Krishna and his consort Radha.

## Shiva Temple

*Kemp Fort, Airport Road, Bangalore 560017*
**Open** *10am to 8pm*
**Admission** *Free*

This recent addition to the city's temple structures is a 65ft tall Shiva statue. An artificial pond resembling the Mansarovar Lake and man made caves with replicas of jyothirlingas is now a popular destination for the devout. Two artificial waterfalls form the backdrop and the statue of Goddess Ganga atop Shiva also spouts water.

## Someshwara Temple

*Ulsoor, Bangalore 560008*
**Open** *5:30am to 12noon and 5:30pm to 9pm*
**Admission:** *Free*

This temple has a history spanning 500 years and is known to be the largest in the city. Its 48-pillared hall is often described as the 'museum of Vijayanagar architecture'.

Tipu's Palace

# Getaways from **Bangalore**

**B**angalore boasts some amazing destinations for day-trippers. Rivers for angling, temples and shrines to pray at, hilltops to gaze from, ancient forts steeped in history and sheer rock faces to slither down are some of the exciting options to choose.

Basic accommodation is available at some places and tenting is a viable option.

It's best to set off early in the day to avoid heavy rush hour traffic within the city. Picnic lunches can be substituted with a meal at a string of cheap restaurants on the way.

These destinations are easy to explore with Bangalore as a base, and means of transport range from conducted tours to taxis. Enjoy your day out!

A hilltop temple in Devarayanadurga

The Folklore Museum at Janapada Loka *(See Pg 461)*

## Nandi Hills
*Kolar District, North of Bangalore*
**Open** *8:30am to 5pm*
**Admission** *Rs 3*

Nandi Hills rises 1,455m above sea level and is surrounded by flat plains of red earth. Its unexpected height earned it a place as the summer retreat of the Tiger of Mysore, Tipu Sultan. Caves, temples and the **Summer Palace** may be found in its sylvan environs. A short ramble through the tree-covered hills will bring you to Amrita Sarovar, the main source of water supply to the hill resort. A little further is the Magazine – a rock where arms and ammunitions were kept during Tipu's reign. Other sights include two ancient **temples** dedicated to Lord Shiva, one at the foot and the other at the top of the hill. At the highest point of the hill sits a colonial-style bungalow built by Sir Mark Cubbon, which has since hosted many celebrities like Mahatma Gandhi, Queen Elizabeth II and heads of SAARC countries in the 1980s. For magnificent views there is **Tipu's Drop** – a 600m high cliff from where condemned convicts were once pushed to their death! Those with children and a tendency to vertigo may give this view a miss. If you have the time, a small detour to Muddenahalli will bring you to the birthplace of the late Sir M Visveswaraya who sowed the seeds for Karnataka's industrialisation. His ancestral home is now a museum. For **paragliding** options, contact KSTDC.

Nandi Hills lies 60 kilometres to the north of Bangalore. The road passes through vineyards and fields of red earth. Buses from the City Bus Stand to Nandi Hills take two hours to reach. Taxis are faster and it makes sense to hire one for the day.

## WHERE TO STAY

### KSTDC Mayura Pine Top
*Tel 0815-2678 624,* **Tariff** *Rs 190 to Rs 700*

### Horticulture Department Guest Houses,
**Tariff** *Rs 275 to Rs 330*
*(For bookings, contact: Special Officer, Nandi Hills, Horticulture Department, Chikkaballapur 562101, or the Director of Horticulture, Lalbagh, Bangalore 560004* **Tel** *2657 9231)*

### Bannerghatta Biological Park
*Anekal Taluk, South of Bangalore*
**Open** *Closed on Tuesday.*
**Admission** *Park fee, Rs 15, Safari ride, Rs 25 (Indians); Park fee, Rs 25, Safari ride, Rs 200 (Foreigners)*

Bannerghatta Biological Park is home to **panthers**, a large variety of avifauna, an amazing collection of reptiles, a **snake park** and a nature camp for children. The 20-minute **safari** allows a glimpse of lions and tigers prowling through the large park. A butterfly park is also underway.

The **zoo** is well stocked and a big hit with children. Elephant rides and life-size models of prehistoric dinosaurs add up to the fun. For the more adventurous sorts, **trekking trails** to Mirza Hill, at a distance of 1.5kms, are laid out. Nearby sights include Uddigebande, which overlooks a deep valley full of vegetative cover and Hajjamana Kallu – a crescent shaped rocky outcrop, featured in movies.

The park lies 25kms south of the city on Bannerghatta Road. Buses ply from all major bus depots and the KSTDC runs conducted tours everyday.

## WHERE TO STAY

### Bannerghatta Nature Camp (Jungle Lodges & Resorts)
*Bannerghatta, Bangalore 560083*
*Tel 2559 7021/7024/7025*
*Fax 2558 6163* **Web** *www.junglelodges.com*
*Tariff Swiss Tent, Rs 750 (Indians), $ 30 (Foreigners); Dormitory, Rs 500 (Indians), $ 20 (Foreigners); Day Visit, Rs 350 (Indians), $ 15 (Foreigners)*

### Cauvery Fishing Camp (Jungle Lodges & Resorts)
*Bheemeshwari Village, on the banks of river Cauvery, south Halagur*
**Open** *6:30am to 8:30am and 3:30pm to 6:30pm*
**Admission** *Restricted*

Serious **anglers** and nature lovers have much to cheer about. This is the site for hooking one of the world's finest game fish – the **mahseer**, in the rugged comfort of camp life. The mahseer is Asia's premier sporting fish and a prize catch for the committed angler who must return it to the water in true sporting tradition, after weighing and photographing it.

Bannerghatta Biological Park

# HERE'S THE ONE PLACE THAT HAS ALL THE FUN.

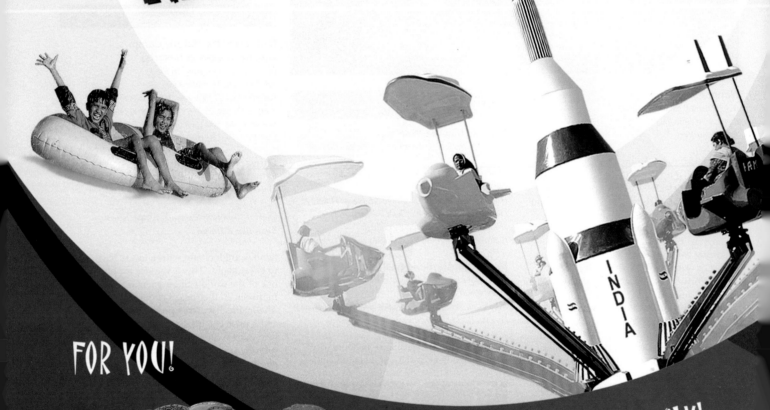

FOR YOU!

YOUR FAMILY!

Cauvery Fishing Camp

At the camp run by Jungle Lodges & Resorts, you can **raft** down the rapids of the rushing Cauvery or sit in a **coracle** absorbing the sights of mountains, gorges and a wealth of flora and fauna. Treks to the nearby hillock afford a panoramic view of the Cauvery flowing through the valley below. Further upstream is Doddamakali Fishing Camp and there is another one downstream at Galibore. There is an ancient Shiva temple nearby, still used by the local Soliga tribals. It takes about two hours to cover the 100km distance on the Kanakpura highway.

## WHERE TO STAY

### Jungle Lodges & Resorts
*Offers both log huts and tented accommodation. The tariff varies for anglers and non-anglers.* **Tel** *2559 7021/ 7024* **Fax** *2558 6163* **Web** *www.junglelodges.com*

### Brindavan
*Whitefield, due east of Bangalore*
**Open** *Darshan is between 7am and 8am and sometimes at 4pm.*
**Admission** *Free*

This is the summer ashram of **Sri Satya Sai Baba**, a famous seer who may be found here from the months of March to May. The **ashram** has a prayer hall with a large bronze idol of Lord Krishna.
Electronic gadgets like cell phones, pagers, cameras, etc are not allowed in the premises. Buses ply from the City Bus Station. Cars and autos are easily available for one way journeys.

### Big Banyan Tree
*Off Mysore Road*
**Open** *Daily*
**Admission** *Free*

Sprawled over a few acres, this 400-year-old botanical wonder in Ramohalli said to be the third **largest banyan tree** in India. You can walk in the dappled light under the canopy of its numerous branches or watch a movie shoot! It's a great picnic spot and especially popular on weekends. KSTDC runs a drive-in-restaurant and there are many small food stalls as well.
A 40-minute drive on the crowded Mysore Road, a turn at the 20th km sign and a further eight kilometre drive will bring you here. Buses from the City Market Depot, Bangalore are rare and hiring a cab is advised.

### Pearl Valley
*Anekal Taluk*
**Open** *All day*
**Admission** *Free*

Pearl Valley is a quiet destination within motorable distance of Bangalore. Hidden in a deep valley cloaked by hills, the falls are an impressive sight during the wet season just after the monsoon. Thin jets of water hurtle down a height of 90m and end in what resembles a pond of pearls, hence the name **Pearl Valley**.
You can get under the cascading falls for an ice-cold shower! Or hike upstream. There is a small shrine of **Lord Shiva** overlooking the falls. KSRTC buses run from Bangalore.

### Mekedatu
*Near Sangama*
**Open** *All day*
**Admission** *Free*

Watch the mighty **Cauvery** squeeze through a deeply chiselled gorge, narrow enough for a goat to leap over. That's how the name Mekadatu, meaning 'goat's leap' came about. Follow its course over a boulder-strewn bed or just sit on a dry rock and enjoy the quiet seclusion of the place. You can also trek to Sangama where the waters of the Cauvery and **Arkavathi** merge. There is a temple dedicated to Sangameshwara at this spot. Mekedatu is best visited in the second half of the year by car.

### Shivaganga
*Near Dobbespet, Nelamangala Taluk, Tumkur District*
**Open** *All Day*
**Admission** *Free*

Shivaganga Hill towers over a small hamlet near Dobbespet. Scale the cone-shaped granite outcrop for picture postcard views. This **1,368m** high hill is said to have four faces: Nandi from the east, Ganesha from the west, a linga from the south and a cobra from the north. A flight of 350 steps leads to the top, passing several mysterious cave temples and a natural spring called **Patalaganga**. The steps lead to two temples: **Gavi Gangadhareshwara cave temple** and the **Honnadevi temple**. The climb although steep is not strenuous thanks to a handrail and frequent beverage

Shivganga

Mekedatu

Avid trekkers and climbers make a beeline to Devarayanadurga perched at a height of 1188m. Set amidst hills and dense forests, Devarayanadurga is dotted with hilltop temples like the **Yoganarasimha** and the **Bhoganarasimha**. The panoramic view of Tumkur town from atop the Devarayanadurga hill is an unusual sight. The **Mahalakshmi temple** at **Goravanahalli** and **Namada Chilume**, a holy natural spring – the source of the river Jayamangali – are the other sights in the area. Legend has it that when Lord Rama struck an arrow into the earth to quench the thirst of his brother Lakshman, this spring shot up.

Jackals, sloth bear, wild boar, deer and 143 species of birds can be seen at the State Forest Reserve.

There are two direct buses from the City Bus Stand to Devarayanadurga. They leave at 7:30am and 8am and the journey takes about an hour and a half. You can check with the driver for the timings of the return trip. Hiring a car for the day is a better option.

stops along the way. At the Gangadhar temple you may witness ghee (clarified butter) turning back into butter, barely 10 minutes after it is offered as abhisheka for the linga. The converted butter is handed out to devotees. Catch any bus travelling on the Tumkur highway and alight at the town of Dobbespet. To reach Shivaganga hire an auto. The entire journey should take an hour. (There are also direct buses from Bangalore to Shivaganga, which run every two hours.) The entire journey should take an hour and there are a number of restaurants along the way.

## Savanadurga

*10kms from Magadi in Bangalore Rural District*
*Open 6am to 5pm*
*Admission Rs 2 (to the Savanadurga State Forest)*

This **hill fortress** was once the hideout of **Kempegowda**, the local chieftain who founded Bangalore in 1537.

There are two hills separated by a deep valley: On the left is **Karigudda** or black hill, covered with greenery and on the right is

**Billigudda**, the barren, white hill. The rocky hilltops afford incredible views. A sheer rockface on one side is great for rock climbing and rappelling. There is even a picturesque lake for boating and the whole area resounds with birdcalls. Except for summer, this is an ideal getaway.

The **Savanadurga State Forest** lies close to the village and you can see a medicinal plant farm and small zoo. **Temples** of **Veerabhadraswamy** and **Narasimha** and the ruins of a 16th century fort built by Kempegowda are set here.

Four buses run daily from Bangalore's City Bus Stand. Alternatively, drive straight to Magadi, a distance of 65kms.

Temple choultries provide very basic accommodation for overnight stays. Cooking facilities are available near the temple.

## Devarayanadurga

*Tumkur District*
*Open Devarayanadurga State Forest Reserve is open from 6am to 6pm everyday*
*Admission Rs 2 for adults*

## Janapada Loka

*Janapada Loka, Bangalore-Mysore Road, Ramanagaram, Bangalore 571511*
*Tel 080-727 1555*
*Open 9am to 1pm and 2:30pm to 5:30pm.*
*Closed on Tuesday.*
*Admission Rs 4*

Janapada Loka houses a stunning collection of 5,000 artefacts celebrating **Karnataka's folk culture**. The 15-acre complex houses museums, an open-air theatre and studio. The museum has drawn from the life and arts of a large number of tribal and rural folk across the state. There is an impressive array of agricultural hunting and fishing implements, weapons, ingenious household gadgets, masks, dolls and shadow puppets.

After a trip to the museum walk over to the Kamat Loka Ruchi, for a taste of food from north Karnataka.

Any Mysore-bound bus (not the non-stop variety) will get you here. Just step off at Ramanagaram town, at the 53rd km.

A C N V L D R V X C C L F J Q

W T I Y U O P K M H K L R E W

Q A S D F G H J U I O P L T Y

Y ( M I S T A K E S ) U B N M L R

A C N V L D R V X C C L F J Q

W T I Y U O P K M H K L R E W

Q A S D F G H J U I O P L T Y

W T I Y U O P K M H K L R E W

Q A S D F G H J U I O P L T Y

W T I Y U O P K M H K L R E W

If you've found any, let us know.

Feel free to share your ideas, your opinions
and suggestions about this book. Simply email your feedback to
response@starkworld.net

Stark World, Infinitum Publishing Pvt. Ltd, 173, 9th Cross, Indiranagar 1st Stage, Bangalore - 560038. Tel: 91-80-51255036

**A to Z Resources**

## AIRPORT / AIRLINES

Both domestic and international terminals are housed in the same building on Airport Road. It is located 13kms east of the City Railway Station and about 9kms from MG Road. Private taxis and auto rickshaws ply between the airport and the rest of the city. A more reliable option is prepaid taxis with counters at the airport that keeps touts at bay: Watch out for taxi touts here! For the rest, Bangalore airport is small, friendly and quite clean with a cafe, bookstore and gift shop. For the persistent mosquitoes, carry repellent especially if you're on a late night flight.

Bangalore is well connected to all the major Indian cities, with daily flights to Mumbai, Kolkata, Delhi, Hyderabad, Chennai, Ahmedabad, Cochin, Goa, Mangalore, Pune and Thiruvananthapuram. Domestic carriers are Indian Airlines, Jet Airways, Air Sahara and Air Deccan. There are direct flights to New York, Singapore, Bahrain, Bangkok, Colombo, Dubai, Jeddah, Frankfurt, Kuala Lumpur, Muscat, Kathmandu, Sharjah and Riyadh operated by Lufthansa, Air India and Singapore Airlines.

### Domestic Airlines

*Indian Airlines 140,141, 2522 6233*
*Jet Airways 2522 0688/1929/0856*
*Air Sahara 2522 0626/0665, 2558 3937*
*Air Deccan 98457 77008*

### International Airlines

*Air India 2522 8601/7747, 2227 7747*
*Air France 2558 9397/9214/7258*
*British Airways 2227 1205/4034*
*KLM Northwest Airlines 2226 9854*
*Malaysian Airlines 2212 2991*
*Royal Nepal Airlines 2559 7878, 2532 7108*
*Lufthansa 2522 9646, 2558 8791*
*Alitalia 2559 1936*
*Cathay Pacific 2226 9745, 2220 2713*
*EI-AI (Israel Airlines) 2227 2575*
*Kuwait Airways 2558 9021/9841/6533, 2559 4243/4244*
*Qantas 2226 4719, 2225 8594*
*Singapore Airlines 2286 7868/7869*
*Sri Lankan Airlines 2207 5020-22*
*Swiss Air 2286 7873/7876*
*United Airlines 2224 4620-22*
*South African Airways 2224 4623*
*Delta Airlines 2227 3439/3440, 2224 4625*
*Scandinavian Airlines 2224 4622*
*Gulf Air 2558 5394/5309*
*Air New Zealand 2224 4624*

## AMBULANCE

Dial 102 for an ambulance if you have a serious medical emergency. However, most hospitals offer prompt ambulance services as well and we carry a list below. For more information see Helplines.

*Ambicare 2332 3560*
*Central Fire Control Room 2225 1780/1786*
*City Corporation (City Area) 2227 7788*
*City Corporation (Civil Area) 2557 1488*
*Indian Red Cross Society 2226 4205/8435*
*Bangalore Hospital 2663 2753*
*Bowring & Lady Curzon Hospital 2663 2753/3494*
*Hosmat 2559 3796/3797*
*Mallya Hospital 2227 7979/7990*
*Manipal Hospital 2526 8901*
*St. Martha's Hospital 2227 4541/5081*
*St. John's Ambulance Association 2222 3384*
*Victoria Hospital 2670 1150/3294*

## ATM

For ready cash you can rely on the city's many ATMs, in all shopping areas and commercial centres. Big banks like Citibank, ICICI, HDFC and HSBC have a presence in almost all areas. Citibank has several on Brigade Road including one outside Niligiri's Supermarket. The Canara Bank ATM on MG Road accepts international cards. Once you leave the busy commercial areas however, ATMs are few and far between. You can use the telephone numbers below to find your closest ATM.

*Citibank 30 Prestige Meridian-II,*
*MG Road, Bangalore 560001*
*Tel 2558 1710, 2559 9855, 2227 2265*
*Web www.citibank.co.in.*

*IDBI 58 Mission Road, Bangalore 560027*
*Tel 2227 9576*
*Web www.idbi.com*

*ICICI ICICI Bank Towers,*
*1 Commissariat Road, Behind Mayo Hall,*
*Bangalore 560001*
*Tel 5129 6007/6509/6000*
*Web www.icicibank.com*

*Corporation Bank 114 MG Road,*
*Bangalore 560001*
*Tel 2558 7940*
*Web www.corpbank.com*

*UTI Bombay Swadeshi Stores Ltd.,*
*99 MG Road, Bangalore 560001*
*Tel 2555 9555*
*Web www.utibank.com*

*HDFC 25/1 Sankara Narayana Building,*
*MG Road Bangalore 560001*
*Tel 2532 0932/0933, 2520 2233*
*Web www.hdfcbank.com*

*HSBC 7 MG Road, Bangalore 560001*
*Tel 2558 5444/5630*
*Web www.hsbc.com*

*Standard Chartered 26 MG Road, Raheja Towers, Bangalore 560001*
*Tel 2558 0632*
*Web www.standardchartered.co.in*

## AUTORICKSHAWS

Autos play the role of taxis in other metros. You can get on and off where you like, no small matter when you consider how crowded some of Bangalore's commercial roads are. The noisy, three-wheeled contraptions appear precarious but are an easy and safe way to get around the city. The metre starts at Rs 10 and increases at the rate of Rs 5 per km. From 10pm to 7am you pay 1.5 to twice the original fare. Be warned though that auto drivers are notorious for haggling and putting up their price, literally! If things get out of hand, report the driver to the nearest policeman. Prepaid autos are available at the City Railway Station.

## AMUSEMENT PARKS

*See section on Entertainment.*

## AYURVEDIC CENTRES

*See section on Health.*

## BANKS

All the major areas are equipped with a bank. They provide fully computerised services including online banking facilities. Nationalised banks like Vijaya Bank, Corporation Bank and Canara Bank are headquartered here, while all others have big offices. You can encash travellers' cheques at Citibank, ICICI, UTI and HDFC. For information see ATMs.

## BOOKS

*See section on Entertainment.*

## BUILDERS

*See section on Real Estate.*

## BUS

The public bus service ferries thousands of people throughout the day and is an inexpensive way of getting around. Mind though, it involves a fair bit of pushing and being pushed and you need to be quick and nimble when getting on and off! Peak hours are not the best time to travel in buses when crowds spill over onto the footboards. Keep an eye out for pickpockets and a firm hold on your belongings. Remember to carry plenty of change. The brown Pushpak buses are a step up in luxury and you can be assured of a seat, but these are few in number. The BTS network is not a great stickler for time so give a half hour here and there in your schedule.

All bus routes begin and end at the City Bus Stand better known as Majestic (for the movie hall in the vicinity). It's right outside the city railway station. Other important terminals are in Shivajinagar and Jayanagar, with smaller ones in every locality. It's best to check timings and places of departure at the terminal's enquiry counter.

For bus travel outside the state, you can choose from state run buses or the slightly more comfortable private ones. At the Majestic stand, only state run buses are allowed, but right outside and further away in equally crowded Kalasipalyam, there is a fleet of private buses humming and revving! The computerised advance booking counter for all KSRTC super deluxe and express buses is located within the bus stand and you can choose from ordinary, semi luxury, super deluxe and sleeper. It's advisable to book long distance journeys in

advance. Private bus bookings can be made across the city at travel agencies and small booking counters. For booking details and enquiry you could call the KSRTC or check the website.

*KSRTC Enquiry 2287 3377*
*Web www.ksrtc.org*

## BUSINESS CENTRES

These readymade offices come with all the trappings – from security men to secretaries. Fully furnished automated cabins to suit individual budgets and tastes are available. You can choose from a variety of options – air-conditioned or non-air conditioned cabins of various sizes, workstations with modular furniture, a cloak room and so on. They offer other conveniences such as ample parking space, security, secretarial assistance to answer your calls and make appointments, peons to take care of administrative work, DTP, fax and equipment.

*DBS Business Centre*
*26 Cunningham Road, Bangalore 560002*
*Tel 2226 7272, 2220 2440*

*Newbridge Business Centres*
*40 Ulsoor Road, Bangalore 560042*
*Tel 2532 5800, 2521 9293,*
*Branches Indiranagar, Koramangala,*
*Ulsoor Road*
*Web www.newbridgebusinesscentre.com*

*Golden Square Executive Centre*
*102 Eden Park 20 Vittal Mallya Road,*
*Bangalore 560001*
*Tel 2224 3860*

*St. Marks Business Centre*
*8 St. Marks Plaza, St. Mark's Road,*
*Bangalore 560001*
*Tel 2227 0506*

*Glenridge Executive Centre*
*32 Alsa Glenridge, Langford Road,*
*Bangalore 560025*
*Tel 2224 6152*

## CABLE

If there's a TV, it's almost certain it will have what is called 'a cable connection' which gives it access to the hundred-odd channels that beam through the day and night. International channels like STAR, BBC, AXN, National Geographic, CNBC, HBO and Discovery are very popular. There are also a slew of Hindi, Kannada, Tamil and Telugu channels that dish out current affairs as well as entertainment programmes.

*Siti Cable Networks*
*39, III Floor, United Mansions, Bangalore 560001*
*Tel 2559 9999, 2558 0214*

*USN*
*Residency Road, Bangalore 560025*
*Tel 2229 1797, 5112 5319*

## CAR RENTALS

*See Taxi*

## CHURCHES

*See section on Spiritual Matters.*

## CLIMATE

Bangalore is best known for its fabulous weather. In between, there are a few summer months when temperatures rise to 38 degrees and winters when it drops to the early teens. The monsoon months are cloudy and early evenings are bound to see some rain.
The city lies at an altitude of 920m and so it's always cool in the shade and scorching in the sun.

 January 27°C - 15°C
February 30°C - 17°C

 March 32°C - 19°C
April 33°C - 21°C

 May 33°C - 21°C
June 29°C - 20°C

 July 27°C - 19°C
August 27°C - 19°C

 September 26°C - 19°C
October 26°C - 17°C

 November 28°C - 18°C
December 26°C - 15°C

## CLUBS

*See section on Entertainment.*

## COURIER & CARGO

Whether it's a document or a dhurrie that you wish to send, courier and cargo agents are easy to spot. There are a number of courier companies, both big and small that deliver packages across the country and overseas as well. It's advisable to stick to the big ones for important deliveries. Parcels heavier than 2.5kgs are sent by cargo. DTDC, Blue Dart, DHL and Professional Couriers provide reliable courier and cargo services and stick to their schedules.

*Professional Couriers 2334 5895/1978*

*DTDC 2535 0414/7813*

*DHL 2558 8855/5905*

*First Flight 2521 3876*

*Blue Dart 2331 7800, 2532 7848*

*EMS Speed Post 2286 1435/0756*

*FedEx 1600-22-6161*

## CREDIT CARDS

Plastic money is widely accepted. All major cards like MasterCard and Visa are accepted at most shops, top-end and mid-range hotels and restaurants. Debit cards, however may or may not be accepted. Smaller shops and budget hotels take only cash.

## CUSTOMS

The usual duty free regulations apply at the Bangalore airport: One litre of alcohol, 200 cigarettes or 50 cigars. Video cameras and laptop computers are also exempt. Cash or travellers cheques exceeding $10,000 should be declared on arrival.

*Web www.customs.gov.in*

## DIAGNOSTIC CENTRES

Most hospitals are equipped with their own diagnostic facilities. But medical diagnostic centres are used to get second opinions or undergo specialised tests. Services like CT, MRI and CAT scan centres, laboratories and X-Ray and Nuclear Barium Test facilities are all available here.

*Manipal Hospital*
*Rustum Bagh, Airport Road,*
*Bangalore 560017*
*Tel 2526 8901-3*

*Elbit*
*6/1 Infantry Road, Bangalore 560001*
*Tel: 2286 0761*

*Medinova Diagnostic Services Ltd.*
*55 Infantry Road, Bangalore 560001*
*Tel: 2286 3455/0513/7244*

*Anand Diagnostic*
*11 Blue Cross Chambers, Infantry Road Cross,*
*Shivajinagar, Bangalore 560001*
*Tel: 2509 6732*

*The Apollo Clinic*
*1ˢᵗ Floor, Sobha Alexander,*
*16/2 Commissariat Road,*
*Near Shoppers' Stop, Bangalore 500095*
*Tel: 5697 3327/8/9*

## DIAL-A-SERVICE

There is a variety of dial-in services that make life easier. You can call Current Booking for tickets to movies playing in any part of town. *(See Tickets)*
Just Dial and Get It have a database with everything from phone numbers to job vacancies. Man Friday, if you haven't guessed, will do odd jobs. From organising parties to paying bills, they do it all. Plumbers, carpenters, postage, courier, bank related work, train, air and bus tickets are just a phone call away. Dial-a-gift is an innovative service that saves you the trouble of agonising over birthday, anniversary and wedding gifts. Called 39, they have a wealth of original gift ideas.

*Just Dial 2333 3333*

*Man Friday 2558 8444*

*Current Booking 2570 5858*

*39 2331 5607*

*Get it 2235 5555*

## DISABILITIES

Sadly, Bangalore is not the greatest city for people with physical disabilities. Few buildings have wheelchair access and footpaths are usually narrow and riddled with cracks.
A private car is the most convenient way to get around the city. Contact Mobility India for queries.

# Helplines

Bangalore has a range of helplines to tackle emergencies of any kind.

You need to dial:

**100** to report a crime.

**101** for the fire brigade.

**102** for an ambulance.

**103** for a mishap on the road or register a traffic complaint.

**1051** and **2226 8888** to alert the cardiac helpline at Jayadeva and Wockhardt hospitals.

**1901338014** to reach the 24-hour diabetic helpline.

**2334 9011** to report a gas leak.

**2353 9574, 2353 9363, 2353 1404** to get in touch with Breakdown 365, a unique help line geared to fix car breakdowns.

**2223 8279** (Samraksha) for queries about AIDS and HIV.

**2526 9307** (Vimochana) if you are a woman in distress.

**2341 1181** (SPCA), **2341 9177** (CUPA) in case of a veterinary emergency.

**2527 0960** for weather forecasts.

*Mobility India*
*1ˢᵗ A Cross, JP Nagar II Phase,*
*Bangalore 560078*
*Tel 2659 7327*
*Web www.mobility-india.org*

## DOCUMENTS

All foreigners should possess a valid visa and passport issued by the Indian embassy. The visa should be registered with a Foreign Registration Office within 15 days of arrival in India. Visas are non-extendable, but 15-day extensions are issued under exceptional circumstances. Foreigners are also required to obtain a protected area permit before visiting the Tibetan settlements between Hunsur and Bylekuppe. They can be obtained at the Ministry of Home Affairs, New Delhi. Health certificates and student cards are optional.

*City Commissioner of Police 2226 0707*
*Web www.bangalorecitypolice.org*

## ELECTRICITY

Blackouts and regular load shedding (when residents are notified about blackouts) are especially common in the summer, so keep a torch or candle at hand. To deal with this capricious power supply, most hotels, restaurants and shops are equipped with a

back-up generator and UPS. If you are bringing any sensitive electrical equipment, like a laptop, a voltage stabiliser, an AC adaptor and a three socket pin are must haves as the electric current is 230-240 volts, AC. Power is provided by the state-run Karnataka Electricity Board and complaints can be registered by calling 1917.

*Bangalore Circle Office 226 0636*

## FAX

Most STD/ISD/PCO booths offer fax services. Receiving faxes costs Rs 10 per page.

## FIRE

Call 101 in the event of a fire. See Helplines.

## FLORISTS

*See section on Shopping.*

## FOREIGN EXCHANGE

*See Money*

## GARDENS

*See section on Entertainment.*

## GOVERNMENT

Websites of important Government Departments and Organisations:

*Karnataka Tourism*
*www.karnatakatourism.org*

*Karnataka State Tourism Development*
*Corporation*
*www.kar.nic.in/kstdc*

*Passport Office, Bangalore*
*www.kar.nic.in/passport*

*Information & Publicity*
*www.karnatakainformation.org*

*Bangalore Telephones*
*www.bangaloretelecom.com*

*Karnataka Police*
*www.karnatakastatepolice.org*

*Bangalore City Police*
*www.bangalorecitypolice.org*

Telephone numbers and email ids of a few Government Officials in Bangalore:

*Commissioner, Bangalore City Corporation*
*(BCC)*
*Tel 2223 7455*
*Email commissioner@blrbmp.com*

*Commissioner, Bangalore Development*
*Authority (BDA)*
*Tel 2336 0843 Email bda@vsnl.com*

*Chairman, Bangalore Water Supply and*
*Sewage Board (BWSSB)*
*Tel 2221 5417*
*Email chmnbwsb@blr.vsnl.net.in*

*Chairman & Managing Director, Karnataka*
*Power Transmission Corporation Limited*
*(KPTCL)*
*Tel 2224 5349, 2221 4342*
*Email cm@keb.gov.in*

*Managing Director, Bangalore Metropolitan*
*Transport Corporation (BMTC)*
*Tel 2222 1124 Email bmtc@blrforward.org*

*Commissioner of Police*
*Tel 2226 0707 Email copblore@rediffmail.com*

*Principal General Manager*
*Bangalore Telecom*
*Tel 2286 8687 Email gmbgtd@vsnl.com,*
*gmbgtd@bangaloretelecom.com*

## HOSPITALS

*See section on Health, Children.*

## HOTELS

*See section on Accommodation.*

## INTERNET

Being the IT capital of India, Bangalore has swift Internet connections and a hoard of Internet cafes. Browsing centres are a dime a dozen and you can surf for Rs 30 an hour or even less at some places.

*Satyam i-way*
*Near Galaxy Theatre, Residency Road*
*Tel 2532 0172*
*Cunningham Road 2238 6896;*
*CMH Road, 2521 5284*

*Reliance Web World*
*Mota Royal Arcade, Brigade Road*
*Tel 3181 3063-68*

*Image Impact*
*1 The Presidency, Cellar Floor,*
*St. Mark's Road, Bangalore 560001*
*Tel 2224 4856, 2221 5607*

## INTERNATIONAL ORGANISATIONS

*Alliance Francaise de Bangalore*
*PB No 108 Thimmaiah Road,*
*Vasantha Nagar, Bangalore 560052*
*Tel 2225 8762, 2226 5390*
*Open 9:30am to 1pm and 4pm to 7pm and*
*9:30am to 1pm on Saturday. Closed on Sunday.*
*Email alfrab@satyam.net.in*

*Indo American Chamber of Commerce*
*205 II Floor, HVS Court,*
*21 Cunningham Road, Bangalore 560052*
*Tel 2220 3366*
*Open 9:30am to 5pm*
*Closed on Saturday and Sunday.*
*Email iaccbang@giasbg01.vsnl.net.in*

*Indo German Chamber of Commerce*
*403 Shah Sultan, Cunningham Road,*
*Bangalore 560052*
*Tel 2226 5650/6497*
*Open 10am to 1pm and 2pm to 5:30pm. Closed*
*on Saturday and Sunday.*
*Email igcchg@vsnl.com*

*Max Mueller Bhavan*
*3 Lavelle Road, Bangalore 560001*
*Tel 2227 5435, 2221 4964*
*Open 9am to 1pm and 2pm to 5:30pm. Closed*
*on Saturday and Sunday.*
*Email gibing@bangalore.goethe.org*

*The British Council*
*23 Prestige Takt, Kasturba Cross Road,*
*Bangalore 560001*
*Tel 2248 9220*
*Open 9am to 5pm. Closed on Sunday.*
*Web www.bclindia.org*

*The Indo British Trade Initiative*
*British Trade Office, 7/4 Thapar Niketan,*
*Brunton Road, Bangalore 560025*
*Tel 2558 6687/8661*
*Open 8:30am to 4pm. Closed on Saturday and*
*Sunday.*

*Indian Institute of World Culture*
*6 BP Wadia Road, Basavanagudi,*
*Bangalore 560004*
*Tel 2667 8581*
*Open 10am to 6pm. Closed on Monday.*

*Indo Japanese Friendship Association*
*Sai Deepa, 2302, 21st Cross, KR Road,*
*Banashankari Road, Bangalore 560070*
*Tel 2658 8968*
*Email miras@hotmail.com*

*Overseas Women's Club of Bangalore*
*(OWC) C/o ITC Hotel Windsor Sheraton &*
*Towers, 25 Golf Course Road,*
*Bangalore 560052*
*Email info@owcbangalore.com*

## LANGUAGE

The local language is Kannada, but you can get by with English, Hindi, Tamil and even a bit of Urdu or Telugu! Most shopkeepers, taxi and auto drivers speak broken, if not fluent Hindi and English. Bangaloreans are a friendly lot and try their best to communicate despite language barriers.

*See box on Useful Kannada Words.*

## LIBRARIES

*See section on Entertainment.*

## 24-HOUR MEDICAL STORES

A string of round-the-clock medical shops have opened in the city and most of them are attached to hospitals. Apart from prescription drugs and over-the-counter medicines, they also stock chocolates and toiletries. However, these pharmacies are restricted to commercial centres and are hard to come by in residential areas.

*Gayathri Hospital*
*91 Magadi Chord Road, Vijayanagar,*
*Bangalore 560040*
*Tel 2335 5201, 2335 2085*

*Khodays Pharma*
*214 Westminster, Cunningham Road,*
*Bangalore 560052 Tel 2228 1540*

*Mallya Hospital*
*2 Vittal Mallya Road, Bangalore 560001*
*Tel 2227 7979*

*Metri Medical*
*30 Fort A Street, Opp. Vani Vilas Hospital*
*Bangalore 560002 Tel 2670 4534*

*Medical Point*
*G216 West Minster, 13 Cunningham Road,*
*Bangalore 560052*

*Manipal Hospital*
*98 Rustom Bagh, Airport Road,*
*Bangalore 560017 Tel 2526 6646*

*Victoria Hospital*
*Near City Market, Bangalore 560001*
*Tel 2262 7471*

*Yellamma Dasappa Hospital*
*25 Andree Road, Shanthi Nagar,*
*Bangalore 560027 Tel 2222 5642*

## MOBILE TELEPHONE

Airtel, Hutch, Spice, BSNL and Reliance are some of the local players who provide a range of affordable cellular services. Post-paid as well as pre-paid packages are offered with 'roaming' facilities. SIM Cards start from Rs 200. They can be bought across the city, at phone booths and Internet cafes and the vendor helps you set them up. Average call rates within India are around Re 3 per minute and international calls can be made for less than Rs 20 a minute. Text messaging gets even cheaper.

*Airtel* 98450 98450

*Spice Telecom* 98440 98440

*Hutch* 98860 98860

*BSNL* 94480 94480

## MONEY

Available denominations are Rs 1,000, Rs 500, Rs 100, Rs 50, Rs 20, Rs 10 and Rs 5 as notes. Coins are available in Rs 5, Rs 2, Rs 1, 50ps and 25ps denomination. 100ps is equal to 1 Rupee. One and two Rupee notes are no longer printed but some may still be in circulation. Private moneychangers are usually open longer hours than banks. For foreign exchange Thomas Cook is a popular choice. AMEX cheques can be encashed at Weizmann Forex on MG Road. Cash advances on all major credit cards are issued at the Bank of Baroda. Check the exchange rates to be doubly sure while making transactions. You can have money transferred back to your account via Thomas Cook and Western Union Bank.

*Thomas Cook*
*55 MG Road, Bangalore 560001*
*Tel 2558 1337/1340*

*Travelex India Pvt. Ltd.*
*G 36 A & B, Brigade Gardens,*
*19 Church Street, Bangalore 560001*
*Tel 5112 7770/7771*

*Weizmann Forex*
*5 Centre Point, Residency Road, Bangalore*
*560025 Tel 2558 2148*

*Western Union*
*1 St. Mark's Road, Bangalore 560001*
*Tel 2558 8691/5684*

## MOVIES

*See Section on Entertainment.*

## NATIONAL HOLIDAYS

All tourist spots managed by the Government remain shut on national holidays. Bangalore celebrates a host of other festivals like Diwali, Christmas and Ramzan. On these occasions banks and government as well as private offices remain closed. However, shops throughout the city function through national holidays and festivals. Tourist spots and most stores remain open on Sunday as well. For more information see National Holidays.
All banks, offices and Government managed tourist spots are shut on National Holidays. The following holidays are observed through the year. Some dates tend to change each year so the months are indicated.

*Independence Day – 15th August*

*Republic Day – 26th January*

*Gandhi Jayanti – 2nd October*

*Dasara – September-October*

*Diwali –- October-November*

*Christmas – 25th December*

*Ramzan – December*

*Makara Sankranthi – February*

*Ambedkar Jayanthi – April*

*Vinayaka Chaturthi – September*

*Bakrid – February*

## NEWSPAPERS

The popular English language dailies include *The Times of India, Deccan Herald, The Hindu, The Asian Age* and *Indian Express* with special Bangalore supplements loaded with city news and events. A string of Kannada newspapers like *Praja Vani, Vijaya Karnataka* and *Kannada Prabha* cover local happenings extensively. Evening newspapers like *Sanje Vani* and *Hi Bengalooru* are popular for their racy coverage of goings-on in the city. Check the Internet for online editions of the dailies.

*The Times of India* www.timesofindia.com

*Deccan Herald* www.deccanherald.com

*Indian Express* www.indian-express.com

*The Asian Age* www.asianage.com

*The Hindu* www.hinduonnet.com

*Vijay Times* www.vijaytimes.com

## PARKS

*See section on Entertainment.*

## PHOTOGRAPHY

Most areas have Fotoflash, Adlabs and Konica outlets that stock film rolls, camera accessories and also develop films. It usually takes a day to develop film and the rate averages at Rs 40 for developing and Rs 5 for each print. Studios in and around MG Road like GK Vale and Whizz have in-house studios where passport size, stamp size and Polaroid photographs are churned out in no time. Memory for digital cameras and video cartridges are available here. For professional print Prabhu Photos and Whizz are the best options.

*Adlabs*
76/1 Mission Road, Bangalore 560027
*Tel* 2297 1431/1432

*Foto Flash*
8 Richmond Circle, Richmond Road,
Bangalore 560025
*Tel* 2297 3053/3054

*G K Vale*
89 MG Road, Bangalore 560001
*Tel* 2558 7546/9429
*Branches* Koramangala, 2550 6545;
Indiranagar, 2529 0203

*Prabhu Photos*
32 Brigade Road, Bangalore 560001
*Tel* 2558 2233/2345

*Whizz*
111-1/2 Dickenson Road, Bangalore 560042
*Tel* 5113 3432/3433

## POLICE

The city has a prompt police force and don't let their bleary eyed looks fool you. Dial 100 to report a crime. The Hoysala patrol vans, a mobile unit of the police, make nightly rounds through the city and can be reached at 103 in case of an emergency. The police force has a strong presence throughout the city with over 65 police stations. The cops on night vigil frown on drivers who consume alcohol – after 10pm travellers on the road are subjected to stringent breath analysis tests.
Recently the All Women's Police Station was set up at Ulsoor to combat gender crimes, from eve teasing to dowry harassment. To keep up with the changing face of crime in the IT Capital, a cyber crime police station has been set up in Mamulpet. The police have been trying to adopt a more pro-active approach to deal with growing crime in the city.

*Web* www.karnatakastatepolice.org

## POST

For those of you who still rely on snail mail, the Indian postal service offers speed post, business post, retail post, express parcel post, money orders, international money transfer and gift

delivery services. The imposing building of the General Post Office (GPO) near Cubbon Park is quite comprehensive. They also have an efficient poste restante service here. You can send international faxes and make phone calls at the Central Telegraph Office. Post you letters before 5pm in the evening if you want them to leave on the same day.

*GPO, Raj Bhavan Road, Bangalore 560001*

## PUBLIC TOILETS

Pay and use toilets across the city come as a relief to travellers. Both Western and Indian-style toilets are available and cleaned after every use. A nominal fee of Rs 2 has to be paid. Be warned though, that clean public toilets are limited to a few areas in the city.

## RADIO

The radio is crackling once again with the entry of FM channels. Star Network's Radio City FM 91 is a favourite and plays predominantly Hindi music packaged with updates of local news and events. AIR also has an FM channel, Rainbow, which plays everything from Hindi music to Western country music. AIR also broadcasts classical music programmes and regular news updates in English, Hindi and Kannada.

## REAL ESTATE

*See section on Real Estate.*

## SMOKING

Smoking is banned in public places by law. This means that theatres, restaurants and even parks are no-smoking zones. However the law isn't strictly enforced.

## SCHOOLS

*See section on Children.*

## SWEETS & SAVOURIES

*See section on Food & Drink.*

## SUPER MARKETS

*See section on Shopping.*

## TAXI

There are both taxis with metres and those without. Hiring one is the most comfortable way of travelling in and around Bangalore. The brave hearted can rent a car without the services of a driver, but beware, roads in Bangalore are not simple perpendicular ribbons and you can get lost very easily in the erratic one ways and winding streets.

## Making a Call

Local landline numbers are 8-digit numbers while mobile numbers are 10-digit numbers.

**From a landline/local telephone:**
To call a local number, dial the 8-digit number directly (For eg., 2529 4822)
To call a mobile, dial the 10 digit number directly (For eg., 98450 98450)

**From a mobile telephone:**
To call a landline/ local number, dial the local code, 080, followed by the 8-digit number (For eg., 080 2529 4822)

To call another mobile, dial the 10-digit number directly (For eg., 98450 98450)

Taxis with metres are known as radio taxis. The ones without may be hired by the hour or number of kilometres. You can also ask for two and four hour options. A self-drive car costs about Rs 800 a day, along with a refundable advance of Rs 10,000. These cars can be taken out of the city as well.

City taxis, radio taxis and spot taxis are just a phone call away. Their speciality is that you are picked up from wherever you call. These taxis operate on the basis of fixed prices and regulated metres. Charges are according to the distance travelled, apart from additional waiting charges of Rs 20 per hour. The metre starts ticking from the point of boarding. They are on call 24 hours a day.

**Taxis for hire**

*Vaibhav on Wheels* 2668 0727

*Dial-a-Car Services* 2526 1737/2622, 2227 6858

*Metro Taxi* 2530 3636/2118/2067

*Europcar* 2221 9502

*Alliance Travels* 2521 3082

*Ambassador Travel Services* 2222 0552/3225

*SRS Travels* 2267 0427/0851/1804

**Radio Taxis**

*Cabs Den* 2248 3879/ 98801 00079

*Gopinath Radio City Taxi* 2332 0152, 2360 5555

*Raj City Taxi* 2333 7777/5666, 2363 4444

*Roman City Taxi* 2548 6606, 2558 1616

*SRP Mobiles* 2678 0022/0044

*Spot City Taxi* 2551 0000

*Sneha Tours & Travels* 2660 4478, 2691 4666

*Surmi Tours & Trade Links* 2323 7191

*Tourist East West* 2225 3377, 2542 2222

*United Motors* 2223 8668

*RK City Taxi* 2312 8888, 2319 9999

## TELEPHONE

Stands for Subscriber Trunk Dialling or telephones that have trunk dialling allow you to call out of Bangalore. The yellow and blue sign saying STD/ISD/PCO may be found all over the

city. Direct, local, interstate and international calls can be made here. Most booths in the heart of the city are open through most part of the night and some have a 'call-back' facility that enables you to receive calls as well. Invariably cheaper than telephone services provided at hotels, a local call costs Rs 2 and a digital metre lets you monitor the price of STD and ISD calls minute to minute. Interstate calls are charged at 'full rate' between 9am and 8pm; the rate halves after 8pm and rates are cheapest between 11pm and 6am. International calls cost an average of Rs 30-50 per minute. A cheaper option is the Net2phone available at most Internet cafes where the charge is Rs 8 per minute for international calls to any country. There are also automated public telephones available in some stores that operate with Rs 1 coins. For any enquiries about changed telephone numbers, dial 1952 or make directory enquiries at 197.
BSNL, Tata Indicom and Touchtel provide telephone connections and services in the city. For more information see Dial-A-Service.

**Some important STD codes**

*Bangalore 080, New Delhi 011, Mumbai 022, Kolkata 033, Chennai 044, Hyderabad 040, Pune 020, Kochi 0484*

**Within Karnataka**

*Belgaum 0831, Bijapur 08352, Chikmagalur 08262, Gulbarga 08472, Hassan 08172, Hospet 08394, Hubli 0831, Karwar 08382, Madikeri 08276, Mangalore 0824, Mysore 0821, Shimoga 08186, Udupi 08252*

## TICKETS

Queuing up for tickets, minutes before the movie begins, is still the most done thing. But some business-savvy theatres have online booking facilities. An organisation called Current Booking delivers tickets at your doorstep if you give them a call. If the film is popular, book in advance. Tickets for plays are available at the venues before the show. For more information see Dial-a-Service.

## TIPPING

It is wise to leave a generous tip if you are returning to the restaurant. Otherwise, tipping is optional, especially when service tax is added. Tips (according to your discretion) are well appreciated in smaller hotels. Porters and bellboys expect a minimum of Rs 10 for their services. Giving alms to beggars is a contentious issue. You could donate money to charitable organisations instead.

## TRAVEL

Travel and tour operators organise an assortment of conducted tour packages that let you explore Karnataka with Bangalore as a base. They offer theme-based packages – hill station tours, temple tours and so on. Regular trips to Mysore, Halebid, Belur, Shravanabelagola, Ooty, Kodaikanal, Hampi and Dharmasthala are conducted. You can also use these agencies to plan your travel, hire a car or make train, bus and airplane reservations on your behalf, for a fee.

---

**Holiday Bliss**
*G-7 Blue Cross Chambers, Infantry Road Cross, Bangalore 560001*
**Tel** *2558 6772, 2532 1433, 2559 1610*
**Web** *www.holidaybliss.co.in*

**Hammock Leisure Holidays Pvt. Ltd.**
*314/1 Vijay Kiran, I Floor, 7th Cross, Domlur Layout, Bangalore 560071*
**Tel** *2535 2877*

**Jungle Lodges & Resorts**
*www.junglelodges.com*

**Karnataka State Tourism Development Corp.**
*www.kar.nic.in/kstdc*

**Karnataka Tourism**
*www.karnatakatourism.org*

**Skyway International Travels**
*1659 10th Main, HAL III Stage JB Nagar, Bangalore 560075*
**Tel** *2520 0001*
**Web** *www.skywaytour.com*

## TRAIN

There are two major train stations in Bangalore – the City Railway Station and the Cantonment Station. The crowded City Station with a sea of people, porters and traffic can be a little intimidating for first timers. The station is equipped with some food stalls, bathrooms and a cloakroom where you can leave your belongings safely. Daily express trains connect Bangalore to all the major south Indian and central Indian cities. Express trains leave for Chennai, Delhi, Hubli, Kolkata and Madurai on a daily basis. Computerised reservations may be made at the City Railway Station with separate queues mapped out for women, foreigners and credit cards users (Rs 30 fee). Book tickets well in advance to avoid being wait listed. Call 131 for general enquiries and 132 for enquiries about reservation.

**Web** *www.southernrailway.org*
*www.indianrailways.gov.in*

**Important trains from Bangalore:**

*To Mumbai, Train No 6530*
**Udyan Express** *Dep. 8pm*

*To Delhi, Train No 2627*
**Karnataka Express** *Dep. 6:30pm*

*To Delhi, Train No 2429*
**Rajdhani Express** *Dep. 6:35pm*

*To Hyderabad, Train No 7686*
**Kacheguda Express** *Dep. 5pm*

*To Chennai, Train No 2658*
**Chennai Mail** *Dep. 10:45pm*

*To Chennai, Train No 2008*
**Chennai Shatabdi Express** *Dep. 4:25pm*

**Enquiries**

| | |
|---|---|
| *General* | – 131 |
| *Reservation* | – 1363, 1362, 1361, 132 |
| *Recorded Information* | – 133 |
| *Arrival. Departure of Trains* | – 131, 2220 0971/0972 |

---

**Railway Stations**

| | |
|---|---|
| *Cantonment* | – 135 |
| *Malleswaram* | – 2334 7651 |
| *Yeshwanthpur* | – 2337 7161/1444 |
| *Bangalore East* | – 2548 5435 |
| *Whitefield* | – 2845 2248 |

**Reservation Counters**

| | |
|---|---|
| *Banashankari* | – 2641 0050 |
| *Indiranagar* | – 2525 9192 |
| *Koramangala* | – 2552 2100 |

## WATER

Avoid tap water for a safe and healthy holiday. Stock yourself with an adequate supply of mineral water while travelling or eating out in small restaurants. Make sure you buy standardised brands like Bisleri, Kinley and Aquafina and return the bottle if the seal has been tampered with. UV-treated and 'Aquaguard' filtered water available in most restaurants is potable. Bangalore does not enjoy a 24-hour water supply, so use it wisely.

---

## Vital Statistics

### Karnataka

*Capital* – Bangalore

*Districts* – 27

*Languages* – Kannada, Tulu, Konkani, Kodava, Hindi and English

*Religions* – Hinduism, Islam, Christianity and Jainism

*Area* – 1,91,791sqkms

*Population* – 5,27,33,958 (2001 census)

*Time* – GMT +5:30

### Bangalore

*Location* – 12° 58' N 177° 35' E

*Altitude* – 919m (3021')

*Population* – 6.8 million

*Green Cover* – 40%

*Area* – 366sqkms

*Languages* – Kannada, Tamil, Telugu, Hindi and English widely spoken

*Rainfall* – 97cm

---

## Useful Kannada Words

**Hello!**
*Namaskara!*

**How are you?**
*Hegiddeera?*

**Fine!**
*Chennagide!*

**Glad to meet you.**
*Nimmannu bheti madi santhosha ayithu*

**What is your name?**
*Nimma hesaru yenu?*

**My name is Raju.**
*Nanna hesaru Raju.*

**Come in.**
*Olage banni.*

**Sit down.**
*Kulithukolli.*

**Stop.**
*Nillisi.*

**Go forward.**
*Munde hogi.*

**Go back.**
*Hinde hogi.*

**Go straight.**
*Seeda hogi.*

**I want to get down here.**
*Naanu illi iliyutheeni.*

**Next stop.**
*Mundina stop.*

**Listen.**
*Keli.*

**Please.**
*Dayavittu.*

**Thank You.**
*Dhanyavaadagalu.*

**Good-bye.**
*Hogibaruve.*

**I want…**
*Nanage beku…*

**Please help me.**
*Dayavittu sahaya maadi.*

**I agree!**
*Sari.*

**It's good!**
*Chennagide!*

**This is very good.** *Idu thumba chennagide.*

**I am sorry**
*Nannannu kshamisi!*

**Lets go!**
*Hogonva!*

**What does this cost?**
*Idara bele yeshtu?*

**Is this water good for drinking?**
*Ee neeru kudiyalu yogyave?*

**Can I make a phone call from here?**
*Naanu illinda phone maada bahuda?*

**Where can I hire a taxi?**
*Taxi yelli siguthade?*

**Where does this road lead?**
*Ee rasthe yellige hoguthe?*

**What is the time?**
*Samaya yeshtu?*

**Please could you tell me where I can find this address?**
*Dayavittu ee vilasa yellide yendu helutheera?*

**Have you eaten?**
*Oota aayitha?*

| | |
|---|---|
| **Morning** | – Beligge |
| **Night** | – Rathri |
| **Yesterday** | – Nenne |
| **Today** | – Eevathu |
| **Tomorrow** | – Nale |
| **Fish** | – Meenu |
| **Vegetable** | – Tarakari |
| **Salt** | – Uppu |
| **Rice** | – Anna |
| **Milk** | – Haalu |
| **Boil** | – Beyisu |
| **Water** | – Neeru |

**Numbers in Kannada**

| | | |
|---|---|---|
| One | – | Ondu |
| Two | – | Yeradu |
| Three | – | Mooru |
| Four | – | Nalku |
| Five | – | Aidu |
| Six | – | Aaru |
| Seven | – | Yelu |
| Eight | – | Yentu |
| Nine | – | Ombathu |
| Ten | – | Hathu |

**Directions in Kannada**

| | | |
|---|---|---|
| Left | – | Yedagade |
| Right | – | Balagade |
| Back | – | Hinde |
| Front | – | Munde |
| Inside | – | Olage |
| Outside | – | Horage |
| North | – | Uttara |
| South | – | Dakshina |
| East | – | Poorva |
| West | – | Pashchima |

**Sizes and Shapes in Kannada**

| | | |
|---|---|---|
| Big | – | Doddadu |
| Small | – | Chikkadu |
| Tall | – | Yettara |
| Wide | – | Agala |
| Narrow | – | Sanna |
| Long | – | Udda |
| Short | – | Gidda |

Peter Colaco's

# Bangalore

## A CENTURY OF TALES

F...
& CA...

Books

# Books on Bangalore

## Network City - Planning the Information Society in Bangalore

James Heitzman – Rs 795
Oxford University Press

Touched by the IT wand, Bangalore has transformed itself into a leading centre of software technology over the last few decades. The book takes a hard nosed look at the development of Bangalore's 'information society'. The evolution of the computer and telecommunications industries, accompanying changes in the educational set-up, the social system, the quality of living and infrastructure and the growth of the social landscape are discussed here.

It is a comprehensive and well researched book, a mixture of business management, communications, information studies and urban planning. With bits of history, sociology and economics thrown in, author James Heitzman (Associate Professor of History, Georgia State University) weaves a book length case study of Bangalore and its rise as a leading networking hub. The author uses extensive information from interviews and archives, presenting case studies on urban planning, public policy formation, economic growth, corporate strategy, technology transfer and culture to support his analyses. Statistics and studies are quoted throughout the book to reinforce the author's views. A largely technical book, it also presents a few interesting insights into Bangalore as a hi-tech city and as a product of the Information Age.

## Bangalore – The Story of a City

Maya Jayapal –Rs 250
East West Books (Madras) Pvt. Ltd.

A staid rendition of the history of Bangalore, it gets all its facts right and there is a sizeable section on present-day Bangalore as well. Author Maya Jayapal tries to pin down the city's elusive charm and the attraction it holds for the new migrant. Walking the tightrope between gushy sentiment and cynicism, Jayapal writes the story of Bangalore without frills and fuss. The changing face of the city, its cosmopolitan lifestyles, the new attitudes and its burgeoning size are themes that run through the book. The transformation of Bangalore is traced from its modest mud fort beginnings to the budding metropolis it is today. Its many faces are analysed: As a mud fort, a British Cantonment, a Garden City and finally Silicon City.

Apart from the sociological commentary the book is a storehouse of information on the geography and architectural landmarks in the city. Markets, parks, trees, bungalows, lakes, churches, temples and mosques, old and new, all find mention in the book. The chapter on major communities in Bangalore and their festivals makes for interesting reading. Maya Jayapal also takes a peek into the future with the concluding chapter, Bangalore Tomorrow discussing its promising growth potential. A must-read for Bangalore-philes.

## Bangalore – A Century of Tales from City & Cantonment

Peter Colaco – Rs 395
Via Media Books

A caricature of Bangalore that tells it like it is. Peter Colaco regales his readers with stories of the City, the Cantonment and what lies between – a compilation of episodes from Bangalore's history minus the boring bits. The city's past comes alive in humorous anecdotes and delightful vignettes in Colaco's tongue-in-cheek writing. But beneath the humorous veneer there are moments of provocative insights into the changing face of the city and its denizens, a note of sadness running through. Newcomers get a taste of life in the city and old-timers derive a few moments of nostalgia.

The author's life and the cityscape run in parallel and the narrative skips happily between the past, present and future. Bangalore is seen through the eyes of many characters – Peter Colaco as a child and adult, his colourful family, the British, the traditional Jayanagar mamis et al feature in the book. The manners and mores of the 'natives', the sahibs and their mems' and even the ghosts that haunted Bangalore make their way into the book. Loosely put together sequences and lively descriptions of the vocabulary of 'fyure Kannada', the ominous divide between the City, the Cant, the music bands and restaurants through the ages follow. There is also a 'then' and 'now' comparison that subtly brings out the sociological changes in the city, written with a hint of irony.

The essays are complemented by quirky watercolour sketches and caricatures by Paul Fernandes.

## Bangalore – Scenes from an Indian City

Gangarams – Rs 1,000

The city is presented in picture postcards, a kaleidoscope of images showing its cosmopolitan face and its earthy charm. People, thoroughfares, parks and slums are captured through the lens of Mahesh Bhat, Clare Arni, Iqbal Mohammed and Clay Kelton, who contribute to the book.

The first chapters provide pertinent facts, figures and demographics. The city's variegated sobriquets and brief information on where to shop, eat and stay is listed. Helpful maps and a blow-by-blow account of Bangalore, from 4000 BC to the present are presented. Interesting bits of trivia are revealed here – Bangalore was the first city in India to get electricity. The year in which Sunday was declared a weekly holiday was 1853!

Noted sociologist MN Srinivas takes a critical look at Bangalore and its future in the introduction to the book. However, the text is just an appendage and the real flavour of the city comes through in the photo essay covering people, places and moods. Particularly striking are the pictures of street children.

## The City Beautiful

TP Issar – Rs 995
TP Issar

TP Issar was the resident expert on all things Bangalore. This is a comprehensive read on Bangalore's skyline and its aesthetic, 'architectural character'. Buildings old and new, but mostly old, find mention in the book. Issar dwells on the metamorphosis of Bangalore, from a garrison town to the chrome and steel city of today.

Colonial bungalows, soaring skyscrapers, heritage buildings and the stories behind their creation, figure through the narrative. The reader is also acquainted with the city's prominent streets and suburbs interspersed with interesting anecdotes and picturesque illustrations. Descriptions of the rambling mansions of Basavanagudi, the European-style buildings of the High Court, Central Library, Vidhana Soudha, Raj Bhavan, Mayo Hall, The Taj West End, Central College, The Bangalore Club, the Indian Institute of Science, BRV Theatre and a catalogue of 250 bungalows from every nook of the city are included. Black and white photographs, line sketches, blue prints and paintings of the tree lined avenues, landmarks and city life add to its appeal.

The book is not meant to be a trip down memory lane, but an attempt to educate the reader about the edifices of the city. Even if you are not too keen about Corinthian balustrades, gate piers or European classical bungalows, the coffee-table-book-feel, colourful photographs and snippets of history will keep you engaged. TP Issar also authored a book on the city's flowering trees and the royal city of Mysore along the same lines.

## An Exemplary Family in Bangalore

Bob Hoekstra & Soumen Chakraborty – Rs 190
Books-for-freedom-Trust

This book is a collection of vignettes and short stories penned by the CEO of Philips Software India, Dr. Bob Hoekstra. Dr. Hoekstra lives and works in Bangalore and all his stories are set here, culled from his experiences in "this fascinating city". The characters have been drawn from everyday life, be it the young IT engineer or the pavement dweller. The anecdotal stories are laced with humour and irony. The city's many faces come through sharply in his matter-of-fact narrative. His descriptions of Bangalore's streets, sounds and sights are particularly poignant and colourful. The stories are accompanied by the sketches of Soumen Chakraborty a long time resident of Bangalore. Hoekstra provides a fresh perspective on life in this bustling metrolpolis – that of an outsider who has made Bangalore his home.

# and Karnataka

## Mysore Royal Dasara

Swami Sivapriya Nanda – Rs 1,800
Abinav Publications

The book is something of a royal coup – written by the prince of Dharampur, the photographs are by the Mysore Maharaja's brother-in-law and the foreword is by the king himself! In the niche of a coffee table book, *Mysore Royal Dasara* uses the theme of the autumnal festival of Dasara to bring together the royalty, rituals and mythology associated with the festival. The unifying thread running throughout is the famed Mysore Dasara celebrated every year at the Mysore Palace. Dazzling photographs displaying the visual grandeur of the nine-day festivities are strewn across all sections.

The significance of Dasara in general and the pivotal role it played in the erstwhile kingdoms of Vijayanagar and Mysore frames the first few chapters of the book. The author's take on the origin of the festival is interesting. The motifs of mother goddess worship, fertility symbolism and the tribal beliefs replete in Dasara are traced.

The author delves into the sacred rites associated with Dasara in the Vijayanagar kingdom. Colourful eyewitness accounts of famous Portuguese, Italian and Dutch travellers are interspersed. Excerpts from the travelogues of Abdur Razak give an especially engaging record of the spectacle of Dasara.

Large sections are devoted to the Mysore Dasara celebrations centred on the king, Srikantadatta Wodeyar. Rare snapshots of the ebullient Mysore Maharaja, his private chambers and glitzy visuals of the lit-up palace are included.

## Karnataka

Mahesh Bhat & UR Ananthamurthy – Rs 1,200
Gangarams

Following the success of his book on Bangalore, *Scenes from a City*, photographer Mahesh Bhat along with Gangarams Publications, has brought out a coffee table book called *Karnataka*. The introductory pages offer facts at a glance, an insight into Karnataka through the ages and a map.

An essay by eminent writer UR Ananthamurthy, titled 'Growing up in Karnataka', provides a fitting introduction to the state. It brings out the diverse characteristics in landscape, cultures and people. Ananthamurthy also speaks of famous Kannadigas through the ages, their contribution to society and interesting anecdotes. Bhat's photographs, taken over a period of ten years, capture seasonal variations, moods, festivals, heritage places and people, telling their own story.

## Hampi – The Fabled Capital of the Vijayanagara Empire

Srinivasachar – Rs 540
Karnataka Archaeology

Brought out by the Department of Archaeology, it has been authored by historian and archaeologist Srinivasachar with photographs by Padma Bhushan award winner TS Satyan. Sweeping pictures, succinct text and colourful maps make this book a comprehensive authority on Hampi, legendary capital of the Vijayanagar kingdom.

A coffee table book of sorts, it makes a refreshing change from the scholarly texts and dry commentary available on the subject. An-easy-to-read history of Vijayanagar spanning the 12th to the 14th centuries, forms the backdrop for the photographs that dominate through the book. The empire's literature, politics, religion and feats in art and architecture are chronicled as well.

The photo essay is a guided tour through the ruins as they stand today. The pictures provide a much-needed visual map of the city, its stark landscape and maze of ruins. Welcome close-ups of the temples, palaces and their stone carvings follow. The crowds of pilgrims and tourists, images of river Tungabhadra at sundown and bustling scenes from the temples and the bazaar make up the rest.

Facts are glossed over – the book is not about the Vijayanagar empire or its kings. The focus is Hampi itself and the attempt is to reconstruct the picture of life in the city as it was and as it exists today.

## Coorg – The Land of the Kodavas

John & Jeanette Isaac – Rs 1,500
Grantha Corporation

Charming Coorg or Kodagu is presented in this visually appealing book by Times reporter Jeanette Issac and United Nations photographer John Isaac. The book is not divided into distinct chapters, but rather flows back and forth between people and places with vivid pictures and simple text.

The pictorial narrative meanders through the idyllic countryside, the sacred Talacauvery and wildlife in Nagarhole. Much is said with pictures and there is a short narrative at the beginning that attempts to demystify the intriguing origin of the Kodavas and the traditions and lifestyle of this enigmatic community. Colourful picture spreads of bougainvillea-strewn roads, lush coffee plantations and the verdant countryside are included. The book is replete with mellow images of the striking Kodava people in their traditional finery and life in the ancestral home or the ainmane. A sociological documentation of their diverse festivals, wedding ceremonies and dances follows, through action-packed photographs and explanatory lines. Ideal for a breezy read without the tedium of heavy information.

## The Land Called South Kanara

William Pais – Rs 2,350
Imageflex Publishers

This large tome catalogues the distinctive heritage of southern coastal Karnataka with glossy photographs and straightforward prose. The spirit of South Kanara or Tulu Nadu as it is called is encapsulated in ten well-wrought chapters that traverse through history, architecture, people, places, sports and festivals. Flipping through the pages the reader gets a vivid picture of the best of its beaches, jungles, monuments and heritage homes.

After a brief introduction to the landscape, Pais dives into a thorough history of South Kanara, going over to its prehistoric and mythical roots, the rule of the Nayakas, the Portuguese, ending with the British invasion. With the right mixture of history and visuals he proceeds to give an interesting account of the large community of Christians living here and their grand old churches. A large chunk of the middle is devoted to the distinctive architecture of the region with subsections on Jain basadis, Hindu temples, church art and the rambling Colonial and village bungalows.

The rich cultural traditions and artistic legacy of the southern coast are described towards the end. The colourful Yakshagana, the macabre Bhootakola, the bustling sights and sounds of the city and the energy of the Kambala buffalo races come alive in candid photographs. In the accompanying text, local beliefs and traditions are explored in some detail, be it the occult practice of serpent worship or tribal lifestyles.

## The Emerald Route

RK Narayan – Rs 200
Penguin Books

The Emerald Route is a travelogue through Karnataka, penned by famed Indian-English writer RK Narayan. Narayan was born in Madras, but Karnataka was his home. It was Mysore that fired his creative imagination and he stayed there all his life. His accounts span the length and breadth of Karnataka, from Belur in the south to Mangalore along the coast and Hampi in the north. Punctuated with interesting anecdotes, his descriptions are lively and colourful. Interspersed within his narrative are historical facts and tales of mythology. Narayan introduces his readers to the distinct flavours, sights and sounds of the region, from Nanjangud bananas and Mysore Mallige to Bangalore's bustling shopping complexes. The book is appended with one-act plays and stories based on Karnataka's folklore.

Ninety thousand reasons why this is the book
for those who wonder why Kerala is God's Own Country.
And the Book for the believers.

moments when you know there's a god. Ninety breathtaking images that captures
vividly, the landscapes, the wildlife and the people of Kerala. A coffee table book that
will make you realise why, National Geographic called Kerala 'one of the ten paradises
of the world'. A collector's item that is sure to turn you into a follower.

To order your copy contact:
Stark World, Infinitum Publishing Pvt. Ltd.  173 Penthouse  9th Cross  Indiranagar  1st Stage  Bangalore 560 038
Tel: +91 80 51255036, 51152105  Fax: +91 80 51255037  Email: response@starkworld.net  www.starkworld.net

Harihar

**Davanagere**

Jagalur

To Dharmavaram

Kanibennur

NH 4

Challkere

Chitradurga

Pavagada

To

Shikaripur

Honnali

Holalkere

NH 13

Dharmapur

NH 4

Hiriyur

Shimoga

Bhadravathi

Channagiri

Hosdurga

Vanivilasa Sagara

Gajanur Dam

Tarikere

Belaguru

Mandagadde
Bird Sanctuary

Bhadra

Bhadra Wildlife
Sanctuary

Birur

Vedavati

N.R.Pura

Kadur

Koppa

Kalahatti Falls

Banavar

Chiknayakanahal

Kemmangundi

NH 206

Baba
Budangiri
Range

Arasikere

Tiptur

Hebbe
Falls

Chikmagalur

Belur

Halebid

Aldur

Turuvekere

Shimsha

Park

Mudigere

Moranadu

Kottigehara

Gonibedu

Hassan

Alur

**Maps**

Dharmasthala

NH 48

Sakleshpur

Channarayapatna

Shravanabelagola

Nagam

Hemavathi

Shiradi

Hole Narsipura

Melkote

Kumara Parvatha

Krishnarajpet

Subramanya

Somvarpet

Saligrama

Cauvery

Sulya

Payaswani

KRS

Cauvery

Abbey
Falls

Nisargadhama

Krishnarajanagara

Ranganathittu
Bird Sanctuary

Mandya

NH 209

Bylekuppe

Periyapatna

Srirangapatna

Arkavathi

Madikeri

Cauvery
Wildlife
Sanctuary

Hunsur

Malavalli

Somanathapur

Shivasamudram
Falls

Muthatti

Cauvery

Bhagamandala

Cauvery

Siddapur

Mysore

NH 212

Bheemeshwari &
Doddamakali Fishing Camp

Virajpet

Lakshman Tirtha

Hampapura

Chamundi
Hills

T. Narasipura

Me

To Cananoor

H.D.Kote

Talakad

Kollegal

Rajiv Gandhi
National Park, Nagarhole

Nanjangud

Yelandur

Irrupu Falls

Kabini

Yelandur

Chamarajanagar

To Manantavadi

Kabini

NH 212

Gundlupet

K Gudi

B.R.Hills
Sanctuary

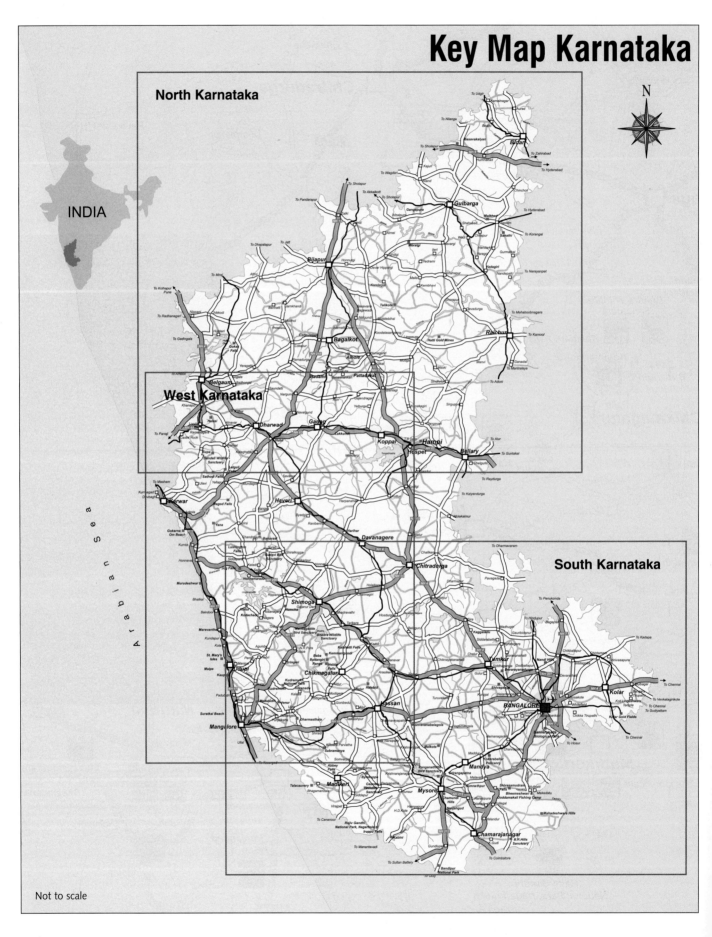

# Key Map Karnataka

**North Karnataka**

**INDIA**

**West Karnataka**

**South Karnataka**

Arabian Sea

Not to scale

# North Karnataka

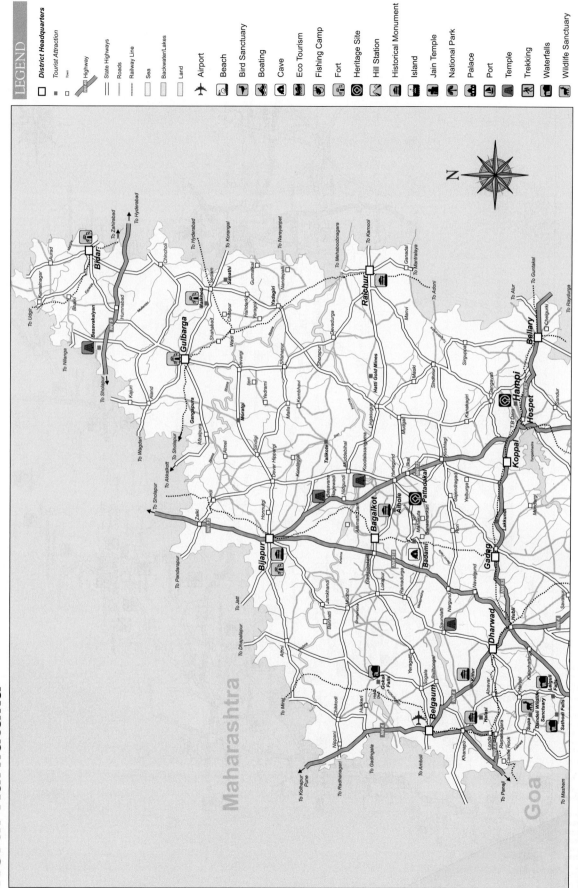

**Scale: 1: 19,00,000**

Maps

# South Karnataka

Scale: 1: 19,00,000

# West Karnataka

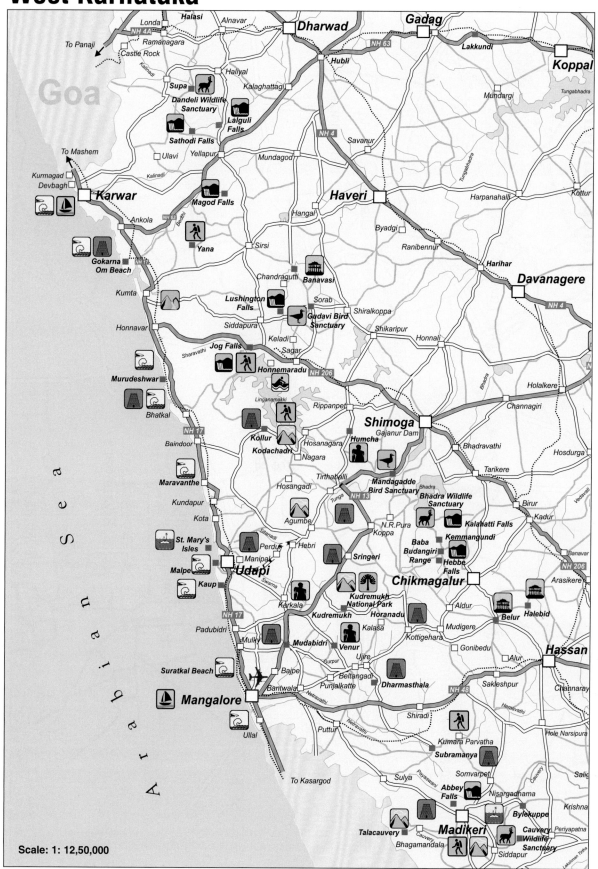

Scale: 1: 12,50,000

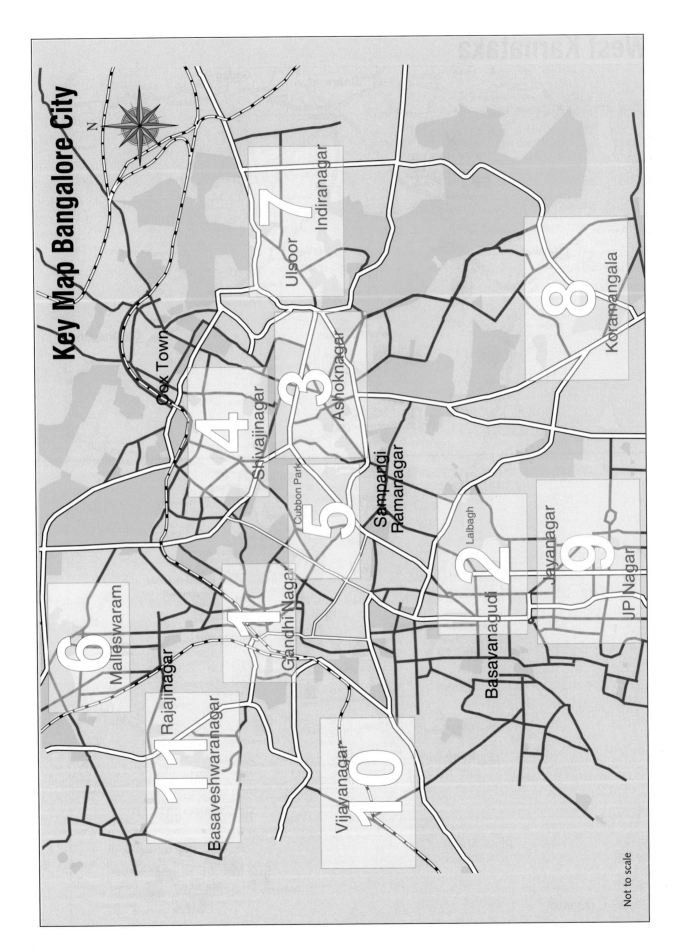

Key Map Bangalore City

# City Bus Stand & Railway Station

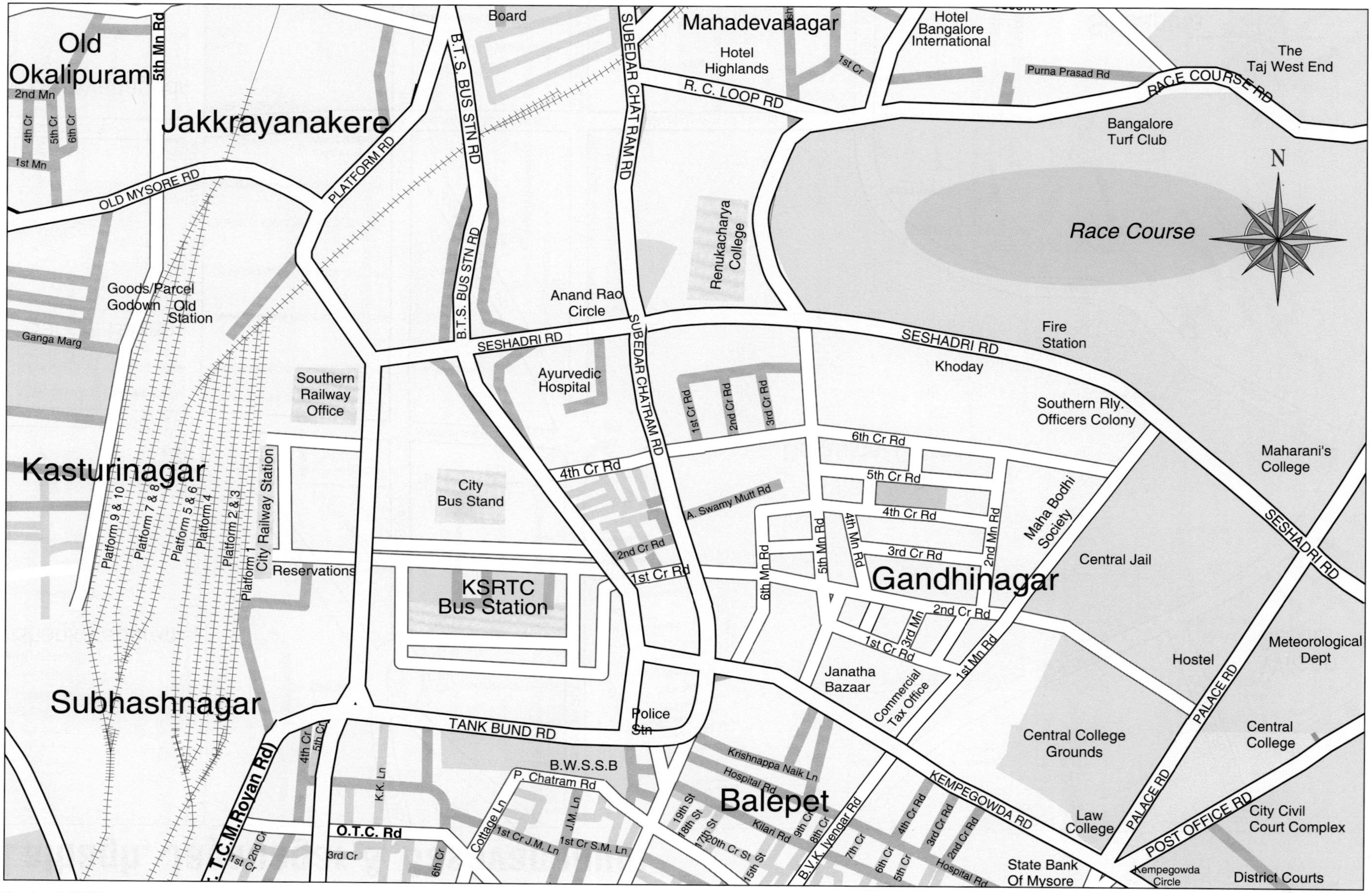

**1**

Old Okalipuram

Jakkrayanakere

Mahadevanagar

Gandhinagar

Balepet

Kasturinagar

Subhashnagar

Race Course

The Taj West End

RACE COURSE RD

Bangalore Turf Club

Purna Prasad Rd

Hotel Bangalore International

1st Cr

R. C. LOOP RD

Hotel Highlands

Maharani's College

SESHADRI RD

Meteorological Dept

Central College

City Civil Court Complex

District Courts

PALACE RD

Hostel

Central Jail

Kempegowda Circle

POST OFFICE RD

PALACE RD

Fire Station

Southern Rly. Officers Colony

Khoday

SESHADRI RD

Maha Bodhi Society

2nd Mn Rd

Central College Grounds

Law College

State Bank Of Mysore

6th Cr Rd

5th Cr Rd

4th Cr Rd

3rd Cr Rd

2nd Cr Rd

1st Mn Rd

KEMPEGOWDA RD

Hospital Rd

4th Mn Rd

5th Mn Rd

3rd Mn

2nd Mn

1st Cr Rd

Commerical Tax Office

Janatha Bazaar

3rd Cr Rd

4th Cr Rd

5th Cr Rd

6th Cr

7th Cr

8th Cr St

9th Cr St

B.V.K. Iyengar Rd

Renukacharya College

3rd Cr Rd

2nd Cr Rd

1st Cr Rd

A. Swamy Mutt Rd

6th Mn Rd

Krishnappa Naik Ln

Hospital Rd

Kilari Rd

15th St

17th St

19th St

18th St

SUBEDAR CHAT RAM RD

SUBEDAR CHATRAM RD

Anand Rao Circle

Ayurvedic Hospital

SESHADRI RD

4th Cr Rd

2nd Cr Rd

1st Cr Rd

Police Stn

B.W.S.S.B

P. Chatram Rd

J.M. Ln

1st Cr S.M. Ln

Board

B.T.S. BUS STN RD

B.T.S. BUS STN RD

City Bus Stand

KSRTC Bus Station

TANK BUND RD

College Ln

1st Cr J.M. Ln

K. K. Ln

O.T.C. Rd

3rd Cr

6th Cr

PLATFORM RD

OLD MYSORE RD

5th Mn Rd

Southern Railway Office

Reservations

City Railway Station

Platform 1

Platform 2 & 3

Platform 4

Platform 5 & 6

Platform 7 & 8

Platform 9 & 10

Goods/ Parcel Godown

Old Station

4th Cr

5th Cr

T.C.M.Royan Rd

1st Cr 2nd Cr

2nd Mn

1st Cr

5th Cr

6th Cr

4th Cr

Ganga Marg

N

# 2

# Lalbagh, Jayanagar & Basavanagudi

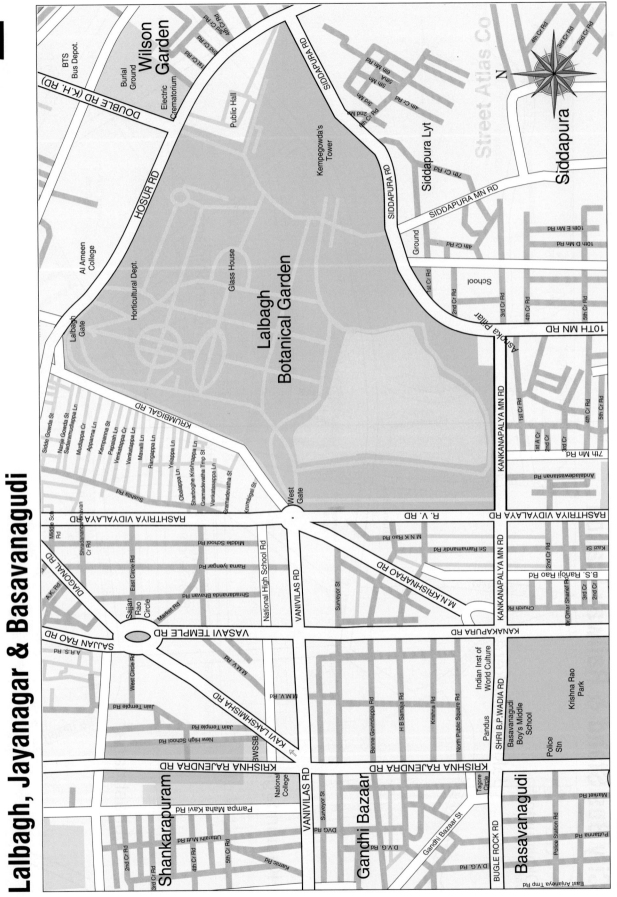

Scale: 1: 9100

Street Atlas Co

**Wilson Garden**

BTS Bus Depot.

Burial Ground

Electric Crematorium

Al Ameen College

Horticultural Dept.

Lalbagh Gate

DOUBLE RD (K.H. RD)

HOSUR RD

Public Hall

Glass House

Kempegowda's Tower

SIDDAPURA RD

SIDDAPURA RD

SIDDAPURA MN RD

Ground

Siddapura Lyt

**Siddapura**

1st Cr Rd
2nd Cr Rd
3rd Cr Rd
4th Cr Rd
5th Mn Rd
6th Mn Rd
5tha Mn

10th E Mn Rd
10th D Mn Rd

School

1st Cr Rd
2nd Cr Rd
3rd Cr Rd
4th Cr Rd
5th Cr Rd

Ashoka Pillar

10TH MN RD

**Lalbagh Botanical Garden**

Sidde Gowda St
Nanje Gowda St
Sadaramudappa Ln
Mudlappa Cr
Appanna Ln
Kempanna St
Venkatappa Cr
Venkatappa Ln
Papaiah Ln
Mavalli Ln
Rangappa Ln
Yelappa Ln
Obalappa Ln
Sharboghe Krishnappa Ln
Gramadevatha Tmp St
Venkatasappa Ln
Bramadevatha St
Krumbigal St

Sushila Rd

KRUMBIGAL RD

West Gate

R. V. RD

KANKANAPALYA MN RD

1st Cr Rd

1st A Cr
2nd Cr
3rd Cr

7th Mn Rd

Andaladewastanan Rd

RASHTRIYA VIDYALAYA RD

RASHTRIYA VIDYALAYA RD

Middle Sch Rd

Shradaranda Bhavan

Shradaranda Cr Rd

Middle School Rd

Rama Iyengar Rd

East Circle Rd

Shradaanda Bhavan Rd

Market Rd

National High School Rd

VANIVILAS RD

Surveyor St

M N K Rao Rd

Sri Ramamandir Rd

M N KRISHNARAO RD

M N KRISHNARAO RD

KANKANAPALYA MN RD

Kazi St

B.S. Ranoji Rao Rd

2nd Cr Rd

Church Rd

Dr. Omar Sharief Rd

3rd Cr
2nd Cr

KANKAPURA RD

DIAGONAL RD

A.K. Rd

Sajjan Rao Circle

SAJJAN RAO RD

A.R.S. Rd

West Circle Rd

Jain Temple Rd

Jain Temple Rd

New High School Rd

BWSSB

KAVI LAKSHMISHA RD

VASAVI TEMPLE RD

KRISHNA RAJENDRA RD

KRISHNA RAJENDRA RD

**Shankarapuram**

National College

3rd Cr Rd
2nd Cr Rd
4th Cr Rd
5th Cr Rd

Pampa Maha Kavi Rd

Uttarahi Mutt Rd

Kamic Rd

VANIVILAS RD

DVG Rd

Surveyor St

**Gandhi Bazaar**

Bennie Govindappa Rd

H B Samaja Rd

Krishna Rd

Krishna Rd

North Public Square Rd

Indian Inst of World Culture

Pandus

SHRI B.P. WADIA RD

Tagore Circle

Gandhi Bazaar St

D.V.G. Rd

BUGLE ROCK RD

D.V.G. Rd

**Basavanagudi**

Basavanagudi Boy's Middle School

Police Stn

Krishna Rao Park

Market Rd

Police Station Rd

Puttanna Rd

East Anjaneya Tmp Rd

**3**

# MG Road, Brigade Road & Residency Road

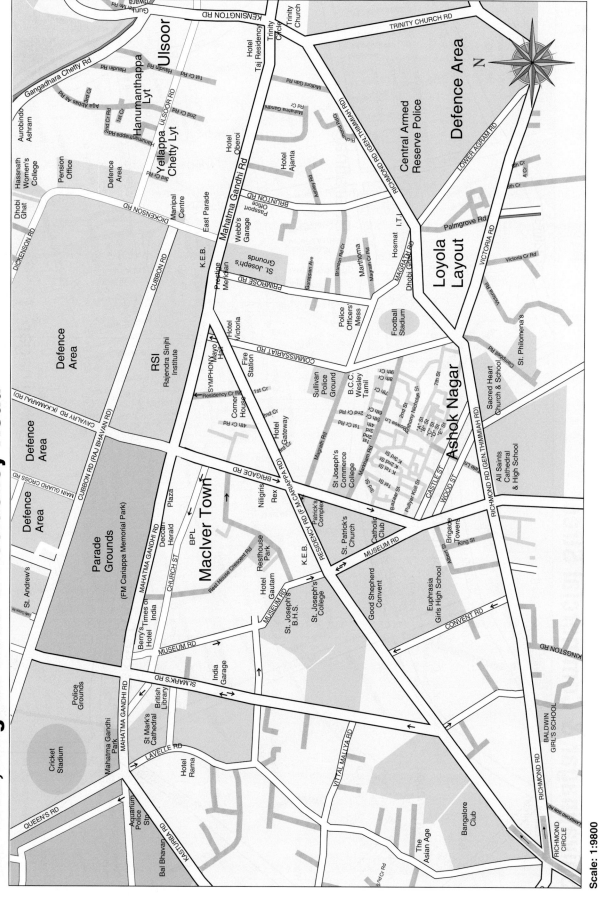

Scale: 1:9800

# Shivajinagar & Commercial Street

**Scale: 1:7500**

# Bangalore City Corporation & Cubbon Park

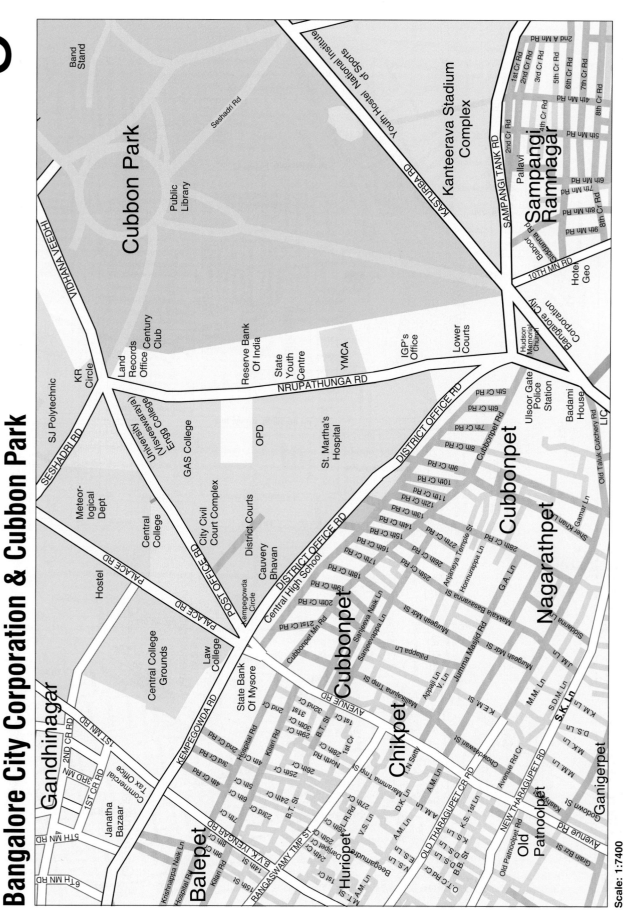

Scale: 1:7400

483

# Malleswaram & Sankey Tank

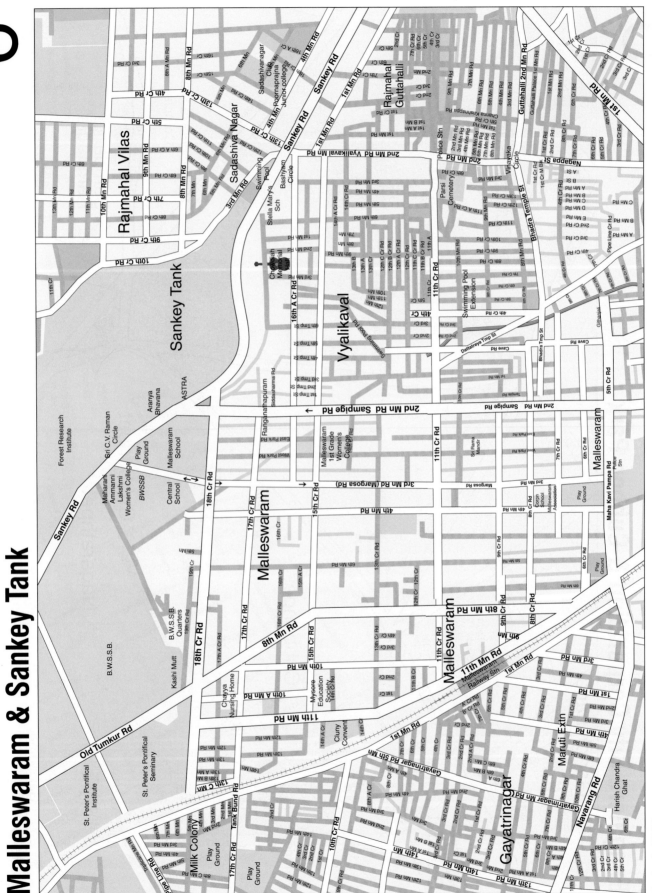

Scale: 1: 10700

# Indiranagar & Ulsoor

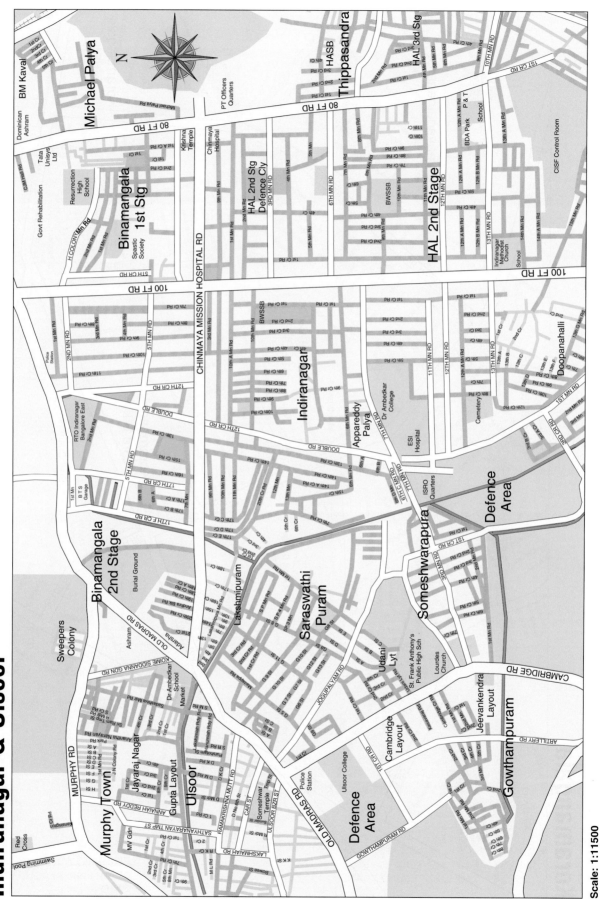

Scale: 1:11500

# Koramangala

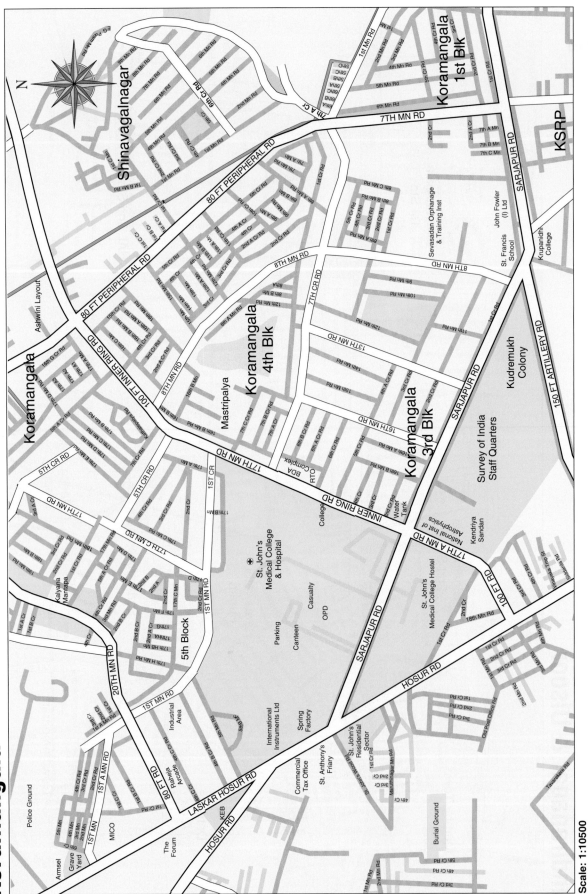

**Scale: 1:10500**

# Jayanagar & JP Nagar

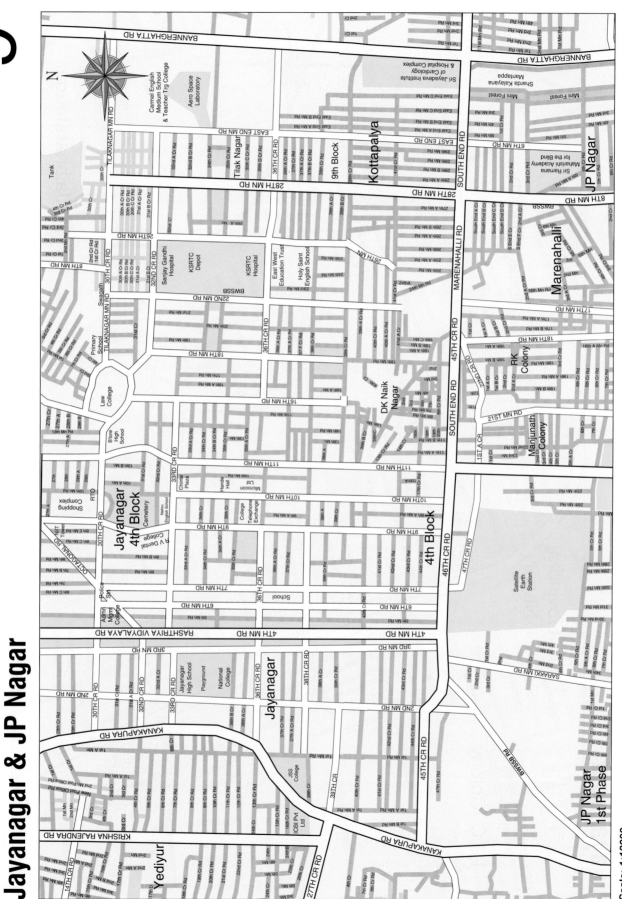

Scale: 1:12000

# Vijayanagar

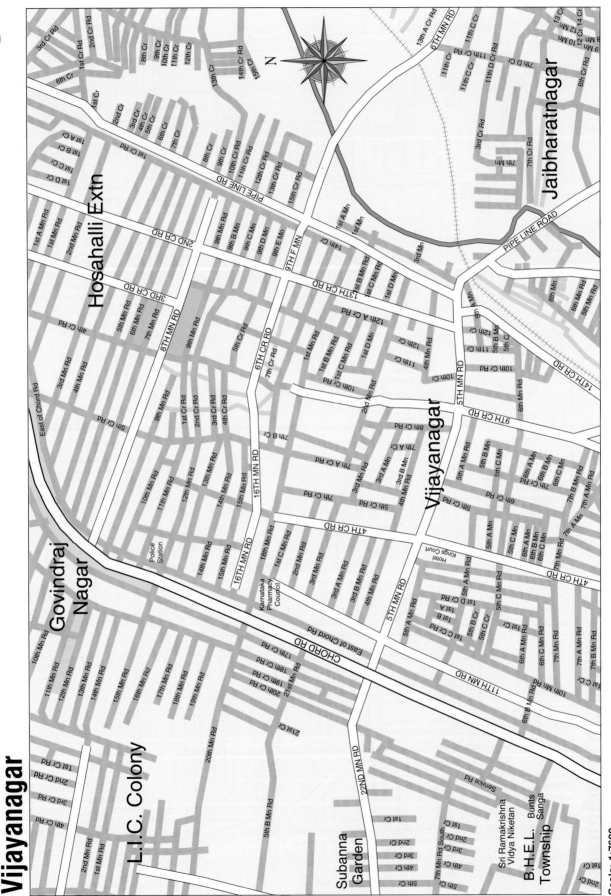

**Jaibharatnagar**

**Hosahalli Extn**

**Govindraj Nagar**

**Vijayanagar**

**L.I.C. Colony**

**Subanna Garden**

**Sri Ramakrishna Vidya Niketan**

**B.H.E.L. Township**

**Bunts Sanga**

Police Station

Karnataka Pharmacy Council

Hotel Kings Court

PIPE LINE ROAD

Scale: 1:7600

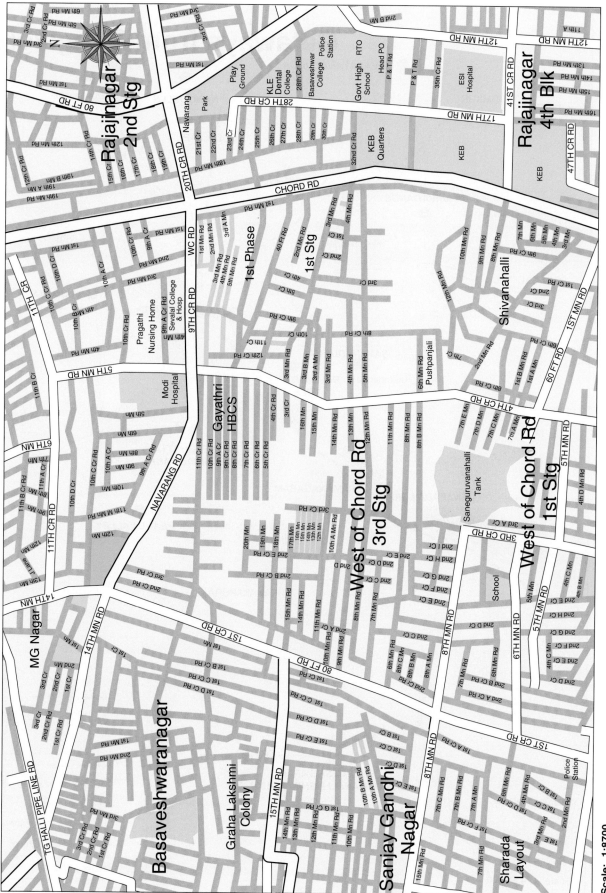

# Rajajinagar & Basaveshwaranagar

**11**

Rajajinagar 2nd Stg

Rajajinagar 4th Blk

Maps

Play Ground

Park

KLE Dental College

Basaveshwar College

Police Station

Govt High School

RTO

Head PO

P & T Rd

P & T Rd

ESI Hospital

KEB Quarters

KEB

KEB

Navarang

CHORD RD

1st Phase

1st Stg

Pragathi Nursing Home

Sevalal College & Hosp.

Modi Hospital

Gayathri HBCS

Shivanahalli

Pushpanjali

West of Chord Rd 3rd Stg

Saneguruvanahalli Tank

West of Chord Rd 1st Stg

MG Nagar

Basaveshwaranagar

Graha Lakshmi Colony

School

Sanjay Gandhi Nagar

Sharada Layout

Police Station

**Scale: 1:8700**

489

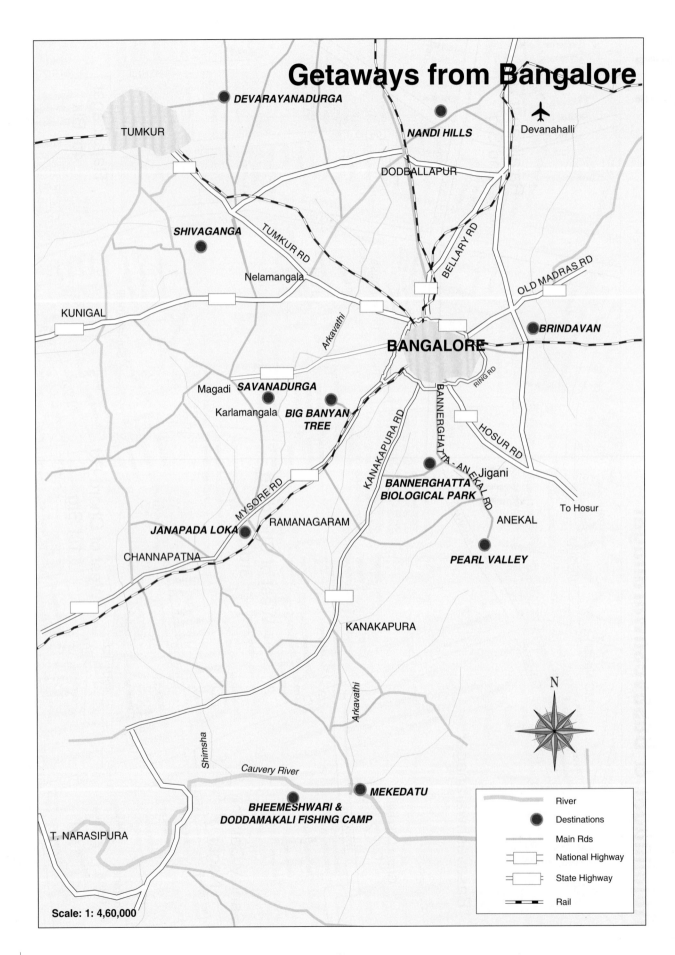

# Getaways from Bangalore

DEVARAYANADURGA

TUMKUR

NANDI HILLS

Devanahalli

DODBALLAPUR

SHIVAGANGA

BELLARY RD

OLD MADRAS RD

Nelamangala

TUMKUR RD

Arkavathi

KUNIGAL

BRINDAVAN

BANGALORE

RING RD

Magadi    SAVANADURGA

Karlamangala    BIG BANYAN TREE

KANAKAPURA RD

BANNERGHATTA - ANEKAL RD

HOSUR RD

Jigani

BANNERGHATTA BIOLOGICAL PARK

Anekal

To Hosur

MYSORE RD

JANAPADA LOKA    RAMANAGARAM

PEARL VALLEY

CHANNAPATNA

KANAKAPURA

Arkavathi

N

Shimsha

Cauvery River

MEKEDATU

BHEEMESHWARI & DODDAMAKALI FISHING CAMP

T. NARASIPURA

| | River |
| | Destinations |
| | Main Rds |
| | National Highway |
| | State Highway |
| | Rail |

Scale: 1: 4,60,000

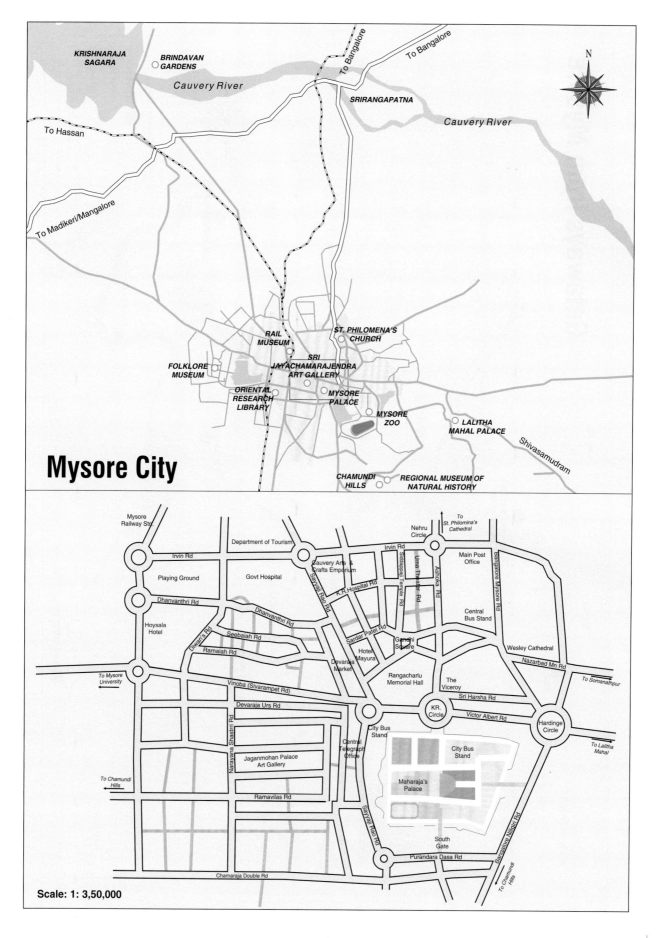

# Mysore City

**Scale: 1 : 3,50,000**

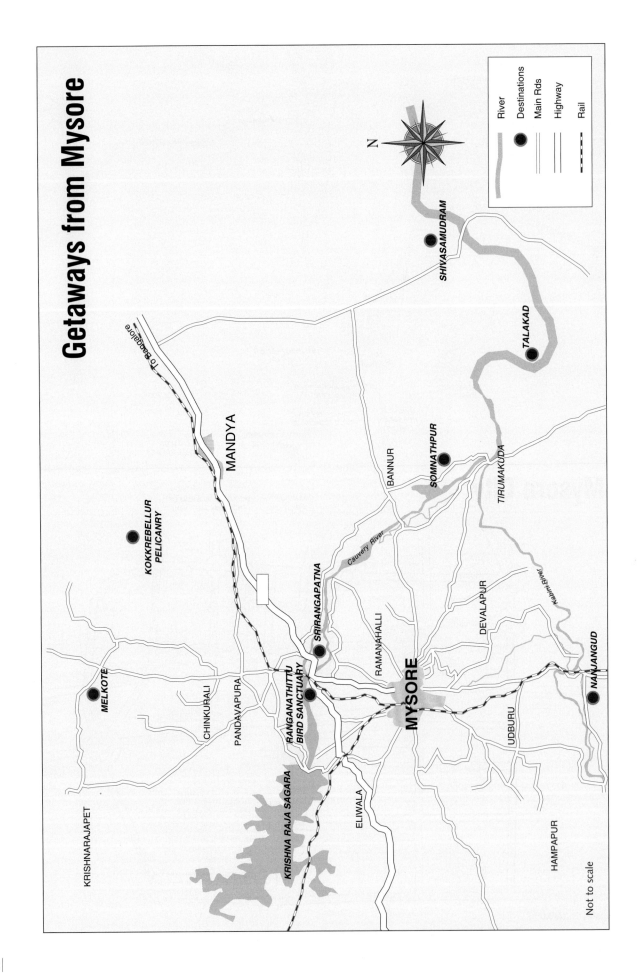

# Getaways from Mysore

**Legend:**
- River
- Destinations
- Main Rds
- Highway
- Rail

N

To Bangalore

MANDYA

KRISHNARAJAPET

MELKOTE

KOKKREBELLUR PELICANRY

CHINKURALI

PANDAVAPURA

KRISHNA RAJA SAGARA

RANGANATHITTU BIRD SANCTUARY

SRIRANGAPATNA

Cauvery River

BANNUR

SOMNATHPUR

SHIVASAMUDRAM

TALAKAD

TIRUMAKUDA

ELIWALA

RAMANAHALLI

MYSORE

DEVALAPUR

Kabini River

UDBURU

NANJANGUD

HAMPAPUR

Not to scale

# Index

## Advertisers Index